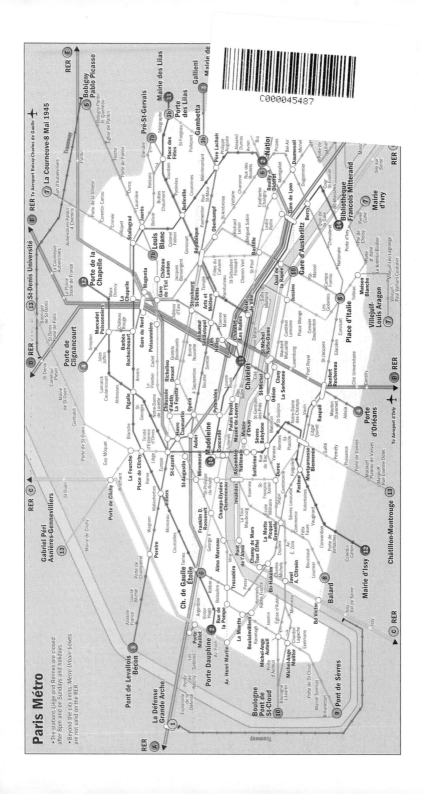

Paris Métro

- The stations Liège and Rennes are closed after 8pm and on Sundays and holidays.
- Beyond the city limits, *Métro Urbain* tickets are not valid on the RER.

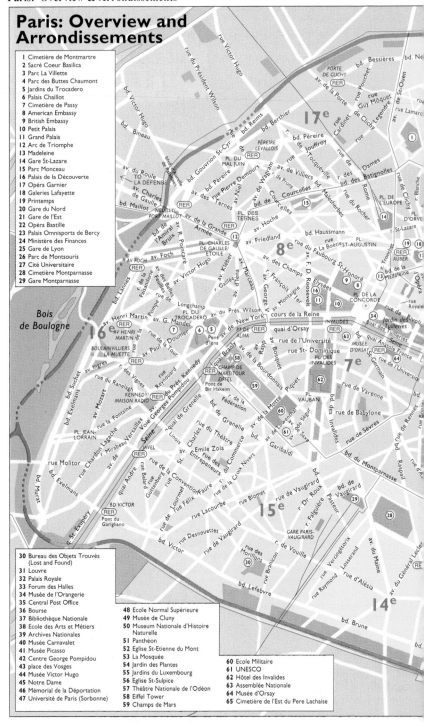

Paris: Overview and Arrondissements

1 Cimetière de Montmartre
2 Sacré Coeur Basilica
3 Parc La Villette
4 Parc des Buttes Chaumont
5 Jardins du Trocadero
6 Palais Chaillot
7 Cimetière de Passy
8 American Embassy
9 British Embassy
10 Petit Palais
11 Grand Palais
12 Arc de Triomphe
13 Madeleine
14 Gare St-Lazare
15 Parc Monceau
16 Palais de la Découverte
17 Opéra Garnier
18 Galeries Lafayette
19 Printemps
20 Gare du Nord
21 Gare de l'Est
22 Opéra Bastille
23 Palais Omnisports de Bercy
24 Ministère des Finances
25 Gare de Lyon
26 Parc de Montsouris
27 Cité Universitaire
28 Cimetière Montparnasse
29 Gare Montparnasse

30 Bureau des Objets Trouvés
   (Lost and Found)
31 Louvre
32 Palais Royale
33 Forum des Halles
34 Musée de l'Orangerie
35 Central Post Office
36 Bourse
37 Bibliothèque Nationale
38 Ecole des Arts et Métiers
39 Archives Nationales
40 Musée Carnavalet
41 Musée Picasso
42 Centre George Pompidou
43 place des Vosges
44 Musée Victor Hugo
45 Notre Dame
46 Mémorial de la Déportation
47 Université de Paris (Sorbonne)

48 Ecole Normal Supérieure
49 Musée de Cluny
50 Museum Nationale d'Histoire
   Naturelle
51 Panthéon
52 Eglise St-Etienne du Mont
53 La Mosquée
54 Jardin des Plantes
55 Jardins du Luxembourg
56 Eglise St-Sulpice
57 Théâtre Nationale de l'Odéon
58 Eiffel Tower
59 Champs de Mars

60 Ecole Militaire
61 UNESCO
62 Hôtel des Invalides
63 Assemblée Nationale
64 Musée d'Orsay
65 Cimetière de l'Est du Pere Lachaise

Bois
de Boulogne

Paris: 1er and 2e

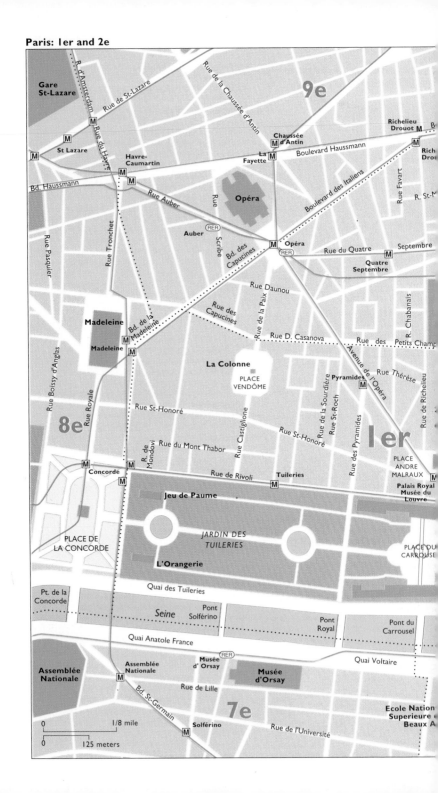

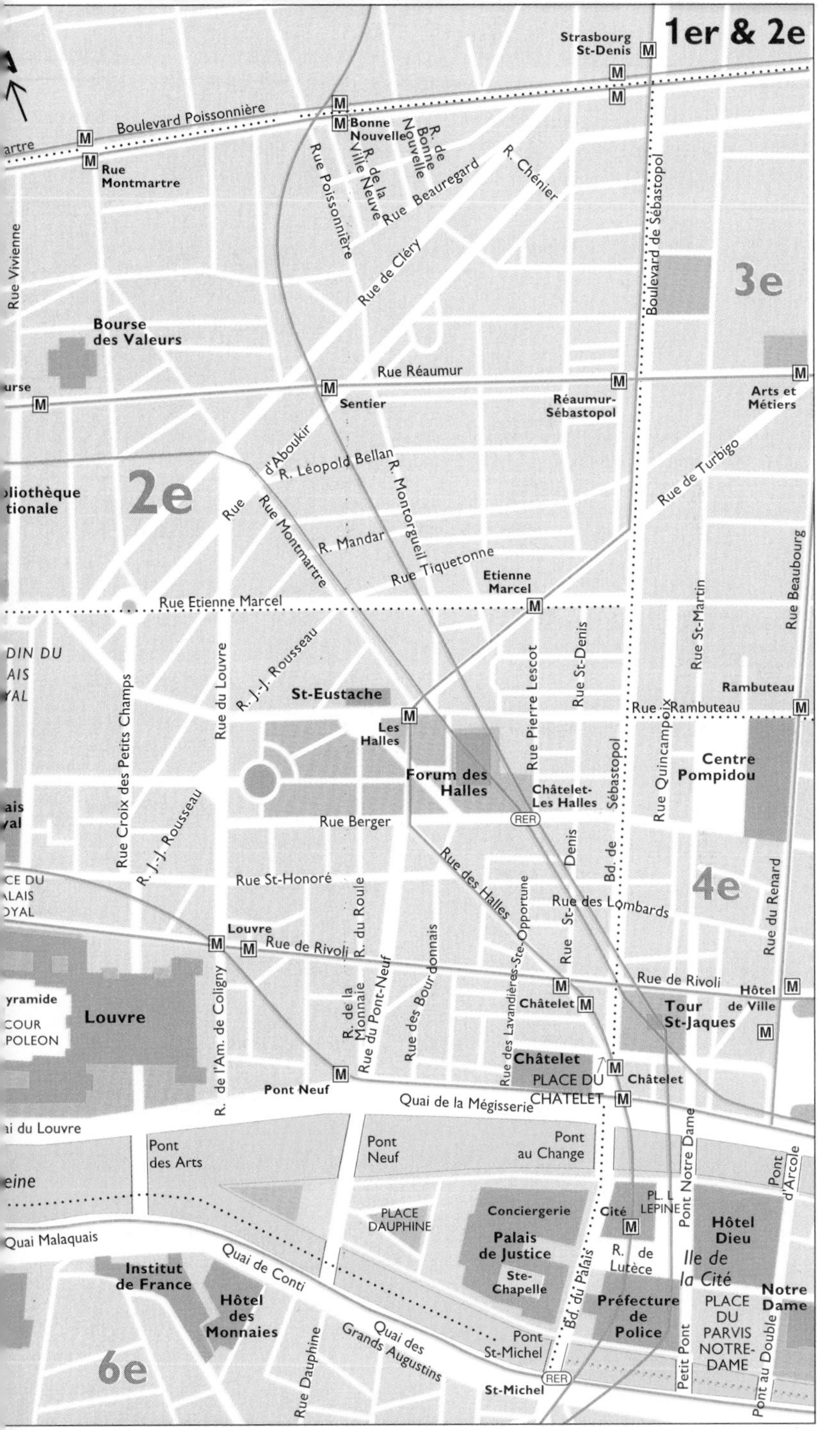

1er & 2e

3e

2e

4e

6e

Strasbourg St-Denis

Boulevard Poissonnière

Bonne Nouvelle
R. de Bonne Nouvelle
R. de la Ville Neuve
Rue Beauregard
R. Chénier

Rue Montmartre

Rue Vivienne

Rue Poissonnière

Rue de Cléry

Boulevard de Sébastopol

Bourse des Valeurs

Rue Réaumur

Sentier

Réaumur-Sébastopol

Arts et Métiers

Bourse

d'Aboukir
R. Léopold Bellan
R. Montorgueil
R. Mandar
Rue Montmartre
Rue Tiquetonne

Bibliothèque nationale

Rue de Turbigo

Etienne Marcel

Rue Etienne Marcel

Rue St-Martin

Rue Beaubourg

JARDIN DU PALAIS ROYAL

Rue du Louvre

R. J.-J. Rousseau

St-Eustache

Rue Pierre Lescot

Rue St-Denis

Les Halles

Rambuteau

Rue Rambuteau

Palais Royal

Rue Croix des Petits Champs

Forum des Halles

Centre Pompidou

PLACE DU PALAIS ROYAL

R. J.-J. Rousseau

Rue Berger

Châtelet-Les Halles
RER

Sébastopol

Rue Quincampoix

Rue St-Honoré

Rue des Halles

Rue St-Denis

Rue des Lombards

Bd. de Denis

4e

Rue du Renard

Pyramide

COUR NAPOLEON

Louvre

Louvre
Rue de Rivoli

R. du Roule

R. de la Monnaie
Rue du Pont-Neuf

Rue des Bourdonnais

Rue de Rivoli

Hôtel de Ville

R. de l'Am. de Coligny

Rue des Lavandières-Ste-Opportune

Châtelet

Tour St-Jaques

Pont Neuf

Châtelet
PLACE DU CHATELET

Châtelet

Quai du Louvre

Quai de la Mégisserie

R.

Seine

Pont des Arts

Pont Neuf

Pont au Change

Pont Notre-Dame

Pont d'Arcole

Quai Malaquais

PLACE DAUPHINE

Conciergerie

Cité

PL. L. LEPINE

Hôtel Dieu

Quai de Conti

Institut de France

Palais de Justice

R. de Lutèce

Ile de la Cité

Ste-Chapelle

Préfecture de Police

PLACE DU PARVIS NOTRE-DAME

Notre Dame

Hôtel des Monnaies

Quai des Grands Augustins

Bd. du Palais

Petit Pont

Pont au Double

Rue Dauphine

Pont St-Michel

6e

St-Michel
RER

Paris: 5e and 6e

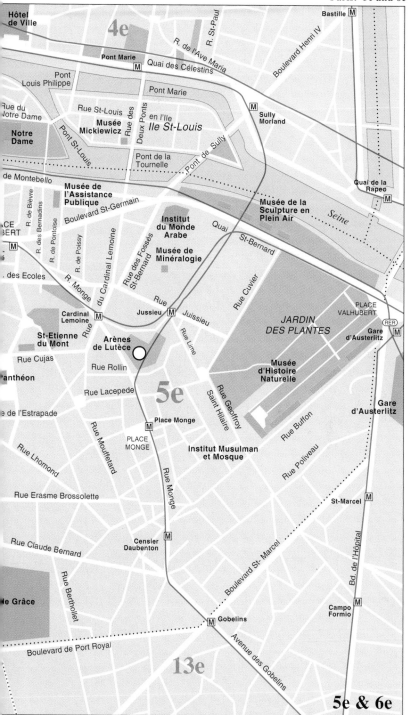

Paris: RER

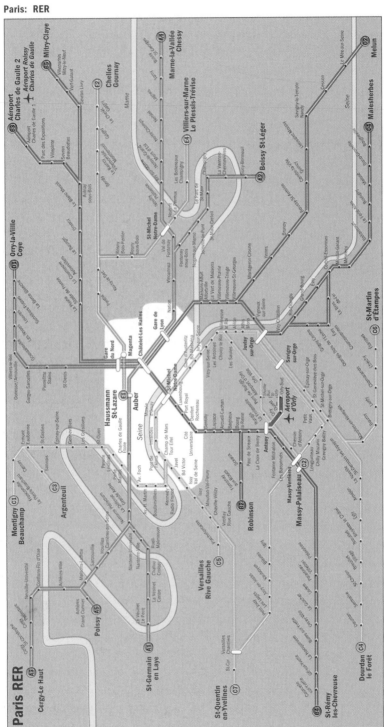

◼ Let's Go writers travel on your budget.

"Guides that penetrate the veneer of the holiday brochures and mine the grit of real life."

—*The Economist*

"The writers seem to have experienced every rooster-packed bus and lunar-surfaced mattress about which they write."

—*The New York Times*

"All the dirt, dirt cheap."

—*People*

◼ Great for independent travelers.

"The guides are aimed not only at young budget travelers but at the independent traveler; a sort of streetwise cookbook for traveling alone."

—*The New York Times*

"Flush with candor and irreverence, chock full of budget travel advice."

—*The Des Moines Register*

"An indispensible resource, *Let's Go*'s practical information can be used by every traveler."

—*The Chattanooga Free Press*

◼ Let's Go is completely revised each year.

"Only *Let's Go* has the zeal to annually update every title on its list."

—*The Boston Globe*

"Unbeatable: good sightseeing advice; up-to-date info on restaurants, hotels, and inns; a commitment to money-saving travel; and a wry style that brightens nearly every page."

—*The Washington Post*

◼ All the important information you need.

"*Let's Go* authors provide a comedic element while still providing concise information and thorough coverage of the country. Anything you need to know about budget traveling is detailed in this book."

—*The Chicago Sun-Times*

"Value-packed, unbeatable, accurate, and comprehensive."

—*Los Angeles Times*

Let's Go Publications

Let's Go: Alaska & the Pacific Northwest 2000
Let's Go: Australia 2000
Let's Go: Austria & Switzerland 2000
Let's Go: Britain & Ireland 2000
Let's Go: California 2000
Let's Go: Central America 2000
Let's Go: China 2000 **New Title!**
Let's Go: Eastern Europe 2000
Let's Go: Europe 2000
Let's Go: France 2000
Let's Go: Germany 2000
Let's Go: Greece 2000
Let's Go: India & Nepal 2000
Let's Go: Ireland 2000
Let's Go: Israel 2000 **New Title!**
Let's Go: Italy 2000
Let's Go: Mexico 2000
Let's Go: Middle East 2000 **New Title!**
Let's Go: New York City 2000
Let's Go: New Zealand 2000
Let's Go: Paris 2000
Let's Go: Perú & Ecuador 2000 **New Title!**
Let's Go: Rome 2000
Let's Go: South Africa 2000
Let's Go: Southeast Asia 2000
Let's Go: Spain & Portugal 2000
Let's Go: Turkey 2000
Let's Go: USA 2000
Let's Go: Washington, D.C. 2000

Let's Go Map Guides

Amsterdam	New Orleans
Berlin	New York City
Boston	Paris
Chicago	Prague
Florence	Rome
London	San Francisco
Los Angeles	Seattle
Madrid	Washington, D.C.

Coming Soon: Sydney and Hong Kong

Let's Go

2000 PARIS

Anna M. Schneider-Mayerson
Editor

Researcher-Writers:
Silas Alben
Judith Batalion
Whitney Bryant

Macmillan

HELPING LET'S GO If you want to share your discoveries, suggestions, or corrections, please drop us a line. We read every piece of correspondence, whether a postcard, a 10-page email, or a coconut. Please note that mail received after May 2000 may be too late for the 2001 book, but will be kept for future editions. **Address mail to:**

Let's Go: Paris
67 Mount Auburn Street
Cambridge, MA 02138
USA

Visit Let's Go at **http://www.letsgo.com,** or send email to:

feedback@letsgo.com
Subject: "Let's Go: Paris"

In addition to the invaluable travel advice our readers share with us, many are kind enough to offer their services as researchers or editors. Unfortunately, our charter enables us to employ only currently enrolled Harvard-Radcliffe students.

Published in Great Britain 2000 by Macmillan, an imprint of Macmillan Publishers Ltd, 25 Eccleston Place, London, SW1W 9NF, Basingstoke and Oxford Associated companies throughout the world
www.macmillan.co.uk

Maps by David Lindroth copyright © 2000, 1999, 1998, 1997, 1996, 1995, 1994, 1993, 1992, 1991, 1990, 1989, 1988 by St. Martin's Press

Published in the United States of America by St. Martin's Press

ISBN: 0 333 77998 3

First edition
10 9 8 7 6 5 4 3 2 1

Let's Go: Paris is written by Let's Go Publications, 67 Mount Auburn Street, Cambridge, MA 02138, USA.

Let's Go® and the thumb logo are trademarks of Let's Go, Inc.
Printed in the USA on recycled paper with biodegradable soy ink.

HOW TO USE THIS BOOK

The platform is moving at the same speed as your Let's Go Travelpod. Hold children by the hand. Please be sure to keep hands and feet inside the vehicle at all times.

"Hello and welcome to the wonderful world of Paris! My name is Monsieur Bleu. Look at what you're holding! That, my friend, is an original copy of *Let's Go Paris: 2000*, the most comprehensive budget guide to be written about my city!

"Our first stop is **History.** This section is a whirlwind tour of Parisian history and culture. It's here that you'll learn about Napoleon's exploits, *Being and Nothingness*, and French New Wave cinema. Now, if you peer out the left window, you'll catch a glimpse of **Essentials.** In this section, you'll learn how to slice through the reams of red tape designed to hamper travel adventures. Snip, snip! Navigating visas, courier companies, and study abroad—it's all here. Out the right window is **Once There,** which explains Paris nitty-gritty—from internet access to shopping protocol.

"A king lives in a château. When he travels, he sleeps wherever he wants. But not you, budget traveler! The **Accommodations** section provides a list of recommended hotels, hostels, and *foyers* in popular locations. We arrange them according to how much we like them; the best are at the top of the list. Be smart and make reservations.

"Parisian meals are known to last all of the day and into the night—to get in on the action, see **Restaurants.** For picnic provisions and spirits, see **Food and Wine.**

"**Let's Go Picks** lists our opinions on some of the best sights, bargains, and revolutions throughout Paris, past and present. When you see a ☒, be happy—it means that the hotel, restaurant, or shop represents the best value, and is worth a trip out of your way.

"**Sights** list the best attractions by arrondissement—the most astounding cathedrals, gardens, historical sites, and holy relics. Dispersed throughout are **suggested itineraries,** recognizable by their black and gray art deco–style boxes, for those anxious to find the best places to kiss or Picasso's old haunts.

"The **Arts and Entertainment** section lists all the hot venues for water-jousting tournaments, Surrealist films, and interpretive dance theater. **Festivals and Seasonal Events** direct you to seasonal action. **Nightlife** catalogues the nocto-scene. The **Shopping** section leads you to. No. Don't Speak. **Daytripping** gives urban warriors a taste of the country.

"As we wrap up this tour, you'll glimpse the **Appendix.** A phrasebook and an expansive menu reader provide the kind of French words you'll need from day to day. In our experience, it's always better to try to speak French, even if you're not proficient. The French will appreciate the effort.

"Finally, while it is our hope that this book helps you make the most of your journey, we also hope you will leave it in the hotel room occasionally and venture out to explore unmapped territory. And we expect that by the time you're done reading, you'll be able to identify all four hundred kinds of French cheese."

Please exit your vehicle in an orderly fashion. Paris is waiting.

No Reservations Needed, Just Show Up!

Bullfrog Bike Tours

Guided English Bike Tours of Paris

Absolutely the BEST way to see Paris!

Meet us here by
the Eiffel Tower.
Look for the Bullfrog Flag.

Nearest Metro Stops

What do we offer?

- 🚲 A 3-4 hour guided English bike tour of Paris and all its famous sites
- 🚲 A relaxed pace allowing you to enjoy the ride
- 🚲 Ride in parks, bike lanes and on sidewalks
- 🚲 Stops every few hundred yards for photos and point of interest information
- 🚲 New city bikes with comfortable seats
- 🚲 A great opportunity to meet other travelers
- 🚲 Informative, enthusiastic and entertaining guides
- 🚲 Rain slickers provided if needed

Times

- 🚲 Times: 11 a.m. and 3:30 p.m.
- 🚲 Season: May 1 – September 15

Cost

- 🚲 130 French Francs or $20 US
- 🚲 Sorry, No credit cards

Don't waste your time...
let us show you EXACTLY what you want to see!

http://bullfrogbikes.com • e-mail: BullfrogBikes @ hotmail.com
Phone: 06-09-98-08-60 "Please read carefully before calling"

CONTENTS

MAPS

LET'S GO PICKS

BEST REVOLUTION: A tough call, with the *communards* and *the* Revolution running neck-and-neck (pun intended). Call us revolutionary, but we'll take the **communards** (see p. 8) for senseless violence, leftism with a vengeance, and sheer destruction. Thanks to all who voted.

BEST PARK: By far, the **Parc de la Villette** (p. 255). Welcome to the future, kiddies.

BEST/WORST CLIMB IN PARIS: Sacré-Coeur (p. 228). Tiny, spiralling, and pitch-black stairs (and so many, so many, whoever knew there were so many) lead you up and up Paris's whitest monument to Paris's highest point, for a view (and a breeze) that is indeed worth it. Go for the comparative study of ubiquitous French graffitti, stay for the holiness.

BEST BAGUETTE: Poujauran (p. 158).

BEST MÉTRO STATION: Châtelet. Not only is it the interchange for all public transportation known to man, but its ever-changing slate of performers (especially around line four) make it worth the five-mile underground hike.

BEST BEVVIES: Pear or **apple cidre** at La Crêperie de Josselin (p. 146), **café glacé** at Le Fumoir (p. 128), **cappuccino** at Le Marais Plus (p. 134), **chocolat chaud** at Café de Flore (p. 139), **water** at Colette (p. 306), **tea** at Le Souk (p. 143), **Chinatown** at China Club (p. 296), **juices** at Apparement Café (p. 134).

MOST UNDERRATED DAYTRIPS: Château de Malmaison (p. 331). The eclectic architecture of the storied Fontainebleau led Napoleon to call it the "house of centuries." Competitive spirits will get a rise out of **Vaux-le-Vicomte** (p. 321); Louis XIV was so jealous of the contractor's aesthetic sensibilities that he killed the man to avoid being upstaged again. (He then hired the designers to build a little place of his own, Versailles.) **Provins** (p. 334) is a beautiful medieval town that captures a sense of history lacking even in Paris's 2000-year-old streets.

BEST PLACE TO BUY CHEAP, ALMOST NICE, SHOES: Place St-Michel (p. 183).

BEST OUTDOOR MARKETS: Marché Biologique (p. 157) is a cut above the rest, featuring organic food that isn't wimpy. Come for the **Marché St-Quentin's** (p. 157) building, but stay for the wide variety of food. The Monge and Mouffetard markets will make backpackers happy (p. 157).

BEST CENTRAL SIGHTS AT NIGHT: Nôtre-Dame's (see p. 164) most spectacular asset is its *derrière*, extravagant flying butresses and all. The best approach is via the Pont St-Louis. Then walk west along the Seine, and cross over the Pont des Arts to get to the **Louvre courtyard** (p. 242). With the pyramid glow reflecting off the pools of water, it is possble to fool someone that you can walk on it. (Note: you cannot fool yourself.)

RESEARCHER-WRITERS

Silas Alben   5ème, 7ème, 15ème, 16ème, 17ème, 18ème

No flash in the pan, Silas spent his summer serving up some of this generation's greatest hits. A closet foodie, he slashed his way through solid food and liquid nightlife in order to find the only spots worthy of a Let's Go recommendation. Through this "anything less than the best is a felony" whirlwind, the guide gained a bakeries section (p. 158), a slimmed-down Daytripping chapter (p. 313), and a list of the best places to smooch in Paris (p. 166). Struggling with the age-old bar-and-arrondissement question, Silas traded overhyped cool for real places with real people, finding places that were "too legit to quit" from the Mouff' to the bowels of Montmartre. As for his thorough, wry writing, well, you can't touch this.

Judith Batalion   3ème, 4ème, 11ème, 12ème, 13ème, 14ème, 20ème

With the height of Napoleon and the might of Napoleon, Judy stormed the Ile de France. Her first conquest was a swampy mess called the Marais (p. 174). Under her veteran tutelage, the section blossomed into accurate, observant commentary. Among her booty: the little-known Musée de l'Art et d'Histoire du Judaisme (p. 258). Next, Judy mastered the nocturnal world, on land and at sea (p. 287). When she arrived at *pâtisseries*, tarts and croissants crumbled at her feet (p. 159). Her final challenge was her greatest triumph: a revitalized, in-the-know shopping section (p. 301). Who needs a batalion when you have Judy?

Whitney Bryant   1er, 2ème, 6ème, 8ème, 9ème, 10ème, 19ème

First, there was the spear. Then the arrow, rifle, and laser. Then there was the Bryant. Somewhere in the middle was an Airtech flight. With sub-molecular precision, Whitney cruised the cobbled streets of Paris armed with digital camera, two years of Let's Go experience, and a better sense of humor than this book has seen in 2000 years. She may be the most bionic weapon this organization has ever launched. Creative, incisive, damn hilarious prose returned to HQ. Medical services were not overlooked (p. 83). Kids were accommodated (p. 275). *Berthillon* consumed. And in the face of adversity, readers deeply served.

ACKNOWLEDGMENTS

Anna, Judy, Whitney, mom, dad, bro, sis, and Wallydog; Matt Anderson, Amanda Brown, Eli Batalion, Melissa Gibson, Hymie and Sara; the Baldy Boy, Moses, Jodinator, Chas, Ash, DrewBoy, Fra' Nicci, 'Squeala, The J-Ator, and Hylas —SA, JB, & WB

Clearly, this book would still be shining in 1999 without the work of three rockin' researcher-writers. A special thanky-thanks goes to Wode—without whom this ray would never be shining. Taya sees smiles in my last-minute tears. Melissa smiles at me. Only Anne Chisholm understands brain food (Vanessa comes close); only Xian grasps the Go history; only Dan bends map "deadlines." Melissa, Jonathan, Valerie, and Ben get apologies for editorial mishaps. A shockingly large *merci* goes to my 11th-hour helpers: Adam, Alex, Elena, Kate, Nic, Olivia, Alice, James, Marshall, Nicole. In the Cité pod, I *was* fabulous—thanks to the love and warmth of ABS, LBD, LCB, EB, and the LCD. Sarah gets a hug from the bottom(less) of my growling stomach. Deirdre lets me hash it all out. Without Emily, I might still be cowering in my apartment. Without my parents, Paris would have been one QE2 ride too far away. My father gives a really good meal a whole new shape. My mother let me sit on the phone in silence; it's the pauses that matter. My uncle is the source of my late-blooming *wanderlust.* My brother knows exactly when to order dessert. In Paris, I found a place of calm and quiet, *frites* and *croques*, with nights of laughter and brass. For this, I thank Adelaide, Vicky, Gaby, Lauren, and Lizzy, who is the real expert on Paris, birthdays, and *marrons glacés.* At Reid Hall, Brune, *les deux* Christines, and Lucille secured my eternal francophilia. Semmy and Stefa were missed; only I was missing. Rachel was there when I needed her. —AMSM

Editor
Anna M. Schneider-Mayerson
Managing Editor
Taya Weiss

Publishing Director
Benjamin Wilkinson
Editor-in-Chief
Bentsion Harder
Production Manager
Christian Lorentzen
Cartography Manager
Daniel J. Luskin
Design Managers
Matthew Daniels, Melissa Rudolph
Editorial Managers
Brendan Gibbon, Benjamin Paloff, Kaya Stone, Taya Weiss
Financial Manager
Kathy Lu
Personnel Manager
Adam Stein
Publicity & Marketing Managers
Sonesh Chainani, Alexandra Leichtman
New Media Manager
Maryanthe Malliaris
Map Editors
Kurt Mueller, Jon Stein
Production Associates
Steven Aponte, John Fiore
Office Coordinators
Elena Schneider, Vanessa Bertozzi, Monica Henderson

Director of Advertising Sales
Marta Szabo
Associate Sales Executives
Tamas Eisenberger, Li Ran

President
Noble M. Hansen III
General Managers
Blair Brown, Robert B. Rombauer
Assistant General Manager
Anne E. Chisholm

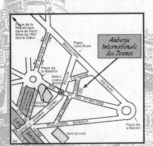

DISCOVER PARIS

Just before dawn, the mist from the Seine drifts lightly into the city, clinging in shreds to stately bridges and capturing Paris in its famed black-and-white essence. Cobbled streets are calm and empty. As pigeons stir the serene quiet in gray smudges of motion, bakeries and pastry shops begin to spin out warm, doughy, flaky treats. In a city known the world over for its pre-eminent cuisine, the morning would be incomplete without the comforting noises and tantalizing smells of the day's first feast.

Paris has many faces, but its soul is rooted in a 2000-year history filled with controversy, decadence, love, revolution, and great food. Some travelers are content with a weekend fling in the city of lights; others take a lifetime to discover its hidden (and not-so-hidden) treasures. The Louvre, the Centre George Pompidou, and the Musée d'Orsay boast some of the most inspiring and well-known artwork in the world, housed in museums that are feats unto themselves; but depending on your mood, happiness could just as well be lurking in a Latin Quarter jazz club, downtown disco, or Left Bank bookstore. This is Paris: brunch in the multi-ethnic, multi-cultural Marais, meet the Mona Lisa's infamous gaze, and dance the night away on the Champs-Elysées.

No matter where you stroll, dance, or tap to the beat, you will be following in the footsteps of someone who came to Paris in search of inspiration and managed to change the world. An entire generation of hungry intellectuals was lured by the call of academic and artistic freedom (not to mention great *croissants*) during and after World War II. A growing community of thinkers and writers flocked to the cafés to argue, write, and drink, hoping for the kind of spark that had inspired genius from Leonardo da Vinci to the revolutionaries of 1789. In the 1940s and 50s Picasso, Sartre, de Beauvoir, and Hemingway took their seats in the cafés of the *6ème* arrondissement; they set the dramatic tone for café life that prevails even today, as great ideas are debated and novels are written under the influence of very potent espresso.

From tiny alleys hiding the world's best bistros to broad avenues flaunting the highest of *haute couture*, from the old stone of the Nôtre-Dame cathedral to the futuristic impulses of the Parc de la Villette, from street performers to the *Comédie Francaise*, from the relics of the first millennium to the celebration of the second, Paris presents itself as both a harbor of tradition and a place of impulse, coyly hiding a discovery around every corner.

FACTS AND FIGURES

- **Population:** 2,152,423
- **Surface area:** roughly 40 sq. mi
- **Most expensive cup of coffee:** US$12
- **Length of the Seine in Paris:** 13 km
- **Total length of tunnels under Paris:** 300 km

HISTORY

ANCIENT PARIS

First settled by the Gallic Parisii clan around 300 BC, the Ile de la Cité offered protection from invaders while the Seine provided fresh water and an easy means of transportation and trade. The conquest of Gaul in 59 BC and of the Parisii island in 52 BC by Julius Caesar's troops intitiated 300 years of Roman rule while catapulting Jules himself to fame, power, and the eventual leadership of the up-and-coming Empire. The Romans, who named the new colonial outpost Lutetia Parisiorum (Latin for "the Midwater-Dwelling of the Parisii"), expanded the city to the Left Bank, building new roads (rue St-Jacques), public baths (Musée de Cluny, p. 254), and gladiatorial arenas (**Arènes de Lutèce**, p. 184), all of which can be seen in remarkably well-preserved ruins in the present-day 5*ème* arrondissement (see **Sights**, p. 182). By AD 360, the Romans had shortened the name of the now-resplendent outpost to Paris. It, and Gaul in general, would remain an integral part of the Empire until its collapse. Rome's legacy includes Catholicism and the French language itself.

Despite Roman prosperity, the advance of **Christianity** and barbarians threatened Roman-pagan rule and provided new heroes, including Paris's first bishop **St. Denis** (Dionysius). He achieved martyrdom after being beheaded in Paris's northern hilltop, Mount Mercury, in AD 260, giving the area its present-day name **Montmartre** (Mount of the Martyr). After the Romans beheaded St-Denis for his attempts to Christianize the city, he allegedly picked up his head and walked north; he collapsed on the site of the current Basilique de St-Denis, the traditional burial-place of France's kings and queens (see **Daytripping**, p. 336).

By the 3rd century AD, the fall of the Empire was imminent. Long-distance trade declined; the army, spread too thin over an enormous area, could not prevent invasions by German delinquents such as the Vandals, Visigoths, and Franks.

When **Attila** and his marauding **Huns** tried to take the city in AD 450, the prayers of **St. Geneviève** reportedly diverted the invaders at Orléans and saved the city, thus making the devout nun Paris's patron saint and giving rise to the belief that Huns don't mess with Nuns (see **Goths**, p. 324).

By the time Rome finally fell in AD 476, Gaul had suffered invasions by Germanic tribes for centuries. Though the honor of sacking the Eternal City was left to the Goths, it was the **Franks** who eventually dominated Gaul and bequeathed it their name. In 476, **King Clovis** of the Franks defeated the Gallo-Romans and took control of Paris, founding France's first royal house (the Merovingians), naming Paris as its capital, and converting the entire city and its invading Franks to Christianity.

300 BC	The Parisii, a Celtic Tribe in Gaul, settle by the Seine on the Ile de la Cité.
52 BC	Caesar invades Gaul. The Romans occupy the Ile de la Cité and call it *Lutetia* and then Paris.
476	King Clovis and the Franks defeat the Romans and make Paris their capital.
768	Charlemagne takes power in Paris.
987	Hugh Capet ascends the throne and tries to unite France's kingdoms.
1163	Construction begins on Nôtre-Dame.
1253	The Sorbonne is founded.
1348-49	The Black Death ravages Paris.
1429	During the Hundred Years War, Jeanne d'Arc tries to liberate Paris.
1572	Catherine de Medici orders the St-Bartholomew's Day Massacre, killing 2000 Protestants.
1643	The Sun King, Louis XIV, takes the throne for 72 years with Versailles as his center court.
1789	The French Revolution.
1793	Napoleon Bonaparte crowns himself Emperor in Nôtre-Dame.
1804	Revolution and the Second Republic.
1848	Baron Haussmann redesigns Paris's boulevards, parks, and arrondissements.
1870	During the Franco-Prussian War, Paris is occupied and defeated.
1889	Eiffel Tower built for World Expo.
1914-18	WWI ends with Treaty of Versailles.
1918-39	Roaring 20s and Depression 30s.
1940	Nazis occupy Paris during WWII; Parisian Jews deported to concentration camps.
1944	Following D-Day, Paris is liberated.
1945	WWII ends; Charles de Gaulle returns.
1954	France's defeat at Dien Bien Phu.
1958	De Gaulle declares the 5th Republic and champions a new constitution.
1962	Algerian War ends France's Colonial Empire in North and West Africa.
1968	May Students' and Workers' Revolt.
1981	François Mitterand elected President and begins his *grands projets* construction program.
1992	France narrowly ratifies the Maastricht Treaty and joins the European Union.
1995	Winter Strikes cripple Paris.
1998	Air France, Train, and Disneyland Paris strikes. France hosts and wins World Cup.

LE COQ The rooster is the symbol of the French people, coming from *gallus* and signifying the Gauls, the progenitors of modern France. From this, we get the conception of the French as proud, war-like people, who arise early, and wake up everyone else. Sometimes, in the press, you will see a reference to *l'Hexagone.* This is another term for France itself, although the reasons behind this are a secret more closely guarded than the recipe for *crème brûlée* (hint: it has to do with the shape of the country). The letters RF, much like the Roman SPQR, stand for République Française, and are often stitched into uniforms, as well as stamped on passports.

The **Merovingian Dynasty** (400-751), named for one of Clovis' predecessors, Merovich, enjoyed almost 300 years of rule before **Pepin the Short's** son, **Charlemagne,** took power in 768 and established the **Carolingian Dynasty** (751-987). On Christmas Day, 800, Charlemagne was crowned Holy Roman Emperor by Pope Leo III. Charlemagne expanded his territorial claims and, although he was illiterate, renewed interest in the art and literature of the ancients, initiating what is known as the **Carolingian Renaissance.** Despite Charlemagne's conquest of most of the Western world, Paris suffered when Charlemagne moved his capital to Aix-la-Chapelle (Aachen, in northwestern Germany). When a wave of invaders consisting of **Viking Normans** and **Muslim Saracens** menaced Europe in the 9th and 10th centuries, Charlemagne's empire fell and France crumbled into fragments.

MEDIEVAL PARIS

As the first millennium approached, France consisted of scores of independent kingdoms, each with its own independent customs, languages, and traditions. The kingdom of France consisted only of the region surrounding Paris, known as the Ile-de-France (and so named because it resembled an island surrounded by the region's many rivers). These medieval kingdoms were organized around the **feudal system,** which bonded peasant-worker vassals to their land-owner lords, who in turn swore allegiance to their kings.

Paris would not return to prominence until the election in 987 of the Count of Paris, **Hugh Capet,** to the throne. Under the rule of the **Capetian Dynasty** (987-1328), Paris flourished as a center of trade, education, and power. Capet's 12th-century descendants attempted to unite the various kingdoms into one centralized country. In 1163, construction began on **Nôtre-Dame cathedral,** which would take over 170 years to complete. The Capetians' most famous king, **Philip II** (1179-1223), expanded Paris's territory, refortified its walls, and paved the city's streets. With the establishment of the University of Paris in 1215 and the Sorbonne later in 1253, Paris reorganized into two distinct parts: the merchant Rive Droite (Right Bank) and the academic Rive Gauche (Left Bank). One of the last Capetians, the holy **Louis IX** (St-Louis), began construction of the **Sainte Chapelle** in 1245, just opposite the rising cathedral of Nôtre-Dame on Ile de la Cité. While new cathedrals inspired **pilgrimages** within France, the **Crusades** (1095-1291) encouraged long-distance travel. Both trade and papal power transferred to France in the 14th century when Pope Clement V moved to Avignon in 1309.

Like most of France's cities, 14th-century Paris suffered the ravages of both the **Black Death** (1348-49) and the **Hundred Years' War** (1337-1453), in which the Burgundians allied with the English against the French and Paris was stuck in the middle. When the last Capetian, **Charles IV,** died in 1328, **Edward III** of England claimed his right to the French throne, his claim was based partly on land in Bordeaux that **Eleanor of Aquitaine** had ceded to England and partly on his relation to the **Duke of Normandy,** whose origins stemmed back to **William the Conqueror** and the **Battle of Hastings** in 1066. Were it not for mythical Joan of Arc, who allied with the Valois King **Charles VII** against **Henry V** of England, Paris might have become an English colony. Instead, Joan of Arc, a French peasant girl from Orléans who heard angelic voices telling her to save France, revitalized the Valois troops, crowned Charles VII king in 1429, and led the Valois to a string of victories. Attempting to win Paris back from the Burgundians in 1429, she was wounded in what is now the 1er arrondissement (see **Sights,** p. 168). Despite her successes, she was captured two years later by the English and burned at the stake in Rouen for heresy. Charles VII recaptured Paris in 1437 and drove the English back to Calais. The **Valois Dynasty** took over where the Capetians left off and moved toward a more unified France.

THE RENAISSANCE

The influence of the **Italian Renaissance** sparked great interest in literature, art, and architecture in 16th-century Paris. In 1527, Charles VII's descendent **François I** commissioned Pierre Lescot to rebuild the **Louvre** in the open style of the Renaissance and to begin work on the **Cour Carrée** (Square Courtyard). François I moved the official royal residence to the new Louvre and invited **Leonardo da Vinci** to his court, where the Italian painter presented **La Jaconde (Mona Lisa)** as a gift to the French king. During the reign of François's successor, **Henri II,** new mansions were added to the **Place des Vosges,** a masterpiece of French Renaissance architecture. However, when Henri II died in the square's Palais des Tournelles in 1563 following a jousting accident, his wife, **Catherine de Medici,** ordered the Tournelles destroyed and began work on the **Tuileries Palace,** the **Pont-Neuf,** and the **Jardins des Tuileries.**

Religious conflict between **Huguenots** (French protestants) and **Catholics** initiated the **Wars of Religion** between 1562 and 1598. After the death of her husband Henri II, Catherine de Medici effectively became France's ruler. A fervent Italian Catholic, she was notoriously ruthless in the savage wars against the French Protestants of the southwest kingdom of Navarre, bordering the Pyrénées.

Influenced by the progressive Humanism of his grandmother **Marguerite de Navarre** (and her Renaissance masterpiece, *The Heptameron*), **Henri de Navarre** agreed to marry Catherine de Medicis's daughter **Marguerite de Valois (Queen Margot)** in an effort to create peace between the two warring kingdoms. But the wedding was a trap. When all of the leading Protestants in France had assembled in Paris for the royal union in 1572, Catherine signaled the start of the St-Bartholomew's Day Massacre. A wild Parisian mob slaughtered some 2000 Huguenots. Henri's life was saved only by a temporary, not-exactly-voluntary conversion to Catholicism. In 1589, Henri de Navarre acceded to the throne as **Henri IV de Bourbon,** ensuring peace, uniting France, and establishing the last of France's royal houses, the **Bourbons.** Upon his ascension to the throne at St-Denis (see **Daytripping,** p. 338), Henri IV waved off the the magnitude of his conversion with the remark, *"Paris vaut bien une messe"* ("Paris is well worth a mass" or, loosely "Paris: what a mess!"). His heart still lay with the Huguenots, though: in 1598, he issued the **Edict of Nantes,** which granted tolerance for French Protestants and quelled the religious wars for almost a century.

Jacques Cartier's discovery of Nouvelle France (Québec) on the North American banks of the St. Lawrence river in 1534, and Samuel de Champlain's establishment of a permanent settlement there in 1608, opened France's chapter on colonial history. This discovery would not only inspire the optimism that characterizes the spirit of the Renaissance but would also ensure France's place with England and Spain in the race for colonial expansion in the centuries to come.

CLASSICISM AND ABSOLUTE MONARCHY

The French monarchy reached its height of power and extravagant opulence in the 17th century. First of the **Bourbon** line, Henri IV succumbed to an assassin's dagger in 1610 and was succeeded by **Louis XIII.** Louis' capable and ruthless minister, **Cardinal Richelieu,** consolidated political power in the hands of the monarch and created the centralized, bureaucratic administration so characteristic of France to this day. He expanded Paris and built the **Palais du Luxembourg** (see **Sights,** p. 186) for the Queen mother, **Marie de Medici,** and the Palais Cardinal, today the **Palais**

Royal, (See **Sights,** p. 170) for himself. This absolutist state, however, strained the already taut social fabric of France as Richelieu manipulated nobles into submission and teased the bourgeoisie with promises of social advancement.

When Richelieu and Louis died within months of each other in 1642, they were succeeded by another king-and-cardinal combo, **Louis XIV** and **Cardinal Mazarin.** Since Louis was only five years old at the time, once again the cardinal took charge, but by 1661 the 24-year-old monarch had decided he was ready to rule alone. Not known for his modesty, Louis adopted the motif of the Sun King and took the motto *'l'état, c'est moi'* ("I am the state"). Following this, he brought a personal touch to national affairs, moving the government to his new 14,000 room palace, **Château de Versailles** (see **Daytripping,** p. 313). Louis made Versailles into a magnificent showcase for regal opulence and noble privilege. The King himself was on display: favored subjects could come to observe him and his Queen rise in the morning, wash, groom, and dine. Royal births were also public events. Louis XIV strove to put down any form of dissent in France, operating on the principle of *"un roi, une loi, une foi"* ("one king, one law, one faith"). Louis reigned for 72 years, revoking the Edict of Nantes in 1685 at the behest of his mistress, and initiating the ruinous **War of the Spanish Succession** (1701-1713). Since the nobles vegetated at court, most didn't even notice their complete loss of political power. From Versailles, Louis XIV commissioned the landscape architect André Le Nôtre to build a wide, tree-lined boulevard called the Grand Cours, today known as the **Champs-Elysées.** The Sun King also built the **Place Vendôme,** and his daughter, the Duchesse de Bourbon, commissioned the **Palais Bourbon,** which today houses the **Assemblée Nationale** (see **Sights,** p. 194).

When Louis finally died in 1715, he had outlasted even his grandsons, and was succeeded by the two-year old **Louis XV.** Coming to its senses, the aristocracy made a grab to reclaim power. Meanwhile, the national debt soared and a series of disastrous wars led to the loss of France's colonies in Canada and India.

The light emanating from the French throne, however, could not eclipse serious domestic problems. The lavish expenditures of Louis XIV and his successors left France with an enormous debt (the improvements to Versailles consumed over half of his annual revenues for many years), and Louis's manipulation of the nobility led to simmering resentment. Part of Louis XIV's decision to move his royal residence to Versailles was his fear of uprising in Paris (see **Daytripping,** p. 313). **Louis XV** continued to live in lavish style at Versailles into the late 18th century. Indifferent to government, Louis XV left the task to his ministers and advisors. As a result, his mistresses Mme de Pompadour and Madame du Barry wielded considerable social and political power.

THE FRENCH REVOLUTION

When **Louis XVI** succeeded to the throne in 1774, the country was in a desperate financial state. While peasants blamed the soon-to-be-*ancien régime* for their mounting debts, the aristo-fat-cats detested the King for his attempts at reform. In 1789, to get out of this no-win situation, Louis XVI called a meeting of the **Estates General,** an assembly of delegates from the three classes of society: aristocrats, clergy, and the bourgeois-dominated **Third Estate.** This anachronistic body had not met since 1614, and after weeks of wrangling over legalities, the Third Estate broke away and declared itself to be the National Assembly. When locked out of their chamber, these delegates moved to the Versailles tennis courts where they swore the **Oath of the Tennis Court** on June 20, 1789, promising to draft a new constitution. Inviting the other Estates to join it, it vowed not to disband until the country had a constitution. The King, while not dismissing the Assembly, sent in troops to intimidate it, inspiring the immortal riposte "the assembled nation cannot receive orders." As rumors multiplied, the initiative passed to the Parisian mob, known as the *sans-culottes* (without breeches) who were angered by high prices for bread and worried by the disarray of the government.

THE REVOLUTION MIGHT BE TELEVISED

The Revolutionaries brought with them, as any successful political regime does, a slew of symbols, paraphenalia, and catchy tunes. In 1789, Lafayette gave us the tricolor, made of three stripes, one each of blue, white, and red. (Random fact: contrary to what your eyes may tell you, the width of each stripe is not the same. The red is larger than the blue, in order to compensate for the different wavelengths of red and blue light.) Everyone worth a 10 Franc coin knows the slogan that was a hit on the dance floor, and matched the beat at beheadings: Liberté, Egalité, Fraternité! A lesser known, and slightly less intimidating icon of the new world order was Marianne, the "muse of the country," whose image is found all over, from city hall sculptures to stamps. Her name, common amongst the commoners, was taken as a symbol of the Revolution's humble roots. She, though a worker, is typically surrounded by curious paraphenalia, like a lion, a tower, a sack of wheat, a Phrygian bonnet, and a baguette (just kidding). And lest we should forget, the Revolution brought a song that will instantly enamor you to Frenchies everywhere: *La Marseillaise.* "*Allons enfants de la Patrie, le jour de gloire est arrivé ...*"

When they stormed the old fortress of the **Bastille** (see p. 209) on July 14th, a destructive orgy exploded across the nation as peasants burnt the records of their debts and obligations. (They had been looking for arms and for political prisoners to liberate, but had found only petty debtors.) The French now celebrate **July 14** *(le quatorze juillet)* as the **Fête Nationale, Bastille Day** (see **Festivals,** p. 282). The Assembly responded in August with the abolishment of feudal privileges and with the **Declaration of the Rights of Man,** which embodied the principles of *liberté, égalité,* and *fraternité.*

Major reforms, like the abolition of guilds and the dismantling of the Church, transformed the nation but could not bring lasting peace to Paris. Cathedrals like Nôtre-Dame and châteaux like Versailles were ransacked and vandalized..

When the petrified king, by now under virtual house arrest, tried to flee the country in 1791 he was arrested and imprisoned; meanwhile, Austria and Prussia mobilized in order to stamp out this democratic disease. In 1793, as the revolutionary armies miraculously defeated the invaders, the radical **Jacobin** faction, led by **Maximilien Robespierre** and his **Committee of Public Safety,** took over the Convention and began a period of suppression and mass execution known as the **Terror.** In January, the Jacobins guillotined the King and his Queen, the much-maligned and misunderstood Austrian, **Marie-Antoinette,** effectively abolishing the monarchy. The ironically named **Place de la Concorde** (Harmony Square) was the site of more than 1300 beheadings (see **Sights,** p. 200). With a **Republic** declared, the *ancien régime* was history.

The Revolution had taken on a radical turn. When the Church refused to be subjugated to the National Assembly, it was abolished and replaced by the oxymoronic **Cult of Reason.** Confusing rationalization with decimalization, a new calendar was introduced with 10-day weeks; though this did not catch on, the Revolutionary **metric** system of measurement is now the international standard. As counter-revolutionary paranoia set in, power lay with the 'incorruptible' **Robespierre** and his McCarthyesque Committee of Public Safety. The least suspicion of royalist sympathy led straight to the gallows; Dr. Guillotine himself did not escape the vengeance of his fearful invention. Fearful of his position, Robespierre ordered the execution of his revolutionary rivals, including the popular **Danton,** before his own denunciation and death in 1794. The **Terror** was over, and power was entrusted to a five-man Directory.

FURTHER READING: THE FRENCH REVOLUTION.
The Oxford History of the French Revolution, William Doyle. Oxford UP (US$15).
A Short History of the French Revolution: 1789-1799, Albert Soboul. Univ. of California Press (US$14).
Citizens: A Chronicle of the French Revolution, Simon Schama (US$26).

NAPOLEON AND EMPIRE

Meanwhile, war continued, as a young Corsican general swept through northern Italy and forced the Austrians to capitulate on his terms. Fearful of his rising popularity, the Directory jumped at **Napoleon Bonaparte's** idea of invading Egypt to threaten the British colonies in India. Though successful on land, the destruction of his fleet at the Battle of the Nile left his disease-ridden army marooned in Cairo. Napoleon responded by abandoning it and hurrying back to France to salvage his political career. Riding a wave of public support, he deposed the Directory, first making himself First Consul of a triumvirate, then Consul for Life in an 1802 referendum, and ultimately **Emperor** in 1804. Napoleon crafted a civil code which would be his most lasting achievement; elements of it remain incorporated into French law today. Though largely faithful to revolutionary ideals, the **Napoleonic Code** bears touches of his autocratic approach to life, re-establishing slavery and requiring wives to show total obedience to their husbands. The code has since been signigicantly revised.

Napoleon also made peace with the Church and reformed the education system, founding the elite Grands Ecoles; but with his popularity contingent on military victory, war remained his specialty. After crushing the Austrians, the Prussians, and the Russians, only Britain remained undefeated, safe in her island refuge.

Napoleon's Paris benefitted from his conquests and booty. With his interest in the ancient Egyptian and Roman worlds, Napoleon brought back countless sculptures from Alexandria and Italy, including the Louvre's *Dying Gladiator* and *Discus Thrower*. He ordered the constructions of the two triumphal Roman arches, the **Arc de Triomphe** and the **Arc du Carrousel,** topping the latter with a gladiatorial sculpture stolen from St. Mark's Cathedral in Venice. Napoleon's many new Parisian bridges, like the **Pont d'Austerlitz,** the **Pont Iéna,** and the **Pont des Arts,** spanned the Seine in elegant style. He ordered the constructionof a neo-Greco-Roman style temple, the **Madeleine,** and he finished the **Cour Carrée** of the Louvre, originally ordered by Louis XIV. But the monument that perhaps best exemplifies Napoleon's Empire style is the **Château de Malmaison** (see **Daytripping,** p. 331). Napoleon and Empress Josephine set the tone for the Empire style, replete with Egyptian motifs and high-waist dresses. Their coronation ceremony was held in Nôtre-Dame and painted by the revolutionary painter **Jacques-Louis David** (and now on display in the Louvre). When Josephine failed to produce an heir, she and Napoleon amicably annulled their marriage, and Josephine moved permanently to Malmaison. The Emperor married **Marie Louise d'Autriche** and his armies pushed east to Moscow.

Napoleon's unravelling came during the Russian campaign of 1812. The Russians withdrew before the advancing *grande armée,* ravaging their own land to deny the enemy food and shelter. After occupying a deserted Moscow, Napoleon was forced to withdraw at the onset of winter. The freezing cold decimated the French ranks, and of the 700,000 men he had led out to Russia, barely 200,000 returned. Napoleon's enemies sensed their time had come, and attacked.

Though ever victorious in battle, Napoleon had lost the support of his war-weary people. In return for abdicating in 1814, he was given the Mediterranean island of **Elba,** and the monarchy was reinstated under **Louis XVIII,** brother of his headless predecessor (**Louis XVII** was Louis XVI's son, who died uncrowned). The story had a final twist: Napoleon, leaving Elba and landing near Cannes on March 26th, 1815, marched northwards to a rapturous reception as the King fled back to England. The adventure of the Hundred Days ended three months later on the field of **Waterloo** in Flanders, Belgium, where the **Duke of Wellington** triumphed as much by luck as by skill. The ex-Emperor threw himself on the mercy of the English, who banished him to remote St. Helena in the south Atlantic, where he died in 1821, probably poisoned by royalist French agents. Popularly regarded as a hero in France, thousands still flock to pay their respects at his grandiose tomb at Les Invalides (p. 252). The **Restoration** of the monarchy followed with Louis XVIII still at the helm, continuing the **Bourbon** dynasty.

REPUBLICS, RESTORATIONS, AND REVOLUTIONS

Though initially forced to recognize the achievements of the Revolution, the rein-stated monarchy soon returned to its despotic ways. When **Charles X** restricted the press and limited the electorate to the landed classes, the people had had enough. Remembering the fate of his brother, Charles abdicated quickly following the **July Revolution** of 1830, and a constitutional monarchy was created under **Louis-Philippe**, Duke of Orleans, whose more modest bourgeois lifestyle garnered him the name "**the citizen king.**" In a symbolic gesture, he kept the Revolutionary tricolor as his flag and his monarchy was constitutional, not absolute. While the middle classes prospered, the industrialization of France created a class of urban poor receptive to the new ideas of **socialism.** When the king and his bourgeois government refused to reform, the people were well practised: there followed the **February Revolution** of 1848 and the declaration of the **Second Republic** with universal male suffrage for the first time. The late Emperor's nephew, **Louis Napoleon,** was elected president. Since the constitution barred him from seeking a second term, he ignored it and seized power in a coup in 1851. Following a referendum in 1852, he declared him-self **Emperor Napoleon III** to popular acclaim. Napoleon III's reign saw the rapid industrialization of Paris, which brought the dangers of a swelling urban popula-tion, pollution, and poverty-stricken living conditions that Balzac's and Hugo's novels describe (see **Literature,** p. 15). Still, during his reign, France's prestige was restored; her factories hummed and **Baron Haussmann** rebuilt Paris, knocking down the medieval street plan (which was conducive to street fighting) and replacing it with grand boulevards along which troops could rapidly be deployed (see **Architecture,** p. 29). Napoleon III also commissioned **Charles Garnier** to design and build the **Opéra,** whose eclectic style stands as the Emperor's finest architec-tural achievement. Despite Napoleon III's extraordinary reconstruction of Paris, his downfall came in July 1870 with the French defeat in the **Franco-Prussian War.**

The confident French did not notice the storm clouds gathering across the Rhine, where **Bismarck** had almost completed the unification of Germany. After tricking the French into declaring war, the Iron Chancellor's troops swiftly over-ran the country. The Emperor was captured and as German armies advanced the **Third Republic** was declared. Paris held out for four months, with the residents so desperate for food that they eventually slaughtered most of the animals in the zoo (see **Sights,** p. 238).

When the government admitted defeat, placing a conservative regime led by **Ado-lphe Thiers** in power, the Parisian mob revolted again in 1871 and declared the Paris **Commune.** For four months, a committee of leftist politicians, the *communards*, (many based in the workers' suburb of Montmartre) assumed power and rejected the Thiers government, which had fled to Versailles. The radical Parisians threw up barricades and declared the city a free Commune. When the city was invaded by vast numbers of French troops in an effort to recapture the city, the *communards* burnt the Hôtel de Ville, the Palais Royal, and Catherine de Medici's Tuileries Palace before retreating ultimately to their last stand in the cemetery of Père Lachaise (see **Sights,** p. 231). The last of the *communards* were shot against the cemetery's **mur des fédérés** on the morning of May 21, 1871. The crushing of the Commune was quick and bloody. Many estimate that over 20,000 Parisians died, slaughtered by their compatriots in about a week. The defeat broke both the power of Paris over the provinces and of the Parisian proletariat over the city.

BELLE ÉPOQUE

After over eighty years of revolutions, violence, and political instability, it is easy to understand why the period of peace, prosperity, and culture that followed between roughly 1890 and 1914 is called the **Belle Epoque** (the Beautiful Period). The colors of the **Impressionists,** the novels of **Proust,** and the **World Expositions** of 1889 and 1900, which gave Paris the **Eiffel Tower,** the **Pont Alexandre III,** the **Grand** and **Petit Palais,** and the first **métro** line, all reflected the optimism and energy of the Belle Epoque. At the same time, however, industrialization and urbanization introduced many new social problems that challenged the Third Republic. Although the government's reforms laid the foundation for the contemporary social welfare state, social tensions continued to grow.

The Third Republic was further undermined by the **Dreyfus affair.** Dreyfus was a Jewish army captain convicted in 1894 on trumped-up charges of treason and then exiled. When the army refused to consider the case even after proof of Dreyfus' innocence was uncovered, France became polarized between the Dreyfusards, who argued for his release (see **Literature,** p. 19), and the reactionary right-wing Anti-dreyfusards, to whom Dreyfus was an unpatriotic traitor regardless of the evidence. The ethnic tensions Zola identified foreshadowed the 20th century conflicts that France would later have to confront in its colonial territories.

WORLD WAR I

After centuries of conflict, the **Entente Cordiale** brought the British and the French into co-operation in 1904. Together with tsarist Russia the three nations of the **Triple Entente** faced the **Triple Alliance** of Germany, Italy and the Austro-Hungarian Empire. Tensions exploded in 1914 when a Serbian nationalist assassinated the Habsburg heir to the Austrian throne, **Archduke Franz-Ferdinand,** in Sarajevo. Germany could have persuaded Austria to exercise restraint but did not. Austria marched on Serbia. Russia, playing the champion of its brother Slavs, responded, and suddenly virtually all of Europe was at war.

After advancing within 50km of Paris, the German offensive stalled at the **Battle of the Marne.** Four years of agonizing trench warfare ensued. Germany's policy of unrestricted submarine warfare on all ships entering European waters provoked the **United States** into entering on the side of the Triple Entente. The entrance of the Americans in 1917 tipped the balance of power in favor of the British and the French (Russia had withdrawn in 1917 in the midst of its own violent revolution), and on November 11, 1918, the fighting ended.

France pushed for crippling reparations from Germany. The Germans were forced to sign the humiliating Treaty of Versailles in the Hall of Mirrors, where the Prussian King Wilhelm I had been crowned Kaiser of the German Reich in 1870 at the end of the Germany's victory in the Franco-Prussian War. The treaty contained a clause ascribing the blame for the war to Germany, and thus lay the foundations for the great resentment that would aid Hitler's rise to power.

THE ROARING 1920S AND THE DEPRESSION 1930S

Parisians poured into the streets and danced with British, Canadian, and American soldiers to celebrate the end of the First World War. Despite the devastation of an entire generation of young men lost in the mustard-gas trenches of Europe, the party would continue into the **roaring 20s,** when artists like **Cocteau, Picasso, Chagall,** and **Man Ray,** intellectuals like **André Gide** and **Colette,** performers like **Josephine Baker,** and expatriates like **Gertrude Stein, Ernest Hemingway, Ezra Pound,** and **F. Scott Fitzgerald** flooded Paris's cafés, dance-halls, and salons.

The party ended with the onset of the **Great Depression** in the 1930s and was exacerbated by the violent right-wing **Fascist demonstrations** of 1934 in which thousands of Parisians marched on Place de la Concorde and stormed the Assemblée Nationale. To combat the Fascists, Socialists and Communists united under **Léon Blum's** left-wing **Front Populaire,** seeking better wages, unionization, and vacation benefits. The Popular Front split over Blum's decision not to aid the Spanish Republicans against the fascist Franco in the Spanish Civil War. The internal tensions betwen the right and the left, fascists and socialists, bourgeois, and workers left France ill-equipped to deal with the dangers of Hitler's rapid rise to power and his impending mobilization on the opposite shores of the Rhine.

WORLD WAR II

After invading Austria, Czechoslovakia, Poland, Norway, and Denmark, Hitler's armies swept through the Ardennes in Luxembourg and blitzkrieged across Belgium and the Netherlands before entering Paris on June 13, 1940. Luckily, curators at theLouvre, sensing the inevitable **Nazi Occupation,** had removed many of its priceless works of art, including the Mona Lisa, and placed them safely into hiding. Photographic images of Nazi footsoldiers and SS troops goosestepping through the Arc de Triomphe are as haunting as the images of shocked Parisians lined up along the Champs-Elysées watching this chilling spectacle of Nazi power. The French signed a truce with the Germans ceding the northern third of the country to the Nazis and designating the lower two-thirds to a collaborating French government set up in Vichy. The puppet **Vichy** government under **Maréchal Pétain** cooperated with Nazi policy, including the **deportation** of over 120,000 French and foreign Jews to **Nazi concentration camps** between 1942 and 1944.

Soldiers broke down doors on the streets surrounding the rue des Rosiers in the largely Jewish neighborhood of the Marais in the 4ème arrondissement and hauled Jewish families to the Vélodrome d'Hiver, an indoor winter cycling stadium, where Jews awaited transportation to French concentration camps like Drancy, in the northeast industrial suburb of Paris near St. Denis, or to camps farther east in Poland and Germany (the **Mémorial de la Déportation** on the Île de la Cité honors those who perished in the Holocaust; see **Sights,** p. 165). France was plagued by many profiteering and anti-Semitic **collaborators** (collabos) who aided the **Gestapo.** Recently, the French government and the Roman Catholic Church in France have acknowledged some responsibility for the deportations and for their moral apathy, but the issue remains controversial.

Despite hardships, Paris's theaters, cinemas, music-halls, and cafés continued to operate, largely for the Nazi soldiers and officers who now flocked to the French capital for rest and relaxation. Many of those restaurants and entertainers who continued to serve and sing for Nazi clients, like the **Moulin Rouge, Maxim's** (see **Sights,** p. 201), **Yves Montand, Maurice Chevalier,** and **Edith Piaf,** would later be criticized as collaborators at the end of the war. French women who took German lovers would, following liberation, have their heads shaved (as film *Hiroshima Mon Amour* illustrates) and be forced to walk in the streets amid the spitting and taunting jeers of their neighbors.

Today France prefers to commemorate the brave men and women of the **Resistance,** who fought in secret against the Nazis throughout the occupation. In Paris, theResistance fighters (or *maquis*) set up headquarters far below the boulevards, in Haussman's **sewers** (see **Museums,** p. 262) and the ancient **catacombs** of the city

---

PARIS IS(N'T) BURNING As the Allied troops made their way to Paris after their successful embarkment on the beaches of Normandy, **Hitler** and the occupying Nazi forces in Paris prepared for a scorched-earth retreat. By August 23, 1944, in obedience to direct orders from Adolf Hitler, *Wehrmacht* engineers had placed mines at the base of every bridge in Paris. Despite Hitler's admiration of Napoleon's monumental tomb in the Invalides (see **Sights,** p. 252) during his smug visit in 1940, more **explosives** were crammed into the basement of the **Invalides,** the **Assemblé Nationale,** and **Nôtre-Dame.** The **Opéra** and **Madeleine** were on the list, and the **Eiffel Tower** was rigged so that it would topple and prevent the approaching Allies from crossing the Seine. A brief order from German commander **Dietrich von Cholitz** would reduce every major monument in Paris—ten centuries of history—to heaps of rubble and twisted iron. Although a loyal Nazi, the cultured general could not bring himself to destroy one of the most beautiful cities in the world. Pestered by Hitler's incessant question, "Is Paris burning?" von Cholitz stalled until the Allies had entered the city and relieved him of his burden. In 1968, he was awarded the French *Légion d'Honneur* for his bravery in the face of a screaming Hitler.

(see **Sights**, p. 217). In London, **General Charles de Gaulle** established the **Forces Françaises Libres** (Free French Forces), declared his **Comité National Français** to be the government-in-exile, and broadcast inspirational messages to his country-man on the BBC (the first of which is now engraved above the **Tomb of the Unknown Soldier** under the Arc de Triomphe). On June 6, 1944, British, American, Canadian, and Québecois troops launched the successful D-Day invasion on the Normandy coast and on August 25th, after four years of occupation, Paris was free. Again, Parisian civilians and Resistance fighters danced and drank with the American, Canadian, and British soldiers who had all worked together to liberate the city. General de Gaulle evaded residual sniper fire to attend mass at Nôtre-Dame and give thanks for the **Liberation of Paris.** His procession down the Champs-Elysées was met with the cheers of thousands of elated Parisians.

After the war, as monuments to French bravery were established in the Musée de l'Armée and the Musée de l'Ordre de la Libération (see **Museums,** p. 259), and as thousands of French Jewish survivors began to arrive at the main Repatriation Center in the **Gare d'Orsay** (see **Museums,** p. 247), there was a great move to initiate change and avoid returning to the social and political stagnation of the pre-war years. General de Gaulle promised new elections once the war's deportees and exiled citizens had been repatriated, and the country drafted a new constitution. In 1946, French women finally gained the right to vote, decades after their fellow English, American, Cuban, South African, Brazilian, Turkish, and Thai suffragists.

POST-COLONIAL PARIS

The **Fourth Republic** was proclaimed in 1944, but its wartime leader de Gaulle quit in 1946, unable to adapt to the deadlock of democratic politics. Like the Third Republic, it lacked a strong executive to keep the country running when the legislature stalemated, and in 14 years saw 25 governments. Despite these problems, the Fourth Republic presided over an economically resurgent France.

The end of the war also signalled great change in France's residual 19th-century **colonial empire.** France's defeat in 1954 at the Vietnamese liberation of **Dien Bien Phu** inspired the colonized peoples of France's other protectorates and colonies, which all gained their **independence** in rapid succession: Morocco and Tunisia in 1956, Mali, Senegal, and the Ivory Coast in 1960. But in Algeria, France drew the line in the sand when Algerian nationalists, backed by the resistance efforts of the **FLN** (Front Libération National), moved for independence. With a population of over one million French *colons* or **pied-noirs** (literally "black feet" French) who were either born in or had immigrated to Algeria, France was reluctant to give up a colony that it had come to regard as an extension of the French *hexagone* (see **Le Coq,** p. 3). The result was the **Algerian War** in 1962,.

The Fourth Republic came to an end in the midst of this chaos overseas. De Gaulle was called out of retirement to deal with the crisis and was voted into power by the National Assembly in 1958. Later that year, with a new **constitution** in hand, the nation declared itself the Fifth Republic. But the Algerian conflict was growing worse. Terrorist attacks in Paris by desperate members of the FLN were met by curfews for North African immigrants. At a peaceful demonstration against such restrictions in 1961, police opened fire on the largely North African crowd, killing hundreds and dumping their bodies into the Seine. Amid the violence in Paris and the war in Algeria, a 1962 referendum reluctantly granted Algeria independence. Almost one hundred years of French colonial rule in Algeria since 1870 abruptly came to an end, and the French colonial empire crumbled in its wake.

But the repercussions of French colonial exploitation continue to haunt Paris, where racial tensions today run high between middle-class French, Arab North Africans, Black West Africans, and Caribbeans, many of whom are second and third generation French citizens.

REBELLION OF 1968

Fiercely nationalist, de Gaulle's foreign policy was a success, delicately playing the USA against the USSR to France's advantage, but his conservatism brought growing domestic problems. In **May 1968**, what started as a student protest against the university system rapidly grew into a full-scale revolt as workers striked in support of social reform. In the spirit of decolonization, revolt, and social change, university students took to the streets, demanding educational and social reform. Frustrated by racism, sexism, capitalism, an outdated curriculum, and the threat of a reduction in the number of students allowed to matriculate, university students seized the Sorbonne. **Barricades** were erected in the **Latin Quarter,** and an all-out student revolt had begun. Students dislodged cobblestones from the streets to hurl at riot police, and their slogan *"Sous les pierres, la plage"* ("under the stones lies the beach") symbolized the freedom of the beach that lay beneath the rock-hard bureaucracy of French institutions. The situation escalated for several weeks. Police used tear gas and clubs to storm the barricades, while students fought back by throwing Molotov cocktails and lighting cars on fire. When 10 million state workers went on strike, paralyzing the country in support of the students, the government deployed tank and commando units into the city.

The Paris revolt—settled, in part, by concessions over university textbooks and curriculum committees—became a model for radical student uprisings in Mexico, Argentina, Québec, and the United States throughout the late 60s and 70s. Less surprising, the Parisian university system was almost immediately decentralized, with various campuses being scattered throughout the city and the nation so that student power could never again come together so explosively as it had in 1968. The National Assembly was dissolved and things looked to be heading for revolution yet again, averted only when fresh elections returned the Gaullists to power. However, the aging General had lost his magic touch, and he resigned following a referendum defeat in 1969.

THE 80S AND 90S: LA HAINE

Three political parties have dominated the French political scene since de Gaulle's resignation in 1969. On the (moderate) right are two parties that formed when de Gaulle's old allies split in 1974: the **Union pour la Démocratie Française (UDF),** led by **Valery Giscard d'Estaing,** and the **Rassemblement pour la République (RPR),** led by **Jacques Chirac.** On the left is the **Parti Socialiste (PS),** in power throughout the 1980s under **François Mitterrand,** and the **Parti Communiste Français (PCF),** which, though influential, holds few seats and little political power.

After de Gaulle's exit, many feared that the Fifth Republic would collapse without its founding father. Yet it endured, though with a different tone. De Gaulle's Prime Minister **Georges Pompidou** won the presidency, with a *laissez-faire* position towards business and a less assertive foreign policy than de Gaulle. In 1974, Pompidou died suddenly, and his conservative (but non-Gaullist) successor **Valéry Giscard d'Estaing** took the presidency. D'Estaing's term saw the construction of the famous **Centre Pompidou** (see **Museums,** p. 251), a center for the arts incorporating galleries and performance space, with a revolutionary design by Richard Rogers and Renzo Piano. This deconstructionist building was turned inside-out, with all the infra-structure, such as service pipes, being used as extra-structural detail, and it marked the beginning of a spate of monumental conceptual architecture in Paris. D'Estaing carried on de Gaulle's legacy by attempting to concentrate on economic development and to increase France's image in international affairs.

In 1981, Socialist **François Mitterrand** took over the presidency and the Socialists gained a majority in the Assemblée Nationale. Within weeks they had raised the minimum wage and added a fifth week to the French worker's annual vacation. Having organized the left into a coherent alliance during the 70s, its political collapse during his presidency forced him to compromise with the right. Mitterrand began his term with widespread nationalization and expanded benefits, but the

PRIVATE! KEEP OUT Mitterrand broke so many hearts during his lifetime that speculation is rife about who wrote the anonymous 1998 novel about an affair with Monsieur le Président, *Un ami d'autrefois* (A Former Friend). Attention focused initially on literary figures such as Françoise Sagan and Francoise Giroud, two well-known writers who led equally renowned live lives with prominent men. Both women denied that they were the late President's "holy prostitute." One French political commentator said: "If all Mitterrand's former mistresses start writing books, then it's a jolly good thing he commissioned the *très grand bibliotheque* (the new national library in Paris)." The most enduring testament to Mitterrand's extramarital affairs is his illegitimate daughter, Mazarine, the fruit of his passion for Anne Pingeot, a museum curator. It was only in 1994, a year before his term ended, that M. Mitterrand appeared with his daughter. Photographs in Paris-Match magazine revealed what the media had known for years, that Mlle Pingeot lived with the President's family in the Elysée Palace. Mazarine Pingeot has stirred bitter controversy by going public to promote her first novel as a way of finally coming to grips with her own identity. The French response? Nobody's perfect. Even the President.

international climate could not support a socialist economy. In the wake of the 1983 recession, the Socialists met with serious losses in the **1986 parliamentary elections**. The right gained control of parliament, and Mitterrand had to appoint the ruthless conservative **Jacques Chirac** as Prime Minister.

At the same time, the **far right** began to flourish under the leadership of **Jean-Marie Le Pen**. He formed the **Front National (FN)** on an anti-immigration platform. The dissolution of France's colonial empire and healthy post-war economy led to the development of a new working class from North Africa and other former colonies. Le Pen was able to capitalize on a racism towards these immigrants that is often phrased—euphemistically—in terms of cultural difference. In the 1986 parliamentary elections, the FN picked up 10% of the vote by blaming France's woes (unemployment in particular) on immigrants and foreigners.

Meanwhile, in this unprecedented power-sharing relationship known as "cohabitation," Mitterrand withdrew to control foreign affairs, allowing Chirac to assume a great deal of domestic power. Chirac privatized many industries, but a large-scale transport strike and widespread terrorism damaged the right, allowing Mitterrand to win a second term in 1988.

The Socialists recovered in the 1988 elections, giving Mitterrand another term (and a victory over Chirac). He proceeded to run through a series of unpopular Socialist governments, one led briefly by **Edith Cresson,** who became France's first woman Prime Minister in 1992 but who was controversial due, in part, to her claim that all Anglo-Saxon men are homosexuals.

Despite controversies over his vast expenditures, Mitterrand's **Grands Projets** plan transformed the architectural landscape of Paris, commissioning multiple projects with modern and grand millennial style. Seeking immortality in stone, steel and concrete, and inspired by Giscard d'Estaing's daring and controversial **Centre Pompidou** (see **Museums**, p. 251), Mitterrand was responsible for the **Musée d'Orsay, Parc de la Villette**, the **Institut du Monde Arabe**, the **Louvre Pyramid**, the **Opéra de la Bastille**, the **Grande Arche de la Défénse**, and the new **Bibliothèque de France.** Although expensive and at times as controversial as the Eiffel Tower was in 1889, Mitterrand's vision for a 21st century Paris has created some of the city's most breathtaking and experimental new architecture. Despite his extraordinary attention to the capital, Mitterrand's other great legacy was his Socialist project to decentralize financial and political power away from Paris and into the hands of local governments outside the Île-de-France. The result was that smaller French cities like Lille and Montpelier became the beneficiaries of new architectural, cultural, and social projects. Mitterrand ensured that Paris would remain the jewel of France, if not its absolute center. The people were more concerned with scandals involving Mitterrand's ministers than his grandiose projects, though, and the left suffered crushing parliamentary defeats in the early 90s which forced him to again appoint a conservative Prime Minister.

In the mid-nineties, Mitterrand admitted to two startling facts. The first was that he had collaborated with the Vichy government in the second world war, before joining the Resistance in 1943. The second, and more shocking, was that he was seriously ill with cancer, and had been since the beginning of his first term as president. (He had been issuing fake health reports for the previous fourteen years.)

In 1995 Mitterrand chose not to run again because of his failing health, and Jacques Chirac was elected to the French presidency. With unemployment at 12.2% at the time of the election, Chirac faced a difficult year. The crisis ended in a massive and prolonged **Winter Strike** by students, bus drivers, subway operators, electricians, and postmen, who protested against budget and benefit cuts proposed by Chirac and his unpopular Prime Minister, **Alain Juppé.** For weeks, Paris was paralyzed and Parisians were forced to walk, bike, and rollerblade to work and to market. Stores kept reduced hours, mail delivery came to a halt, and occasional blackouts and ubiquitous traffic jams plagued the city. Despite hardships, many Parisians were glad to see the spirit of 1968 still alive and to rediscover their neighbors, local cafés, and corner markets while grounded in their neighborhoods by the transport strikes.France moved slowly into 1996, recovering from the strike and mourning François Mitterrand, who died in early January. Later that year, President Chirac was denounced around the globe for conducting underground **nuclear weapons tests** in the **South Pacific.**

RECOMMENDED READING: FRANÇOIS MITTERRAND.
Dying Without God: François Mitterrand's Meditations on Living and Dying,
Fran-Olivier Giesber. Arcade (US$13).

The ascendancy of the right was short-lived; in 1997, Chirac dissolved the parliament, only to find the election returning a socialist parliament. Chirac was forced to accept his one-time presidential rival **Lionel Jospin** as Prime Minister. As the head of the Socialist majority in the Assemblée Nationale, Jospin was appointed in 1998. Though Chirac will remain in office until 2002 at least, the left is firmly in control of France (and most of western Europe), although voters are prone to conservatism, especially regarding the European Union. Chirac's Gaullist **RPR** is the dominant conservative party, with Jospin's **PS** leading the socialist left. Anti-immigrant resentment escalated in 1993 when Interior Minister Charles Pasqua proposed there be "zero immigration" and initiated the "Law Pasqua," which gave the police greater freedom to interrogate (and intimidate) immigrants in France. A recent split between Le Pen and his deputy has caused a fragmentation of the far right, with two different **FN** parties competing for the extremist vote.

One of the most important challenges in the 80s and 90s has been the question of European integration. Despite France's support of the creation of the **European Economic Community (EEC)** in 1957, the idea of a unified Europe has met considerable resistance. Since the inception of the 1991 **Maastricht Treaty,** which significantly strengthened economic integration by expanding the 13-nation EEC to the more closely knit **European Union (EU),** the French have manifested profound unease about further integration, as many fear a loss of French national character and autonomy. Hoping that a united Europe would strengthen cooperation between France and Germany, Mitterrand led the campaign for a "Oui" vote in France's 1992 referendum on the treaty. This position lost him prestige; the referendum scraped past with a 51% approval rating. The **Schengen agreement** of 1995 created a 6-nation zone without border controls. 1999 saw the extension of this zone to the entire EU bar the U.K., Ireland, and Denmark, as well as the birth of the European single currency, the **Euro.** Some historians believe this "shared sovereignty" marks but the first step toward an ultimate political union.

The good news is that immigrants, their children, and grandchildren are changing the face of France. Arabic expressions like *kif-kif* ("it's all the same") have become accepted parts of spoken French, black performers like MC Solaar and Teri Moïse top the French music charts, and multi-ethnic restaurants have changed the way Paris thinks about French cuisine. For a better idea of the racial climate in France, see **Post-Colonial Francophone Literature** (p. 21), **Post-Colonial Paris** (p. 11) **Film,** or rent Mathieu Kassovitz's films *La Haine* and *Café Au Lait.*

LITERATURE

MEDIEVAL AND RENAISSANCE LITERATURE

Medieval France, however, produced an extraordinary number of literary texts, starting at the beginning of the 12th century with popular **chansons de gestes,** stories written in verse that recount tales of 8th-century crusades and conquests. The most famous of these, the **Chanson de Roland** (1170), dramatizes the heroism of Roland, one of Charlemagne's soldiers, killed in battle in the Pyrenées in 778. While *chansons de geste* entertained 12th century masses, the aristocracy preferred more refined literature extolling knightly honor and courtly love, such as the *Lais* (narrative songs) of **Marie de France,** the *romans* (stories) of **Chrétien de Troyes,** and Béroul's adaptation of the Irish legend of **Tristan et Iseult.**

During the 13th century, popular satirical stories called **fabliaux** celebrated the bawdy and scatalogical with tales of cuckolded husbands, saucy wives, and shrewd peasants. **Villehardouin's** and **Froissart's** historical chronicles stand in contrast to the mythical **Queste du Saint Graal** *(Quest for the Holy Grail)*, **La Mort d'Artu** *(Death of King Arthur)*, and Guillaume de Lorris and Jean de Meung's tract on courtly love, the **Roman de la Rose.** The 14th and 15th centuries produced the feminist writings of **Christine de Pisan,** the ballads of **François Villon,** and comic theater like the hilarious **Farce de Maître Pathelin.**

The Renaissance in France produced literary texts that challenged Medieval notions of courtly love and Christian thought. Insired by Boccaccio's *Decameron* and the Italian Renaissance, Marguerite de Navarre's *Héptaméron* employed pilgrim stories to explore the innovative ideas of Humanism. **Calvin's** humanist treaties criticised the Catholic Church and opened the road to the ill-fated Protestant Reformation in France. With Jacques Cartier's founding of Nouvelle France (Québec) in North America in 1534, French writers began to expand their perspectives on themselves and the world. **Rabelais's** fantastical *Gargantua and Pantagruel* imaginatively explored the world from giants' point of view, and **Montaigne's** *Essais* pushed the boundaries of individual intellectual thought. While the poetry of **Ronsard** and **Du Bellay,** the memoirs of **Marguerite de Valois,** and the works of **Louise Labé** contributed to the Renaissance's spirit of optimism and change, they also expressed anxiety over the atrocities of the 16th-century Wars of Religion.

SEVENTEENTH-CENTURY CLASSICISM

The founding of the **Académie Française** in 1635 gathered 40 men to regulate and codify French literature, language, and rhetoric. The rules and standards they set loosely at this time would soon solidify into rigid regulations, launching the "Classical" age of French literature. The Académie has ever since acted as the church of classical French letters (for more on the Académie, see **Sights,** p. 189).

Seventeenth-century French literature was not as rigid as the Académie, however. In the realm of philosophy, French thinkers reacted to the skepticism that had arisen in the wake of Humanism by establishing the foundations of **Rationalism,** which championed logic and order. As science emerged from the shadows of religion, **René Descartes** placed his trust firmly in logic and set out to understand the world. The greatest of French philosophers, in his 1637 *Discourse on Method* Descartes proved his own existence with the irrefutable deduction "I think, therefore I am." A gifted mathematician, the father of analytical geometry also introduced the notation 'x' for an unknown quantity. Opposed to Descartes was the equally diverse genius of **Blaise Pascal**. After a youth misspent inventing the mechanical calculator and the science of probabilities, he became a devotee of Jansenism, a Catholic reform movement which railed against the worldliness of the Jesuit-dominated Church. Retiring from public life, he expounded the virtues of solitude in his best-known work, the *Pensées* (1658). **La Rochefoucauld's** *Maximes* painted a more pessimistic view of man's relationship to the world. **La Fontaine's** *Fables* and **Charles Perrault's** *Contes de ma mère l'oye* (Fairy Tales of Mother Goose) explored right and wrong in more didactic and deceivingly childish ways with such tales as La Fontaine's *Le Corbeau et le Renard* (The Fox and the Crow) and Perrault's *Cendrillon* (Cinderella).

Also Jansenist was the classically-oriented tragedian **Jean Racine**, whose *Phèdre* (1677) is considered by many to be the greatest play of French literature. His comic counterpart, **Molière,** satirized the social pretensions of his age in comedies of manner, which combined classical structures with hilarious farce. Molière's comedies, such as *L'Ecole des femmes, Le Misanthrope, L'Avare, Le Malade imaginaire*, and *Tartuffe*, use back-talking servants, comic dialogue, farce, and caricature to poke even more fun at French society. Even at the court of Versailles, where many of his plays were first performed to the accompaniment of music by Lully, Molière used comedy to express his own hilarious version of social criticism. Molière's actors formed the basis for the the **Comédie Française**, the world's oldest national theatre company which still produces the definitive versions of French classics in at its theatre in Paris (see **Arts and Entertainment**, p. 269). Molière himself died in 1673, during a performance of his satire on hypochondria, *L'Invalide Imaginaire* (The Imaginary Invalid).

THE ENLIGHTENMENT

The tensions created in French society under Louis XIV would give rise to a period of intense philosophical activity in the years leading up to the Revolution. This **Enlightenment** was dominated by the intellectual and literary activity of three men; **Charles-Louis de Montesquieu, Voltaire,** and **Jean-Jacques Rousseau.** The oldest of the three, Montesquieu achieved recognition in 1721 for the *Persian Letters*, a compelling and damning picture of Parisian culture seen through the eyes of two visiting Persians. This was followed in 1748 by *The Spirit of Laws*, which revolutionized political theory by its emphasis on the principles rather than the institutions of government. Meanwhile, Voltaire (whose real name was François Marie Arouet) illuminated the entire century with his insistence on liberty and tolerance. A period of exile across the Channel in 1726-1728 laid the basis for his seminal *Philosophical Letters* (1734), an exposition of the merits of the English constitution. Voltaire's reputation as a writer rests on his short stories, or *contes*, such as *Candide* (1758), a comic refutation of the optimistic philosophy that "all is for the best in the best of all possible worlds." In the same year he chose to live at Ferney on the Franco-Swiss border; with enemies in high places all over Europe, he found it expedient to be able to switch country at short notice. Even more unwelcome were the ideas of **Jean-Jacques Rousseau.** Whilst Voltaire and Montesquieu proposed progressive reforms, Rousseau thought that society needed to be entirely reshaped. In *On the Social Contract* (1762), he opens with the statement that "man was born free, but he is everywhere in chains", and proceeds to develop his utopian vision. Asserting that only in solitude can true freedom be realized, he proposed the total subjugation of people to the state. Able to act upon the united "general will" of its people, the republic itself could act as a free, lone super-being.

Voltaire and Rousseau were both members of the *philosophes* (philosophers), a diverse group of thinkers bent upon social reform. They were led by **Denis Diderot,** who directed the landmark *Encyclopédie* in collaboration with the scientist **Jean d'Alembert.** This enormous undertaking aimed to encompass the entire body of human knowledge, with contributions from all the leading French intellectuals of

NOBLESSE OBLIGE In early July, 1789, the Marquis de Sade shouted to the crowds to storm the Bastille, where he had been incarcerated for his sexual perversions. Unfortunately for him, he was transferred to an insane asylum just days before the mob took his advice. In fact, he had already been sentenced to death and executed in 1772—though only in effigy, since he had fled the Kingdom. Taking refuge in his château at Lacoste, in the Lubéron, de Sade and his wife preyed upon local women until he was finally imprisoned in 1777. He spent the next 13 years writing plays and novels, such as *120 Days of Sodom*. Released in 1790, he spoke on behalf of the Revolution but was condemned to death again (for moderatism of all things!); he was saved this time by the fall of Robespierre. Finally, with Napoleon in charge, he was forced to play a submissive role, and remained in captivity until his death in 1814. Though his wholesale abuse of the peasantry might seem to rank among the worst excesses of the *ancien régime*, others detect in his amorality the ultimate expression of the intellectual liberation of the Enlightenment.

the time; of the 35 volumes published between 1752 and 1780, Diderot edited 28. Somehow he also found time to write novels, including *Rameau's Nephew*, in which he questions the meaning of virtue via the life of the good-for-nothing nephew of **Jean-Philippe Rameau** (see **Music**, p. 30)

The Enlightenment's search for an ideal society inspired stories of fantastic journeys. While **Bernardin de St-Pierre's** *Paul et Virginie* depicted love as an idyllic Roccoco painting, the **Marquis de Sade's** *Philosophy in the Boudoir* and **Laclos's** *Les Liaisons Dangereuses* explored darker sides of the erotic. **Beaumarchais's** plays *The Marriage of Figaro* and the *The Barber of Séville* foreshadowed the Revolution and the end of aristocratic and monarchical excess.

After a century of philosophical fomentation, from an intellectual standpoint the Revolution seemed inevitable. Concerned more with the implementation of the *philosophes'* agenda rather than its further development, this time of social upheaval saw little in the way of new political thought. Amid the turmoil, science rapidly advanced, despite the suppression of the Academy of Sciences in 1793. The suppression was opposed by **Antoine-Laurent Lavoisier**, the "father of modern chemistry," who demonstrated that oxygen (which he named) was indispensable for respiration. His political activism led him to the guillotine in 1794. **Pierre-Simon de Laplace**, another friend of Lavoisier, set troubled minds to rest in 1787 when he demonstrated the stability of the solar system, but he had a far greater effect on world history as an examiner for the Artillery corps. Impressed with a young Corsican cadet's mathematical skill, Laplace recommended Napoleon Bonaparte for a commission in the army.

ENLIGHTENMENT BACKLASH

The 19th century saw an emotional reaction against Enlightenment rationality. Though anticipated in some ways by Rousseau, the expressive ideals of **Romanticism** first came to prominence in Britain and Germany rather than analytically minded France. One of the first essays into the Romantic era in France came with the publication of **François-René de Chateaubriand's** novel *Attala* (1801) inspired by the time he spent waiting out the excesses of the revolution with native Americans around Niagara falls. Goethe and the German Romantics were greatly admired by the stylish **Mme de Staël**, whose *Delphine* (1802) and *Corinne* (1807) reflect upon the injustices of being a talented woman in a chauvinist world. It was during this time that the novel became the pre-eminent literary medium, with such great writers as **Stendhal** and **Balzac**, but it was **Victor Hugo** who dominated the Romantic age. While his novels *The Hunchback of Notre-Dame* (1831), and *Les Misérables* (1862) have achieved near-mythical status, he was also a prolific playwright and poet. An early blow for feminism was struck by **Aurore Dudevant**. After leaving her husband and her childhood home of La Châtre in 1831, she took the pen-name **Georges Sand** and started a

REBEL WITHOUT A CAUSE The life of **Arthur Rimbaud** makes most modern teen idols seem as adventurous as Trappist monks. During the Franco-Prussian war of 1870, the 16-year old Rimbaud ran away from home to start a revolution, but was foiled when he was arrested at the train station for traveling without a ticket. Undeterred, a year later he ran away again to defend the Paris Commune, abandoning it only days before it was suppressed. The politically disillusioned Rimbaud put his trust in the pen rather than the sword, and set out to change the world through poetry. By abandoning traditional forms, trusting to his visions, and torturing himself to achieve new experiences he aimed to "derange all the senses." The confident 17-year-old sent some verses to Paul Verlaine, who was so impressed that he invited Rimbaud to stay with him. Arriving in Paris in 1871, Rimbaud seduced the older man who abandoned his wife and child; after two years they separated acrimoniously, with Verlaine shooting Rimbaud in the wrist. In 1875, at the ripe old age of twenty-one, Rimbaud abandoned poetry and set off to explore the world. Traveling to Indonesia and Egypt, he settled down to a peaceful career running guns into Ethiopia. Cancer forced his return to France in 1891, and he died that year in Marseille. Fame came during his absence after Verlaine, believing him dead, published the works of "the late Arthur Rimbaud," and today he is recognized as one of the greatest French poets.

successful career as a novelist, condemning the social conventions which bound women into unhappy marriages in books such as *Valentine* (1832). Sand was as famous for her scandalous lifestyle as for her prose, with a string of high-profile relationships, including a 10 year dalliance with Frédéric **Chopin** (see **Music**, p. 31).

Normandy also provided the setting for **Gustave Flaubert**'s Realist novel *Madame Bovary* (1856), in which the author developed his characters' psychology through detailed descriptions of their experiences. Prosecuted for immorality in 1857, Flaubert was narrowly acquitted. Six months later, **Charles Baudelaire** was not so lucky; the same tribunal fined him 50 francs. The poet gained a reputation for obscenity, despite the fact that the condemned work, *The Flowers of Evil*, is now recognized as the most influential piece of French poetry of the 19th century.

Baudelaire participated in the 1848 revolution, and his radical political views closely resembled those of the anarcho-socialist innovator **Pierre-Joseph Proudhon.** Born in poverty, Proudhon's sharp mind won him a scholarship to college at Besançon and then Paris. There, in 1840, he published the leaflet *What is Property?* His inflammatory reply was that "property is theft." Put on trial in 1842, he only escaped punishment because the jury refused to condemn ideas it could not understand. A pivotal figure in the history of socialism, Proudhon inspired the *syndicaliste* trade-union movement of the 1890s. An more optimistic philosophy was provided by the **Positivism** of **Auguste Comte.** Comte anticipated that science would give way to a fully rational explanation of nature. Science certainly demonstrated a great deal of progress at the time; **Louis Pasteur** showed that disease and fermentation were both caused by micro-organisms; famous for his milk **pasteurization** process, he also solved the problem of transporting beer long distances without its spoiling. (Pasteur's institute is now a museum; see **Sights**, p. 220.)

Like artistic Impressionism, Symbolism reacted against stale conventions and used new techniques to capture instants of perception. Led by Stéphane Mallarmé and Paul Verlaine, the movement was instrumental in the creation of modern poetry as we understand it today, particularly through the work of the precocious Arthur Rimbaud (see graybox below). In 1880, a loose grouping of novelists proclaimed the birth of Naturalism, a development of Realism in which attempted to use a scientific, analytic approach to dissect and reconstruct reality. Obscure in theory, in practice there is little to unite the works of such writers as Emile Zola and Guy de Maupassant. Zola, who went to school with Cézanne, defended the maligned Impressionists during his early days as a journalist, but his life work was Les Rougon-Macquart, a 20-novel series which uses the life of the title family to examining every aspect of French life during the Second Empire.

BELLE ÉPOQUE TO WWII

Works that confronted the **Dreyfus Affair's** anti-Semitism, like Zola's *J'accuse*, lay the foundation for a whole new literature in France that would explore issues of individual identity—including sexuality, gender, and ethnicity—in 20th century France. The decadence and social snobbery of the turn of the century was captured by **Marcel Proust** in the seven-volumes of *Remembrance of Things Past* (1913-1927). Revolutionary in technique, this autobiographical portrait of upper-class society during the Belle Epoque inspires a fanaticism which puts Star Wars to shame. Like most serious French authors of the time, Proust published in the influential *Nouvelle Revue Française*. Founded in 1909, this journal rose to prominence under the guidance of **André Gide,** who won the Nobel Prize in 1947 for morally provocative novels such as *The Counterfeiters* (1924). Throughout his career, Gide was engaged in rivalry with Catholic revivalist **Paul Claudel.** Claudel struggled unsuccessfully to persuade Gide that divine grace would eventually overcome greed and lust, the basic theme behind plays such as *The Satin Slipper* (1924).

Like Proust, Gide and **Colette** wrote frankly about homosexuality. Proust's portraits of Belle Epoque Parisians in *Sodom and Gomorrah*, Gide's homerotic novels like *l'Immoraliste*, and Colette's sensual descriptions of 20s opium dens and 30s cabarets in *Le pur et l'impur* and *La Vagabonde* inspired later 20th-century feminist and homoerotic writing, like **Jean Genet's** *Querelle* (1947), **Monique Wittig's** *Les Guerillères* (1967), and **Hervé Guibert's** *Fou de Vincent (Crazy about Vincent)*.

A leading member of the avant garde, **Guillaume Apollinaire** vocally supported innovation in all the arts, which was amply present in his own work. Two of his anthologies stand out; the well-loved *Alcools* (1913) and the innovative *Calligrammes* (1918), in which he created visual poems (or 'calligrams') by using words to draw out pictures on the page.

As in art, film, dance, and music, 20th-century French literature moved toward abstraction. Inspired by Marcel Duchamp and the nonsensical art movement called Dadaism, the theatrical collaborations of choreographer Diaghelev, set-designer Picasso, composer Satie, and writer **Jean Cocteau** during WWI laid the foundation for even further abstraction following the war. In France, Dada took a literary bent under the influence of Romanian born **Tristan Tzara,** whose poems of nonsensically scrambled words attacked the structure of language. Tzara's colleagues **André Breton** and **Louis Aragon** soon became dissatisfied with the anarchy of Dada, and set about developing a more organized protest. This burst upon the world in 1924 with the publication of Breton's first *Surrealist Manifesto*, in which he expounded its guiding principal: the artistic supremacy of the subconscious. What was not created consciously was difficult to understand consciously, though, and most Surrealist poetry defies analysis. Surrealism exercised a great influence on later absurdist French theater, such as **Eugène Ionesco's** *Rhinocéros*, expatriate **Samuel Beckett's** *Waiting for Godot*, and **Sartre's** *No Exit*.

Meanwhile, the rising threat of Nazi Germany spurred a call to arms by writers, led by the indomitable **André Malraux**. Active in the Chinese and Spanish civil wars, the former supplied the subject for his masterpiece, *The Human Condition* (1933). Another adventurer, **Antoine de Saint-Exupéry**, used his experiences as an early aviation pioneer to create classics such as the *The Little Prince* (1943).

EXISTENTIALISM AND FEMINISM

The period following the war was intellectually dominated by **Jean-Paul Sartre**, Grand High Master of **Existentialism**. This held that life, in itself, was meaningless; only by choosing and then committing yourself to a cause could existence take on a purpose. Sartre committed his own ideas to the stage, dominating French theatre in the 1940s and 1950s. In *No Exit* (1946), four people in a small room discover they are there for eternity: as they find out, *"L'enfer, c'est les autres"* (Hell is other people). Sartre's *Being and Nothingness*, became a kind of Existentialist

SECOND, WITHOUT SEX Everyone knows that Simone de Beauvoir and Jean-Paul Sartre went together like peanut butter and jelly, but there was a slightly eccentric current to their bond, one that went far beyond a box-lunch simile. They met after Jean-Paul had failed his exam at the Ecole Normale Supérieure (see p. 183). She, beautiful, and he, less than beautiful (to put it politely), studied together constantly in the following year, and spent most of their free time watching Westerns at the cinema. The following time around, big, bad Jean-Paul came in first on the exam, and Simone just behind in second place (how this affected her feminist writings, no one can say). Their intense friendship, purported to be purely Platonic throughout, lasted a lifetime. When Sartre died, de Beauvoir lied upon his corpse overnight, so distraught was she.

manifesto, which declared that God is dead and that it is the absurd that governs our lives. He also wrote four novels, but dissatisfied with his work, he abandoned the medium to his companion **Simone de Beauvo**ir. Existentialist and seminal feminist, de Beauvoir made waves with *The Second Sex* (1949), an essay attacking the myth of femininity.

Its famous statement, "One is not born, but becomes a woman" inspired a whole generation of second-wave **feminism** in the 50s, 60s and 70s. With their exploration of feminine and gender identity, writers like **Marguerite Duras** *(L'Amant)*, **Nathalie Sarraute** *(Tropismes)*, **Marie Cardinal** *(Les Mots Pour le Dire)*, **Christine Rochefort** *(Les Stances à Sophie)*, **Hélène Cixous** *(Le Rire de la Méduse)*, **Luce Irigaray** *(Ce Sexe Qui n'en est Pas Un)*, and **Marguerite Yourcenar** *(Le Coup de Grace)*, the first woman member of the Académie Française, sparked feminist movements in France and abroad. The founding of the publishing house *Des Femmes* (see **Books,**) in the 70s ensured that French women writers would continue to have a means of expressing themselves in print.

Though **Albert Camus** is often classed with Sartre, he could scarcely be more different. Born into poverty in Algeria, Camus edited the Resistance newspaper *Combat* while Sartre was working under censorship in occupied Paris. Camus' existentialism was marked by a sense of decency; commitment was not enough if it was unfair to others. He achieved fame with his debut novel *The Outsider* (1942), which tells the story of a dispassionate social misfit condemned to death for an unrepentant murder. Camus' play *Caligula* (1945) was an early example of **Anti-Theatre,** whose adherents laid bare the strangeness of life and exposed the inadequacies of language. During the 50s, the existentialists met at the cafés of Montparnasse to discuss the absurd world around them.

In Irish emigré **Samuel Beckett**'s *Waiting for Godot* (1953), two men wait and wait, without knowing why or for whom. *Rhinoceros* (1960), by Romanian immigrant **Eugène Ionesco,** portrays the protagonist's perplexity as everyone else turns into a horned african mammal.

LATE TWENTIETH CENTURY

Experimentation with narrative and perspective in the 50s and 60s led to the creation of the **nouveau roman** (the new novel), which abandoned conventional narrative techniques and created new ones, such as *sous conversation* (what people think as they converse). Among its best known exponents were Sarraute, Duras, and **Alain Robbe-Grillet** *(Projet pour une révolution à New York)*. .

From the 70s to the 90s, criticism, theory, and philosophy have exerted a great influence over literary, political, and intellectual life in France. To many, **Postmodernism** is just another French fashion, unduly mimicked by provincial thinkers everywhere. To the French intelligentsia, however, postmodernism is often associated with America, the land of superficial, eclectic mass cultural. In *The Postmodern Condition: A Report on Knowledge*, **Jean François Lyotard,** who is not a ballerina by trade, nonetheless turned a routine report commissioned by the

Canadian government into an artful, spinning and whirling manifesto of postmodernism, arguing that modernist thought was too stable and thus constraining. It was not long before a slew of French thinkers were hashing out the problems of contemporary life, discussing our audio-visual, information intensive world in terms of paradoxes and word-games. Literary theory was profoundly affected by the notion of **deconstruction,** whereby an author's text is rigorously examined for unconscious writing habits that often undermine the author's intentions. The founder of this method was the famous **Jacques Derrida,** who would have done well to deconstruct his own surname. Over recent decades, Postmodern discourse and its cousin, **Poststructuralism,** have continued to flourish, and the French tendency to turn intellectuals into celebrities has had many personalities to lionize or deride. In the 60s, as **Sartre's** cigarette smoke ceased to cloud up cafés and classrooms, the postmodernists moved in. Among the greatest of these thinkers are historical "archaeologist" **Michel Foucault,** thinker turned sci-fi fan **Jean Baudrillard,** and more recently the feminist body **Hélène Cixous.** To many, these intellectuals and their colleagues represent the most important thinking done in the post-war world.

The 80s and 90s have also seen the emergence of new writers in France such as **Annie Ernaux** and **Hervé Guibert,** as well as a growing number of works by authors of North African origin, such as **Mehdi Charef's** *Le thé au harem d'Archi Ahmed* (1983). Late 20th-century political conflicts over immigrants, racism, and xenophobia have renewed interest in post-colonial Francophone literatures.

POSTCOLONIAL FRANCOPHONE LITERATURE

In the 20th century, many voices have emerged from France's former colonies and protectorates in the **Antilles** (Martinique and Guadeloupe), the **Carribean** (Haiti), **North America** (Québec), **North Africa** (the **Maghreb:** Algeria, Tunisia, Morocco), and **West Africa** (Senegal, Mali, Ivory Coast, Congo, and Cameroon). Although written in French, these novels, poems, and plays speak out against France's colonial exploitation, from the conquest of the Antilles and Carribean in the 16th-18th centuries and the occupation of North and West Africa in the 19th century to decolonization in the 1960s and the emergence of independent states (see **History,** p. 11).

Beginning in Paris in the 1920s with the foundation of the **Négritude** movement by African and Antilles intellectuals **Aimé Césaire** (Martinique) and **Léopold Sédar Senghor** (Senegal), Francophone literature began to flourish. Césaire's *Cahiers d'un retour au pays natale* and Senghor's *Anthologie de la poésie nègre et malgache* attempted to define a shared history and identity among black peoples in Africa, the Caribbean, the Antilles, and North America. Their work and the subsequent founding of the press **Présence Africaine** (see **Shopping,** p. 309) inspired generations of Francophone intellectuals on both sides of the Atlantic, the most celebrated of whom is **Franz Fanon** *(Les Damnées de la Terre)* from the Antilles.

While France relinquished its protectorates Morocco and Tunisia with relatively little resistance in the 1950s, its refusal to part with Algeria, where over one million French *pied noirs* resided, erupted into the Algerian War in 1960s (see **History,** p. 11). As a result, much Maghrebian writing is marked by a search for cultural identity, a conflict between colonial and post-colonial history, and a desire to create new and independent states. Some of the most prolific of these writers are **Assia Djébar** *(Les Femmes d'Alger dans Leur Appartement)* from Algeria; **Driss Charibi** *(La Civilisation...Ma Mère!)* from Morocco; and **Albert Memmi** *(La statue de sel)* from Tunisia. North African immigration to France in the 70s, 80s, and 90s has had a profound impact on French language, culture, and politics. Many second- and third-generation Maghrebian writers in France, such as **Mehdi Charef** *(Le thé au harem d'Archi Ahmed)* have written about *beur* (slang for an Arab resident of France) culture, racism, and the difficulties of cultural assimilation.

The Indochinese victory against the French at Dien Bien Phu in 1954 offered a brief period of colonial liberation before the Vietnam War again brought occupation, exploitation, and violence. While many Vietnamese writers have abandoned the linguistic weight of their colonial past, some like **Linda Lê** *(Calomnies)* continue to write in French about issues of cultural identity and contemporary politics.

Québecois writers have struggled to maintain their linguistic and cultural identity. Since the *Révolution Tranquille* (Quiet Revolution) in the 1960s, the combined work of the *FLQ* (Front du Libération du Québec), the *Parti Quebecois*, the *Loi 101* (a law promoting the French language in Québec and making English illegal), and the Québecois people to gain independence from Anglophone Canada has inspired generations of Québecois writers, such as **Michel Tremblay** *(Les Belles Soeurs)* and **Gaston Miron** *(L'Homme Rapaillé).*

FURTHER READING: LITERATURE. After WWI, a "lost generation" of literati moved to Paris from Ireland, England, and America—**James Joyce, Ernest Hemingway, Ford Maddox Ford, Ezra Pound, Gertrude Stein,** and **F. Scott Fitzgerald** among them. Above all, the expatriates sought a freedom in Paris they could not find at home, a sentiment best summed up by Gertrude Stein's famous statement, "America is my country, but Paris is my hometown."

This spirit has governed much of Paris's 19th- and 20th- century expatriate writers. For those who want to read about Paris through their eyes, or through those of some famous native Parisians, the following list may be helpful:

Anglophones: **Charles Dickens's** *Tale of Two Cities,* **Henry James's** *The Ambassadors* and *The American,* **Ernest Hemingway's** *A Moveable Feast,* **James Baldwin's** *Giovanni's Room,* **Henry Miller's** *Tropic of Cancer,* **Anaïs Nin's** *Journals,* **Gertrude Stein's** *Autobiography of Alice B. Toklas,* **Somerset Maugham's** *The Moon and Sixpence,* **George Orwell's** *Down and Out in Paris and London,* and **Ned Rorem's** *Paris Diary.* **Patrick Suskin's** big hit *Perfume: The Story of a Murderer,* tells the tale of an olfactorily-blessed homicidal maniac. **Art Buchwald's** recent memoirs, *I'll Always Have Paris* and *Leaving Home* recount his stories of post-WWII Paris after the Liberation. One of the most elegant expatriate portraits of Paris is **Edmund White** and **Hubert Sorin's** *Our Paris: Sketches from Memory.*

Frenchies: **Victor Hugo's** *Les Misérables,* **Emile Zola's** *Nana* and *Thérèse Racquin,* **Honoré de Balzac's** *Old Goriot* and *Cousin Bette,* **Eugène Sue's** *Les Mystères de Paris,* **Marcel Proust's** *Remembrance of Things Past,* **Colette's** *The Pure and the Impure* and *The Vagabonde,* **Celine's** *Journey to the End of the Night,* and **Simone de Beauvoir's** *Mandarins.*

FINE ARTS

ROMAN COINS, MEDIEVAL MASTERPIECES

Gallo-Roman artifacts, coins, torques, and sculptures that have survived the centuries now rest in the Musée Carnavelet (see **Museums,** p. 258). Much of Paris's surviving **Medieval** art reflects religious and spiritual virtues. Stunning stained glass and intricate stone facades at **Chartres** (see **Daytripping,** p. 323), **Sainte-Chapelle,** and **Nôtre-Dame,** among other churches, retold biblical stories for the benefit of the (usually illiterate) medieval churchgoer. Replicas of Parisian and provincial ecclesiastical masonry can be seen at close range in the Musée National des Monuments Français (see **Museums,** p. 264), while brilliant stained glass and intricate tapestries, like the **Lady with the Unicorn,** are displayed in the **Musée de Cluny** (see **Museums,** p. 254). The rise of monasteries brought the art of illumination to its height, as monks added ornate illustrations to the manuscripts they recopied. The Cluny, the Musée Marmottan (see **Museums,** p. 259), and the Chantilly Museum (see **Daytripping,** p. 330) display detailed manuscripts in gold-leaf and brilliant blues, including the Chantilly's **Très Riches Heures du Duc de Berry,** an illuminated prayer book whose portrayal of country peasants ushered in the naturalism of the **Northern Renaissance.**

THE RENAISSANCE

Inspired by the painting, sculpture, and architecture of the **Italian Renaissance,** 16th-century France imported its styles from Italy. François I brought the best Italian artists up north to decorate his palace at Fontainebleau. **Leonardo da Vinci** came and brought the **Mona Lisa (La Jaconde)** as a royal gift to the French monarch at the Louvre, where she still resides today. Later, under Louis XIV, French art flourished. **Nicolas Poussin** elaborated the theory of the "grand manner," with its huge canvases and panoramic subjects taken from mythology and history. The French **Académie Royale,** founded in 1648, came to value this style above all others, and all subsequent French painters had to contend with these weighty "academic" precepts. Claude Lorraine's idyllic landscapes defined the Académie's landscape tradition. In 1725, the Académie inaugurated annual **Salons,** held in the vacant halls of the Louvre. Sober scenes of everyday life by Chardin and Greuze stood in contrast to the flamboyant pastel Rococo colors of Boucher and Fraggonard, whose work covered the gold-embossed salons and bedrooms of the aristocracy with flying cherubs and mischievous escapades (see p. 24). **Watteau** painted the *fêtes* and secret *rendez-vous* of the aristocracy, and **Elisabeth Vigée-Lebrun** painted the French nobility, like Marie-Antoinette, with a charm that years later earned her great success with the court of Russia.

When François I inherited a strong, united country in 1515, the time had come for France's initiation into the new artistic universe. Exposed to the Renaissance during his Italian campaigns, the King invited the greatest living artists to work in France, including **Leonardo da Vinci** and **Il Rosso.** At his new palace of **Fontainebleau** (1527; see **Daytripping,** p. 321), Italian designers and French craftsmen laid the foundations for the French Renaissance style. The **Ecole de Fontainebleau** combined Italian and Flemish influence with a French sensibility in the works of father-and-son team **Jean and François Clouet.** Known for its subtle eroticism, the Fontainebleau school shared the Renaissance movement away from religious subjects toward scenes of courtly life and classical mythology.

Baroque sculpture also centered around Versailles, from **Giradon's** outdoor *Apollo Tended by the Nymphs* (1666), to **Antoine Coysevox**'s busts reflected in the Hall of Mirrors. Baroque painting became a clear favorite after **Simon Vouet** returned from Rome in 1627, but he was soon obscured by the genius of **Nicolas Poussin.** Poussin, who spent the majority of his career in Rome, is crediting with developing the **Academic** style, espoused by the *Académie Royale* after its foundation in 1648. Under style dictator Le Brun, the Academy became the sole arbiter of taste in all matters artistic.

JACQUES-LOUIS DAVID
Unlike many artists, Jacques-Louis David bridged the gap between the *ancien régime,* the French Revolution, and Napoleon's Empire without losing his head. David managed to survive and prosper by ingeniously painting with the times. From his pre-revolutionary paintings **(The Tennis Court Oath),** to his neo-classical revolutionary paintings **(The Oath of the Horatii, The Defeat at Thermopylae, The Rape of the Sabine Women, The Death of Socrates,** and **The Death of Marat)** that praise the Republican virtues of the Revolution using Greek and Roman themes (see **Musée du Louvre,** p. 242), David honored the mob and the monarch of the moment. When the **Louvre** opened the royal collection to the public in 1793, David used mirrors to amplify the sight angles of his work and to increase his favor with the new leaders of the Revolution. In the early days of the First Empire, David changed allegiance, moved to the camp of Napoleon, and painted **The Coronation of Napoleon.** Napoleon's love of Egyptian, Roman, and Greek motifs reflected his admiration for Roman emperors. David was one of the first to exploit this new iconography, which, along with the Empress Josephine's high-waist dresses, came to be known as the **Empire style.**

The early 18th century brought on the **Rococo** style. Reacting against the formal simplicity of Baroque ideals, its asymmetric curves and profusion of ornamentation were perhaps more successful in the **Louis XV style** of interior design than architecture. Catering to the tastes of the nobility, **Antoine Watteau** and **François Boucher** painted playful pastoral landscapes and scenes from courtly life.

Napoleon's reign saw an entrenchment of Neo-Classicism as he used the artistic language of ancient Rome to buttress the image of his reign. **Jacques-Louis David** created giant canvases on Classical themes, painting in a clear style which sacrificed atmosphere for detail and design. Perhaps his most famous work is the *Le Sacre de Napoleon (Coronation; 1807)*, depicting the moment Napoleon crowned himself Emperor. In the decorative arts, the **Empire style** recalled the days of Anthony and Cleopatra, as Roman models were supplemented by a frenzy inspired by Napoleon's Egyptian exploits.

CLASSICAL AND ROMANTIC SCHOOLS

While the Romantic movement scarcely affected French architecture, its influence in the visual arts was immense. Even though Ingrès took up the neo-classical mantle of David after the latter's death in 1825, his interest in medieval and religious themes betrayed the Romantic taste for all things Gothic. His most celebrated work, the sensuous reclining nude of *La Grande odalisque* (1814; now in the **Musée du Louvre,** p. 242), prefigures the oriental fascination of his younger contemporary **Eugène Delacroix.** A master of Romantic art, Delacroix's dramatic shading and masterly use of color contrasts sharply with Ingres restrained, academic painting. The bold brushwork seen in *La Liberté guidant le peuple (Liberty Leading the People; 1830; also in the Louvre)* would prepare the way for Impressionism later in the century. Still, Ingres's sinuous lines and sensual surfaces contrast with Delacroix's emphasis on brilliant colors, dramatic movement, and emotional excess in works like the orientalist *Death of Sardanopolous* (see the **Musée du Louvre,** p. 242 and **Musée d'Orsay,** p. 247). **Théodore Géricault** exploited the dramatic effects of Romanticism with darker and ominous overtones in his famous painting *The Raft of the Medusa* (also in the Louvre). Meanwhile the invention of **photography** by Parisians **Nièce** and **Daguerre** provided a new artistic medium, sparking an intense debate over the relative merits of painting and photography.

Disillusioned with Napoleon III and the Second Empire, artists and writers like Nadar and Baudelaire gathered in the cafés of the Latin Quarter and starved proudly in the garrets of Paris. Like the itinerant gypsies after which they were named (and the Puccini opera that depicted them, *La Bohème*), the **Bohemians** proclaimed for themselves a life free from normal conventions. While urban Bohemians starved in the attics of Paris, artists like **Jean-François Millet** and **Henri Rousseau** followed the **Romantic** urge to escape to nature, retreating to **Barbizon** to paint the Fontainebleau forest and the French peasantry (see **Musée d'Orsay,** p. 247). Influenced by the social-utopian theories of Charles Fourier, **Gustave Courbet** rejected Academic historical painting in favor of a "living art" that would portray what he saw around him. With France's growing 19th-century colonial empire in North and West Africa, Indochina, and the Antilles, orientalism and the exotic became inspirations for fashion, painting, and the decorative arts. Painters like **Jean-Léon Gérôme** and later **Paul Gauguin** created lush scenes of Turkish baths, snake-charmers, and Tahitian villagers. Responding to this new obsession with orientalism or *chinoiserie*, Japanese *ukiyoe* prints, Chinese lacquered furniture, and East Asian silks, kimonos, and vases decorated Parisian homes from 1853 on.

IMPRESSIONISM

While Neoclassicists and Romantics treated themes far removed from everyday life, in the 1830s a group of painters settled near Fontainebleau to paint nature as they saw it. Led by **Théodore Rousseau** and **Jean-François Millet**, the artists of the

Ecole de Barbizon celebrated the land and the humble life of those who worked it. In the 1850s, this grew into the **Realist** movement under **Gustave Courbet,** whose treatment of everyday subjects on a grand scale shocked the public. When his painting *The Artist's Studio* (now in the Louvre) was rejected by the Universal Exhibition of 1855, he responded by opening his own "Pavilion of Realism." The tempestuous seascapes he painted around Etretat, Normandy would profoundly influence the young Edouard Manet (see below).

As the Indusrial Revolution spread its arm across France, a rapidly evolving society called for an art better able to deal with its incessant change. In the 1860s, the young **Edouard Manet** began to move away from Realism when he found the handling of his subject of more interest than the fidelity of its reproduction. The small group of artists who clustered around him came to be known as the **Impressionists,** and they were united more by this emphasis on visual effect itself rather than any particular style or technique. The sunny landscapes of **Claude Monet,** the rosy-cheeked faces of **Pierre-Auguste Renoir,** and the working scenes of **Camille Pisarro** all combine prosaic, contemporary subjects with a sense of immediacy and freshness. They achieved this new revolutionary style by painting outside, directly from life, rather than in the studio from sketches. Accustomed to the smooth surfaces and clear-cut lines of Academic painting, critics objected to the rough brushwork and blurry quality of the Impressionists. **Edouard Manet's** *Déjeuner sur l'Herbe* was refused by the Salon of 1863 due to its almost-x-rated content; it was later shown at the **Salon des Refusés,** along with 7000 other rejected salon works (see **Musée d'Orsay,** p. 247).

Many modern viewers are surprised to learn that Impressionism was once considered shocking art. In 1874, a group of young radicals lead by **Monet** and **Pissarro** established an independent exhibition, which included Monet's *Impression: Soleil Levant.* A snide critic derogatorily labeled its creator an "Impressionist." Monet and his colleagues adopted this name, and the show became an annual event. Urban Impressionist paintings, like **Dégas's** *Le verre d'absinthe* and **Caillebotte's** *Rue de Paris, temps de pluie,* focused on cafés, boulevards, cabarets, and ballets. At the same time, the Impressionists' credo of *plein air* painting inspired Monet's *Water Lilies.*

But the first law of art states that every movement inspires an equal and opposite reaction, and in the 1880s and 1890s the **Post-Impressionists** concentrated their technical explorations in search of solidity and permanence, pushing painting further toward abstraction. Meanwhile, **Pointillists** like **Seurat** explored a highly scientific type of dot-matrix painting, with works made up of tiny dots in primary colors to build up a final image and in *La Grande Jatte* (1885) millions of such points bathe his picture in a natural light unattainable by conventional techniques. **Paul Cézanne** created solidity and mass using geometric forms and a limited palette; his technique was so painstakingly slow that he had to use artificial fruit for his still lifes. Also drawn to Provence was the dutch painter **Vincent van Gogh,** whose expressive personal style of swirling brush strokes and intense colors left the viewers of his own time cold. In sculpture, **Auguste Rodin** and his student, muse, and lover **Camille Claudel** focused on a highly energetic, muscular shaping of bronze and stone. Rodin finally achieved fame and notoriety at the age of 35, when critics accused him of casting *The Age of Bronze* (1877) directly from a live model. His influence on the course of sculpture, though, would come from later works such as the towering *Balzac* (1898). Rather than a lifelike portrayal of the novelist, the coarse modeling of Rodin's broodily draped figure paves the way for abstraction (see **Musée Rodin,** p. 247).

During the last decades of the 19th century, Bohemia had moved outside Haussmann's city to the cabarets and cafés of **Montmartre**—an oasis for artists and bourgeois alike from the sterility of the modern city below. **Toulouse-Lautrec** captured the spirit of the Belle Epoque in the vibrant silkscreen posters that covered Paris as well as in his paintings of brothels, circuses, and can-can cabarets. **Art Nouveau** transformed architecture, furniture, lamps, jewelry, fashion, book illustrations, and even the entrances to the Paris métro (see the **Musée d'Orsay,** p. 247).

TWENTIETH CENTURY

When the Mona Lisa was stolen from the Louvre in 1907, the police arrested writer-critic Guillaume Apollinaire (see p. 19), having noticed the interest shown in it by his friend Pablo Picasso. The most prolific artist of the twentieth century, **Picasso** developed a bewildering number of styles during his 80 year career. Arriving in Paris in 1900, in 1907 he shot to notoriety for *Les demoiselles d'Avignon*, which shocked both for its illicit subject (the title referred to a street in Barcelona's red light district) and for the angular treatment of the figures which presaged **Cubism**. Developed by Picasso and **Georges Braque,** this radical movement was really a continuation of Cézanne's geometric approach; by presenting the subject from many different angles at once, the artist tried to capture the whole three-dimensional object on a flat plane. Cubist painting sought to represent the idea of an object rather than the object itself. The word 'Cubism' was coined by Picasso's friend and great rival **Henri Matisse.** In a 1905 trip to Collioure in the Languedoc, struggling with pointillism, Matisse abandoned it and started squeezing paint from the tube directly onto the canvas. Shocked Parisian critics called the artists associated with the expressive new style *Fauves* (wild animals), and the name stuck. While **Fauvism** made only a brief splash on the canvas of time, Matisse's art remained a vibrant celebration of life; in mature works such as *The Dance* (1931-32) his mastery of line and color animate the composition to create a sense of movement and joy (see **Musée d'Art Moderne de la Ville de Paris,** p. 258).

   Marcel Duchamp added an element of dynamic movement to Cubism with his *Nude Descending a Staircase*. **Utrillo** and **Man Ray** formed part of the same set, while **Eugène Atget,** a photographer who documented the streets and store-fronts of Paris, provided Picasso and his friends with photographic "sketches" to use as a basis for their art. **Marc Chagall's** Cubist fairy-tale pictures of his native Russian villages anticipated Surrealism.

   The first world war shattered Europe's complacency, and a generation of young artists turned their backs on a world descending into chaos. Appearing first in Zurich, this nihilistic anti-art movement became known under the nonsense name of **Dada** (or **Dadism**). Already in 1913 Duchamp had exhibited *Bicycle Wheel*, a bicycle wheel on a stool. The first of his 'ready-mades,' by exhibiting commonplace objects Duchamp started off the whole but is it art? question. Horrified by the slaughter of the war, Duchamp switched from painting futurist machine-worshiping images to leading the Dadaists, a group of artists who focused on nonsense and non-art. Duchamp drew a mustache on a picture of the Mona Lisa to mock the institutions that led to the deaths of an entire generation of young men during the war, and the Dadaists exhibited a urinal titled *La Fontaine* to graphically illustrate the relationship of art to mass-produced industrial objects and the ready-made iconography of the 20th century.

   Like Dadaism, Surrealism rejected all traditional notions of art, but it was fundamentally a constructive movement, plumbing the hidden creative depths of the mind. The paintings of **René Magritte**, **Joan Miró**, **Max Ernst** and **Salvador Dalí** produced disturbing images of fallen angels, disfigured bodies, and melting clocks, reaching a far larger public than his own work. Rather than directly expressing the subconscious, the dreamlike fantasies of surrealist art aim to unsettle and liberate the unconscious creativity of the viewer. See p. 19 for the parallel movements in literature.

   During the 30s, photographers like **Brassaï** and **Kertész,** both emigrants from Hungary, recorded the streets and *quartiers* of Paris, especially Montmartre, in black and white. In 1937, Picasso exhibited **Guernica** in the Spanish pavilion of the Paris International Exposition. Depicting the bombing of a Basque town during the Spanish Civil War, *Guernica* provided one of the century's most moving condemnations of the horrors of war.

   As the Germans advanced on Paris, the masterpieces of the Louvre were evacuated to basements and gardens in Paris and the provinces. Within days of the German entry into Paris, the invaders filled the Opéra and the theaters, which staged uncontroversial farces to avoid offense. Braque and Picasso just kept painting, and musicians pulled out their Wagner and Beethoven scores. On May 27, 1943, hundreds of "degenerate" paintings by **Miró, Picasso, Ernst, Klee,** and **Léger** were destroyed in a bonfire in the garden of the Jeu de Paume. Tens of thousands of masterpieces belonging to Jewish collectors were appropriated and shipped to Germany. Only recently have serious inquiries into **stolen Nazi art** been addressed, as investigations into annulled Jewish bank accounts in Switzerland become a focus of public attention. Later 20th-century experiments in photography, installation art, video, and sculpture, such as Pierre et Gilles's exploitation of kitsch and camp in their iconographic and homoerotic photography, can be seen in the permanent collections and temporary exhibitions of the **Centre Pompidou** and the **Fondation Cartier pour l'Art Contemporain** (see **Museums,** p. 261).

ARCHITECTURE

ROMAN BATHS AND MEDIEVAL CATHEDRALS

The **Romans** rebuilt Paris in the image of their own city, with vineyards, baths, arenas, and the north-south rue St-Jacques/St-Martin, a road that led to Rome and that was a prototype for the major Parisian axes of today. The remnants of Roman Paris can be found in the partially reconstructed **Arènes de Lutèce,** the **baths** of the **Hôtel de Cluny,** and the residential **excavations** in the square in front of Nôtre-Dame. An early type of architecture modeled after Roman basilicas blossomed into the massive **Romanesque cathedrals** of the 11th century. The oldest parts of **St-Germain-des-Prés** show the immense walls and semicircular arches characteristic of this style. Prosperity in the 12th century allowed the invention of a new, far more ornate architectural style—the **Gothic.**

In their quest for height, master builders developed the ribbed vault, small rectangular vaults supported by diagonal arches and strung together in series to create the main nave. **Nôtre-Dame-de-Paris** (started 1163; p. 163) is an example of the early Gothic style, but it is with the cathedral of **Chartres** (built 1194-1220; p. 323) that the art reached maturity. The use of flying buttresses, exterior supports which leap from the side-aisles to support the nave, allowed ceilings to soar up to 15 meters into the air. With the walls freed of structural duties, they could be filled with windows, so that from within the ceiling appears to float above on a sea of shimmering stained glass. Dominating the ends of the nave, the circular rose window became common in the 13th century, and the way in which the 'petals' radiate out from the centre gave its name to the **Rayonnant** style. This emerged around 1230, when the ultimate height limit of stone vaulting was reached and attention turned from structural innovation towards decoration. Windows became still larger and the supporting stone was carved into delicate tracery; a delectable example is the **Sainte-Chapelle** (finished 1248; p. 165), with an almost continuous glass curtain on three sides of the chapel. From this period, Paris also gained the **Basilique de St-Denis,** Europe's first Gothic cathedral (see **Daytripping,** p. 334).

King Philippe Auguste made Paris into a defensive capital, responding to regular raids by beginning work on the fortress of the **Louvre** and building the first walls around the city. The 12th century also saw the basic segregation that still characterizes the city's geography: Philippe Auguste's construction established political and ecclesiastical institutions on the **Île de la Cité,** academic ones on the **Left Bank,** and commercial ones on the **Right Bank.** By the 14th century, Paris's 80,000 inhabitants made it one of the great cities of Europe; at the same time, the 100 Years' War with the English and Burgundians threatened the city's lifeblood. To cope with the danger, Charles V replaced the earlier wall with a larger wall on the Right Bank, guarded by the new **Bastille** fortress. Although destroyed in the 17th century, the wall's path can be followed down boulevard St-Martin and boulevard Beaumarchais (the northern and eastern edges of the 3*ème* arrondissement).

RENAISSANCE CHÂTEAUX

French Renaissance architecture, though perfected at **Fontainebleau,** had been developing since the 16th century. Gunpowder had made nonsense of medieval siege tactics, and as war moved to the battlefield once fearsome châteaux could be transformed into stately pleasure domes. The style reached maturity in the 1540s, as architects succeeded in combining the influences of antiquity and the Italian High Renaissance with local needs and traditions. François I had his nest at Fontainebleau, Catherine de Medici had hers at Blois and Chenonceau. Although both repeatedly promised to renovate the Louvre and move back into the city, nothing came of it except Catherine's **Palais Tuileries** which was destroyed by Revolutionaries in the 19th century anyway. Henri IV had different plans; after fighting for almost four years to get into Paris, he was not about to leave. He changed the face of Paris, building the **Pont Neuf** and the **Place des Vosges.** He widened the roads and banned merchant overflow into the streets to accommodate carriages. His efforts were not quite enough; obstacles blocking the street slowed his carriage and enabled François Ravaillac to leap in and assassinate him in 1610. Merchants constructed the first lavish **Hôtel de Ville** (see **Sights,** p. 180).

The 17th century found France at the acme of cultural power, as **Louis XIII** and **Louis XIV** recognized the power of art to project an image of unchallenged royal authority. With the court established in the Île de France, Paris became the screen on which they projected their grandeur. **Baroque** architecture was introduced from Italy by Louis XIII's mother, **Marie de Medici,** who commissioned the **Palais de Luxembourg** (1615; p. 186), but it reached its peak with the château of **Vaux-le-Vicomte** (1657; p. 332), which brought architect Louis **Le Vau,** artist Charles **Le Brun** and landscaper Louis **Le Nôtre** together for the first time. Louis XIV was so impressed with their work that he commissioned them to build him a new palace at **Versailles** p. 313). When Le Vau died, architectural responsibility for the palace passed to **Jules Hardouin-Mansart,** François' great-grand-nephew, who had gained fame for his church at **Les Invalides** (1675; p. 252). Under the approval of his egocentric master, the size of the palace was more than tripled until it could house a quarter of the king's retinue of 20,000. Louis XIV banned Gothic architecture; Italianate domes popped up across the city's skyline.

REVOLUTIONARY VANDALS AND NAPOLEONIC MONUMENTS

Not too surprisingly, destruction outweighed construction during the French Revolution. Most of its impressive architectural achievements were temporary: an artificial mountain on the Champ de Mars, a cardboard Neoclassical interior for Notre-Dame, and sundry plaster statues of Liberty. More lasting were the various defacements, especially of churches and kings' statues. Like Louis XIV and Marie Antoinette, the biblical kings of Nôtre-Dame's grand **portals** all lost their heads, which were rediscovered only in 1977 and are now on display at the Musée de Cluny (see **Museums,** p. 254). Versailles was ransacked and **vandalized.** However, the Jacobins developed parts of the city previously owned by the Church and the nobility.

Napoleon made further improvements in the early 19th century; he planned cemeteries, dug sewers, numbered houses, widened the streets, and carried the artistic riches of a continent to the Louvre. Such decadent art could not long escape the attentions of the interfering *philosophes*, and under the thundering criticism of Diderot and company, the playful Rococo style gave way to severe **Neoclassicism,** exemplified by **Jacques-Germain Soufflot's** grandiose Eglise Ste-Geneviève (1757). Ste-Geneviève was deconsecrated during the Revolution and re-dedicated as the **Panthéon** to the *"great men of the fatherland."* It now serves as the fitting final resting place of **Voltaire** and **Rousseau** (see p. 184)

The Neoclassical agenda was best fulfilled in the two architectural monuments dedicated to the Empire's glory. The **Eglise de la Madeleine** (see p. 201), a giant imitation of a Greco-Roman temple, was commissioned in 1806 as a shrine to the Empire's *Grande Armée* (Great Army); however, this role was quickly taken over by the imposing **Arc de Triomphe** (see p. 198), begun in the same year but not finished until 1836. Napoleon also had a château built for Josephine at **Malmaison** (see p. 331). See **History,** p. 7 for more on the fiesty General.

NINETEENTH CENTURY: HAUSSMANIZATION

Despite revolution and political instability, the 19th century was a prosperous time for Parisian architecture. The government's decision that France's major railroads should all terminate in Paris guaranteed that the city would thrive as the center of manufacturing, a magnet attracting thousands of migrants from the provinces. Industrialization made many living quarters more pleasant: glass became cheap and windows proliferated. But unchecked growth continued to swamp improvements, and many of Paris's one million people lived in congested slums.

In the realm of architecture alone, Neoclassicism reigned throughout the 19th century. While the romantically-inspired **Gothic revival**, rampant in England, had its French disciples (notably the "great restorer" **Viollet-le-Duc,** 1814-1879), the dominant Ecole de Beaux Arts taught a strictly classical curriculum. Innovation came through the back door, as the use of iron for buildings allowed vast spaces to be spanned; in the **Bibliothèque Ste-Geneviève** (1838), Henri Labrouste used an iron framework to fashion a light, airy reading room in an otherwise wholly classical building. The ultimate expression of 19th-century classicism is to be found in **Charles Garnier's** Paris opera house (1862-1875; p. 203), a vast, ornate stone fantasy. The **Opéra Garnier** was part of **Baron Georges Haussman's** grand redesign of the capital in the 1860s.

Although traces of the past abound, parts of pre-19th-century Paris would be virtually unrecognizable to a modern visitor. Today's city is the Paris remade under the direction of Haussman. From 1852 to 1870, Haussmann transformed Paris from an intimate medieval city to a centralized modern metropolis. Commissioned by Napoleon III to modernize the city, Haussmann tore long, straight boulevards through the tangled clutter and narrow alleys of old Paris, creating a unified network of **grands boulevards.** These avenues were designed not only to increase circulation of goods and people but also to make Paris a work of art, reflecting the elegance of Second Empire style. Not incidentally, the wide avenues also impeded insurrection, limiting once and for all the effectiveness of street barricades. Haussmann redesigned the Bois de Boulogne (see **Sights,** p. 234) and the Bois de Vincennes (see **Sights,** p. 238), as well as the **Parc des Buttes de Chaumont** (see **Sights,** p. 230).

The changes during this period were momentous. The city doubled its area and Haussmann shifted the boundaries of the 20 existing *quartiers*, establishing Paris's present organization into **20 arrondissements** (see **Orientation,** p. 72). Five of Paris's seven hills were leveled; only **Montmartre** and the **Montagne Ste-Geneviève** remain. Twelve thousand structures were destroyed to create 136km of straight avenues. Sweeping away the medieval tangle of streets, Haussmann replaced them with tree-lined avenues bordered by majestic buildings; the wide sidewalks he created permitted the establishment of outdoor cafés and kiosks, and encouraged that peculiarly Parisian form of entertainment, **flânerie;** the art of walking with no purpose but to see and be seen. The transformation of Paris continued into the early 20th century. Traffic circles, ubiquitous **pissoirs** (public urinals), and electrical lamps symbolized the city's modernity.

Architecture finally reawoke as engineers began taking matters into their own hands. In 1876, **Gustave Eiffel** together with architect **Louis-Auguste Boileau** designed a new building for **Au Bon Marché,** the world's first department store, creating large skylit interior spaces in which to display merchandise. Nicknamed the "magician of iron," Eiffel is most famous for the star exhibit of the Universal Exhibition of 1889, a certain tower that bears his name (see **Sights,** p. 190). Twice as tall as any other building in the world, its framework construction excited violent passions; most Parisians thought it unspeakably ugly, not to mention unstable. A century later, of course, it stands as the best-loved landmark in France. Truly a monumental figure, Eiffel also designed the internal structure of the Statue of Liberty. The World Expositions of 1889 and 1900 inspired the **Métropolitain** subway system and the **Grand** and **Petit Palais** (see **Museums,** p. 259).

TWENTIETH-CENTURY MODERNISM AND SUBURBAN MISERY

Paris survived both World Wars fundamentally unscathed. In the interwar period, a few radical architects began to focus on new building materials. A Swiss citizen who lived and built in Paris, Charles-Edouard Janneret, known as **Le Corbusier,** was a pioneer in the new material of reinforced concrete. A prominent member of the **International School**, Le Corbusier dominated his field from the 1930s until his death in 1965, and is famous for such buildings as the *Unité d'habitation* in Marseille (1947). Following his principles, the building itself is raised on stilts, while the absence of ornamentation brings out the essential qualities of its concrete construction. Housing 1600 people on 16 stories, the original design featured two shopping streets, a roof garden and an outdoor theatre.

During the postwar years, architects began to make buildings that would stand out rather than blend in. Most of the changes were made in the outer arrondissements, like the 13*ème* and the 17*ème*, leaving the historic core intact. The old marketplace of **Les Halles**, now a subterranean shopping mall, was torn down, and the *quais* of the Left Bank, like those of the Right, were almost converted into expressways—acts that inspired popular calls for conservation.

The city's history of expansion into the surrounding territory dates back to the emergence of working-class districts *(faubourgs)* in the late 18th century. In the 19th century, rail lines and trolleys made the suburbs more inviting. During the 50s and 60s, the government sponsored housing developments and a plan for a ring of "new towns" surrounding Paris, including **Marne-la-Vallée,** where **Disneyland Paris** is located. The 50s also initiated the construction of large housing projects or **HLMs** *(habitations à louer modéré)*, concrete monstrosities originally intended as affordable housing, but which have become synonymous with suburban misery, racism, and the exploitation of the immigrant poor.

TWENTIETH-CENTURY FUTURISM

The 80s and 90s produced some of Paris's newest, most controversial, and experimental masterpieces. Inspired by President Giscard d'Estaing's daring **Centre Pompidou** in the late 70s, President Mitterrand initiated his famous 15-billion-franc *Grands Projets* program to provide a series of modern monuments at the dawn of the twenty-first century (see p. 12). As Paris rounds the Millenium and enters the 21st century, new projects such as the renovation of the Centre Pompidou will continue to transform the capital. The **ZAC** project *(zone d'aménagement concerte)* plans to build a new university, sports complex, public garden, and métro in the 13*ème*, Paris's most rapidly redeveloping arrondissement.

MUSIC

The early years of music in Paris date back to the Gregorian chant of 12th-century monks in Nôtre-Dame. Other early highlights include the 13th century ballads of Medieval troubadours, the Renaissance masses of **Josquin des Prez** (c.1440-1521), the Versailles court opera of **Jean-Baptise Lully** (1632-87), the organ fugues of **Jean-Philippe Rameau** (1683-1764).

When the Rousseauist **Robespierre** came to power, he declared the necessity of forging a single will for the people. Meanwhile the people rallied to the strains of revolutionary music, such as **Rouget de Lisle**'s *War Song of the Army of the Rhine*. Composed in 1792 to rally French forces fighting the Prussians, it was taken up with gusto by volunteers from Marseille; dubbed the *Marseillaise*, it became the national anthem in 1795.

Paris in the 19th century enjoyed its status as a center of European musical influence. With the rise of the middle class in the early part of the 19th century came the spectacle of **"grand opera,"** as well as the simpler **opéra comique.** These styles later merged and culminated in the *über*-Romantic **lyric opera,** a mix of soaring arias, exotic flavor, and tragedy (usually death). **Gounod's** *Faust* (1859), **Saint-Saëns's** *Samson et Dalila* (1877), **Bizet's** *Carmen* (1875), and **Berlioz's** *Les Troyens* (1856-58) are all examples of this style. Berlioz is also renowned for his *Symphonie Fantastique* (1830), a paradigm of Romantic composition and a not-so-subtle semi-autobiographical account of the composer's unrequited love for the Irish actress Harriet Smithson.

Paris was a musical center for non-French composers as well. Half French, half Polish, **Frédéric Chopin** (1810-1849) started composing at the age of seven, and his mature work transcends the Romantic style. Though during the early 19th century French music remained under the influence of Beethoven, by the 1830s Paris had again become the musical centre of Europe. There Chopin mixed with the Hungarian **Franz Liszt,** the Austrian **Felix Mendelssohn,** and the French **Hector Berlioz.** Berlioz's unconventional compositional style gave birth to the modern orchestra by requiring a far greater range of musicians; his *Requiem* (1837) is scored for 166 musicians and a chorus of 290, as well as four brass sections placed around the concert hall. It was to handle such a complex orchestra that Berlioz developed the dictatorial conducting style that persists today. He also espoused the Romantic notion of **program music,** which uses careful instrumentation to narrate a story such as in the *Symphonie Fantastique* (see above). Chopin's harmonic explorations and Liszt's dramatic flourishes are characteristic elements of **Romantic** music.

For now, music remained aloof from the influence of Impressionism; the densely expressive sounds of the **Post-Romantics** took their cue from Wagner's operatic exploits across the Rhine. The composers **César Franck** and **Camille Saint-Saëns,** both wrote symphonic poems. A development of Romantic program music, these single-movement orchestral works aimed to evoke a scene more than narrate a story; a well-loved example is Saint-Saëns *Carnival of the Animals* (1886). Saint-Saëns's pupil **Gabriel Fauré** gained universal exposure when his *Requiem* was chosen as the theme music of the 1998 World Cup.

As in other arts, music at the turn of the 20th century began a new period of intense, often abstract invention. One of the most beloved of these composers is **Claude Debussy** (1862-1918). Though his style is called **Impressionist,** this owes more to Debussy's admiration for the visual movement than any application of its methods. His instrumental works *Prélude à l'après-midi d'un faune* (1894) and *La Mer* (1905), as well as his opera *Pelléas et Mélisande* (1902), use tone color and non-traditional scales to evoke moods. Though often classified with Debussy, Ravel's music shows great versatility; his free use of Spanish rhythms betrays his Basque origins, while a trip to North America opened his eyes to the possibilities of jazz. When a listener screamed "but he is mad!" at the 1928 premiere of his most famous work, the platinum-single, mood-enhancing *Boléro*, the composer retorted, "Aha! She has understood." **Erik Satie,** born in Honfleur in 1866, composed in a sarcastic, anti-sentimental spirit, also in striking contrast to that of Debussy.

FEEL THE BEAT Royal composer Jean-Baptiste Lully's death is one of the saddest, strangest tales in music history. Before the advent of the conducting baton, leaders of musical ensembles used a long, pointed stick to keep time. During a performance celebrating Louis XIV's recovery from illness in 1687, Lully accidentally stabbed himself in the foot with his stick. He died later that year of gangrene.

Each summer from 1909 to 1929, musicians and artists alike eagerly awaited the summer season of the Ballets Russes. Under the leadership of **Sergei Diaghilev,** the Russian dance company astounded audiences with the dancing of **Vaslav Nijinsky** and the music of **Igor Stravinsky,** whose ballet *The Rite of Spring* caused a riot at its 1913 premiere (see p. 203 for the theater). Violently dissonant and rhythmic, the piece sounded the clarion call for the modernist movement. No less shocking was the first night of *Parade* in 1917, organized jointly by Diaghilev and the multi-talented Jean Cocteau. In this landmark event, Erik Satie's score used sirens and typewriters, Pablo Picasso provided the costumes and decoration; poet and critic Guillaume Apollinaire coined the word 'surreal' to describe its effect.

The disconcerting influence of Surrealism bypassed the public of the 1920s, who were busy throwing themselves into the wild excesses of the post-war *années folles*. In the Great Depression which followed, the avant-garde reasserted itself on the public consciousness, and an audience weary of fifty years of shock tactics was grateful for the relative peace of a new neoclassicism. The young members of the Group of Six, led by **Francis Poulenc** and **Darius Milhaud,** attracted concertgoers with their lighthearted, melodic style. Milhaud developed **polytonality** by scoring music simultaneously in a number of keys; an early example is the jazzy *The Bull on the Roof* (1918). His *Création du monde* (1924) took some of the first tentative steps on the part of European music to come to terms with jazz.

Already famous for his monochromatic *Blue* paintings, in 1960 **Yves Klein** presented *The Monotone Symphony*. In this performance piece three naked models painted the wall blue with their bodies, while the artist conducted an orchestra on one note for 20 minutes. Somewhat less messy, though no less radical, is the music of composer **Pierre Boulez** (born 1925). Boulez was an adept of the **Neo-serialist** school, which uses the 12-tone system developed in the 1920s by Austrian Arnold Schoënberg. Always innovative, Boulez's work includes aleatory music, partial compositions which leave their completion to the performer, but his greatest influence on modern music has been as director of IRCAM, a centre for avant-garde music in Paris. Paris remains a hotbed for composition in the post-electronic European tradition, anchored by the **IRCAM** institute in the Pompidou Museum (see **Museums,** p. 251).

Boulez's earlier work owes a debt to his teacher, the late **Olivier Messaien** (d. 1992). Messaien suffered from synesthesia, a sensory disorder which confuses sound and vision; different harmonies appeared to him in different colors, and this dual perception affected his composition. He was also fascinated by birdsong; both these influences are seen in *Chronochromie* (1960). Another of Messaien's students was **Iannis Xenakis.** Xenakis's music uses computers to coordinate and even compose music according to advanced mathematical techniques. Xenakis was an engineer by training, and his first major composition, *Metastasis* (1954), was a translation into sound of the design of the Philips Pavilion in the 1958 Brussels Exposition.

With the exception of fashionable Existentialism, the public remained unimpressed by the stream of unintelligible innovation gushing from the fount of French intellectualism in the 50s. They were far happier with the songs of crooner Charles **Aznavour** and the unregrettable Edith **Piaf.** Similarly, **Jacques Brel's** and Juliette Greco's popular *chansons* charmed smoky cabarets in the 1960s. Some of Paris's most famous song divas, Piaf, the Egyptian-born **Dalida,** and the Québecoise **Fabienne Thibeault** have now made way for such new *chanteuses* as **Patricia Kaas, Isabelle Boulay,** and the seductive **Mylène Farmer.**

JAZZ

France has been particularly receptive to **jazz** and on the whole recognized its artistic integrity sooner than the United States. In the 1930s, French musicians copied the swing they heard on early Louis Armstrong sides, but the 1934 Club Hot pair of violinist **Stéphane Grapelli** and stylish Belgian-Romany guitarist **Django Rein-**

hardt were already innovators. After WWII, the stream of American musicians to Paris began to flow. A jazz festival in 1949 brought the young **Miles Davis** across the pond for a dreamy April in Paris and a romance with actress Juliette Greco. Pianist **Bud Powell,** drummer **Kenny Clarke,** and others found the respect, dignity, and gigs accorded them there too attractive to leave. American jazz players like **Duke Ellington** played clubs like the Left Bank hotspot, **Le Caveau de la Huchette** (see **Nightlife,** p. 300), and jazz classics like **Davis's** *April in Paris* helped the city's rain-slicked streets take on their saxophonic gloss. Pianist **Jacky Terrasson** has recently taken giant steps to earn the helm of the late and beloved **Michel Petrucciani.** You may catch him at **Au Duc des Lombards** (see **Nightlife,** p. 299).

ROCK, HIP-HOP, AND TODAY'S SCENE

In the late 50s and the 60s, a unique French take on American rock emerged: the movement was termed, in a stroke of onomatopoetic brilliance, **yé-yé.** Teen idols like **Johnny Hallyday** and **François Hallyday** took the limelight, and the youth-oriented **Salut les Copains** was the movement's rag. In the 70s bands came and went, but in the 80s a number of solid groups emerged. Look for recordings by **Téléphone, Marquis de Sade, Indochine,** or **Les Rita Mitsouki.**

In recent years, ethnic hybrids have had a huge influence on French pop music. Check out **Alabina, Karim Kacel, Cheb Kalad,** and **Mano Negra** for examples of African raï. Techno has not had the following in France that it's had elsewhere on the continent, but for some progressive-syntho fun, **Air,** has been widely exported in the last year. Another phenomenally successful export has been the French disco house sound, with the 70s-influenced (and occasionally 70s-sampling) tunes of **Daft Punk, Bob Sinclar,** and **Cassius** burning up dance floors across the world. Daft Punk's *Homework* album, Cassius's *1999* album, and Stardust's *Music Sounds Better With You* single are probably the best embodiment of the sound. Or just attend Respect, at Queen on Wednesday nights (see **Nightlife,** p. 295). Renowned **DJ Dimitri from Paris** combines house with touches of lounge, while the **Micronauts** and their acid house sound continue to be in demand as remixes. The Source label is one of the major underground dance music labels in France. Recent pop hits have come from groups like **Les Nubians, Les Négresses Vertes, Autour de Lucie, Dolly, Louise Attaque** and soloists like **Axel Renoir, Etienne Daho,** and the Québecois **Jean LeLoup.** French R&B stars **Native** and **Teri Moïse** top the charts along with rap stars like **MC Solaar, Liaison Dangereuses, Manau, Passithe,** and controversial **NTM** (Nique Ta Mère), and the more recent **KDD** (Kartel Double Dentente), whose lyrics speak out against urban crime, racism, and anti-immigrant prejudice in France.

The bulk of popular music played on French radio will be familiar to anglophone travelers, despite a 1996 law requiring that **francophone music** make up 40% of radio stations' playlists—much of that quota gets filled between 1 and 6 AM. The problem facing French music is not so much one of quality as of distribution; it still has a strong following in France outside the mainstream, but most of the music industry in France is in the hands of multinational corporations.

FILM

Not long after he and his brother Louis presented the world's first paid screening in a Paris café in 1895, **Auguste Lumière** remarked, "The cinema is a medium without a future." In defiance (or occasional consent) of this statement, the French have striven to reveal the broadest possibilities of film. The trick cinema of magician-turned-filmmaker **Georges Méliès** astounded audiences with "disappearing" objects, but gave way by 1908 to an emphasis on narrative. At 14 minutes in length, and with 30 scenes, Méliès's *Journey to the Moon* (1902) was the first motion picture to realize the story-telling possibilities of the medium. **Max Linder's** physical comedy spoke volumes through the silent medium.

Paris was the Hollywood of the early days of cinema, dominating production and distribution worldwide. However, WWI stunted French growth and allowed the Americans to sink their claws in for good, in France as elsewhere. Still, the creative climate in France was fertile: new movements in art engaged with film and yielded the slapstick *Entr'acte* (1924) by **René Clair,** starring that grand-Dada of impertinence, **Marcel Duchamp,** and **Luis Buñuel's** *Un Chien Andalou* (1928), a marvel of jarring associations featuring **Salvador Dalí.** The Dane **Carl Dreyer's** *Passion of Joan of Arc* (1928) exhibits a passion for close-ups of the faces of actress **Falconetti's** Joan and her accusers.

Although the first world war allowed Hollywood to wrest celluloid dominance from a shattered Europe, in the 1920s and 1930s French cinema was the most critically acclaimed in the world under such great directors as **Jean Renoir,** son of the Impressionist painter. *La Grande illusion*, which he directed in 1937, is a powerful anti-war statement; set in the prisoner of war camps of World War I, it is a desperate plea for humanity released in the shadow of Nazi Germany.

The 1930s brought the transition to sound, crowned by **Jean Vigo's** *Zero for Conduct* (1933). This dark yet lyrical story of boarding school rebellion prefigured the growth of **Poetic Realism** under **Marcel Carné** and writer **Jacques Prévert** (*Daybreak*, 1939), with its concern for the gritty lives of the working class, epitomized in the masculine **Jean Gabin** and the unflappable **Arletty.** **Jean Renoir** balanced social criticism with a gentle humanism, revealing in *The Rules of the Game* (1939) the erosion of the French bourgeoisie and hinting at his country's malaise at the doorstep of war. Censorship during the Occupation led to a move from political films to nostalgia and escapist cinema. Yet Carné and Prévert's epic *Children of Paradise* (1943-5) finds in 1840s Paris the indomitable spirit of the French.

After the War, **Jean Cocteau** carried the poetic into the fantastic with *Beauty and the Beast* (1946) and *Orphée* (1950). The surrealist *Beauty and the Beast* featured an early use of special effects to show the monster changing into a handsome man. However, popular French taste went in for lush, well-buffed productions. A group of young intellectuals gathered by critic **André Bazin** for the magazine **Cahiers du Cinéma** took issue with this "cinema of quality." Encouraged by government subsidies, in 1959 they swapped pen for the camera. **François Truffaut's** *The 400 Blows* and **Jean-Luc Godard's** *Au Bout du Souffle* (Breathless) were joined the same year by **Alain Resnais's** *Hiroshima, Mon Amour* (written by Marguerite Duras) and sounded the clarion call of the **French New Wave (Nouvelle Vague).** Aznavour starred in François Truffaut's *Shoot the Piano Player* (1960). While Truffaut was the driving force behind this group of young critics-turned-directors, it was **Jean-Luc Godard** who made the movement his own. Godard's *Au Bout du Souffle* which Truffaut produced, was shot without a script, relying instead on improvisation from sketches Godard worked out between rehearsals. Three years earlier, a star was born when **Jean Vadim** sent the incomparable **Brigitte Bardot** shimmying naked across the stage in *And God Created Woman.*

Other directors associated with the New Wave are **Jean Rouch** (*Chronicle of a Summer*, 1961), **Louis Malle** (*The Lovers*, 1958), **Eric Rohmer** (*My Night with Maud*, 1969), **Agnès Varda** (*Cléo from 5 to 7*, 1961), and **Chris Marker** (*La Jetée*, 1962). These directors are loosely unified by their interest in the newly mobile camera, the rupture of the categories of fiction and documentary, the fragmentation of linear time and the ways of memory, the thrill of youth and speed, cars, and noise, and Hitchcock and Lang's American films (mainly gangsters and westerns). The filmmaker as *auteur* (author) or essayist remains a dominant notion in French film and has coined the term *"Art et Essai"* to describe what anglophones call "Art Cinema."

Godard emerged as the New Wave oracle through the 60s. His collaborations with actors **Jean-Paul Belmondo** and **Anna Karina,** including *Vivre Sa Vie* (1962) and *Pierrot le Fou* (1965), inspired a generation of filmmakers. *Weekend* (1967), a descent into anarchy and cannibalism which concludes with the Lumière-invoking intertitle, "The End of Cinema," marks the proximity of contemporary film and radical politics and presages the national events of May 1968 (see **History,** p. 12).

New Wave directors dominated though the 70s, although the movement became increasingly disparate. Even so, the biggest-grossing film of the decade was a middle-brow comedy, **Gérard Oury's** *Les Adventures de Rabbi Jacob* (1973).

The world impact of French cinema in the 60s brought wider recognition of French film stars in the 70s and 80s, such as the stunning **Catherine Deneuve** *(Belle de jour, Les Parapluies de Cherbourg)*, gothic priestess **Isabelle Adjani** *(La Reine Margot)*, and the omnipresent **Gérard Depardieu** *(Danton, 1492, Camille Claudel)*, as well as **Juliette Binoche** *(Blue)* and **Julie Delpy** *(Europa, Europa)*.

An extraordinary range of new French films have found wide release abroad, are now available on video, and can serve as a wonderful introduction to French culture. Comedies like Edouard's Molinaro's campy *La Cage aux Folles* (1975), Colline Serraud's *Trois hommes et un couffin* (Three Men and a Baby, 1985), and Luc Besson's action thriller *Nikita* (1990) have all inspired American remakes, while more recent comedies like Jean-Marie Poiré's *Les Visiteurs* (1992) and François Ozon's *Sitcom* (1998) imitate and poke fun at American B-comedies and television sitcoms. Jean-Jacques Beineix's *Betty Blue* (1985), Claude Berri's *Manon des Sources* (1986) and *Jean de Florette* (1986), Louis Malle's WWII drama *Au Revoir les Enfants* (1987), Marc Caro and Jean-Pierre Jeunet's dystopic *Delicatessen* (1991), and Krzysztof Kieślowski's three colors trilogy, *Blue* (1993), *White* (1994), and *Red* (1994), have all become instant classics of 80s and 90s French cinema.

Some of the most explosive recent French films are the production of *cinéma beur*, the work of second-generation North Africans coming to terms with life in the HLMs (housing projects) of suburban Paris. Rich with graffiti art and rap music, films like **Mehdi Charef's** *Le Thé au harem d'Archi Ahmed* (1986) and **Mathieu Kassovitz's** *La Haine* (1995) expose the horrors of urban racism. Facing up to a history of colonialism, meanwhile, is a recent preoccupation, as in **Claire Denis's** *Chocolat* (1987). The art cinema continues to prosper under **Marcel Hanoun** *(Bruit d'Amour et de Guerre*, 1997) and **Jacques Doillon** *(Ponette*, 1997).

France's powerful influence on other Francophone cinema has produced such important post-colonial films as Gillo Pontecorvo's *The Battle of Algiers* (Algeria, 1966), Sembène Ousmane's *Xala* (Senegal, 1974), and Québecois films such as Denys Arcand's *Declin de l'empire américain* (1986) and *Jésus de Montréal* (1990), and Michel-Marc Bouchard's *Les Feluettes* (Lilies, 1997).

Several recent French films have begun to explore the issue of gay identity and sexual orientation, including Belgian Alain Berliner's transgender tragicomedy *Ma vie en rose* (1997). Cédric Klapisch's hilarious *Chacun cherche son Chat* (1996) painted gay and straight life in the hip *quartier* of the Bastille. Astérix and Obélix (Gérard Depardieu) were reunited in live-action to battle the toops of Caesar in *Asterix et Obelix Contre Cesar* (1999).

The French government subsidizes the film industry as part of French culture, but American studios, which dominate the French market, call it "unfair." Paris retains a vibrant film culture. Foreign films are normally dubbed into French; watch out for listings marked *version originale* (V.O.) to see an English language film graced by French subtitles.

ESSENTIALS

FACTS FOR THE TRAVELER

WHEN TO GO

In August, tourists move in and Parisians move out on vacation (for other vacation days see **Festivals and Seasonal Events,** p. 280). Smaller hotels, shops, and services may close—when tourists flood those that remain open, frustration is about the only thing available to all. Still, if you avoid the Champs-Elysées, Versailles, and the Eiffel Tower, August can be pleasingly calm. While summer heat does nothing to soften the blow of Paris's pollution, high temperatures usually don't hit until July; June is notoriously rainy. In the fall, the tourist-madness begins to calm down. Despite winter temperatures and rain, there is little snow. In the off season airfares and hotel rates drop, travel is less congested, and museum lines are short (although Sunday lines are *never* a pretty sight).

Avg Temp (low/high)	January		April		July		October	
	°C	°F	°C	°F	°C	°F	°C	°F
Paris	0/6	32/43	5/16	41/61	13/24	55/75	6/15	43/59

DOCUMENTS AND FORMALITIES

ENTRANCE REQUIREMENTS.

Passport (p. 38). Required for citizens of Australia, Canada, Ireland, New Zealand, South Africa, the USA and the U.K.

Visa (p. 41). For stays of under 90 days, required of citizens of South Africa. For stays over 90 days, a visa is also required of citizens of Australia, Canada, New Zealand and the USA.

Work Permit (p. 40). Required for citizens of Australia, Canada, New Zealand, South Africa, and the USA.

Driving Permit (p. 82). Required for all those planning to drive. You must be at least 18 years old to drive in France.

CONSULAR SERVICES ABROAD

Always call ahead; different services will have their own hours of opening. Most of the listed hours are for visa concerns. Most are also open during the afternoon but only for reserved appointments; call in the morning to schedule one.

Australia, Consulate General, Level 26 St. Martins Tower, 31 Market St., Sydney NSW 2000. Tel. (2) 926 157 79, www.france.net.au/site/administration/consulats/sydney/index.htm. Open M-F 9am-1pm.

Canada, Consulate General, 1 pl. Ville Marie, 26th floor, Montréal QC H3B 4. Tel. (514) 878 4385, www.consulfrancemontreal.org. Open M-F 8:30am-noon. Consulate General, 25 rue Saint-Louis, Québec QC GIR 3Y8. Tel. (418) 694 2294, www.consulat-france-qc.org/Accueil.htm. Open M-F 9am-12:30pm.Consulate General, 130 Bloor St. West, #400, Toronto-Ontario M5S 1N5. Tel. (416) 925 8041, web.idirect.com/~fs1tto/index.htm. Open M-F 9am-1pm.

Ireland, French Embassy, Consulate Section, 36 Ailesbury Rd., Ballsbridge, Dublin 4. Tel. (1) 260 16 66, www.ambafrance.ie. Open M-F 9am-noon.

New Zealand, French Embassy and Consulate, 34-42 Manners St. PO box 11-343, Wellington. Tel. (4) 802 7793, www.ambafrance.net.nz.

South Africa, French Embassy and Consulate, 807 George Ave. Arcadia, Pretoria 0083. Tel. (12) 429 7030, www.france.co.za. Open M-F 8:30am-12:30pm and 2-5pm. Consulate, 2 Dean St., PO box 1702 8001 Cape Town. Tel. (21) 4 231 575. Open M-F 9am-12:30pm.

United Kingdom, Consulate General, 21 Cromwell Rd., London SW7 2 EN. Tel. (171) 838 2000, www.ambafrance.org.uk/db.phtml?id=consulat. Open M-W 8:45am-3pm, Th-F 8:45am-noon.

United States, Consulate General, 4101 Reservoir Rd. NW, Washington DC 20007. Tel. (202) 944-6000, www.france-consulat.org/dc/dc.html. Open 8:45am-12:30pm.

CONSULAR SERVICES IN PARIS

An embassy houses the offices of the ambassador and his or her staff and deals mostly with international business and treaty negotiation, whereas a consulate contains all facilities for dealing with nationals. Call before visiting any of these offices; various services have different hours of availability. Visa services tend to be available only in the morning. If you find yourself in serious trouble, call your country's embassy or consulate; they should be able to provide legal advice and may be able to advance you some money in a dire emergency. The consulate can also give you lists of local lawyers and doctors, notify family members of accidents, and give information on how to proceed with legal problems. Don't expect them to get you out of every scrape, though: you must always abide by French law while in France, and if you are arrested, the consulate can do little but point you toward a lawyer. Dual citizens of France cannot call on the consular services of their second nationality for assistance.

Australian Embassy and Consulate, 4 rue Jean Rey, 15ème (tel. 01 40 59 33 00; www.austgov.fr). M: Bir Hakeem. Open M-F 9:15am-noon and 2-4:30pm.

Canadian Embassy and Consulate, 35 Ave. Montaigne, 8ème (tel. 01 44 43 29 00). M: Franklin-Roosevelt or Alma-Marceau. Open 9am-noon and 2-5pm. Consular services: by appointment. Open M-F 2-4:30pm. **Generale Delegation of Quebec,** 66 rue Pergolèse, 16ème (tel. 01 40 67 85 00). Open 9am-5:30pm.

Irish Embassy and Consulate, 12, av. Foch, 16ème (tel. 01 44 17 67 48; for passport services fax 01 44 17 67 50). M: Argentine. Open 9:30am-noon, but phone lines are open until 5:30pm. Consular services: at same location but entrance is at 4 rue Rude. Open M-F 9:30am-noon; telephone 9:30am-1pm and 2:30-5:30pm.

New Zealand Embassy and Consulate, 7ter, rue Leonardo da Vinci, 16ème (tel. 01 45 00 24 11; fax 01 45 01 26 39). M: Victor-Hugo. Open M-F 9am-1pm and 2-5:30pm.

South African Embassy, 59, quai d'Orsay, 7ème (tel. 01 53 59 23 23; fax 01 47 53 99 70). M: Invalides. Open M-F 9am-noon.

British Embassy, 35, rue du Faubourg-St-Honoré, 8ème (tel. 01 44 51 31 00; fax 01 44 51 31 27; www.amb-grandebretagne.fr). M: Concorde or Madeleine. Consulate, 16, rue d'Anjou (same phone). M: Concorde. Open M-F 9:30am-12:30pm and 2:30-5pm. Visa bureau open M-F 9:30am-12:30pm.

United States Embassy, 2, av. Gabriel, 8ème (tel. 01 43 12 22 22; fax 01 42 66 97 83). M: Concorde. Open M-F 9am-6pm. Consulate, 2, rue St-Florentin, 1er (tel. 01 43 12 48 76, 01 43 12 23 47 for automated information). Open M-F 9am-3pm. Closed for both American and French holidays.

PASSPORTS

REQUIREMENTS. Citizens of Australia, Canada, Ireland, New Zealand, South Africa, the U.K., and the U.S. need valid passports to enter France and to re-enter their own country. France does not allow entrance if the holder's passport expires in under three months after the expected date of departure; returning home with an expired passport is illegal, and may result in a fine.

PHOTOCOPIES. It is a good idea to photocopy the page of your passport that contains your photograph, passport number, and other identifying information, along with other important documents such as visas, travel insurance policies, airplane tickets, and traveler's check serial numbers, in case you lose anything. Carry one set of copies in a safe place apart from the originals and leave another set at home. Consulates also recommend that you carry an expired passport or an official copy of your birth certificate in a part of your baggage separate from other documents.

LOST PASSPORTS. If you lose your passport in France, immediately notify the local police and the nearest embassy or consulate of your home government. To expedite replacement, you will need to know all information contained in the lost passport and show identification and proof of citizenship. In some cases, a replacement may take weeks to process, and it may be valid only for a limited time. Any visas stamped in your old passport will be irretrievably lost. In an emergency, ask for immediate temporary traveling papers that will permit you to re-enter your home country. Your passport is a public document belonging to your nation's government. You may have to surrender it to a foreign government official, but you are entitled to get it back in a reasonable amount of time.

NEW PASSPORTS. All applications for new passports or renewals should be filed several weeks (or months) in advance of your planned departure date. Most passport offices do offer emergency passport services for an extra charge, however. Citizens residing abroad who need a passport or renewal should contact their nearest embassy or consulate.

Australia Citizens must apply for a passport in person at a post office, a passport office, or an Australian diplomatic mission overseas. Passport offices are located in Adelaide, Brisbane, Canberra, Darwin, Hobart, Melbourne, Newcastle, Perth, and Sydney. New adult passports cost AUS$126 (for a 32-page passport) or AUS$188 (64-page), and a child's is AUS$63 (32-page) or AUS$94 (64-page). Adult passports are valid for 10 years and child passports for 5 years. For more info, call toll-free (in Australia) 13 12 32, or visit www.dfat.gov.au/passports.

Canada Application forms are available at all passport offices, Canadian missions, many travel agencies, and Northern Stores in northern communities. Passports cost CDN$60, plus a CDN$25 consular fee, are valid for 5 years, and are not renewable. For additional info, contact the Canadian Passport Office, Department of Foreign Affairs and International Trade, Ottawa, ON, K1A 0G3 (tel. (613) 994-3500; www.dfait-maeci.gc.ca/passport). Travelers may also call 800-567-6868 (24hr.); in Toronto, (416) 973-3251; in Vancouver, (604) 586-2500; in Montreal, (514) 283-2152.

Ireland Citizens can apply for a passport by mail to either the Department of Foreign Affairs, Passport Office, Setanta Centre, Molesworth St., Dublin 2 (tel. (01) 671 13 63; fax 671 1092; www.irlgov.ie/iveagh), or the Passport Office, Irish Life Building, 1A South Mall, Cork (tel. (021) 27 25 25). Obtain an application at a local Garda station or post office, or request one from a passport office. Passports cost IR£45 and are valid for 10 years. Citizens under 18 or over 65 can request a 3-year passport that costs IR£10.

New Zealand Application forms for passports are available in New Zealand from most travel agents. Applications may be forwarded to the Passport Office, P.O. Box 10526, Wellington, New Zealand (tel. 0800 22 50 50; www.govt.nz/agency_info/forms.shtml).

Standard processing time in New Zealand is 10 working days for correct applications. The fees are adult NZ$80, and child NZ$40. Children's names can no longer be endorsed on a parent's passport—they must apply for their own, which are valid for up to 5 years. An adult's passport is valid for up to 10 years.

South Africa South African passports are issued only in Pretoria. However, all applications must still be submitted or forwarded to the applicable office of a South African consulate. Tourist passports, valid for 10 years, cost around SAR80. Children under 16 must be issued their own passports, valid for 5 years, which cost around SAR60. Time for the completion of an application is normally 3 months or more from the time of submission. For further information, contact the nearest Department of Home Affairs Office (www.southafrica-newyork.net/passport.htm).

United Kingdom Full passports are valid for 10 years (5 years if under 16). Application forms are available at passport offices, main post offices, and many travel agents. Apply by mail or in person to one of the passport offices, located in London, Liverpool, Newport, Peterborough, Glasgow, or Belfast. The fee is UK£31, UK£11 for children under 16. The process takes about four weeks, but the London office offers a five-day, walk-in rush service; arrive early. The U.K. Passport Agency can be reached by phone at (0870) 521 04 10, and more information is available at www.open.gov.uk/ukpass/ukpass.htm.

United States Citizens may apply for a passport at any federal or state courthouse or post office authorized to accept passport applications, or at a U.S. Passport Agency, located in most major cities. Refer to the "U.S. Government, State Department" section of the telephone directory or the local post office for addresses. Passports are valid for 10 years (5 years if under 18) and cost US$60 (under 18 US$40). Passports may be renewed by mail or in person for US$40. Processing takes 3-4 weeks. For more info, contact the U.S. Passport Information's 24-hour recorded message (tel. (202) 647-0518) or look on the web at http://travel.state.gov/passport_services.html.

THE EUROPEAN UNION AND THE TRAVELER. Traveling between the fifteen member states of the **European Union** (EU) has never been easier, especially for EU citizens. Citizens of EU member states need only a valid state-issued identity card to travel within the EU, and have right of residence and employment throughout the Union, though some regulations do apply (see **Visas and Work permits**, p. 41). **Freedom of mobility** within the EU was established on May 1st 1999; henceforth, with the exception of the UK, Ireland and Denmark, border checks will be abolished at internal EU borders. However travelers should always carry a passport or EU-member issued identity card as police controls may still be carried out. Over the next five years, immigration and visa policies will be start to be made on a Union-wide basis.

There are **no customs** at internal E.U. borders (travelers arriving in one EU country from another by air should take the **blue channel** when exiting the baggage claim), and travelers are free to transport whatever legal substances they like across the Union provided they can demonstrate that it is for personal (i.e. non commercial) use. In practice this means quantities in excess of 800 cigarettes, 10L of spirits, 90L of wine (60 of sparkling wine) and 110L of beer—quite enough for most people! Correspondingly, on June 30th, 1999, **duty-free was abolished** for travel between EU member states. Those arriving in the EU from outside will still have a duty-free allowance. January 1st 1999 saw the launch of the **Euro**, a common currency for 11 of the EU nations. While it exists only in electronic form as yet, in the future it will mean far fewer money-changing headaches for travelers in Europe (see **Money**, p. 43).

The 15 member states of the EU are: Austria, Belgium, Denmark, Finland, France, Germany, Greece, Ireland, Italy, Luxembourg, the Netherlands, Portugal, Spain, Sweden, and the United Kingdom.

ESSENTIALS

ESSENTIALS

VISAS AND WORK PERMITS

French visas are valid for travel in any of the states of the EU common travel area (the entire Union except the UK and Ireland, plus Iceland and Norway); however if the primary object of your visit is a country other than France you should apply to their consulate for a visa. **British** and **Irish** citizens do not require a visa to visit, reside in, or work in France; however there are some formalities to complete for stays of over 90 days (see below).

All visitors to France are required to register their presence with the Police in the town in which they are staying; this is normally done automatically by hotels and hostels, and when signing a lease with a landlord.

VISITS OF UNDER 90 DAYS

Citizens of South Africa need a **short-stay visa;** citizens of Australia, Canada, New Zealand and the USA do not need visas. To apply for a short-stay visa, your passport must be valid for three months after you intend to leave France. In addition to the application form you require 2 passport-sized photos, proof of a hotel reservation or an organized tour, or, if you intend to stay with relatives or friends, a certificate of accommodation stamped by the police station or town hall (2 copies), a return ticket and proof of medical insurance. A single/multiple entry visa for 30 days or under costs 165F; for 31-90 days, the cost is 195F for single entry, or 230F for multiple entry. Apply for a visa at your nearest French consulate; short-stay visas for South African nationals usually take 2 days to process. Visa fees are payable in local currency according to an exchange rate determined by the consulate.

VISITS OF OVER 90 DAYS

All non-EU citizens require a **long-stay visa** for stays of over 90 days. These need to be applied for well in advance, and require no less than eight copies of the application form and eight passport photos, along with proof of residence in your home country, proof of sufficient financial means to support you during your stay in France, proof of medical insurance, and proof that you do not have a criminal record. Visas can take two months to process and cost 650F. Visa fees are payable in local currency according to an exchange rate determined by the consulate. U.S. Citizens can take advantage of the Center for International Business and Travel (CIBT) (tel. 800-925-2428), which will secure visas for travel to almost all countries for a variable service charge.

Within 60 days of their arrival, all foreigners (including EU citizens) who plan to stay over 90 days must apply for a **residence permit** *(carte de séjour);* apply at the local *préfecture, mairie,* or *commissariat;* in Paris go to the *préfecture de Police.* You must show sufficient resources to support yourself for the duration of your stay. Unemployed EU citizens are given 90 days from their entry to France to find employment; if they succeed they will be issued with a residence permit valid for 10 years and automatically renewable after that; if they do not, but can show proof of financial independence, they will be issued with a permit valid for 5 years. All other foreign nationals cannot work without applying for a work permit (see below). Residence permits are issued free of charge to EU citizens: otherwise they cost 220F. In addition non-EU citizens must take a medical examination before being issued a card; these cost 360F for students and 1050F for others.

STUDY AND WORK PERMITS

Only EU citizens have the right to work and study in France without a visa. Others wishing to study in France must apply for a special student visa, for which you will need proof of admission to a French university, proof of financial independence, and proof of medical insurance. Foreigners studying in France must apply for a residence permit within two months of their arrival. Non EU citizens wishing to work in France must have a firm offer of employment before applying for a visa; the employer should arrange for an official work contract to be sent to you, which must be presented upon arrival in France. You must also apply for a residence permit within 8 days of your arrival. For **au-pairs**, **scientific researchers**, and **teaching assistants**, special rules apply; check with your local consulate. In all cases you must have a firm offer of employment before applying for a visa. For more information, see **Alternatives to Tourism**, p. 65).

IDENTIFICATION

French law requires that all people carry a form of official identification—either a passport or an EU government-issued identity card. The police have the right to demand to see identification at any time and you risk running a large fine if you do not comply. Minority travelers, especially black and Arab travelers, should be especially careful to carry proof that they are in France legally. In general when traveling it is advisable to carry two or more forms of identification, including at least one photo ID. A passport combined with a driver's license or birth certificate usually serves as adequate proof of your identity and citizenship. Many establishments, especially banks, require several IDs before cashing traveler's checks. Never carry all your forms of ID together, however; you risk being left entirely without ID or funds in case of theft or loss. It is useful to carry extra passport-size photos to affix to the various IDs or railpasses you may acquire, although photo booths can be found in just about every métro station.

STUDENT AND TEACHER IDENTIFICATION. The **International Student Identity Card (ISIC)** is the most widely accepted form of student identification. Flashing this card can procure you discounts for sights, theaters, museums, meals, buses, and other services. Present the card wherever you go, and ask about discounts even when none are advertised. The international identification cards are preferable to institution-specific cards because the tourism personnel in France are taught to recognize the former. Cardholders have access to a toll-free 24hr. ISIC helpline whose multilingual staff can provide assistance in medical, legal, and financial emergencies overseas (tel. 800-626-2427 in the U.S. and Canada; elsewhere call collect (181) 666 90 25).

Many student travel agencies around the world issue ISICs, including STA Travel in Australia and New Zealand; Travel CUTS in Canada; USIT in Ireland and Northern Ireland; SASTS in South Africa; Campus Travel and STA Travel in the U.K.; Council Travel, Let's Go Travel, STA Travel, and via the web (www.council-travel.com/idcards/index.htm) in the U.S.; and any other travel agency with a student focus. You can also write to Council for a copy. The card is valid from September of one year to December of the following year and costs AUS$15, CDN$15, or US$20 (UK£?). Applicants must be at least 12 years old and degree-seeking students of a secondary or post-secondary school. Because of the proliferation of phony ISICs, many airlines and some other services require additional proof of student identity, such as a signed letter from the registrar attesting to your student status that is stamped with the school seal or your school ID card. The **International Teacher Identity Card (ITIC)** offers the same insurance coverage, and similar but limited discounts. The fee is AUS$13, UK£5, or US$20. For more information on these cards, contact the **International Student Travel Confederation (ISTC)**, Herengracht 479, 1017 BS Amsterdam, Netherlands (from abroad call 31 20 421 28 00; fax 421 28 10; email istcinfo@istc.org; www.istc.org).

YOUTH IDENTIFICATION. The International Student Travel Confederation also issues a discount card to travelers who are 25 years old or younger but not students. Known as the International Youth Travel Card (IYTC; formerly the GO25 Card), this one-year card offers many of the same benefits as the ISIC, and most organizations that sell the ISIC also sell the IYTC. A brochure that lists discounts is free when you purchase the card. To apply, you will need either a passport, valid driver's license, or copy of a birth certificate, and a passport-sized photo with your name printed on the back. The fee is US$20.

CUSTOMS

ARRIVING IN FRANCE. Upon entering France from a non-EU country, you must declare items which exceed the legal allowance and pay duty on them as established by French customs law. Keeping receipts for purchases made abroad will help establish values when you return. It is wise to make a list, including serial numbers, of any valuables that you carry with you from home; if you register this list with customs before your departure and have an official stamp it, you will avoid import duty charges and ensure an easy passage upon your return. Be especially careful to document items manufactured abroad.

RECLAIMING VALUE-ADDED TAX. Most purchases in France include a 20.6% value-added tax (TVA). Non-EU residents (including EU citizens who reside outside the EU) can in principal reclaim the tax on purchases for export worth over 1200F made in one store. Only certain stores participate in this *vente en détaxe* refund process; ask before you pay. You must show a non-EU passport or proof of non-EU residence at the time of purchase, and ask the vendor for a tripartite form called a *bordereau de vente à l'exportation;* make sure that they fill it out, including your bank details. When leaving the country, present the receipt for the purchase together with the completed form to a French customs official. If you're at an airport, look for the window labeled *douane de détaxe*, and be sure to budget at least an hour for the intricacies of French bureaucracy. On a train, find an official or get off at a station close to the border. Once home, you must send a copy back to the vendor within 6 months; eventually the refunds will work their way into your account. Some shops exempt you from paying the tax at the time of purchase; you must still complete the above process. Note that food products, tobacco, medicine, unmounted precious stones, cars, means of transportation (i.e. bicycles and surfboards), and "cultural goods" do not qualify for a TVA refund.

GOING HOME. Upon returning home, you must declare all articles acquired abroad exceed the allowance established by your country's customs service, and pay duty on them. There is normally a smaller allowance for goods and gifts purchased at **duty-free** shops abroad; if you exceed this you must declare and pay duty and possibly sales tax on them as well. "Duty-free" merely means that you need not pay a tax in the country of purchase. Note that from June 30th, 1999, Duty Free has been abolished for trips starting and ending within the EU For more specific information on customs requirements, contact the following information centers:

Australia Australian Customs National Information Line 1 300 363; www.customs.gov.au.

Canada Canadian Customs, 2265 St. Laurent Blvd., Ottawa, ON K1G 4K3 (tel. (613) 993-0534 or 24hr. automated service 800-461-9999; www.revcan.ca).

Ireland The Collector of Customs and Excise, The Custom House, Dublin 1 (tel. (01) 679 27 77; fax 671 20 21; email taxes@revenue.iol.ie; www.revenue.ie/customs.htm).

New Zealand New Zealand Customhouse, 17-21 Whitmore St., Box 2218, Welington (tel. (04) 473 69 09; fax 473 77 30; www.customs.govt.nz).

South Africa Commissioner for Customs and Excise, Private Bag X47, Pretoria 0001 (tel. (012) 314 99 11; fax 328 64 78).

United Kingdom Her Majesty's Customs and Excise, Custom House, Nettleton Road, Heathrow Airport, Hounslow, Middlesex TW6 2LA (tel. (0181) 910 36 02/35 66; fax 910 37 65; www.hmce.gov.uk).

United States U.S. Customs Service, Box 7407, Washington D.C. 20044 (tel. (202) 927-6724; www.customs.ustreas.gov).

MONEY

Money may be the root of all evil, but in Paris it's a necessary one. Even a modest daily budget will probably fall between 250-300F. Still, if you stay in hostels and prepare your own food, expect to spend anywhere from 100-140F per person per day. Hotels start at about 130F per night for a double room, while a basic sit-down meal with wine costs 65F. Personal checks from home will meet with blank refusal, and even travelers checks are not widely accepted outside tourist-oriented businesses; moreover, many establishments will only accept franc- or euro-denominated travelers checks. The bottom line is, carry enough cash to take you through the day, and take care.

THE EURO. On January 1, 1999, 11 countries of the European Union, including France, officially adopted the **euro** as their common currency. Euro notes and coins will not be issued until January 1st 2002, and until that time the Euro will exist only in electronic transactions and travellers cheques. On June 1st, 2002 the Franc will be entirely withdrawn from circulation and the Euro will become the only legal currency in France. *Let's Go* lists all prices in French Francs, as these will still be most relevant in 2000. However, all French businesses must by law quote prices both in Francs and euros.

Travelers who will be passing through more than one nation in the euro-zone should note that exchange rates between the 11 national currencies were irrevocably fixed on January 1, 1999. Henceforth, Bureau de Change will be obliged to interchange euro-zone currencies at the official rate and with **no commission,** though they may still charge a nominal service fee. Euro-denominated traveler's checks may also be used throughout the euro-zone, and can also be exchanged commission-free throughout the 11 euro nations.

The **11 euro countries** are: Austria, Belgium, Finland, France, Germany, Ireland, Italy, Luxembourg, the Netherlands, Portugal, and Spain. Updated information on the euro can be found on the EU's website at www.europa.eu.int/.

CURRENCY AND EXCHANGE

The national currency of France is the *franc français* or French Franc (abbreviated to FF or just F), though it has now been superseded by the **euro** (symbol €; see above for more information). Each franc is divided into 100 **centimes**. The franc is available in brightly colored 50F, 100F, 200F and 500F notes, smart two-tone 10F and 50F coins, as well as silvery 5F, 2F, 1F and ½F coins and pale copper 5, 10 and 20 *centimes* pieces. There are a still a few old 20F notes around, too.

The currency chart below is based on published exchange rates from August 1999, except for the Euro rate which is fixed permanently at the value given. For a quick conversion into US dollars, note that one euro is approximately equal to one dollar. However since its introduction the euro has shown a tendency to slide against the dollar, losing almost 15% of its value in the six months following its launch. If this trend continues, travelers may want to think twice before changing all their money into francs (or euros) before departure.

EURO€1 = 6.55957 FF
US$1 = 6.15 FF
CDN$1 = 4.13 FF
UK£1 = 9.92 FF
IR£1 =8.33 FF
AUS$1 = 4.01 FF
NZ$1 = 3.26 FF
SAR1= 1.00 FF

1F = EURO€0.152449
1 FF = US$0.16
= CDN$0.24
= UK£0.10
= IR£0.12
= AUS$0.25
= NZ$0.31
= SAR1.00

ESSENTIALS

Money From Home In Minutes.

If you're stuck for cash on your travels, don't panic. Millions of people trust Western Union to transfer money in minutes to 165 countries and over 50,000 locations worldwide. Our record of safety and reliability is second to none. For more information, call Western Union: USA 1-800-325-6000, Canada 1-800-235-0000. Wherever you are, you're never far from home.

www.westernunion.com

WESTERN UNION | MONEY TRANSFER®

The fastest way to send money worldwide:

As a general rule, it's cheaper to convert money in France. It's good to bring enough foreign currency to last for the first 24-72 hours of a trip to avoid being penniless after banking hours or on a holiday. Travelers living in the U.S. can get foreign currency from the comfort of their home; **Capital Foreign Exchange,** tel. 888-842-0880, or **International Currency Express,** tel. 888-278-6628, will deliver foreign currency (for over 120 countries) or traveler's checks overnight (US$15) or second-day (US$12) at competitive exchange rates.

Watch out for commission rates and check newspapers for the standard rate of exchange. Banks generally have the best rates. Since you lose money with each transaction, convert in large sums. Also, using an ATM card or a credit card (see p. 46) will normally get you better rates. If you use traveler's checks or bills, carry some in small denominations (US$50 or less), especially for times when you are forced to exchange money at disadvantageous rates. At the same time, exchanging large sums at one time (though never more than is safe to carry around) to minimize losses on commission and ATM withdrawal fees. Yes, this is rocket science.

Beware of *bureaux de change* at airports, train stations, and touristy areas such as the Champs-Elysées, which generally have less favorable rates. Going off the beaten path may stretch your dollar. Many, but not all, banks will exchange money from 9am-noon and 2-4:30pm. Banks near the Opéra, however, exchange money from 9am-5pm during the week and have 24-hour exchange machines.

American Express, 11, rue Scribe, 9ème (tel. 01 47 77 79 33; fax 01 47 77 74 57). M: Opéra or Auber. Across from the back of the Opéra. Tolerable exchange rates and long lines in summer, especially M and F-Sa. No commission. Cardholders can cash US$1000 in personal checks from a U.S. bank every 21 days; bring your passport. The office receives moneygrams and holds mail for cardholders or for those with AmEx Traveler's Checks. English spoken. Open M-F 9am-6:30pm, Sa 10am-5:30pm, exchange counters only Su 10am-5pm.

Thomas Cook, 73, av. des Champs-Elysées, 8ème (tel. 01 45 62 89 55; fax 01 45 62 89 55). M: Franklin D. Roosevelt. If you do not have an AmEx card, you can receive moneygrams at over 30 Thomas Cook locations in Paris. Contact the Champs-Élysées branch for more info. English spoken. Open daily 9am-10pm. Branch for money exchange near Tourist Office at 125, av. des Champs-Elysées.

At Tourist Office, Main office on the Champs-Elysées offers competitive rates with no commission. (See **Tourist Offices,** p. 85).

TRAVELER'S CHECKS

Traveler's checks are one of the safest and least troublesome means of carrying funds, since they can be refunded if stolen. Several agencies and banks sell them, usually for face value plus a small percentage commission. A number of places in France, only accept traveler's checks in francs or euros, so keep that in mind when buying your checks. (Members of the American Automobile Association, and some banks and credit unions, can get American Express checks commission-free; see **Driving Permits and Insurance**). **American Express** and **Visa** are the most widely recognized. If you're ordering checks from a bank, do so well in advance, especially if you are requesting large sums. American Express offices often sell traveler's checks in major currencies over the counter.

Each agency provides refunds if your checks are lost or stolen, and many provide additional services, such as toll-free refund hotlines in the countries you're visiting, emergency message services, and stolen credit card assistance.

In order to collect a **refund for lost or stolen checks,** keep your check receipts separate from your checks and store them in a safe place or with a traveling companion. Record check numbers when you cash them, leave a list of check numbers with someone at home, and ask for a list of refund centers when you buy your checks. Never countersign your checks until you are ready to cash them, and always bring your passport with you when you plan to use the checks.

American Express: Call 800 251 902 in Australia; in New Zealand 0800 441 068; in the U.K. (0800) 52 13 13; in the U.S. and Canada 800-221-7282. Elsewhere, call U.S. collect 1-801-964-6665; www.aexp.com. American Express traveler's checks are available in France. Checks can be purchased for a small fee (1-4%) at American Express Travel Service Offices, banks, and American Automobile Association offices. AAA members can buy the checks commission-free. American Express offices cash their checks commission-free (except where prohibited by national governments), but often at slightly worse rates than banks. *Cheques for Two* can be signed by either of two people traveling together. The booklet *Traveler's Companion* lists travel office addresses and stolen check hotlines for France.

Citicorp: Call 800-645-6556 in the U.S. and Canada; in Europe, the Middle East, or Africa, call the London office at 44 171 508 7007; from elsewhere, call U.S. collect 1-813-623-1709. Traveler's checks in 7 currencies. Commission 1-2%. Guaranteed hand-delivery of traveler's checks when a refund location is not convenient. Call 24hr.

Thomas Cook MasterCard: From the U.S., Canada, or Caribbean call 800-223-7373; from the U.K. call (0800) 622 101; from elsewhere, call 44 1733 318 950 collect. Checks available in 13 currencies. Commission 2%. Thomas Cook offices cash checks commission-free, and their offices are widespread in France.

Visa: Call 800-227-6811 in the U.S.; in the U.K. (0800) 895 078; from elsewhere, call 44 1733 318 949 and reverse the charges. Locations and other information provided.

CREDIT CARDS

Credit cards are generally accepted in all but the smallest businesses in Paris. Major credit cards can be used to extract cash advances in francs from associated banks and cash machines throughout France. Credit card companies get the wholesale exchange rate, which is generally 5% better than the retail rate used by banks and other currency exchange establishments. The most commonly accepted cards, in both businesses and cash machines, are **Visa** (also known as **Carte Bleue**), and **MasterCard** (also called **Eurocard**). Heavy surcharges keep small businesses out of the **American Express** loop. American Express cards do work in some ATMs, as well as at AmEx offices and major airports.

French-issued credit cards are fitted with a micro-chip (such cards are known as *cartes à puces*) rather than a magnetic strip *(cartes à piste magnétiques);* in untouristed areas, cashiers may attempt (and fail) to scan the card with a micro-chip reader. In such circumstances you should ask for a more senior staff member who (hopefully) will know to swipe your card through the magnetic strip reader. If in doubt, explain: say *"Ceci n'est pas une carte à puce, mais une carte à piste magnétique"* (This card does not have a microchip, but a magnetic-strip).

All ATM machines require a **Personal Identification Number (PIN).** Ask your credit card company for a PIN before you leave; without it, you will be unable to withdraw cash outside your home country. If you already have a PIN, make sure it will work in France. Credit cards often offer an array of other services, from insurance to emergency assistance. Check with your company to find out what is covered.

CREDIT CARD COMPANIES. Visa (U.S. tel. 800-336-8472) and **MasterCard** (U.S. tel. 800-307-7309) are issued in cooperation with individual banks and some other organizations. **American Express** (U.S. tel. 800-843-2273) has an annual fee of up to US$55, depending on the card. Cardholder services include the option of cashing personal checks at AmEx offices, a 24-hour hotline with medical and legal assistance in emergencies (tel. 1-800-554-2639 in U.S. and Canada; from abroad call U.S. collect 1-202-554-2639), and the American Express Travel Service. Benefits include assistance in changing airline, hotel, and car rental reservations, baggage loss and flight insurance, sending mailgrams and international cables, and holding your mail at one of the more than 1700 AmEx offices around the world. The **Discover Card** (U.S. tel. 800-347-2683; outside U.S., call 801-902-3100) offers small cash-back bonuses on most purchases, but is not widely accepted in France.

CASH CARDS

24-hour **Cash machines** (also called **ATMs**) are widespread in France. Depending on the system that your home bank uses, you can probably access your own personal bank account whenever you need money. ATMs get the same wholesale exchange rate as credit cards. Despite these perks, do some research before relying too heavily on automation. There is often a limit on the amount of money you can withdraw per day (usually about US$500, depending on the type of card and account), and computer networks sometimes fail. Your home bank may also charge a fee for using ATM facilities abroad.

The two major international money networks are **Cirrus** (U.S. tel. 800-4-CIRRUS (424-7787)) and **PLUS** (U.S. tel. 800-843-7587 for the "Voice Response Unit Locator"). The PLUS system works in most Visa ATMs. Institutions supporting PLUS are: Crédit Commercial de France, Banque Populaire, Union de Banque à Paris, Point Argent, Banque Nationale de Paris, Crédit du Nord, Gie Osiris, and ATMs in many post offices. To locate ATMs around the world, use www.visa.com/pd/atm or www.mastercard.com/atm..

ATM ALERT. All automatic teller machines require a four-digit **Personal Identification Number (PIN),** which credit cards in the United States do not always carry. You must ask your credit card company to assign you one before you leave. Without this PIN, you will be unable to withdraw cash with your credit card abroad. Also, if your PIN is longer than four digits, ask your bank whether the first four digits will work, or whether you need a new number. There are no letters on the keypads of most European bank machines, so work out your PIN here: QZ correspond to 1, ABC correspond to 2; DEF to 3; GHI to 4; JKL to 5; MNO to 6; PRS to 7; TUV to 8; and WXY to 9. If you mistakenly punch the wrong code into a French ATM three times it will eat your card. If you **lose your card** in Paris, call for help at the following numbers, all of which have English-speaking operators: **Mastercard** (tel. 08 00 90 13 87); **Visa** (tel. 08 00 90 20 33); **American Express** (tel. 01 47 77 72 00).

GETTING MONEY FROM HOME

AMERICAN EXPRESS. Cardholders can withdraw cash from their **checking** or **current accounts** at any of AmEx's major offices and many of its representatives' offices, up to US$1000 every 21 days (no service charge, no interest). AmEx also offers Express Cash at any of their ATMs in France. Express Cash withdrawals are automatically debited from the Cardmember's checking account or line of credit. AmEx Green card holders may withdraw up to US$1000 in a seven day period. There is a 2% transaction fee for each cash withdrawal, with a US$2.50 minimum/ $20 maximum. To enroll in Express Cash, Cardmembers may call 800 CASH NOW (227-4669) in the U.S.; outside the U.S. call collect 1-336 668 5041.

WESTERN UNION. Travelers from the U.S., Canada, and the U.K. can wire money abroad through Western Union's international money transfer services. In the U.S., call 800 325 6000; in the U.K., call 0800 833 833; in Canada, call 800 235 0000. You can send money to any Western Union office; there are some located in French post offices. The rates for sending cash are generally US$10-11 cheaper than with a credit card, and the money is usually available at the place you're sending it to within an hour.

U.S. STATE DEPARTMENT (U.S. CITIZENS ONLY). In emergencies, U.S. citizens can have money sent via the State Department. For US$15, they will forward money within hours to the nearest consular office, which will disburse it according to instructions. The office serves only Americans in the direst of straits abroad;

non-American travelers should contact their embassies for information on wiring cash. Check with the State Department or the nearest U.S. embassy or consulate for the quickest way to have the money sent. Contact the Overseas Citizens Service, American Citizens Services, Consular Affairs, Room 4811, U.S. Department of State, Washington, D.C. 20520 (tel. 202-647-5225; nights, Sundays, and holidays 647-4000; fax (on demand only) 647-3000; http://travel.state.gov).

TAXES

All goods and services bought in France include a **Value Added Tax (TVA)** in the purchase price; this must also be included in all advertised or posted prices. The standard rate is 20.6%, although foodstuffs are taxed at 5.5% and newspapers and medicines 2.1%. Non-EU residents may be able to reclaim part of the tax they have payed on leaving the country: see **Reclaiming value-added tax,** p. 42.

Hotels may levy a *taxe de séjour* (see **Accommodations,** p. 98).

HEALTH

Common sense is the simplest prescription for good health while you travel. Travelers complain most often about their feet and their gut, so take precautionary measures: drink lots of fluids to prevent dehydration and constipation, wear sturdy, broken-in shoes and clean socks, and use talcum powder to keep your feet dry. To minimize the effects of jet lag, "reset" your body's clock by adopting the time of your destination as soon as you board the plane.

BEFORE YOU GO

There is no shortage of pharmacies in Paris, and almost everything for minor health problems, from headaches to hangovers, is readily available (see **Health and Help,** p. 91). Some travelers swear by their own compact **first-aid kit,** containing bandages, aspirin or other pain killer, antibiotic cream, a thermometer, a Swiss army knife with tweezers, moleskin, decongestant for colds, motion sickness remedy, medicine for diarrhea or stomach problems (Pepto Bismol tablets and Immodium), sunscreen, insect repellent, and burn ointment. **Contact lens** wearers should bring an extra pair, a copy of the prescription, a pair of glasses, extra solution, and eyedrops. People with **asthma** or **allergies** should be aware that Paris has visibly high levels of air pollution, particularly during the summer, and that non-smoking areas are almost nonexistent. Call 01 44 59 47 64 for updated information on air quality and pollution levels in Paris. (Open M-F 9am-5:30pm.) Consider bringing an over-the-counter antihistamine, decongestant, inhaler, etc., since there may not be a French equivalent with the correct dosage.

In your **passport,** write the names of any people you wish to be contacted in case of a medical emergency, and also list any **allergies** or medical conditions you would want doctors to be aware of. Allergy sufferers might want to obtain a full supply of any necessary medication before the trip. Matching a prescription to a foreign equivalent is not always easy, safe, or possible. Carry up-to-date, legible prescriptions or a statement from your doctor stating the medication's trade name, manufacturer, chemical name, and dosage. While traveling, be sure to keep all medication with you in your carry-on luggage.

AIDS, HIV, STDS

Acquired Immune Deficiency Syndrome (**AIDS; SIDA** in French) is a major problem in France. Paris is the AIDS capital of Europe. There are as many heterosexuals infected as homosexuals, and more women infected than men. The easiest mode of HIV transmission is through direct blood-to-blood contact with an HIV-positive person; *never* share intravenous drug, tattooing, or other needles. The most common mode of transmission is sexual intercourse. You can greatly reduce the risk by using latex condoms; these are widely available in France (see **Birth Control,** p. 49). For counseling and information resources, see p. 85.

For more information on AIDS, call the **U.S. Centers for Disease Control's** 24-hour hotline at 800-342-2437. Council's brochure, *Travel Safe: AIDS and International Travel,* is available at all Council Travel offices and at their website (www.ciee.org/study/safety/travelsafe.htm).

Sexually transmitted diseases (STDs) such as gonorrhea, chlamydia, genital warts, syphilis, and herpes are easier to contract than HIV, and some can be just as deadly. When having sex, condoms may protect you from certain STDs, but oral or even tactile contact can lead to transmission.

BIRTH CONTROL

Contraception is readily available in most pharmacies (for some 24-hr pharmacies, see p. 84). To obtain **condoms** in France, visit a pharmacy and tell the clerk, *"Je voudrais une boîte de préservatifs"* (zhuh-voo-DRAY oon BWAHT duh PREY-zehr-va-TEEF). The French branch of the International Planned Parenthood Federation, the **Mouvement Français pour le Planning Familiale** (MFPF; tel. 01 42 60 93 20), can provide more information. Women on the pill should bring enough to allow for possible loss or extended stays. Bring a prescription, since forms of the pill vary a good deal. Women who use a diaphragm should bring enough contraceptive jelly. Though condoms are increasingly available, you might want to bring your favorite brand before you go, as availability and quality vary.

NO PRÉSERVATIFS ADDED Having invented the French kiss and the French tickler, the speakers of the language of love have long had *savoir faire* in all things sexual—safety included. French pharmacies provide 24-hour condom (*préservatif* or *capote*) dispensers. In wonderful French style, they unabashedly adorn the sides of buildings on public streets and vending machines in the métro. When dining out, don't ask for foods without *préservatifs* or mistake your raspberry compote for a *capote*. Funny looks will greet you, as the French have not yet caught on to the international craze for condom-eating, and will think you a bit odd.

WOMEN'S HEALTH

Abortion is legal in France, where the abortion pill, RU-486, was pioneered. However, if you are in Paris for a short stay, it may not be available to you. In any case, the MFPF and the Centre de Planification et d'Education Familiale (see **Health and Help,** p. 83 and **Women Travelers,** p. 60) can provide referrals and other information. Women who need an abortion while abroad should contact the International Planned Parenthood Federation, European Regional Office, Regent's College Inner Circle, Regent's Park, London NW1 4NS (tel. (171) 487 7900; fax 487 7950; email info@ippf.org; www.ippf.org), for more information.

SAFETY AND SECURITY

SELF DEFENSE

There is no sure-fire set of precautions that will protect you from all of the situations you might encounter when you travel. A good self defense course will give you more options in dealing with the unexpected. **Impact, Prepare,** and **Model Mugging** can refer you to local self defense courses in the United States (tel. 800-345-5425) and Vancouver, Canada (tel. (604) 878-3838). Workshops (2-3 hours) start at US$50 and full courses run US$350-500. Courses are for both women and men.

FINANCIAL SECURITY

PROTECTING YOUR VALUABLES

To prevent easy theft, don't keep all your valuables (money, important documents) in one place. Label every piece of luggage both inside and out. **Don't put a wallet with money in your back pocket.** Never count your money in public and carry as little as possible. If you carry a purse, buy a sturdy one with a secure clasp, and carry it crosswise on the side, away from the street with the clasp against you. A **money belt** is the best way to carry cash; you can buy one at most camping supply stores. A **neck pouch** is equally safe, although far less accessible. Keep some money separate from the rest to use in an emergency or in case of theft.

PICKPOCKETS

In city crowds and especially on public transportation, **pickpockets** are amazingly good at their craft. Rush hour is no excuse for strangers to press up against you on the métro. If someone stands uncomfortably close, move to another car and hold your bags tightly. Be alert in public telephone booths. If you must say your calling card number, do so very quietly; if you punch it in, make sure no one can see you.

DRUGS AND ALCOHOL

A meek "I didn't know it was illegal" will not suffice. Possession of **drugs** in France can end your vacation abruptly; convicted offenders can expect a jail sentence and fines. Never bring any illegal drugs across a border. It is vital that **prescription drugs,** particularly insulin, syringes, or narcotics, be accompanied by the prescriptions themselves and a statement from a doctor and left in original, labeled containers. In France, police may stop and search anyone on the street—no reason is required. Also, a positive result of the gentlemanly drinking age (16) is that public drunkenness is virtually unseen, even in younger crowds. In general, raucous chest-beating and sidewalk stumbling will earn the disdain of locals.

INSURANCE

Travel insurance generally covers four basic areas: medical/health problems, property loss, trip cancellation/interruption, and emergency evacuation. Be sure to check whether your regular insurance policies extend to travel-related accidents; even if they do, you may consider purchasing travel insurance if the cost of potential trip cancellation/interruption or emergency medical evacuation is greater than you can absorb.

US residents' **Medical insurance** (especially university policies) often covers costs incurred abroad; check with your provider. **Medicare does not cover foreign travel.** Canadians are protected by their home province's health insurance plan for up to 90 days after leaving the country; check with the provincial Ministry of Health or Health Plan Headquarters for details. **Homeowners' insurance** (or your family's coverage) often covers theft during travel and loss of travel documents (passport, plane ticket, railpass, etc.) up to US$500.

ISIC and **ITIC** provide basic insurance benefits, including US$100 per day of in-hospital sickness for a maximum of 60 days, US$3000 of accident-related medical reimbursement, and US$25,000 for emergency medical transport (see **Identification,** p. 41). This might sound like a lot, but in reality won't even cover a major operation. Cardholders have access to a toll-free 24-hour helpline whose multilingual staff can provide assistance in medical, legal, and financial emergencies overseas (tel. 800-626-2427 in the U.S. and Canada; elsewhere call the U.S. collect 713-267-2525. **American Express** (tel. 800-528-4800) grants most cardholders automatic car rental insurance (collision and theft, but not liability) and ground travel accident coverage of US$100,000 on flight purchases made with the card.

Prices for travel insurance purchased separately generally run about US$50 per week for full coverage, while trip cancellation/interruption may be purchased separately at a rate of about US$5.50 per US$100 of coverage.

INSURANCE PROVIDERS. Council and **STA** (see p. 54 for complete listings) offer a range of plans that can supplement your basic insurance coverage. Other private insurance providers in the **U.S. and Canada** include: **Access America** (tel. 800-284-8300; fax 804-673-1491); **Berkely Group/Carefree Travel Insurance** (tel. 800-323-3149 or 516-294-0220; fax 294-1095; info@berkely.com; www.berkely.com); **Globalcare Travel Insurance** (tel. 800-821-2488; fax 781-592-7720; www.globalcare-cocco.com); and **Travel Assistance International** (tel. 800-821-2828 or 202-828-5894; fax 828-5896; email wassist@aol.com; www.worldwide-assistance.com). Providers in the **U.K.** include **Campus Travel** (tel. (01865) 258 000; fax 792 378) and **Columbus Travel Insurance** (tel. (0171) 375 0011; fax 375 0022). In **Australia** try **CIC Insurance** (tel. 9202 8000; fax 9202 8220).

PACKING

Pack lightly; the rest is commentary. You can buy anything you'll need in Paris. One tried-and-true method of packing is to set out everything you think you'll need, then pack half of it—and twice the money, if you can. Pack your favorite clothes. There is no one specific way to dress in Paris, but everyone dresses like they mean it (see **Blending In,** p. 96).

For a long stay in Paris, you might prefer a suitcase to a backpack. If you'll be on the move frequently, go with the pack. Bring along a small daypack for carrying lunch, a camera, and valuables (see **Protecting Your Valuables,** p. 50).

WASHING CLOTHES

Laundromats are listed on p. 87, but sometimes it may be cheaper and easier to use a sink. Bring a small bar or tube of detergent soap, a small rubber ball to stop up the sink, and a travel clothesline.

ELECTRIC CURRENT

In France, electricity is 220 volts AC, enough to fry any 110V North American appliance. 220V Electrical appliances don't like 110V current, either. Visit a hardware store for an adapter (which changes the shape of the plug) and a converter (which changes the voltage). Don't make the mistake of using only an adapter (unless appliance instructions explicitly state otherwise).

CONTACT LENSES

Machines which heat-disinfect contact lenses will require a small converter (about US$20) to 220V, as well as a plug adapter. Consider switching temporarily to a chemical disinfection system, but check with your lens dispenser; some lenses may be damaged by a chemical system. Lens care supplies may be expensive and difficult to find, so bring enough for your entire vacation.

FILM

Expect to pay at least US$4 for a 24-exposure ISO200 35mm color film. If you're not a serious photographer, you might want to consider bringing a **disposable camera.** Airport carry-on X-ray machines should not affect film speeds of 400 and under; always pack film in your carry-on luggage, since higher-intensity X-rays are used on checked luggage.

OTHER USEFUL ITEMS

It's always a good idea to carry a first-aid kit (see **Health,** p. 48). Other useful items include: an umbrella; sealable plastic bags (for damp clothes, soap, food, shampoo, and other spillables); alarm clock; waterproof matches; plastic water bottle; string (makeshift clothesline and lashing material); towel; padlock; whistle; rubber bands; flashlight; cold-water soap; earplugs; electrical tape (for patching tears); tweezers; garbage bags; a small calculator for currency conversion; a pair of flip-flops for the shower; a money-belt for carrying valuables; deodorant; razors; tampons; and condoms (see **AIDS, HIV, and STDs,** p. 49). For more tips, see *The Packing Book*, by Judith Gilford (Ten Speed Press; $9), and *Backpacking One Step at a Time* (Harvey Manning. Vintage; $15).

KEEPING IN TOUCH

MAILING TO PARIS

Airmail letters under 1 oz. between the US and France take 4 to 7 days and cost US$0.60 20g letters from Canada cost CDN$0.95. Allow at least 5 working days from Australia (postage AUS$1.00 for up to 20g) and 3 days from Britain (postage UK£0.30 for up to 20g). Envelopes should be marked "air mail" or *"par avion"* to avoid slow surface mail. There are several ways to arrange pick-up of letters sent to you while you are abroad. See **Receiving Mail in Paris,** p. 93.

If regular airmail is too slow, **Federal Express** (U.S. tel. for international operator 800-247-4747; UK 0800 123 800; Australia 13 26 10; Ireland 1800 535 800; South Africa 011 923-8000; New Zealand 0800 733 339) can get a letter from New York to Paris in two days for a whopping US$25.50; rates among non-U.S. locations are prohibitively expensive (overnight from London to Paris, for example, costs upwards of UK£36). Using a **U.S. Global Priority Mail** flat-rate envelope, a letter from New York would arrive within four days and would cost US$5.

Surface mail is by far the cheapest and slowest way to send mail. It takes one to three months to cross the Atlantic and two to four to cross the Pacific—appropriate for sending large quantities of items you won't need to see for a while. When ordering books and materials from abroad, always include one or two **International Reply Coupons (IRCs)**—a way of providing the postage to cover delivery. IRCs should be available from your local post office and those abroad (US$1.05)

CALLING PARIS

TO CALL FRANCE DIRECT FROM HOME, DIAL:

1. The international access code of your home country. **International access codes** include: Australia 0011; Ireland 00; New Zealand 00; South Africa 09; U.K. 00; U.S. 011. Country codes and city codes are sometimes listed with a zero in front (e.g., 033), but after dialing the international access code, drop successive zeros (with an access code of 011, e.g., 011 33).
2. 33 (France's country code).
3. The 10-digit French number **minus the first zero**.

Thus if a number was listed as 01 23 45 67 89, you would dial the international access code followed by 33 1 23 45 67 89.

BILLED CARDS. Calls are billed either collect or to your account. **MCI World-Phone** also provides access to MCI's Traveler's Assist, which gives legal and medical advice, exchange rate information, and translation services. Other phone companies provide similar services to travelers. **To obtain a calling card** from your national telecommunications service before you leave home, contact the appropriate company below.

USA: AT&T (tel. 888-288-4685); **Sprint** (tel. 800-877-4646); or **MCI** (tel. 800-444-4141; from abroad dial the country's MCI access number).

Canada: Bell Canada **Canada Direct** (tel. 800-565-4708).

U.K.: British Telecom **BT Direct** (tel. (800) 34 51 44).

Ireland: Telecom Éireann **Ireland Direct** (tel. (800) 250 250).

Australia: Telstra **Australia Direct** (tel. 13 22 00).

New Zealand: Telecom New Zealand (tel. (800) 000 000).

South Africa: Telkom South Africa (tel. 09 03).

PREPAID CARDS. You can buy prepaid cards at home or in France (see p. 91) which can be used anywhere in the world; the number of varieties available is bewildering but beware that the cheaper the calls offered, the more likely you are to have trouble getting through. Most major telecommunications companies issue them too; these are generally widely available in news agents and travel stores. Common prepaid cards you can buy at home include the Telstra **PhoneAway** (Australia), the Telecom Eireann **Ireland Direct Prepaid**, AT&T **Global Prepaid Card** (USA), the Telecom New Zealand **talkaway**, and the Canada Direct **Hello!.**

GETTING THERE

BY PLANE

When it comes to airfare, a little effort can save you a bundle. If your plans are flexible enough to deal with the restrictions, courier fares are the cheapest. Tickets bought from consolidators and standby seating are also good deals, but last-minute specials, airfare wars, and charter flights often beat these fares. The key is to hunt around, to be flexible, and to persistently ask about discounts. Students, seniors, those under 26 and those who plan ahead should never pay full price for a ticket.

DETAILS AND TIPS

Timing: Airfares to France peak between June and September, while Easter and Christmas are also expensive periods in which to travel. Most cheap fares require a Saturday night stay. Flexibility is usually not an option for the budget traveler; traveling with an "open return" ticket can be pricier than fixing a return date when buying the ticket and paying later to change it. Most budget tickets, once bought, allow no date or route changes to made; student tickets sometimes allow date changes for a price.

Checking in: Whenever flying internationally, pick up tickets for international flights well in advance of the departure date, and reconfirm by phone within 72 hours of departure. Most airlines require that passengers arrive at the airport at least two hours before departure. One carry-on item (max 5kg) and two pieces of checked baggage weighing up to 60Kg total is the norm for non-courier intercontinental flights; for flights within Europe, the checked baggage allowance is normally 20Kg, regardless of the number of pieces.

Fares: Round-trip fares to Paris from the U.S. range from US$250-400 (during the off-season) to US$200-700 (during the summer) From Australia, count on paying between AUS$1600 and AUS$3000, depending on the season. From New Zealand, fares start at about NZ$5000 and climb to $9000. Flights from the U.K. to France are a comparative snip at UK£80-UK£140 for London-Paris, while a return flight from Dublin to Paris can cost as little as IR£120 return.

BUDGET AND STUDENT TRAVEL AGENCIES

A knowledgeable agent specializing in flights to Europe can make your life easy and help you save, too, but agents may not spend the time to find you the lowest possible fare—they get paid on commission. Students and under-26ers holding **ISIC and IYTC cards** (see **Identification**, p. 41), respectively, qualify for big discounts from student travel agencies. Most flights from budget agencies are on major airlines, but in peak season some may sell seats on less reliable chartered aircraft.

Campus/Usit Youth and Student Travel (www.usitcampus.co.uk). In the U.K. call (0171) 730 34 02; in North America call (0171) 730 21 01; worldwide call (0171) 730 81 11. Offices include: 19-21 Aston Quay, O'Connell Bridge, **Dublin** 2 (tel. (01) 677-8117; fax 679-8833); 52 Grosvenor Gardens, **London** SW1W 0AG; New York Student Center, 895 Amsterdam Ave., **New York,** NY, 10025 (tel. 212-663-5435; email usitny@aol.com). Additional offices in Cork, Galway, Limerick, Waterford, Coleraine, Derry, Belfast, and Greece.

Council Travel (www.counciltravel.com). U.S. offices include: Emory Village, 1561 N. Decatur Rd., **Atlanta,** GA 30307 (tel. 404-377-9997); 273 Newbury St., **Boston,** MA 02116 (tel. 617-266-1926); 1160 N. State St., **Chicago,** IL 60610 (tel. 312-951-0585); 10904 Lindbrook Dr., **Los Angeles,** CA 90024 (tel. 310-208-3551); 205 E. 42nd St., **New York,** NY 10017 (tel. 212-822-2700); 530 Bush St., **San Francisco,** CA 94108 (tel. 415-421-3473); 1314 NE 43rd St. #210, **Seattle,** WA 98105 (tel. 206-632-2448); 3300 M St. NW, **Washington, D.C.** 20007 (tel. 202-337-6464). **For U.S. cities not listed,** call 800-2-COUNCIL (226-8624). Also 28A Poland St. (Oxford Circus), **London,** W1V 3DB (tel. (0171) 287 3337), **Paris** (144 41 89 89), and **Munich** (089 39 50 22).

CTS Travel, 44 Goodge St., **London** W1 (tel. (0171) 636 00 31; fax 637 53 28; email ctsinfo@ctstravel.com.uk).

STA Travel, 6560 Scottsdale Rd. #F100, Scottsdale, AZ 85253 (tel. 800-777-0112 fax 602-922-0793; www.sta-travel.com). A student and youth travel organization with over 150 offices worldwide. Ticket booking, travel insurance, railpasses, and more. U.S. offices include: 297 Newbury Street, **Boston,** MA 02115 (tel. 617-266-6014); 429 S. Dearborn St., **Chicago,** IL 60605 (tel. 312-786-9050); 7202 Melrose Ave., **Los Angeles,** CA 90046 (tel. 323-934-8722); 10 Downing St., **New York,** NY 10014 (tel. 212-627-3111); 4341 University Way NE, **Seattle,** WA 98105 (tel. 206-633-5000); 2401 Pennsylvania Ave., Ste. G, **Washington, D.C.** 20037 (tel. 202-887-0912); 51 Grant Ave., **San Francisco,** CA 94108 (tel. 415-391-8407). In the U.K., 6 Wrights Ln., **London** W8 6TA (tel. (0171) 938 47 11 for North American travel). In New Zealand, 10 High St., **Auckland** (tel. (09) 309 04 58). In Australia, 222 Faraday St., **Melbourne** VIC 3053 (tel. (03) 9349 2411).

Travel CUTS (Canadian Universities Travel Services Limited), 187 College St., Toronto, Ont. M5T 1P7 (tel. 416-979 2406; fax 979 8167; www.travelcuts.com). 40 offices across Canada. Also in the U.K., 295-A Regent St., **London** W1R 7YA (tel. 0171 255 19 44).

Wasteels, Victoria Station, London, U.K. SW1V 1JT (tel. (0171) 834 70 66; fax 630 76 28; www.wasteels.dk/uk). A huge chain in Europe, with 203 locations. Sells the Wasteels BIJ tickets, which are discounted (30-45% off regular fare) 2nd class international point-to-point train tickets with unlimited stopovers (must be under 26); sold only in Europe.

Other organizations that specialize in finding cheap fares include:

Cheap Tickets (tel. 800-377-1000, www.cheaptickets.com) flies worldwide to and from the U.S. Choose itineraries by destination, price, and airline.

Travel Avenue (tel. 800-333-3335) rebates commercial fares to or from the U.S. and offers low fares for flights anywhere in the world. They also offer package deals, which include car rental and hotel reservations, to many destinations.

COMMERCIAL AIRLINES

The commercial airlines' lowest regular offer is the **APEX** (Advance Purchase Excursion) fare, which provides confirmed reservations and allows "open-jaw" tickets. Generally, reservations must be made 7 to 21 days in advance, with 7- to 14-day minimum-stay and up to 90-day maximum-stay restrictions, and hefty cancellation and change penalties (fees rise in summer). Book peak-season APEX fares early, since by May you will have a hard time getting your desired departure date. Although APEX fares are not the cheapest possible fares, they will give you a standard against which you can compare bargain fares. Low-season fares should be appreciably cheaper. **Air France** (tel. 0 802 802 802 in France; from abroad call +33 8 36 64 08 02; www.airfrance.com) is France's national airline, connecting France to the world. If flying in tricolor glory will make your vacation, it may be worth paying a bit more.

 BUYING TICKETS OVER THE INTERNET. There are many advantages to browsing for travel bargains on the Web. Many airline sites offer special last-minute deals to internet customers, and you can make leisurely selections at any hour of the day or night. Make sure that the site uses a secure server before handing over any credit card details. **STA online** (www.sta-travel-com) offers student-rate flights and insurance. **Travelocity** (www.travelocity.com) offers a comprehensive range of services including flights and car hire. **Cheaptickets** (www.cheaptickets.com) offers just that, with a minimum of hassle and free browsing before you buy. At **Priceline** (www.priceline.com) you choose how much you want to pay, though you are obliged to buy the ticket if it finds one; be prepared for antisocial hours and odd routes.

TRAVELING FROM NORTH AMERICA

Basic round-trip fares to Paris range from US$250-700. Standard commercial carriers like American and United will probably offer the most convenient flights, but they may not be the cheapest, unless you manage to grab a special promotion or airfare war ticket. You will probably find flying one of the following "discount" airlines a better deal, provided that one of their departure points works for you.

Icelandair (tel. 800-223 5500; www.centrum.is/icelandair) has last-minute offers and standby fares on some flights between North America and Europe. Reservations must be made within three days of departure.

Finnair (tel. 800-950-5000; www.us.finnair.com). Cheap round-trips from San Francisco, New York, and Toronto through Helsinki.

TowerAir (tel. 800-348-6937; www.towerair.com). Departs from Los Angeles, Miami, New York, and San Francisco.

United Airlines (tel. 800-538 2929 for international reservations; www.ual.com). Mammoth US carrier offers last-minute special 'E-fares' deals available only online.

Air France 162 flights per week between the US and France. See above for details.

TRAVELING FROM THE UK AND IRELAND

Because of the myriad of carriers flying between the UK and the continent, we have only included discount airlines or airlines with cheap specials here. Also try the **Air Travel Advisory Bureau** in London (tel. (020) 76 36 50 00; www.atab.co.uk), which provides free referrals to specialist travel agencies and consolidators who offer discounted airfares out of major UK airports.

Aer Lingus (tel. (01) 886 88 88; www.aerlingus.ie). Return tickets from Dublin to Paris, (IR£99-149); and from Cork, Shannon, Galway, Sligo, and Kerry (IR£99-199).

British Midland (Belfast (01232) 241188; Dublin (01) 283 0700; London (0345) 554554 tel. (0870) 607 0555 for reservations; U.S. tel. (800) 788-0555; www.british-midland.com) has services from Belfast, Dublin, Edinburgh, Glasgow, Leeds, London, Manchester, Teesside. Prices start at UK£45 one-way.

Debonair Airways (tel. (0541) 50 03 00; www.debonair.co.uk). Return tickets from London(UK£73-143).

KLM (tel. (0870) 507 40 74; www.klmuk.com) Cheap return tickets from London.

TRAVELING FROM AUSTRALIA AND NEW ZEALAND

Air New Zealand (tel. (0800) 35 22 66; www.airnz.com). From Auckland and elsewhere.

Qantas Air (Australia tel. 13 13 13); www.qantas.com.au). Flights from Australia and New Zealand for around AUS$2400.

Singapore Air (Australia tel. (02) 93 50 01 00; New Zealand tel. 379 32 09; www.singaporeair.com). Flies from Auckland, Sydney, and Melbourne.

Thai Airways (Australia tel. (1300) 65 19 60; New Zealand tel. (09) 377 02 68; www.thaiair.com). From Auckland, Sydney, and Melbourne.

TRAVELING FROM SOUTH AFRICA

Air France (tel. (011) 880 80 40; www.airfrance.com). From Johannesburg.

British Airways (tel. (011) 441 86 00; www.british-airways.com/regional/sa). From Johannesburg and Cape Town from SAR3100.

Lufthansa (tel. (011) 484 47 11; www.lufthansa.com). From Johannesburg and CapeTown.

OTHER CHEAP ALTERNATIVES

AIR COURIER FLIGHTS

Couriers help transport cargo on international flights by guaranteeing delivery of the baggage claim slips from the company to a representative overseas. Generally, couriers must travel light (carry-ons only) and deal with flight restrictions. Most flights are round-trip only with short, fixed-length stays (usually one week) and a limit of a single ticket per issue. Most operate only out of the biggest U.S. cities. You must be over 21 (in some cases 18), have a valid passport, and procure your own visa, if necessary. Groups such as the **Air Courier Association** (tel. 800-282-1202; www.aircourier.org) and the **International Association of Air Travel Couriers**, 220 South Dixie Hwy., P.O. Box 1349, Lake Worth, FL 33460 (tel. 561-582-8320; email iaatc@courier.org; www.courier.org) provide their members with lists of opportunities and courier brokers worldwide for an annual fee. For more information, consult *Air Courier Bargains* by Kelly Monaghan (The Intrepid Traveler, US$15) or the *Courier Air Travel Handbook* by Mark Field (Perpetual Press, US$10).

CHARTER FLIGHTS

Charters are flights a tour operator contracts with an airline to fly extra loads of passengers during peak season. Charters can sometimes be cheaper than flights on scheduled airlines, some operate nonstop, and restrictions on minimum advance-purchase and minimum stay are more lenient. However, charter flights fly less frequently than major airlines, make refunds particularly difficult, and are almost always fully booked. Schedules and itineraries may also change or be cancelled at the last moment (as late as 48 hours before the trip, without a full refund), and check-in, boarding, and baggage claim are much slower. As always, pay with a credit card if you can, and consider traveler's insurance against trip interruption.

Discount clubs and **fare brokers** offer members savings on last-minute charter and tour deals. Study their contracts closely; you don't want to end up with an unwanted overnight layover. **Travelers Advantage,** Stamford, CT (tel. 800-548-1116; www.travelersadvantage.com; US$60 annual fee includes discounts, newsletters, and cheap flight directories) specializes in European travel and tour packages.

STANDBY FLIGHTS

Traveling standby requires considerable flexibility in the dates and cities of your arrival and departure. Companies that specialize in standby flights don't sell tickets, but the promise that you will get to your destination (or near your destination) within a certain window of time (anywhere from 1-5 days). Do not be surprised if you are stranded for several days, especially during tourist high season. You may only receive a refund if all available flights which depart within your date-range from the specified region are full. Future travel credit is always available.

Carefully read agreements with any company offering standby flights, as tricky fine print can leave you in the lurch. To check on a company's service record, call the Better Business Bureau of New York City (tel. 212-533-6200). It is difficult to receive refunds, and clients' vouchers will not be honored when an airline fails to receive payment in time.

Airhitch, 2641 Broadway, 3rd Fl., New York, NY 10025 (tel. 800-326-2009 or 212-864-2000; fax 864-5489; www.airhitch.org) and Los Angeles, CA (tel. 310-726-5000). In Europe, the flagship office is in Paris (tel. 147 00 16 30) and the other one is in Amsterdam (tel. 312 06 26 32 20). Several offices in Europe, round-the-clock info line, and a rating system that gives you your approximate probability of getting on a flight. Flights to Europe cost US$159 each way when departing from the Northeast, $239 from the West Coast or Northwest, $209 from the Midwest, and $189 from the Southeast. Travel within Europe is also possible, with rates ranging from $79-$139.

TICKET CONSOLIDATORS

Ticket consolidators, or **"bucket shops,"** buy unsold tickets in bulk from commercial airlines and sell them at discounted rates. The best place to look is in the Sunday travel section of any major newspaper, where many bucket shops place tiny ads. Call quickly, as availability is typically extremely limited. Not all bucket shops are reliable establishments, so insist on a receipt that gives full details of restrictions, refunds, and tickets, and pay by credit card. For more information, check the website **Consolidators FAQ** (www.travel-library.com/air-travel/consolidators.html) or the book *Consolidators: Air Travel's Bargain Basement*, by Kelly Monaghan (Intrepid Traveler, US$8).

BY BUS

British travelers may well find buses the cheapest way of getting to Paris, with return fares starting around UK$50. Obviously, the bus trip will also entail a ferry trip or occasionally a descent into the Channel Tunnel; these are included in the price of a ticket. On the downside, buses take far longer than trains and planes, and are far more susceptible to delays.

Eurolines, 4 Cardiff Rd., Luton LU1 1PP (tel. (08705) 14 32 19; fax (01582) 40 06 94; in London, 52 Grosvenor Gardens, Victoria; (tel. (01582) 40 45 11); email welcome@eurolines.uk.com; www.eurolines.co.uk). Europe's largest operator of international coach services. A Eurolines Pass offers unlimited 30-day (under 26 and over 60 UK£159; 26-60 UK £199) or 60-day (under 26 and over 60, UK£199, 26-60 UK£249) travel between 30 major tourist destinations. Roundtrip fares between London and Paris start at UK£49. Eurolines also offers **Euro Explorers,** seven complete travel loops throughout Europe with set fares and itineraries.

BY BOAT

Ferries across the English Channel *(La Manche)* link France to England and Ireland. The most popular route is also the shortest, between Dover and Calais, with departures every hour. Hoverspeed (see below) offers high-speed hovercraft and catamaran links on the same route, catering to claustrophobes in a hurry; the fastest link between the two countries is undoubtedly via the Channel Tunnel (see p. 59). All the ferries cater both to car and foot passengers, and the French ports all have excellent rail and autoroute connections to the national networks. The following details are based on **one-way** trips; Almost all companies offer reduced rates for stays of 5 days or less. Check with travel agents or the following companies.

SHORT CROSSINGS

P&O Stena Line: reservations tel. 0990 980 980 (UK); 08 02 01 00 20 (France). Weather and availability tel. 01304 863 603 (UK). Website www.posl.com. **Dover-Calais:** every 45 minutes 7am-1am and hourly through the night. Foot passengers UK£24; car with two people UK£105-143; car and up to 8 passengers UK£108-148.

SeaFrance: reservations tel. 08705 711 711 (UK); www.seafrance.co.uk. **Dover-Calais:** 16 departures daily. Foot passengers UK£15; car and driver UK£80; UK£1 additional passengers.

Hoverspeed: reservations and bookings tel. 08705 240 241 (UK); 03 21 46 14 54 (France). High speed hovercraft and catamaran services. Service is suspended in rough weather. **Dover-Calais:** 35-50min., 12-20 per day. Foot passengers UK£25-30; car and driver UK£104-140; car and 2 passengers UK£105-145. **Folkestone-Boulogne:** 55 minutes, 3-4 daily. Foot passengers UK£25; Car and driver UK£94-130; car and 2 passengers UK£95-135. **Newhaven-Dieppe:** 2hr., 2-3 per day. Foot passengers UK£25; Car and driver UK£114-153; car and 2 passengers UK£115-160.

ENGLAND AND IRELAND TO BRITTANY AND NORMANDY

Brittany ferries: Tel. 0870 90 12 400 (UK); 08 03 82 88 28 (France); www.brittanyferries.co.uk. **England to France. Portsmouth-Caen:** 6hr., 1-3 per day, 140-290F, 410-1280F with car. **Portsmouth-St-Malo:** 8¾hr., 1-2 per day, none on Fridays during low season; foot passengers 150-320F; 50F extra for bikes in high season; 480-1460F with car. **Plymouth-Roscoff:** 6hr., 1 per week during low season, 1-3 per day otherwise, foot passengers 140-300F; 50F extras for bike in high season; 440-1340F with car. **Poole-Cherbourg:** 4¼hr., 1-2 per day, none on weekends during low season, foot passengers 140-290F; 50F extra for bike in high season; 410-1280F with car. **Ireland to France. Cork-Roscoff:** 14hr., foot passengers 340-650F; 100-150F extra for bike; 1040-2770F with car. 10% student discount on all standard fares. Special prices available for roundtrip tickets with a set return date.

P&O European ferries: tel. 0870 2424 999 (UK); 01 44 51 00 51 (France); www.poef.com. **Portsmouth-Le Havre:** 2-3 per day Jan. 1-Dec. 23rd; special schedule applies Dec. 24-Dec. 31. **Portsmouth-Cherbourg:** 5-7 per day Mar. 20- Dec. 23; 1 per day Jan. 1- Mar. 19; special schedule from Dec. 24-Dec. 31. Both crossings 5½hr., 8hr. at night; foot passenger UK£18-32; car and two people UK£78-142; additional car passengers UK£7. The high-speed Superstar Express also operates between Portsmouth and Cherbourg (2¾hr.); call for details.

Irish Ferries: tel.01 638 3333 (Ireland); 01.42.66.90.90 (France). www.irishferries.ie. Summer services **Rosslare-Cherbourg** and **Rosslare-Roscoff;** destination alternates every two days. Foot passengers IR£45-85, students and seniors IR£41-71; car and two passengers IR£129-309; additional passengers IR£5-32. Cabins from IR£26.

BY CHANNEL TUNNEL

Though still dogged by huge debts, the Channel Tunnel is increasing in popularity every year as people have overcome their fears of traveling for 27 miles under the sea. Undoubtedly the fastest, most convenient and least scenic route from England to France, the 'Chunnel' offers two types of service. **Le Shuttle** is a drive-on train service which ferries cars and coaches between Folkestone and Calais; **Eurostar** is the high-speed train which links London to Paris and Brussels, with stops at Ashford in England and Calais and Lille in France. On the Eurostar, traveling at close to 150mph, the whole journey takes a snappy three hours. What's more, you board and exit the train right in the middle of each city—no added transportation time or cost is needed. Trains leave London Waterloo for Gare du Nord, where you can catch the metro and the RER. It is prudent to buy your ticket a week in advance. You must check-in at the station at least **20 minutes before departure.** Attach the nifty and required tag to all baggage items (available at terminals and travel agencies). You are allowed to transport two bags and one carry-on; you will be required to pay 90F for each additional piece of baggage. Enquire at Eurostar ticket offices or at Campus Travel in London for special promotions.

Eurostar: Reservations tel. 01233 61 75 75 (UK); 01 49 70 01 75 (France); www.eurostar.co.uk. Eurostar tickets can also be bought at most major travel agents. **London-Paris Gare du Nord:** 3hr., 18-23 departures daily. roundtrip fares: UK£249 standard; under 25 UK£79; over 60 UK£119; child (4-11) UK£55; restricted fares from UK£79. **London-Disneyland Paris:** 3hr., 1 per day, departing UK in the morning, returning early evening. Round-trip UK£89-119; youth UK£79; child UK£59. Slightly fewer departures from Ashford; fares are same as for London departures.

Le Shuttle: tel. 0800 096 9992 (UK); 03 21 00 61 00 (France); www.eurotunnel.co.uk. 20 min.; 1-3 departures per hour. Services run throughout the night. Roundtrip prices for car and all passengers: day UK£110-150; Economy (open) UK£219-299; minibreaks (5-day return) UK£139-195.

ACCOMMODATIONS

General information on **hostels** follows below; see the Chapter **Accommodations,** p. 98 for the full range of options.

HOSTELS

Hostels are generally dorm-style accommodations, often in single-sex large rooms with bunk beds, although some hostels do offer private rooms for families and couples. They sometimes have kitchens and utensils for your use, bike or moped rentals, storage areas, and laundry facilities. There can be drawbacks: some hostels close during certain daytime "lock-out" hours, have a curfew, don't accept reservations, and/or impose a maximum stay. In France, a bed in a hostel will average around100-120F.

For their services and lower rates at member hostels, hostelling associations, especially **Hostelling International (HI),** can definitely be worth joining. HI hostels are scattered throughout France, and many accept reservations via the International Booking Network (tel. (02) 9261 1111 from Australia, 800-663-5777 from Canada, (01629) 581 418 from the U.K., (01) 301 766 from Ireland, (09) 379 4224 from New Zealand, 800-909-4776 from U.S.; www.hiayh.org/ushostel/reserva/

ESSENTIALS

ibn3.htm) for a nominal fee. HI's umbrella organization's web page lists the web addresses and phone numbers of all national associations and can be a great place to begin researching hostelling in a specific region (www.iyhf.org). Other comprehensive hostelling websites include www.hostels.com and www.eurotrip.com/accommodation. To join HI, contact one of the following organizations in your home country:

Australian Youth Hostels Association (AYHA), 422 Kent St., Sydney NSW 2000 (tel. (02) 9261 1111; fax 9261 1969; email yha@yhansw.org.au; www.yha.org.au). One-year membership AUS$44, under 18 AUS$13.50.

Hostelling International-Canada (HI-C), 400-205 Catherine St., Ottawa, ON K2P 1C3 (tel. 800-663-5777 or (613) 237-7884; fax 237-7868; email info@hostellingintl.ca; www.hostellingintl.ca). One-year membership CDN$25, under 18 CDN$12; 2-yr. CDN$35.

An Óige (Irish Youth Hostel Association), 61 Mountjoy St., Dublin 7 (tel. (01) 830 4555; fax 830 5808; email anoige@iol.ie; www.irelandyha.org). One-year membership IR£10, under 18 IR£4, families IR£20.

Youth Hostels Association of New Zealand (YHANZ), P.O. Box 436, 173 Cashel St., Christchurch 1 (tel. (643) 379 9970; fax 365 4476; email info@yha.org.nz; www.yha.org.nz). One-year membership NZ$24, ages 15-17 NZ$12, under 15 free.

Hostelling International South Africa, P.O. Box 4402, Cape Town 8000 (tel. (021) 24 2511; fax 24 4119; email info@hisa.org.za; www.hisa.org.za). One-year membership SAR50, under 18 SAR25, lifetime SAR250.

Scottish Youth Hostels Association (SYHA), 7 Glebe Crescent, Stirling FK8 2JA (tel. (01786) 891 400; fax 891 333; email info@syha.org.uk; www.syha.org.uk). Membership UK£6, under 18 UK£2.50.

Youth Hostels Association of England and Wales (YHA), 8 St. Stephen's Hill, St. Albans, Hertfordshire AL1 2DY, England (tel. (01727) 855 215 or 845 047; fax 844 126; email yhacustomerservices@compuserve.com; www.yha.org.uk). One-year membership UK£11, under 18 UK£5.50, families UK£22.

Hostelling International Northern Ireland (HINI), 22-32 Donegall Rd., Belfast BT12 5JN, Northern Ireland (tel. (01232) 324 733 or 315 435; fax 439 699; email info@hini.org.uk; www.hini.org.uk). One-year membership UK£7, under 18 UK£3, families UK£14.

Hostelling International-American Youth Hostels (HI-AYH), 733 15th St. NW, Suite 840, Washington, D.C. 20005 (tel. 202-783-6161 ext. 136; fax 783-6171; email hiayhserv@hiayh.org; www.hiayh.org). One-year membership US$25, over 54 US$15, under 18 free.

SPECIFIC CONCERNS

WOMEN TRAVELERS

Women traveling alone, or even with other women, and even in busy areas, can expect to be hassled by men, especially at night. Women should exercise caution, maintain a confident gait, and avoid direct eye contact with intimidating men. Parisian women often respond to verbal harassment with an icy stare, but you should do your best to avoid conflict. Speaking to *drageurs* (as the French call them), even to say "NO!", is only to invite a reply, but if you feel threatened don't hesitate to call out to others or to draw attention to yourself. A loud *"laissez-moi tranquille!"* (LAY-say mwa trahnk-EEL; "leave me alone!") or *"au secours!"* (awe-S'KURE; "help!") will embarrass them and hopefully send them on their way. Harassment can be minimized by making yourself as inconspicuous as possible; see **Blending In,** for tips. Wearing a conspicuous **wedding ring** may dissuade unwanted overtures. Even a mention of a husband waiting back at the hotel may be enough in some places to discount your potentially vulnerable, unattached appearance.

Let's Go: Paris lists crisis numbers on p. 83. **In an emergency, dial 17 for police assistance**. Carry a **whistle** or an air horn on your keychain, and don't hesitate to use it in an emergency. An **IMPACT Model Mugging** self-defense course will not only prepare you for a potential attack, but will also raise your level of awareness of your surroundings as well as your confidence (see **Self Defense,** p. 49). Women also face some specific health concerns when traveling (see **Women's Health,** p. 49).

Women exploring on their own inevitably face additional safety concerns, but it's easy to be adventurous without taking undue risks. If you are concerned, consider staying in hostels which offer single rooms that lock from the inside. Communal showers in some hostels are safer than others; check before settling in. Stick to central accommodations and avoid solitary late-night walks or travel. For more information, see the *Handbook for Women Travellers*, Maggie and Gemma Moss (Piatkus Books; US$15).

TRAVELING ALONE

There are many benefits to traveling alone, among them greater independence and challenge. You will have greater opportunity to interact with the residents of the region you're visiting. Without distraction, you can write a great travel log in the grand tradition of Mark Twain, John Steinbeck, and Charles Kuralt.

On the other hand, any solo traveler is a more vulnerable target of harassment and street theft. Lone travelers need to be well-organized and look confident at all times. Try not to stand out as a tourist, and be especially careful in deserted or very crowded areas. Maintain regular contact with someone at home who knows your itinerary.

A number of organizations supply information for solo travelers, and others find travel companions for those who don't want to go alone. A few are listed here.

Connecting: Solo Traveler Network, P.O. Box 29088, 1996 W. Broadway, Vancouver, BC V6J 5C2, Canada (tel. 604-737-7791; email info@cstn.org; www.cstn.org). Bi-monthly newsletter features going solo tips, single-friendly tips and travel companion ads. Annual directory lists holiday suppliers that avoid single supplement charges. Advice and lodging exchanges facilitated between members. Membership US$25-35.

Travel Companion Exchange, P.O. Box 833, Amityville, NY 11701 (tel. 516-454-0880 or 800-392-1256; www.travelalone.com). Publishes the pamphlet *Foiling Pickpockets & Bag Snatchers* (US$4) and *Travel Companions*, a bi-monthly newsletter for single travelers seeking a travel partner (subscription US$48).

FURTHER READING: TRAVELING ALONE.
Traveling Solo, Eleanor Berman. Globe Pequot (US$17).
The Single Traveler Newsletter, P.O. Box 682, Ross, CA 94957 (tel. 415-389-0227). 6 issues US$29.

OLDER TRAVELERS

In Paris, most museums, concerts, and sights offer reduced prices for visitors over 60. If you don't see a senior citizen price listed, ask, and you may be delightfully surprised. Tour buses and Seine-river boat tours, such as the **Bateaux Mouches** (see **Tours,** p. 162) enable you to see a large number of sights without walking great distances. *Let's Go: Paris* tries to list at least one hotel in every arrondissement that is accessible to those with limited mobility (see **Travelers with Disabilities,** p. 62). When booking your hotel, ask for a room on the first floor or inquire about access to the lift. We've also tried to list at least one mid-priced quality hotel in each arrondissement so you can avoid the sometimes noisy young crowd at the hostels.

Agencies for senior group travel are growing in enrollment and popularity. These are only a couple:

Elderhostel, 75 Federal St., Boston, MA 02110-1941 (tel. 617 426 7788 or 877 426 8056; email registration@elderhostel.org; www.elderhostel.org). Programs at colleges, universities, and other learning centers in Europe on varied subjects lasting 1-4 weeks. Must be 55 or over (spouse can be of any age).

Walking the World, P.O. Box 1186, Fort Collins, CO 80522 (tel. 970 498 0500; fax 970 498 9100; email walktworld@aol.com; www.walkingtheworld.com), sends trips to France.

> **FURTHER READING: OLDER TRAVELERS.**
> *No Problem! Worldwise Tips for Mature Adventurers,* Janice Kenyon. Orca Book Publishers (US$16).
> *Unbelievably Good Deals and Great Adventures That You Absolutely Can't Get Unless You're Over 50,* Joan Rattner Heilman. Contemporary Books (US$13).

BISEXUAL, GAY, AND LESBIAN TRAVELERS

Next to London, Amsterdam, and Berlin, Paris has one of the largest gay populations in Europe. Despite homophobia and the ravages of AIDS, Paris' gay and lesbian communities are vibrant, politically active, and full of opportunities for fun. Listed below are contact organizations, mail-order bookstores, and publishers which offer relevant materials (see also **Women Travelers,** p. 60).

International Gay and Lesbian Travel Association, 4331 N. Federal Hwy., #304, Fort Lauderdale, FL 33308 (tel. 954-776-2626 or 800-448-8550; fax 954-776-3303; email IGLTA@aol.com; www.iglta.com). An organization of over 1350 companies serving gay and lesbian travelers worldwide. Call for lists of travel agents, accommodations, and events.

International Lesbian and Gay Association (ILGA), 81 rue Marché-au-Charbon, B-1000 Brussels, Belgium (tel./fax 32 2 502 24 71; email ilga@ilga.org; www.ilga.org). Not a travel service. Provides political information, such as homosexuality laws of individual countries.

> **FURTHER READING: BISEXUAL, GAY AND LESBIAN TRAVELERS.**
> *Spartacus International Gay Guide.* Bruno Gmunder Verlag. (US$33).
> *Damron's Accommodations* and *The Women's Traveller.* Damron Travel Guides (US$14-19). For more information, call 415 255 0404 or 800 462 6654 or check their website (www.damron.com).
> *Ferrari Gay Paris, Ferrari Guides' Gay Travel A to Z, Ferrari Guides' Men's Travel in Your Pocket,* and *Ferrari Guides' Women's Travel in Your Pocket.* Ferrari Guides (US$14-18). For more information, call 602 863 2408 or 800 962 2912 or check their website (www.q-net.com).

TRAVELERS WITH DISABILITIES

Many of Paris's museums and sights are fully accessible to wheelchairs and some provide guided tours in sign-language. Unfortunately, budget hotels and restaurants are generally ill-equipped to handle the needs of handicapped visitors. Handicapped accessible bathrooms are virtually non-existent among hotels in the one-to-two star range and many elevators could double as shoe-boxes. Change is slowly coming to Paris. The invaluable brochure *Paris-Ile-de-France for Everyone* (available in English for 60F at most tourist offices and through the CNRH (see below), and 80F from abroad) lists accessible sites, hotels, and restaurants as well as indispensable practical tips.

Let's Go: Paris tries to list at least one wheelchair-accessible hotel in each arrondissement. Please see "handicapped accessible" in the index for a full list of **handicapped accessible hotels.** Take note that the hotels described as such in this book are those with reasonably wide (but not regulation size) elevators or with ground-floor rooms wide enough for wheelchair entry. To ask restaurants, hotels, railways, and airlines if they are wheelchair accessible, say: *"Etes-vous accessibles aux fauteuils roulants?"* (ET VOO ax-es-EEB-luh OH foh-TOY roo-LONT?). If transporting a **seeing-eye dog** to France, you will need a rabies vaccination certificate issued from home.

The RATP and its personnel are generally well equipped to assist blind or deaf passengers. Very few métro stations are wheelchair-accessible, but RER lines A and B are. For a guide to métro accessibility, pick up a free copy of the RATP's brochure, *Handicaps et déplacements en région Ile-de-France* (tel. 01 36 68 41 41 for help in English), which provide a list of stations equipped with escalators, elevators, and moving walkways. Public buses are not yet wheelchair accessible except for line 20, which runs from Gare de Lyon to Gare St-Lazare. Taxis are required by law to take passengers in wheelchairs. The following offer transport for the motion impaired: **Airhop** (tel. 01 41 29 01 29; open M-F 8am-noon and 1:30am-6pm) **Le Kangourou** (tel. 01 47 08 93 50; open M-F 9am-6pm) and **GiHP**, 24 ave. Henri Barbusse, 93000 Bobigny, (tel. 01 41 83 15 15; open M-F 7:30am-8pm) can help you get to and from the airports (See **To and From the Airports,** p. 74).

Those with disabilities should inform airlines and hotels of their disabilities when making arrangements for travel; some time may be needed to prepare special accommodations. Call ahead to restaurants, hotels, parks, and other facilities to find out about the existence of ramps, the widths of doors, the dimensions of elevators, etc. The following organizations provide information or publications that might be of assistance:

L'Association des Paralysées de France, Délégation de Paris, 22, rue de Père Guérion, 13ème (tel. 01 40 78 69 00). M: Place d'Italie. Publishes *Où ferons-nous étape?* (85F), which lists French hotels accessible to persons with disabilities. Open M-F 9am-12:30pm and 2-5:30pm.

Audio-Vision guides, at Parisian theaters such as the Théâtre National de Chaillot, 1, pl. Trocadéro, 11 Novembre, 16ème (tel. 01 53 65 31 00), the Comédie Française, 2, rue de Richelieu, 1er (tel. 01 44 58 15 15), and the Théâtre National de la Colline, 15, rue Malte-Brun, 20ème (tel. 01 44 62 52 00). Spoken service for the blind or vision-impaired, which describes the costumes, sets, and theater design.

Comité National Français de Liaison pour la Réadaption des Handicapés (CNFLRH), 236bis, rue de Tolbiac, 13ème (tel. 01 53 80 66 66; fax 01 53 80 66 67; www.hand-itel.org). Publishes *Paris-Ile-de-France for Everyone,* an English-language guide to hotels and sights with wheelchair access (60F in France, 80F from abroad).

Mobility International USA (MIUSA), P.O. Box 10767, Eugene, OR 97440 (tel. 541 343 1284 voice and TDD; fax 541 343 6812; email info@miusa.org; www.miusa.org). Sells *A World of Options: A Guide to International Educational Exchange, Community Service, and Travel for Persons with Disabilities* (US$35).

The following organizations arrange tours or trips for disabled travelers:

Access Travel, 16 Haysewater Ave., Astley, Lancs. M29 7BL, UK (tel. 01942 888 844) is a specialized tour operator which arranges vacations in France for disabled travelers.

Directions Unlimited, 720 N. Bedford Rd., Bedford Hills, NY 10507 (tel. 800 533 5343; in NY 914 241 1700; fax 914 241 0243; email cruisesusa@aol.com). Specializes in arranging individual and group vacations, tours, and cruises for the physically disabled. Group tours for blind travelers.

FURTHER READING: TRAVELERS WITH DISABILITIES.
Access in Paris, Gordon Couch. Quiller Press (US$12).
Wheelchair Through Europe, Annie Mackin. Graphic Language Press (760 944-9594; email niteowl@cts.com) (US$13).
Global Access (www.geocities.com/Paris/1502/disabilitylinks.html) has links for disabled travelers in France.

MINORITY TRAVELERS

Despite Paris's extraordinary diversity, its large African, Maghreban, East Asian, and South Asian populations, and its wealth of multi-ethnic restaurants and cultural events, racism is as big a problem here as it is in London, Sydney, and New York. Immigrants are frequently blamed for France's high unemployment rate and expensive state welfare system, though socioeconomic studies do not support such claims (see **History**, p. 13). However, French prejudice is more cultural than color-oriented; the most common complaint is that immigrants do not adopt French culture and customs. Minority travelers are likely to be treated simply as foreigners; it wasn't for nothing that James Baldwin and Charles Mingus fled the U.S.A. for Paris in the 1950s.

Those of Arab, North African, or West African descent may face suspicious or derogatory glances from passersby. Should you confront race-based exclusion or violence, you should make a formal complaint to the police. We encourage you to work through either SOS Racisme or MRAP in order to facilitate your progress through a confusing foreign bureaucracy.

S.O.S. Racisme, 28, rue des Petites Ecuries, 10ème (tel. 01 53 24 67 67). Occupied primarily with helping illegal immigrants and people whose documentation is irregular. They provide legal services and are used to negotiating with police.

MRAP (Mouvement contre le racisme et pour l'amitié entre les peuples), 43, bd. Magenta, 10ème (tel. 01 53 38 99 99 or 01 53 38 99 88). Handles immigration issues and monitors racist publications and propaganda.

TRAVELERS WITH CHILDREN

Regardless of the fact that Paris offers a dizzying array of sights, sounds, and above all, smells, those traveling with children will need to plan their day's ahead. Children, whose legs and attention spans are generally shorter than those of adults, will soon tire and cease to care who painted the Mona Lisa, or who used to hang out in the Latin Quarter.

Thankfully, there are a plethora of sights and attractions that are just for kids in Paris. For a Let's Go thumb in the right direction, see **Kids**, p. 275. A good way to plan the day with children is in bite-sized segments, allowing for an afternoon nap (especially in the August heat), and frequent, strategic breaks for the other great pacifier: Parisian sweets (for more on this, your secret weapon, see p. 160). The other good news is that while the French might love to hate you, the attitude barrier does not apply to little ones, who will most often be accommodated in restaurants, cafés, and (heaven forbid) bars. Cheaper restaurants and chains often have children's menus. Hotels generally have a minimal charge for an extra bed or cot, called a *lit supplementaire*. Travelers with babies should have no problem finding the necessary supplies in supermarkets and pharmacies.

The Paris magazine *L'Officiel des Spectacles* (2F) has a section entitled *Pour Les Jeunes* that lists exhibits, programs, and movies appropriate for children (see **Newspapers and Listings**, p. 95).

FURTHER READING: TRAVELERS WITH CHILDREN.
Trouble Free Travel with Children, Vicki Lansky. Book Peddlers (US$9).

DIETARY CONCERNS

France may be the country of gastronomy, but sometimes it seems so caught up in its own eating traditions that those with special dietary requirements can feel left behind. Eating out can be difficult for **vegetarians** and almost impossible for **vegans**—to Parisians, the idea of someone who eats neither meat nor cheese may verge on the incomprehensible. Both are most likely to find something palatable at ethnic restaurants. Try eating at Tunisian, Moroccan, Indian, Vietnamese, and Chinese restaurants, which offer couscous, rice, and vegetable platters. If you don't eat eggs or dairy products, you should clearly state this fact to the server. Sometimes if you inform the server that you are vegetarian, he or she may be able to substitute main dishes with salads or other vegetarian appetizers or side dishes. Though the French are very fond of salads, be especially careful to make sure the *patron* understands that you want neither ham nor fish nor chicken livers nor cheese with your greens. Health food stores, called *diététiques* or *maisons de régime*, are expensive. Health food products are called *produits diététiques*. For more information about vegetarian travel, contact:

North American Vegetarian Society, P.O. Box 72, Dolgeville, NY 13329 (tel. 518 568 7970; email navs@telenet.com; www.cyberveg.org/navs/). Publishes Transformative Adventures, a guide to vacations and retreats (US$15).

In Paris, **kosher** delis, restaurants, and bakeries abound in the 3*ème* and 4*ème* arrondissements, particularly on rue des Rosiers and rue des Écouffes. Contact the **Union Libéral Israélite de France Synogogue** (see **Religious Services,** p. 87) for more information on kosher restaurants. For a list of vegetarian and kosher restaurants, see **Restaurants by Type,** p. 128. If you are strict in your observance, you may have to prepare your own food.

FURTHER READING: DIETARY CONCERNS.
The Vegan Travel Guide. The Vegan Society. (US$15).
The Jewish Travel Guide lists synagogues, kosher restaurants, and Jewish institutions in over 80 countries. Vallentine-Mitchell Publishers, Newbury House 890-900, Eastern Ave., Newbury Park, Ilford, Essex, UK IG2 7HH (tel. 020 8599 8866; fax 599 09 84). It is available in the US ($16) from ISBS, 5804 NE Hassallo St., Portland, OR 97213-3644 (tel. 800 944 6190).

ALTERNATIVES TO TOURISM

STUDY

Every year, thousands of people from all over the world descend on France to study, whether for a few weeks of French language immersion or to enroll in an advanced degree program. In response to this demand, hundreds of institutions have mushroomed, offering courses to cater to every taste. You don't even need to speak French to get a degree; in 1999, in a bid to bolster the long-term standing of France (and earn a little foreign currency on the side), the French government announced a program to offer certain degree courses in English to overseas students.

All non-EU citizens need a **study visa** if they intend to spend more than three months studying in France, while everyone will need a residency permit. As long as you have been accepted onto a course and can show proof of financial independence, you should have no trouble getting a study visa. For details, see **Visas and Work Permits,** p. 41.

FRENCH UNIVERSITIES

French universities (except for the Grandes Ecoles; see below) must admit anyone holding a *baccalaureat* (French school-leaving certificate) or a recognized equivalent to their first year of courses (British A-levels or 2 years of college in the US). Non-native French speakers must also pass a written and oral language test. At the end of the first year, exams separate the wheat from the chaff. The cream of the academic crop go to the elite **Grandes Ecoles** after passing notoriously difficult entrance exams which require a year of preparatory schooling in themselves.

French universities are far, far cheaper than American equivalents, including programs offered by US universities in France; however, expect to pay at least 2500F per month in living expenses. EU citizens studying in France can take advantage of the **SOCRATES** program, which offers grants to support inter-European educational exchanges. Most UK and Irish universities will have details of the grants and the application procedure available. The universities and organizations listed below can supply further information and help organize an academic program in France.

If you are already fluent in French, direct enrollment in a French university can be more rewarding than a class filled with Americans. It can also be up to four times cheaper, although you may not receive academic credit at home. After 1968, the **Université de Paris** split into 10 independent universities, each at a different site and offering a different programs. The Sorbonne, now the Université de Paris IV, devotes itself to the humanities. Contact the cultural services office at the nearest French consulate. As a student at a French university, you will receive a student card *(carte d'étudiant)* upon presentation of your residency permit and a receipt for your university fees. In addition to standard student benefits, many additional benefits are administered by the **Centre Régional des Oeuvres Universitaires et Scolaires (CROUS)**. Founded in 1955 to improve the living and working conditions of students, CROUS welcomes foreign students. The brochure *Le CROUS et Moi* lists addresses and info on student life. Pick up their guidebook *Je Vais en France* (free), in French or English, from any French embassy.

Agence EduFrance, 173 bd. St-Germain, 6ème (tel. 01 53 63 35 00; www.edufrance.fr) is a one-stop resource for foreigners thinking about studying for a degree in France. Information on courses, costs, grant opportunities and student life in France. Website available in English, with a downloadable questionnaire that will prepare a tailor-made list of contacts.

The British Council, 11 Portland Place, London W1N 4EJ (tel. 020 7930 8466; fax 020 7389 3199; www.britishcouncil.org) has information on educational exchanges between the UK and France, and also administers the SOCRATES educational exchange program in Britain.

Université Paris-Sorbonne, 1, rue Victor Cousin, 75230 Paris Cedex 05 (Tel. 01 40 46 22 11; fax 01 40 46 25 88; www.paris4sorbonne.fr), the grand-daddy of French universities, was founded in 1253 and is still going strong. Inscription into degree courses cost about 2500F per year. Also offers programs for US students lasting 3-9 months.

American University of Paris, 31 Avenue Bosquet, 7ème (Tel. 01 40 62 06 00; www.aup.fr) offers US-accredited degrees and summer programs taught in English at its Paris campus. Tuition and living expenses total about US$28,000 per year.

LANGUAGE SCHOOLS

Language schools are offered in the summer by many French universities, while independent organizations run language classes throughout the year. The American University in Paris also runs a summer program (see above for contact details). For more information on language courses in France, contact your national **Institut Français,** official representatives of French Culture attached to French embassies around the world (contact your nearest French embassy or consulate for details). The Canadian version has created a fantastic **clickable map** of language schools in France at www.ambafrance.org:80/COURS/index_eng.html. Other well-known schools include

Alliance Française, Ecole Internationale de Langue et de Civilisation Françaises, 101, bd. Raspail, 6ème, Paris or 75270 Paris Cedex 06 (tel. 01 45 44 38 28; fax 01 45 44 89 42; email afparis_ecole@compuserve; http://www.paris.alliancefrancaise.fr). M: Nôtre-Dame-des-Champs. Instruction all levels, with specialized courses in legal and business French. From 1400F per month for evening classes (1¾hr. per day) to 3200F per month for an intensive course (4hr. per day). MC, V.

Cours de Civilisation Française de la Sorbonne, 47, rue des Ecoles, 5ème (tel. 01 40 46 22 11; fax 01 40 46 32 29; www.fle.fr/sorbonne/). Offers instruction at all levels in the French language, together with a comprehensive lecture program of French cultural studies taught by professors of the Sorbonne. Must be at least 18 and have completed high school. Semester- and year-long courses during the academic year, and 4-, 6-, 8-, and 11-week summer programs. **AIFS** (see above) arranges housing and meals.

Institut de Langue Française, 3, ave. Bertie Albrecht, 8ème (tel. 01 45 63 24 00; fax 01 45 63 07 09; http://www.instlanguefr.com). M: Charles de Gaulle-Etoile. Language, civilization, and literature courses (2 weeks, 20 hours per week course 3000F).

Institut Parisien de Langue et de Civilisation Française, 87, bd. de Grenelle, 15ème (tel. 01 40 56 09 53; fax 01 43 06 46 30; email institut.parisien@dial.oleane.com). M: LaMotte-Picquet-Grenelle. French language, fashion, culinary arts, and cinema courses (intensive language courses 10, 15 (1050F per week), 25 (1750F per week) hours per week).

 FURTHER READING: STUDY ABROAD.

Academic Year Abroad. Institute of International Education Books (US$45).
Vacation Study Abroad. Institute of International Education Books (US$40).
Peterson's Study Abroad Guide. Peterson's (US$30).

WORK

Anyone hoping to come to France and slip easily into a job will face a tough reality on their arrival. French unemployment stubbornly remains above 10%, and unqualified foreigners are unlikely to meet with much sympathy from French employers.

OPTIONS FOR WORK

Non-EU citizens will find it well-nigh impossible to get a work permit without a firm offer of a job; networking will prove your best bet for (illegal) employment. Students have two special options: Au pair employment (see below), and part-time work during the school year or summer. Those registered at a French university may get work permits for the summer with a valid visa, a *carte étudiant*, and proof of a job. After an academic year in France, Americans with a student *carte de séjour* can find part-time work if they will be enrolled at a French university in the fall. Check the French embassy's *Employment in France for Students* (see **French Government Information Offices,** p. 70). Full-time students at a US universities can apply to work permit programs run by **Council on International Educational Exchange (Council)** and its member organizations. For a US$225 application fee, Council can procure three- to six-month work permits and a handbook to help you find work and housing. Among other options for legal, gainful employment are **Au- pair** positions, which offer lodging, board and a small stipend to young men and women in return for childcare and household chores. You are very unlikely to land a job teaching English in France unless you have a **TEFL** (Teaching of English as a Foreign Language) certificate or equivalent and a couple of years experience. If you are an experienced English teacher, though, you can try for an official position as a **Teaching Assistant** in a French school: contact your national French embassy for details. For more information on visas, see **Study and Work Permits,** p. 92.

EU citizens can work in France without a visa or work permit, though they will need a **residency permit** (see p. 40). Those without an offer of employment have a grace period of three months in which to seek work; during this time they are eligible for social security benefits. To receive benefits, you must arrange it in advance with your local social security office before leaving for France; beware that French bureaucracy often takes three months just to process the paperwork. If you do not succeed in finding work in that time, you must return home unless you can prove your financial independence. By law, all EU citizens must be given equality of opportunity when applying to jobs not directly related to national security, so theoretically if you speak French you have as much chance of finding a job as an equivalently qualified French person.

Students can also check with their university's French language department, which may have connections to jobs abroad.

AU PAIR

Open to men and women, 18-30 years old with some knowledge of French, the au pair position involves child care and light housework for a French family while enrolled at a French school or university. Talking with children can be a great way to improve your French, but looking after them can be strenuous. Know in advance what the family expects of you. Expect to receive room, board, and a small stipend. Au pair jobs (usually 6-18 months) can be arranged through individual connections, but make sure you have a contract detailing hours per week, salary, and accommodations. Check with the French Embassy (see **French Government Information Offices,** p. 70) and the following organizations for more info.

L'Accueil Familial des Jeunes Etrangers, 23, rue du Cherche-Midi, 6ème (tel. 01 42 22 50 34; fax 01 45 44 60 48). M: Sèvres-Babylone. Arranges summer and 6-10 month au pair jobs (placement fee 680F for EU, 800F for non-EU). Will help switch families if you are unhappy. They can find you a room in exchange for 12hr. of work per week, or room and board for 18hr. of work (you must have a student visa). Also arranges similar jobs for non-students, which require 30hr. of work per week, in exchange for room, board, employment benefits, and a métro pass.

Childcare International, Ltd., Trafalgar House, Grenville Place, London NW7 3SA (tel. 020 8906 3116; fax 020 8906 3461; email office@childint.demon.co.uk; www.child-int.demon.co.uk) offers au pair positions in France. Provides information on qualifications required and local language schools. The organization prefers a long placement but does arrange summer work. UK£80 application fee.

TEACHING ENGLISH

Post a sign in markets and schools stating that you are a native speaker, and scan the classified ads of local newspapers, where residents sometimes advertise for language instruction. Securing a position will require patience and legwork. Because the job market is more accessible to British teachers, Americans will find the job search particularly difficult.

International Schools Services, Educational Staffing Program, P.O. Box 5910, Princeton, NJ 08543 (tel. 609 452 0990; fax 609 452 2690; email edustaffing@iss.edu; www.iss.edu). Recruits teachers and administrators for American and English schools in France. All instruction in English. Applicants must have a bachelor's degree and two years of relevant experience. Nonrefundable US$100 application fee. Publishes The ISS Directory of Overseas Schools (US$35).

Office of Overseas Schools, A/OS Room 245, SA-29, Dept. of State, Washington, D.C. 20522 2902 (tel. 703 875 7800; fax 703 875 7979; email overseas.school@state.gov; http://state.gov/www/about_state/schools/). Keeps a list of schools abroad and agencies that arrange placement for Americans to teach abroad.

PROFESSIONAL TEACHING

For non-French citizens, teaching positions are possible only at private schools. Private preparatory schools, such as the British School of Paris (tel. 01 39 76 32 21), American School of Paris (tel. 01 41 12 82 82), Marymount International (tel. 01 46 24 10 51), and the International School of Paris (tel. 01 42 24 09 54) may have openings for qualified teachers, particularly in the natural sciences.

FINDING WORK ONCE THERE

Check help-wanted columns in French newspapers, especially *Le Monde, Le Figaro*, and the English-language *International Herald Tribune*, as well as *France-USA Contacts*, a free weekly circular filled with classified ads, which can be picked up in Yankee hangouts. Many of these jobs are "unofficial" and therefore illegal (one risks deportation), but many people find them convenient because they often don't ask for presentation of a work permit. However, the best tips on jobs for foreigners come from other travelers. Be aware of your rights as an employee, and always get written confirmation of your agreements. Youth hostels frequently provide room and board to travelers willing to help run the place.

In Paris, start your job search at the **American Church,** 65 Quai d'Orsay, 7*ème* (tel. 01 40 62 05 00) which posts a bulletin board (view M-Sa 9am-10pm) full of job and housing opportunities targeting Americans and anglophiles (open M-Sa 9am-10pm). Those with ambition and an up-to-date résumé, in both French and English, should stop by the **American Chamber of Commerce in France,** 21 av. George V, 1st floor, 8*ème* (tel. 01 40 73 89 90; fax 01 47 20 18 62; open M-F 9am-5pm), an association of American businesses in France. Your résumé will be kept on file for two months and placed at the disposal of French and American companies. Chamber of Commerce membership directories can be browsed in the Paris office (library open Tu and Th 10am-12:30pm; admission 50F). Filled with practical info on working as an American abroad, it is useful to have it sent to you before your arrival in France. The **Agence Nationale Pour l'Emploi (ANPE),** 4, impasse d'Antin, 8*ème* (tel. 01 43 59 62 63; fax 01 49 53 91 46; www.enpe.fr), has specific info on employment. Remember to bring your work permit and, if you have one, your *carte de séjour.* (Open M-W and F 9am-5pm and Th 9am-noon.) The **Chambre de Commerce et d'Industrie de Paris,** 27, ave. de Friedland, 8*ème* (tel. 01 55 65 55 65; fax 01 55 65 77 68; M: George V), provides the pamphlet *Foreigners: Starting Up Your Company in France* (48F). Their library at 16, rue Chateaubriand, is also a good resource. (Open M-F 9am-6pm. Admission 30F.) The **Centre d'Information et de Documentation Jeunesse (CIDJ),** 101, quai Branly, 15*ème* (tel. 01 44 49 12 00; fax 01 40 65 02 61), an invaluable state-run youth center provides info on education, résumés, employment, and careers. English spoken. Jobs are posted at 9am on the bulletin boards outside. (Open M-F 9am-6pm; Sa 9:30am-1pm.)

VOLUNTEER

Volunteering can provide an opportunity to meet people and to receive free room and board. International firms, museums, art galleries, and non-profit organizations like UNESCO may have unpaid internships available.

REMPART, 1, rue des Guillemites, 4*ème* (tel. 01 42 71 96 55; fax 01 42 71 73 00). Offers summer and year-long programs geared toward protecting the French heritage. Restores churches, monuments, and the environment. Anyone 15 or over is eligible. Programs cost 40-50F per day, plus a 220F insurance fee.

Club du Vieux Manoir, 10, rue de la Cossonnerie, 1*er* (tel. 01 45 08 80 40 or 03 44 72 33 18). Offers year-long and summer programs, as short as 15 days, restoring castles and churches throughout France. Anyone 15 or over is eligible. Programs cost 80F per day, plus 90F application fee.

United Nations Educational, Scientific, and Cultural Organization (UNESCO), (www.unesco.org.). If your visit to UNESCO (see **Sights,** p. 191) leaves you ready to serve a greater cause, the organization offers unpaid internships of three to six months for university graduates. You must speak either French or English and be a citizen of a member country; if you aren't, you can try through a university. For more information check the website above or write, to the attention of your country's delegation, to UNESCO PER-Staff Training Section, 1 rue Miollis, 75732 Paris.

Service Civil International Voluntary Service (SCI-VS), 814 NE 40th St., Seattle, WA 98105 (tel./fax 206 545 6585; email sciivsusa@igc.apc.org). Arranges placement in work camps in Europe for those age 18 and over. Local organizations sponsor groups for physical or social work. Registration fees US$50-250, depending on the camp location.

> **FURTHER READING: VOLUNTEER OPPORTUNITIES.**
> *How to Get a Job in Europe,* Robert Sanborn. Surrey Books (US$22).
> *The Alternative Travel Directory,* Clayton Hubbs. Transitions Abroad (US$20).
> *International Directory of Voluntary Work,* Victoria Pybus. Vacation Work
>   Publications (US$16).

OTHER RESOURCES

FRENCH GOVERNMENT INFORMATION OFFICES

Tourism is France's largest industry, and the French government gladly provides prospective visitors with free and sundry brochures from their official tourist offices in most anglophone countries (see also **French Consulates,** p. 36).

French Government Tourist Office: Call for free info packets including the helpful *France Discovery Guide* and the tourist paper *France Insider's News.* **U.S.:** 444 Madison Ave., 16th floor, New York, NY 10022 (tel. (212) 838-7800); 676 N. Michigan Ave., #3360, Chicago, IL 60611 (tel. (312) 751-7800); 9454 Wilshire Bd., #715, Beverly Hills, CA 90212 (tel. (310) 271-6665); **Québec (Canada):** 1981 Ave. McGill College, #490, Montréal, Québec H3A 2W9 (tel. (514) 288 4264); **U.K.:** 178 Piccadilly, London W1V OAL (tel. (0171) 629 1272). **Ireland:** 10 Suffolk St., Dublin 2 (tel. (01) 679 0813). **Australia:** 6 Perth Ave., Yarralumla, Canberra (tel. (02) 6216 0100); 25 Bligh St., Sydney, NSW 2000 (tel. (02) 9231 5244). **New Zealand:** contact the Australian branch or the Consular Section of the French Embassy at 1 Willeston St., Wellington (tel. (64) 4 4720 200).

Cultural Services of the French Embassy: U.S., 972 Fifth Ave., New York, NY 10021 (tel. (212) 439-1400). U.K., 23 Cromwell Rd., London SW7 2EL (tel. (0171) 838 20 55). General information about France including culture, student employment, au pair jobs, and educational possibilities.

USEFUL PUBLICATIONS

The following is a very small selection of thousands of books published about France. Many of them may only be available on order or from a specialist travelers' bookstore: check local listings to see if there is one near you. Otherwise, all books can be ordered over the internet from Amazon (www.amazon.com).

GENERAL BACKGROUND

French or Foe? Getting the Most Out of Visiting, Living and Working in France, Polly Platt. Distribooks Intl, 1998 (US$16.95). A popular guide to getting by in France.

Fragile Glory: A Portrait of France and the French, Richard Bernstein, 1991 (US$14.95). A witty look at France by the former New York Times Paris bureau chief.

Paris Inside Out, David Applefield. Houghton Mifflin, 1994 (US$16.95). A fount of information that does a great job of demystifying Paris and Parisians.

Wicked French, Howard Tomb. Workman, 1989 (US$4.95). A hilarious guide to everything you really didn't need to know how to say in French.

ESSENTIALS

SUPPLEMENTARY TRAVEL BOOKS

A Traveller's Wine Guide to France, Christopher Fielden. Traveller's Wine Guides, 1997. (US$18). Exactly what it says it is, by a well-known oenophile.

Michelin Green Guides, Michelin. Around US$20. The authoritative guide to France, this series covers the country in 24 regional books with unbeatable information on towns and sights. You'll still need your trusty *Let's Go* for all your practical information, accommodations, and food needs.

Traveller's Literary Companion: France, Ed. John Edmonson. Passport Books, 1997 (US$17.95). For those rare times when *Let's Go* doesn't reach that literary high, these 120 extracts from great French writers provide another perspective on France.

THE WORLD WIDE WEB

The Web is catching on in France in a big way, making it an ever more useful resource for travelers as businesses realize the advantages of cyberspace. Websites relevant to specific concerns and businesses mentioned above are given in the relevant sections.

OFFICIAL FRENCH SITES AND TOURIST INFORMATION

Maison de la France (www.maison-de-la-france.com:8000/) is the main government tourist site. Up-to-date information on tourism in France, including a calendar of festivals and major events, regional info with links to local servers, and a host of tips on everything from accommodation to smoking laws. English version available.

France Diplomatie (www.france.diplomatie.fr/) is the French department of Foreign affairs site, with information on visas and other official matters as well as comprehensive presentations on French history, culture, geography, politics and current affairs. Most information is available in English.

OTHER FRENCH RESOURCES

Nomade (www.nomade.fr) and **French Excite** (www.excite.fr) are a popular French search engines—though they're not very useful if you can't read French.

TF1 (www.TF1.com) is the home page of France's most popular TV station, and with news, popular culture, weather and traffic reports in French.

Météo-France (www.meteo.fr) has 2-day weather forecasts and maps for France.

Foreign Language for Travelers (www.travlang.com) can help you brush up on your French language skills or learn a few words before you go.

The Paris Pages (www.paris.org) offer an impressive amount of information on sights, entertainment, nightlife, and current events as well as an interactive map of monuments and museums and a huge page of links to other Paris web pages.

City of Paris (www.paris-france.org) is the official website of the City of Lights. It offers information on visiting, studying, and living in Paris.

Paris Free Voice (www.parisvoice.com) is the magazine for English-speaking Parisians, offering up-to-date info on current events, movies, concerts, theater, and the latest expositions, cafés, and hotspots.

Pariscope (www.pariscope.fr) is the website of the weekly magazine sold in all Paris kiosks, listing movies, clubs, plays, concerts, and restaurants. Similar to the Paris Free Voice but in French.

GENERAL TRAVEL RESOURCES

Let's Go (www.letsgo.com) is where you can find our newsletter, information about our books, up-to-the-minute links, and more.

 FURTHER READING: THE WORLD WIDE WEB.
Travel Planning Online for Dummies, Noah Vadnai. IDG Books. (US$25).

ONCE THERE

ORIENTATION

Flowing from east to west, the Seine River crisscrosses the heart of Paris. The Ile de la Cité and neighboring Ile St-Louis sit at the geographical center of the city, while the Seine splits Paris into two large expanses—the Rive Gauche (Left Bank) to its south and the Rive Droite (Right Bank) to its north. In the time of Louis XIV, the city had grown to 20 *quartiers*. Modern Paris is divided into 20 *arrondissements* (districts) that spiral clockwise around the Louvre.

> **ÈME?** The French equivalent of "th" (e.g. fourth or fifth) is *ème*. When you *see* an arrondissement referrred to as 16ème, the proper pronunciation is to add "iemme" to the French number (for a list of these, see the **Appendix**, p. 340). So 16ème is *seizième*, not sixteenthieme. The exception is 1st. The French abbreviation is 1er *(premier)*.

RIVE GAUCHE (LEFT BANK)

The *"gauche"* in Rive Gauche once signified a secondary, lower-class lifestyle, the kind flaunted by the perennially impoverished students who stayed there. Today, the Left Bank is the traveler's first choice for accommodations because of the cachet of its alternative, bookish crowd, the allure of its inexpensive restaurants and fashionable cafés and bars.

The **Latin Quarter,** focused on the **Sorbonne** and actually encompassing the **5ème arrondissement** and parts of the **6ème,** has been home to students for centuries. The boundary between the 5*ème* and the 6*ème,* **boulevard St-Michel,** overflows with cafés, cinemas, boutiques, and bookstores. As you head southeast from here, hotel prices fall. Farther east, the neighborhood around **pl. de la Contrescarpe,** at the center of the 5*ème,* is more intimate and even cheaper. A cornucopia of ethnic restaurants graces **rue Mouffetard,** the indisputable culinary heart of the 5*ème.*

Crossing bd. St-Michel and running east-west, **boulevard St-Germain** in the **6ème arrondissement** practically defines **St-Germain-des-Prés,** a neighborhood that has turned the sidewalk café into an art form and amused everyone from Rimbaud to Sartre. Tiny restaurants with cheap *menus,* however, snuggle around rue de Buci, rue Dauphine, rue du Seine, and especially **rue Grégoire de Tours,** as do street markets with fresh produce.

Don't stay in the **7ème** for the view or for the party atmosphere. A civil servant heaven filled with traveling businesspeople, the 7*ème* proffers pricey, small rooms that promise but don't necessarily provide views of the Eiffel Tower. The military and ministerial 7*ème* houses "serious date" restaurants but little in the way of affordable food, other than in markets like the one on **rue Cler.**

Montparnasse, where the chic 6*ème* meets the commercial **14ème arrondissement** just south of the Latin Quarter, attracted expatriates in the 1920s. Picasso, Hemingway, and Stein kicked up their heels in the cafés and *crêperies* of this locale. Today, areas near the fashionable **boulevard du Montparnasse** maintain their glamor, while adjoining blocks are more residential. Sex shops and sleazy nightlife dominate the northern end of av. du Maine. East of the 14*ème,* in the **13ème,** Paris's "Chinatown" overflows with cuisine from Vietnam, Laos, Thailand, and Cambodia.

The expansive **Parc des Expositions,** just outside the Porte de Versailles at the southern tip of the **15ème,** attracts executives in the winter. In summer, hotels scramble for guests, and tourists can sometimes haggle with the district's hotel owners.

RIVE DROITE (RIGHT BANK)

The first four arrondissements comprise what has historically been central Paris and contain the oldest streets and residences in the city. Still, because of the Left Bank's appeal, hotels here may have unexpected vacancies. In general, hotel prices rise with proximity to the Louvre and the Opéra, and supermarkets and inexpensive restaurants are fewer and farther between than elsewhere.

Paris's royal past is conspicuous in much of the **1er,** home to the Louvre. Chanel and the Banque de France set the scene; the few budget hotels lurking here are rarely accompanied by budget accoutrements (laundromats, grocery stores, etc.). Although above ground the 1*er* is one of the safest areas in Paris, the métro stops are best avoided at night, when the tunnels of M: Châtelet and Les Halles are claimed by drug dealers and other unsavory types.

Devoid of its own sights, the **2ème arrondissement** is within easy walking distance of the Marais, the Centre Pompidou, the Louvre, the Palais-Royal, Notre-Dame, and more. Many cheap little restaurants and hotels populate this mostly working-class area and make it an excellent place to stay. Although the eastern end of rue St-Denis is a center of prostitution and pornography, its seediness does not spill out very far.

Absolutely *the* place to live in the 17th century, the **Marais,** in the **3ème** and **4ème arrondissements,** has regained its swish, thanks to 30 years of extensive renovations. Once-palatial mansions have become exquisite museums, and the tiny twisting streets have been adopted by fashionable boutiques and galleries. The area shelters some terrific accommodations at reasonable rates. Prices drop as you head north through the 4*ème* into the 3*ème*. **Rue des Rosiers,** in the heart of the 4*ème*, is the focal point of the city's Jewish population. Superb kosher delicatessens neighbor Middle Eastern and Eastern European restaurants. The area is lively on Sundays, when other districts shut down. The Marais has also recently become the center of gay Paris.

The **8ème arrondissement** is home to the world-famous and much-visited **av. des Champs-Elysées.** Don't expect inexpensive eateries amid embassies and *haute couture* salons but rather many of Paris's most famous restaurants. For the most part, budget travelers should visit the 8*ème's grands boulevards* and then dine elsewhere.

The **9ème arrondissement** links some of Paris's most affluent and touristed quarters with less popular and affluent ones. There are plenty of hotels, but many to the north are used for the local flesh trade. Nicer but not-so-cheap hotels are available near the respectable and central bd. des Italiens and bd. Montmartre.

For most visitors, the **10ème** means little more than Gare de l'Est and Gare du Nord. A flock of inexpensive hotels roosts near the stations, but the area is far from sights and nightlife and is somewhat unsafe. Use special caution west of pl. de la République along rue du Château d'Eau. Don't write the 10*ème* off, though. Good, cheap ethnic restaurants abound, and some areas make for pleasant wandering.

Five métro lines converge at M: République and three at M: Bastille, making the **11ème arrondissement** a transportation hub and mammoth center of action, the hangout of the young and electric. Budget accommodations line these streets and are likely to have space. The Bastille area hums with nightlife; it's rough, but mostly safe. At night, be wary in the pickpocket-strewn pl. de la République.

The **12ème arrondissement** is generally safe (though be careful around Gare de Lyon); the streets around the Bois de Vincennes offer some of the city's most pleasant places to stay, but are removed from the city center.

Wealthy and residential, the museum-spattered **16ème arrondissement** is a short walk from the Eiffel Tower but a 20-minute métro ride to the center. Hotels here are relatively luxurious and apt to have vacancies. Restaurants are scarce and upscale. The **17ème** combines the elegance of its western neighbor with the sordidness of pl. Pigalle, to the east; some of its hotels cater to prostitutes, others to visiting businesspeople. Safety is an issue where it borders the 18*ème*, especially near pl. de Clichy.

ONCE THERE

The area known as **Montmartre** owes its reputation to the fame of artists who lived there. Hotel rates rise as you climb the hill to the Basilique Sacré-Coeur. Food near the church and pl. du Tertre is pricey. Downhill and south at seedy pl. Pigalle, hotels tend to rent by the hour. At night avoid M: Anvers, M: Pigalle, and M: Barbès-Rochechouart; use M: Abbesses instead.

The **19ème** and **20ème arrondissements** are by no means central; apart from the Parc de la Villette in the 19*ème* and Père-Lachaise in the 20*ème*, expect at least a half-hour métro ride to the city's sights. The 19*ème's* Parc des Buttes-Chaumont is great for picnics and jogs. Although cheap high-rises dot the hillsides, a few charming streets preserve an old-Paris feel. Two-star hotels here are a good bet if you're stuck without a bed. Rue de Belleville can be dangerous at night.

A **map** of Paris is essential if you plan to do any serious strolling. Pick up a free, updated métro map, that includes bus lines and the RER, in any métro station. Each métro station has a map of its neighborhood, with a street index. The Streetwise Paris map folds up in your pocket and includes a street index, a métro map, and an inset map of Montmartre (US$5.95). The Michelin series *Paris: Atlas par arrondissements* is probably the most comprehensive pocketable map you are going to find, looking something like Paris's own *A to Z*.

TO AND FROM THE AIRPORTS

ROISSY-CHARLES DE GAULLE

Most transatlantic flights land at **Aéroport Roissy-Charles de Gaulle,** 23km northeast of Paris. As a general rule, Terminal 2 serves Air France and its affiliates; for info call the 24-hour English-speaking information center (tel. 01 48 62 22 80).

RER. The two cheapest and fastest ways to get into the city from Roissy-Charles de Gaulle are by RER or bus. To take the RER train, first take the free shuttle bus from Terminal 1, gate 28, Terminal 2A gate 5, Terminal 2B gate 6, or Terminal 2D gate 6 to the Roissy train station. From there, the RER B3 (one of the Parisian commuter rail lines) will transport you to central Paris. To transfer to the métro, get off at Gare du Nord, Châtelet-Les-Halles, or St-Michel, which are both RER and métro stops. To go to Roissy-Charles de Gaulle from Paris, take the RER B3, any train with a name starting with the letter "E," to "Roissy," which is the end of the line. Then change to the free shuttle bus (RER departs every 20min.; 5am-12:30am; duration 30--35min., bus 10min.; 48F).

SHUTTLE BUS. Taking a shuttle bus the whole distance is somewhat simpler than the RER, and takes about the same time. One choice is the **Roissybus** (tel. 01 48 04 18 24) which runs from in front of the American Express office on rue Scribe, near M: Opéra, to gate 10 of Terminal 2A (which also serves terminal 2C), to gate 12 of Terminal 2D (which also serves Terminal 2B), and to gate 30 of Terminal 1, arrivals level (departs every 15min. to airport 5:45am-11pm, from airport 6am-11pm, 45min., 45F).

The second shuttle bus option is the Daily **Air France Buses** (tel. 01 41 56 89 00), which run to two areas of the city. Line 2 runs to and from the Arc de Triomphe (M: Charles de Gaulle-Etoile) at 1, Av. Carnot (every 20min., 5:50am-11pm; 35min.; one-way 60F, round-trip 105F), and to and from the pl. de la Porte de Maillot/Palais des Congrès (M: Porte de Maillot) on bd. Gouvion St-Cyr (same schedule and prices). Line 4 runs to and from r. du Commandant Mouchette in front of the Méridien Hotel, near the **Gare Montparnasse** (M: Montparnasse-Bienvenue; to the airport every 30 min. from 7am-9pm, one-way 70F, round-trip 120F); and to and from **Gare de Lyon** (M: Gare de Lyon), at 20, bd. Diderot (same schedule and prices). The shuttle stops at or between the terminals 2A-2F, and at terminal 1 on the arrivals level, outside exit 34. **Tickets** can be purchased on the bus itself. Call 01 41 56 89 00 for recorded information, available in English, on all Air France airport shuttles.

DOOR-TO-DOOR SERVICE. While the RER B and shuttle buses are the cheapest means of transportation, it can be a somewhat harrowing experience to navigate the train and métro stations if you are loaded down with heavy baggage. As **taxis** are exorbitantly expensive (250-280F to the center of Paris), shuttle vans are the best option for door-to-door service. **Airport Shuttle** (tel. 01 45 38 55 72) charges 120F for one person, 89F per passenger for two or more, for Roissy-CDG or Orly. **Paris Shuttle** (tel. 01 43 90 91 91) charges 85F per passenger for two or more, to Roissy-CDG or Orly. Paris Airports Service (tel. 01 49 62 78 78) charges 115F for one, and 135F for two passengers to Orly; to Roissy-CDG the charge is 145F for one, and 180F for two. Expect the shuttle van ride to take between one hour and 90 minutes from the center of Paris.

ORLY

Aéroport d'Orly (tel. 01 49 75 15 15 for info, in English 6am-11:45pm), 18km south of the city, is used by charters and many continental flights.

RER. From Orly Sud gate H or gate I, platform 1, or Orly Ouest arrival level gate F, take the shuttle bus known as **Orly-Rail** (every 15min; 5:40am-11:15pm) to the **Pont de Rungis/Aéroport d'Orly** train stop where you can board the **RER C2** for a number of destinations in Paris (call RATP at 08 36 68 77 14 (French) or 08 36 68 41 14 (English) for info; every 15min., 6am-11pm; 25min.; 35F). The **Jetbus** (every 12min.; 5:45am-11:30pm; 22F), provides a quick connection between Orly Sud-gate H-platform 2, or Orly Ouest arrival level gate C and M: Villejuif-Louis Aragon on line 7 of the métro.

BUS. Another option is the RATP **Orlybus,** which runs to and from métro and RER stop Denfert-Rochereau, 14ème. Board at Orly Sud gate H, platform 4 or Orly Ouest level 0, gate J (M-F every 13min., Sa-Su every 16-20min.; 6am-11pm; 30F takes 30 min.). **Air France Buses** run between Orly and **Gare Montparnasse**, 36, rue du Commandant Mouchotte, 6ème (M: Montparnasse-Bienvenüe), and the Invalides Air France agency, pl. des Invalides (departs every 12min. from 6am to 11pm; 30 min. ride; 45F one-way, 75F round-trip). Air France shuttles stop at Orly Sud, gate J and Orly Ouest, gate E, arrivals level.

ORLYVAL. The RATP also runs **Orlyval** (tel. 01 43 46 14 14), a combination of métro, RER, and VAL rail shuttle. To get to Orly, buy an Orlyval ticket (57F), take the métro to Gare du Nord, Châtelet-Les-Halles, or St-Michel and change to the RER B. Make sure that the station Antony-Orly is lit up on the changing schedule panel next to the track (see **Getting Around,** p. 79). Get off at Antony-Orly and transfer to the VAL train. Reverse these instructions to enter the city from Orly. From the airport, buy a ticket at an RATP office (Ouest gate W level 1; sud gate K). Note that weekly or monthly cards are not valid for Orlyval. (VAL trains run from Antony to Orly M-Sa 6am-8:30pm and Su and holidays 7am-11pm; trains arrive at Orly Ouest 2min. after reaching Orly Sud. Orly to Antony every 7min. M-Sa 6am-10:30pm and Su 7am-10:57pm; 30min. from Châtelet.)

DOOR-TO-DOOR SERVICE. See the listing for **Roissy-Charles de Gaulle** for information on **shuttle van service.** More expensive **Taxis** from Orly to town cost at least 120F during the day, 160F at night and on weekends. Allow at least 45 minutes for the trip, as traffic can be heavy.

TO AND FROM THE TRAIN STATIONS

Each of Paris's six train stations is a veritable community of its own, with resident street people and police, *cafés*, *tabacs*, banks, and shops. Locate the ticket counters *(guichets)*, the platforms *(quais)*, and the tracks *(voies)*, and you will be ready to roll. Each terminal has two divisions: the *banlieue* and the *grandes lignes.* **Grandes lignes** depart for and arrive from distant cities in France and other countries—each of the six stations serves destinations in a particular region of France or Europe. Trains to the **banlieue** serve the suburbs of Paris and make frequent stops. Within a given station, each of these divisions has its own ticket counters, information booths, and timetables; distinguishing between them before you get in line will save you hours of frustration. **Don't forget to "composter" your ticket** (time-stamp it) at the orange machines on the platform before boarding the train, or you may be slapped with a heavy fine. All train stations are reached by at least two métro lines; the métro stop bears the same name as the train station. For **train information** or to make reservations, call the SNCF at 08 36 35 35 35 (3F per min.), or use Minitel 3615 SNCF (see **Vive la Technologie,** p. 93) 7am to 10pm daily. The SNCF line is perpetually busy (try in the evening). You can also book tickets at a local travel agency. There is a free telephone with direct access to the stations on the right-hand side of the Champs-Elysées tourist office. In addition, there are yellow **ticket machines** known as Billetterie at every train station; if you know your PIN, you can use a MasterCard, Visa, or American Express to buy your own tickets. MasterCard and Visa are also accepted at the ticket booths. Some cities can be accessed by both regular trains and **trains à grande vitesse** (**TGV;** fast speed trains). TGVs are more expensive but much faster; they also require reservations that cost a small fee. Regular trains require no reservations; this means that tickets for regular trains can be used as far after purchase date as you wish, although they must be used within 24 hours of being stamped.

SNCF offers a wide range of discounted roundtrip tickets for travelers in France which go under the name **tarifs Découvertes**—you should rarely have to pay full price. While further discounts are available with the purchase of special card, for those under 25, children, and adults traveling together should always receive at least. Get a calendar from a train station detailing *période bleue* (blue period), *période blanche* (white period) and *période rouge* (red period) times and days; blue gets the most discounts, while red gets none. Even without the cards, all of the above groups are automatically entitled to lesser reductions (usually 25% rather than 50%).

Note: The following prices are the **undiscounted fares** for one-way, second-class tickets unless otherwise noted. Summer schedules are listed. In general, prices, and number of trips per day, vary according to the day of the week, season, and other criteria. A word on **safety:** each terminal shelters its share of thieves. Gare du Nord and Gare d'Austerlitz become rough at night, when drugs and prostitution emerge. It is not advisable to buy tickets in the stations except at official counters.

Gare du Nord: Trains to northern France, Britain, Belgium, the Netherlands, Scandinavia, the Commonwealth of Independent States, and northern Germany (Cologne, Hamburg). To: Brussels (18 per day (spring), 2hr., 287F); Amsterdam (15 per day, 5hr., 378F); Cologne (7 per day, 5-6hr., 364F); Boulogne (5 per day, 2½hr., 180F); Copenhagen (1 direct, 3 indirect per day, 16hr., 1265F); London (by the Eurostar chunnel, approx. 17 per day, 2hr., 350-1080F).

Gare de l'Est: To eastern France (Champagne, Alsace, Lorraine), Luxembourg, parts of Switzerland (Basel, Zürich, Lucerne), southern Germany (Frankfurt, Munich), Austria, and Hungary. To: Zürich (4 per day, 6hr., 418F); Munich (6 per day, 8hr., 685F); and Vienna (5 per day, 14hr., 970F).

Gare de Lyon: To southern and southeastern France (Lyon, Provence, Riviera), parts of Switzerland (Geneva, Lausanne, Berne), Italy, and Greece. To: Geneva (5 per day, 3½hr., 508F); Florence (4 per day, 11hr., 655F); Rome (4-5 per day, 12hr., 630F); Lyon (23 per day, 2hr., 295-398F); Nice (12 per day, 6hr., 340-945F); Marseille (13 per day, 4-5hr., 373F).

Gare d'Austerlitz: To the Loire Valley, southwestern France (Bordeaux, Pyrénées), Spain, and Portugal. (TGV to SW France leaves from Gare Montparnasse.) To: Barcelona (2 per day, 9hr., 500-810F) and Madrid (1 per day, 12-13hr., 530-850F).

Gare St-Lazare: To Normandy. To: Caen (29 per day, 2hr., 154F); Rouen (17 per day, 1hr., 103F).

Gare Montparnasse: To Brittany, and the TGV to southwestern France. To: Rennes (33 per day, 2-2½hr., 283F).

TO AND FROM THE BUS STATIONS

Most international buses to Paris arrive at **Gare Routière Internationale du Paris-Gallieni,** at M: Gallieni but just outside Paris at 28, av. du Général de Gaulle, Bagnolet 93170. **Eurolines** (tel. 08 36 69 52 52; Minitel 3615 Eurolines; www.eurolines.fr) sells tickets to most destinations in France and neighboring countries. Pick up schedules for departures from the station or their office at 55, rue St-Jacques, 5ème. M: Maubert-Mutualité. The bus is typically cheaper than the train, about 50% of the full train fare for London, Brussels, and Amsterdam. It takes longer on most routes.

GETTING AROUND PARIS

PUBLIC TRANSPORTATION

The **RATP (Régie Autonome des Transports Parisiens)** coordinates an efficient and stylishly designed network of subways, buses, and commuter trains in and around Paris. For information on the services and many facets of RATP, contact the **La Maison de la RATP,** right above M: Gare de Lyon, the **Bureau de Tourisme RATP,** pl. de la Madeleine, 8ème (tel. 01 40 06 71 44; M: Madeleine; open M-Sa 8:30am-6:45pm, Su 6:30am-1pm), or the **RATP helpline** (tel. 08 36 68 77 14; 2,33F per minute; open daily 6am-9pm; www.ratp.fr). English spoken. For wheelchair or seeing-impaired métro services see **Travelers With Disabilities,** p. 62.

If you're staying in Paris for several days a weekly *(hebdomadaire)* or monthly *(mensuel)* **Carte Orange** pass can be very economical. To get your ID-style pass, bring an ID photo (taken by machines in most major stations for 25F) to the ticket counter, ask for a *carte orange* with its plastic case, and then purchase your handsome *carte orange hebdomaire* (80F) or equally swanky *carte orange mensuel* (271F). Think of your *carte orange* as your most useful souvenir. These cards have specific start and end dates (the weekly ones run Monday to Sunday, and the monthly start at the beginning of the month) and often can't be bought in the middle or end of the month or week. All prices quoted here are for passes in Zones 1 and 2 (the métro and RER in Paris and suburbs), and work on all métro, bus, and RER modes of transport. If you intend to travel to the distant 'burbs, you'll need to buy RER passes for more zones (up to 5).

If you're only in town for a day or two, a cheap option is the **Mobilis** pass (32F for a one day pass in zones 1 and 2; tel. 01 53 90 20 20), which provides unlimited métro, bus, and RER transportation within Paris. If you expect to do a ton of sightseeing, consider buying one of the métro passes designed for tourists. At 70F for two days, the **Paris Visite** tourist tickets are valid for unlimited travel on bus, métro, and RER and discounts on sightseeing trips, bicycle rentals, and more; they can be purchased at the airport or at métro and RER stations. These passes are also available for longer durations, but the discounts you receive from them do not outweigh how much more costly they are than a plain old *carte orange* or Mobilis pass. No matter which *coupon* you have, write the number of your *carte* on your *coupon* before you use it.

Individual tickets for the RATP cost 8F each, or can be bought in a carnet of 10 for 52F. Each métro ride takes one ticket, and the bus takes at least one, sometimes many more, depending on how many connections you make, and the time of day.

MÉTRO

Inaugurated in 1898, the *Paris Métropolitain* (métro) is one of the world's oldest and most efficient subway systems. Stations are marked with an "M" or with the *"Métropolitain"* lettering designed by art nouveau pioneer Hector Guimard (See **Sights**, p. 224). Trains run frequently, and connections are easy, even if they require a three mile walk from one platform to the next. The first trains start running around 5:30am; the last ones leave the end-of-the-line stations (the *"portes de Paris"*) for the center of the city at about 12:15am. For the exact departure times of the last trains, check the poster in the center of each station marked *Principes de Tarification* (fare guidelines), or the white sign with the platform's number and direction. Transport maps are posted on train platforms and near turnstiles; all have a *plan du quartier* (map of the neighborhood). Connections to other lines are indicated by orange *correspondance* signs, exits by blue *sortie* signs. Lines are numbered (1 is the oldest), but referred to by their final destinations. Transfers are free if made within a station, but it is not always possible to reverse direction on the same line without exiting the station and using another ticket.

WELCOME TO THE FUTURE In the fall of 1998, the RATP unveiled its newest métro line, Line 14, Météor, connecting the new Bibliothèque Nationale to Madeleine. Paris's first new métro line since 1936 is now working in all its computerized glory, for you see, it has no drivers, only a computerized program that speeds it, with no jolts or starts, from station to station. This is all well and good, but what if one really *wants* to accidentally land in someone's lap?

Each trip on the métro requires one ticket. Tickets can be bought individually (8F), but a *carnet* of 10 (52F) is more practical and economical. Don't buy tickets from anyone except the people in the ticket booths. To pass through the turnstiles, insert the ticket into the small slit in the metal divider just to your right as you approach the turnstile. It disappears for a moment, then pops out about a foot farther along, and a little green or white circle lights up, reminding you to retrieve the ticket. If a small electric whine sounds and a little red circle lights up, your ticket is not valid; take it back and try another. **Hold onto your ticket** until you exit the métro, past the point marked **Limite de Validité des Billets;** a uniformed RATP *contrôleur* (inspector) may request to see it on any train. If caught without one, you must pay a hefty fine. Also, any *correspondances* (transfers) to the RER require you to put your validated (and uncrumpled) ticket into a turnstile. Otherwise you might need to buy a new ticket in order to exit. There is no longer first-class métro service; any cars still marked "1" are waiting to be repainted. Some trains require you to lift up a small metal handle, or push a small rectangular green button in order to enter or exit the train. Keep this in mind, or find yourself alone, weeping bitterly, on the subway platform. A word on being helpful to people who have "lost" their ticket and need to get through an entrance or exit: while it may seem a small matter to allow someone to follow you through the gate, be warned that **thieves** often use this strategy to insinuate their way into your bag or pocket. A word on vermin: many a station is full of furry friends, apparently overgrown mice, who run in the gutters behind the chairs—keep your eyes open.

Do not count on buying a métro ticket home late at night. Some ticket windows close as early as 10pm, and many close before the last train is due to arrive. Always have one ticket more than you need. Stay away from the most **dangerous stations** (Barbès-Rochechouart, Pigalle, Anvers, Châtelet-Les-Halles, Gare du Nord, Gare de l'Est). Despite the good neighborhoods in which some of these stops are located, they are frequented by troublemakers looking to prey on tourists. When in doubt, take a taxi. If you choose to walk home, stay on well-lit streets.

RER

The RER *(Réseau Express Régional)* is the RATP's local suburban train system, which passes through central Paris. Introduced in 1969, the RER runs through deeper tunnels at higher speeds. Within the city, the RER travels much faster than the métro. There are five RER lines, marked A-E, with different branches designated by a number, such as the C5 line to Versailles-Rive Gauche. The brand-spanking-new line, the E is called the Eole (Est-Ouest liaison express), and links Gare Magenta to Gare Haussman St-Lazare. The principal stops within the city, which link the RER to the métro system, are Gare du Nord, Nation, Charles de Gaulle-Etoile, Gare de Lyon, and Châtelet-Les-Halles on the Right Bank and St-Michel and Denfert-Rochereau on the Left Bank. To check for the right train, watch the electric signboards next to each track. These signs list all the possible stops for trains running on that track. Be sure that the little square next to your destination is lit up. There are two transit classes on RER trains. Unless you indicate otherwise, you'll be sold a second-class ticket. Every RER car is marked "1" or "2"; second-class ticket holders are excluded from first-class cars under penalty of fine. Second-class tickets cost 8F within the city and are the same ones used for the métro or bus. To get to the suburbs, you'll need to buy special tickets (10-38F one-way). You'll need your ticket to *exit* RER stations. Insert your ticket just as you did to enter, and pass through. The RER runs, as does the métro, from 5:30am-1am daily.

BUS

Because the métro is efficient, convenient, and so damn stylish, the Parisian bus system is often neglected by both locals and visitors. Though slower and often more costly than the métro (one ticket takes you as far as you want on one line, but connections between bus lines require a new ticket), bus rides can be cheap sight-seeing tours and helpful introductions to the city's layout. The RATP's free *Grand Plan de Paris* includes, among other things, a map of the bus lines for day, evening, and night time. This can be had in any métro station. The free bus map *Autobus Paris-Plan du Réseau* is available at the tourist office and at all métro information booths. The routes of each line are also posted at each stop. Buses with three-digit numbers come from or are bound for the suburbs, while buses with two-digit numbers travel exclusively within Paris. Buses with numbers in the 20s come from or are bound for Gare St-Lazare, in the 30s Gare de l'Est, in the 40s Gare du Nord, in the 70s Châtelet/Hôtel de Ville (with exceptions), in the 80s Luxembourg (with exceptions), and in the 90s Gare Montparnasse.

Bus tickets are the same as those used in the métro, and can be purchased either in métro stations or on the bus from the driver. Enter the bus through the front door and punch your ticket by pushing it into the machine by the driver's seat. If you have a *carte orange* or other transport pass (Paris Visite, Mobilis, etc.), flash it at the driver. Inspectors may ask to see your ticket, so hold onto it until you get off. Should you ever wish to leave the earthly paradise that is the RATP autobus, just press the red button and the *arrêt demandé* sign will magically light up.

Most buses run daily 6:30am to 8:30pm, although those marked **Autobus du Soir** continue until 1am. Still others, ominously named **Noctambus,** run all night. Night buses (3 tickets needed, 4 if you use 2 buses, all travel passes valid) start their runs to the *portes* of the city from the "Châtelet" stop and leave M-Th every hour on the half hour from 1:30 to 5:30am, every half hour from 1-5:30am F and Sa. Buses departing from the suburbs to Châtelet run every hour on the hour 1 to 6am. Noctambuses I through M, R, and S have routes along the Left Bank en route to the southern suburbs. Those marked A through H, H, P, T, or V will have routes on the Right Bank, going north. Look for bus stops marked with a bug-eyed moon. Ask at a major métro station or at Gare de l'Est for more information on Noctambuses.

For more detailed diagrams of all bus routes, consult the *Plan de Paris par Arrondissement* (see **Orientation,** p. 72). The RATP *Grand Plan de Paris* includes legible maps of all Parisian bus routes and numbers. Some of the principle bus routes are listed below.

Bus #20: From Gare de Lyon to Gare Saint-Lazare; République, Bastille. A trip down the grands boulevards. Many have open back platform.

Bus #21: From Gare Saint-Lazare to Ponte de Gentilly; the Louvre, Pont Neuf, Châtelet, St-Michel.

Bus #29: From Gare Saint-Lazare to Porte de Montepoivre; the Centre Pompidou, Bastille. Intrepid ride through narrow streets of the Marais. Most have open back platform.

Bus # 38: Porte d'Orléans to Gare de l'Est; Centre Pompidou, Notre Dame, the Sorbonne, Jardins du Luxembourg, to the Catacombes.

Bus # 69: Champs de Mars to Gambetta; Musée d'Orsay, the quais, Châtelet, Hotel de Ville, Bastille, Père Lachaise Cemetery.

Bus #82: From Neuilly to the Jardins du Luxembourg; Montparnasse, Ecole-Militaire, Invalides, Champs-de-Mars, Tour Eiffel.

Bus #83: From Friedland Haussman to Porte d'Ivry; Gare des Invalides, pl. des Ternes, (34-45min.). Paris's finest real estate and views of the quais. Most have open back platform.

Bus #87: Champs de Mars to Port Reuilly; St-Sulpice, Cluny, Odéon, Latin Quarter, Ile-St-Louis, Bastille, Gare de Lyon.

Bus #95: From Tour Montparnasse past St-Germain-des-Prés, the Louvre, Palais Royal, the Opéra, and to Montmartre, near Sacré-Coeur (50min.).

In addition, a special tourist bus, **Balabus,** stops at virtually every major sight in Paris (from Gare de Lyon to Bastille, St-Michel, Louvre, Musée d'Orsay, Concorde, Champs-Elysées, Charles-de-Gaulle-Etoile, Porte Maillot, Pont de Neuilly, Grande Arche de La Défense, about 1¼hr.). Balabus costs 1-3 tickets, depending how far you ride (3 for the full loop) and runs April 2 to September 24 on Sundays and holidays. The first bus leaves Grande Arche de la Défense at 12:30pm and Gare de Lyon at 1:30pm; the last bus leaves Grande Arche at 8pm and Gare de Lyon at 8:30pm. Buses run about every 20 minutes. Each bus stop is marked Balabus (Bb).

TAXIS

Taxis in Paris are expensive. Rates vary according to time of day and area, but they're never cheap. **Tarif A,** the basic rate, is in effect in Paris 7am to 7pm (4F per km). **Tarif B** is in effect Monday to Saturday 7pm to 7am, all day Sunday, and during the day from the airports and immediate suburbs (5F83 per km). **Tarif C,** the highest, is in effect from the airports 7pm to 7am (7F16 per km). In addition, there is a *prix en charge* (base fee) of about 13F. All taxis have lights on their roofs indicating the rate being charged. Should you call a taxi rather than getting one at a taxi stand, the base fee will increase according to how far away you are and how long it takes the driver to get there. For all cabs, stationary time (at traffic lights and in traffic jams) costs 120F per hour. Additional charges (6F) are added for luggage over 5kg, a fourth adult, or for taxis leaving from train stations and taxi stops. Taxis can and refuse to take more than three people. For tipping see p. 97. Taxis are cheapest on weekdays in the daytime.

If you must take a taxi, try to pick one up at a train station or taxi stand, called *arrêt taxis,* usually found near bus stops. Calling a radio-cab (**Alpha Taxis,** tel. 01 45 85 85 85; **Taxis Radio Etoile,** tel. 01 41 27 27 27; **Taxis G7,** tel. 01 47 39 47 39; **Taxis Bleus,** tel. 01 49 36 10 10; or **Taxis 7000,** tel. 01 42 70 00 42) is more expensive. If you have a complaint, or have left a personal belonging behind, contact the taxi company, or write to **Service des Taxis de la Préfecture de Police,** 36, rue des Morillons, 75015 (tel. 01 55 76 20 00; M: Convention). Ask the driver for a receipt; if you file a complaint, record and include the driver's cab license number.

BY CAR

CARS

Irwin Shaw writes, "One driver out of every twelve in Paris has killed a man. On foot, the Parisian is as courteous as the citizen of any other city. But mounted, he is merciless." The infamous rotary at the Arc de Triomphe is particularly nightmarish: police are stationed on the Champs-Elysées side to keep unwitting tourists from walking directly across eight lanes of traffic to the Arc. As a rule, the fastest and biggest car wins. **Priorité à droite** gives the right of way to the car approaching from the right, regardless of the size of the streets, and Parisian drivers make it an affair of honor to take this right even in the face of grave danger. Drivers are not allowed to honk their horns within city limits unless they are about to hit a pedestrian, but this rule is often broken. The legal way to show discontent is to flash the headlights. If you don't have a map of Paris marked with one-way streets, the city will be impossible to navigate. Parking is hard to locate and garages are expensive. Foreigners need a passport, a valid license that is at least one year old, and a credit card to rent in Paris; an international license is not required. The following prices are for economy, standard (stick-shift) transmission cars *with* insurance.

FINDING YOUR WHEELS

RENTALS. You can **rent** a car from a U.S.-based firm (e.g. Avis, Budget, or Hertz) with European offices, from a European-based company with local representatives (e.g. Europcar), or from a tour operator (e.g. Auto Europe, Europe By Car, or Kemwel Holiday Autos) which will arrange a rental for you from a European company at its own rates. Multinationals offer greater flexibility, but tour operators often strike better deals. Expect to pay at least US$150 per week, plus 20.6% tax, for a teensy car; you'll probably have to purchase insurance as well (see below). Generally automatic gearboxes are unavailable on the cheaper cars, and cost extra; most Europeans prefer the performance and economy of stick-shifts. Reserve well before leaving for France and pay in advance if at all possible. It is always significantly less expensive to reserve a car from the U.S. than from France. Always check if prices quoted include tax, unlimited mileage and collision insurance; some credit card companies will cover this automatically. Ask about discounts and check the terms of insurance, particularly the size of the deductible. Non-Europeans should check with their national motoring organization (like AAA or CAA) for international coverage. Ask your airline about special fly-and-drive packages; you may get up to a week of free or discounted rental. The minimum age for renting in France is usually 21; those under 25 will often have to pay a surcharge. At most agencies, all that's needed to rent a car is a valid drivers' license and proof that you've had it for a year. You can rent cars in Paris from the following rental agencies:

Rent-a-Car, 79, rue de Bercy, 12ème (tel. 01 43 45 15 15; fax 01 43 45 65 00). For a Fiat Panda with unlimited miles: 221F per day during the week; 462F per weekend (F after 5pm to M 10am); 1617F per week. Min. age 23 with 2-year old license. Open M-F 8:30am-7pm. Call for other locations. MC, V.

Inter Touring Service, 117, bd. Auguste Blanqui, 13ème (tel. 01 45 88 52 37; fax 01 45 80 89 30). M: Glacière. 225F (with 300km free) per day, (450F with 700km free) per weekend, (1260F with 2000km free) per week. Min. age 21 with 1-year license.

Autorent, 98, rue de la Convention, 15ème (tel. 01 45 54 22 45; fax 01 45 54 39 69). M: Boucicaut. Also at 36, rue Fabert, 7ème (tel. 01 45 55 12 54). M: Invalides. Rents Fiat Pandas for 280F per day (250km included), 550F per weekend (F noon-M 9am; 700km included); 1800F with unlimited mileage. Some cars with **automatic transmission.** Open M-F 8:30am-7pm, Sa 8:30am-noon. AmEx, MC, V.

PERMITS AND CAR INSURANCE

INTERNATIONAL DRIVING PERMIT (IDP). Those in possession of a valid EU-issued driving license are entitled to drive in France with no further ado. Whilst others may be legally able to drive in France on the strength of their national licenses for a few months, not all the police know; it's safest to get an International Driving Permit (IDP), which is essentially a translation of your regular license into 10 languages, including French. The IDP, valid for one year, must be issued in your own country before you depart; motoring organizations cannot issue IDPs valid in their own country. You must be 18 years old to receive the IDP. The IDP is an addition, not a replacement, for your home license, and is not valid without it. An application for an IDP usually needs to include one or two photos, a current local license, an additional form of identification, and a fee.

Australia: Contact your local Royal Automobile Club (RAC) or the National Royal Motorist Association (NRMA) if in NSW or the ACT (tel. (08) 9421 4298; www.rac.com.au/travel). IDP AUS$15.

Canada: Contact any Canadian Automobile Association (CAA) branch office in Canada, or write to CAA, 1145 Hunt Club Rd., Suite 200, K1V 0Y3 Canada. (tel. 613-247-0117; fax 247-0118; www.caa.ca/CAAInternet/travelservices/internationaldocumentation/idptravel.htm). IDP CDN$10.

New Zealand: Contact your local Automobile Association (AA) or their main office at Auckland Central, 99 Albert St. (tel. (9) 377 4660; fax 302 2037; www.nzaa.co.nz.). IDP NZ$8.

South Africa: Contact your local Automobile Association of South Africa office or the head office at P.O. Box 596, 2000 Johannesburg (tel. (11) 799 1000; fax 799 1010). IDP SAR28.50.

U.S.: Visit any American Automobile Association (AAA) office or write to AAA Florida, Travel Related Services, 1000 AAA Drive (mail stop 100), Heathrow, FL 32746 (tel. 407-444-7000; fax 444-7380). You do not have to be a member of AAA to receive an IDP; cost US$10.

CAR INSURANCE. EU residents driving their own cars do not need any extra insurance coverage in France. For those renting, paying with a gold credit card usually covers standard insurance; if your home car insurance covers you for liability, make sure you get a **green card,** or **International Insurance Certificate** to prove it. If you have a collision abroad, the accident will show up on your domestic records if you report it to your insurance company. Otherwise, be prepared to shell out US$5-10 per day for insurance on a rental car. Leasing should include insurance and the green card in the price. Some travel agents offer the card; it may also be available at border crossings.

TWO-WHEELERS

During the métro strike of December 1995, bike stores sold out to car-less Parisians, and the community of cyclists dreaming of an autoless Paris became more vocal. The government promised that 1997 would bring 50km of Parisian streets reserved for motorless wheels. Nonetheless, if you have never ridden a bike in heavy traffic, don't use central Paris as a testing ground. The Bois de Boulogne and the Bois de Vincennes should be more your speed (see **Participatory Sports,** p.

276). Bicycles can be transported on all RER lines, but not on the métro. Ask for a helmet and inquire about insurance.

Paris à velo, c'est sympa! 37, bd. Bourdon, 4ème (tel. 01 48 87 60 01). M: Bastille. Rentals available with a 2500F (or credit card) deposit. See also **Tours,** p. 162. 24hr. rental 150F; 9am-7pm 80F. ½day (9am-2pm or 2pm-7pm) 60F.

La Maison du Vélo, 11, rue Fénelon, 10ème (tel. 01 42 81 24 72). M: Poissonière. Follow rue Lafayette in the direction of traffic. Rue Fénelon runs along the left side of the St-Vincent de Paul church. "The English speaking bike store in Paris." Sells new and used bikes, repairs all models. Rent mountain or hybrid bikes at 90F per day. 2000F deposit. Open Tu-Sa 10am-7pm.

Paris-Vélo, 2, rue de Fer-à-Moulin, 5ème (tel. 01 43 37 59 22). M: Censier Daubenton. Bike rental 90F per day with 2000F deposit includes accident insurance. See also **Tours,** p. 162. Open M-Sa 10am-12:30pm and 2pm-7pm.

Active Bike, 20, rue Acacias, 17ème (tel. 01 40 55 02 02; fax 01 48 25 30 88). M: Charles de Gaulle-Étoile. From the Arc, walk to the end of av. Carnot and turn left. Rents scooters starting at 200F per day, 950F per week with 6000F deposit required.

HEALTH AND HELP

Should you require a house call for a condition not requiring hospitalization, you can call any of the S.O.S. numbers listed below. Request documentation (including diagnoses) and receipts to submit to your home insurance company for reimbursement. Any of these S.O.S. services can make referrals for internists, dentists, optometrists, and ophthalmologists in your arrondissement.

EU citizens can get reciprocal health benefits, entitling them to a practitioner registered with the state system, by filling out a **E111** or **E112** form before departure; this is available at most major post offices. They will generally treat you whether or not you can pay in advance. EU citizens studying in France also qualify for long-term care. Other travelers should ensure they have adequate medical insurance before leaving; if your regular **insurance** policy does not cover travel abroad, you may wish to purchase additional coverage. With the exception of Medicare, most health insurance plans cover members' medical emergencies during trips abroad; check with your insurance carrier to be sure. (For more information, see **Insurance,** p. 50.)

If you need a doctor **(un médecin),** call the local hospital for a list of nearby practitioners. If you are receiving reciprocal health care, make sure you call a **honoraires opposables** doctor, who will be linked to the state health care system. They may not charge more than 110F for a consultation at their surgery, and this amount is reimbursable. Doctors described as **honoraires libres** are free to charge whatever they like, and their fees will not be reimbursed under reciprocal health care agreements. If they find something wrong, you will soon discover that French doctors prescribe more medication per patient than any others in the world (on average twice as much as British doctors); you may find yourself paying a lot for prescription drugs. Note that the same medicines may go under different names in France from your home country; check with your doctor before you leave.

 To reach the **police,** dial 17. In a **medical emergency,** dial 15. The **rape crisis hotline** is 0 800 05 95 95.

Ambulance (SAMU): tel. 15. Outside of Paris, call 01 45 67 50 50.

Fire: tel. 18. Firefighters are called *les Pompiers* in French. A fire is *un feu.*

Police: tel. 17. For emergencies only. Each arrondissement also has its own *gendarmerie* (police force) to which you should take your non-emergency concerns.

Poison: tel. 01 40 05 48 48. In French, but some English assistance is available.

ONCE THERE

Rape: SOS Viol (tel. 0 800 05 95 95) is the national rape hotline, which offers counseling, medical and legal advice, emotional support, and referrals. Open M-F 10am-7pm.

Doctors: SOS Médecins (tel. 01 47 07 77 77) and **Urgences Médicales de Paris** (tel. 01 48 28 40 04) will make house calls. **Centre Médicale Europe,** 44 rue d'Amsterdam, 9ème(tel. 01 42 81 93 33). M: St-Lazare. All kinds of physicians under one roof, charging minor fees (110F consultation fee for foreigners). Open M-F 8am-7pm, Sa 8am-6pm. Appointments advisable.

Hospitals: Hospitals in Paris are numerous and efficient. Unless your French is exceptionally good, you'll have the best luck at one of the anglophone hospitals. **Hôpital Américain de Paris,** 63, bd. Victor Hugo, Neuilly (tel. 01 46 41 25 25). M: Port Maillot, then bus #82 to the end of the line. In a suburb of Paris. Employs almost entirely English-speaking personnel (all doctors and most staff), but much more expensive than the mega-cheap French hospitals. You can change U.S. dollars at the in-hospital *bureau de change* or use their ATM. Regardless, this is probably the only place in France you will be able to get a proper American insurance claim form and have it filled out, so your chances of reimbursement are higher than anywhere else. Has the full gamut of specialists, state-of-the-art facilities (including dental services), and helpful staff. **Hôpital Franco-Britannique de Paris,** 3, rue Barbès, in the Parisian suburb of Levallois-Perret (tel. 01 46 39 22 22). M: Anatole-France. Considered a French hospital. Has some English-speakers, but don't count on it.

Pharmacies: Pharmacie des Halles, 10, bd. de Sébastopol, 1er (tel. 01 42 72 03 23). M: Châtelet-Les-Halles. Open M-Sa 9am-midnight, Su noon-midnight. **Pharmacie Dhéry,** in the Galerie des Champs, 84, av. des Champs-Elysées, 8ème (tel. 01 45 62 02 41). M: George V. Open 24hr. Also provides the **Pharma Presto** service, which delivers prescription medicines (and non-prescriptions, if you're a smooth talker) for 120F from 8am-6pm, and 180F from 6pm-8am. **Grande Pharmacie Daumesnil,** 6, pl. Félix-Eboué, 12ème (tel. 01 43 43 19 03). M: Daumesnil. Visible as you exit the métro. Open 24hr. **Pharmacie Européenne,** 6, pl. de Clichy, 9ème (tel. 01 48 74 65 18). M: Place de Clichy. Open 24hr. **Pharmacie Opéra Capucines,** 6, bd. des Capucines, 9ème (tel. 01 42 65 88 29). M: Opéra. Open M-Sa 8am-12:30am, Su 10pm-12:30am. AmEx, MC, V. Every arrondissement should have a **pharmacie de garde** (pharmacy on call), which will open in case of emergencies. The locations change, but the name of the nearest one is posted on each pharmacy's door.

PHARMACISTS. Perhaps the easiest thing to do if you are a foreigner and get sick in Paris is to head for the pharmacy. Each arrondissement has a rotating system of 24-hour pharmacies *(pharmacies de garde).* The police will be able to tell you which one is open on any given night, and at night and on Sundays pharmacies post a list on their door of those on duty. Like in England, French pharmacies have a monopoly on dispensing medication (often stronger in France than in other countries), and are staffed by highly trained individuals who assist you in dealing with your symptoms, whatever they might be. You can often avoid the time and money spent in going to a doctor by dealing with a pharmacist, as they can also provide basic services, like bandaging a wound, for a small fee. In the event that you require a doctor's care, the pharmacist can provide you with a list of doctors in the arrondissement ranging from gynecologists to general-care practitioners.

Women's Health: Mouvement Français pour le Planning Familial (MFPF), 10, rue Vivienne, 2ème (tel. 01 42 60 93 20). M: Bourse. Counseling and medical evaluations in French on family planning concerns. Appointment required to see a generalist (115F) or a gynecologist (255F). No appointment required to obtain the morning-after pill (10F donation). All fees can be Open M-F 9:30am-5:30pm (hours are variable during the summer so call in advance). Note that on Friday, the clinic is held at 94, Blvd. Massana, 13ème on the first floor of the Tour Mantoue, door code 38145 (tel. 01 45 84 28 25).

It's a big world.

And we've got the network to cover it.

Use **AT&T Direct**® Service
when you're out exploring the world.

Global
connection
with the AT&T
Network

AT&T
direct
service

Exploring the corners of the earth? We're with you. With the world's most powerful network, **AT&T Direct**® Service gives you fast, clear connections from more countries than anyone,* and the option of an English-speaking operator. All it takes is your AT&T Calling Card. And the planet is yours.

For a list of AT&T Access Numbers, take the attached wallet guide.

*Comparison to major U.S.-based carriers.

AT&T Access Numbers

Austria ●	0800-200-288	Egypt ●(Cairo)	510-0200
Albania ●	00-800-0010	(Outside Cairo)	02-510-0200
Armenia ●▲	8◆10111	Estonia	800-800-1001
Bahrain	800-000	Finland ●	9800-100-10
Belgium ●	0-800-100-10	France	0-800-99-0011
Bulgaria ▲	00-800-0010	Germany	0800-2255-288
Croatia	0800-220111	Greece ●	00-800-1311
Czech Rep. ▲	00-42-000-101	Hungary ●	00-800-01111
Cyprus ●	080-90010	Ireland ✓	1-800-550-000
Denmark	8001-0010	Israel	1-800-94-94-949

Italy ●	172-1011	Russia ●▲	
Luxembourg †	0-800-0111	(Moscow) ▶	755-5042
Macedonia, F.Y.R. of ○		(St. Petersburg) ▶	325-5042
	99-800-4288	Saudi Arabia ◇	1-800-10
Malta	0800-890-110	South Africa	0-800-99-0123
Monaco ●	800-90-288	Spain	900-99-00-11
Morocco	002-11-0011	Sweden	020-799-111
Netherlands ●	0800-022-9111	Switzerland ●	0-800-89-0011
Norway	800-190-11	Turkey ●	00-800-12277
Poland ●▲	00-800-111-1111	U.K. ▲❖	0800-89-0011
Portugal ▲	0800-800-128	U.K. ▲❖	0500-89-0011
Romania ●	01-800-4288	U.A. Emirates ●	800-121

FOR EASY CALLING WORLDWIDE

1. Just dial the AT&T Access Number for the country you are calling from.
2. Dial the phone number you're calling. *3.* Dial your card number.

For access numbers not listed ask any operator for **AT&T Direct**® Service. In the U.S. call 1-800-331-1140 for a wallet guide listing all worldwide AT&T Access Numbers.

Visit our Web site at: www.att.com/traveler
Bold-faced countries permit country-to-country calling outside the U.S.

●   Public phones require coin or card deposit.
▲   May not be available from every phone/payphone.
▶   Additional charges apply outside the city.
◇   Calling available to most countries.
▲   Await second dial tone.
✓   Use U.K. access number in N. Ireland.
❖   If call does not complete, use 0800-013-0011.
†   Collect calling from public phones.
○   Public phones require local coin payment through the call duration.

When placing an international call *from* the U.S., dial 1 800 CALL ATT.

© 1999 AT&T

M: Porte Ivry. **Centre de Planification et d'Education familiale,** 27, rue Curnonsky, 17ème (tel. 01 48 88 07 28). M: Porte de Champerret. Provides free consultations in French on family planning, abortion, cervical and breast cancer, and referrals for gynecologists. You must call first for an appointment. Open M-F 9am-5pm.

AIDS: AIDES, 247, rue de Belleville, 20ème (tel. 01 44 52 00 00). M: Télégraphe. One of the oldest and most prominent AIDS public service organizations in France, AIDES runs a 24hr. hotline with info in French and English (tel. 0 800 84 08 00). Office open M-Sa 9am-6pm and Su 2-6pm. The **Free Anglo-American Counseling Treatment and Support (FACTS)** hotline (tel. 01 44 93 16 69) at the American Church also provides HIV/AIDS support in English M, W, and F 6-10pm.

HIV: 43, rue de Valois, 1ème (tel. 01 42 61 30 04). M: Palais-Royal or Bourse. Testing and treatment for STDs. Free consultations. Syphilis tests (free), plasma and chlamydia tests (300F), and free and anonymous HIV testing includes mandatory counseling. Call for appointments. English-speaking doctors available. Open M-F 9am-7pm. HIV testing also available at 218, rue de Belleville, 20ème (tel. 01 47 97 40 49). M: Télégraphe. Also at 3, rue de Ridder, 14ème (tel. 01 45 43 83 78; M: Plaisance; Free, anonymous HIV tests M-F noon-6:30pm, Sa 9:30am-noon). Mandatory counseling, some English spoken. Results in 1 week.

Alcoholics Anonymous: 3, rue Frédéric Sauton, 5ème (tel. 01 46 34 59 65). M: Maubert-Mutualité. A recorded message in English will refer you to several numbers you can call to talk to telephone counselors, and information on daily meetings in the American Church. Daily meetings.

Drug Problems: Hôpital Marmottan, 17-19, rue d'Armaillé, 17ème (tel. 01 45 74 00 04). M: Charles de Gaulle Étoile or Argentine. Not an emergency service, but a general hospital that specializes in drug problems. For consultation or treatment, open M, W-Th noon-7pm, F 10am-7pm, and Sa noon-6pm; Aug. M-F only.

Emotional Health: Services and aid are provided by a number of organizations. Try calling **SOS Crisis Help Line: Friendship** (tel. 01 47 23 80 80). English-speaking. Support and information for the depressed and lonely. Open daily 3-11pm. For personalized crisis-control and counseling (for anything from pregnancy to homesickness), the American Church (see **English-Language Religious Services,** p. 87) offers the **International Counseling Service (ICS)** (tel. 01 45 50 26 49), which provides access to psychologists, psychiatrists, social workers, and a clerical counselor. First consultation is free; payment thereafter is negotiable. Open M-F 9:30am-6pm, Sa 9:30am-1pm. The office is staffed irregularly July-Aug. but will respond if you leave a message on its answering machine. Call for an appointment.

Dentists: SOS Dentaire, 87 bd. Port-Royal (tel. 01 43 37 51 00). RER: Port-Royal. Open daily 8am-11:45pm for emergencies involving your mouth.

Eyeglasses or Contacts: S.O.S. Optique Lunettes (tel. 01 48 07 22 00) will provide 24hr-assistance should you break or lose your glasses or contact lenses and will come to your house, free of charge, should you be unable to leave.

Ophthamologist: S.O.S. Oeil (tel. 01 40 92 93 94), 24hr. ophthalmology advice.

SERVICES

TOURIST OFFICES

Though packed in the summer, the following offices are usually able to keep the wait down to an hour at most. Lines are worst in the afternoon. All offices stock brochures, maps, and pamphlets. For 20F, they will help you find a room in a one-star hotel, 25F for a two-star, 40F for a three-star, and 8F for hostels, but they can only arrange for a room the day of your arrival. The central branch exchanges currency at decent rates with no commission and always has English-speaking representatives.

Bureau d'Accueil Central: 127, av. des Champs-Elysées, 8ème (tel. 08 36 68 31 12, 2.23F per minute; www.paris-touristoffice.com). M: Charles-de-Gaulle-Étoile. English-speaking staff. Mobbed in summer. Open daily 9am-8pm.

Bureau Gare de Lyon, 12ème (tel. 01 43 43 33 24). M: Gare de Lyon. Open M-Sa 8am-8pm.

Bureau Tour Eiffel, Champs de Mars, 7ème (tel. 01 45 51 22 15). M: Champs de Mars. Small office. Open May-Sept. daily 11am-5pm.

Orly, Sud: Near gate H (tel. 01 49 75 00 90). **Orly, Ouest:** Near gate F (tel. 01 49 75 01 39). Both open daily 6am-11:30pm.

Roissy-Charles de Gaulle: Near gate 36 arrival level (tel. 01 48 62 27 29). Open daily 7am-10pm.

BUDGET TRAVEL OFFICES

Centre Régional des Oeuvres Universitaires (CROUS), 39, av. Georges Bernanos, 5ème (general tel. 01 40 51 36 00, lodging tel. 01 40 51 37 17, or 01 40 51 36 99). RER: Port-Royal. Info on student dormitory housing in Paris (from 2 days-1 year) and on university restaurants throughout the city that offer simple but filling and cheap meals. Lodging information office is open M-F from 1-5pm, center is open M-F 9am-5pm and (See **Restaurants,** p. 127).

Council on International Educational Exchange (CIEE), 1, pl. de l'Odéon, 6ème (tel. 01 44 41 74 99; fax 01 43 26 97 45; infofrance@ciee.org). M: Odéon. Answers questions about work and study abroad, and offers mail service, phone service, and computers for use in the office. The library has useful info on jobs, travel, and housing, but is only available to students registered as Council participants (Open M-F 3am-6:30pm). Information and Orientation meetings Fridays at 12:30am. Register in Paris (1800F) or contact your CIEE office at home before you leave. Open M-F 9am-6pm.

Council Travel, 1, pl. Odéon, 6ème (tel. 01 44 41 89 80; fax 01 40 51 89 12; CouncilTravelFrance@ciee.org). M: Odéon. English-speaking travel service for people under 26. Books flights, and sells train tickets, BIJ/Eurotrain tickets, guidebooks, and ISICs (60F with current student ID). Replaces lost Council Travel tickets. Open M-F 9:30am-6:30pm and Sa 10am-5pm.

Office de Tourisme Universitaire (OTU), 2, rue Malus, 5ème (tel. 01 44 41 74 74). M: Place Monge; and 119, rue St-Martin, 4ème (tel. 01 40 29 12 12). A French student-travel agency offering reduced train and plane tickets for students under 26. Bring an official form of ID, like passport or birth certificate. Also sells ISICs (60F) and BIJ tickets. English spoken. Open M-F 10am-6:30pm, St-Martin branch open Sa 10am-5pm.

LIBRARIES

Anybody can visit French libraries; to borrow books, you need a passport ID and two proofs of French residency (phone and electricity bills, *carte de séjour*). General public libraries are located in every arrondissement and are listed in the phone book under *bibliothèque*. Universities and museums often have libraries which are open to the public.

Bibliothèque National de France, France's national library includes a branch at 66-68, rue de Richelieu, 2ème (tel. 01 47 03 81 26), the new monstrous François Mitterrand branch at 11 quai François Mauriac, 13ème (tel. 01 53 79 59 59, M: Quai de la Gare or Bibliothèque), and the Bibliothèque de l'Opéra, in the Opéra at 8 rue Scribe, 9ème (tel. 01 47 42 07 02, M: Opéra). Readers card 20F per day, 200F per year.

Bibliothèque Publique, in the Centre Pompidou, 4ème (tel. 01 44 78 12 33). M: Rambuteau. Books in English cannot be checked out. Open M and W-F noon-10pm, Sa-Su 10am-10pm.

Bibliothèque Marguerite Durand, 79, rue Nationale, 13ème (tel. 01 45 70 80 30). M: Nationale. Paris' women's library has books and archives concerning women and feminism in France. Free. Open M-Sa 2-6pm.

ONCE THERE

FOR ENGLISH BOOKS

The American Library, 10, rue Général Camou, 7ème (tel. 01 53 59 12 60; email: 100142.1066@compuserve.com). M: Ecole Militaire. The largest English library in Paris. 5-10F book sale every spring—call in March for the exact dates. Membership 570F per year, student 460F, summer 240F, day entry 70F. Open Tu-Sa 10am-7pm.

The British Council Library, 9-11, rue Constantine, 7ème (tel. 01 49 55 73 23; fax 01 49 55 73 02). M: Invalides. Library has a large selection of English books, CD-ROMS, audio and video tapes, and internet services. Membership 250F per year, 130F for 6 months; student rate 200F per year, 110F for 6 months; day entry (cannot borrow books) 30F. Open M-Tu and Th-F 11am-6pm, W 11am-7pm. Closed in August.

Bibliothèque Publique, see above.

ENGLISH-LANGUAGE RELIGIOUS SERVICES

American Church in Paris, 65, quai d'Orsay, 7ème (tel. 01 40 62 05 00). M: Invalides or Alma-Marceau. A community center and a church. Bulletin boards list jobs, rides, apartments, and personals. Publishes *Free Voice*, a free English monthly listing cultural events and classified (ads 80F for 30 words). Services Su at 11am, followed by coffee. Counseling service (tel. 01 45 50 26 49), call for an appointment. Open M-Sa 10:00pm, Su 9am-7:00pm. Free concerts Sept.-June Su 6pm. AA, AL-ANON, and FAACTS (HIV support) meetings. Orientation for newcomers to Paris in Oct. Flea market 1st Sa of each month (2-5pm).

St. Michael's Church (Anglican and Episcopalian), 5, rue d'Aguesseau, 8ème (tel. 01 47 42 70 88). M: Concorde. Services in English Su at 10:30am and 6:30pm. Bulletin boards list jobs, accommodations, and events. Open M-Tu and Th-F 10am-1pm and 2-5:30pm. **American Cathedral (Anglican and Episcopalian),** 23, av. George V, 8ème (tel. 01 53 23 84 00). M: George-V. English services daily at 9am. Open M-F 9am-5pm.

St. Joseph's Church (Catholic), 50, av. Hoche, 8ème (tel. 01 42 27 28 56). M: Charles de Gaulle-Etoile. Mass in English M-F 8:30am, Sa 6:30pm, Su 9:45, 11am, 12:15am and 6:30pm; July-Aug. Su mass at 10am, 12:15am, and 6:30pm. Open M-Sa 10am-6pm.

Buddhist Temple, Centre de Kazyn Dzong, route de la ceinture du lac Daumesnil, 12éme (tel. 01 40 04 98 06). M: Porte Dorée. A Buddhist temple and meditation center. Meditations Tu-F 9:30-10:30am, 6pm, 7:30pm, Sa-Su 10am-noon, 2:30-5:30pm.

Mosque de Paris, Institut Musulman (Muslim Institute), pl. de l'Ermite 5ème (tel. 01 45 35 97 33); M: Place Monge. A gorgeous mosque, this is also a community center with tea house, restaurant, and *hamman*. Open Sa-Th 9am-noon and 2-6pm.

Union Libéral Israélite de France (Jewish), 24, rue Copernic, 16ème (tel. 01 47 04 37 27). M: Victor-Hugo. Services F at 6pm and Sa at 10:30am, mostly in Hebrew with a little French. English-speaking rabbi stays after the service to chat. Services in the evenings and mornings of High Holy Days; call for info. Open M-Th 9am-noon and 2-6pm, F-Sa 9am-noon.

Eglise Russe (Russian Eastern Orthodox), also known as **Cathédrale Alexandre-Nevski,** 12, rue Daru, 8ème (tel. 01 42 27 37 34; M: Ternes). Open Tu, F and Su 3-5pm. Services (in French and Russian) Su at 10am.

LAUNDRY, ETC.

Dry cleaners are also best found through neighborly recommendation, exploration, or the yellow pages. Key search word: *nettoyage à sec* or *pressing*. Dry cleaners are also called *teintureries*. Many dry cleaners also offer simple tailoring services. **Buci Pressing,** 7, rue Ancienne Comédie, 6ème (tel. 01 43 29 49 92; M: Odéon) offers reasonably priced dry cleaning and services: pants 25F, blazers 30F, hemming from 70F (open M-Sa 8am-7:30pm; tailoring on Tu and F). **Pressing de Seine,** 67, rue de Seine, 6ème (tel. 01 43 25 74 94; M: Odéon), is another good option. Dry cleaning runs 25-90F; most hemming and sewing is under 100F (open M-Sa 8am-

7:15pm; MC,V). **Pressing Villiers,** 93, rue Rocher, 8ème (tel. 01 45 22 75 48; M: Villiers), does not offer tailoring but will dry-clean pants 39F, dresses 65F, and blazers 47F (open M-Sa 8am-7:30pm).

Laundromats or *laveries* are not difficult to find. Some have self-serve dry-cleaners (60F). All charge about 5F for 8-12min. in the dryer *(séchoir)* and 2-5F for detergent. Laundromats are listed by area in the yellow pages. Some include: **LaveauClaire**, 119, rue Charenton, 11ème (6kg load 18F, 10kg 30F; Open daily 7am-9pm), **Lavage**, 69, rue de Bac, 6ème (6kg load 25F, 12kg load 35F; Open daily 7:30am-9pm), **Lav' Club**, 19, rue Pergolese, 16ème (9kg load 27F, 18kg load 50F; Open daily 7:30am-9pm), **Laverie Primus**, 87, rue Didot, 14ème (7kg load 25F, 10kg load 40F, 16kg load 50F).

For **shoe repairs,** look for neighborhood *cordonniers*, like **Oziel Emile,** 4, rue Lobineau, Marché St Germain (tel. 01 46 34 58 05; M: St-Germain-des-Prés; open Tu-F 8:30am-1pm and 4-7:15pm, Sa 8:30am-1pm).

GROOMING SERVICES

It's hell finding a new stylist in a new city, but Paris is the center of style and fashion. Remember, Paris is the city that coiffed Marie-Antoinette and created the Pompadour. **Hair Salons** are a dime a dozen in Paris. The best way to find a reliable one is, of course, to ask a friend for a recommendation. Should that option not be available, you should scout the *coiffeurs* of your arrondissement for economical options or check the *pages jaunes'* five pages of listings by arrondissement under the subject heading *coiffeurs.*

A number of coiffures in the Marais style a young clientele and even offer student discounts. The coiffeurs at **Space Hair**, 10, rue Rambuteau, 3ème (tel. 01 48 87 28 51; M: Rambuteau) cut and shampoo amidst disco balls and loud techno. Many coiffures coiffe here, and it is easy to get a same-day appointment. Cut and style women 195F, men 150F, 15% discount for students and for everyone between 9-11am; open Tu-F 9am-11pm, Sa 9am-10pm, M noon-10pm. **Planet Hair**, 01 48 87 38 86; M: Rambuteau) is smaller and slightly more down to earth, but also services a young clientele. Women cut and style 250F, men 150F, student discount 20%; open Tu-W and F-Sa 10am-8pm, Th noon-9pm.

COMPUTER SERVICES

If you're in need of new **hardware,** head to **Surcouf,** 139, av. Daumesnil, 12ème (tel. 01 53 33 20 00; M: Gare de Lyon; www.surcouf.fr). From the métro walk up bd. Diderot and turn right onto av. Daumesnil. Surcouf also sells **software,** from French spell-checkers to Adobe. Prices are competitive. **Computer repair** tends to be expensive (400F per hr.). (Open M-Sa 10am-7pm.) Dozens of little less-expensive computer repair stores have opened up across the street from Surcouf along av. Daumesnil. For your basic computer **software** needs, head to the **FNAC Forum des Halles,** 1, rue Pierre Lescot 1er, level 3 (tel. 01 40 41 40 00; M: Châtelet-Les-Halles; open M-Sa 10am-7:30pm), or the branch at 74, av. Champs-Elysées, 8ème (tel. 01 53 53 64 64; M: Franklin D. Roosevelt; open M-Sa 10am-midnight, Su noon-midnight).

If you are in Paris for more than a month, expect to do substantial emailing, and do not have **Internet access** at work or school, it is probably more economical to invest in a cheap modem and to procure the services of an **Internet provider** rather than to trek several times a week to the expensive cyber-cafés in Paris. One of the simplest ways of connecting to the Internet through your home is via **Wanadoo** (www.wanadoo.fr), (tel. 08 01 63 34 34), France Telecom's very own Internet server. Dial 14 for the France Telecom office nearest you. There you fill out the Wanadoo form, pick up your connection software kit, and you're ready to go. Unlimited internet connection is as low as 45F per month. Wanadoo's basic configuration requirements are a 486PC with Windows 3.1 or 95 or a 7.1 Macintosh system; 8-16 MB of RAM; and a modem of 14.4 kbps. (Open M-F 9am-7pm, Sa 11am-

7pm.) To contact **America Online** in Paris for connection inquiries, call 01 69 19 94 50. For **Compuserve** (50 connections per month at 70F; unlimited service at 135F/month) call toll-free 0803 009 000.

BANKING

If you are planning a long-term stay in Paris and have a permanent address and a letter of support from your bank at home, you can open an account at any convenient financial institution and obtain an ATM card drawn on your French account. Most foreign banks can wire money to French accounts (for US$30-40 per transfer). Required minimum balances vary but are usually not steep for residents. Non-resident bank accounts require a hefty opening deposit and a high minimum balance (50,000F). Banks' main offices (often located near the Opéra) have foreign affairs departments that deal with such issues. Note that *compte courant* means current account, *compte d'épargne* means savings account, *compte sur livret* means deposit account, and *relève de compte* means account statement.

WOMEN'S RESOURCES

In Paris, the following women's centers can provide information on events, counseling, women's health, and birth control. Note you need a prescription from a *gynocologue* or a *généraliste* for both the pill and the morning-after pill. Consult the groups below for a referral (also see **Health: Birth Control and Abortion,** p. 49).

Maison des Femmes, 163, rue de Charenton, 12ème (tel. 01 43 43 41 13; fax 01 43 43 42 13). M: Gare de Lyon. This woman-only space offers seminars, self-defense classes, discussion groups, political action projects, and resources for women, as well as information about women events and organizations throughout Paris. Carries feminist journals, *Marie pas clair* and *Paris Feministe* in the center's library, which hosts a café and on Fridays (7:30-10pm).Open M-Tu and Th 9am-1pm, W and F 3-7pm, library open W 6-8pm.

GAY AND LESBIAN RESOURCES

In Paris, visit the gay and lesbian bookstores **Les Mots à la Bouche,** an excellent resource for travelers just arriving in the city (see **Books and Magazines,** p. 309). Consult the encyclopedic **Guide Gai** (79F, at Paris newsstands), with almost 400 pages of information in French and English about gay hotels, restaurants, nightlife, organizations, and services throughout France. The hip magazine **Têtu** (stubborn) provides smart articles all in French on fashion, culture, events, and the latest in queer *chic*. **Le Guide Paris Soirées** (29F) offers nearly 100 pages of listings in French for gay, lesbian, and trans (-sexual or -vestite) clubs, restaurants, and other establishments. The monthly **Illico** is probably the best source of info for gay men (9F at newsstands). For information on HIV, AIDS, and safer sex, call the 24-hour free and anonymous AIDS information hotline, **SIDA Info Service** (tel. 0 800 84 08 00); for AIDS info in English, call **Factsline** (tel. 01 44 93 16 69; M, W and F 6-10pm). Unless otherwise stated, the following centers and hotlines are primarily French-speaking, with some degree of English spoken. Other Parisian organizations that may be useful include:

Centre Gai et Lesbien, 3, rue Keller, 11ème (tel. 01 43 57 21 47; fax 01 43 57 27 93). M: Ledru Rollin or Bastille. Serves as an info hub of gay services and associations in Paris. Café, library, and a monthly exhibit of gay-related art. Open M-Sa 2-8pm, Sa 2-7pm.

ACT-UP PARIS, 45, rue de Sedene, 11ème (tel. 01 48 06 13 89). M: Bréguet-Sabin. The Paris chapter of ACT-UP (the AIDS Coalition to Unleash Power) meets Tu 7:30pm at l'Ecole des Beaux Arts, rue Bonaparte, 6ème, M: St-Germain-des-Près, to discuss HIV, AIDS, and homophobia.

Centre du Christ Libérateur (métropolitan Community Church), 5, rue Crussol, 11ème (tel. 01 48 05 24 48 or 01 39 83 13 44). M: Oberkampf. Founded by Pasteur Doucé, this center provides advice and counseling for gay and lesbian people.

Fréquence Gaie/Radio Orient, 98.2FM (tel. 01 40 13 88 00), a 24hr. gay and lesbian radio station providing news, information, and block-rocking beats in French and English.

Maison des Femmes, 163, rue de Charenton, 12ème (tel. 01 43 43 41 13). Info and cultural center for lesbians and bisexual women. Open W and F 4-7pm, Sa 5-7pm. Women's café F 8pm-midnight.

S.O.S. Homophobie (tel. 01 48 06 42 41). A hotline for gay, lesbian, and bisexual concerns. Takes calls Sept.-June M-F 8-10pm; July-Aug. Tu-F 8-10pm.

Ecoute Gaie (tel. 01 44 93 01 02). A crisis hotline, similar to SOS Homophobie, but staffed by mostly men. M 8-10pm, Tu and F 6-10pm, and W 7-10pm.

MINORITY RESOURCES

Paris has a number of institutes, bookstores, and community centers which can provide visitors with information on cultural events, programs, and histories of Paris's immigrant communities. The bookstore and publishing house **Présence Africaine** is most famous for having first published the Martiniquais poet Aimé Césaire's poetry in the 1920s. Today, the bookstore stocks thousands of titles on West African and Caribbean literature, politics, philosophy, and culture, and serves as an unofficial center for information on Paris's African and Caribbean communities (see **Books and Magazines**, p. 309). While jazz clubs like the **Duc des Lombards** have hosted African-American jazz musicians like Ella Fitzgerald, Louis Armstrong, Thelonius Monk, and Miles Davis for decades, **Hayne's Bar**, founded by LeRoy Haynes in 1947, is a center for African-American expatriates and a former hangout for James Baldwin and Richard Wright (see **Jazz**, p. 299 and **Restaurants**, p. 130). Paris's North African communities have reshaped French identity itself. In addition to the city's Tunisian, Algerian, and Moroccan neighborhoods, mosques, restaurants, and shops, the **Institut du Monde Arabe** offers exhibitions, events, lectures, and films on Arab culture both in Paris and in the Maghreb (see **Museums**, p. 259). Paris's Vietnamese and Cambodian neighborhoods share the 13ème and 19ème with their Chinese and Laotian, Indian and Pakistani neighbors. The following centers have valuable information about history and cultural events for their communities:

Association des Trois Mondes, 63bis, rue du Cardinal Lemoine, 5ème (tel. 01 42 34 99 09). M: Cardinal-Lemoine. Audiovisual presentations and cinema of Arab, Latin American, African, and Asian communities. Immigration information. Tu-F 2-6pm.

Centre Culturel Algérien, 171, rue de la Croix-Nivert, 15ème (tel. 01 45 54 95 31). M: Boucicault. Periodicals, exhibits on Algeria, Islam, immigrant communities. M-F 9am-5pm. Closed Aug.

Agence pour le développement des relations interculturelles, 4, rue Réne-Villermé, 11ème (tel. 01 40 09 69 19). M: Père-Lachaise. Information on immigration, intercultural relations, Parisian racial politics. M, W, Th 9:30am-1pm, 2-6pm; F 9:30am-1pm, 2-5pm.

Centre Culturel Coréen, 2, av. d'Iéna, 16ème (tel. 01 47 20 84 15). M: Iéna. Information on meetings in South Korean community, contemporary Korean literature collection. M-F 9:30am-12:30pm, 2:30-6pm.

Centre Culturel Égyptien, 111, bd. St Michel, 5ème (tel. 01 46 33 75 67). M: Luxembourg. Displays and meetings on Egyptian culture, literature. M-F 10am-7pm, Sa 3-7pm. Closed Aug.

Maison de l'Asie, 22, av. du Président Wilson, 16ème (tel. 01 53 70 18 46). M: Iéna. Displays on history and civilizations of Asia. Events for East and South Asian communities. M-F 9am-6pm.

KEEPING IN TOUCH

PHONES

CALLING HOME FROM FRANCE

A **calling card** is the most convenient way to call home from abroad, but it's not always cheaper. There are two basic types. In the first, the card is issued free or for a small charge, but calls are billed either to your home account or to the person you are calling. It's lucky that you won't see the bill until you get home, as calls with these cards can be ruinously expensive. On no account use them for calls inside France or to other countries than the issuing one, since you'll probably be charged for a call back to your home country and then out again to the person you're calling. Far cheaper are prepaid cards, in which you buy a card which contains a certain amount of call time. The former is more convenient and is better if you don't expect to be using it much, but the latter is often cheaper for long calls. If you are using a public pay phone in France, you will still need to insert a functioning *Télécarte* (see below) to make your call; however it will not be billed. Many tiny *épiceries* and *restos* offer lesser-known cards like the *Phonepass*, which give greater rates (3hr. to US or 4hr. to the UK, 100F). The best way to find these is to look for posters listing rates in windows.

BILLED CARDS. To call home with a calling card, contact the France operator for your service provider. The local access numbers from France are: **AT&T:** 0 800 99 00 11; **Sprint:** 0 800 99 00 87; **MCI WorldPhone Direct:** 0 800 99 00 19; **Canada Direct:** 0 800 99 00 16 or 0 800 99 02 16; **BT Direct:** 0 800 99 02 44; **Ireland Direct:** 0 800 99 03 53; **Australia Direct:** 0 800 99 00 61; **Telecom New Zealand Direct:** 0 800 99 00 64; **Telkom South Africa Direct:** 0 800 99 00 27.

PREPAID CARDS. For general information, see **Prepaid Cards,** p. 53. You can also buy prepaid cards in France; the most popular is the **Carte Intercall Monde,** available in most *tabacs* and news agents. These are available in 50F and 100F denominations, and give up to 75% off standard French international call rates.

DIRECT DIAL. If you must use a pay phone, prepare yourself in advance with a fully-charged *Télécarte* (see below), and be ready to watch the numbers drop. Calls are cheaper between 7pm and 8am Monday to Friday, noon-midnight Saturday and all Sunday. Expect to pay about 3F per minute to the UK, Ireland and North America, and about 10F per minute to Australia and New Zealand. Use only public *France Télécom* pay phones, as private ones often charge more. Although convenient, in-room hotel calls invariably include an arbitrary and sky-high surcharge (as much as US$10).

If you do dial direct, you must first insert a *Télécarte* (see **calling within France** below), then dial 00 (the international access code for France), the country code and then number of your home. **Country codes** include: Australia 61; Ireland 353; New Zealand 64; South Africa 27; U.K. 44; U.S. and Canada 1. Note that when calling the UK from abroad you should drop the first zero of the area code.

Telephone rates are reduced Monday to Friday 7pm-8am, noon Saturday to Monday 8am for calls to the EU; M-F 7pm-1pm, and all day Sa and Su to the U.S. and Canada. Remember time differences when you call—Paris is one hour ahead of Greenwich Mean Time and six hours ahead of New York (Eastern Standard Time) (For more on this, see the **Appendix,** p. 340.)

CALLING COLLECT. The expensive alternative to dialing direct or using a calling card is using an international operator to place a **collect call** (also called reverse-charges; *faire un appel en PCV* in French). An English-speaking operator from your home nation can be reached by dialing the appropriate service provider (see **Billed Calls,** p. 91), and they will typically place a collect call even if you don't possess one of their phone cards.

PHONE HOME. A small digital screen on the phone will issue a series of simple commands; press the small button marked with a British flag to get instructions in English. Follow them, or face *"assimilation."* A call is *un coup de téléphone* or *un appel;* to dial is *composer;* a collect call is made *en PCV* (pay-say-vay); a person-to-person call is *avec préavis. Décrochez* means pick up; you will then be asked to *patientez* (wait) before you can put your card in. Only when you are told *numérotez* or *composez* should you dial. *Racrochez* means "hang up," and generally means you've done something wrong. If you want to make another call, don't hang up at the end of the first one; just press the green unlabeled button. On some *Télécarte* phones, you need to *fermer le volet* (pull down the lever above the card slot), and wait for a dial tone. Most pay phones receive incoming calls. The number is on a sticker inside the booth, prefaced by *ici le.*

CALLING WITHIN FRANCE

Almost all French pay phones accept only stylish microchip-toting phonecards called **Télécartes;** in many cafés and bars, some phones are still coin-operated; some also take credit cards. You may purchase the card in two denominations: 49F for 50 *unités,* and 97F for 120 *unités,* each worth anywhere from six to 18 minutes of conversation. The *Télécarte* is available at post offices, métro stations, and *tabacs.* Don't buy cards from street vendors who recycle discarded cards and cheat you. If your credit isn't good at home, the 120 *unités Télécarte* will serve you well (call to the U.K. 20min. for 120 units; call to the U.S. or Canada 12min. for 120 units). Emergency and collect calls require neither coins nor *Télécartes.*

Phone numbers in Paris and the Ile-de-France require **01** in front, in the northwest of France **02,** in the northeast **03,** in the southeast and Corsica **04,** and in the southwest **05.** Emergency calls and numbers beginning with **0 800** (formerly 05) are free. Most numbers beginning with **08** (formerly 36) are expensive (the equivalent of 900 numbers in the U.S.).

Directory information: tel. 12. English rarely spoken.

International information: 00 33 12 + country code (Australia 61; Ireland 353; New Zealand 64; U.K. 44; U.S. and Canada 1).

International Operator: tel. 00 33 11.

MAIL

SENDING MAIL HOME

Post offices are marked on most Paris maps by their abstract flying-letter insignia; on the streets, look for the yellow and blue PTT signs. In general, post offices in Paris are open Monday to Friday 8am to 7pm (they stop changing money at 6pm) and on Saturday 8am to noon, though the **Poste du Louvre,** 52, rue du Louvre, 1*er* (tel. 01 40 28 20 40 for postal info, 01 40 28 20 00 for telegrams; M: Louvre; closes daily 6:20-7am) is open almost 24 hours, and takes MasterCard and Visa. Buy stamps at *tabacs* or from vending machines inside major post offices to save time.

Air mail between Paris and North America takes five to ten days and is fairly dependable. Send mail from the largest post office in the area. To airmail a 20g (about 1 oz.) letter or postcard from France to the U.S. or Canada costs 4F40, to Australia or New Zealand 5F20. It is vital to distinguish your airmail from surface mail by labeling it clearly **par avion.** To airmail a **package,** you must complete a green customs slip. In France there are two grades of express mail: letters sent **prioritaire** cost the same as regular airmail letters and arrive within four or five days to North America, although anything heavier than a letter will cost more than regular airmail; **chronopost** arrive in one to three days at a soaring cost of 230F for a letter. Chronopost is only available until 6pm in most post offices, until 8pm at major branches; call 0 800 43 11 00. You must go up to a window for *prioritaire* or chronopost. No worries about how much postage to use, as the caring, idiot-proof machines in the lobbies of most post office hold your hand through the process, weighing your package/letter, and printing out a sticker with the right amount of postage. Group hug, anyone?

The **aerogramme**, a sheet of fold-up, pre-paid airmail paper, requires no envelope and costs more (5F to the U.S. or Canada, no enclosures allowed). **Registered mail** is called *avec recommandation* and costs between 26 and 30F, depending upon where the mail is going. To be notified of a registered letter's receipt, ask for an *avis de réception* and pay an additional 8F. **Surface mail** is by far the cheapest way but takes one to three months to cross the Atlantic. It's adequate for getting rid of books or clothing you no longer need; a special book rate makes this option even more economical.

For mail to the U.S., **Federal Express** (tel. 0 800 12 38 00), delivers the next business day, and even on **Saturdays.** They rob you blind (360F to send a 500g package, with a 98F surcharge for Saturdays). Call Monday through Friday before 5pm for pick up, or drop it off in their location at 2, rue du 29 Juillet, between Concorde and rue du Rivoli in the 1er. Open M-Sa 9am-7pm, but drop it before 4:45pm for next-day delivery.

RECEIVING MAIL IN PARIS

There are several ways to arrange pick-up of letters sent to you by friends and relatives while you are abroad. If you do not have a mailing address in Paris, you can receive mail through the **Poste Restante** system, handled by the 23-hour Louvre post office (see above). To ensure the safe arrival of your letters, they should be addressed with your last/family name in capital letters, followed by a comma and your first name, followed by *Poste Restante*, the address of the specific post office, and Paris, FRANCE. You will have to show your passport as identification and pay 3F for every letter received.

General Delivery: Mail can be sent to France through **Poste Restante** (the French phrase for General Delivery) to almost any city or town with a post office. Address *Poste Restante* letters to: GRUNITZKY, Yannick; Poste Restante: Recette Principale; [750xx where xx is the arrondissement you want to send to, e.g. 06 for the 6ème, 016 for the 16ème] PARIS; FRANCE; mark the envelope 'hold'. When picking up your mail, bring a form of photo ID, preferably a passport. There is generally a small charge per item to pick up, which in many cases is overlooked anyway. If the clerks insist that there is nothing for you, have them check under your first name as well.

VIVE LA TECHNOLOGIE
In certain hotels and restaurants you may notice a dusty little gray box, marked by a few ring stains and perhaps buried under some old newspapers, but otherwise an eminently useful member of the computer age. Minitel is what the French invented during the 1980s while the rest of the world was working on the Internet. Today, it seems like a dinosaur: a computer system with the power of a Commodore 64 provides telephone numbers, addresses, on-screen newspapers, the weather, train schedules, and ticket info. The French are kind of rabid about their allegiance to Minitel. Consult your Minitel guide. Please do not touch the Minitel. The Minitel is only for emergency use or daily functions. Do not ever confuse the two. Remember the Minitel is part of you or at the very least part of all of us. The Minitel won the war, old man. Eat up your crêpes and... <transmission garbled>

If you have a listed telephone number, you can lease your own from the phone company. But at 2F per minute, Minitel could break your budget before you're even aware of it. Use the little yellow Minitel machines in post offices for directory enquiries, including the Poste du Louvre and Poste des Champs-Elysées (see **Mail,** p. 92); bring a *Télécarte*. Dial 3611, wait for the beep, then press *Connexion*, then type the name and city of the personage or company you seek, then press *Envoi*. This service costs 37 centimes a minute, after the first three minutes.

American Express: AmEx's travel offices throughout the world will act as a mail service for cardholders if you contact them in advance. Under this free **Client Letter Service,** they will hold mail for up to 30 days and forward upon request. Address the letter in the same way shown above. Some offices will offer these services to non-cardholders (especially those who have purchased AmEx Travelers Cheques), but you must call ahead to make sure. **American Express,** 11, rue Scribe, 75009, Paris (tel. 01 47 77 79 59) holds mail, after which they return it to the sender. This service is free with presentation of your American Express traveler's checks or card. To have it held longer, write "Hold for x days" on the envelope. The envelope should be addressed with your name in capital letters, "c/o American Express: Client Mail" printed below your name. Open M-F 9am-6pm, Sa 9am-5pm.

FAXES

Most Parisian post offices have public **fax** machines, called *télécopieurs* or *faxes*. Rates to the U.S. are approximately 45F for the first page, 25F per page after that.

INTERNET ACCESS

While major French companies and institutions boast websites and Internet access, students are rarely given a university account. As a result, widespread cyber culture is still lagging in Paris, although it looms on the horizon like a tsunami of technocracy. In the meantime, for those addicts who desire that binary fix, there are options. **Cybercafe Guide** (www.cyberiacafe.net/cyberia/guide/ccafe.htm#working_france) can help you find cybercafés in France and all over the world. Cybercafés tend to be expensive. Your best strategy is to compose email letters on your laptop or home computer, then download and send them at the café. Save them to a disk as a text or word processing program file, then they can be opened on the café computer, and cut and pasted into your email. This will reduce your login time and your expense. Some tourist offices (see **Tourist Offices,** p. 85, and, supposedly, smell-mecca Sephora, p. 306) has free internet access. Definitely, many a hostel has access in its lobby, but prepared for slow connections, lengthy lines, and comparatively high fees.

WebBar, 32, rue de Picardie, 3ème (tel. 01 42 72 66 55). M: République. With leather chairs, a funky bar, and industrial decor, one of coolest (too cool?) spots to surf. Live music, poetry nights, and salsa dancing on Mondays. Internet 40F per hr., 300F for 10hr. Open M-F 8:30am-2am, Sa-Su 11am-2am.

Cyber Cube, 5, rue Mignon, 6ème (tel. 01 53 10 30 50). M: St-Michel or Odéon. From either métro, take rue Danton, from which rue Mignon branches off. The first thing you should know is that it is not really a cube. The second is that you will most likely have to wait for one of their Macs or PCs with all the fixings (telnet, FTP, Word, and a plethora of design programs). B & W printing 1F per page. Internet 1F per min. For students, 200F for 5 hours or 300F for 10 hours. Open M-Sa 10am-10pm. Also in the 11ème at 12, rue Daval (tel. 01 49 29 67 67). M: Bastille.

Hammam Café, 4, rue des Rosiers, 3ème (tel. 01 42 78 04 45). M: St-Paul. No longer a *hammam,* as steam doesn't mix well with computers. Salads, pasta, and Ben and Jerry's ice cream. Internet 1F per min. Live music 2-3 times per week. Saunter downstairs to link up or upstairs for music. Open Su-Th noon-midnight, F noon-4pm, Sa sundown-2am.

Le Jardin de l'Internet, 79, bd. St-Michel, 5ème (tel. 01 44 07 22 20). RER: Luxembourg. Friendly English-speaking staff. Coffee 7F, hot chocolate 10F, sandwiches 13-19F. Internet 1F per min., 25F for 30min., 48F for 1hr., 190F for 5 hours. Open M-Sa 9am-11pm, Su 11am-10pm.

Luxembourg Micro, 83, bd. St-Michel, 5ème (tel. 01 46 33 27 98). RER: Luxembourg. Not far from the main gates of the Jardin Luxembourg lies this quaint little wonder of modern technology, with some of the cheapest net rates in town. 0.75F per minute, 23F for half an hour, 45F for an hour. Membership cards: 100F for 2.5 hours, 180F for 5 hours, and 275F for 10 hours. Open M-Sa 9am-9pm.

Café Orbital, 13, rue du Médicis, 6ème (tel. 01 43 25 76 77). M: Odéon or buses #21, 38, or 84-86. France's first cyber café offers telnet, newsgroups, the Web, and computers whose large screens are positioned so that anyone behind you can read your email— a real cyber community. Internet 1F per min. but beware the 30min. minimum, 55F per hr. Students may get a *Carte Sidérante:* 200F for 5hr., 300F for 10hr. Open M-Sa 10am-11pm, Su noon-8pm.

AMAC, 141, bd. du Montparnasse, 6ème (tel. 01 55 42 10 60). M: Vavin. Also in the 5ème at 4, rue de la Sorbonne (tel. 01 55 42 10 60). M: St-Michel. Despite the name, this smallish internet joint has mostly PCs, all of which are very fast and new. 5F for 5minutes, 50F for an hour. Student cards: 200F for 5 hours, 350F for 10 hours, 600F for 20 hours. In the 6ème open M-Sa 9am-7:30pm, in the 5ème open M-F 9am-7pm, Sa 1-7pm.

THE MEDIA

TELEVISION AND RADIO

Television makes up for the lack of national papers. For most of the post-war period, French television was in the hands of a state-run monopoly, but in the mid-80s several public stations were privatized. **TF1,** now the most popular station in France, was privatized in 1986. For the stubbornly intellectual, there is the public channel **ARTE.** Cable TV is also available, while pay channel **Canal Plus** shows recent films and live sporting events. TV Guides are the most popular publications in France, with **Télé 7 jours** leading the pack while **Télérama** provides commentary not only on TV but also on culture in general. French **radio** went commercial in 1984, though the success of large conglomerates means few stations remain independent. National stations include **Fun Radio** for teens; **Skyrock,** a noisy and provocative rock station; and **Nostalgie,** adult-oriented with quiz shows and emotional music. Public stations include **France-Inter,** a quality general interest station, and **France Info,** an all-news station.

NEWSPAPERS AND LISTINGS

The weeklies *Pariscope* (3F) and *Officiel des Spectacles* (2F) are the most comprehensive listings of movies, plays, exhibits, festivals, clubs, and bars. *Pariscope* also includes an English-language section called *Time Out Paris.* The tourist office's free monthly *Where: Paris* highlights exhibitions, concerts, walking tours, and events. The Mairie de Paris, 29, rue de Rivoli, 4ème (tel. 01 42 76 42 42; M: Hôtel-de-Ville) publishes the free monthly *Paris le Journal* with articles about what's on around the city. On Wednesday *Le Figaro* includes *Figaroscope,* a supplement about what's happening in Paris. *Free Voice,* a monthly English-language newspaper published by the American Church (see **English-Language Religious Services,** p. 87), and the bi-weekly *France-USA Contacts (FUSAC)* list jobs, housing, and information for English speakers and are available for free from English-speaking bookstores, restaurants, and travel agencies throughout Paris.

French newspapers are a rich source of day-to-day politics, culture, and debate for those who read French. *Libération* (7F), a socialist newspaper, offers comprehensive news coverage of world events. Heavy on culture, including theater and concert listings, *"Libé"* has excellent, controversial, and thought-provoking editorials. Readers with a penchant for politics will disappear behind a copy of *Le Monde* (7F50), decidedly centrist with a tendency to wax socialist. *Le Figaro* (7F) leans to the right, with an entire section of financial news. *Le Parisien* (5F) and *France-Soir* (4F) are tabloids with occasional scoops in the political and social arenas. *La Tribune* (7F) is France's *Wall Street Journal.* The Communist Party puts out *L'Humanité* (7F) for the good of the people. For a run-down of the latest on rap, hip-hop, industrial, and pop, fashion trends, and Paris street–culture, pick up a copy of the well-designed and snidely amusing magazine *Technik Art* (18F), a monthly *communiqué* (in French) for the Parisian dandy. Gay and lesbian readers should consult *Têtu* (30F) for the latest in French queer politics, fashion, and events. For an English-language run-down of world events, financial news, and sports, read the *International Herald Tribune* (10F).

There are two **newsstands open 24 hours:** 33, av. des Champs-Elysées, 8*ème*, M: Franklin D. Roosevelt; 2, bd. Montmartre, 9*ème*, M: Rue Montmartre.

WHEN IN PARIS

While some would attempt to argue that the Parisian version of "etiquette" is none at all, there are indeed many a cultural nuance, the knowledge of which will help ease your transition into the City of Light.

AUGUST (AND EVERYTHING AFTER) AND HOURS

Be aware that Parisians clear out of their beloved city for nearly the entire month of August: consequently, most things shut down, and anglophones flood the city's monuments. As for hours of opening *(horaires)*, most restaurants and some other small business close for "lunch," which clocking in at a hefty three hours, must include a sizable nap as well (typically noon-3pm). Many establishments and most museums are closed on Mondays, and other hours are characteristically protean: calling ahead is always a good idea.

BLENDING IN

Try to blend in as much as possible. The French tend to dress more conservatively than people in other countries. Shorts shouldn't be too short, nor should they feature strategically ripped butt areas. Usually skirts or dresses for girls are more appropriate and just as good in hot weather. Don't worry about overdressing, you probably won't be; Parisians are very stylish, even students and young people dress well when going out. Closed shoes, solid colored pants or jeans, and plain T-shirts or button-down shirts are ideal, not baggy pants and torn jeans.

CHURCH ETIQUETTE

Surprising as it may seem, churches are indeed places of worship before they are tourist attractions. That said, it is important to keep proper conduct in mind, including mode of dress. Cutoffs, tight, short, bare shouldered, sloppy, or dirty are words that should never be used in describing what you are wearing into a church. Do not walk into the middle of a mass unless you plan to give an impromptu homily. Do not take flash photographs (or any pictures, preferably), and don't walk directly in front of the altar unless directed to do so.

DRIVING

The French have a not undeserved reputation for aggressive, dangerous driving. Still, while they will zoom past slow cars or space cadets, they will in all likelihood not hit you. Parisians jaywalk for sport. See also **Cars,** p. 81.

FLOORS

Keep in mind that the French call the ground floor the *rez-de-chaussée* and start numbering with the first floor above the ground floor *(premier étage)*. The button labeled "R" and not "1" is typically the ground floor. This system can cause unpleasant surprises, when your fourth "floor hotel" room is in reality above the tree line.

GREETINGS AND SALUTATIONS

Although the Parisian concept of customer service leaves much to be desired, there is no end to the pleasantries that one encounters whenever entering or exiting a business, restaurant, or hotel. Always, always say *"Bonjour Madame/Monsieur"* when you come in, and *"Au Revoir"* when you leave, or face an even icier reception than is the norm. If you bump into someone on the street or while awaiting/pushing your way into transportation, always say *"Pardon or Excusez-moi."* The proper way to answer the phone is *"Âllo,"* but if you use this on the street, your cover will be blown.

POCKET CHANGE

Cashiers and tellers will constantly ask you *"Avez-vous la monnaie?"* ("Do you have the change?) as they would rather not break your 1000F note for a pack of gum. If you don't have it, smile ever-so-sweetly and say *"Non, désolée."* Number 274 on the list "Things I Wish I Had Packed:" a coin purse.

PUBLIC RESTROOMS

The streetside public restrooms in Paris are worth the 2F they require. For this paltry sum, you are guaranteed a clean restroom, as these magic machines are self-cleaning after each use. This kind of cleanliness should not be expected in your average cafe, as they tend to have the squat toilets that foreigners rarely have the joy of encountering. In addition, don't feel you have to buy something in order to use the restroom. Just march right in there, and if someone says something, feign frontal lobotomy.

SAFETY AND SECURITY

Personal safety in France is on a par with the rest of Western Europe, with a far lower rate of violent crime than the US. As big cities go, Paris is relatively safe. It's best not to be complacent, though, especially since tourists are often seen as (and often are) easy victims. Be especially careful on public transport at rush hour and on the way to and from the airport. Theft is also common on métro line number one and at department stores; never leave your wallet, passport or credit card on the counter. Exercise caution and common sense—keep bags closed and under your arm if possible and be particularly vigilant in crowded areas - and you increase your chances of a trouble-free holiday.

   Certain areas of Paris can be rough at night, including Les Halles and the Bastille area. Travelers should not walk around Pigalle, Barbès-Rochechouart, Montmartre, rue St-Denis in the *2ème*, or Belleville alone at night. In general, the northern and eastern arrondissements are less safe than the southern and western ones, and the Right Bank less safe than the Left. Be especially aware when in the arrondissements outside the typical tourist loop. In an emergency, dial 17 for police. The distribution of people can reveal a great deal about the relative safety of the area; look for children playing, women walking in the open, and other signs of an active community. If you are traveling alone, be sure that someone at home knows your itinerary and never admit that you're traveling alone. *Ça va sans dire:* When walking at night, stick to busy, well-lit streets and avoid dark alleyways, parks, parking lots, and deserted areas. Keep in mind that a district can change character drastically between blocks. Whenever possible, *Let's Go* warns of unsafe neighborhoods, but always use your noggin'.

TIPPING

Service is always included in meal prices in restaurants and cafés, and in drink prices at bars and clubs; look for the phrase *service compris* on the menu or just ask. If service is not included, tip 15-20%. Even when service is included, it is polite to leave extra *monnaie* (change) at a café, bistro, restaurant, or bar—a few francs for a glass of wine, 5% for a meal.

ACCOMMODATIONS

> In those days the hotel was one of the many damp, plain hostelries made for tourists, chiefly American, of very modest means who, if they were like me would always remember how the exotic bidet, positioned solidly in the drab bedroom, along with the toilet far down the ill-lit hallway, virtually defined the chasm between Gallic and Anglo-Saxon cultures.
>
> —William Styron, *Darkness Visible*

In Paris, budget accommodations fall into three categories: hotels, hostels, and *foyers*. Hotels are comfortable, afford complete privacy and independence, and are often the cheapest option for those traveling in couples or small groups. *Foyers* are semi-permanent student communities that become available for shorter-term stays in the summer. (For information on hostels, see p. 59.) Hostels and *foyers* are the least expensive option for people traveling alone. **High season** in Paris falls from May to October and prices might increase during this time; the peak of high season is July and August.

Be aware that the city of Paris has a **Taxe de Séjour** of approximately one to five francs flat-rate per person per night; this does not have to be included in advertised or quoted prices, but must be listed along with the room price on the back of the hotel room door.

It is advisable to check for this as well as other add-on expenses such as direct telephone service (some hotels will even charge you for collect calls) before making a reservation. Likewise, **always insist on seeing a room first,** even if the proprietor is not amenable. Hotels and hostels are ranked according to qualities such as charm, friendliness, convenience, and value for money; particularly outstanding establishments are awarded the Let's Go thumb pick ().

TYPES OF ACCOMMODATIONS

HOSTELS AND FOYERS

> **A HOSTELER'S BILL OF RIGHTS.** There are certain standard features that we do not include in our hostel listings. Unless we state otherwise, you can expect that every hostel has: no lockout, no curfew, a kitchen, free hot showers, secure luggage storage, and no key deposit.

Many of Paris's hostels don't bother with many of the restrictions—sleepsheets, curfews, and the like—that characterize most hostels in the world; they do have maximum stays, age restrictions, lockouts and occasional curfews, but often these restrictions are flexible. Accommodations usually consist of single-sex rooms with two to eight beds, but you may be asked whether you're willing to be in a co-ed room. You will likely need to share a room with strangers.

Foyers, on the other hand, are intended for university students or workers during the academic year, and are available for short- or long-term stays during the summer. *Foyers*, often comprised of single rooms, offer the security and privacy of a hotel while providing the lower prices and camaraderie of a youth hostel.

To stay in a **Hostelling International (HI)** hostel, you must be a member (see **Accommodations**, p. 59). If you show up at an HI hostel without a membership card, the hostel should issue you a blank card with space for six validation stamps. Each night you'll pay a nonmember supplement (19F) and earn one Guest Stamp. Get six stamps and you're a member. Membership purchased this way costs 114F, so it's cost-efficient for prospective hostelers to become members before leaving home. Most student travel agencies issue HI cards on the spot, or you can contact a national hostel organization (see **Student and Budget Travel Agencies,** p. 54). Another benefit of an HI membership is HI's recently instituted International Booking Network, whereby you can reserve a room in advance. Information on French hostels can also be obtained on the web at www.fuaj.fr.

Despite the hype, there are only six official HI hostels and HI affiliates in Paris. Most of the hostels and *foyers* in the city are privately run organizations, usually with services comparable to those at HI and often preferable to the HI hostels because of their more central locations.

HOTELS

Small Parisian hotels are a long-time institution in this city; they are almost all proudly shabby, and some have eccentric character. Hotels offer total privacy, no curfew, and (usually) concerned managers. Most importantly, they routinely accept reservations. Budget hotels in Paris are not significantly more expensive than their hostel and *foyer* counterparts. Groups of two, three, and four may find it more economical to stay in a hotel since, unlike hostels, hotels rent doubles by the room and not by the body.

The French government employs a ratings system which graces hotels with zero to four stars depending on the services offered, the percentage of rooms with bath, and other such indicators. Most hotels listed by *Let's Go* are zero, one- or two-star, with a smattering of inexpensive three-stars. Expect to pay at least 120F for a single room and 150F for a double.

If you want a room with twin beds, make sure to ask for *une chambre avec deux lits* (a room with two beds); otherwise you may find yourself in *une chambre avec un grand lit* (room with a double bed). In our listings, doubles refer to rooms with one full-size bed; two-bed doubles refer to the rare room with two separate (usually twin) beds. Breakfast in hotels normally runs 25-40F extra, with coffee or hot chocolate, bread and croissants; you'll probably get a better deal at a local café. Rooms in cheap hotels normally have no en suite facilities; they are to be found on the hallway. Occasionally you will have to pay extra for a hot shower (10-25F), and some very cheap hotels have no washing facilities at all. *Let's Go* notes if this is the case. Otherwise, rooms may come with a variety of add-ons: *avec bidet-lavabo* means a sink and a bidet, but no toilet; *avec WC* or *avec cabinet* means with sink and toilet; *avec douche* means with shower; and *avec salle de bain* is with a full bathroom. Most bathrooms also have a *bidet*, a low toilet-like apparatus which is intended for cleaning genitalia; no matter how desperate you are, do not use a bidet as a toilet. If your room has no shower, you'll usually have to pay extra (15-25F) for the hall shower key. All French hotels display on the back of each room's door a list showing the prices of rooms, breakfast and any residency tax. It is illegal to charge you more than is shown, though you can try to bargain for a lower rate if you are staying longer than a few days. It is illegal to hang laundry out the window or from balconies, although the law is rarely enforced.

Unfortunately, most hotels in Paris are not handicapped accessible—if this is an important consideration for you, you should ask before booking. See 'handicapped accessible' in the index of this book for a list of hotels with accessibility.

RESERVATIONS

Make reservations at least two weeks in advance, and up to a couple of months in advance for the summer. English may not be spoken at some smaller places, but this shouldn't dissuade a non-French-speaker from calling; most proprietors are used to receiving calls from non-French-speakers. Phrases which are helpful for making a room reservation in French are included in the appendix (p. 340). If the place where you wish to reserve a room asks for a deposit, they usually expect you to fax them your credit card number. Ask about a hotel's cancellation policy before giving a credit card number and whether or not your card will be billed. If

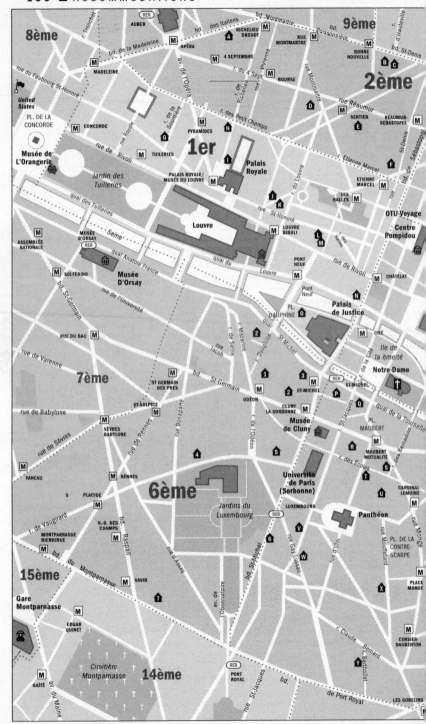

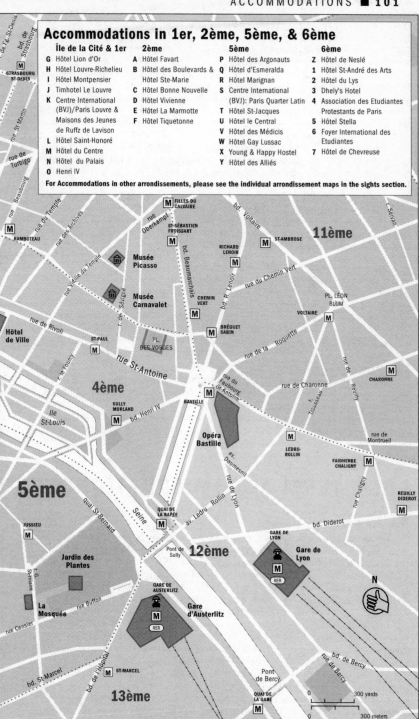

Accommodations in 1er, 2ème, 5ème, & 6ème

Île de la Cité & 1er
- G Hôtel Lion d'Or
- H Hôtel Louvre-Richelieu
- I Hôtel Montpensier
- J Timhotel Le Louvre
- K Centre International (BVJ)/Paris Louvre & Maisons des Jeunes de Ruffz de Lavison
- L Hôtel Saint-Honoré
- M Hôtel du Centre
- N Hôtel du Palais
- O Henri IV

2ème
- A Hôtel Favart
- B Hôtel des Boulevards & Hôtel Ste-Marie
- C Hôtel Bonne Nouvelle
- D Hôtel Vivienne
- E Hôtel La Marmotte
- F Hôtel Tiquetonne

5ème
- P Hôtel des Argonauts
- Q Hôtel d'Esmeralda
- R Hôtel Marignan
- S Centre International (BVJ): Paris Quarter Latin
- T Hôtel St-Jacques
- U Hôtel des Médicis
- V Hôtel le Central
- W Hôtel Gay Lussac
- X Young & Happy Hostel
- Y Hôtel des Alliés

6ème
- Z Hôtel de Neslé
- 1 Hôtel St-André des Arts
- 2 Hôtel du Lys
- 3 Dhely's Hotel
- 4 Association des Etudiants Protestants de Paris
- 5 Hôtel Stella
- 6 Foyer International des Etudiantes
- 7 Hôtel de Chevreuse

For Accommodations in other arrondissements, please see the individual arrondissement maps in the sights section.

you can avoid leaving a number (which is often times the case if you just send written confirmation or say you don't have one) do so in case you don't like the hotel upon your arrival. Either way, make sure the fax is clear about your anticipated dates and type of room (single, quad with shower, etc.).

If you decide to leave Paris before you intended, or if you want to switch hotels, don't expect to get back all of your deposit. On the flip side, if you change your plans before you even get started, you should certainly call and cancel your reservation; the hotel proprietor will be turning away others who are willing to pay for the spot you're not intending to use. If you plan to arrive late, call and ask a hotel to hold a room for you.

Once in Paris, the **Office du Tourisme** on the Champs-Elysées or one of its other bureaus should be able to find you a room, although the lines may extend to the horizon and the selections are not necessarily among the cheapest (see **Tourist Offices,** p. 85). If you have difficulty finding accommodation in the popular and central Latin Quarter or Marais, check our listings in the outlying arrondissements where rooms are often cheaper, and usually only a 20-minute métro ride to most sights. The following booking offices, located near major métro lines, are also frequently crowded, but their English speaking staff can arrange for stays in hostels and budget hotels throughout the city.

La Centrale de Réservations (FUAJ-HI), 4, bd. Jules Ferry, 11ème (tel. 01 43 57 02 60; fax 01 40 21 79 92). M: République. Follow the rue du Faubourg du Temple away from pl. de la République until you reach the park-like entity that divides bd. Jules Ferry in two. Cross to far side and turn right—La Centrale is half a block up on your left. One of the best ways to secure a bed in a hostel (115F per night per person). Provides same-day reservations in one of their affiliated youth hostels or budget hotels—a total of 10,000 beds in and around the city. The earlier you show up the better. Books beds for groups throughout France and Europe, arranges excursions, and procures plane and bus tickets. Open 24hr.

OTU-Voyage (Office du Tourisme Universitaire), 119, rue St-Martin, 4ème (tel. 01 40 29 12 12; see **Budget Travel Offices,** p. 86). Across the pedestrian mall from the Pompidou. Even in the busiest months, OTU-Voyage guarantees "decent and low-cost lodging" in Residence Bastille (see p. 116) and hotels for same-day reservation and immediate use. You must pay the full price of the *foyer* room when making your reservation, even before seeing the room. Employees speak English and other foreign languages. 10F service charge. Also at 2, rue Malus, 5ème (tel. 01 44 41 74 74). M: Place Monge. Open M-F 10am-6:30pm, St-Martin branch open Sa 10am-5pm.

LONG-TERM ACCOMMODATIONS

STUDENT

For travelers planning a summer, semester, or academic year visit to Paris, student housing is available in the dormitories of most French universities. Contact the **Centre Régional des Oeuvres Universitaires (CROUS)** for more information. Additional lodging is available on a month-to-month basis at the **Cité Universitaire** (15, bd. Jourdan, 14ème; tel. 01 44 16 64 00; M: Cité Universitaire; for information write to M. le Délégué Général de Cité Universitaire de Paris, 19, bd. Jourdan, 75690 Paris Cedex 14). Over 30 different nations maintain dormitories at the Cité Universitaire, where they board their citizens studying in Paris. In summer, dorms lodge anyone on a first-come, first-served basis. Reserve a bed months in advance—at least by April for June and July; if it is closer to the summer, try calling anyway. Some kitchens are available. (Singles 2000-3000F per month.)

To stay in the American House write to Fondation des Etats-Unis, 15, bd. Jourdan, 75690 Paris Cedex 14 (tel. 01 53 80 68 82). Rates vary according to demand: in summer 2900F per month; cheaper off season. (Office open M-F 9-5pm.) The **restaurant** in the Maison Internationale offers decent fare at rock-bottom prices.

RENTING AN APARTMENT

If you plan to stay in Paris for a longer period of time, consider renting an apartment. Although rent is high and utilities are expensive, apartments offer convenience, privacy, and a kitchen. Call, fax, write, or visit **Allô Logement Temporaire,** 64, rue du Temple, *3ème* (tel. 01 42 72 00 06; fax 01 42 72 03 11; email alt@claranet.fr; M: Hôtel-de-Ville; open M-F noon-8pm). This helpful, English-speaking association charges a membership fee of 300F if they succeed in finding an apartment for you, which is followed by an additional charge of 200F per month. The company suggests writing or calling before you leave for France. Be sure to leave a phone or fax number where you can be reached easily as vacancies come and go very quickly.

Alternatively, consult the French Department at your local university; it may be able to connect you with students abroad who want to sublet. Remember that short-term rentals, usually more expensive per month than longer rentals, can be difficult to procure, especially in winter months. The **internet** can provide listings on Paris apartments, but these often tend to be more expensive places advertised by wealthy Parisians with computers and internet access. Surf the web to get a sense of the housing market before you go (see **Other Resources,** p. 71).

If possible, stay in a hotel or hostel your first week in Paris and find an apartment while you're there. This process will allow you to see what you're getting. Among the best places to look are the bulletin boards in the **American Church** (see **Essentials,** p. 87). Those upstairs tend to advertise long-term rentals, while those downstairs list short-term, often cheaper, arrangements. A smaller list of apartments to rent or share can be found at the bookstore **Shakespeare and Co.** (see **Books and Magazines,** p. 307). Check listings in any of the English-French newsletters like **Paris Voice** or **France-USA Contacts (FUSAC),** a free publication found in English bookstores and restaurants throughout Paris. FUSAC is also distributed in the U.S. (FUSAC, P.O. Box 115, Cooper Station, New York, NY 10276; tel. (212) 929 2929; fax 255 5555; fusac@club-internet.fr). It includes an extensive section of classified ads, in which anglophones offer apartments for rent or sublet. *De Particulier à Particulier* is a French publication which comes out on Thursdays and lists an extensive selection of available housing, as does the Tuesday *Le Figaro.*

Subletting is technically illegal, but many choose to do so anyway. Those who do sublet should work out a written agreement with the landlord, defining all of their mutual expectations regarding security deposits, utilities, maintenance, and rent. This document will help to avoid any misunderstandings. The original renter may require cash payments to avoid paying heavy taxes, and utilities and mailbox are likely to remain under the renter's name. The subletter may need to tell the building superintendent or *concierge* that he or she is merely a guest, relative, or friend of the renter.

HOME EXCHANGE AND RENTALS

Home exchange offers the traveler various types of homes (houses, apartments, condominiums, villas, even castles in some cases), plus the opportunity to live like a native and to cut down dramatically on accommodation fees—usually only an administration fee is paid to the matching service. On the other hand, you have to give up your own castle to someone else while you're away. Once you join or contact one of the exchange services listed below, it is then up to you to decide with whom you would like to exchange homes. Most companies have pictures of member's homes and information about the owners. A great site listing many exchange companies can be found at www.aitec.edu.au/~bwechner/Documents/Travel/Lists/HomeExchangeClubs.html. If you're unwilling to hand your house over to strangers, **home rentals** can still work out much cheaper than hotels for larger groups. Both home exchanges and rentals are ideal for families with children, or travelers with special dietary needs.

HomeExchange, P.O. Box 30085, Santa Barbara, CA 93130 (tel. 805-898-9660; email admin@HomeExchange.com; www.homeexchange.com.

Intervac International Home Exchange, 230 bd. Voltaire, 75011 Paris (tel. 01 43 70 21 22; fax 01 43 70 73 35; www.intervac.com).

The Invented City: International Home Exchange, 41 Sutter St., #1090, San Francisco, CA 94104 (in the U.S. tel. 800-788-2489, elsewhere 415-252-1141; fax 252-1171; email invented@aol.com; www.invented_city.com). For US$75, you get your offer listed in 1 catalog and unlimited access to the club's database containing thousands of homes for exchange.

HOTELS, HOSTELS, AND FOYERS

ÎLE DE LA CITÉ

Henri IV, 25, pl. Dauphine (tel. 01 43 54 44 53). M: Cité. Walk toward the Conciergerie and turn right on bd. du Palais, left on quai de l'Horloge, and left at the front of the Conciergerie onto pl. Dauphine. One of the best-located hotels, Henri IV is also one of the least expensive. Named in honor of Henri IV's printing presses which once occupied the 400-year-old building, the hotel has charming views of the tree-lined pl. Dauphine. Simple, attractive furnishings. Showers 15F. Reserve 1 month in advance. Singles 125-160F; doubles 170-205F, with shower 250F; triples 240-265F; quads 290F.

FIRST ARRONDISSEMENT

In the shadow of the Louvre, much of the 1er remains true to its regal past. Cartier, Chanel, and the Banque de France set an intimidating mood for the budget traveler. Don't let the financiers and ladies-who-lunch scare you away: a few budget options remain. Those who stay near Châtelet-Les-Halles will revel in the central location but should use a safer métro station at night.

Hôtel Montpensier, 12, rue de Richelieu (tel. 01 42 96 28 50; fax 01 42 86 02 70). M: Palais-Royal. Walk around the left side of the Palais-Royal to rue de Richelieu. Clean rooms, lofty ceilings, and brightly colored decor welcome the clientele. Its good taste distinguishes it from most hotels in this region and price range. Brightly lit lounge with stained-glass ceiling. Small elevator. TVs in rooms with shower or bath. Shower 25F. Reserve 2 weeks in advance. Breakfast 37F in lounge or bedroom. AmEx, MC,V. Singles/doubles 310F, with toilet and shower 420F, with toilet, bath, and sink 510F. Extra bed 80F.

Hôtel Lion d'Or, 5, rue de la Sourdière (tel. 01 42 60 79 04; fax 01 42 60 09 14). M: Tuileries or Pyramides. From M: Tuileries walk down rue du 29 Juillet away from the park and turn right on rue St-Honoré then left on rue de la Sourdière. Carpeted rooms are clean and quiet. You'll hear the bells toll from nearby Eglise St-Roch but little else. Phone and TV in most rooms. Friendly staff speaks English. Breakfast 35F. 5% discount for stays of more than 3 nights. AmEx, MC, V. Singles 230F, with shower 350F; doubles with shower 450F, with bath and toilet 480F. Extra bed 60F.

Hôtel Saint-Honoré, 85, rue St-Honoré (tel. 01 42 36 20 38 or 01 42 21 46 96; fax 01 42 21 44 08). M: Louvre, Châtelet, or Les Halles. From M: Louvre, cross rue de Rivoli on rue du Louvre and turn right on rue St-Honoré. Recently renovated, with new reception, breakfast area, and comfortable rooms with firm beds and a dashing black and mauve color scheme. Friendly, English-speaking staff, and young clientele. Fridge access. All rooms have shower and toilet, and most have TVs. Breakfast 29F. Reserve by fax or phone and confirm the night before. AmEx, MC, V. Singles 290F; doubles 320-350F, with bathtub 380F; triples and quads 480F.

Hôtel Louvre-Richelieu, 51, rue de Richelieu (tel. 01 42 97 46 20; fax 01 47 03 94 13). M: Palais-Royal. See directions for Hôtel Montpensier, above. Plastic flowers and faux Monet prints decorate these smallish rooms with radios, phones, and a view of the bustling thoroughfare. Doubles in converted attic are an oasis of taste—muted flowered wallpaper, pine furniture, and skylight (but no view). English spoken. Breakfast 35F. Showers 10F. Reserve 3 weeks ahead in summer. MC, V. Singles 190-210F, with shower or bath and toilet 280-345F; doubles 230F, with shower or bath and toilet 420F; triples with shower and toilet 490F. Extra bed 50F.

Hôtel du Palais, 2, quai de la Mégisserie (tel. 01 42 36 98 25; fax 01 42 21 41 67). M: Châtelet-Les-Halles. Located by the Seine at the corner of pl. du Châtelet and quai de la Mégisserie, all rooms (except those on top floor) have splendid views of the river and are within earshot of the traffic below. Very basic rooms with high ceilings on first floor; tiny sky-lit rooms with funky eaves on top floor. A good choice if you don't mind steep stairways. Breakfast 30F. Reserve 3 weeks in advance. AmEx, MC, V. Singles with shower 283F, with shower or bath and toilet 353F; doubles with shower 326F, with shower and toilet 356F, with bath and toilet 386F; triples 429F; large quad 462F; quint with 2-sink bathroom and huge windows 535F. Extra bed 70F.

Hôtel du Centre, 20, rue du Roule (tel. 01 42 33 05 18; fax 01 42 33 74 02). M: Châtelet-Les-Halles or Pont Neuf. From M: Pont Neuf take rue de la Monnaie toward Les Halles straight onto rue du Roule. If inexpensive accommodations and central location are your overriding concerns, the Hôtel du Centre is the place for you. Most rooms have soft beds, red carpets, and TVs. Breakfast 30F. Reserve 2 weeks in advance. AmEx, MC, V. Singles or doubles with shower and toilet, 356F. Extra double bed 30% extra.

Timhotel Le Louvre, 4, rue Croix des Petits-Champs (tel. 01 42 60 34 86; fax 01 42 60 10 39). M: Palais-Royal. From the métro, cross rue de Rivoli to rue St-Honoré; take a left onto rue Croix des Petits-Champs. Though part of a chain, this 2-star hotel offers the only wheelchair-accessible rooms at reasonable prices in the 1er. Clean and modern rooms with bath, shower and cable TV. Great location next to the Louvre. AmEx, MC, V. Singles 580F; doubles 680F.

HOSTELS AND FOYERS

Centre International de Paris (BVJ)/Paris Louvre, 20, rue J.-J. Rousseau (tel. 01 53 00 90 90; fax 01 53 00 90 91). M: Louvre or Palais-Royal. From M: Louvre take rue du Louvre away from river then turn left on rue St-Honoré and right on rue J.-J. Rousseau. Courtyard hung with brass lanterns and strewn with brasserie chairs. 200 beds. Bright, dorm-style rooms with 2-10 beds per room. 2-course lunch or dinner 40F, 4-course 60F. English spoken. Breakfast and showers included. 24hr. reception. Weekend reservations up to 1 week in advance. Reserve by phone only. Rooms held only 10min. after your expected check-in time; call if you'll be late. 120F.

Maisons des Jeunes de Rufz de Lavison, 18, rue J.-J. Rousseau (tel. 01 45 08 02 10). M: Louvre or Palais-Royal. Located next door to above hostel. During the academic year, it's a private residence for male college students. In summer (mid-June to mid- Aug.) it's a co-ed foyer, primarily for long-term stays. Quiet, spacious, and sunny rooms for 50 students. Flower-filled, open-air courtyard. During winter, dinner is provided. Shower and breakfast included. 4-night min. stay. Reception 9am-7pm. No curfew. Reservations starting June 15; 1 night's payment required. Singles 160F; doubles 280F. Monthly: singles 4,000F; doubles 6,800F.

SECOND ARRONDISSEMENT

The *2ème* is within walking distance of the Marais, the Centre Pompidou, and the Louvre. The relatively safe western half shows some of the money that comes through the Bourse des Valeurs daily. However, try not to stray too far into the northeastern quarter past rue d'Aboukir, especially near seedy rue St-Denis. We're not saying the place is teeming with peep shows and prostitutes, but if you're looking for *"relaxation complète"* for 200F, this area would be an enticing option.

Hôtel Vivienne, 40, rue Vivienne (tel. 01 42 33 13 26; fax 01 40 41 98 19). M: Rue Montmartre. Follow the traffic on bd. Montmartre past the Théâtre des Variétés and turn left on rue Vivienne. From its hardwood-floored reception area to its spacious rooms with armoires, hair dryers, phones, and TVs, this hotel reconciles gracious living with budget rates, good with evil, black with white. Some balconies, beamed ceilings, and views across the Paris rooftops. Elevator. Breakfast 40F. MC, V. Singles and doubles with shower 370-450F; doubles 515F; 3rd person under 10 free, over 10 add 30%.

Hôtel Bonne Nouvelle, 17, rue Beauregard (tel. 01 45 08 42 42; fax 01 40 26 05 81). M: Bonne Nouvelle. From the métro follow traffic down rue Poissonnière and turn left on rue Beauregard. Antique-crammed lobby is an oasis from the questionable neighborhood to the east of the hotel. Rooms are variable, with those on the top floors boasting rooftop views and skylights. All rooms have TVs, hairdryers, and tidy bathrooms with toilet, shower, or bath. Tiny elevator. Breakfast 35F, in room 35F. Reserve by credit card. MC, V. Singles 330-390F; doubles 380-430F; triples 500-600F; quads 590-690F.

Hôtel des Boulevards, 10, rue de la Ville Neuve (tel. 01 42 36 02 29; fax 01 42 36 15 39). M: Bonne Nouvelle. From the rue Poissonnière métro, turn right on rue Poissonnière then left on rue de la Lune and right onto rue de la Ville Neuve. This route avoids the X-rated movie theater on rue de la Ville Neuve, the one blemish in an otherwise decent area. Quiet, aqua rooms with TVs, phones, and wooden wardrobes. Bag storage in the basement. Reserve 2 weeks ahead and confirm with credit card deposit. 10% *Let's Go* discount. AmEx, MC, V. Singles and doubles 210-230F without shower, 235-285 with; double with bath 320F; third person add 60F.

Hôtel Tiquetonne, 6, rue Tiquetonne (tel. 01 42 36 94 58; fax 01 42 36 02 94). M: Etienne Marcel. Walk against traffic on rue de Turbigo; turn left on rue Tiquetonne. Near Marché Montorgueil *and* St-Denis's sex shops, this affordable 7-story hotel is a study in faux finishes: from fake-marble corridors to "I-can't-believe-it's-not-wood" doors. Elevator. Breakfast (25F) served in room. Hall showers 30F. Closed Aug. and 1 week at Christmas. MC, V. Singles with shower 143-213F; doubles with shower and toilet 246F.

Hôtel La Marmotte, 6, rue Léopold Bellan (tel. 01 40 26 26 51). M: Sentier. From the métro take rue Petit Carreaux (the street market) and then turn right at rue Léopold Bellan. Reception located in ground-floor bar of a modern building. Quiet, spacious rooms with TVs, phones, marmots, and safe-boxes. Many restaurants nearby. Breakfast 25F. Shower 15F. Reserve 2-3 weeks ahead. AmEx, MC, V. Singles and doubles 180-220F, with shower 270-300F; 2-bed doubles 320F.

Hôtel Favart, 5, rue Marivaux (tel. 01 42 97 59 83; fax 01 40 15 95 58). M: Richel Drout. From the métro turn left down bd. des Italiens and left on Marivaux. On a quiet street in a good location. Rooms are sizeable and some boast textured wallpaper, mirrored ceilings, views of the Opéra Comique, or all of the above, for sensory overload. All rooms have a TV, phone, shower, toilet, and hair dryer. One handicapped accessible room on first floor with a very large bathroom. Large elevator. Breakfast included. AmEx, MC, V. July-Aug. singles 450F, doubles 555F; Sept.-June 630F, 665F, triples 790F.

Hôtel Ste-Marie, 6, rue de la Ville Neuve (tel. 01 42 33 21 61; fax 01 42 33 29 24). M: Bonne Nouvelle. Located next to Hôtel des Boulevards. Renovated. Rooms feature candy-striped walls, Pepto-pink bedspreads, new mattresses, and clean bathrooms. All rooms with phones, TVs in rooms with baths. Breakfast 25F, free for children. Showers 10F. 10% discount for stays over 7 days. AmEx, MC, V. Singles 220F, with bath 280F; doubles 270F, 340F; triples with shower and toilet 470F.

THIRD ARRONDISSEMENT

Once the home of Paris's noblest families, the 3ème's many 17th-century mansions now house a number of budget accommodations. These well-located and relatively inexpensive hotels cluster in the 3ème's noisy, commercial northwest—particularly around rue de Turbigo, where hotels sidle up to Paris's garment district.

Hôtel de Roubaix, 6, rue Greneta (tel. 01 42 72 89 91; fax 01 42 72 58 79). M: Réaumur-Sébastopol or Arts-et-Métiers. From M: Réaumur-Sébastopol, walk opposite traffic on bd. de Sébastopol and turn left on rue Greneta or take bus #20 from Gare de Lyon to St-Nicolas des Champs. Run by helpful, advice-dispensing staff, this well-kept hotel features clean rooms with flowered wallpaper and new bathrooms. Large breakfast room and 2 lounges. All rooms have shower, toilet, telephone, locker, and TV. 53

rooms, some noisy. Breakfast included. MC, V. Singles 305-330F; doubles 370-410F; triples 415-480F; quads 500F; quints 525F.

■ **Hôtel du Séjour,** 36, rue du Grenier St-Lazare (tel./fax 01 48 87 40 36). M: Etienne-Marcel or Rambuteau. From M: Etienne Marcel follow the traffic on rue Etienne-Marcel, which becomes rue du Grenier St-Lazare. One block from Les Halles and the Centre Pompidou, this hotel is mid-renovation; ask for a new room. Most rooms are bright, with large windows. 20 rooms. Showers 20F. Reception 7am-10:30pm. Singles 180F; doubles 260F, with shower and toilet 320F, third person 150F extra.

Hôtel Bellevue et du Chariot d'Or, 39, rue de Turbigo (tel. 01 48 87 45 60; fax 01 48 87 95 04). M: Etienne-Marcel. From the métro, walk against traffic on rue de Turbigo. A beautiful Belle Epoque lobby, with bar and breakfast room, gives this hotel a spiffy feel. Clean and modern rooms, some on a quiet courtyard. All have phones, TVs, toilets, and baths. Slanted ceilings on the top floor rooms make them the prettiest. 59 rooms. Singles 315F; doubles 350F; triples 425F; quads 460F.

Hôtel Picard, 26, rue de Picardie (tel. 01 48 87 53 82; fax 01 48 87 02 56). M: Temple. From the métro, walk against traffic down rue du Temple, take the first left on rue du Petit Thouars, and at the end of the street turn right. Next door to cyber café WebBar (p. 94). Simple pastel rooms; TVs in rooms with showers. Elevator. Breakfast 30F. Hall showers 20F. Apr.-Sept. reserve 1 week ahead. Tax 5F. MC, V. 10% *Let's Go* discount. Singles 210F, with shower and toilet 260F; doubles 250-270F, 330F; triples 520F.

Hôtel de Bretagne, 87, rue des Archives (tel. 01 48 87 83 14). M: Temple. From the métro, walk opposite traffic on rue du Temple, then turn left on rue de Bretagne and right onto rue des Archives. Steps away from a small park, the cheaper rooms are small and simple, while steeper ones have TVs and are more spruced. 25 rooms. Breakfast in room 30F. Reserve by phone 1 week in advance; after 7pm for an English receptionist. Singles 160F-320F; doubles 200-370F; triples 330-500F; quads 440-600F.

Hôtel Paris France, 72, rue de Turbigo (tel. 01 42 78 00 04, reservations 01 42 78 64 92; fax 01 42 71 99 43). M: République or Temple. From M: République take rue de Turbigo. The large lobby has soft sofas and a big TV. Some rooms have TV, phone, hair dryer and locker. Some noisy rooms but those on the top floor are renovated and bright with balconies, clean bathrooms, and super views. Elevator. Sunny breakfast 30F. AmEx, MC, V. Singles 250-405F; doubles 320-560F; triples 445-615F.

FOURTH ARRONDISSEMENT

The 4ème is a great place to live and an ideal base for tourists. The plethora of bars in the neighborhood make going out easy and worry-free. Even if you venture past the arrondissement, all the nightbuses in Paris converge in the 4ème at M: Châtelet. Note that many hotels are on quiet streets, so it's a great place to stay even if you're not nocturnal.

■ **Grand Hôtel Jeanne d'Arc,** 3, rue de Jarente (tel. 01 48 87 62 11; fax 01 48 87 37 31; www.hoteljeannedarc.com). M: St-Paul or Bastille. From M: St-Paul walk opposite traffic on rue de Rivoli and turn left on rue de Sévigné then right on rue de Jarente. On a quiet side-street in the Marais, the Jeanne d'Arc's stylish rooms all have showers, toilets, and TVs. 2 rooms on the ground floor are wheelchair accessible. Elevator. Breakfast 35F. Reserve 2 months in advance. MC, V. Singles 300-400F; doubles 305-500F; triples 540F; quads 600F. Extra bed 75F.

Castex Hôtel, 5, rue Castex (tel. 01 42 72 31 52; fax 01 42 72 57 91). M: Bastille or Sully-Morland. Exit M: Bastille on bd. Henri IV and take the 3rd right on rue Castex. Spotless rooms in this family-run hotel look onto the street or the courtyard. TV room. Check-in 1pm. All rooms with telephone and sink. Breakfast 30F. Reserve by sending a fax with a credit card number 1 month in advance. MC, V, AmEx. Singles 240-290F; doubles 320-360F; triples 460F. Extra bed 70F.

Hôtel de Nice, 42bis, rue de Rivoli (tel. 01 42 78 55 29; fax 01 42 78 36 07). M: Hôtel-de-Ville. Walk opposite traffic on rue de Rivoli for about 4 blocks; the hotel is on the left. Rooms feature colorful bed covers and wallpaper, and all have TVs, toilets, and phones. A few have balconies with great views. Lots of sun, but hot in the summer (fans are provided). Elevator. Breakfast 35F. Rooms ready at 2pm, but you can leave your bags earlier. Check out 11am. Reserve by fax or phone with 1 night's deposit 1 month ahead for summer. MC, V. Singles 380F; doubles 500F; triples 630F. Extra bed 130F.

Hôtel Andréa, 3, rue St-Bon (tel. 01 42 78 43 93; fax 01 44 61 28 36). M: Hôtel-de-Ville. Follow traffic on rue de Rivoli and turn right on rue St-Bon. On a quiet street 2 blocks from Châtelet. Clean and comfortable rooms with phones. Elevator. Rooms with shower also have TV. Top floor rooms have balconies. Breakfast 30F. Hall showers 20F. Reserve 3 weeks in advance by fax or phone with a credit card number. MC, V. Singles 250F, with toilet and shower 325F; doubles 260F, with toilet and shower 360F; triples 435F; quads 500F.

Hôtel Practic, 9, rue d'Ormesson (tel. 01 48 87 80 47; fax 01 48 87 40 04). M: St-Paul. Walk opposite the traffic on rue de Rivoli then turn left on rue de Sévigné and right on rue d'Ormesson. A clean hotel on a cobblestone square in the heart of the Marais. Rooms are modest, but renovated rooms have TVs and hairdryers. English spoken. Breakfast 25F. Reserve by fax 2-4 weeks in advance. AmEx, MC, Visa. Singles 200F; doubles 280-400F. Extra bed 80F.

Hôtel de la Place des Vosges, 12, rue de Birague (tel. 01 42 72 60 46; fax 01 42 72 02 64; www.france-hotel-guide.com/h75004placedesvosges.htm). M: Bastille. Take the 3rd right off rue St-Antoine. Only steps away from pl. des Vosges (and once a stable for the royal horses), the location can't be beat. Plush red carpets, dark wood, and exposed beams give the small rooms charm. TVs in all rooms. Very professional staff. Rooms on higher floors get a bit hot in summer. Elevator. Breakfast included. Reserve by fax 2 months ahead with one night's deposit; your credit card will be charged 10 days prior to your arrival. MC, V. Singles 365-385, with bath 475-485F; doubles 405-425, with bath 545-560F; 1 small quad 860-880F, with bath 695-710F.

HOSTELS

Hôtel des Jeunes (MIJE) (tel. 01 42 74 23 45; fax 10 40 27 81 64; www.mije.com; email MIJE@Wanadoo.fr) books beds in Le Fourcy, Le Fauconnier, and Maubuisson (see below), 3 small hostels located on cobblestone streets in old Marais residences. The most picturesque and best-located youth accommodations around. No smoking. English spoken. Internet 1F per minute at Le Fourcy. Public phones and free lockers (with a 2F deposit). Ages 18-30 only. 7-day max. stay. Reception 7am-1am. Lockout noon-3pm. Curfew 1am. Quiet after 10pm. Breakfast (served 7:30-10am), shower, and sheets included. Arrive before noon the first day of reservation (call in advance if you'll be late). Groups may reserve 1 year in advance. Individuals should reserve at least 1 month in advance. Restaurant La Table d'Hôtes (at Le Fourcy) offers an entrée with drink and coffee and 3-course "hosteler special" (52F). Open M-F 11:30am-1:30pm and 6:30-8:30pm. 4- to 9-bed dorms 140F; singles 220F; doubles 340F; triples 450F.

Le Fourcy, 6, rue de Fourcy. M: St-Paul or Pont Marie. From M: St-Paul, walk opposite the traffic for a few meters down rue François-Miron and turn left on rue de Fourcy. Hostel surrounds a large courtyard ideal for meeting travelers or for open-air picnicking. Light sleepers should avoid rooms on the social courtyard. Elevator.

Le Fauconnier, 11, rue du Fauconnier. M: St-Paul or Pont Marie. From M: St-Paul take rue du Prevôt, turn left on rue Charlemagne, and turn right on rue du Fauconnier. Ivy-covered building steps away from the Seine and Ile St-Louis. Spacious 4-bed rooms, some doubles, some singles.

Maubuisson, 12, rue des Barres. M: Hôtel-de-Ville or Pont Marie. From M: Pont Marie, walk opposite traffic on rue de l'Hôtel de Ville and turn right on rue des Barres. A half-timbered former girls' convent that looks out onto a silent street by the St-Gervais monastery. Smaller 2- to 7-bed rooms with nice views. Elevator.

FIFTH ARRONDISSEMENT

The 5ème has many of the best budget lodgings in the city. Hotel and hostel owners here often bend over backwards to help clueless Anglo tourists, despite being inundated by them due to the ample attractions of the Latin Quarter. Most of these hotels could easily fill up at twice their summer rates; therefore the key to getting a room is to **reserve well in advance**—from one week in the winter to two months in the summer. If foresight eludes you, don't despair: same-day vacancies occur at even the most popular hotels. In the fall, the return of students means more competition for *foyers*.

Hôtel d'Esmeralda, 4, rue St-Julien-le-Pauvre (tel. 01 43 54 19 20; fax 01 40 51 00 68). M: St-Michel. Walk along the Seine on quai St-Michel toward Nôtre-Dame then turn right at parc Viviani. Rooms have an old feel, with solid, rustic chairs and desks. Some reveal views of the park, the Seine, and Nôtre-Dame. Breakfast 40F. Singles 160F, with shower and toilet 320F; doubles 420-490F; triples 550F; quads 600F.

Hôtel St-Jacques, 35, rue des Ecoles (tel. 01 44 07 45 45; fax 01 43 25 65 50). M: Maubert-Mutualité. Turn left on rue des Carmes, then left on rue des Ecoles. Regal rooms at reasonable rates, with balconies, large windows, and TVs. Street noise ranges from low to moderate. English spoken. Elevator. Breakfast 35F. AmEx, MC, V. Singles 250F, with shower and toilet 480F; doubles 420-580F; triples 560-650F.

Hôtel des Argonauts, 12, rue de la Huchette (tel. 01 43 54 09 82; fax 01 44 07 18 84). M: St-Michel. With your back to the Seine, take the first left off bd. St-Michel onto rue de la Huchette. Above a Greek restaurant of the same name. Clean, modern rooms, with new linoleum floors. Courtyard rooms are quiet for tourist ghetto location. Breakfast 25F. AmEx, MC, V. Singles with shower 250F; doubles with shower and bath 350-400F.

Hôtel le Central, 6, rue Descartes (tel. 01 46 33 57 93). M: Maubert-Mutualité. From the métro walk up rue de la Montaigne Ste-Geneviève. Great location near rue Mouffetard and the Pantheon. Crooked stairs lead to bright, newly painted rooms with discount furnishings. Higher floors have views of Right Bank. Rooms on pl. Contrescarpe somewhat noisy. All rooms have showers. Singles 160-213F; doubles and triples 236-266F.

Hôtel Marignan, 13, rue du Sommerard (tel. 01 43 54 63 81 or 01 43 25 31 03). M: Maubert-Mutualité. From the métro turn left on rue des Carmes then right on rue du Sommerard. Spacious, bright, and quiet pastel rooms. Owner welcomes everyone from backpackers to families to families in backpacks. Free laundry, access to kitchen. Breakfast 20F. No credit cards; reserve ahead by check. Singles 240F; doubles 320-450F; triples 420F-560F; quads 500-670F.

Hôtel des Alliés, 20, rue Berthollet (tel. 01 43 31 47 52; fax 01 45 35 13 92). M: Censier-Daubenton. From the métro, walk 20min. down rue Monge toward bd. Port-Royal and turn right on rue Claude Bernard and left on rue Berthollet. Far back in the arrondissement, but close to the markets and shops of rue Mouffetard. The rooms are large and bright, with quality furnishings. Breakfast 28F. Hall showers 15F. MC, V. Singles 180F, doubles and triples 235-320F.

Hôtel Gay Lussac, 29, rue Gay-Lussac (tel. 01 43 54 23 96; fax 01 40 51 79 49). M: Luxembourg. From the métro walk down rue Gay-Lussac to rue St-Jacques. Stately old rooms, some with fireplaces. A bit worn, but with good beds. Elevator. Breakfast included. Singles 185F; doubles 320-350F; triples 450-480F; quads 570F.

Hôtel des Médicis, 214, rue St-Jacques (tel. 01 43 54 14 66). M: Luxembourg. From the métro turn right on rue Gay-Lussac and then left on rue St-Jacques. Rickety old place which shuns right angle geometry; perhaps that's why Jim Morrison slummed here (room #4) for three weeks in 1971. Some guests have ensconced themselves in the time-worn rooms for more than five years. Has personality, which the owner happily preserves. Reception 9am-11pm. No reservations in summer; arrive early in the morning and hope for a vacancy. Singles and doubles 180-190F.

ACCOMMODATIONS

HOSTELS AND FOYERS

■ **Centre International de Paris (BVJ): Paris Quartier Latin,** 44, rue des Bernardins (tel. 01 43 29 34 80; fax 01 53 00 90 91). M: Maubert-Mutualité. Walk with traffic on bd. St-Germain and turn right on rue des Bernardins. 138 beds. Immense ultra-modern hostel with a shiny cafeteria. A friendly, boisterous crowd congregates in the huge common area. Kitchen, TV, and message service. Showers in rooms. Breakfast included. Lockers 10F. 24hr. reception. Check-in before 2:30pm. Reserve well in advance and confirm, or arrive at 9am to check for often available rooms. Check-out 9am. 2-, 4-, and 10-bed dorms 120F; singles 150F.

■ **Young and Happy (Y&H) Hostel,** 80, rue Mouffetard (tel. 01 45 35 09 53; fax 01 47 07 22 24). M: Monge. From the métro, cross rue Gracieuse and take rue Ortolan to rue Mouffetard. A lively hostel in the heart of the student quarter, serving cheap beer with a smile. Clean rooms, basic but cheerful. Lockout 11am-5pm. Curfew 2am. Breakfast included. Sheets 15F. Towels 5F. Reserve with 1 night's deposit or show up at 8am. Commission-free currency exchange. Laundry nearby. MC, V. Dorms 117F, 97F off-season; doubles 137F, 117F off-season.

SIXTH ARRONDISSEMENT

The 6ème combines the bohemian caché, intellectual panache, and thriving artistic culture of the *quartier latin* and injects a healthy dose of tourism. Budget hotels are sparse in this neighborhood, but the following exceptions provide surprising bargains. Travelers with disabilities will find few budget options, however, and should look to the nearby 7ème.

■ **Hôtel de Neslé,** 7, rue du Neslé (tel. 01 43 54 62 41; fax 01 43 54 31 88). M: Odéon. Walk up rue Mazarine, take a right onto rue Dauphine and then take a left on rue du Neslé. Fantastical and absolutely sparkling, the Neslé stands out in a sea of nondescript budget hotels. The recently renovated, ultra-clean rooms feature Moroccan tiles or other theme accoutrements with murals depicting the history of Paris. For a treat, book the double room with Turkish *hammam* steam bath (500F). No reservations accepted: come the morning you intend to stay around 10am. Singles 175F; doubles 350-500F.

■ **Dhely's Hotel,** 22, rue de l'Hirondelle (tel. 01 43 26 58 25; fax 01 43 26 51 06). M: St-Michel. Just steps from pl. St-Michel and the Seine on a cobblestone way, the Dhely's wood paneling, flower boxes, modern facilities, and quiet location make for a pleasant stay. TV and phones in rooms. Breakfast 35F. Hall showers 25F. Each night must be paid in advance. Reserve in advance with deposit. AmEx, MC, V. Singles 200F; doubles 290F, with shower 380F; triples 370F, with shower 490F. Extra bed 100F.

■ **Hôtel du Lys,** 23, rue Serpente (tel. 01 43 26 97 57; fax 01 44 07 34 90). M: Odéon or St-Michel. From either subway stop, take rue Danton; rue Serpente is a side street. With a no-holds-barred floral decorating theme, sky lights, chintz drapes, and fluffy bedspreads, this hotel feels like a warm English country house, or at least something from *Better Homes and Gardens*. All rooms include bath or shower, TV, phone, and hair dryer. Visa. Singles 490F; doubles 520F; triples 620F.

Hôtel de Chevreuse, 3, rue de Chevreuse (tel. 01 43 20 93 16; fax 01 43 21 43 72). M: Vavin. Walk up bd. du Montparnasse in the direction opposite the Tour and turn left on rue de Chevreuse. Now under new management, this hotel is only getting better and better. Clean, quiet rooms with TV and Ikea furniture. Breakfast 35F. Reserve one week in advance and confirm by fax. MC, V. Singles 235F; doubles 295F, with shower, TV, and toilet 355F, with full bath 395F; triples with full bathroom and TV 535F.

Hôtel St-André des Arts, 66, rue St-André-des-Arts (tel. 01 43 26 96 16; fax 01 43 29 73 34; email hsaintand@minitel.net). M: Odéon. From the métro, take rue de l'Ancienne Comédie, walk one block, and take the first right on rue St-André-des-Arts. Centrally located, the hotel has a helpful staff who run a busy ship. Discounts for those willing to wear skipper costume. The rooms aren't fancy, but the bathrooms are new. High ceilings make up for smaller rooms. All rooms have showers, sinks, and toilets. Breakfast included. MC, V. Singles 330-370F; doubles 474-514F; triples 581F; quads 648F.

Hotel Stella, 41, rue Monsieur-le-Prince (tel. 01 40 51 00 25; fax 01 43 54 97 28). M: Odéon. This perhaps overly homey hotel takes the exposed beam look to a whole new level, sporting some woodwork reportedly several centuries old. Some of the triples have pianos in the room, for those who need one. All of the rooms have a shower and toilet, for those who need one. Reserve in advance, with deposit. No credit cards. Singles 250F; doubles 300F; triples 450F; quads 500F.

HOSTELS

Foyer International des Etudiantes, 93, bd. St-Michel (tel. 01 43 54 49 63). RER: Luxembourg. Across from the Jardin du Luxembourg. Marbled reception area, library, TV lounge, kitchenettes, laundry facilities, and spacious rooms, all fitted with elegant wood paneling and some with balconies. Breakfast and shower included. July-Sept. hotel is coed, open 24hr.; Oct.-June women only. Reserve in writing two months in advance, and as early as January for the coed summer months (e.g. January). 300F deposit if confirmed. 10am check-out. Call ahead or arrive at 10am to check for no-shows. No credit cards. Two-bed dorms 120F; singles 170F. Monthly: 2030F; 2990F.

Association des Etudiants Protestants de Paris, 46, rue de Vaurigard (tel. 01 43 54 31 49 or 01 53 10 21 00; fax 01 46 34 27 09; email aepp.resa@worldnet.fr; home.worldnet.fr/aepp). M: Odéon or RER: Luxembourg. From Odéon, go left up rue Condé and then right on Vaugirard. Overlooking the Jardin de Luxembourg, the Association lets its simple, tiered rooms to people aged 18-26. Part summer hostel, part university residence, the building includes a kitchen, lounge, and washing machines. Breakfast included. To stay for more than 7 days, make reservations 2 weeks in advance. No reservations for fewer than 7 days, but call ahead or show up at 10am the same day. 10F membership fee charged on arrival, plus 100F key deposit. Call, write, or email to request a long-term application (due before May 30). MC, V. Dorms 82F; singles 100-120F; doubles 190-200F. Monthly 2100F.

SEVENTH ARRONDISSEMENT

With no hostels and few budget options, the quiet 7ème attracts mainly business travelers, older couples, and families. Most reasonably priced hotels are near Place de l'Ecole Militaire; expect telephones and TVs, breakfast in bed, bathtubs, and a short walk to the tallest thing in Paris.

🏠 **Grand Hôtel Lévêque,** 29, rue Cler (tel. 01 47 05 49 15; fax 01 45 50 49 36; www.hotel-leveque.com; email info@hotelleveque.com). M: Ecole-Militaire. Take av. de la Motte-Picquet to lovely rue Cler. 3-star quality: nice furnishings, pretty decor, TV in all rooms. Safe in room (10F). Breakfast 35F. Reserve one month ahead. AmEx, MC, V. Singles 270F; doubles with shower and toilet 380-400F, 2-bed doubles with shower, sink, and toilet 400-450F; triples with shower and toilet 550F.

🏠 **Hôtel Malar,** 29, rue Malar (tel. 01 45 51 38 46; fax 01 45 55 20 19). M: Latou-Maubourg. From the métro, follow traffic on bd. de la Tour Maubourg, turn left on rue St-Dominique, and then right on rue Malar. Family resort feel in a classy neighborhood. All rooms have TVs, telephones, showers, and hairdryers. Breakfast 35F. AmEx, MC, V. Reserve one month ahead. Singles 295F-370F; doubles 350F-500F. Extra bed 100F.

Royal Phare Hôtel, 40, av. de la Motte-Picquet (tel. 01 47 05 57 30; fax 01 45 51 64 41). M: Ecole-Militaire. Next to the métro stop on a busy street, near a few other hotels of similar quality and higher rates. Small, tidy, colorful rooms with TVs, phones, and hair dryers. Friendly reception. Breakfast 35F (7-10am in room or in lobby). Reserve 1 week ahead during the summer with 1 night's deposit. AmEx, MC, V. Singles with shower and toilet 320-380F, with bath and toilet 415F; doubles 365-440F. Extra bed 100F.

Hôtel Eiffel Rive Gauche, 6, rue du Gros Caillou (tel. 01 45 51 24 56; fax 01 45 51 11 77; email eiffel@easynet.fr). M: Ecole-Militaire. Walk up av. de la Bourdonnais, turn right on rue de la Grenelle, then left on Gros Caillou. On a quiet street, this family-run hotel is a favorite for anglophone travelers. Dali paintings with pink, aqua, and brown decor. All with cable TV, phone; upper floors see top of Eiffel. Breakfast buffet served 8-

11am in the large peach dining area (40F) or in your room (47F). Hall showers 15F. AmEx, MC, V. Singles 240-435F; doubles 280-480F; triples 460-570F. Extra bed 90F.

Hôtel de la Paix, 19, rue du Gros-Caillou (tel. 01 45 51 86 17; fax 01 45 55 93 28). M: Ecole Militaire. Across from Hôtel Eiffel Rive Gauche (above), it's the cheapest of the bunch with amusing white-and-tan 70s decor. Small, but pleasant and clean. Friendly reception. Breakfast 32F. Reserve one week ahead. Singles 180F, with shower 255F; doubles with shower 320F, plus toilet 350F-395F.

Hôtel du Champ de Mars, 7, rue du Champ de Mars (tel. 01 45 51 52 30; fax 01 45 51 64 36; www.adx.fr/hotel-du-champ-de-mars; email stg@club-internet.fr). M: Ecole-Militaire. Just off av. Bosquet. If you are willing to pay, this hotel may be the most *chic* for your money. Flower-boxed and gardened, like a country house in Provence with pretty blues and yellows. All rooms have phone and satellite TV. Breakfast 35F, served in rooms or elegant downstairs salon 7-10am. Reserve one month ahead and confirm with 1 night's deposit by credit card. Small elevator. AmEx, MC, V. Singles with shower 375F, with large bed and bath 405F; doubles with shower 380F, with bath 410-440F; triples with bath 525F.

Hôtel Kensington, 79, av. de la Bourdonnais (tel. 01 47 05 74 00; fax 01 47 05 25 81). M: Ecole Militaire. Walk north up av. Bosquet, turn left on rue de Grenelle and then right on av. de la Bourdonnais. Compact rooms with pastel paisley wallpaper have TV, shower or bath, and toilet. Brisk, professional service. Elevator. Breakfast 30F, served 7:30-11am in dining room or bedroom. Reserve with 1 night's deposit. AmEx, MC, V. Singles with shower 310F, with bath 490F; doubles 400F, 490F. Extra bed 80F.

Hôtel de France, 102 bd. de la Tour Maubourg (tel. 01 47 05 40 49; fax 01 45 56 96 78). M: Ecole Militaire. Directly across from the Hôtel des Invalides. Owners eager to give advice on Paris (in English, Spanish, or French). Beyond the purple-painted halls you'll find sparkling, clean rooms. Some rooms have spectacular views of the *Eglise du Dôme* and the Invalides. There are two wheelchair accessible rooms (500F), a portable ramp, and a wide elevator. All rooms with phone and cable. Breakfast 35F. AmEx, MC, V. Singles 395F; doubles 500F; connecting rooms for 4-5 persons 800-860F.

EIGHTH ARRONDISSEMENT

The 8*ème* is more for jet-setters than for budget travelers. While you might spot a movie star dining at Fouquet's or hopping into a car outside Christian Dior, you'll be hard-pressed to find comfortable, affordable lodging nearby. If you must sleep near the Champs, the following shouldn't break the bank.

Hôtel Europe-Liège, 8, rue de Moscou (tel. 01 42 94 01 51; fax 01 43 87 42 18). M: Liège. From the métro, walk down rue d'Amsterdam and turn left on rue de Moscou. Very pleasant, quiet, and reasonably priced hotel with newly painted rooms. Many restaurants nearby. All rooms have TV, hair dryer, phone, showers, or baths. 2 handicapped-accessible rooms on the ground floor, soon to be fully wheelchair accessible. Breakfast 35F. AmEx, MC, V. Singles 370F; doubles 480F.

Hôtel d'Artois, 94, rue La Boétie (tel. 01 43 59 84 12 or 01 42 25 76 65; fax 01 43 59 50 70). M: St-Philippe de Roule. From the métro take a left and go down on rue La Boétie. A stone's throw from the Champs-Elysées and next to a 4-star. A bit worn, but with spacious bathrooms and large bedrooms. Plant-filled lobby and incense-scented breakfast room. English spoken. Elevator. Breakfast 28F. Hall showers 22F. MC, V. Singles 255F, with shower 365F, with bath and toilet 405F; doubles 290F, with shower 440F; triples with bath and toilet 580F.

Hôtel Madeleine Haussmann, 10, rue Pasquier (tel. 01 42 65 90 11; fax 01 42 68 07 93). M: Madeleine. From the métro walk up bd. Malesherbes and turn right on rue Pasquier. A bit expensive given the simplicity of the rooms but understandable in light of the location and proximity to the Madeleine, pl. de la Concorde, and the Opéra. Clean, recently redecorated rooms with shower or bath, TV, phone, and hairdryers. Ask for handicapped accessibility. Buffet breakfast 40F. July 15-Sept. 1, singles 600F; doubles 650F; triples 760F; and one quad 800F; off-season 460F, 470F, 560F, 660F.

HOSTELS AND FOYERS

UCJF (Union Chrétienne de Jeunes Filles, YWCA), 22, rue Naples (tel. 01 53 04 37 47; fax 01 53 04 37 54). M: Europe. From the métro take rue de Constantinople and turn left onto rue de Naples. Organized, well-kept, homey environment **for women only.** Spacious, quiet rooms, hardwood floors, large beds. Large oak-paneled common room with fireplace, TV, VCR, books, theater space, and family-style dining room. June-Aug. 3-day min. stay; Sept.-May longer stays for women ages 18-26 (age flexible). All guests pay 30F YWCA membership fee, as well as 50F (for 1-week stays) or 100F (for stays of 1 month or more) processing fee. Reception open M-F 8am-12:30am, Sa-Su 9am-12:30pm and 1:30pm-12:30am. Guests permitted until 10pm; men not allowed in bedrooms. Curfew 12:30am (ask for key, 200F deposit). Kitchen, laundry. Singles 155F; doubles 280F; triples 420F. Weekly: singles 950F; doubles 1560F. Monthly, including demi-pension: singles 3100F; doubles 5400F; triples 7320F. Breakfast and dinner included. Also at 168, rue Blomet, 15ème (tel. 01 56 56 63 00; fax 01 56 56 63 12); M: Convention. Men should contact the YMCA Foyer Union Chrétienne de Jeunes Gens, 14, rue de Trévise, 9ème (tel. 01 47 70 90 94).

Foyer de Chaillot, 28, av. George V (tel. 01 47 23 35 32; fax 01 47 23 77 16). M: George V. From the métro make a right down av. George V and walk about 3 blocks (on the opposite side of the street) until you see a high-rise silver office building called Centre Chaillot Galliera. The foyer is on the 3rd floor. Spacious, upscale, dorm-like environment for **professional women only.** Residents must be working or hold an internship and be between the ages of 18-25; min. one-month stay. Modern and impeccable rooms. Singles all have a sink, while doubles have shower and sink. Toilets and additional showers in each hall. Large common rooms equipped with stereo and TV. Fully equipped kitchens. Guests permitted until 10pm. 2100F deposit required to reserve a room along with an application and a description of your activities in Paris. Breakfast and dinner included M-F. Singles 3450 per month; doubles 6000F per month.

NINTH ARRONDISSEMENT

The 9ème's proximity to the sights of the 2ème, 8ème, and 18ème makes it an ideal base. The hotels of the southern 9ème are generally safe and clean, but many along the northern edge serve clients paying by the hour. Avoid the areas around M: Pigalle and M: Barbès-Rochechouart. However, just a few streets south of bd. de Clichy and rue Pigalle, the neighborhood shifts from a red-light district to a quiet and diverse residential quarter.

Hôtel Beauharnais, 51, rue de la Victoire (tel. 01 48 74 71 13). M: Le Peletier. Follow traffic on rue de la Victoire and look for flower boxes, since there is no Hotel sign and the lobby looks like someone's sitting room. The witty and gregarious Mme Bey dispenses helpful advice in English, German, and French and is particularly kind to young travelers. Each cozy room is dressed in antiques and mirrors. Breakfast 30F. No credit cards. Let's Go rates, sometimes only available for stays of two or three days: Doubles with shower 320F; triples with shower 490F.

Hôtel Chopin, 10 bd. Montmartre or 46, passage Jouffroy (tel. 01 47 70 58 10; fax 01 42 47 00 70). M: Grands Boulevards. Inside a lovely passage listed on the historical registry. Very clean, very new rooms, decorated in a style that does not say budget hotel. Some lucky rooms even have a view of the Musée Grevin's wax studio. All rooms have TV, phone, and fans. Quiet. Breakfast 40F. AmEx, MC, V. Singles with shower 355F, with shower and WC 405-455F; doubles with shower and WC 450-520F; triples with shower and WC 595F.

Hôtel des Arts, 7, Cité Bergère (tel. 01 42 46 73 30; fax 01 48 00 94 42). M: Rue Montmartre. Walk uphill on rue du Faubourg- Montmartre, turn right on Cité Bergère (there is a large sign outside the alleyway that leads there). A family hotel with small, pleasant rooms on a quiet pedestrian street. Completely renovated in the summer of 1999. Popular with businesspeople. All rooms have shower, TV, and hair dryers. Elevator. Breakfast 33F. AmEx, MC, V. Singles 360-380F; doubles 380-400F; triples 530F.

Perfect Hôtel, 39, rue Rodier (tel. 01 42 81 18 86; fax 01 42 85 01 38). Across from the Woodstock Hostel, see directions below. While not living up to its name perfectly, this hotel offers clean, workable rooms with great views from the upper floors, and phones. Elevator. Affable, English-speaking receptionist will show you the way. Singles and doubles with hall shower 180-205F; triples with bath 265F. AmEx, MC, V.

HOSTELS AND FOYERS

🔲 **Woodstock Hostel,** 48, rue Rodier (tel. 01 48 78 87 76; fax 01 48 78 01 63). M: Anvers or Gare du Nord or bus #85 (probably the best way). From M: Anvers, walk against traffic on pl. Anvers, turn right on av. Trudaine and then left on rue de Rodier. From M: Gare du Nord turn right on rue Dunkerque (with the station at your back); at pl. de Roubaix, veer left on rue de Maubeuge, veer right on rue Condorcet, and turn left on rue Rodier. A 15min. walk. A nice hostel, located near Gare du Nord, Gare de l'Est, and Sacré Coeur. Cleaner than Yasgur's farm ever was, with quiet, affordable rooms. Communal kitchen, safety deposit box, and fax. The courtyard looks nicer than most cafés. Showers free (and clean). Call ahead to reserve a room. MC, V. Apr.-Oct. 4-person dorms 97F; doubles 107F. Sept.-May dorms 87F; doubles 97F.

TENTH ARRONDISSEMENT

Catering to the traffic that pours through Gare de l'Est and Gare du Nord, a number of inexpensive hotels have set up shop in the 10ème. After dark, beware of the Gare du Nord, rue du Faubourg St-Denis and bd. de Magenta, and near M: Barbès.

Hôtel de Milan, 17, rue de St-Quentin (tel. 01 40 37 88 50; fax 01 46 07 89 48). M: Gare du Nord. Follow rue de St-Quentin from Gare du Nord; the hotel is on the right-hand corner of the 3rd block. An antique wooden elevator ascends the center of a spiral staircase. The well-kept rooms are slightly more expensive than other 10ème hotels, but the location right next to the Gare du Nord is very convenient for Euro-stars. Breakfast 20F. Hall showers 18F. MC, V. Singles 160-280F; doubles 186-266F; triples 429F.

Hôtel Moderne du Temple, 3, rue d'Aix (tel. 01 42 08 09 04; fax 01 42 41 72 17). M: Goncourt. Walk with the traffic on rue du Faubourg du Temple then turn right on rue d'Aix; the hotel is on the left. Located on a quiet street, this Czech-owned hotel has immaculate and tastefully decorated rooms, some overlooking a courtyard. Breakfast 23F. AmEx. Singles 120-140F, with shower 170F, with shower and WC 220F; doubles 160, with shower 190F, with shower and WC 240F; triples 180, with shower 280F, with shower and WC 320F.

Hôtel Palace, 9, rue Bouchardon (tel. 01 40 40 09 46 or 01 42 06 59 32; fax 01 42 06 16 90). M: Strasbourg/St-Denis. Walk against traffic on bd. St-Denis until the small arch; follow rue René Boulanger on the left, then turn left on rue Bouchardon. The privacy of a hotel with the rates of a hostel. Cheerful rooms face a green courtyard. Laundry and market next door. Breakfast 20F. Shower 20F. Reserve 2 weeks ahead. MC, V. Singles 133F; doubles 146-236F; triples 362F; quad 415F.

Cambrai Hôtel, 129bis, bd. de Magenta (tel. 01 48 78 32 13; fax 01 48 78 43 55). M: Gare du Nord. Follow traffic on rue de Dunkerque to pl. de Roubaix and turn right on bd. de Magenta. The hotel is on the left. A homey, family-owned hotel close to the gare. Clean, airy rooms with natural light, high ceilings, and TVs. Breakfast 45F. Showers 20F. MC, V. Singles 170-210F, with shower 270F, with shower and WC 290F; doubles 340F; triples 500F; family suite 550F is also wheelchair accessible.

Hôtel Lafayette, 198, rue Lafayette (tel. 01 40 35 76 07; fax 01 42 09 69 05). M: Louis Blanc. Walk opposite the traffic lane closest to you on rue Lafayette; hotel is on the left. Small, clean, no-frills rooms near the Canal St-Martin. Two handicapped accessible rooms. Breakfast 20F. Hall showers 20F. AmEx, MC, V. Singles 120F; doubles 160-195F, with shower 240F.

Hôtel Sibour, 14, rue Sibour (tel. 01 46 07 20 74; fax 01 46 07 37 17). M: Gare de l'Est. Go down bd. Strasbourg and then turn left on rue Sibour. Functional, smallish rooms near the Gare de l'Est, if location is a priority. All have telephones and televisions. Breakfast 25F. Showers 15F. AmEx, MC, V. Rooms for one or two people 195F, with shower 225F, with shower and WC 285F.

ELEVENTH ARRONDISSEMENT

The 11ème is short on sights but long on nightlife and budget accommodations. Inexpensive hotels cluster around the Opéra Bastille, providing easy access to nightclubs, bars, and cafés. More budget options cluster near pl. de la République, a transportation hub. The 11ème's hotels tend to have vacancies in July and August, although its large youth hostels are popular year-round.

Hotel Moderne, 121, rue de Chemin-Vert (tel. 01 47 00 54 05; fax 01 47 00 08 31). M: Père Lachaise. A few blocks from the métro along rue de Chemin-Vert, on the right. Newly renovated, modern, bright, and clean. Reserve by fax or phone with credit card number. MC, V. Prices likely to go up given new look. Singles 120F, with shower 200F, with shower and toilet 250F; double 140F, 245F, 250F.

Hôtel Rhetia, 3, rue du Général Blaise (tel. 01 47 00 47 18; fax 01 48 06 01 73). M: Voltaire. From the métro, take av. Parmentier and turn right on rue Rochebrune then left on rue du Général Blaise. In a calm and quiet neighborhood, some rooms overlook a park; others, a courtyard. Clean rooms with lacquered furniture and narrow single beds. Breakfast 15F. Hall showers 10F. Reception daily 7:30am-10pm. Singles 180, with shower 220F; doubles 200F, 240F; triples 240F, 290F.

Hôtel Beaumarchais, 3, rue Oberkampf (tel. 01 53 36 86 86; fax 01 43 38 32 86). M: Oberkampf. Exit on rue de Malte and turn right on rue Oberkampf. Newly renovated with bright, trendy furniture, whitewashed walls, clean bathrooms, Matisse and Kandinsky prints, and TVs. Beautiful salmon-colored lobby and courtyard. Small elevator. A/C. Slightly more expensive, but a great price for what you get. AmEx, MC, V. Singles 350-450F; doubles 550F; suites 700. Breakfast 35F, in room 45F.

Plessis Hôtel, 25, rue du Grand Prieuré (tel. 01 47 00 13 38; fax 01 43 57 97 87). M: Oberkampf. From the métro, walk north on rue du Grand Prieuré. 5 floors of clean, bright rooms. Rooms with showers have hairdryers, fans, TVs and a few balconies. TV, drink vending machines, and leather chairs in the comfortable lounge. 10% discount after 3rd night. Elevator. Hearty "American" breakfast 38F. Open Sept.-July. AmEx, MC, V. Singles 195F, with shower and toilet 280, with bath 295F; doubles 215F, with shower and toilet 325F, with bath 350F.

Hôtel Nôtre-Dame, 51, rue de Malte (tel. 01 47 00 78 76; fax 01 43 55 32 31; email hotelnotredame@wanadoo.fr). M: République. Walk down av. de la République and take a right on rue de Malte. Tidy, renovated rooms with tasteful, bright decor and decent beds. Cheerful lounge. Elevator. All rooms with TV, shower, and toilet. Showers 20F. Breakfast (35F) served in your room or in the salon. Reserve 1 month ahead. MC, V. Singles 200-370F; doubles 190F, with shower 280F, with shower or bath and toilet 330F; 2-bed doubles 380F.

Hôtel de Nevers, 53, rue de Malte (tel. 01 47 00 56 18; fax 01 43 57 77 39). M: Oberkampf or République. From M: République, walk down av. de la République and take a right on rue de Malte. Spotless, spacious rooms. Ask for a room on a high floor, away from the noise of the street. Guests have access to a refrigerator. Elevator. Pets welcome. Breakfast 25F, served in room. Hall showers 20F. 24hr. reception. Reserve 2 weeks ahead by credit card. MC, V. Singles and doubles 180F, with shower 235F, with shower and toilet 260-275F; triples with shower and toilet 335F; quads with shower and toilet 410F. Extra bed 50F.

Hôtel de Belfort, 37, rue Servan (tel. 01 47 00 67 33; fax 01 43 57 97 98). M: Père-Lachaise, St-Maur, or Voltaire. From M: Père-Lachaise, take the rue de Chemin-Vert and turn left on rue Servan. 15min. from pl. de la Bastille. Dim corridors and clean, functional rooms with industrial carpets and plain peach walls. All rooms with shower, toilet, TV and phone. Elevator. Breakfast (served 7:30-9:30am) 20F. MC, V. *Let's Go* special: 115F per person per night in doubles, triples, and quads.

Luna-Park Hôtel, 1, rue Jacquard (tel. 01 48 05 65 50, reservations 01 48 05 01 21; fax 01 43 38 07 56). M: Parmentier. Turn right on rue Oberkampf and walk against traffic, then left on rue Jacquard. Colorful, spacious rooms in decent condition on a quiet street near Oberkampf nightlife. Laundromat next door. Breakfast 25F. Showers 15F. To reserve a room, send a check covering your first night. Singles 140F; doubles with TV 170F, with shower and toilet 220F; triples with shower and TV 270F; quads 320F.

HOSTELS AND FOYERS

■ **Auberge de Jeunesse "Jules Ferry" (HI),** 8, bd. Jules Ferry (tel. 01 43 57 55 60; fax 01 43 14 82 09). M: République. Walk east on rue du fbg. du Temple and turn right on the far side of bd. Jules Ferry. Wonderfully located in front of park and next to pl. de la République. Clean rooms with 100 bunk beds and sinks. Some doubles with big beds. Crowded, friendly, party atmosphere. Smiling staff. Breakfast (served 7-9:15am) and showers included. Lockers 10F. Sheets 5F. Laundry (20F wash, 10F dry). Flexible 4-night max. Airport shuttle 89F. Internet access in lobby (1F per min.). 24hr. dining room and reception. Lockout 10am-2pm. No curfew. No reservations, so arrive by 8am. If there are no vacancies, the hostel can book you in one of its sister hostels. MC, V. 4- to 6-bed dorms 120F; doubles 250F.

Résidence Bastille, 151, av. Ledru Rollin (tel. 01 43 79 53 86; fax 01 43 79 35 63). M: Voltaire. Walk across the pl. Léon Blum and head south onto av. Ledru Rollin. Less crowded and more subdued than most hostels. Modern building. Some triples and quads have their own bathrooms. Friendly staff. 2-4 wooden bunks per room. About 150 beds. Ages 18-30. Couples accommodated in doubles. Breakfast (7:30-10am), showers, and sheets included. Lockers available from 9am-6pm (20F). 5-night max stay. Internet 1F per min. Reception daily 7am-10pm. Lockout noon-4pm. Flexible 1am curfew. Reservations by fax 10-15 days in advance. 10% reduction with ISIC or GO25. MC, V over 200F. Wheelchair accessible. Mar.-Oct. 125F; Nov.-Feb. 110F.

TWELFTH ARRONDISSEMENT

The area around the Gare de Lyon has a wealth of budget hotels. This neighborhood is within walking distance of Bastille nightlife and even the Marais. However, be careful at night. In the 12ème's southeast corner, hotels are far enough from central Paris to be both cheap and quite comfortable. They also provide easy access to the Bois de Vincennes (see **Sights,** p. 238).

Mistral Hôtel, 3, rue Chaligny (tel. 01 46 28 10 20; fax 01 46 28 69 66). M: Reuilly-Diderot. Walk west on bd. Diderot and take a left onto rue Chaligny. One of the best deals in Paris. A spectacularly clean, mostly renovated hotel. Each room is unique, with quality furniture from chandeliers to wicker headboards. The owner's mom pays attention to detail—fresh maps in the rooms. All rooms have TV and phone. Parking. 19 rooms. Breakfast 35F, served in rooms or downstairs. Hall showers 15F. Call 7am-midnight to reserve 2 weeks in advance and confirm in writing or by fax (a deposit is required). AmEx, MC, V. Singles 205F, with shower 250F; 1-bed doubles 210F, with shower 260F; 2-bed doubles with shower 290F; triples with shower and toilet 340F; quads with shower and toilet 400F. Tax 3F.

Hôtel de Reims, 26, rue Hector Malot (tel. 01 43 07 46 18; fax 01 43 07 56 62). M: Gare de Lyon. Take bd. Diderot away from the tall buildings and make a left onto rue Hector Malot. Charming proprietress tends to this hotel, which, despite day-glo bedspreads and signs of aging, still feels like a cozy French grandmother's house. 27 rooms. Breakfast 30F. Reserve by phone 1 week in advance and confirm in writing or by fax. MC, V. Singles 180F, with shower 250F; doubles 220F, with shower 262F, with shower and toilet 280F; triples with shower 300F.

Nièvre-Hôtel, 18, rue d'Austerlitz (tel. 01 43 43 81 51). M: Gare de Lyon or Quai de la Rapée. From Gare de Lyon walk away from the train station on rue de Bercy and take a right on rue d'Austerlitz. The austere entry of the recently redone hotel belies pleasant, cheerful rooms. Resident cat presides at the entrance. High-ceilinged rooms with spotless bathrooms. 27 rooms. Breakfast 20F. Hall showers free for Let's Go readers. Call for reservations and confirm in writing. MC, V. Singles 160F; doubles 200F, with shower 260F, with toilet 300F. Tax 3F.

Hôtel Printania, 91, av. du Dr. Netter (tel. 01 43 07 65 13; fax 01 43 43 56 54). M: Porte de Vincennes. Walk west on the cours de Vincennes and turn left on av. du Dr. Netter. 25 spotless rooms with brown, office-like carpets and formica headboards. 9 renovated rooms have TV, toilet, and shower. One-flight climb to elevator. Breakfast (28F) served in room. Reserve by phone or fax with credit card number or cheque deposit. AmEx, MC, V. Doubles 180F, with shower and toilet 240F, with TV 260F, renovated 280F; triples 360F.

Hôtel de l'Aveyron, 5, rue d'Austerlitz (tel. 01 43 07 86 86; fax 01 43 07 85 20). M: Gare de Lyon. Walk away from the train station on rue de Bercy and take a right on rue d'Austerlitz. On a quiet street. Small, clean, unpretentious rooms with aged wallpaper, Paris posters, and beds. Leather and chrome lounge with a huge TV. Fridge available. Friendly, English-speaking staff is eager to make suggestions on local spots. 26 rooms. Breakfast 20F. Reserve early. MC, V. Singles and doubles 185F, with shower 225F, with shower and toilet 260F; triples 240F, with shower and toilet 315F; quads with shower and toilet 360F.

Palym Hôtel, 4, rue Emile-Gilbert (tel. 01 43 43 24 48; fax 01 43 41 69 47). M: Gare de Lyon. Rue Emile-Gilbert runs parallel off bd. Diderot, directly across from the train station. A bright, clean hotel with cheery yellow and green lobby, gleaming brass fixtures, and modern rooms. Rooms on the 6th floor are small. As befits a two-star, all rooms have TV and phone, as well as shower and toilet. Elevator. Big friendly dog. Wheelchair accessible. Breakfast 30F. Pets 30F. Reserve with credit card number by fax. MC, V. Singles 330-360F; doubles 360-390F; triples or quads 530F. Extra bed 100F. Tax 5F.

FOYERS

Centre International du Séjour de Paris: CISP "Ravel," 6, av. Maurice Ravel (tel. 01 44 75 60 00; fax 01 43 44 45 30). M: Porte de Vincennes. Walk east on cours de Vincennes then take the first right on bd. Soult, left on rue Jules Lemaître, and right on av. Maurice Ravel (15 min. walk). Associated with CISP "Kellerman" in the 13ème and just as cool. Large rooms (most with 4 or fewer beds), art exhibits, auditorium, and access to outdoor municipal pool next door (25F). Self-serve restaurant open daily 7:30-9:30am, noon-1:30pm, and 7-8:30pm. Full-service restaurant open noon-1:30pm and 7:30-9:30pm. Internet 10F per 10min. Breakfast, sheets, and towels included. 1-month max. stay. Reception daily 7:30am-1:30am. Curfew 1:30am. Reserve a few days ahead by phone. MC, V. Dorms with shower 143F; singles with shower, toilet, and phone 191F; doubles with shower, toilet, and phone 322F.

THIRTEENTH ARRONDISSEMENT

On the cusp of revitalization, the 13ème has little in the way of established hotels. But there are some *foyers* and hostels with extremely reasonable prices and easy access to the métro.

HOSTELS AND FOYERS

Association des Foyers de Jeunes: Foyer des Jeunes Filles, 234, rue de Tolbiac (tel. 01 44 16 22 22; fax 01 45 88 61 84; www.foyer-tolbiac.com). M: Glacière. Walk east on bd. Auguste Blanqui, turn right on rue de Glacière, then left on rue de Tolbiac. Large, modern *foyer* for women (ages 18-30) most of whom are workers and students here for semi-permanent stays. Excellent facilities include kitchens, TV, laundry, gym, library, and cafeteria. Helpful staff. 242 rooms. Showers and breakfast (M-Sa 6:30-8:30am) included. There are usually vacancies in summer. For short-term reservations fax or call a few days ahead; for long-term, 3-4 months ahead. MC, V. Sunny singles 120F. 3245F per month, breakfast and dinner included. 30F registration fee (good for 1 year).

CISP "Kellerman," 17, bd. Kellerman (tel. 01 44 16 37 38; fax 01 44 16 37 39; email 100616.2215@compuserve.com; www.cisp.asso.fr). M: Porte d'Italie. Cross the street and turn right on bd. Kellerman. Affiliated with CISP "Ravel" in the 12ème, this 392-bed hostel resembles a spaceship on stilts. Located in a drab area, but close to Cité Universitaire and the métro. Impeccably clean with TV room, laundry, and cafeteria (open daily noon-1:30pm and 6:30-9:30pm). Mostly bunk beds. Breakfast included (7-

9:30am). Lockout 1:30-6:30pm. Wheelchair accessible. MC, V. A good place to try for last-minute reservations. 2-4 bed dorms 124F; 8-bed dorms 100F; singles 142F, with shower and toilet 172F; doubles 248F, with shower and toilet 284F. Tax 1F.

Maison des Clubs UNESCO, 43, rue de Glacière (tel. 01 43 36 00 63; fax 01 45 35 05 96). M: Glacière. Walk east on bd. Auguste Blanqui and take a left on rue de la Glacière. Enter through the garden on the right. Conveniently located near the 5ème, this hostel offers small, clean rooms. Common space is limited. Helpful management. 90 rooms. Showers and breakfast included (7:45-9am). Reception 7am-2am. Check-out 10am, but the front desk can hold your bags for the day. Curfew 2am. Hosts many groups, so reservations recommended. Singles 170F; doubles 290F; triples 375F.

FOURTEENTH ARRONDISSEMENT

Just south of the 6ème, the 14ème combines an almost central location with cheaper-than-chi-chi prices. The neighborhood does not afford Paris's most outstanding views, but its busy, safe streets and interesting history make it a pleasant place to stay.

■ **Hôtel de Blois,** 5, rue des Plantes (tel. 01 45 40 99 48; fax 01 45 40 45 62). M: Mouton-Duvernet. From the métro, turn left on rue Mouton Duvernet then left on rue des Plantes. One of the better deals in Paris. Glossy wallpaper, ornate ceiling carvings, velvet chairs, and an iron spiral staircase. TVs, phones, hair dryers, and big, clean bathrooms. Laundromat across the street. Nightbus stops at métro. 24 rooms. Breakfast 27F. Reserve 10 days ahead. AmEx, MC, V. Singles 230F; doubles 240-280F, with shower 270F, with bath 320-360F; triples 360F.

Ouest Hôtel, 27, rue de Gergovie (tel. 01 45 42 64 99; fax 01 45 42 46 65). M: Pernety. Walk against traffic on rue Raymond Losserand and turn right on rue de Gergovie. A clean hotel with modest furnishings, but excellent rates and friendly staff. Breakfast 20F. Hall shower 20F (sometimes long waits). MC, V. Singles with small bed 120F; singles with larger bed and doubles 160F, with shower 220F; 2-bed doubles 200F, with shower 230F.

Hôtel du Parc, 6, rue Jolivet (tel. 01 43 20 95 54; fax 01 42 79 82 62; www.hotelduparc.com). M: Edgar-Quinet. Facing the Tour Montparnasse, turn left on rue de la Gaîté, right on rue du Maine, then right on rue Jolivet. Creative color schemes and floral wallpaper. Windows open onto the courtyard or a park. Well-lit rooms with TVs, phones, hair dryers. Does not accept big groups. 32 rooms. Breakfast 30F. Shower 20F. AmEx, MC, V. Singles and doubles 260F; triples with shower 450F.

Hôtel Broussais, 3, rue Ledion (tel. 01 40 44 48 90; fax 01 40 44 96 76). M: Plaisance. From the corner of Raymond Losserand and Alésia, walk east on rue d'Alésia away from the tall orange building towards rue des Suisses. Continue on Alesia, turn right on rue Didot, and veer left onto rue Ledion (12min). Tasteful beige rooms are simple but clean. All have TVs, phones, showers, and toilets. Single rooms are small. Nightbus stops at Porte D'Orléans métro. 25 rooms. Breakfast 30F. Reserve 3 weeks ahead. AmEx, MC, V. Singles 240F; doubles 280F.

Hôtel du Midi, 4, av. René-Coty (tel. 01 43 27 23 25; fax 01 43 21 24 58). M: Denfert-Rochereau. From the métro, take av. Général Leclerc to pl. de l'Abbé Migne, where the catacombs are, then turn right on av. René-Coty. Popular with business travelers, but serving many students over the summer, this hotel features marble bathrooms, hair dryers, TVs, pants straighteners, fridges, and jacuzzis. Renovations (to be completed Dec. 2000) will bring a pool and a dry cleaner. Nightbus J stops at Place D'Enfer across the street. Breakfast 38F. Parking 58F per day. Reserve 10-15 days in advance. AmEx, MC, V. Singles with shower 298F; doubles with shower and toilet 328-408F; doubles with bath 498-600F; 3-4 person room 498-600F; large suite 800F. Tax 5F per night.

HOSTELS AND FOYERS

FIAP Jean-Monnet, 30, rue Cabanis (tel. 01 43 13 17 00; fax 01 43 13 17 07). M: Glacière. From the métro, take bd. Auguste-Blanqui, turn left on rue de la Santé and then right on rue Cabanis. This 500-bed international student center, which caters primarily to groups, offers well-furnished rooms with toilet and shower. The concrete complex contains a game room, TV rooms, laundry room, sunlit piano bar and café, restaurant, outdoor terrace, and *discothèque*. Lobby kiosks post events and tourist info. Nightbus stops at Denfert-Rochereau métro. Breakfast included, but add 10.50F for buffet. Curfew 2am. Reserve 2-4 weeks in advance. Be sure to specify if you want a dorm bed, or else you will be booked for a single room. 50F deposit per person per night in cheque or credit card. MC, V. 8-bed dorms 133F; singles 287F; doubles 376F; triples 492F; quads 656F. Some rooms wheelchair accessible.

FIFTEENTH ARRONDISSEMENT

Anglo-American hostels offer good options when the more central arrondissements fill up. The budget hotels of the 15*ème* are not a particularly attractive bunch, but they'll do when the hostels are booked or a single room is desired. Off the main tourist track, most will have vacancies in July and August. Hotel breakfast is 20F-40F, but you would do better to visit a bakery or café.

Hôtel Printemps, 31, rue du Commerce (tel. 01 45 79 83 36; fax 01 45 79 84 88). M: La Motte-Picquet-Grenelle. In the middle of a busy, bourgeois neighborhood surrounded by shops (including Monoprix) and restaurants, this hotel is clean and cheap. Breakfast 20F. Hall showers 15F. Reserve 3-4 weeks ahead. MC, V. Singles or doubles 150F, with shower 190F; 2-bed doubles with shower and toilet 230F.

Pacific Hôtel, 11, rue Fondary (tel. 01 45 75 20 49; fax 01 45 77 70 73). M: Dupleix or Av. Emile Zola. Two-star quality at one-star prices, this hotel is easily the most elegant of the bunch. Quiet street, laundromat on rue Violet. MC, V. Singles with toilet 200F, with shower 262F; doubles 260F, 318F; triples 370F.

Hôtel Camélia, 24, bd. Pasteur (tel. 01 47 83 76 35 or 01 47 83 69 91; fax 01 40 65 94 98). M: Pasteur. Next to the métro and surrounded by shops and cafés, this one-star hotel offers plain, clean rooms. No elevator. Extra bed 50F. MC, V. Singles or doubles 210F, with shower and TV 300F.

Mondial Hôtel, 136, bd. de Grenelle (tel. 01 45 79 73 57 or 01 45 79 08 09; fax 01 45 79 58 65). M: La Motte-Picquet-Grenelle. Conveniently located next to the loud elevated métro. Ask for a room off the street. Basic facilities, 10 min. walk from the Eiffel Tower. Breakfast 20F. Hall showers 10F. Extra bed 73F. MC, V. Singles 183F, with shower 223F; doubles 206F, 246F.

Nainville Hôtel, 53, rue de l'Eglise (tel. 01 45 57 35 80; fax 01 45 54 83 00). M: Félix Faure or Charles Michels. Similar to Pacific Hôtel but more ragged at the edges. Above a nondescript café, the rooms range in quality so take a look first. The park next door is a nice bonus. Hall shower 25F. MC, V. Single or double with sink 215F, with shower 300F, with shower and toilet 370F.

Practic Hôtel, 20, rue de l'Ingénieur Keller (tel. 01 45 77 70 58; fax 01 40 59 43 75). M: Charles-Michels. From pl. Charles Michels, walk up rue Linois, turn left on rue des 4-Frères Peignot, then turn right on rue de l'Ingénieur Keller. Rooms with a modern feel. AmEx, MC, V. Singles or doubles 250-295F, with shower and toilet 350F; 2-bed doubles with shower and toilet 400F; triples 490F.

Hôtel de la Paix, 166, bd. de Grenelle (tel. 01 44 49 63 63; fax 01 45 66 45 27). M: Cambronne. On a busy street, this large hotel is like Hôtel Printemps but more expensive. Some lucky winners get a bedside bidet. 200F deposit for phone in room. English spoken. MC, V. Wheelchair accessible. Singles with sink 185F, with shower and toilet 275F-310F; doubles 200F; 3- to 4-person suites 550F.

HOSTELS AND FOYERS

Three Ducks Hostel, 6, pl. Etienne Pernet (tel. 01 48 42 04 05; fax 01 48 42 99 99). M: Félix Faure. Walk against traffic on the left side of the church; the hostel will be on your left. Aimed at young Anglo fun-seekers, the Three Ducks wants you to rock with them at the in-house bar until the 2am curfew—probably the best late-night option in the 15th. 15min. from the Eiffel Tower, offers a kitchen, lockers, and 2- to 8-bed dorm rooms. Laundromat and groceries nearby on rue du Commerce. Shower, breakfast included. Sheets 15F, towels 5F. Reserve with credit card deposit, several days ahead in peak season. MC, V. Mar.-Oct. 117F; Nov.-Feb. 97F.

Aloha Hostel, 1, rue Borromée (tel. 01 42 73 03 03; fax 01 42 73 14 14). M: Volontaires. Walk against traffic on rue de Vaugirard; turn right on rue Borromée. More tranquil and private than the 3 Ducks, with similar clientele. Music and drinks in the café. Breakfast included. Safety deposit boxes. Sheets 15F, towels 10F. Reception 8am-2am. Lockout 11am-5pm. Curfew 2am. Reserve a week ahead in peak season with credit card deposit. MC, V. Mar.-Nov. dorms 107F; doubles 127F; Dec.-Feb. 97F, 117F.

La Maison Hostel, 67b, rue Dutot (tel. 01 42 73 10 10). M: Volontaires. Cross rue de Vaugirard on rue des Volontaires and make the second right. Proceed two blocks. Recently opened, the hostel has new furnishings and provides excellent doubles and clean 2- or 3-bed dorms in a quiet neighborhood. All rooms have a shower and toilet. Breakfast included (8-9:30am). The doubles come with sheets; otherwise, sheets 15F to rent, with towels 5F. Reception 8am-2am. Lockout 11am-5pm. Curfew 2am. Internet access. Access to full kitchen. Reserve 1 month in advance. In summer 2- and 3-bed dorms 117F, doubles 137F; off-season 107F, 127F. MC, V.

SIXTEENTH ARRONDISSEMENT

Wealthy and residential, the 16ème may inconvenience budget tourists on several counts. Though close to the Eiffel Tower, it remains a 20-minute métro ride away from the more famous museums, sights, and nightlife. It also has few of the grocery stores, affordable restaurants, and cafés abundant elsewhere in the city. However, hotels here are luxurious and have vacancies even in the high season.

Hôtel Résidence Chalgrin, 10, rue Chalgrin (tel. 01 45 00 19 91; fax 01 45 00 95 41). M: Argentine. Walk down av. de la Grande Armée toward the Arc de Triomphe, turn right on rue Argentine, then turn right on rue Chalgrin. Charming and quiet with ornate woodwork and Louis XVI chairs. Welcoming matron has found and refinished every antique lamp, armoire, and headboard herself, and no 2 spacious rooms are alike. All rooms have cable TV and phone. Breakfast 30F. AmEx, MC, V. Singles and doubles 240-260F, with toilet and shower 280-350F; triple suite 470F. Extra bed 30F.

Villa d'Auteuil, 28, rue Poussin (tel. 01 42 88 30 37; fax 01 45 20 74 70). M: Michel-Ange-Auteuil. Walk up rue Girodet and turn left on rue Poussin. At the lip of the Bois de Boulogne, on a peaceful street laced with antique shops and restaurants. A genteel and proper hotel. Spacious, high-ceilinged rooms have graceful wooden-framed beds and tasteful decor. All rooms have a shower, toilet, phone, and TV, and face the street or a garden. Breakfast 30F. 10% discount for *Let's Go* travelers. MC, V. Singles 290-300F; doubles 340-350F; triples 415F.

Hôtel Ribera, 66, rue La Fontaine (tel. 01 42 88 29 50; fax 01 42 24 91 33). M: Jasmin. Walk down rue Ribera to its intersection with rue La Fontaine. Pink and blue rooms, some with marble fireplaces and floor-to-ceiling windows. Gender politics aside, blue rooms tend to be nicer. Rooms with shower have TV. Breakfast 28F. 10% discount July 15-Aug. 31. AmEx, MC, V. Singles 220F, with shower 260F; doubles 250F, with shower 290-350F.

Hôtel Keppler, 12, rue Keppler (tel. 01 47 20 65 05; fax 01 47 23 02 29). M: George V or Kléber. From George V turn left on av. Bassano and take the fourth right onto rue Keppler. Efficient two-star hotel near the Champs-Elysées; sports tan-and-blue rooms with high ceilings. Breakfast 30F. AmEx, MC, V. Same price for 1 or 2 people: twin bed with shower 430F, with bath or TV 460F; 2 single beds with bath 480F; 3 single beds 550F.

SEVENTEENTH ARRONDISSEMENT

The 17ème offers a spectrum from the elegance of the 16ème to the sleaze of the 18ème. Some of its hotels cater to visiting businessmen, others to prostitutes, some to both. Safety is a concern where the 17ème borders the 18ème, especially on bd. des Batignolles and near pl. de Clichy. Most of the hotels listed are near the safer southern border with the 16ème. Though far from the Latin Quarter and sights, these are worth checking when the more central arrondissements are filled.

Hôtel Riviera, 55, rue des Acacias (tel. 01 43 80 45 31; fax 01 40 54 84 08). M: Charles-de-Gaulle-Etoile. Walk north on av. MacMahon, then turn left on rue des Acacias. Close to the Arc de Triomphe, this budget hotel wins on location. Modern, quiet, pastel rooms have comfortable beds, TVs, and hairdryers. Elevator. Breakfast 30F. Reservations encouraged, by phone or fax. AmEx, MC, V. Singles with shower 290F; doubles with shower or bath and toilet 400-440F; triples with shower and toilet 510F.

Hôtel Belidor, 5, rue Belidor (tel. 01 45 74 49 91; fax 01 45 72 54 22). M: Porte Maillot. Go north on bd. Gouvion St-Cyr and turn right on rue Belidor. Dim halls give way to quiet rooms with floral wallpaper circa 1976 and Mondrian carpets. Most rooms face a quiet, tiled courtyard. Breakfast included. Open Sept.-July. MC, V. Singles 230F, with shower and toilet 340F; doubles with sink 260F, with bath and toilet 370F; 2-bed doubles with toilet 360F; with shower and toilet 450F; triples 390F.

Hôtel Jouffrey, 28, passage Cardinet (tel. 01 47 54 06 00; fax 01 47 63 83 12). M: Malesherbes. Follow rue Cardinet across bd. Malesherbes and rue de Tocqueville and turn left into passage Cardinet. Quiet neighborhood in the *coiffure* district, which, while fairly safe, is far from the métro (10min.). Simple, clean brown rooms. TVs and direct-line phones in every room. One room is fully handicapped-accessible, once you clear the first two steps into the hotel. Dogs welcome. All rooms with shower and toilet. Breakfast 30F, in room 35F. MC, V. Singles 290F; doubles 330-380F.

Hôtel Champerret Héliopolis, 13, rue d'Héliopolis (tel. 01 47 64 92 56; fax 01 47 64 50 44). M: Porte de Champerret. Turn left of av. de Villiers. Clean and bright rooms, with a charming breakfast terrace. TVs, phones, hairdryers. Close to the métro, with many restaurants and cafés nearby. One fully handicapped-accessible bedroom with a large bathroom. Breakfast 38F.Singles 385F; doubles 450-495F; triples 580F.

EIGHTEENTH ARRONDISSEMENT

Montmartre has two types of lodging bargains. One is the dirt-cheap hotels south of rue des Abbesses and Sacré Coeur which are clean and fairly safe. Ask to see your room first and beware of side streets which become dark and deserted by night. The other type, up on the hill west of Sacré Coeur, is more expensive but offers fantastic cafés nearby and long views over the city. First and foremost, do not walk alone at night. Also, avoid M: Pigalle and M: Barbès-Rochechouart at night, use M: Abbesses instead.

Hôtel Caulaincourt, 2, sq. Caulaincourt (tel. 01 46 06 42 99; fax 01 46 06 48 67). M: Lamarck-Caulaincourt. Walk up the stairs to rue Caulaincourt and proceed to your right, between nos. 63 and 65. Formerly artists' studios (some remain), these large, simple rooms have great light and wonderful views, whether onto the courtyard grove of trees or the northwestern portion of the city. In a very pleasant neighborhood, it's one of the best values around. Reserve up to one month in advance. MC, V. Singles with shower 190F, with shower and toilet 240F, with bath and toilet 270F; doubles 40F more, triples 80-100F more. 5 rooms with sink 145F for one person, 180F for two.

Hôtel André Gill, 4, rue André Gill (tel. 01 42 62 48 48; fax 01 42 62 77 92). M: Abbesses. Walk downhill on rue des Abbesses and turn right on rue des Martyrs and left on rue André Gill. A refuge from the noise and seediness of bd. de Clichy. Slightly garish red rooms, but quite comfortable for the price. Elevator. Breakfast 25F. Hall showers 25F. AmEx, MC, V. Singles 180F; singles or doubles with breakfast 240F, with shower 390F, with bath 390F; triples with bath and breakfast 530F.

Grand Hôtel de Clermont, 18, rue Veron (tel. 01 46 06 40 99). M: Abbesses. Clean and very basic rooms, not much beyond a thick-mattressed bed. But the prices are quite noteworthy. Hall shower 15F. The bar downstairs has bohemian character, and offers guests a 48F menu. Be a little wary around the neighborhood at night. Reserve two weeks ahead. MC, V. Singles with sink and toilet 100-120F; doubles with sink 160F.

Style Hôtel, 8, rue Ganneron (tel. 01 45 22 37 59; fax 01 45 22 81 03). M: Pl. de Clichy. Walk up av. de Clichy and make a right onto Ganneron. Next to the cemetery, after which lies a pretty section of Montmartre. Two buildings; the newer is closer to the street, with larger rooms, nice wood floors and armoires. Older building is quieter, with slightly worn rugs and phones that only receive calls. All rooms with shower and toilet. MC, V. Single 270F, double 295F, triple or quad 340F. Extra bed 30F.

HOSTELS AND FOYERS

Village Hostel, 20, rue d'Orsel (tel. 01 42 64 22 02; fax 01 42 64 22 04; email village@levillage-hostel.fr; www.levillage@levillage-hostel.fr). M: Anvers. Go uphill on rue Steinkerque and turn right on rue d'Orsel. Right in the midst of the heavy tourist traffic to Sacré Coeur, but clean and cheap. Doubles and 3- to 8-bed dorms are bright orange, yellow, and green, though not particularly spacious. Sheets 15F. Towel 5F. Curfew 2am. Lockout 11am-4pm. TV, stereo, and internet access in the lounge. Every room has toilet and shower. 1- to 2-week max. stay. Same-day reservations only—call at 7:30am when reception opens. MC, V. Dorms 120-150. 1-bed double 294F, 2-bed 310F with sheets.

NINETEENTH ARRONDISSEMENT

The 19ème is far from central. Unless you've come to Paris just to visit this arrondissement's excellent parks, the Parc de la Villette and Parc des Buttes-Chaumont, you'll have to commute to your sightseeing. However, the métro line Marie des Lilas-Châtelet will zip you quickly to the center, should you find yourself in Paris in high-season, or seeking a room at rock-bottom prices.

Rhin et Danube, 3, pl. Rhin et Danube (tel. 01 42 45 10 13; fax 01 42 06 88 82). M: Danube or bus #75 from Châtelet. Steps from the métro in a residential, hilly area. Well-maintained rooms, most of which look onto the picturesque *place*. All rooms have kitchens with fridges, dishes, and coffeemakers. Hair dryers, shower, WC, and color TVs. MC, V. Singles 220F; doubles 350F; triples 430F; quads 500F.

Hôtel du Parc Buttes Chaumont, 1, pl. Armand Carrel (tel. 01 42 08 08 37 or 01 42 08 86 89; fax 01 42 45 66 91). M: Laumière or buses #75 or 60. From the métro follow rue Laumière to its end at pl. Armand Carrel. Now a 3-star hotel, the pleasant but not-quite-budget Hôtel du Parc is steps away from the Parc des Buttes-Chaumont. Modern, clean, and quiet rooms come with comfy beds, A/C, TVs, phones, toilets, and hair dryers. Rec room with pool table. Top floor rooms have a great view. Elevator, handicap access. All rooms with shower. Breakfast 45F in lounge or your room. Reserve 2 weeks ahead. AmEx, MC, V. Singles 420F; doubles 490F; triples 600F.

Crimée Hôtel, 188, rue de Crimée (tel. 01 40 36 75 29 or 01 40 35 19 57; fax 01 40 36 29 57). M: Crimée. By the métro at the corner of rue de Flandre. In the northern, commercial 19ème, near restaurants and shops and close to La Villette. Sparkling lobby doubles as a breakfast room. Sparkling rooms double as your sleeping quarters. Modern, smallish rooms with hairdryers, TVs, radios, A/C, toilets, and showers. Elevator. Breakfast 32F. AmEx, MC, V. Singles 260F; doubles 290F; triples 320F; quads 420F.

La Perdrix Rouge, 5, rue Lassus (tel. 01 42 06 09 53; fax 01 42 06 88 70). M: Jourdain. To your left if you are facing the church at the métro exit. So close to the métro that you could fall in from the front door. Small, unluxurious, but clean rooms with TV and toilet. Some rooms overlook the church. Pink formica headboards and office carpeting. Elevator. Breakfast 30F. Reserve by fax. AmEx, MC, V. Singles with shower 285F; doubles with shower 320F; triples with bath 385F.

TWENTIETH ARRONDISSEMENT

Though farther from the sights of central Paris, the primarily residential 20*ème* offers greater availability and cheaper prices than hotels in other *quartiers*.

Hôtel Printana, 355, rue des Pyrénées (tel. 01 46 36 76 62). M: Jourdain. From rue du Jourdain take a left on rue des Pyrénées; hotel is on the right. Kind and devoted proprietors don't speak English but do offer refurbished rooms. Elevator. Breakfast 25F. Reserve 10-15 days in advance. Singles with toilet 145F; doubles with toilet 210F, with shower 245F; triples with shower and toilet 300F.

Eden Hotel, 7, rue Jean-Baptiste Dumay (tel. 01 46 36 64 22; fax 01 46 36 01 11). M: Pyrénées. Off rue de Belleville. Turn right from the métro. Eden is an oasis of hospitality, with good value for its two stars and clean rooms with TVs and toilets. Elevator. Breakfast 28F. Bath or shower 25F. Hotel tends to be busier during the week; reserve rooms by fax 1 week in advance. MC, V. Singles 195F; doubles 240F, with shower and toilet 270-295F. Extra bed 60F.

Hôtel Dauphine, 236, rue des Pyrénées (tel. 01 43 49 47 66; fax 01 46 36 05 79). M: Gambetta. Walk north on rue des Pyrénées. Far from luxurious on the 2-star hotel spectrum, with sparsely furnished, yet homey, pastel rooms with TV, phone, hair dryer, and the occasional fridge. Some noise from bustling street vendors. Breakfast served 7-10am (25F). Reserve rooms 1 week in advance. AmEx, MC, V. Singles with shower 250F; doubles with shower 260F, with bath 300F. Extra bed 70F.

HOSTELS AND FOYERS

Auberge de Jeunesse "Le D'Artagnan" (HI), 80, rue Vitruve (tel. 01 40 32 34 56; fax 01 40 32 34 55; email paris.le-d'artagnan@fuaj.org). M: Porte de Bagnolet or Porte de Montreuil. From Porte de Bagnolet, walk south on bd. Davout and make a right on rue Vitruve. A big, modern complex surrounded by highrises, but with a festive, busy feel. 440 beds. Restaurant (open 7-10:30pm), bar (open 8pm-2am; happy hour 9-10pm, occasional live music), internet station (1F per min.), and a small cinema (free films nightly). Breakfast and sheets included. Large lockers (10F per day). Laundry 15F per wash, 5F per dry. Reception 24hr. Lockout noon-3pm. Reservations by fax or email a must; hostel is packed Feb.-Oct. 2-8 bed dorms 115F.

RESTAURANTS

For most Parisians, life is about eating, with this activity comprising approximately twenty-three hours of every day. With bakeries and restaurants on every corner and dozens of open-air markets, food is a high-profile, high-quality affair. Most French meals are the result of trips to specialty cheese, meat, bread, and fruit stores, with some assembly required. This practice is probably the easiest, tastiest, and cheapest way for those new to French food to dive in. Eating establishments range from the famous repositories of *haute cuisine*, where the chef is a star and Michelin is licking his boots, to the corner brasserie, which can often delight and sometimes nauseate. The variety is astounding. *Gauche* or gourmet, French or foreign, fancy or cheap, you can dine on Tibetan soups or Thai noodles, Algerian couscous or Moroccan tea, Peruvian beans or Senegalese fish. Inexpensive French *bistros* and *crêperies* offer the breads, cheeses, wines, pâtés, *pôtages*, and pastries that are central to French cuisine.

FRENCH CUISINE

Italian monarch Catherine de Medici brought the tradition of **haute cuisine** from Florence, along with her cooks, who taught the French to appreciate the finer aspects of sauces and seasonings. Great 19th-century chefs made fine food an essential art of civilized life and much of their wisdom on sauces and glazes is collected in the voluminous *Larousse Gastronomique*, a standard reference for French chefs today.

The style made famous in the U.S. by Julia Child is **cuisine bourgeoise,** quality French home-cooking. A glance through her *Mastering the Art of French Cooking I & II* will give you ideas for dishes to try in France. Simple meals in this genre are *steak-frites* (steak and fries), *poulet rôti* (roasted chicken), *soupe à l'oignon*, *boeuf bourguignon*, and *lapin poêlé* (fried rabbit), and can be found on just about every corner in Paris. Both *haute cuisine* and *cuisine bourgeoise* rely heavily on the **cuisine de province** (also called *cuisine campagnarde*) by creating sophisticated versions of regional cuisine. Trendy **nouvelle cuisine,** consisting of tiny portions of delicately cooked, artfully arranged ingredients with light sauces, became popular in the 1970s.

French **meat** is not all **frogs** *(grenouille)* and **snails** *(escargots)*, although these tasty morsels both make great appetizers (frog really does taste like chicken, and snails taste like mussels; however, most of what they taste like is the garlic butter sauce in which they are usually cooked). It is true that the French tend to eat a wider variety of creatures than most Anglo-Saxons. *Tripes* (bovine stomach-lining) cooked in herbs is well-loved by many but doesn't go over as well with foreigners; the sausage version is called *andouille* or *andouillette*. Rabbit *(lapin)* is fairly common, as is broiled puppy *(chiot rôti)*. Although not all steaks are *tartare* (raw minced beef), most red meat is served quite rare unless you request otherwise. France's many coastal provinces, such as Brittany, Normandy, and Provence, have given French cuisine wonderful selections of **fish** *(poisson)* and **seafood** *(fruits de mer)*. Unless clearly marked *filet*, the fish will most likely arrive eyes, tail, top hat, and all.

Vegetables may be overcooked by some standards. Maybe this is to compensate for the meat, the central aspect of most chef's oeuvre, being kind of bloody. Usually served with vinaigrette or hollandaise, French asparagus *(asperges)* is a white, stumpy version of the matchstick you've come to love. *Haricots verts* (green beans) are a svelte and tastier cousin of the ones your mother made you eat. Restaurants often serve *frites* (french fries) or *pommes de terre gratins*, potatoes sliced, doused with cream, butter, and cheese, and baked. **Bread** is served with every meal. It is perfectly polite to use a piece of bread to wipe your plate.

Charles de Gaulle argued in 1951 that "the French will only be united under the threat of danger. No one can simply bring together a country that has 265 kinds of cheese." There are, in fact, over 400. With extraordinary variety, French **cheeses** *(fromages)* fall into three main categories. Cooked cheeses include *beaufort* and *gruyère*. Veined cheeses, such as *bleu* and *roquefort*, gain their sharp taste from the bread molds that are encouraged to grow on them. Soft cheeses, like *brie* and *camembert*, round out a basic cheese tray. Tangy *fromages de chèvre* (goat cheeses) come in two forms: the soft, moist, and crumbly *frais*, and the sharp *sec* (dry). Sheep aren't just for wool: the aforementioned *roquefort* comes from the tasty *lait* of those who go "baaa."

Among *charcuterie* (cold meat products), the most renowned is pâté, a spread of finely minced liver and/or other meats. Often a house specialty, it comes in hundreds of varieties, some highly seasoned with herbs. *Pâté de campagne* (from pork) is chunky, while *pâté de foie* (liver) is soft and velvety.

For many trim Parisians a **salad** is a regular, hefty *plat* (main dish) in itself and thus can come with more cheese, cold cuts, fish, and bread than greens and veggies. Dressing also tends to be a must, so be sure to say you want it separately or not at all. If you need food on the run, you can avoid the dreaded McDonald's and its French doppelganger Le Quick by grabbing an easy *panini* or baguette sandwich (12-20F) at most *boulangeries*, *pâtisseries*, or sidewalk food stands. An excellent budget meal, baguette sandwiches are fresh and substantial and can come with ham, sausage, chicken, tomato, lettuce, and different cheeses. *Panini* are a toasted Italian version that looks flat and pasty before being pressed.

Immigrant communities have shaken up the traditionally spiceless French culinary scene. In addition to ubiquitous Greek *gyro* sandwiches, there are a number of outstanding Moroccan, Algerian, Tunisian, Senegalese, Ivory Coast, and Caribbean restaurants in Paris. Many bistros have menus with foreign dishes or visiting chefs. North African couscous is the most assimilated foreign dish. Chinese, Thai, Vietnamese, Cambodian, Korean, Tibetan, Japanese, Indian, and Pakistani restaurants, especially in the "Chinatowns" of the 9*ème*, 13*ème*, and 19*ème*, offer many affordable and delicious vegetarian options.

DINING IN PARIS

A restaurant meal in France can seem like quite a drawn-out affair, one you may not want to indulge in more than once a day for the sake of time, money, or digestive harmony. Traditional French food is very meat-based and liable to give one a heavy feeling, particularly on hot, humid days of sight-seeing. While there are some very good restaurants catering to tourists, most of them (identifiable by large placard sidewalk menus in five languages) are frighteningly unauthentic and expensive. The best way to go is to supplement one daily splurge on the best three-course menu your budget can support with picnics and snacks assembled from bakeries, cheese shops, greengrocers, and butchers. Although it takes some courage to order from these specialty food shops when you don't know the names, a little gesturing and practice will soon give you access to the best bargain of a trip to Paris.

The French breakfast *(le petit déjeuner)* is usually light, consisting of bread, croissants, or *brioches* (buttery breads) with jam and butter, plus an espresso with hot milk *(café au lait)* or a hot chocolate (*le chocolat*, often served in a bowl, or *bol*). The most enjoyable breakfasts are those had at leisurely cafés on bustling squares, or from delectable *boulangerie* goods transported to gardens and parks. Unless they are particularly charming, avoid hotel dining rooms.

Lunch *(le déjeuner)*, the largest meal of the day, is served between noon and 2:30pm in most restaurants, though some cafés and restaurants in tourist areas will stay open through the day. Restaurants are most crowded from 1-2pm when everyone takes their lunch break. During the lunch hour some shops, businesses, and government offices close; linger over a two-hour lunch a few times and you'll be hooked too.

Dinner *(le dîner)* begins quite late. Most restaurants open at 7pm, with 8:30pm the typical time to dine; revelers sometimes extend their meals into the early morning. A complete French dinner includes an *apéritif*, an *entrée* (appetizer), *plat* (main course), salad, cheese, dessert, fruit, coffee, and a *digestif* (after-dinner drink, typically a cognac or other local brandy, such as *calvados* from Normandy). There are five major *apéritifs: kir*, a blend of white wine with *cassis*, a black currant liqueur (*kir royale* substitutes champagne for the wine); *pastis*, a licorice liqueur diluted with water; *suze*, which is fermented *gentiane*, a sweet-smelling mountain flower that yields a wickedly bitter brew; *picon-bière*, beer mixed with a sweet liqueur; and martinis. The French usually take wine with their restaurant meals. You might hear the story of the famous director who dared to order a Coke with his 1500F meal; he was promptly kicked out of the restaurant by the head chef. Of him it was said, *"Il manque de savoir vivre"*—he doesn't know how to live.

Most restaurants offer *un menu à prix fixe* (fixed-price meal) that costs less than ordering *à la carte*. Importantly, lunch *menus* are often cheaper than dinner menus—if there is a pricier restaurant that you'd particularly like to try, consider going for lunch. The *menu* may include an *entrée* (appetizer), a main course *(plat)*, cheese *(fromage)*, and dessert (see **Appendix**, p. 342, for translations of common dishes). Some also include wine or coffee. For lighter fare, try a *brasserie*, which has a fuller menu than a café but is more casual than a restaurant. If you want to eat in true French manner, hold your fork face down in your left hand, your knife in the right and leave them there. The French also tend to cut one morsel of food and eat it right away, instead of first chopping up your entire steak or quiche and eating with the fork alone. But whatever. Does it really matter *how* you eat, as long as you aren't a vulgar pig?

Mineral water is everywhere; order sparkling water (*eau pétillante* or *gazeuse*) or flat mineral water (*eau plate*). Ice cubes (*glaçons*) are rare. To order a pitcher of tap water, ask for *une carafe d'eau fraîche*. Finish the meal with espresso (*un café*), which comes in lethal little cups with blocks of sugar. When *boisson compris* is written on the menu, you are entitled to a free drink (usually wine) with the meal. You will usually see the words *service compris* (service included), which means the tip is automatically added to the check (*l'addition*). Otherwise you should tip 15-20%.

WINE

In France, **wine** is not a luxury, it's an everyday pleasure. During WWI, French infantry pinned down by heavy shell-fire subsisted on the barest of rations: bread and wine. This is where we get the term "random fire." When France sent its first citizen into orbit on a Soviet space craft, he took the fruit of the vine with him. Wine is an institution in France and is served at almost every occasion. The character and quality of a wine depend upon the climate, soil, and variety of grape from which it is made. Long, hot, and fairly dry summers with cool, humid nights create the ideal climate (for love, and wine). White wines are produced by the fermentation of grapes carefully crushed to keep the skins from coloring the wine. The fermentation of rosés allows a brief period during which the skins are in contact with the juice; this period is much longer with red wines.

Wine-producing regions are sprinkled throughout the country. The Loire Valley produces a number of whites, with the major vineyards at Angers, Chinon, Saumur, Anjou, Tours, and Sancerre. Cognac, farther south on the Atlantic coast, is famous for the double-distilled spirit of the same name. Centered on the Dordogne and Garonne Rivers, the classic Bordeaux region produces red and white Pomerol, Graves, and sweet Sauternes. *Armagnac*, similar to cognac, comes from Gascony, while Jurançon wines come from vineyards higher up the slopes of the Pyrénées. Southern wines include those of Languedoc and Roussillon on the coast and Limoux and Gaillac inland. The vineyards of Provence on the coast near Toulon are recognized for their rosés. The Côtes du Rhône from Valence to Lyon in the Rhône Valley are home to some of the most celebrated wines of France, including Beaujolais. Burgundy is especially famous for its reds, from the wines of Chablis and the Côte d'Or in the north to the Mâconnais in the south. Alsatian whites tend to be spicier and more pungent. Many areas produce sparkling wines, but the only one that can legally be called "Champagne" is distilled in the Champagne area surrounding Reims. Several of the wine bars listed below have tasting when the *nouveau* edition of their specialty wine comes out, like *le beaujolais nouveau* on the third Thursday of November.

There is a specific wine for every meal, and every occasion, but there are draconian, high-society rules for which. Don't worry, as going by what tastes you like is probably best. White wines tend to be lighter, drier, and fruitier. They go with fish, and many of the white dessert wines, like Barsac, Sauternes, or Coteaux du Layon are great with fruit. Red wines tend to be heavier, more fragrant, and considerably older. Red meat and red wine is a fine combination.

France passed the first comprehensive wine legislation in 1935, and since then the *Appellation d'Origine Controlée* regulations (*AOC*, or "controlled place of origin" laws) have ensured the quality and fine reputation of French wines. All wines are categorized according to place of origin, alcohol content, and wine-making practices; only about 16% of French wines are deemed worthy of the top classification. Categories include *Vins Délimités de Qualité Supérieure* (*VDQS*, or "restricted wines of superior quality") and *Vins de Pays* (country wines). Still, a budget traveler in France will often be pleasantly surprised by even the least expensive of *vins de tables* (table wines), which are what most folk drink.

When confused about which wine to choose, simply ask. Most waiters in good restaurants and employees in wine shops will be more than happy to recommend their favorites to you. Or fall back on the *vin de maison* (house wine) of the restaurant, but beware, as they can sometimes be bitter, grainy little numbers. Wine bars will let you sample expensive wines by the glass (see **Wine Bars**, p. 152). Realize that you are already a wine expert. Despite all the pretentious talk surrounding the color, vintage, bouquet, and year, a good wine is the wine you like.

UNIVERSITY RESTAURANTS

For travelers or long-term visitors strapped for cash, university restaurants provide cheap and dependable, although crowded, meals. Students can purchase meal tickets at each restaurant location while food is being served (tickets 14F50 if you are a French or German student; 23F50 if you have an ISIC). The following university restaurants are most convenient, but the list is not nearly exhaustive. They open on a rotating schedule during the summer and on weekends; it is extremely important to get a schedule before showing up. Note that opening hours are also different during the summer and on weekends. For more information—summer and weekend schedules, a list of other restaurant locations—visit **CROUS (Centre Regional des Oeuvres Universitaires et Scolaires)**, 39, av. Georges Bernanos, 5*ème* (tel. 01 40 51 37 10, M: Port-Royal; open M-F 9am-5pm).

Most of the following offer a cafeteria style choice of sandwiches, regional and international dishes, grilled meats, and drinks: **Bullier,** 39, av. Georges Bernanos, 5*ème* (M: Port-Royal; open 8am-4:30pm); **Cuvier-Jussieu,** 8bis, rue Cuvier, 5*ème* (M: Cuvier-Jussieu; open 9am-4:15pm); **Censier,** 31, rue Geoffroy St-Hilaire, 5*ème* (M: Censier-Daubenton; open 11am-3pm); **Châtelet,** 10, rue Jean Calvin, 5*ème* (M: Censier-Daubenton; open 8-11am); **Assas,** 92, rue d'Assas, 6*ème* (M: Port-Royal or Nôtre-Dame-des-Champs; open 7:45am-6:15pm); **Mabillon,** 3, rue Mabillon, 6*ème* (M: Mabillon; open 11:30am-3:30pm and 6:30-8:30pm); **Grand Palais,** cours la Reine,

8ème (M: Champs-Elysées Clemenceau; open 11:30am-2pm and 6:15-7:45pm); **Cit-eaux,** 45, bd. Diderot, 12ème (M: Gare de Lyon; open 11:30am-2:30pm); **C.H.U. Pitié-Salpetrière,** 105, bd. de l'Hôpital, 13ème (M: St-Marcel; open 8am-4:30pm); **Dareau,** 13-17, rue Dareau, 14ème (M: St-Jacques; open 11:30am-2pm); **C.H.U. Necker,** 156, rue de Vaugirard, 15ème (M: Pasteur; open 9am-4pm); **Dauphine,** av. de Pologne, 16ème (M: Porte Dauphine; open 8am-6pm).

RESTAURANTS

Do not approach French dining with the assumption that chic equals *cher*. Recent economic hard times have led to the return of the *bistro*, a more informal, less expensive, often family-run restaurant. Even more casual are *brasseries*. Often crowded and action-packed, *brasseries* are best for large groups and high spirits. The least expensive option is usually a *crêperie*, a restaurant specializing in the thin Breton pancakes filled with various meats, cheeses, chocolates, fruits, and condiments. Surprisingly, you can often eat at a *crêperie* for the price of a fast-food chain. A number of North African restaurants also serve affordable couscous dishes. At *nouveau* bistros French, Mediterranean, Asian, and Spanish flavors converge in a setting that is usually modern and artistic.

The French eat lunch at 1pm and dinner at 9pm—avoid these times to avoid crowds, although you may be eating alone. Note that the French sit longer at dinner than Americans do. The check *(l'addition)* may be a long time in coming—spending two hours in a restaurant is not unusual. If you are particularly pleased with the service, feel free to leave a small cash tip as a sign of your gratitude (anywhere from a few francs to 5% of the check), but don't feel obligated. The initials BC mean *boisson compris*, drink included; BNC, or *boisson non-compris*, means the opposite.

A note about the organization of the following section: the restaurants we suggest are arranged both by type and by location. **Restaurants By Type** provides a list of restaurants followed by an arrondissement label; turn to **Restaurants By Location** for the full write-up. The latter groups restaurants by arrondissement, then ranks them in order of value: the top entry may not be the cheapest, but it will be the best in its price range and area. Restaurants are ranked according to the following price scale: $ means under 70F for a full, usually 2-course meal; $$ means 70-110F for a 2- or 3-course meal; $$$ means over 100F for a 2- or 3-course meal.

RESTAURANTS BY TYPE

ALL-YOU-CAN-EAT
Restaurant Natacha	16ème
Lao-Thai	19ème

AMERICAN
Coffee Parisien	6ème
Haynes Bar	9ème

BASQUE
Chez Gladines	13ème

BISTRO
Les Fous de l'Isle	*Ile St-Louis*
Le Petit Bofinger	4ème
Le Divin	4ème
Le Temps des Cérises	4ème
Restaurant Perraudin	5ème

Au Pied de Fouet	7ème
Restaurant du Bourgogne	10ème
Au Trou Normand	11ème
Chez Paul	11ème
Le Bistrot du Peintre	11ème
Le Square Trousseau	12ème
La Route du Château	14ème
Le Café du Commerce	15ème
Le Zéphyr	20ème

BRUNCH
Le Fumoir	1er
Le Dénicheur	2ème
Le Loup Blanc	2ème
En Attendant Pablo	3ème
L'Apparement Café	3ème

Les Fous de l'Isle	*Ile St-Louis*
Amnésia Café	4ème
Café Beaubourg	4ème
🐌 Le Loir dans la Théière	4ème
Les Enfants Gâtés	4ème
Le Troisième Bureau	11ème
James Joyce Pub	17ème
L'Endroit	17ème

CAFÉS
See below for full listings.

CAMBODIAN, THAI, AND VIETNAMESE

Le Lotus Blanc	7ème
Indochine	13ème
La Lune	13ème
Lao Thai	13ème
Wassana	18ème
Lao Thai	19ème

CARIBBEAN

Babylone Bis	2ème
Le Rocher du Diamant	12ème

CORSICAN

Sampieru Corsu	15ème

CREOLE

🐌 Papou Lounge	1er
Babylone Bis	2ème
La Théière dans Les Nuages	4ème
Chez Lucie	7ème

CRÊPERIE

La Crêpe Rit du Clown	6ème
Crêperie Saint Germain	6ème
Crêperie de Josselin	14ème
Ty Breiz	15ème

EASTERN EUROPEAN

Chez Marianne	4ème
Un Saumon à Paris	11ème

FRENCH

L'Epi d'Or	1er
Restaurant Chez Max	1er
Le Loup Blanc	2ème
Le Hangar	3ème
Le Réconfort	3ème
🐌 Au Gamin de Paris	4ème
Au Petit Fer à Cheval	4ème
L'Excuse	4ème

Le Grizzli	4ème
Le Tapis Franc	4ème
Le Vieux Comptoir	4ème
Au Bistrot de la Sorbonne	5ème
Café Le Volcan	5ème
L'Apostrophe	5ème
Le Truffière	5ème
Restaurant Perraudin	5ème
La Cambuse	6ème
Le Machon d'Henri	6ème
Le Petit Vatel	6ème
🐌 La Varangue	7ème
Le Club des Poètes	7ème
La Menu de Margot	8ème
Occitanie	11ème
Chez Paul	11ème
🐌 Pause Café	11ème
L'Ebauchoir	12ème
Le Temps des Cérises	13ème
Café du Commerce	13ème
Au Rendez-Vous Des Camionneurs	14ème
Le Colvert	14ème
Le Jeroboam	14ème
Les Petites Sorcières	14ème
L'Armoise	15ème
Restaurant Les Listine	15ème
Chez Ginette	18ème
Refuge des Fondues	18ème
Chez Claude et Claudine	18ème
Rendez-Vous des Chauffeurs	18ème
Le Baratin	20ème

FRIGHTENING CLOWN THEME

La Crêpe Rit du Clown	6ème
🐌 Le Clown Bar	11ème

GREEK

🐌 Sans Frontières	6ème
Le Colvert	14ème
Chez François	15ème
Mozlef	15ème

INDIAN

Le Réconfort	3ème
Kamala Inde	6ème
Nirvana	8ème
Sarangiu Anarkali	9ème
La Ville de Jagannath	11ème

IRISH

The James Joyce Pub	17ème

RESTAURANTS

ITALIAN

Pizza Sicilia	1er
Signorelli	1er
La Castafiore	Ile St-Louis
Le Jardin des Pâtes	5ème
Pizzéria King Salomon	9ème
Piccola Italia	15ème

JAPANESE

Japanese Barbecue	2ème

KOSHER

⧄ l'As du Falafel	4ème
Café des Psaumes	4ème
Pizzéria King Salomon	9ème

MALAYSIAN

Chez Foong	15ème

MEXICAN AND TEX-MEX

Mexi and Co.	5ème
Ay, Caramba!	19ème

MEDITERRANEAN

Café Med	Ile St-Louis

MIDDLE EASTERN

⧄ Chez Omar	3ème
Le Réconfort	3ème
Chez Marianne	4ème
l'As du Falafel	4ème
Café des Psaumes	4ème
⧄ Sans Frontières	6ème
Byblos Café	16ème

NORTH AFRICAN

Café Moderne	11ème
Le Souk	11ème
P'tit Cahoua	13ème
L'Atlantide	18ème
⧄ Café Flèche d'Or	20ème

OPEN LATE (MIDNIGHT OR LATER)

⧄ Papou Lounge	1er
L'Epi d'Or	1er
⧄ Le Dénicheur	2ème
Babylone Bis	2ème
Le Hangar	3ème
⧄ l'As du Falafel	4ème
Café des Psaumes	4ème
Chez Marianne	4ème
L'Apostrophe	5ème
Crêperie Saint Germain	6ème
Le Club des Poètes	7ème

⧄ Haynes Bar	9ème
Chez Paul	11ème
Chez Gladines	13ème
⧄ Le Samson	13ème
N'Zadette-M'foua	14ème
Casa Tina	16ème
The James Joyce Pub	17ème

OUTDOOR DINING

Le Hangar	3ème
Chez Marienne	4ème
Le Grizzli	4ème
Le Bistrot du Peintre	11ème
Le Patio Provençal	17ème

PERUVIAN

Restaurant Pachamama	3ème

PROVENÇALE

Le Divin	4ème
Grannie	7ème
Occitanie	11ème
Au Produits du Sud-Ouest	11ème
Restaurant Les Listines	15ème
Le Patio Provençal	17ème

QUÉBECOIS

Equinox	4ème

RUN BY A GURU

⧄ La Victoire Suprême du Coeur	1er
Chez Papa	14ème

SANDWICH SHOPS

⧄ Così	6ème
Guen maï	6ème
⧄ Antoine's: Les Sandwichs des 5 Continents	8ème
Vitamine	8ème
Barry's	8ème
Deli's Café	9ème
Le 25ème Image	10ème

SPANISH

La Casita Tapas	1er
Casa Tina	16ème

TIBETAN

Le Singe d'Eau	8ème

TRENDY INTELLIGENTSIA

⧄ Le Fumoir	1er
L'Apparement Café	3ème
Les Enfants Gâtés	4ème

Café de Flore	6ème	Le Grenier de Notre Dame	5ème
Le Sélect	6ème	Le Jardin des Pâtes	5ème
🖾 Café de l'Industrie	11ème	Guen maï	6ème
Chez Paul	11ème	Le Kitch	11ème
Le Troisième Bureau	11ème	Phinéas	14ème
La Folie en Tête	13ème	Aquarius Café	14ème
		Au Grain de Folie	18ème
TURKISH		Rayons de Santé	18ème
Le Cheval de Troie	12ème		
Aux Îles des Princes, 17ème		**WEST AND EAST AFRICAN**	
		Babylone Bis	2ème
VEGETARIAN		🖾 Paris-Dakar	10ème
🖾 La Victoire Suprême du Coeur	1er	À la Banane Ivoirienne	11ème
Aquarius	4ème	N'Zadette-M'foua	14ème
Piccolo Teatro	4ème	Le Dogon	10ème

RESTAURANTS BY LOCATION

ÎLE DE LA CITÉ

The best places to refresh close to the sights of Ile de la Cité are the **cafés** on the peaceful pl. Dauphine, serving lunch for 60-75F.

ÎLE ST-LOUIS

Due to the exorbitant costs associated with shipping food the vast distances from the mainland, most of the restaurants on Ile St-Louis are very expensive. For the most part, budget travelers in search of bargain *menus* had better look elsewhere. However, the following restaurants are worth a splurge.

Les Fous de l'Isle, 33, rue des Deux-Ponts (tel. 01 43 25 76 67). M: Pont Marie. A mellow café-bistro for the neighborhood crowd that displays the work of local artists and has evening concerts of varying genre (Brazilian, *chansons françaises*) every 2nd Tuesday, save July and Aug. Appetizers 30-65F. Salads 50-65F. Entrées like *croustillant de saumon* and *nois de St-Jacques aux fruits de la passion* 60-98F. Open Tu-F noon-11pm, Sa 6-11pm, Su noon-7pm for brunch. MC, V. $$

Café Med, 77, rue St-Louis-en-l'Ile (tel. 01 43 29 73 17). M: Pont Marie. The siren song of *crèmes caramels* and quiches sitting on a pie rack in the window draws in passersby to this sunny and otherwise standard little restaurant. Thankfully, the prices will not force you to lash yourself to the mast. Menu (59F) includes entrées like *taboulé maison*, *plats* like lasagna or quiche lorraine, and dessert. Loud enough that you couldn't be blamed for wanting to plug your ears. Open M-Sa 12-4:30pm and 6:30-11pm. $

La Castafiore, 27, rue St-Louis-en-l'Ile (tel. 01 43 54 78 62). M: Pont Marie. A chic Italian restaurant with salmon stucco walls and lighting so dim, and seating so intimate, you just might take a nap on the table while awaiting your homestyle Italian cuisine. Appetizers (60-78F), pastas (58-72F), meat entrées (78-98F). Sample 2-course lunch *menu*: *soupe à l'oignon* with *penne arrabbiata* (59-62F). Dinner *formule* 98F. Prices after 8:30pm are very high. Open daily noon-3pm and 7-11pm. AmEx, MC, V. $$

CAFÉS

M'ile Saveurs, 47, rue St-Louis-en-l'Ile (tel. 01 43 26 77 11). M: Pont Marie. Good for a drink or snack on the island, as many of the other similar cafés adjust their prices in honor of the influx of summer tourists. Slice of quiche, 15F, croissant, 4F50. Open M-Th 8:30am-8pm, F-Sa 8am-around 10pm, depending upon the time of year. MC, V.

FIRST ARRONDISSEMENT

The arcades overlooking the Louvre along rue de Rivoli are filled with the chic and expensive, but tea or *chocolat chaud* at a *salon de thé* (see p. 152) are affordable treats. Traditional restaurants cluster around the Palais-Royal while Les Halles features cheaper, louder eateries offering everything from fast-food to four-course Italian feasts. Near Les Halles, the rue St-Denis's thoroughly respectable restaurants coexist with thoroughly respectable sex shops. During daylight hours, travelers should consider these eateries welcome bargains, but we advise steering clear of the area after dark.

■ **Papou Lounge,** 74 rue J.-J. Rousseau (tel. 01 44 76 00 03). M: Les Halles. Walk toward the church St-Eustache, then take a right onto rue Coquillère, then a right on rue J.-J. Rousseau. With its house music, black and white tile floors, and voodoo dolls on the walls, the Papou is a cross between a Tahitian lounge and a French café. Salads like endive and apple (40F) appear with substantial plates like beef brochette with tomatoes, rice, and green beans (70F). Watch out for the *boudin:* it's wickedly good, and purple. Gourmet hamburgers (48-55F), salmon burger (52F), cold beer (16-20F). Daily special 55F. Open daily 10am-2am with nonstop food service. MC, V.

■ **La Victoire Suprême du Coeur,** 41, rue des Bourdonnais (tel. 01 40 41 93 95). M: Châtelet. Follow traffic on rue des Halles then turn left on rue des Bourdonnais. Run by the devotees of the guru Sri Chinmoy who have both body and soul in mind when creating dishes like *gratinée aux champignons* (mushrooms and green beans in a rich cheese sauce). Never mind that the color photos on the wall of their Yul Brynner-esque guru up to his elbows in dough or playing gleefully with children are a little weird. It is vegetarian, and very tasty. The lassi shakes are to die for (35F). All-day 3-course *formule* 89F. Entrées 47-67F. Open M-F noon-2:30pm and 6:30-10pm, Sa noon-10pm.

L'Epi d'Or, 25, rue J.-J. Rousseau (tel. 01 42 36 38 12). M: Louvre or Les Halles. Walk toward St-Eustache then take the second right after the church onto rue J.-J. Rousseau. A small restaurant open to the street in the summer and decorated with tasteful antiques and tasteful journalists from the nearby *Le Figaro* offices. The staff is charming and the food is excellent. 3-course *menu* served until 9pm (105F). Main courses from 90F. Housemade *foie gras à canard* appetizer (26F) and *entrecôte bordelaise* (rib steak; 105F). Open Sept.-July M-F noon-2:15pm and 7:30-11:30pm, Sa 7:30-11:30pm. Last orders at midnight. Closed 1 week in Feb. Reservations recommended. MC,V.

Signorelli, 35, rue St-Honoré (tel. 01 40 13 91 41). M: Les Halles. From Les Halles, head down rue St-Honoré toward the Louvre. The restaurant takes its name from the many copied paintings of Luca Signorelli, Michelangelo's master, that hang on its walls. Daily *menu* 78F. Pastas include homemade tortellini with prosciutto (69-82F). Desserts like chocolate fondue with orange-infused cream (49F). If you're daring, tackle *La Torre del Moro* (coffee with brandy, 56F). Open M-F and Su noon-3pm and 7-10:30pm, Sa 7-10:30pm. AmEx, MC, V.

Pizza Sicilia, 26, rue de Beaujolais (tel. 01 42 96 93 55). M: Palais-Royal. On the corner of Montpensier and Beaujolais just north of the Palais. A budget gastronomic gem. Friendly Italian-style service, low prices, and good food. Try the *tortellini aux champignons* (tortellini with mushrooms, 47F), margherita pizza (39F), or *zuppa inglese* (23F). Open M-Sa noon-2:30pm and 7-11:30pm. MC, V.

Restaurant Chez Max, 47, rue St-Honoré (tel. 01 45 08 80 13). M: Châtelet. Owner Max Reytet is a real charmer, piloting the smooth course of his fire-engine red restaurant overlooking the street below. Check out the *gambas flambée* star of the 3-course *menu* which includes wine (135F). Open M-F noon-2pm and 7:30-1:30am, Sa 7:30pm-1:30am. AmEx, MC, V.

CAFÉS

■ **Le Fumoir,** 6, rue de l'Admiral Coligny (tel. 01 42 92 05 05). M: Louvre. Directly across from the Louvre sits this awesome café, where decidedly untouristy types drink their chosen beverage in deep green leather sofas. Part bar, part tea house in feel, Le Fumoir serves the best brunch in Paris (take that, Marais! 120F), smoked-salmon sandwiches (37F), and coffee (15F). Open Su-Th 11am-midnight, F-Sa 11am-2am. AmEx, MC, V.

SECOND ARRONDISSEMENT

Wedged between the wide boulevards of the 9*ème* and the affluence of the 1*er* near the Louvre, the 2*ème* provides inexpensive meals to tourists exploring this and neighboring *quartiers*. Rue Montorgueil is lined with excellent bakeries, fruit stands, and specialty stores (see **Food Markets**, p. 156), and side streets like rue Marie Stuart and rue Mandar hide some worthwhile dining options. The Passage des Panoramas and Passage des Italiens showcase fast, cheap food.

🖟 **Le Dénicheur,** 4, rue Tiquetonne (tel. 01 42 21 31 01). M: Etienne-Marcel. Walk against traffic on rue de Turbigo and turn left on rue Tiquetonne. Decorated like a sinkhole for bric-a-brac, this restaurant is full of lawn gnomes for sale, excellent food, and an affable crowd. Are upside-down Christmas trees sacrilegious? Only *le dénicheur* (antique hunter) knows. 2-course *menu* 50-55F; 3-course *menu* with coffee 70F. Omelettes, sandwiches, and quiches all 35F. Sunday brunch (80F). Tea and brioche served all day (16F). Open daily noon-3:30pm and 7:30pm-2am.

Babylone Bis, 34, rue Tiquetonne (tel. 01 42 33 48 35). M: Etienne-Marcel. Walk against traffic on rue de Turbigo and turn left onto rue Tiquetonne. Popular with artists who come for Antillean and African specialties. With zebra skins on the walls, banana leaves on the ceiling, and loud *zouk* playing, this restaurant tends to get wild. Josephine Baker, wherefore art thou? Specialties include *aloko* (bananas flambéed in liqueur, 35F), *beignets de banane* (banana fritters, 50F), and *poulet braisé* (braised, lime-marinated chicken, 80F). Cocktails 35F. Dinner served all night. Open daily 8pm-7am. MC, V.

Le Loup Blanc, 42, rue Tiquetonne (tel. 01 40 13 08 35). M: Etienne-Marcel. Walk against traffic on rue de Turbigo and turn left on rue Tiquetonne. Artistic renderings of buff men look down on the multitudes of men eating *boeuf* here. Specializes in grilled and marinated meats. Entrées with choice of sides 55-98F. The Loup Blanc mixed grille allows you to sample 4 kinds of meats (mmm, cardamom chicken livers) and sides (66-82F). The vegetarian *salades mosaiques* includes salad and 4-6 sides (49-65F). Sunday brunch 75-95F. Open M-Sa noon-3pm and 8pm-midnight, Su 11am-4:30pm. Visa.

Japanese Barbecue, 60, rue Montorgueil (tel. 01 42 33 49 61). M: Sentier. Follow rue Réaumur and turn right on rue des Petits-Carreaux, which becomes rue Montorgueil. Yeee haaaa! Konichiwa! Get them little doggie-sans, and roll 'em in seaweed! All *menus* with broth and rice, some with salad. Grill *menus* (73F), sushi/sashimi *menus* (77-120F), lunch *menus* (47-60F), vegetarian *menu* includes miso soup, salad, and entrée (66F). Open daily noon-3pm and 7-11:30pm.

CAFÉS

Au Vide Gousset, 1 rue Vide-Gousset (tel. 01 42 60 02 78). M: Bourse. This café fits its neighborhood, full of suits from the Bourse and Agence France Presse, and upscale shoppers from nearby pl. des Victoires. Nevertheless, it feels *very* Parisian, with lace curtains and overpriced coffee. Open M-F 8am-7:30pm. Closed Aug.

THIRD ARRONDISSEMENT

The restaurants of the upper Marais, sometimes tucked away in courtyards and alleys, offer Peruvian, Tibetan, Middle Eastern, and French cuisine. A number of kosher take-aways and restaurants are located around the intersection of rue du Vertbois and rue Volta. Dinner can be pricey, but lunchtime *menus* are good deals.

Le Hangar, 12, impasse Berthaud (tel. 01 42 74 55 44). M: Rambuteau. Take the Impasse Berthaud exit from the métro. Tucked in an alley near the Centre Pompidou, Le Hangar is bright and intimate, serving French specialties, such as *foie gras de canard poêlé* (fried goose liver, 88F). Appetizers 30-58F. Large selection of wine (bottles 58-460F). Open M 7pm-midnight, Tu-Sa noon-3:00pm and 7pm-midnight. $$$

En Attendant Pablo, 78, rue Vieille-du-Temple (tel. 01 42 74 34 65). M: Hotel de Ville. From rue de Rivoli, turn left on rue Vieille-du-Temple. This intimate combination *pâtisserie*/lunch café serves enormous salads (58F), and *tartines* (spreads). Lunch *menu*

RESTAURANTS

with *tarte salée* 53F; Sunday brunch 89-109F. Large selection of fresh fruit juices (25F) and many pastries embracing chocolate (30F). Open W-Su noon-6pm. MC, V. $

Le Réconfort, 37, rue de Poitou (tel. 01 42 76 06 36). M: St-Sébastien-Froissart. Walk along rue du Pt-Aux-Choux until it turns into rue de Poitou. A hyper-eclectic, swank eating experience. French, Indian, and Middle Eastern tastes. Entrées such as *concombre à la crème et aux herbes* (34F) are delicate and light, as are large-portioned *plats* like the *salade de poulet tikka* (59F). Lunch menu (69-89F). Open M-Th noon-2pm and 8:15-11pm, F noon-2pm and 8:15-11:30pm, Sa 8:15-11:30pm, Su 8:15-11pm. $$$

Taxi Jaune, 13, rue Chapon (tel. 01 42 76 00 40). M: Arts-et-Métiers. Walk along rue Beaubourg and turn left onto rue Chapon. When the kind patron displays their art on his walls, artists thank him in taxi-art. Here's a little secret: the food is worth a lot more. Adhering to a fry-as-little-as-possible policy, this comfy joint serves dishes that are light and piquant. Entrées hover around 30F; plats around 85F. Copious lunch *menu* 72F. Open M-F noon-2:30pm and 7:30pm-2am, food served until 11pm. $$$

🕮 **Chez Omar,** 47, rue de Bretagne (tel. 01 42 72 36 26). M: Arts et Métiers. Walk along rue Réamur, away from rue Saint Martin. Rue Réamur turns into rue de Bretagne. Couscous madness. Adrenaline and heaps of Middle Eastern food form the landscape in this Art-Deco-ish, mirrored restaurant. Couscous with vegetables 60F, lamb 70-98F, chicken 70F. Open M 7:30-11:30pm, Tu-Su noon-3pm and 7:30-11:30pm. $-$$

Restaurant Pachamama, 2, impasse Berthaud (tel. 01 48 87 88 22). M: Rambuteau. Take the Impasse Berthaud exit. Peruvian cuisine, salsa music, and low prices make this bar/restaurant very hot. Small and intimate. Generous lunch (55F). Try the spicy *Aji de Gallima* (chicken with cheese sauce, 45F). Open Tu-Su noon-11pm. $$

La Baromètre, 17, rue Charot (tel. 01 48 87 04 54). This crowded and animated neighborhood restaurant, wine bar, and favorite lunch spot serves big portions of hearty food. Large selection of salads including *Salade Auvergnate*, with blue cheese, egg, croutons, and nuts (44F). Daily plates 60-62F. Open M-F 7am-9pm. $-$$

CAFÉS

🕮 **Le Marais Plus,** 20, rue des Francs-Bourgeois (tel. 01 48 87 01 40). The relaxed *salon de thé* of this wacky toy store and funky gift and book shop, has tables which function as display counters and exhibit toys, baby clothing, cutlery, and numerous other tchatchkes. Hot and iced teas 25F, cappuccino with divine froth 25F, selection of salads 60F, *tartes salées* and *crudités* 50F. Open daily noon-6:30pm.

L'Apparemment Café, 18, rue des Coutures St-Gervais (tel. 01 48 87 12 22). M: St-Paul. Next to the Picasso Museum, this hip café offers coffee (12F), designer salads (45F), and Sunday brunch in comfortable cushioned chairs. You may want to move in. Open M-F noon-2am (lunch until 2pm), Sa 4pm-2am, Su 12:30pm-midnight. MC, V.

FOURTH ARRONDISSEMENT

In the 4*ème*, old mansions, galleries, and cafés serve *brunch*, a late-Sunday-morning meal invented by gay men in the 7th century. Rue des Rosiers is the promised land of Eastern European and Israeli bakeries, delis, and restaurants, not all of which are kosher (see **Specialty Stores,** p. 155).

Au Petit Fer à Cheval, 30, rue Vieille-du-Temple (tel. 01 42 72 47 47). M: Hôtel-de-Ville or St-Paul. Head down rue de Rivoli against traffic and turn left onto rue Vieille-du-Temple. An oasis of *chèvre*, kir, and *gauloises*. A local crowd that knows a good thing when they find it. Invisible from the front, a few tables huddle behind the bar, where you can order the life-changing *chèvre chaud* salad with prosciutto and toasted bread (50F). Sandwiches 20-35F. Desserts 25-34F. Open M-F 9am-2am, Sa-Su 11am-2am. $-$$

Le Vieux Comptoir, 8, rue de Birague (tel. 01 42 72 55 36), directly behind pl. des Vosges. M: Bastille. Funky little restaurant and wine bar. Duck with roasted peaches (75F) or chocolate mousse with *grappa* (Italian liqueur 39F). Regional wines (18F per glass). Lunch *formule* (79F), dinner *formule* (109F). Open daily noon-3pm and 7-11pm. $$

Le Tapis Franc, 12, rue Pecquay (tel. 01 44 59 86 72). M: Rambuteau. Follow the traffic on rue Rambuteau, take the second right on rue Pecquay. In 1930s Paris, *les tapis* (rugs) was slang for the popular bistros of Montmartre. *Franc* described places frequented by artists and prostitutes. When the government closed Paris's brothels in 1950, bistros took over as fronts for these dislocated "employees." Today, Le Tapis sells only fine French cuisine, but is still eccentric and entertaining. The place is small, but the portions are enormous. Dinner *menu* 80F, lunch *plats* 45F, salads 40F, *entrées* 45F. Open daily noon-2:30pm and 7-11:30pm. MC, V. $$

■ **L'As du Falafel,** 34, rue des Rosiers (tel. 01 48 87 63 60). M: St-Paul. Go with the traffic a few steps down rue de Rivoli, make a right on rue Pavée; turn left on rue des Rosiers. This kosher falafel stand and restaurant displays pictures of Lenny Kravitz, who credited this cheerfully decorated place with "the best falafel in the world, particularly the special eggplant falafel with hot sauce." Go his way with the falafel special (25F), lamb *shawerma* (32F), or sauteed chicken with curry sauce (32F). Open Su-Th 11:30am-11:30pm. MC, V. $

Equinox, 33-35, rue des Rosiers (tel. 01 42 71 92 41) M: Hôtel-de-Ville. Between Café Amnésia and Au Petit Fer à Cheval, Equinox serves Québecois specialties like *tourtière* (a meat pie) and desserts made with imported *sirop d'érable* (maple syrup). Equinox is a center of the hip Parisian Québecois scene, sponsoring cultural events along with the Librairie du Québec (see **Books,** p. 309) and the Association Paris-Québec (see **Festivals,** p. 280). *Entrée* and *plat* 130F, with dessert 150F, *plat* and dessert 115F. The adjacent, mostly-male **Okhawa** café serves cheaper Québecois daily dishes (50F). Montréal hamburger 55F. Restaurant and café open daily 10am-2am. $-$$$

■ **Au Gamin de Paris,** 51, rue Vieille-du-Temple (tel. 01 42 78 97 24). M: St-Paul. Walk along rue de Rivoli, turn right on rue des Ecouffes, left on rue des Rosiers, and right onto rue Vieille-du-Temple. A relaxed, but keenly awake, resto-bar. Young 'uns feast on copious platters. The *filet de boeuf sauce au miel et pommes sautées* (beef in honey sauce with sauteed potatoes, 98F) is sweet, spicy, and scrum-diddly-umptious. The *tartin flambée* is explosive (39F). Open daily noon-2am. Visa, MC. $$$

Le Petit Bofinger, 6, rue de la Bastille (tel. 01 42 72 05 23). M: Bastille. Rue de la Bastille runs directly off pl. de la Bastille. Schmancy Bofinger's baby brother offers affordable, totally classic cuisine. Steak tartare is a once-and-future special (79F). Finish off with a dessert like poached peaches with cassis (30F). Such a steal, the lunch *formule* is like robbing the cradle (95F). Open daily noon-3pm and 7pm-midnight. $$

Chez Marianne, 2, rue des Hospitalières-St-Gervais (tel. 01 42 72 18 86). M: St-Paul. Follow rue de Rivoli a few steps and turn right on rue Pavée; turn left on rue des Rosiers and right on rue des Hospitalières-St-Gervais. Central European canteen. Sample 4, 5, or 6 specialties (55F, 65F, or 75F), including tzatziki, falafel, and tarama. Homemade desserts like strudel (30F) and *vatrouchka*, a white cheese cake (35F). Reservations recommended. Take-out available. Open daily 11am-12:30am. MC, V. $-$$

Piccolo Teatro, 6, rue des Ecouffes (tel. 01 42 72 17 79). M: St-Paul. Walk with the traffic down rue de Rivoli and take a right on rue des Ecouffes. A romantic vegetarian hideout. Lunch and dinner *menus* (52F, 90-115F) feature *tempeh au curry* (solid grains sauteed in a curry sauce) with assorted veggies. Appetizers 30-65F. Entrées 50-70F. A *kir* on the house for *Let's Go* readers. Open W-Su noon-3pm and 7-11pm. AmEx, MC, V. $$

Le Divin, 41, rue Ste-Croix-de-la-Bretonnerie (tel. 01 42 77 10 20). M: Hôtel-de-Ville or Rambuteau. Walk away from the Hôtel de Ville on rue du Temple and turn right on rue Ste-Croix-de-la-Bretonnerie. Go South, young man, where sun and cheer bounce off the walls as fabulous *Provençal* specialties such as *carré d'agneau rôti au miel et au romarin* (lamb cubes roasted with honey and rosemary, 82F) get passed around. *Menu* 89F. Vegetarian platters 52-59F. Open Tu-Sa noon-2pm and 7:30-11:30pm, Su 7:30-11pm. Closed for lunch in July and Aug. AmEx, MC, V. $$

Café des Psaumes, 14-16, rue des Rosiers (tel. 01 48 04 74 77). M: St-Paul. Next to l'As du Falafel, above. A lip-smacking kosher restaurant. Falafel plate (59F) or falafel sandwich (25F). *Couscous douceur* (couscous with beef, raisins, chick peas, almonds, and cinnamon, 85F). Open Su-Th 11am-midnight, F noon-sundown. MC, V. $-$$

RESTAURANTS

Aquarius, 54, rue Ste-Croix-de-la-Bretonnerie (tel. 01 48 87 48 71). M: Hôtel-de-Ville. Walk away from the Hôtel de Ville on rue du Temple and turn right on rue Ste-Croix-de-la-Bretonnerie. Also at 40, rue de Gergovie, 14ème (tel. 01 45 41 36 88). A new-age zone with smoke-free air, an occult library, and fresh vegetarian dishes like homemade yogurt (62F). Lunch and dinner *menus* (64, 95F) feature a cold dish, hot dish, and dessert. Open M-Th noon-10:15pm, F-Sa noon-10:30pm. MC, V. $-$$

Le Grizzli, 7, rue St-Martin (tel. 01 48 87 77 56). M: Châtelet. Walk along Quai de Gesvres and turn left onto St-Martin. More cuddly than grizzli, this unpretentious classic bistro serves meticulously prepared food. Its outdoor seating on a pedestrian road located near the Seine and its affordable prices make it attractive to many tourists, although the bistro retains an authentic feel. The *marbré de lentiles vertes et cocos au vinaigre de xères*, a vegetarian pâté (48F), and the *saumon à l'ardoise* (79F) are especially tasty. Open M-Sa noon-3pm and 7-11pm. $$-$$$

La Théière Dans Les Nuages, 1, rue Cloche Perce (tel. 01 44 54 04 72). M: St-Paul. Walk with traffic on rue de Rivoli and turn right onto this small pedestrian street; the restaurant is at the top of the stairs. Tasty Creole eats such as *salade énergétique,* with apples, cheese, and nuts (35F) and *picadinho,* a beef, corn, and banana dish (52F). Sunny staff. Open M 7-11:30pm, Tu-Sa noon-3pm and 7-11:30pm. $$

Le Petit Gavroche, 15, rue Ste-Croix-de-la-Bretonnerie (tel. 01 48 87 74 26). M: St-Paul. Walk with traffic along rue de Rivoli, turn right onto rue Bourg-Tibourg and left onto rue Ste-Croix-de-la-Bretonnerie. This comfortably tattered bistrot serves a mixed clientele diehard regulars and Marais hipsters. Simple, quick, and cheap! 3-course lunch *menu* 45F; *entrées* 20-30F, *plats* 50F, desserts 20F. Open daily noon-2:30pm and 7-10pm. $

L'Excuse, 14, rue Charles V (tel. 01 42 77 98 97). M: St-Paul. Walk against traffic on rue de Rivoli, turn right onto the narrow rue St-Paul, and then left onto Charles V. For those seeking a serious splurge, deluxe is the name of the game at this magical bistro. In other words. The 185F dinner *menu* is well worth it. Lunch *menu* 120-150F. Specialities include *roulé de sole à l'étuvée* (braised sole rolled with layers of tomato, basil, and cream of vanilla, 169F). Open M-Sa noon-2pm and 7:30-11pm. $$$+

CAFÉS

Les Enfants Gâtés, 43, rue des Francs-Bourgeois (tel. 01 42 77 07 63). M: St-Paul. Walk against traffic on rue de Rivoli, turn left onto rue Pavée and right on rue Francs-Bourgeois. A sexy, yet lovable, spot to brood and linger. Coffee 15F, brunch 95-170F, Berthillon ice cream 36F. Open W 8am-8pm, Tu and Th-Su 8am-midnight.

Café Beaubourg, 100, rue St-Martin (tel. 01 48 87 63 96). M: Hôtel-de-Ville. If you close one eye, you might only see the occasional model. Luckily, this simple, sleek cavern also draws tourists, families, and comrades. Legendary bathrooms. Coffee 16F, hot chocolate 26F, breakfast 65F, brunch 110F. Open daily 8am-1am. AmEx, MC, V.

Amnésia Café, 42, rue Vieille-du-Temple (tel. 01 42 72 16 94). M: Hôtel de Ville. In the heart of the Marais, the Amnésia's wood interior and plush sofas attract a largely gay crowd on Saturday nights and a mixed scene for Sunday brunch (40-130F). Other options include the swank smoked salmon *Salade Nordique* (65F), espresso (11F), and *kir* (20F). Open daily 10am-2am. MC, V.

Okhawa Café, 33-35, rue des Rosiers (tel. 01 42 71 92 41) M: Hôtel-de-Ville. Mostly male. See **Restaurants,** p. 135, for the full listing.

La Belle Hortense, 31, rue Vieille-du-Temple (tel. 01 48 04 71 60). M: St-Paul. Bar/bookstore. Coffee 7-11F. See **Nightlife, p. 293,** for full listing.

FIFTH ARRONDISSEMENT

With the student population demanding inexpensive but proper meals at all hours, the 5ème is geared toward the budget gourmand. The main drag is rue Mouffetard (the Mouff'), and the side streets off pl. de la Contrescarpe. Cheap restaurants of dubious quality cluster around rue de la Huchette and rue Galande. For authentic Vietnamese and Chinese fare, see the row of restaurants at 29-35 rue Lagrange.

▧ **Savannah Café,** 27, rue Descartes (tel. 01 43 29 45 77). M: Cardinal Lemoine. Follow Cardinal Lemoine uphill, make a right on rue Clovis, and walk one block. Offers "selections from around the world," and prepares them delicately. Dishes include eggplant caviar, taboule, lamb curry, and traditional French cuisine. Lunch and dinner *menus* (75F, 137F). Open M 7-11pm, Tu-Sa noon-2:30pm and 7-11pm. MC, V. $$$

La Truffière, 4, rue Blainville (tel. 01 46 33 29 82). M: Place Monge. Follow rue Monge downhill to a left on rue Lacépède, and proceed through Pl. Contrescarpe. In a cozy stone house, one of the few serious restaurants near the Mouff'. Bargain lunch *menus* (90F and 120F) featuring southwestern French cuisine like mussels with saffron and terrine of scallops. Interesting full *menu* a steep 240F. Reservations recommended. Open Sept.-June Tu-Su noon-2:30pm and 7-11pm; July-Aug. closed Su. MC, V. $$$

▧ **Au Jardin des Pâtés,** 4, rue Lacépède (tel. 01 43 31 50 71). M: Jussieu. From the métro, walk up rue Linné and turn right on rue Lacépède. Organic gourmet pastas with a variety of vegetables and sauces, including *pâtés de seigle* (ham, white wine, and sharp *comté* cheese, 56F), fill the menu. Many vegetarian offerings. Appetizers 19-31F, entrées 39-77F. Reservations recommended. Open Tu-Su noon-2:30pm and 7-11pm. MC, V. $

Restaurant Perraudin, 157, rue St-Jacques (tel. 01 46 33 15 75). M: Luxembourg. From the métro, take rue Royer Collard to rue St-Jacques. Classic bistro, popular among the academes for its traditional French dishes like Burgundy beef stew (59F); few vegetarian options. Come early to avoid crowds. 3-course lunch *menu* (63F). Appetizers 41F, entrées 59F, desserts 28-36F, wine 9F. Not *haute cuisine,* but solid fare. Open Tu-F noon-2:15pm and 7:30-10:15pm, M and Sa 7:30-10:15pm. $$

L'Apostrophe, 34, rue de la Montagne Ste-Geneviève (tel. 01 43 54 10 93). M: Maubert-Mutualité. Walk down bd. St-Germain with traffic and turn right on rue de la Montagne Ste-Geneviève. This small, candle-lit restaurant offers traditional and creative French food at reasonable prices. Lunch (65F) and dinner (85F) *menus.* Open M-Th 5pm-12:30am, F-Sa 5pm-2am. MC, V. $$

Mexi and Co., 10, rue Dante (tel. 01 46 34 14 12). M: Maubert-Mutualité. Follow bd. St-Germain against traffic to rue St-Jacques and make a sharp right. Feels like a northern Mexico highway stop, and just as refreshing given its tourist ghetto surroundings. Sidle up to the big kitchen table among shelves of spices and sauces. Burritos (40F), tortillas (56F), quesadillas (30F) all mouth-watering and not too heavy. Count 80F for a big meal. Open daily 10:30am-midnight. $

Le Grenier de Nôtre Dame, 18, rue de la Bûcherie (tel. 01 43 29 98 29). M: St-Michel. Walk along quai St-Michel to quai de Montebello; turn right on rue Lagrange and left on rue de la Bûcherie. Macrobiotic and vegetarian specialties with a contemporary French spin. 3-course *menus* (75F, 78F, and 105F). Delicious polenta with stir-fried vegetables (75F). Open M-Th noon-2:30pm and 7-11pm, F-Su noon-11pm. MC, V. $$

Au Bistrot de la Sorbonne, 4, rue Toullier (tel. 01 43 54 41 49). M: Luxembourg. Follow bd. St-Michel towards the Seine and make a right on rue Soufflot. Make the second left. *Menus* at 95F and 140F will delight you with gourmet dishes like goat cheese-walnut salad, steak with bearnaise sauce, and chestnut ice cream. Open M-Sa noon-2:30pm and 7-11pm. MC, V. $$

CAFÉS

Café de la Mosquée, 39, rue Geoffrey St-Hilaire (tel. 01 43 31 38 20). M: Censier Daubenton. In the Mosquée de Paris, this cool café, with decorative tiles, white-marble floors, and tropical shade trees offers mint tea (10F) and *Mahgrebin* pastries such as *kadaïf* (10F). Indulge yourself with an afternoon in the *hammam* (men on Tu and Su; women M, Tu, Th, Sa). Café open daily 10am-midnight.

SIXTH ARRONDISSEMENT

Tiny restaurants with rock-bottom prices jostle each other for space and customers in the area bounded by bd. St-Germain, bd. St-Michel, and the Seine, making this area an excellent quadrangle to wander in search of a filling meal. Rue de Buci harbors bargain Greek restaurants and a rambling daily street market, while rue Gregoire de Tours has the highest density of cheap restaurants (think greasy spoons, not 4-star gems). More options can be found along the streets near the Odéon métro stop.

■ **Coffee Parisien,** 4, rue Princesse (tel. 01 43 54 18 18). M: Mabillon. Meant to emulate a Parisian café plunked down in NYC, the walls are covered with smiling JFKs and Americana, as is the menu. This may be the last resort for those needing a bagel with lox and cream cheese (80F), nachos (45F), and a hot fudge sundae (45F) all in one sitting. God Bless la France! Open daily noon-midnight. $$

■ **Cosi,** 54, rue de Seine (tel. 01 46 33 35 36). M: Mabillon. This sandwicherie's product is enormous, tasty, and inexpensive. The opera piped into the pleasant eating area makes it even better. Tomato, Mozzarella, Roquette (38F), desserts (20F). Open daily noon-midnight. $

■ **Sans Frontières,** 19, rue du Regard (tel. 01 45 48 87 67). M: St-Placide. A Greco-Persian restaurant whose classy interior makes it look like a pricey brasserie. It is delightfully cheap, the portions are large, and the food is well done. Lunch menu 65F, dinner menu 95F or 120F. All have a *meze* plate (appetizer samples) that is a meal in and of itself (hummus, tzatziki, eggplant, the works), as well as a main course and dessert. Very kind staff keeps the techno hits coming. Open daily noon-2:30pm and 7-11pm. MC, V. $$

La Cambuse, 8, rue Casimir Delavigne (tel. 01 43 26 48 84). M: Odéon. Veer right off pl. de l'Odéon. This 6-table family restaurant serves up ample amounts of *soupe à l'oignon, boeuf bourguignon,* or *coq au vin.* Expect hearty servings. The 3-course *menu* (100F) includes a starter, a daily *plat* like duck terrine, and desserts such as *crème caramel.* Dig the enormous cheese plate. Open M-Sa noon-2:30pm and 7-10:30pm. Reserve ahead. May be closed in Aug. MC, V. $$

La Crêpe Rit du Clown, 6, rue des Canettes (tel. 01 46 34 01 02). M: Mabillon. Despite the vaguely frightening clown motif, this *crêperie* won't make you feel like crying on the inside. *Formule* 63F, with a meal crêpe, a dessert crêpe or ice cream, and a drink. Crêpes 35-42F, salads 24F on up (choose your ingredients). Open M-Sa noon-11:30pm. MC, V. $

Crêperie Saint Germain, 33, rue St-André-des-Arts (tel. 01 43 54 24 41). M: St-Michel. Jazz plays amid a Moroccan mosaic of disco balls, beaded lampshades, terra cotta tables, and earthenware plates. The house specializes in filling wheat-flour *crêpes noirs,* like the Chihuahua (guacamole, black olives, and salad, 39F) or the Manhattan (ground beef, cheese, tomatoes and a fried egg, 56F), and sweet dessert crêpes (26-56F). A 49F *menu* (served until 6pm) includes 2 simple crêpes and a glass of *cidre,* but bring a friend; there's a 110F minimum. Open daily noon-1am. AmEx, MC, V. $

Guen maï, 2bis, rue de l'Abbaye (tel. 01 43 26 03 24). M: Mabillon. Next to St-Germain-des-Prés. A combination store and lunch-only restaurant serving vegetarian, *biologique* (organic), and macrobiotic food (no eggs, butter, or refined sugars) alongside freshly squeezed juices and organic wines. Robust house-made *gratin de tofou* (26F) and vegetable tart (24F) highlight the *plats du jour* (64F). Go early to be guaranteed a spot in this ultra-popular place. Store (which sells all-natural products and some organic fruits and vegetables) open M-Sa 9am-8:30pm. Restaurant open M-Sa 11:45am-3:30pm. MC, V. $

Le Machon d'Henri, 8, rue Guisarde (tel. 01 3 29 08 70). M: Mabillon. A staple of traditional cooking in the area, the ever-changing menu packs in yupparisians and sundry locals. Ever popular is the *gigot d'agneau,* and the *gratin dauphinois.* Appetizers 35-40F, *plats* 70-80F. Open M-Sa noon-2:30pm and 7-11:30pm. $$

Kamala-Inde, 13, rue Monsieur-le-Prince (tel. 01 40 51 73 27). M: Odéon. An incense-scented refuge near St-Germain-des-Prés, Kamala's ample portions bring in the South Asian community for well-priced fare. The 59F lunch *menu* consists of a vegetarian appetizer, a curry or fish masala and dessert. Other specialties include lamb curry (72F) and basmati with saffron, veggies, almonds, and raisins (65F). Open Su-Th noon-2:30pm and 7-11pm, F, Sa noon-2:30pm and 7-midnight. AmEx, MC, V. $

Le Petit Vatel, 5, rue Lobineau (tel. 01 43 54 28 49). M: Mabillon. From the métro, follow traffic on bd. St-Germain, turn right on rue de Seine, and then take the second right onto rue Lobineau. The recently improved Le Petit Vatel still abides with Mediterranean French specialties such as the Catalan *pamboli* (bread with puréed tomatoes, ham, and cheese) at low, low prices. The 60F lunch *menu* includes appetizer, main course, and dessert. There is always a vegetarian option. Take-out available. Open Tu-Sa noon-3pm and 7-11pm. MC, V. $

> # COUNTER CULTURE Café drinks are cheaper at the *comptoir* (or *zinc*) than seated inside the *salle* or on the *terrasse*. Both of these prices should be posted. Aside from coffee, other popular café drinks include *citron pressé*, freshly squeezed lemon juice (with sugar and water on the side). Cafés also serve *croques monsieur* (grilled ham-and-cheese sandwiches), *croques madame* (the same with a fried egg), and assorted omelettes.

CAFÉS

Aux Deux Magots, 6, pl. St-Germain-des-Prés (tel. 01 45 48 55 25). M: St-Germain-des-Prés. Sartre's second-choice café and Simone de Beauvoir's first, it was here that the couple first met. Home to literati since 1885, Aux Deux Magots is now a favorite among Left Bank youth and tourists, primarily the latter. Named after 2 Chinese porcelain figures *(magots)*, this café has high ceilings, gilt mirrors, and Art Deco café decor. Jokes about maggots will get you thrown out. Coffee (23F), *café crème* (26F), hot chocolate (33F), and pastries (12-24F). Open daily 7am-1:30am. AmEx, V.

Café de Flore, 172, bd. St-Germain (tel. 01 45 48 55 26). M: St-Germain-des-Prés. It was here, in his favorite hangout, that Jean-Paul Sartre composed *L'être et le néant (Being and Nothingness)*. Apollinaire, Picasso, Breton, Thurber, and Prévert also sipped their brew here. Making jokes about the pronunciation of Prévert will get you kicked out. Enjoy your drink on the terrace, Brigitte Bardot's favorite spot. Espresso 34F, tea 34F, *salade Flore* 68F, pastries 31-50F. Open daily 7am-2am. MC, V.

Le Procope, 13, rue de l'Ancienne Comédie (tel. 01 40 46 79 00). M: Odéon. Founded in 1686, making it the first café in the world. Voltaire drank 40 cups per day here while writing *Candide,* and his table remains what the owners call "a festimony of permanence." Marat came here to plot the Revolution and dodge the police. Figurines of other famous regulars line the café's back wall. History has its price—a 299F *menu*. Coffee 14F, beer 21-28F. Open daily 11am-2am.

Le Séléct, 99, bd. du Montparnasse (tel. 01 45 48 38 24). M: Vavin. Across the street from La Coupole. Trotsky, Satie, Breton, Cocteau, and Picasso all frequented this swank bistro/café. Today, the maudlin still gather. Coffee 6.50F at the counter, *café au lait* 35F, teas 22-25F, and hot chocolate 35F. Open daily 7am-3am. MC, V.

Café Mabillon, 164, bd. St-Germain (tel. 01 43 26 62 93). M: Mabillon. Dark, sleek, and conspicuous. See **Nightlife,** p. 294 for full listing.

SEVENTH ARRONDISSEMENT

The wealthy 7*ème* does not boast many budget options; look elsewhere (like the nearby 15*ème*) for inexpensive dining. Moderately priced gourmet restaurants, aimed at lawyers and government officials on lunch break, are more the norm. Some of the grocers and bakeries, including The Real McCoy and Veggie, have small tables for inexpensive eat-in. The restaurants below are worth the small splurge.

🔖 **La Varangue,** 27, rue Augereau (tel. 01 45 05 51 22). M: Ecole-Militaire. Turn right on rue de Grenelle from av. de la Bourdonnais, then take a left onto rue Augereau. Intimate atmosphere and varied menu replete with freshness. Lunch *menu* (55F) and dinner *menus* (77 and 98F) include dishes such as eggplant, chicken, and tomato tart, wine or cider, and dessert. *Grandes salades* with fresh vegetables (45F) and other vegetarian offerings. Open M-F noon-2:30pm and 7-10pm. Dinner reservations recommended. AmEx, MC, V. $$

▨ **Au Pied de Fouet,** 45, rue de Babylone (tel. 01 47 05 12 27). M: Vaneau. A small but well-known bistro, once frequented by Cocteau. Excellent place to try French home-cooking such as *confit de canard* (duck casserole, 60F) at bargain prices. Appetizers 13-20F, entrées 45-65F, dessert 15F. Open M-F noon-2:30pm and 7-9pm, Sa noon-2:30pm. $$

Grannie, 27, rue Pierre Leroux (tel. 01 43 34 94 14). M: Vaneau. Pretty yellow-and-blue dining room, particularly friendly atmosphere for the cool 7*ème*. Food ranges from decent to very good. Lunchtime *formules* include meat or fish of the day with salad and coffee (58F) or with salad, appetizer, and wine (80F). Wine 15-30F per glass. Open M-F noon-1:30pm and 7:30-10pm, Sa 7:30-10:30pm. MC, V. $$

Le Club des Poètes, 30, rue de Bourgogne (tel. 01 47 05 06 03). M: Varenne. Walk up bd. des Invalides toward the esplanade, turn right on rue de Grenelle and then left onto rue de Bourgogne. With a fisted salute and a *"Vive la poésie,"* Jean-Pierre Rosnay welcomes you to his club, established in 1961 to "make poetry contagious and inevitable." Beginning at 10pm, a troupe of readers including Rosnay and his wife grace your ears with the great French poets. Not cheap (100-150F for dinner with wine), but fun, with a good dose of culture. 96F lunch *menu*. Open M-Sa noon-3pm and 8pm-1am. AmEx, MC, V. $$

Chez Lucie, 15, rue Augereau (tel. 01 45 55 08 74). M: Ecole-Militaire. The newcomer on a street of competitive restaurants, in a small but lively room. Offers inventive creole cuisine including gumbos, crab, and chicken with lime and ginger. Three-course *menus* at 98F, 148F, with entrées 65-98F à la carte. Desserts like dark chocolate cake with rum (40F). Open M-Sa noon-2:30pm and 7:30-11:30pm. $$

Le Lotus Blanc, 45, rue de Bourgogne (tel. 01 45 55 18 89). M: Varenne. This Vietnamese restaurant, replete with banquettes in burgundy velvet and warm polished wood, is a neighborhood favorite as yet undiscovered by the throngs visiting the nearby Musée Rodin. For 59F the lunchtime *formule* serves up filling main dishes like caramelized pork or ginger chicken with rice, and dessert. Other dishes include spicy shrimp and cashews (63F) and curried squid (47F). Menu available in English. Open M-Sa noon-2:30pm and 7:30-11pm. $$

CAFÉS

Café du Marché, 38, rue Cler (tel. 01 47 05 51 27). M: Ecole-Militaire. This is the main location on delightful rue Cler for whiling away the afternoon hours amid bustling bakeries and produce markets. Good range of croissants, *brioches*, and a reasonable cup of coffee (12-22F). Open M-Sa 7am-midnight, Su 8am-4pm. MC, V.

EIGHTH ARRONDISSEMENT

The 8*ème* is as glamorous and expensive as one might expect of Paris. In fact, most of the charm of this arrondissement lies in its gratuitous extravagance. If you're not interested in participating in such exuberant wastefulness, there are some affordable restaurants to be found, especially on side streets around rue La Boétie.

▨ **Antoine's: Les Sandwichs des 5 Continents,** 31, rue de Ponthieu (tel. 01 42 89 44 20). M: Franklin D. Roosevelt. Walk toward the Arc de Triomphe on the Champs-Elysées then turn right on av. Franklin D. Roosevelt and left on rue de Ponthieu. This sandwich shop offers up a 35F meal (*panini*, yogurt, and a drink) on bread that is probably worth 35F on its own. The Buffalo sandwich (barbecued chicken and melted cheese on hearty bread, 27F) is not quite French cuisine. An incredible deal for the 8*ème*. Desserts and ice-cream bars 12-18F. Beer 12-18F. Take-out available. Open M-Sa 8am-7pm. $

La Table de Margot, 40, rue Ponthieu (tel. 01 53 96 06 88). M: Franklin D. Roosevelt. Follow directions to Antoine's above. Head here with your parents or to impress a date: French staples well done, with flattering lighting. Meat and fish entrées 67-69F, salads 56-58F. *Menu* includes appetizer or salad, kir, and a choice of entrée (89F). Open daily 11:30am-3pm and 7-10:30pm. AmEx, MC, V. $$

Le Singe d'Eau, 28, rue de Moscou (tel. 01 43 87 72 73). M: Europe. Monkey-waiters serve proper Tibetan cuisine in a very colorful dining room. Steven Seagal couldn't be wrong. Appetizers 18-40F, entrées 45-55F. Lunch *menu* 65F. Plenty of vegetarian options. English spoken. Open Sept.-July M-Sa noon-3pm and 7-11pm. AmEx, MC, V. $

Barry's, 9, rue de Duras (tel. 01 40 06 02 27). M: Champs Elysées-Clemenceau. From the métro, cross the Champs-Elysées and walk straight up av. Marigny to pl. Beauvau, take a sharp right onto rue du fbg. St-Honoré and turn left on rue de Duras. Head to Barry's to refuel after window-shopping on rue du fbg. St-Honoré. A clean, quiet, airy self-serve sandwich emporium with *panini* (22-32F), sandwiches (25-32F), and salads (39-55). Open M-F 11am-3pm. $

Vitamine, 20, rue de Bucarest (tel. 01 45 22 28 02). M: Liège. From the métro, walk up rue de Moscou. The restaurant is on the 1st corner on your right. Overlooking the lively pl. Dublin, with an outdoor summer terrace. Straightforward self-serve place with low-priced sandwiches and salads. English spoken. Sandwiches with excellent bread 13-20F, salads 22-35F. *Plats du jour,* such as mousaka with salad 35F. Several vegetarian selections. Open M-F 8am-4pm. $

CAFÉS

Fouquet's, 99 av. des Champs-Elysées (tel. 01 47 2370 60). M: George V. It is indeed filled with French stars of song and screen, but it is also filled with American tourists; the two groups rarely mix. Beneath its red awning rests classic French decor and snobbery so "French" that it seems like a caricature of itself. James Joyce dined here (and look what it did to him). Bank-breaking coffee and a chance to be seen, 25F. Entrées 90-140F. Open daily 8am-1am; food served noon-3pm and 7pm-midnight. AmEx, MC, V.

Bar des Théâtres, 6 av. Montaigne (tel. 01 47 23 34 63) M: Alma-Marceau. Pretentious people; unpretentious café. See p. 294 for full listing.

Fauchon, 26, pl. de la Madeleine (tel. 01 47 42 60 11). M: Madeleine. Primo, pricey snacks. See p. 155 for full listing.

Hédiard, 21, pl. de la Madeleine (tel. 01 43 12 88 88). M: Madeleine. Gourmet goodies. See p. 155 for full listing.

NINTH ARRONDISSEMENT

Except for a few gems, meals close to the Opéra cater to the after-theater and movie crowd and can be quite expensive. For truly cheap deals, head farther north. Displaced by the projectile force of the city's skyrocketing prices, many immigrants have found a home here, providing visitors to the 9*ème* with affordable North and West African, Latin American, and Middle Eastern delicacies.

Haynes Bar, 3, rue Clauzel (tel. 01 48 78 40 63). M: St-Georges. Head uphill on rue Nôtre-Dame-de-Lorette and turn right on rue H. Monnier and then right on rue Clauzel to the end of the block. The first African-American owned restaurant in Paris (1947), a center for expatriates and a former hangout for crazy kats like Louis Armstrong, James Baldwin, and Richard Wright. Very generous portions for under 100F. Soul food like fried chicken and fresh-baked corn bread (70F), Sister Lena's BBQ spare ribs (80F), and T-bone steak (90F): all served with creole rice, and red or string beans. New Orleans jazz piano Friday nights. Closed Aug. Open Tu-Sa 7pm-midnight. AmEx, MC, V. $$

Deli's Café, 6, rue du Faubourg-Montmartre (tel. 01 48 24 24 04). M: Rue Montmartre. A small, affordable café with great sandwiches like chicken curry on spinach or tomato bread (16-21F), *panini* (18-23F), and *brioches* (25F). Open daily 7am-2am.

Sarangui, Anarkali, 4, pl. Gustave Toudouze (tel. 01 48 78 39 84). M: St-Georges. Walk uphill on rue Nôtre-Dame-de-Lorette and branch right onto rue H. Monnier. On a secluded cobble-stone square. This north Indian restaurant is best in the summer when you can sit outside on the plaza. Tandoori, curry, *biryani* dishes (50-80F), chicken and lamb (55-75F), and veggie dishes (30-40F). Lunch *menus* 60-72F. Open June-Aug. Tu-Sa noon-2:30pm and 7-11:30pm, Su-M 7pm-11:30am; Sept.-May Tu-Sa noon-2:30pm and 7-11:30pm. AmEx, MC, V. $

Pizzéria King Salomon, 46, rue Richer (tel. 01 42 46 31 22). M: Cadet or Bonne Nouvelle. From M: Cadet descend rue Saulner and turn right on rue Richer. A popular kosher pizzeria in the heart of the 9ème's small Jewish community. The King Salomon (58F) pizza is cut in half, so that whoever cares more about the pizza gets to keep it. Individual pizzas 42-58F. Take-out available. Open Su-Th 11:30am-3pm and 6:30pm-midnight, Sa 6:30pm-midnight. $

CAFÉS

Café de la Paix, 12, bd. des Capucines (tel. 01 40 07 32 32). M: Opéra. On the left as you face the Opéra. This institution just off rue de la Paix (the most expensive property on French Monopoly) has drawn a classy crowd since it opened in 1862. There is a reason *paix* is pronounced "pay": coffee 26F, *café crème* 28F, ice cream 40-59F. The restaurant inside is twice as *cher*, with *menus* around 300F. Open daily 10am-1:30am.

Le Café Zephyr, 12 bd Montmartre (tel. 01 47 70 80 14). M: Grands Boulevards. An interesting café next to the Musée Grevin, founded by Auvergnats in love with Africa. Come for the North African decor, stay for the waiters in weird denim/red suspender outfits. Open M-Sa 8am-2am, Su 10am-8pm. MC, V.

TENTH ARRONDISSEMENT

While many tourists never see more of the 10ème than their Gare du Nord layover allows, those who venture out will find French, Indian, and African restaurants with reasonable prices. Catering to locals rather than tourists, these restaurants offer some of Paris's more colorful culinary creations. Passage Brady overflows with cheap Indian *restaux* and rue Lafayette with Japanese delights.

Paris-Dakar, 95, rue du fbg. St-Martin (tel. 01 42 08 16 64). M: Gare de l'Est. Senegalese cuisine served with West African charm (including mesmerizing Senegalese dance videos on the bar). Lunch *menu* (59F), dinner *menu* (129F), and African *menu* (179F) feature *tiébou dieune* (fish with rice and veggies) and the house drink *bissap*, made from the African flower *oseil rouge* and fresh mint, among other unique alimentations. Open Tu-Th and Sa-Su noon-3pm and 7pm-2am, F 7pm-2am. MC, V.

Le Dogon, 30, rue René Boulanger (tel. 01 42 41 95 85). M: République. Follow bd. St-Martin from the métro; rue René Boulanger is on your right. Named after the owner's hometown in Mali, this West African restaurant is steps away from pl. de la République. White walls, batiks, and animal pelts serve as the backdrop for curries, couscous, and affordable lunch *menus* (55F). Popular bar in the evening. Open M-F noon-3pm and 7pm-1am, Sa-Su 7pm-1am. MC, V.

Restaurant du Bourgogne, 26, rue des Vinaigres (tel. 01 46 07 07 91). M: Jacques Bonsergent. Walk with traffic on rue de Lancry, bear left on rue Jean and turn left on rue des Vinaigres. With wood-beam ceilings, red-checkered tablecloths, and family-style seating, this recently-renovated bistro is a provincial classic. Lunch *menu* (50F) and dinner *menu* (55F). Open M-F noon-2:15pm and 7-11pm, Sa noon-2:15pm. Closed August.

La 25ème Image, 9, rue Récollets (tel. 01 40 35 80 88). M: Gare de l'Est. Near the Canal St-Martin, this colorful café-gallery offers light salads and creative sandwiches (38-50F) for those waiting for a train. Open M-F 10am-midnight. MC, V.

ELEVENTH ARRONDISSEMENT

Like trailer-trash to a hog-fry, Tex-Mex, burger, and pizza chains have sprung up around the mall-like Opéra Bastille. However, a number of reasonably priced tapas bars as well as African, Asian, and French spots lie along rue Charonne, rue Keller, rue de Lappe, and rue Oberkampf. These play to play to a hip crowd.

Un Saumon à Paris, 32, rue de Charonne (tel. 01 49 29 07 15). M: Ledru-Rollin. Walk up av. Ledru Rollin and turn left onto rue de Charonne. In a school of its own, this Polish-Russian smoked fish and caviar bar masterminds fresh salmon and trout smoked in more ways than you ever dreamed possible (48-70F). Perojkis (44F), strudel (35F) and a selection of over 15 Vodkas. Especially tasty is the *saumon sauvage fumé à chaud* (hot smoked salmon, 68F). Bargain 3-course lunch *menu* 69F. Open M-Sa 10:30am-3:30pm and 6pm-1am, Su 6pm-1am. $$

Le Kitch, 10, rue Oberkampf (tel. 01 40 21 94 19). M: Oberkampf or Filles du Calvaire. Despite the dollar-store decor, this restaurant-bar catches a hip crowd with affordable, tasty, primarily vegetarian dishes. Gazpacho 29F, vegetarian lasagna 52F. Open M-F 11am-3pm and 8pm-2am, Sa-Su 8pm-2am. $

Le Bistrot du Peintre, 116, av. Ledru-Rollin (tel. 01 47 00 34 39). M: Ledru-Rollin. Walk up av. Ledru-Rollin. The luscious dark wood, curvaceous mirrors, and floral tiles of this original Art Nouveau bistro are a treat. The classic menu includes omelettes (32-35F) and duck with sauteed potatoes, the house specialty (69F). Entrées 48-82F and desserts 18-33F. Open M-Sa 7am-2am, Su 10am-8pm. MC, V. $$-$$$

Chez Paul, 13, rue de Charonne (tel. 01 47 00 34 57). M: Bastille. Go east on rue du Fbg. St-Antoine and turn left on rue de Charonne. Timeless (read: black-and-white) late-night hangout whose crowd ranges from neighbors to pretty young things. Friendly staff. *Escargots* (38F), steak with pepper, cognac, and potatoes (78F). Open Sept.-July daily noon-3pm and 7pm-2am, food served until 12:30am. AmEx, MC, V. $$-$$$

La Ville de Jagannath, 101, rue St-Maur (tel. 01 43 55 80 81). M: St-Maur. Walk along av. de la République and turn right onto St-Maur. Near Oberkampf, this colorful and incense-filled Indian restaurant serves vegetarian lunch (50F) and dinner (90, 130, 160F) *menus* with curries, daal, rice, and yogurt. Open Su-Th 7:30-11:30pm, F-Sa 7:30-12:30pm. Amex, MC, V. $$-$$$

Le Souk, 1, rue Keller (tel. 01 49 29 05 08). M: Ledru-Rollin. Walk up av. Ledru Rollin, turn left onto rue de Charonne and make an immediate right onto rue Keller. Bags of spices, mud walls, oil lamps, and blue pottery amid Arabic specialties. Entrées 38-75F; grilled meat dishes 85-88F. The Souk is also a late-afternoon *salon de thé*. Open Tu-Su noon-2:30pm and 7:30pm-midnight. Tea 3-9pm. Amex, MC, V. $$$

Café Moderne, 19, rue Keller (tel. 01 47 00 53 62). M: Ledru-Rollin. Walk up av. Ledru Rollin, turn left onto rue de Charonne and make an immediate right onto rue Keller. The laid-back sibling of the 3ème's Chez Omar (see p. 134). Make molehills out of the mounds of meat and steaming coucous (70-98F). The *salade maison* entrée (55F) is large enough for two. Open M-F noon-2:30pm and 7-11:30pm, Sa-Su 7-11:30pm. $$

Occitanie, 96, rue Oberkampf (tel. 01 48 06 46 98). M: Parmentier. In the heart of the Oberkampf district. Potatoes, cheese, sausage, and plaid successfully recreate the rustic south. Lunch *formule* 52-59F. Dinner *menus* 65-198F. Entrées 66-110F. Open mid-Aug. to mid-July M-F noon-3pm and 7:30-11pm, Sa 7:30-11pm. AmEx, MC, V. $$$

Au Trou Normand, 9, rue Jean-Pierre Timbaud (tel. 01 48 05 80 23). M: Oberkampf. Walk north on rue de Malte until it intersects rue Jean-Pierre Timbaud. Possibly the cheapest bistro in Paris, the Norman's friendly feel and 29F *steak frites* hook youthful regulars. Appetizers 10-15F, *plats du jour* 30F, desserts 9-10F. Open Sept.-July M-F noon-2:30pm and 7:30-11pm, Sa 7:30-11pm. $

La Banane Ivoirienne, 10, rue de la Forge-Royale (tel. 01 43 70 49 90). M: Faidherbe-Chaligny. Walk west on rue du Fbg. St-Antoine and turn right on rue de la Forge-Royale. Ivory Coast prints and *plats*. Entrées 60-80F. Dinner *menus* (95-140F). Live African music every Friday. Open Tu-Sa 7pm-midnight. MC, V. $$

CAFÉS

🔖 **Café de l'Industrie,** 16, rue St-Sabin (tel. 01 47 00 13 53). M: Breguet-Sabin. A huge and happy-ning café graced with neo-colonial touches and black-and-white prints. The Industrie swells with a trendy, but not pouty, crowd. Coffee 10F, *vin chaud* 24F, salads 45-58F; prices increase by 4F after 10pm. Open Su-F 10-2am, serves food noon-12:30pm.

🔖 **Pause Café,** 41, rue de Charonne (tel. 01 48 06 80 33). M: Ledru-Rollin. Walk along av. Ledru Rollin and turn left onto rue de Charonne. Once a people-drooling, name-dropping, terrace-posing sort of joint, Pause enters the millennium as a downbeat and friendly colorful café. This still-cool bar had a starring role in the recent film *Chacun Cherche Son Chat*. Excellent salads (40-50F) and cheap beer (15F). Open M-Sa 7:45am-2am, Su 8:30am-8:30pm. MC, V.

Le Troisième Bureau, 74, rue de la Folie-Méricourt (tel. 01 43 55 87 65). M: St-Ambroise. A funky café-bar. Relaxed mix of bar regulars and younger hipsters. Coffee 9F, Sunday brunch noon-5pm (85F). Open daily 10am-2am.

TWELFTH ARRONDISSEMENT

The 12*ème* is a good place to give your wallet a break. Although a number of restaurants are cluttered around pl. de la Bastille, others are located discretely throughout the arrondissement.

L'Ebauchoir, 45, rue de Citeaux (tel. 01 43 42 49 31). M: Faidherbe-Chaligny. Walk down rue de Faubourg St-Antoine, turn left on rue de Citeaux. Great balance of funky and French. Try the *foie de veau au miel et au coriandre* (veal liver with honey and coriander, 80F). Appetizers 30-60F, main courses 75-100F, desserts 25-40F. Open M-Th noon-2:30pm and 8-10:30pm, F-Sa noon-2:30pm and 8-11pm. $$

Le Cheval de Troie, 71, rue de Charenton (tel. 01 43 44 24 44). M: Bastille. Sneak into this restaurant like the famed Trojan horse, its namesake, and pillage the menu. Serving savory Turkish food in an authentic setting, the Cheval's lunch *formule* can't be beat. For only 55F, feast on an appetizer like *coban saleta*, with fresh cucumbers, tomatoes, and feta; a main course like *imam bayildi* (stuffed eggplant); and dessert such as rice pudding and *Sigara Bogregi* (feta, egg, and mint fried inside flaky pastry, 54F). Dinner *menu* 92F. Open M-Sa noon-2:30pm and 7-11:30pm. MC, V. $$

Le Square Trousseau, 1, rue Antoine-Vollon (tel. 01 43 43 06 00). M: Ledru-Rollin. This beautiful Belle Epoque bistro is well worth the small splurge that gets you innovative French cuisine. Sample roast chicken with 3 marinades (85F) or duck with olive purée (95F) with a glass of wine (15F and up). Save room for desserts like Grand Marnier soufflé with raspberry *coulis* (40F). Watch for the movie crews; the Trousseau has appeared in more than a few French films. Open daily noon-2:30pm and 8-11:15pm. AmEx, MC, V. $$$

Les Broches à l'Ancienne, 21, rue St-Nicolas (tel. 01 43 43 26 16). M: Ledru-Rollin. Walk along rue de Fbg. St-Antoine towards the Bastille column and turn left onto St-Nicolas. A shrine to all things rotisserie: meats and culture. Chicken, lamb, and a rollicking good time are always on the menu (72-88F). *Menu* 170F. Dinner and performance 135F; reserve ahead. Open Tu-Sa 12:30am-2:30pm and 8-11pm; M 12:30am-2:30pm. Jazz concerts on Fridays. $$$

THIRTEENTH ARRONDISSEMENT

The 13*ème* is a budget gourmand's dream. The Butte aux Cailles's restaurants and bars fill with the young and high-spirited; scores of Vietnamese, Thai, Cambodian, Laotian, and Chinese restaurants cluster in Paris's "Chinatown," south of pl. d'Italie on av. de Choisy, a large North African community offers Moroccan, Tunisian, and Algerian specialties in the restaurants near the St-Marcel métro.

BUTTE AUX CAILLES

Café du Commerce, 39, rue des Cinq Diamants (tel. 01 53 62 91 04). M: Pl. d'Italie. Take bd. Auguste Blanqui and turn left onto rue des Cinq Diamants; on the corner of rue Jonas. Funky place with a fruit-i-ful menu brought together by the jovial restaurant owner. Dinner *menus* (65, 89, 120F) include *éventail d'avocat aux framboises* (avocado with strawberries) and *entrecote sauce roquefort* with special sautéed potatoes. Bargain lunch *menu* 47-50F. Open daily 11:30am-3pm and 7pm-2am. Reservations recommended on weekends. AmEx, MC, V. $$

Le Samson, 9, rue Jean-Marie Jégo (tel. 01 45 89 09 23). M: Pl. d'Italie. Take rue Bobillot and turn right on rue de la Butte aux Cailles and then right on rue Jean-Marie Jégo.

Arty, mellow, and jam-packed. Homemade sausages flambéed in whiskey (40F) and *tagliatelle* with smoked salmon (49F). Lunch (68F) and dinner (78F) *menus*. Open M-F noon-3pm and 8pm-midnight, Sa 8pm-midnight. $$

Chez Gladines, 30, rue des Cinq Diamants (tel. 01 45 80 70 10). M: Pl. d'Italie. Take bd. Auguste Blanqui and turn left onto rue des Cinq Diamants; on the corner of rue Jonas. Serves southwestern French and Basque specialties on long wooden tables with red-checked tablecloths. Hearty main courses like *escalope de veau montagnarde* (country ham with cheese and mushroom sauce, 72F), salads (32-57F), and *escargots* (55F). Wines by the glass (14-16F). Open Sept.-July daily 9am-2am. $$

Le Temps des Cérises, 18-20, rue de la Butte aux Cailles (tel. 01 45 89 69 48). M: pl. d'Italie. Take rue Bobillot and turn right on rue de la Butte aux Cailles. Local restaurant cooperative hosts films and art events. Solid lunch (58F) and dinner (118F) *menus* include *pâté de foie* and *boudin* sausage with apples and *crème fraiche*. Open M-F 11:45am-2:15pm and 7:30-11:45pm, Sa 7:30-11:45pm. AmEx, MC, V. $$

🔲 **Chez Paul,** 22, rue de la Butte aux Cailles (tel. 01 45 89 22 11). M: Pl. d'Italie. Take rue Bobillot and turn right on rue de la Butte aux Cailles. The chicest of the Butte aux Cailles venues, Chez Paul has the recipe for success: a lovely terrace, bins of candy, and fashionable dishes such as the *assiette de cochonaille chaud* (warm pig plate including tail, groin, ear, and cheek, 80F). Open M-Sa noon-2:30pm and 7:30pm-midnight, Su noon-3pm and 7:30pm-midnight. Reservations recommended. $$$

Au P'tit Cahoua, 39, bd. St-Marcel (tel. 01 47 07 24 42). M: St-Marcel. Under a tent worlds away from Paris, this kitchen spins fabulous *magrebin* meals. The lunch *menu* (65F) offers *tabouli* or *briouats au thon* (tuna in a flaky pastry), chicken, olive, and lemon *tajine*, or *couscous merguez* (a spicy sausage). Various *tajines* (85-95F) and couscous (85-115F) entrées. Finish with fig, date, and apricot pastries (40F for a plate). Open M-F and Su noon-3pm and 7:30-11pm, Sa 7:30-11pm. MC, V. $$-$$$

CHINATOWN

Indochine, 41, av. de Choisy (tel. 01 45 85 55 00). M: Porte de Choisy. Through the green-trim and glass patio lies a long dining room. Friendly staff, and popular with local Vietnamese residents. House specialty Bo Bún (rice vermicelli, vegetables, and grilled beef, 38F), Phô soup specialties (36-40F), and desserts (17F). Open M and W-F noon-3pm and 7-11pm. MC, V. $-$$

La Lune, 35 av. de Choisy (tel. 01 45 84 89 61). M: Port de Choisy. An enormous selection of Vietnamese, Thai, Cambodian, and Chinese food in a restaurant adorned with laterns, wall paintings and plants, and possessing more character than many of its neighbors. Most dishes 30-45F. Open Th-Tu noon-2pm and 7-11pm. $-$$

CAFÉS

Cafés by day turn into bars by night. For the full listings, see **Nightlife,** p. 296.

Les Oiseaux de Passage, 7, passage Barrault (tel. 01 45 89 72 42). M: Corvisart. Art exhibits and live music.

La Folie en Tete, 33, rue de la Butte aux Cailles (tel. 01 45 80 65 99). M: Corvisart. A place to read magazines and write novels.

Le Merle Moqueur, 11, rue de la Butte aux Cailles (tel. 01 45 65 12 43). M: Corvisart. Cooler than the shade.

FOURTEENTH ARRONDISSEMENT

The 14*ème* is bordered at the top by the busy bd. du Montparnasse, which is lined with restaurants ranging from Tex-Mex chains to classic "untouched" cafés. Rue de Montparnasse, which intersects with the boulevard, teems with charming and reasonably priced *crêperies* (*menus* 40-70F). The central and pedestrian rue Daguerre is lined with vegetarian-friendly Asian, Mediterranean, and French restaurants (*menus* 40-60F). While the southern half of the arrondissement is mostly residential, a concentration of good-value restaurants (*menus* 50-80F) cluster on rue Didot.

RESTAURANTS

Phinéas, 99, rue de l'Ouest (tel. 01 45 41 33 50). M: Pernety. Follow the traffic on rue Pernety and turn left on rue de l'Ouest. Specializing in *tartes sucrées et salées* made before your eyes, this delightful restaurant doubles as a comic book shrine. Fantasy dining is completed by elaborate candelabras and a suspended glimmering gold crown. Entrées include vegetarian options (58-80F). Desserts include *tarte citron* (10-36F). Open Tu-Sa 9am-noon for take-away and noon-11:30pm. for sit-down meals. AmEx, MC, V. $$

Chez Papa, 6, rue Gassendi (tel. 01 43 22 41 19). M: Denfert-Rochereau. Walk down Froidevaux along the cemetery and the restaurant will be on the left at the intersection of Froidevaux and Gassendi. As Louis XIV might have said, *"le restaurant c'est moi"* (see **History,** p. 4). In this bustling delish eatery, Papa-nalia is the name of the game. Papa portraits and articles line the walls, and special Papa dishes fill the menu. *Escargots Papa* are prepared with a mushroom, tomato, cream, cantal cheese and butter sauce (54F). The best deal is the *salade boyarde* which contains lettuce, potatoes, ham, cantal, and *bleu de brebis* (36F). *Menu* served until 10pm on weekdays (55F). The nearby cemetery need not provoke fear: Papa is immortal. Also located in the 8ème, 10ème, 14ème, and 15ème. Open M-Sa noon-1am. $

Le Colvert, 129, rue du Château (tel. 01 43 27 32 56). M: Pernety. Follow traffic on rue Raymond Losserand and turn right on rue du Château. Offers French mediterranean cuisine such as *confit de canard aux baies roses* (duck pâté with bayberries, 85F). Affordable lunch (65F) and dinner *menus* (89F). Small and often busy, so dinner reservations are advised. Open M-F 10:30am-3pm and 7-11:30pm, Sa 7-11:30pm. MC, V. $$

La Route du Château, 123, rue du Château (tel. 01 43 20 09 59). M: Pernety. Walk with traffic on rue Raymond Losserand until it crosses rue du Château. The romantic Parisian bistro *par excellence:* mood lighting, lace curtains, courteous service, and exquisite food. Specialties include *lapin* (rabbit) sautéed in cider and mustard (80F). Appetizers 32-50F, entrées 80-95F, dinner *menu* (85F). Open M 7pm-midnight, Tu-Sa noon-2pm and 7pm-midnight. AmEx, MC, V. $$

Au Rendez-Vous Des Camionneurs, 34, rue des Plantes (tel. 01 45 40 43 36). M: Alésia. Cross av. du Maine, walk down rue du Moulin Vert, and turn right onto rue des Plantes. This vibrant local watering hole for artists and young couples. The *menus* consist of simple, delicately prepared dishes (76F). The *crousti tomate fromage entrée* is hearty and filling (26F), and the *truit* (trout) is soft and savoury (52F). Reservations recommended. Open M-F noon-2:30pm and 7:30-9:30pm. Closed Aug. $$

Les Petites Sorcières, 12, rue Liancourt (tel. 01 43 21 95 68). M: Denfert-Rochereau. Walk along av. de Général Leclerc, turn right onto rue Daguerre, left onto rue Boulard, and right onto Liancourt. The witch theme—however amusing—is secondary to the quality of the dishes. *Entreés* include *céleri rémoulade et haddock aux pommes* (creamed celery with haddock and apples, 48F). *Plats* include *confit d'épaule d'agneau au cumin* (lamb conserve with cumin, 88F). Open M-F noon-2pm and 8-11pm, Sa 8-11pm. $$$

N'Zadette-M'foua, 152, rue du Château (tel. 01 43 22 00 16). M: Pernety. Walk with the traffic on rue Raymond Losserand, and turn right on rue du Château. Congolese cuisine. *Sourire Congolais* (fish, tomato, pineapple, cream, and cucumber appetizer, 42F) and *maboke* (meat or fish cooked in banana leaves, 69F) served with a smile. Entrées (54-88F). *Menu* 85F. Open daily 7pm-2am. MC, V. $$

Aquarius Café, 40, rue de Gergovie (tel. 01 45 41 36 88). M: Pernety. Walk against traffic on rue Raymond Losserand and turn right on rue de Gergovie. A vegetarian oasis. The "mini mixed grill" dish includes tofu sausages, wheat pancakes, brown rice, and vegetables in a mushroom sauce (65F). Aquarius salad with goat cheese, vegetable pâté, and potato salad (55F). Desserts are light and feel almost healthy (16-35F). Open M-F noon-2:15pm and 7-10:30pm, Sa noon-2:15 and 7-11:45pm. AmEx, MC, V. $$

Crêperie de Josselin, 67, rue du Montparnasse (tel. 01 43 20 93 50). M: Edgar Quinet. On a street full of *crêperies*, this small restaurant stands out. Locals crowd the wood-paneled dining room with Breton lace coverings, table lamps, colorful wall mosaics and a collection of ceramics. Le Petit Josselin next door accommodates the overflow. Outstanding food at reasonable prices: crêpes *salées* 22-70F and *sucrées* 22-42F. Open Tu-F noon-2pm and 6-11:45pm, Sa-Su noon-midnight. $$

Au Produits Du Sud-Ouest, 21-23 rue d'Odessa (tel. 01 43 20 34 07; fax 01 45 38 53 95). M: Edgar Quinet. Bd. Edgar Quinet intersects with rue d'Odessa right near the métro stop; the restaurant is at the intersection. A specialty *confit* (conserve) shop by day, the rustic and casual bistro, decorated with sports trophies and plaid, is a lively dinner spot. The menu displays a snapshot of a smiling cow, and features a wide selection of typical southwestern meat *confits*. *Confit au canard* 65F. Lunch special *plat du jour* and coffee or wine 32F. Open Tu-Sa noon-2pm and 7-11pm. $$

CAFÉS

La Coupole, 102, bd. du Montparnasse (tel. 01 43 20 14 20). M: Vavin. Half-café and half-restaurant, La Coupole's Art Deco mirrors, chairs, tiled floors, and tables have hosted Lenin, Stravinsky, Hemingway, and Einstein. The menus are expensive, but you can probably still afford coffee (11F), hot chocolate (21F) or a *croque monsieur* (28F). Also, from 10:30pm on, the awesome three-course *"Menu* Faim de Nuit" includes dishes such as oysters, steak tartare with french fries and salad, and a lemon tart (132). Open M-Th 7:30am-2am, F 9:30pm-4am, Sa 3-7pm and 9:30pm-4am. Dancing on the weekends. MC, V.

Le Dôme, 108, bd. du Montparnasse (tel. 01 43 35 25 81). M: Vavin. The elegant 1920s marble tables, gilded mirrors (with engravings of flappers), and stained glass make it one of the best and most expensive cafés in town. Coffee 15F, sandwiches 22F. Open daily 8am-midnight. AmEx, MC, V.

FIFTEENTH ARRONDISSEMENT

Cheap, easy bistros and brasseries trip over each other on rue du Commerce, rue de Vaugirard, bd. de Grenelle, and near Gare Montparnasse. Inexpensive Middle Eastern eateries abound—**Mozlef** at 18, rue de l'Arrivée, and **Samaya** at 31, bd. de Grenelle, are two of the best (both open daily noon-midnight). Asian food also has a presence; locals lunch at Thai **Phetburi,** also at 31, bd. de Grenelle (open M-Sa noon-2:45pm and 7-11:15pm). Restaurants off of the main avenues rely on reputation, so they deserve the extra time it takes to get there.

Restaurant Les Listines, 24, rue Falguière (tel. 01 45 38 57 40). M: Falguière. Upscale cuisine that won't break the bank. Pretty interior with delicately prepared seafood and meat dishes. Appetizers 35F, 79F menu and Loire Valley wines (14-21F). Open M-F noon-2:30pm and 7-10pm, Sa noon-2:30pm. AmEx, MC, V. $$

Chez François, 106, rue St-Charles (tel. 01 45 77 51 03). M: Charles Michels. An exciting, motley *menu* (Greek mushrooms, rabbit Niçoise, pear pastry, cheese and wine, 70F) keeps locals fiending. Open M-Sa noon-2:30pm and 7-10:30pm. MC, V. $$

Chez Foong, 32, rue Frémicourt (tel. 01 45 67 36 99). M: Cambronne. Walk across pl. Cambronne; turn left onto Frémicourt. Superb Malaysian kitchen serves fresh entrées like *ikan pais bernyiur* (grilled fish in banana leaves with coconut, 59F) and exquisite coconut sweet potato pastries (35F). Lunch and dinner *menus* include appetizer, entrée, rice, and dessert (56F, 78-85F). Open M-Sa noon-2:30pm and 7-11pm. MC, V. $$

Café du Commerce, 51, rue du Commerce (tel. 01 45 75 03 27). M: Commerce. Since 1921, this brasserie has offered great food amidst lush courtyard greenery. The bistro *menu* (82F) and dinner *menu* (117F) feature smoked salmon with fresh cream, lamb with herbs, and chocolate mousse all destined to delight. Reservations recommended on weekends. Open daily noon-midnight. AmEx, MC, V. $$

L'Armoise, 67, rue des Entrepreneurs (tel. 01 45 79 03 31). M: Commerce. Walk to the end of Commerce and take a right. Gourmet restaurant worth a splurge. 3-course *menu*, mainly seafood, allows one to test drive dishes otherwise inaccessible to the budget traveler: crayfish and salmon with lemon and herbs, lamb with pâté, and crème brûlée (148F). Open M-F noon-2:30pm and 7-10pm, Sa noon-2:30pm. MC, V. $$$

Ty Breiz, 52, bd. de Vaugirard (tel. 01 43 20 83 72). M: Pasteur. Authentic Breton *crêperie* is a little slice of Quimper, from the fine and filling crêpes to the provincial friendliness of the waitstaff. Dinner crêpes from 17F to 51F, including the 41F *savoyarde* (cheese, bacon, onions, potatoes). Dessert crêpes 16-43F. Show them your *Let's Go* and get a free *kir breton*. Open M-Sa 11:45am-2:45pm and 7-10:45pm. MC, V. $$

Sampieru Corsu, 12, rue de l'Amiral Roussin. M: Cambronne. Walk into the pl. Cambronne and take a left on rue de la Croix Nivert, then turn left on rue de l'Amiral Roussin. A Corsican types out copies of his Communist journal while his wife warmly invites you to share a table with other members of the *lumpenproletariat*. Eat your fill of roast chicken and pay according to your means, though the suggested price for the copious 3-course *menu* is cheap (45F, pâté, cheese plate, and wine included). Open M-F 11:45am-1:30pm and 6:30-9:30pm. $

Piccola Italia, 70, rue de Vouillé (tel. 01 48 42 51 88). M: Plaisance. Follow rue d'Alésia under the bridge. Cute pasta place across the street from an historic bathhouse sporting the national motto. This corner of the city feels like the old neighborhood, with good prices to boot (50-55F for most dishes). Open daily noon-2:30pm and 7-midnight. MC, V $$

CAFÉS

🔖 **Aux Artistes,** 63, rue Falguière (tel. 01 43 22 05 39). M: Pasteur. Follow Pasteur away from the rails for two blocks and make a right. One of the arrondissement's coolest spots. Funky red walls, neo-Impressionist oeuvres, and a Hawaii license plate on the wall? Here, it all makes sense. Modigliani used to come here from the nearby Cité des Artistes (see **Sights,** p. 220). You can get a full meal too: lunch *menu* at 56F, dinner 78F. Open M-F noon-12:30am, Sa noon-2pm. MC, V. $$

SIXTEENTH ARRONDISSEMENT

If you are staying in the 16*ème*, eat elsewhere, as budget restaurants have a hard time staying open here. Make a gourmet picnic from the many fine food shops on rue Passy and av. Mozart, or the open-air markets on av. du Président Wilson, rue St-Didier, and at the intersection of rue Gros and rue La Fontaine (see **Food Markets,** p. 156). A good bet for restaurants is on rue de l'Annonciation, running perpendicular between rue de Passy and rue de Raynouard or on rue de Lauriston, close to Etoile.

🔖 **Casa Tina,** 18, rue Lauriston (tel. 01 40 67 19 24). M: Charles-de-Gaulle-Etoile. Walk up av. Victor Hugo, turn left on rue Presbourg and right on rue Lauriston going uphill. An upbeat Spanish restaurant—think bullfights, Hemingway, Gypsy Kings—decorated with painted tiles and vintage posters. Serves up tapas (18-89F), sangria, paella in an 89F lunch *menu*. 110F tapas *menu*. Open daily noon-2:30pm and 7-11pm. Reservations recommended. AmEx, MC, V. $$

Byblos Café, 6, rue Guichard (tel. 01 42 30 99 99). M: La Muette. Walk down rue Passy one block and turn left on rue Guichard. A Lebanese restaurant/*traiteur* in a bright, contemporary dining room. Hors d'oeuvres: *tabouli, moutabal* (pureed eggplant with sesame paste), and a variety of hummus dishes. Grilled meats and chicken 70-86F. Vegetarian meals include beautiful salads like the moussaka (eggplant in olive oil, tomato sauce, hummus, and onions, 34F). Takeout available for 10-20% less. Open daily noon-2:30pm and 7-10:30pm. AmEx, MC, V. $$

CAFÉS

Torréfaction de Passy, 28, rue de l'Annonciation (tel. 01 42 88 99 90). M: Passy. Walk up rue de Passy; at pl. de Passy, turn left on rue de l'Annonciation. Primo coffee beans from South and Central America give some of the richest brews in the city. Even at 12-28F a cup, an excellent proposition. Open M 9am-1pm, Tu-Sa 9am-7:30pm. MC, V.

SEVENTEENTH ARRONDISSEMENT

Far from the tourists, no restaurant in the 17*ème* can survive without a strong rapport with the locals. However, the variety of neighborhoods here implies an equal variety of cuisine. The best area to look for cheap eats, whether trendy and light or traditional and hearty, is in Batignolles, extending northward from rue des Dames.

Good options also exist between Parc Monceau and the Arc de Triomphe, among the many faceless, overpriced brasseries. Rue de la Jonquière (M: Guy-Môquet) is lined with Moroccan, Tunisian, and Algerian shops and restaurants.

Le Patio Provençal, 116, rue des Dames (tel. 01 42 93 73 73). M: Villiers. Follow rue de Lévis away from the intersection and turn right on rue des Dames. On the sunny terrace, indoors among green arbors, vines, and dried lavender, this restaurant serves staples of southern French cuisine: tomatoes, eggplants, olives, thyme, fish, and wine. Ample *grandes assiettes* (57-65F) or half-portions (37-45F). Desserts like chocolate draped with raspberry purée (34-37F). Often very busy, making service a bit slow and reservations necessary. Open M-F noon-2:30pm and 7pm. MC, V. $$

Restaurant Natacha, 35, rue Guersant (tel. 01 45 74 23 86). M: Porte Maillot. Take bd. Gouvion St-Cyr past the Palais de Congrès and turn right on rue Guersant. Follow the gray flannel suits to this local favorite. Extraordinary lunch selection: all you can eat buffet with hors d'oeuvres, fish, grilled meat, and desserts (85F). Smaller 2-course *menu* 65F. Dinner *formule* 110F. Open M-F noon-2:30pm and 7:30-11pm, Sa 7:30-midnight. Reservations recommended. MC, V. $$

🖼 **The James Joyce Pub,** 71, bd. Gouvion St-Cyr (tel. 01 44 09 70 32). M: Porte Maillot. Take bd. Gouvion St-Cyr past Palais de Congrès. Upstairs from the pub itself is a restaurant with stained-glass windows depicting scenes from Joyce's novels. It is no surprise that this Irish pub is the busiest in Paris. The spectacular brunch on Sundays (noon-3pm) is a full Irish fry: eggs, bacon, sausage, mushrooms, black and white puddings, beans, chips, and coffee (65F). Regular menu selections include Bunratty Boxty potatoes (30F), Ballybunion bacon with cabbage (55F), and Cu Chulann's chicken (75F). Downstairs, the pub pulls pints of what Joyce called "...Ghinis. Foamous bomely brew bebattled by bottle gagerne de guergerre..." Also serves as a tourist office for English speaking ex-pats. Televised sporting events and monthly concerts bring crowds; weekly advertisement in *Pariscope* lists times. Open daily 6am-2am. MC, V. $$

Aux Îles des Princes, 96, rue de Saussure (tel. 01 40 54 01 03). M: Wagram. Turn left off av. de Villiers onto rue Jouffroy then left again onto rue de Saussure. A hopping Turkish dinner spot specializing in charcoal-grilled lamb, beef, and chicken brochettes (40-70F). The moustached owner speaks a bit of French and no English, but hand gestures and patience will get you lunch and dinner *menus* (45-90F). Bottles of Turkish wine 60-65F. Reservations recommended. Open M-F noon-3:30pm and 6-11pm, Sa 6pm-midnight, Su noon-3:30pm. V, MC. $$

CAFÉS

🖼 **L'Endroit,** 67, pl. du Dr-Félix-Lobligeois (tel. 01 42 29 50 00). M: Rome. Follow rue Boursault to rue Legendre, and make a right. As cool during the day as it is at night. The 4-course Sunday brunch (12:30-3:30pm, 98F) heads a long menu featuring tandoori chicken (78F) and club sandwiches (54F). See **Nightlife**, p. 298 for the full listing.

EIGHTEENTH ARRONDISSEMENT

During the siege of Paris in 1814, Russian cossacks occupied Montmartre. They came to call the restaurants, where they grabbed quick bites between battles, *bistro* (Russian for "quick"). The Russians are gone, but the tourists are here in force, particularly around pl. du Tertre and pl. St-Pierre. Charming bistros and cafés are common between rue des Abbesses and rue Lepic. In addition to the listings below, **Chez Louisette** and **Au Baryton,** which are located within the St-Ouen flea market just north of the 18ème, offer *moules marinière, frites,* and live French *chanson* entertainment (see **Markets,** p. 311).

🖼 **Chez Ginette,** 101, rue Caulaincourt (tel. 01 46 06 01 49). M: Lamarck-Caulaincourt. Upstairs from the métro. An unspoiled slice of Montmartre, in an airy wedge-shaped room livened up by music at night. Locals come for inventive and inexpensive French cooking, like monkfish with prawn sauce (98F), eggplant stuffed with goat cheese

RESTAURANTS

(50F), and more conventional meat and fish dishes (78-98F), along with omelettes and salads (38-55F) on the diverse menu. Open M-Sa noon-2:30pm and 7:30pm-2am. Closed Aug. MC, V. $$

🖾 **Le Soleil Gourmand,** 10, rue Ravignan (tel. 01 42 51 00 50). M: Abbesses. Facing the church in pl. des Abbesses, go to the right end and take the rightmost of the three streets that diverge there. Arty ambience: imprinted cast-iron chairs, tiled table tops, paintings and scribbles on the walls, resident intellectuals. Perfect when you've OD'd on *coq au vin* and *boeuf bourgignon*, this *salon de thé* offers lighter fare including five-cheese tart with salad (58F), oriental seafood salad (65F), and delectable house-baked cakes and crumbles (30-44F). Open daily 12:30-2:30pm and 8:30-11pm. $$

Rayons de Santé, 8, pl. Charles Dullin (tel. 01 42 59 64 81). M: Abbesses or Anvers. From M: Abbesses, follow rue Yvonne le Tac away and turn right on rue des Trois Frères and left into pl. Charles Dullin. Serious about vegetarian cooking, they delight with vegetable tarts and omelettes imbued with spinach and leeks, seitan with paprika sauce (29-31F), or whole wheat couscous and soy sausage (35F). Excellent goat cheese on toast (26F). One fish dish: broiled cod (39F). Various fruit juices at 14F. Open Su-Th 9am-3pm and 6:30-10pm, F 9am-3pm; call ahead in the summer. $

Rendez-vous des Chauffeurs, 11, rue des Portes Blanches (tel. 01 42 64 04 17). M: Marcadet-Poissoniers. Walk one block north on bd. des Barbés and make a right. Off the beaten track, it maintains its earthy character despite rave reviews for an ambitious 65F menu served lunch and 7:30-8:30pm. Appetizers (18-30F) like apple with rabbit pâté and entrées (40-90F) like *canard bourgogne* keep 'em coming back. Open Th-Tu noon-2:30pm and 7:30-11pm. $

Au Grain de Folie, 24, rue la Vieuville (tel. 01 42 58 15 57). M: Abbesses. Like eating at home, except that you can have dessert even if you don't finish your asparagus casserole. Ranging from palatable to tasty, the dishes are various permutations of couscous, hummus, lentils, beans, and veggie pies and stews in portions so huge that eating *à la carte* may be cheaper than the 2-course *menu* (100F). Appetizers, including avocado in roquefort sauce, 20-40F. Entrees 50-70F. Desserts, like frozen bananas in hot chocolate, 25-40F. Open daily 12:30-2:30pm and 7-11pm. $$

Refuge des Fondues, 17, rue des Trois Frères (tel. 01 42 55 22 65). M: Abbesses. Walk down rue Yvonne le Tac and take a left on rue des Trois Frères. A narrow, red-painted room with two long tables and an ambience somewhat like a cabaret. Only two main dishes: *fondue bourguignonne* (meat fondue) and *fondue savoyarde* (cheese fondue). The wine is served in baby-bottles with rubber nipples; leave your Freudian hang-ups at home. *Menu* with *apéritif*, wine, appetizer, fondue, and dessert (92F). Reserve or show up early. Open W-M 7pm-2am. Closed for part of July and Aug. $$

Wassana, 10, rue Ganneron (tel. 01 44 70 08 54). M: Pl. Clichy. Walk up av. de Clichy and make the fifth right. Big pink dining room serving delicious Thai food five minutes from the corpse of Stendhal. Lunch menus (65, 85F), and a dinner menu (130F) include fish and lemon soup, chicken in coconut milk sauce, and sautéed beef with ginger and mushrooms. Appetizers 35-49F, entrées 48-75F. Open M-F noon-2:30pm and 7:30-11pm. $$

CAFÉS

🖾 **Le Sancerre,** 35, rue des Abbesses (tel. 01 42 58 08 20). M: Abbesses. Classic Montmartre café with some interesting dishes, from chili con carne (49-80F) to hearty crêpes *maison* (25-35F). Terrace. Open daily 7am-2am.

🖾 **Halle St-Pierre,** a quiet café open the same hours as its **Musée d'Art Naïf Max Fourny** (see **Museums,** p. 260), with assorted coffee and tea (7-20F), cookies, brownies, and cakes (15F), salads, and the major French newspapers. A very pleasant setting unnoticed by the tourists outside.

La Petite Charlotte, 24, rue des Abbesses. M: Abbesses. Pretty pink and blue café serving a 38F breakfast of croissant, coffee, and *orange pressée*, with 58-64F lunch *menus*. In-house *pâtisserie* with ice cream, and a nice terrace on the pl. des Abbesses. Open Tu-Su 9am-8pm.

NINETEENTH ARRONDISSEMENT

The ethnically diverse 19*ème* offers great budget dining options, especially in "Little Chinatown" where Chinese, Vietnamese, Thai, and Malaysian restaurants cluster along Rue de Belleville (M: Belleville). Greek sandwich shops line av. Jean Jaurès and rue de Crimée. The Parc des Buttes-Chaumont is a winning spot for a picnic lunch and a worthy place to jog it off.

Lao-Thai, 34, rue de Belleville (tel. 01 43 58 41 84). M: Belleville. Thai and Laotian specialties on an all-you-can-eat buffet with 12 different dishes, rice, and dessert. Perfect for the poor and hungry traveler. Lunch M-F 49F, Sa-Su 55F. Dinner Su-Th 74F, F-Sa 80F. Open Tu-Su noon-2:30pm and 7-11:15pm. MC, V. $

L'Atlantide, 7, av. de Laumière (tel. 01 42 45 09 81). M: Laumière. Exotic rugs and lattice wooden screens welcome you to this elegant Algerian restaurant, which is surprising, as they are *inanimate objects*. Starters 30-52F, *couscous* 56-102F, veggies 70-80F. Open M-Sa 7pm-midnight, Su noon-3pm and 7pm-midnight. MC, V. $$

Ay, Caramba!, 59, rue de Mouzaïa (tel. 01 42 41 23 80; fax 01 42 41 50 34). M: Pré-St-Gervais. From the métro, turn right on rue Mouzaïa. With piñatas and a Mariachi band, Ay, Caramba! fits right in this quiet, residential, French neighborhood. Good Mexican menu includes *fajitas* and *tacos* (84-89F), *Nachos caramba* (chips, cheese, *pico de gallo*, guacamole, and choice of beef, chicken, or chile, 43F). Margaritas 43F. Adjoining Tex-Mex grocery and liquor store. Restaurant open M-Th 7:30-11pm, F-Sa noon-2:30pm and 7:30-11pm. AmEx, MC, V. $$

TWENTIETH ARRONDISSEMENT

A traditional meal amid Belleville's cobblestones is a welcome breath of fresh air from Paris's crowded center. Further, a number of trendy cafés and bistros, such line rue St-Blaise in the south of the arrondissement.

Café Flèche d'Or, 102, rue de Bagnolet (tel. 01 43 72 04 23). M: Alexandre-Dumas. Follow rue de Bagnolet until it crosses rue des Pyrénées; café is on right. Near the Porte de la Réunion gate of Père Lachaise cemetery, this bar, performance space, and café is housed in a defunct train station and sits on a windowed terrace overlooking the old tracks. North African, Caribbean, and South American cuisine make love, not war, with nightly jazz, ska, folk, samba, and post-rock concerts (10-25F); frequent puppet shows; and occasional Sunday morning psychology cafés hosted by clinical psychologists. Lunch *formule* 69F, dinner *menus* 110-125F. Open Tu-Su 10am-2am, M 6pm-2am; lunch served Tu-Su noon-2:30pm, dinner served daily 8pm-midnight. MC, V (100F minimum). $$

Le Zéphyr, 1, rue Jourdain (tel. 01 46 36 65 81). M: Jourdain. Walk along Belleville and turn left onto rue Jourdain. An authentic Parisian bistro. Excellent food: check. Charismatic service: check. 1930s vintage decor: check plus. Unique dishes include *ravioli d'aubergine et cumin à la vinaigrette de menthe* (eggplant ravioli with cumin and mint vinaigrette, 48F). 4-course dinner *menu* 160F. If dinner seems expensive, try the lunch *menu* for 72F. Open M-F noon-2pm and 8-11pm, Sa 8-11pm. Busy at dinner time; reservations recommended. MC, V. $$$

Dalmier, 29, rue St-Blaise (tel. 01 43 72 16 95). M: Porte de Bagnolet. From the métro, follow rue de Bagnolet, then turn left on rue St-Blaise. Nestled into a cobbled street in the old Charonne neighborhood, Dalmier is a combination *pâtisserie* and restaurant where you can squeeze in with the midday regulars for some good, down-home *cuisine familiale*. Lunch *menu* 62F. Open M-Sa noon-7pm. $-$$

CAFÉS

Trattoria Courts Metrages, 1, rue des Envierges (tel. 01 47 97 08 40). M: Pyrénées. This Italian restaurant-café-bar is pleasantly hidden on a quiet road across from Parc de Belleville. Its outdoor terrace affords a magnificent view of Paris that includes many of the city's major sights. Coffee 12F. Open daily 11am-midnight. Lunch served noon-2pm, dinner 8pm-midnight, crowded bar after 10pm.

WINE BARS

Although wine bistros have existed since the early 19th century, the budget-friendly, wine-by-the-glass bar emerged only a few years ago with the invention of a machine that pumps nitrogen into the open bottle, protecting wine from oxidation. Rare wines, expensive by the bottle, have become affordable by the glass. Expect to pay 20F for a glass of high-quality wine. The owners carefully select the wines that constitute their *caves* (cellars) and are usually available to help out less-knowledgeable patrons. The wine shops in the **Nicolas** chain are reputed for having the world's most inexpensive cellars, although Nicolas himself owns the fashionable and expensive wine bar **Jeroboam**, 42, rue Artois, 8ème (tel. 01 42 89 29 75; M: Opéra). For a crash-course on French wine, see **Wine**, p. 126.

■ **Le Clown Bar**, 114, rue Amelot, 11ème (tel. 01 43 55 87 35). M: Filles du Calvaire. There are many imitators, but there is only one Clown Bar. Across from the Cirque d'Hiver, and frequented by real live carnies, this place is very cool and very popular. By the glass starts at 15F. Open M-Sa noon-3:30pm and 7pm-1am. MC, V.

Jacques Mélac, 42, rue Léon Frot, 11ème (tel. 01 43 70 59 27). M: Charonne. A family-owned wine bar and bistro. In Sept., Mélac lets children harvest, tread upon, and extract wine from grapes grown in vines hanging from the bar's storefront—call ahead for the exact date and don't miss the party. The Mélac wines sold here, however, come from his vineyard. Wine 18F per glass. Entrees include *gigot d'agneau* (69F). Jacques has a real sense of humor. Open Sept.-July M 9am-5pm, Tu-F 9am-midnight. MC, V.

Au Sauvignon, 80, rue des Sts-Pères, 7ème (tel. 01 45 48 49 02). M: Sèvres-Babylone. At the corner of rue de Sèvres and rue des Sts-Pères. Specializes in wines from the Loire valley. Articles and caricatures paper the walls to show the national recognition received by the owner for wines sold here. Lively crowd of well-groomed thirty-some-things. Come here the third Thursday in Nov. to sample the newest Beaujolais. Wine from 21F per glass. Open M-Sa 8:30am-9pm. Visa.

Willie's Wine Bar, 13, rue des Petits Champs, 1er (tel. 01 42 61 05 09). M: Palais-Roy-ale. Behind the Palais. This English bar has been popular since opening in 1980. Exposed wood beams, chic decor, and huge windows looking out onto the Palais and apartment of author Colette. International clientele. Huge selection of French wines (30-50F a glass). Open M-Sa noon-2:30pm and 7pm-1am. MC, V.

SALONS DE THÉ

T'ien Yi Heng said, "one drinks tea to forget the sound of the world." For Paris's upper middle class, this appears to be very true, with these latter-day salons springing up in the gentrified and gentrifying parts of town. Paris's *salons de thé* (tea rooms) provide low-key refinement and an afternoon respite not only for the ladies-who-lunch but also for an increasingly younger set. Service is often slow, so relax over a *tisane* (herbal tea), or sip an invigorating *menthe* (mint) or *tilleul-menthe* (lime blossom and mint). And don't forget the pastries.

■ **Angelina's**, 226, rue de Rivoli, 1er (tel. 01 42 60 82 00). M: Concorde or Tuileries. Audrey Hepburn's favorite. Belle Epoque paintings, gold-leaf interiors, and an atmo-sphere of propriety dampen all sounds but the clink of teacups. Afternoon tea (33F) and pastries (6-35F). The *chocolat africain* (hot chocolate, 36F) and *Mont Blanc* (meringue with chestnut cream, 36F) are house specialties. Open M-F 9am-7pm, Sa-Su 9:30am-7:30pm. AmEx, MC, V.

■ **Le Loir Dans la Théière**, 3, rue des Rosiers, 4ème (tel. 01 42 72 90 61). M: St-Paul. Named "The dormouse in the teapot" after the character in *Alice in Wonderland*, this bohemian salon serves curiouser and curioser caramel and jasmine tea (20F), coffees (12-30F), cakes and tarts (38-48F), and Sunday brunch (120F). Open daily noon-6:30pm. MC, V.

Ladurée, 16, rue Royale, 8ème (tel. 01 42 60 21 79). M: Concorde. Also at 75, av. des Champs-Elysées, 8ème (tel. 01 40 75 08 75), M: FDR. Typically intimidating for the Champs-Elysées, this tea-house sells chocolates galore in its adjunct store, most notably the large chocolate *macarons* (22F). Nearly as rich as the women sipping tea in the salon is Ladurée's hot chocolate. Open daily 8:30am-7pm.

Marriage Frères, 30, rue du Bourg-Tibourg, 4ème (tel. 01 42 72 28 11). M: Hôtel de Ville. Also at 13, rue des Grands Augustins, 6ème (tel. 01 40 51 82 50), M: St-Michel. Founded by 2 brothers who found British tea shoddy, this elegant salon offers 400 varieties of tea (35-41F), sandwich plates (55F), and cakes (40F). Tea *menu* (sandwich, pastry, and tea, 115F). The **Musée de Thé** upstairs chronicles Marriage Frères's imperialist forays into the Orient. Museum and salon open daily 10:30am-7:30pm; lunch M-Sa noon-4pm, brunch Su 12:30-7:30pm. AmEx, MC, V.

Muscade, 36, rue de Montpensier, 1er (tel. 01 42 97 51 36). M: Palais-Royale. In the Palais-Royale's northwest corner, Muscade is an expensive restaurant that becomes an affordable *salon de thé* in the afternoon. With mirrored walls and art by Cocteau (who lived above), Muscade is ideal for Sunday afternoons. 26 kinds of tea (22F) and an assortment of pastries (30F). Open M-Sa 3-6pm, Su 3-7pm.

FOOD AND DRINK

Something you can never do too often is assemble inexpensive meals yourself with staples such as cheese, pâté, wine, bread, and chocolate. Having learned its lesson in the Revolution, the government controls bread prices, so you can afford to indulge with every meal. Do as the French do: go from one specialty shop to another to assemble a picnic (most are closed between 1 and 4pm), or find an outdoor market *(un marché)*. A *charcuterie*, the French version of a delicatessen, offers cooked meats, pâtés, quiches, and sausages. *Crémeries* sell dairy products, and the corner *fromagerie* may stock over 100 kinds of cheese. *Boulangeries* sell several varieties of bread; buy in the morning or just before mealtimes, when the baguettes are steaming hot. Sometimes within the *boulangerie*, a *pâtisserie* sell pastries, and a *confiserie* stocks candy and ice cream. You can buy your produce at a *primeur*. *Boucheries* sell all kinds of meat and poultry, as well as roast chicken. For an adventurous carnivore, a *chevalier* sells horse-meat (look for the gilded horse-head over the door). A *traiteur* is a combination of a *charcuterie* and a *boulangerie*, they often sell *plats cuisinés* (prepared meals). Note that French storeowners are fantastically touchy about people touching their fruits and vegetables; unless there's a sign outside the corner store that says *libre service*, ask inside before you start handling the goods displayed.

The *baguette* is the long, crisp, archetypal French loaf, which, at about 5F, has kept many a budgeteer afloat on treks through Paris. The *bâtard* has a softer crust, the smaller *ficelle* a thicker, harder crust. *Pain de campagne*, made with whole wheat flour, is heavier inside than a baguette. *Pain complet* is a whole-grain loaf, and *pain à six céréales* is made with six grains. The cheap, government-subsidized bread you buy from a nameless bakery in Paris may well be the best you have ever eaten; make it your staple.

French pastry is far more interesting than the mere croissant. Breakfast pastries include the delectable *pain au chocolat* (croissant or *brioche* with chocolate) and *croissant aux amandes* (almond croissant). More elaborate choices are flans (egg-based, custardy cakes) and fruit tarts, including the *chausson aux pommes*, a light pastry with apple filling (see **Pastries,** p. 159). Many *gâteaux* (cakes) were invented in the 19th century, such as the chocolate-and-espresso *opéra* and the many-layered, cream-filled *millefeuilles*. *Gâteau Paris-Brest*, a cream-filled delight, is the only dessert named for a round-trip on the SNCF. *Clafoutis*, although it sounds like some kind of infection, is actually a moist kind of coffee cake, usually made with cherries. All of these pastries can be eaten in the afternoon with tea or after dinner as a dessert. Also good (or rather, divine) with tea are crumbly cookies like *macarons* and *madeleines*.

Supermarchés (supermarkets) have it all under one roof, although they make shopping less interesting. In some, it is up to you to weigh your produce, bag it, and label it: electronic weighing machines can be found next to the produce bins. If you're in the mood for a five-and-dime complete with men and women's clothing, photocopiers, telephone cards, and a supermarket, go to any of the **Monoprix** and **Prisunics** that litter the city (48 in Paris to be exact). For a listings of Monoprix and Prisunics throughout the city enter any one and ask for *Le Guide*. They are usually open during the week until 9pm, although the Prisunic at 52, av. Champs-Elysées, is open until midnight. Also look for the smaller chains such as **Franprix**, **Shopi**, and **Casino**. Starving students and travelers-in-the-know swear by the ubiquitous **Ed l'Epicier** and **Leader Price**. Buy in bulk and watch the pile of francs you save grow; it's possible to end up paying 30-50% less than you would elsewhere. Two of Ed's drawbacks: no non-Ed brands (alas, no Nutella), and some stores do not carry produce. **Picard Surgelés**, with 50 locations in the city, stocks every food ever frozen—from crêpes to calamari. Most branches offer free delivery.

Epiceries (grocery stores) also carry staples, wine, produce, and a bit of everything else. Open-air markets, held at least once a week in various arrondissements, remain the best places to buy fresh fruit, vegetables, fish, and meat. Competition is fierce, prices are low. Finally, you can grab simple food items, cigarettes, and lotto tickets at any corner *dépaneur* (convenience store).

SPECIALTY STORES

Alléosse, 13, rue Poncelet, 17*ème* (tel. 01 46 22 50 45). M: Ternes. An immense and exquisite selection of cheeses, perfect for classy evenings and extravagant sandwiches. Be prepared to pay for quality to match the store's strong smell. Open Tu-Sa 9am-1pm and 4-7pm, Su 9am-1pm. MC, V.

Androuet, 19, rue Daguerre, 14*ème* (tel. 01 43 21 19 09). Amid the artisanal works on display in galleries along rue Daguerre is this gallery of cheese. The brightly colored cheeses, intricately designed and displayed, are decorated in patterns of leaves or layers of raisins (*vendangeur*, 26.50F per piece). Open Tu-F 9am-1pm and 3:30-8pm, Sa 9am-8pm, Su 9am-1:30pm.

Confiserie Rivoli, 17, rue de Rivoli, 4*ème* (tel. 01 42 72 80 90). M: St-Paul. Candyland! Tubs of Haribo candy 50F. *Let's Go* does not recommend eating too many gummies. Open M-Sa 10am-7pm.

Ecouffes Alimentation S. Benchetrit, 16, rue des Ecouffes, 4*ème* (tel. 01 48 87 75 32). M: St-Paul. Walk in the direction of traffic down rue de Rivoli and turn right on rue des Ecouffes. Kosher staples: packaged goods, frozen meats, dairy products (*camembert* and Philadelphia cream cheese), and wine, much of it imported. Not too expensive. Shabbat candles, too. Open Su-Th 8am-8pm, F 8am-5pm. MC, V.

Fauchon, 26, pl. de la Madeleine, 8*ème* (tel. 01 47 42 60 11). M: Madeleine. A cross between a billionaire's supermarket and a museum, this most famous of Parisian food emporiums carries it all, from hard liquor to soft bread. Tuxedoed attendants float about the store helping clients find their favorite pâté and *galettes*. The best chocolate *macarons* in the known universe. Great food items for gifts, including packaged jams and *madeleines* in fancy Fauchon tins (see **Gift Ideas,** p. 306). As in most upscale *traiteurs* and *pâtisseries*, choose your items, have them written up by the walking attendants, take the slip to the cashier to pay, and then pick up your packages with the attendant. Open M-Sa 9:40am-7pm. AmEx, MC, V.

Finkelsztajn's, 27, rue des Rosiers, 4*ème* (tel. 01 42 72 78 91), and 24, rue des Ecouffes, 4*ème* (tel. 01 48 87 92 85). M: St-Paul. Eastern European nosh to-go-go, from strudel to latkes (13F). Gargantuan sandwiches 30-45F. Champion cheesecake 15F. Rue des Rosiers open Sept.-July W-Th 10am-2pm and 3-7pm, F-Su 10am-7pm; rue des Ecouffes open Aug.-June, M-Tu 10am-1:30pm and 3-7pm, F 9am-7:3-pm, Sa 10am-7:30pm, Th, Su 9am-1pm and 2-7pm.

Goldenberg, 69, av. de Wagram, 17*ème* (tel. 01 42 27 34 79). M: Ternes. This distinguished gourmet delicatessen sells Eastern European and Middle Eastern food, including pastrami, olives, and sausages, all priced for their chic customers. Some products are kosher, some are not; be sure to ask. Pastries (cheesecake, strudel, baklava, etc.) 10-25F each. Also doubles as an expensive café (bagel with cream cheese and lox 95F). Open daily 8:30am-11pm. MC, V.

La Grande Epicerie, 38, rue de Sèvres, 6*ème* (tel. 01 44 39 81 00). M: Sèvres-Babylone. This food annex to Bon Marché, one of Paris's most illustrious department stores, sells overpriced French ingredients. The produce arrangements are a work of art together with the extensive wine section. Sells the whole gamut for gourmands, as well as everyday eggs and milk, for those who simply can't be bothered with regular grocery stores. Open M-Sa 8:30am-9pm. AmEx, MC, V.

Hédiard, 21, pl. de la Madeleine, 8*ème* (tel. 01 43 12 88 88). M: Madeleine. The second most famous gourmet food store in Paris, curiously located on the opposite side of the square. Especially strong in wine and produce. It is, of course, all ungodly expensive. Open M-Sa 8am-10pm. AmEx, MC, V.

Jardin de Vie, 13, rue Brézin, 14ème (tel. 01 45 43 54 98). M: Mouton Devernet. Stocks healthy versions of your favorite French delicacies, from wine to boxed *croque tofu* (16F). Small selection of organically grown vegetables, natural beauty products, and household items. Health and nutrition advice is always available. Open in summer Tu-Sa 10am-7:30pm.

Aux Quatre Saisons, 5, rue Tardieu, 18ème (tel. 01 42 54 61 20). M: Anvers or Abbesses. From M: Anvers walk up rue Steinkerque and turn left onto pl. St-Pierre, which becomes rue Tardieu. This small health-food shop is filled with organic vegetables, fruit juices, and a variety of snack foods to energize your climb up Montmartre. Soy drink 11-13F, vegetable pasta 12F. Recipe booklets 11F. Open M 3:30-7:30pm, Tu-Sa 9:30am-1pm and 3:30-7:30pm. MC, V.

The Real McCoy, 194, rue de Grenelle, 7ème (tel. 01 45 56 98 82). American café and bodega for those who can't do without Total, Fruit by the Foot, and BBQ sauce (40F). Club, BLT sandwiches 24-30F, shakes 26F. Open daily 10am-8pm. AmEx, MC, V.

■ **Tang Frères,** 44 or 48, av. d'Ivry, 13ème (tel. 01 45 70 80 00). M: Porte d'Ivry. Look for no. 44 and go down a few steps to this huge grocery in the heart of Chinatown; or look for no. 48 and follow the sign through a parking lot to the much larger Tang next door. Rice, spices, teas, soups, and noodles in bulk. Sexy selection of exotic fruit. Stocks canned goods and high-quality, hard-to-find Eastern and Western produce. Cheap Asian beers (Sapporo and Kirin 7.80F), rice wines, and sake. There's also a butcher, a restaurant, a café, and a gourmet shop. No. 44 open M-Sa 10am-8:30pm; no. 48 open Tu-F 9am-7:30pm and Sa-Su 8:30am-7:30pm.

Thanksgiving, 14, rue Charles V, 4ème (tel. 01 42 77 68 29). M: St-Paul or Pont Marie. Don't leave home without it. American junk food (tortilla chips, Pop Tarts, and Snapple) at a premium (23, 35, and 20F). Adjacent restaurant. Open Tu-Sa 11am-7pm, Su 11am-6pm. Remember to bring your Visa (or MC), because they don't take...

Veggie, 38, rue de Verneuil, 7ème (tel. 01 42 61 28 61). M: Rue du Bac. Follow rue de Bac toward the Seine and turn right onto rue de Verneuil. Small health-food store has seen a future in organic grains, vegetables, spreads, and soy products for 25 years. Takeout or eat-in options include fresh carrot juice (15F), sandwiches (15F), and vegetable pies. Open M-F 10:30am-2:30pm and 4-7:30pm; snack bar open noon-2:30pm.

WINE STORES

For more info on what to buy and where to drink while out, see **Wine**, p. 126 and **Wine Bars**, p. 152.

Nicolas, 132, bd. Raspail, 6ème (tel. 01 43 26 64 36). M: Vavin. When you think of France, you think of wine, and so will Mom. But the overwhelming variety can be difficult to sort through. At Nicolas, the super-friendly English-speaking staff is happy to help you pick the perfect Burgundy and pack it in travel boxes with handles. Wines 20-250F. Numerous branches throughout the city. Open M-F 10am-6pm. AmEx, MC, V.

Les Caves Augé, 116 bd. Haussmann, 8ème (tel. 01 45 22 16 97). M: St-Augustin. The oldest wine-seller (or should we say cellar?) in Paris is somewhat intimidating, but hyper-knowledgeable. Not for the faint of pocketbook. Open M 1-7:30pm, Tu-Sa 9am-7:30pm. AmEx, MC, V.

Les Caves Taillevent, 199 rue Faubourg-St-Honoré, 8ème (tel. 01 45 61 14 09). M: Charles-de-Gaulle-Etoile. A dizzyingly large number of bottles in this giant wine emporium, which has tastings. Hail Bacchus! Open M 2-8pm, Tu-Sa 9am-7:30pm. Closed first 2 weeks of Aug. AmEx, MC, V.

FOOD MARKETS

In the 5th century, ancient Lutèce held the first market on what is now Ile de la Cité. More than a millennium and a half later, markets exude conviviality and neighborliness in every arrondissement, despite the ongoing growth of the *supermarché*. Most are open two to six days per week (always on Sunday), although the vendors often have stores nearby, open daily. The freshest products are often sold by noon, when many stalls start to close up. Quality and price can vary significantly from one stall to the next; you might want to stroll through the market before selecting your purchases.

Marché rue Montorgueil, 2ème. A center of food commerce and gastronomy since the 13th century, the marble-cobbled Mount Pride Market is composed of a number of wine, cheese, meat, and produce shops.

Marché Port Royal, 5ème. M: Censier-Daubenton. Make a right on bd. du Port-Royal in front of the Hôpital du Val de Grâce and make a right. Toward the intersection of bd. du Port-Royal. Colorful, fun, and busy. Some people with limited vocabularies might call it quaint. Find your favorite fresh produce, meat, fish, and cheese here; other tables are loaded with shoes, cheap chic, and housewares. Open Tu, Th, and Sa 8am-1:30pm.

Marché Mouffetard, 5ème. M: Monge. Walk through Pl. Monge and follow rue Ortolan to rue Mouffetard. Cheese, meat, fish, produce, and housewares sold here, and a few bakeries of high reputation. Open Tu-Su 8am-1:30pm.

Marché Monge, 5ème. M: Monge. Strong on produce and breads, but with all the basics, including Vietnamese and African prepared foods. Open W, F, Su 8am-1:30pm.

Marché Biologique, on bd. Raspail between rue Cherche-Midi and rue de Rennes, 6ème. M: Rennes. French New-Agers peddle everything from organic produce to 7-grain bread and tofu patties. Prices are higher than at other markets, perhaps due to the clientele, perhaps due to higher quality (depends on the booth). Open Su 7am-1:30pm.

Marché Raspail, on bd. Raspail between rue de Cherche-Midi and rue de Rennes, 6ème. M: Rennes. Small, open-air meat and produce market. A few household appliances (lamp shades and the like). Open Tu and F 7am-1:30pm.

Marché St-Quentin, 85bis, bd. de Magenta, 10ème. M: Gare de l'Est or Gare du Nord. Outside: a massive construction of iron and glass, built in 1865, renovated in 1982, and covered by a glorious glass ceiling. Inside: stalls of all varieties of produce, meat, cheese, seafood, and wine. Open Tu-Sa 8am-1pm and 4-7:30pm, Su 8am-1pm.

Marché Bastille, on bd. Richard-Lenoir from pl. de la Bastille north to rue St-Sabin, 11ème. M: Bastille. Fruit, cheese, veggies, exotic mushrooms, bread, meat, and cheap housewares stretch from M: Richard Lenoir to M: Bastille. Expect to spend at least an hour here. Popular as a Sunday morning family outing. Open Th and Su 7am-1:30pm.

Marché Popincourt, on bd. Richard-Lenoir between rue Oberkampf and rue de Jean-Pierre Timbaud, 11ème. M: Oberkampf. An open-air market close to many hotels. The street fills with fresh, well-priced perishables (fruit, cheese, groceries, bread). Less expensive than the Marché Bastille. Open Tu and F 8am-1:30pm.

Marché Beauvau St-Antoine, on rue d'Aligre between rue de Charenton and rue Crozatier, 12ème. M: Ledru-Rollin. One of the largest Parisian markets, with the cheapest produce in the city—for a reason. Browse before buying—quality is wildly variable. Also visit the market's large tag sale. Produce market open Tu-Sa 8am-1pm and 3:30-7:30pm, Su 8am-1pm. Tag sale open daily 8am-1pm. Busiest on weekends.

Marché de Grenelle, on bd. de Grenelle from rue de Lourmel to rue de Commerce, 15ème. M: Dupleix. A very popular open-air market with the market standards (meat, fish, fruit, veggies, cheese) as well as cookies, candies, flowers, housewares, and clothing. Open W and Su 8am-1:30pm.

Marché Président-Wilson, on av. Président-Wilson between rue Freycinet and pl. d'Iéna, 16ème. M: Iéna or Alma-Marceau. An excellent alternative to the 16ème's exorbitant restaurants. Competitively priced agricultural and dairy products as well as meat and fish. Spectacular flower stalls. Clothing, table linens, and other household goods available. Open W and Sa 8:30am-1pm.

Marché Gros-la-Fountain, 16ème. M: Ranelagh. Follow traffic on rue de l'Assomption then turn right on rue de la Fontaine. Loads of fish, cheese, vegetables, and flowers at competitive prices. Open Tu and F 8am-1pm.

Marché des Batignolles, 96, rue Lemercier, 17ème. M: Brochant. Turn left off rue Brochant onto rue Lemercier. An indoor market with all the usual food groups at fair, though not fantastic, prices. The complex also contains a small supermarket for the items on your shopping list that aren't animal or vegetable. Open Tu-F 8am-12:30pm and 4-7:30pm, Sa 8am-1pm and 3-7:30pm, Su 8am-1pm.

Marché Berthier, on bd. de Reims between rue de Courcelles and rue du Marquis d'Arlandes, along pl. Ulmann, 17ème. M: Porte de Champerret. Turn left off bd. Berthier onto rue de Courcelles then right on bd. de Reims. Hard-selling meat and vegetable vendors needn't try so hard—this market probably has the cheapest produce in Paris. Keep an eye out for North African and Middle Eastern specialties like fresh mint, Turkish bread, and baklava. Open W and Sa 8am-1pm.

Marché Dejean, rue Dejean, 18ème. M: Château-Rouge. Follow the rising numbers on rue Poulet and turn right on rue Dejean. A small selection of vegetables, fruit, meat, and fish catering to the mostly African neighborhood with specialties like yams and ginger roots. Surrounding streets are filled with shops selling music, fabric, and sculpture. Open Tu-Sa 7:30am-7pm, Su 7:30am-1pm.

BAKERIES

One of the daily staples of French life is the flaky, golden baguette, as well as the visit to the *boulangerie* to procure it. The *artisan boulanger* holds himself to as high a standard as any in the food craft, and government-controlled prices oblige you to taste his handiwork as often as possible. Ranging from the airy *ficelle* to the dark and hearty *pain de compagne*, bread comes in dozens of flavors to suit every purpose, be it sandwich, cheese platform, soup sopper-upper, or stand-alone pacifier for growling stomachs. Alongside it you'll find croissants, *petits pains*, and pastries crafted into flaky, creamy, chocolate and fruit-filled masterpieces. If the name escapes you, point to what you desire as politely as possible and you'll soon be in a crusty, doughy wonderland.

Boulangerie Julien, 75, rue St-Honoré, 1er (tel. 01 42 36 24 83). M: Pont-Neuf. Old shop selling breads with a sweet, hearty, doughy quality. Good variety of salad and sandwich options, as well as almond, hazelnut, and fruit pastries. Show up around noon for some of the freshest bread you'll taste. Open M-Sa 6:30am-8pm.

Boulangerie Martin, 40, rue St-Louis-en-l'Isle, 4ème (tel. 01 43 54 69 48). M: Pont-Marie. A picturesque bakery on the Ile St-Louis which makes one of the best baguettes in the city, the *Martin*, truly a masterpiece out of the oven. The pastries aren't too shabby either. Open Tu-Sa 7am-1pm and 3-7:30pm.

Maison Kayser, 8, rue Monge, 5ème (tel. 01 44 07 01 42). M: Maubert-Mutualité. Very high quality all around—wide range of breads, croissants (5-8F), fruit tarts (apricot, apple, rhubarb, etc.). A big serving of flan is just 7F. Open W-M 7am-8pm.

Poilâne, 8, rue Cherche-Midi, 6ème (tel. 01 45 48 42 59), off bd. Raspail. M: Sèvres-Babylone. Tiny shop that services the huge bakery responsible for Paris's most famous bread. Fragrant, crusty sourdough loaves are baked all day in wood-fired ovens. Unlike the baguette, these circular loaves don't come cheap; priced by weight, a loaf usually costs 38-45F. For just a taste, ask for a *quart* (a quarter-loaf), about 11F. Can also be bought by the slice *(tranche)*. Open M-Sa 7:15am-8:15pm.

Poujauran, 20, rue Jean-Nicot, 7ème (tel. 01 47 05 80 88). M: La Tour-Maubourg. Various country and herb breads, in addition to the standards; miniatures sold also. Tarts, cookies, and confections of superior quality as well. Open Tu-Sa 8:30am-8:30pm.

Beurre et Cacao, 35, rue de l'Annonciation, 16ème (tel. 01 42 24 00 55). M: Passy. From the métro, walk up rue de Passy; at pl. de Passy, turn left on rue de l'Annonciation. Top-quality *pâtisserie* on a pretty pedestrian street, fortunately out of view of McDonald's. Shoppers take a break to enjoy the tantalizing array of cakes, pies, tarts, breads, tea, and ice cream on the large terrace. Open Tu-Su 8am-7:30pm. MC, V.

Paul, 4, rue Poncelet, 17ème (tel. 01 42 27 80 25). M: Ternes. Folks come to purchase this upscale bakery's mystically aromatic crusty loaves, baked in wood-fired ovens. Bite-sized samples 4-5F. Pastries 5-14F. 25F *menu* includes a sandwich, dessert, and drink. Open M-Sa 7:30am-7:30pm, Su 7:30am-1:30pm.

Noailly, 36, rue Lepic, 18ème (tel. 01 46 06 10 92). M: Abbesses. Not a huge selection, but high quality spurred by the high competition nearby. Country breads (in the shape of animals), fruit pies, cakes, and tarts are all in abundance. Open Tu-Su 7am-8pm.

YOUR DAILY BREAD Among the 1300 *boulangeries* in Paris, how to separate the wheat from the chaff? Start with the definition. According to the craft, a baguette must weigh between 250 and 300 grams, measuring about 70cm in length and 6cm in diameter. The crust must be smooth and golden, ready to crackle under moderate finger-pressure (ask for it *"bien cuit"*). The underside, or "sole," should never be charred; beware also a honeycomb imprint, indicating accelerated cooking in a rotating oven—the taste will be cut short as well. The inside should be light and soft, subtly doughy and salty. The true connoisseur eats at least one whole baguette per day (twice the national average) for enough practice to judge for herself.

PASTRIES

Paris's pastries and chocolates are fail-safe cure-alls for the any ailment. Recently, American desserts—like brownies and coökies (koo-KEES)—have gained a strong following among Parisians but more traditional vices like the *tarte au chocolat* deservedly remain local favorites. Neighborhood *pâtisseries* or *confiseries* will satisfy any sweet tooth, but for serious sugar-lovers, the *crème de la crème* in specialty sweets can be found sprinkled throughout the city. Most *pâtisseries* also sell savory items, including sandwiches and quiches.

Gérard Mulot, 76, rue de Seine, 6ème (tel. 01 43 26 85 77). M: Odéon or St-Sulpice. Classic service, outrageous selection of handmade pastries, from flan to marzipan with virtually any kind of fruit. Sample heaven on earth, Mulot's *macaron*. Individual *tartes* 15F; eclairs 13F. Open Th-Tu 7:15am-8pm.

Le Nôtre, 48, av. Victor Hugo, 16ème (tel. 01 45 02 21 21). M: Victor Hugo. Also at 15, bd. de Courcelles, 8ème (tel. 01 45 63 87 63); and 121, av. de Wagram, 17ème (tel. 01 47 63 70 30). A small chain that sells wonderful pastries (17-30F) throughout the city. Join the local children pointing out their choices to *maman*. Buttery croissants (5F). Most branches open daily 9am-9pm. AmEx, MC, V.

Au Panetier, 10, pl. des Petits Pères, 2ème (tel. 01 42 60 90 23). M: Bourse. Known for its wide selection of breads, the modest and beautifully tiled Au Panetier—one of the oldest pastry shops in Paris—also creates delectable and affordable tarts (10-12F). Open M-F 10am-7pm.

Dalloyau, 5, bd. Beaumarchais, 4ème (tel. 01 48 87 89 88). M: Bastille. Stapled into the mind of every *gourmand* in Paris, Dalloyau is the first name in special occasion. Pricey, but exquisitely crafted and aesthetically delightful pastries (20-30F). Divine *macarons* (18F). 6 branches throughout Paris. Open Tu-Su 8:30am-7:45pm.

La Bague de Kenza, 106, rue St-Maur, 11ème (tel. 01 43 14 93 15). M: St-Maur. An Algerian *pâtisserie* serving a wide selection of tasty sweet and savory pastries (8-18F). The *cocas* are spicy and are stuffed with vegetables (8F). Open M-Th, Fr-Sa 9am-10pm, Su 10am-10pm.

Ladurée, 16, rue Royale, 8ème (tel. 01 42 60 21 79) M: Concorde, and at 75, av. des Champs-Elysées, 8ème (tel. 01 40 75 08 75). M: FDR. See full listing, p. 153.

Fauchon, 26-30, pl. de la Madeleine, 8ème (tel. 01 47 42 60 11). M: Madeleine. Melt-in-your-mouth chocolate *macarons* (21F). See **Groceries,** p. 155 for the full listing.

CHOCOLATE

Much like the fierce, warring Parisii tribe that first settled Paris in 250 BC, the current tribe of *chocolatiers* that controls the collective sweet tooth of the city comprises of bellicose, proud, and powerful individuals. Whether hailing from *Omnia Gallia* or the *Pays Bas*, the following establishments proudly purvey the gooiest of gooey confections, *tartes* so delicate that they might be worth their 300F price tags, and chocolate so dark that you will stare into the abyss.

■ **La Maison du Chocolat,** 8, bd. de la Madeleine, 9ème (tel. 01 47 42 86 52). M: Madeleine. Also at other locations, including 52, rue François 1er, 8ème (tel. 01 47 23 38 25). The whole range of milk to dark, and, for those tired of the usual consumption of solid chocolates, La Maison offers a mysterious distilled chocolate essence drink. Standard solid bar, 28-39F. Open M-Sa 9:30am-7pm. MC, V.

Debauve et Gallais, 30, rue des St-Pères, 7ème (tel. 01 45 48 54 67). M: St-Germain-des-Près. Also at 33, rue Vivienne, 2ème (tel. 01 40 39 05 50). M: Bourse. A "chocolate pharmacy" founded in 1800 by confectioner Sulpice Debauve. Need something for your nerves? They prescribe two almond milk chocolates, from among 40 flavors. Select your own *bouchée* (mouthful) for 18F. Beware: there is no treatment for sugar shock. Open M-Sa 9am-7pm. MC, V.

Jadis et Gourmande, 88 bd. de Port-Royal, 5ème (tel. 01 43 26 17 75) M: Raspai, or 49bis, ave Franklin-Roosevelt, 8ème (tel. 01 42 25 06 04). M: FDR. *The* place to buy chocolate Eiffel Towers, Santas, and thermometers: kind of like one-stop shopping. 33,60F for 100g. Open M 1-7:30pm, Tu-Sa 10:30am-7:30pm. MC, V.

Peltier, 66, rue de Sèvres, 7ème (tel. 01 47 83 66 12 or 01 47 34 06 62). M: Vaneau or Duroc. Also at 6, rue St-Dominique, 7ème (tel. 01 47 05 50 0). M: Solférino. A famous and famously self-congratulatory *chocolatier*. Nonetheless, great desserts. The house specialty, a *tarte au chocolat,* is more gooey than rich (16F). Open M-F 9:30am-8pm, Sa 9am-8pm, Su 8:30am-6:45pm. MC, V 150F min.

ICE CREAM

■ **Berthillon,** 31, rue St-Louis-en-l'Ile, 4ème (tel. 01 43 54 31 61), on Ile-St-Louis. M: Cité or Pont Marie. The best and most famous ice cream and sorbet in Paris. Choose from dozens of *parfums* (flavors), ranging from passion fruit and gingerbread to the standard chocolate. Singles 9F; doubles 16F; triples 20F. Sitting down is more expensive (double 32F), but you would probably be willing to sell your children to pay for this stuff: it's that good. Since lines are quite long in summer, look for stores nearby that sell Berthillon products; the wait is shorter and they're open in late July and Aug., when the main outfit shuts down. A list of the six stores is posted on the Berthillon window after it closes. Open Sept.-July 14; takeout W-Su 10am-8pm; eat-in W-F 1-8pm, Sa-Su 2-8pm. Also closed 2 weeks both in Feb. and Apr.

■ **Jadis et Gourmante,** 39, rue des Archives, 3ème (tel. 01 48 04 08 03). M: Rambuteau. Some of the richest ice cream in town. Also a *chocolaterie,* see p. 160. 1 scoop 10F, 2 scoops 15F, 3 scoops 20F. Open M 1-7:30pm, Tu-Sa 10:30am-7:30pm.

Pascal le Glacier, 17, rue Bois-le-Vent, 16ème (tel. 01 45 27 61 84). M: La Muette. Walk one block down against traffic on av. Mozart and make a left. Tangy and diverse sorbets, including particularly mouth-watering plum and mango. Rich dark chocolate rivals Berthillon's. 1 scoop 13F, 2 scoops 20F. Open Tu-Sa 10:30am-7pm. MC, V.

Etoile Manquante, 34, rue Vieille-du-Temple, 4ème (tel. 01 42 72 48 34). M: St-Paul. One of the row of bar-cafés that line rue Vieille-du-Temple, this one also serves takeout cones. While you're there, examine the starry ceiling and biomorphic wall displays, and excuse yourself to the sensational bathrooms. Open daily 10am-2am.

Dammann's, 20, rue du Cardinal Lemoine, 5ème (tel. 01 46 33 61 30). M: Cardinal Lemoine. Stylish tea house scoops 25 innovative flavors of ice cream and sorbet, such as After-Eight, Tiramisu, and Almond Milk. Open summer M-Sa 11:30am-8pm; winter 11:30am-6pm.

Raimo, 59-61, bd. de Reuilly, 12ème (tel. 01 43 43 70 17). M: Daumesnil. A large, traditional father-son-run *glacier,* Raimo serves everything from user-friendly cones of piña colada (10-25F) to sit-down projects like the *vacherin framboise* with cookies, almonds, meringue, raspberry sauce, and chantilly. Nearly 100 exquisite and unique flavors of *glaces* and sorbet. Open Tu-Su 9am-midnight.

Glacier Calabrese, 15, rue d'Odessa, 14ème (tel. 01 43 20 31 63). M: Edgar Quinet. Homemade *glace* flavors include mint, chamomile, and a very spicy ginger. Single 6.5F. Waffle cone add 0.5F. Open daily 10am-midnight.

SIGHTS

> Paris is an ocean. Sound it: you will never touch bottom.
> Survey it, report on it! However scrupulous your surveys and reports, however
> numerous and persistent the explorers of this sea may be, there will always
> remain virgin places, undiscovered caverns, flowers, pearls, monsters—there will
> always be something extraordinary.
> —Honoré de Balzac, *Père Goriot*, 1834

For all its grandeur, Paris is a small city. In just a few hours you can walk from the heart of the Marais in the east to the Eiffel Tower in the west, passing many of the city's principal monuments. You don't have a true sense of Paris until you know how close medieval Nôtre-Dame is to the modern Centre Pompidou, or the *quartier latin* of students to the Louvre of kings. With a map and comfortable shoes, you are ready to see Paris from ground-zero. The city is particularly manageable if explored by arrondissement.

TOURS

Although walking is one of the best ways to see the city, mechanized transport and multimedia spectacles may be just the thing for tired feet.

Parisbus (tel. 01 42 30 55 50) runs bus tours with English-language commentary that last over two hours. The ticket is good for unlimited trips on two consecutive days; you can spend as much time as you want at any of the sights (Trocadéro, Eiffel Tower, Louvre, Nôtre-Dame, Musée d'Orsay, Opéra, Champs-Elysées, and the Grand Palais) then hop on the next bus. Tickets 125F, students 100F, children 60F. For a fraction of the cost, some public bus lines offer less formal tours of Paris's sights (see **Buses**, p. 79).

Paristoric, 11bis, rue Scribe (tel. 01 42 66 62 06; www.paris-story.com), M: Opéra. A high-tech slide show montage showing highlights of Paris's monuments and cultural history with narrative and musical accompaniment. Covering two-millennia in 45 minutes, the show contextualizes the city within history, art, and architecture, so that you'll never confuse Neoclassical with Renaissance again. Shows daily on the hour Nov.-Mar. 9am-8pm, Apr.-Oct. 10am-8pm. Available in English. Admission 50F, students and children 30F, under 6 and the second child in a family free.

Bullfrog Bike Tours, (tel. 06 09 98 08 60; email BullfrogBikes@hotmail.com; bullfrogbikes.com). This may be your only chance to have Texans show you the sights of Paris. Good for those new to the city, these 3-4hr. bike tours take you from the Eiffel Tower to the Louvre and back, at a relaxing pace. Tours May 1-Sept. 15 meet every day on the Champ de Mars in front of the Eiffel Tower (look for the flag) at 11am and 3:30pm. Rain or shine. No reservations needed. Night tours also available. Tickets 130F or $20US.

Paris à velo, c'est sympa!, 37, bd. Bourdon, 4ème (tel. 01 48 87 60 01). M: Bastille. Leads 3hr. tours (look out, Gilligan!) from Bastille to Parc La Villette, to the Champs-Elysées, to Montmartre, and other destinations. Call days in advance to request tours in English and for larger groups (tours 10am, 3pm; 170F, under 26 150F). Rentals available with a 2500F (or credit card) deposit. 24hr. rental 150F; 9am-7pm 80F. ½day (9am-2pm or 2pm-7pm) 60F.

Paris-Vélo, 2, rue de Fer-à-Moulin, 5ème (tel. 01 43 37 59 22). M: Censier Daubenton. Tours in English for groups of 10 or more, which any number of riders may join. 150F per person, 26 and under 120F. Open M-Sa 10am-12:30pm and 2pm-7pm.

Bateaux-Mouches (tel. 01 42 25 96 10; info line 01 40 76 99 99) provide 1½-hour tours in English. (M: Alma-Marceau). Departures every 30min. 10am-11pm from the Right Bank pier near Pont d'Alma. Tickets 40F, ages 4-14 20F, under 4 free.

Vedette Pont-Neuf boats (tel. 01 46 33 98 38) are another option, with commentaries in French and English. (M: Pont-Neuf or Louvre). 1hr. Departures daily at 10:30am, 11:15am, noon, and every 30min. between 1:30 and 6:30pm. Leave from the Pont Neuf landing. Tickets 50F, under 12 25F.

Canauxrama, 13, quai de la Loire, 19ème (tel 01 42 39 15 00; fax 01 42 39 11 24). A glide down the minor artery of the **Canal St-Martin** trades the multilingual bullhorn and search lights for a subdued, shady river ride. Reservations required.

SEINE ISLANDS

ÎLE DE LA CITÉ

If any place could be called the heart of Paris, it is this slip in the river. Île de la Cité sits in the very center of the city and indeed at the very center of the Île de France, the geographical region surrounding Paris and bordered by the Seine, the Marne, and the Oise Rivers (see the map for **Daytripping,** p. 313). All distance points in France are measured from the *kilomètre zéro*, a circular sundial on the ground in front of Nôtre-Dame.

In the 3rd century BCE, when it was first settled, the Ile de la Cité *was* Paris (see **History,** p. 1). In the 6th century, when Clovis crowned himself king of the Franks, he adopted the oft-contested island as the center of his domain. At that time, Clovis ordered that work begin on the Eglise St-Etienne, the island's first Christian church, constructed over the ruins of a Roman temple. Six centuries later the basilica was razed to make room for Nôtre-Dame. In the 12th century work also commenced on the Ste-Chapelle under the direction of Bishop Maurice Sully. Completed in the 14th century, the cathedral is one of the most famous and beautiful examples of medieval architecture. Nowadays the island is swamped with tourists, but tranquility may be found at Pl. Dauphine and the Pont-Neuf park. For an overview of this area, refer to the color **map** of the **Fifth and Sixth Arrondissements** in the front of this book.

CATCHING THE WORM ON ÎLE DE LA CITÉ

■ Get to **Nôtre-Dame** (p. 163) early to beat the crowds, then visit the equally impressive **Ste-Chapelle** in the Palais de Justice (p. 165). After a round-trip jaunt over the **Pont Neuf** (p. 166) visit the eerily delightful **Conciergerie** (p. 166).

NÔTRE-DAME

We climbed the spiral staircase. Atop this cathedral, I expected to see Quasimodo around some corner. "It's marvelous, marvelous" I kept exclaiming to myself. "Isn't it sir?" the fat woman replied, brimming with pride at being the concierge of Nôtre-Dame. "You don't see that anywhere else. We're at the heart of Paris. It beats the Eiffel Tower, doesn't it?"

—Georges Brassaï, *Paris of the 30s,* 1932

*M: Cité. Tel. 01 42 34 56 10. **Open** M-F 8am-6:45pm, Sa-Su 8am-7:45pm. **Towers** open Apr.-Sept. 10am-6pm, Oct.-Mar. 10am-5pm. Free. **Tours** in English begin at the booth to the right as you enter, W and Th noon, Sa 2:30pm; in French M-F at noon, Sa at 2:30pm. **Free.** Confession can be heard in English. Roman Catholic masses celebrated daily. Treasury open M-Sa 9:30am-6pm; last ticket at 5:30pm. **Admission** 15F, students and ages 12-17 10F, 6-12 5F, under 6 free. High Mass with Gregorian chant is celebrated Sunday at 10am, with music at 11:30am, 12:30, and 6:30pm. **Crypt** open daily Apr.-Sept. 10am-6pm; Oct.-Mar. 10am-5pm; last ticket sold 30min. before closing. **Admission** 35F, students 23F, under 12 free.*

In 1163, Pope Alexander III laid the cornerstone for the **Cathédrale de Nôtre-Dame-de-Paris** over the remains of a Roman temple. The most famous and most trafficked of the Cité's sights, this massive structure was completed 200 years later in 1361. Around this time, three other cathedrals also dedicated to the Virgin Mary were built in the Paris basin. Nôtre-Dame was used particularly for royal marriages, most notably that of Henri of Navarre to Marguerite de Valois (see **History**, p. 4); royal burials were reserved for St-Denis (see **Daytripping**, p. 338), coronations for Reims (although Henri VI was crowned at Nôtre-Dame in 1431), and the most important relics for Ste-Chapelle (see below, p. 165). Nevertheless, Notre-Dame took pride of place in the public's attention.

Hence it was the setting for Joan of Arc's trial for heresy in 1455, and Napoleon's papal coronation in 1804. Revolutionary secularists renamed the cathedral Le Temple de la Raison (The Temple of Reason). During this time the Gothic arches were hidden behind plaster facades of virtuous Neoclassical design. Though reconsecrated after the Revolution, the building fell into disrepair and was used to shelter livestock. Victor Hugo's wildly popular 1831 novel *Nôtre-Dame-de-Paris* (The Hunchback of Notre-Dame) revived the cathedral's popularity enough to inspire Napoleon III and Haussmann to invest time and money in its restoration. The modifications by Eugène Viollet-le-Duc (including a new spire, the gargoyles, and a statue of himself admiring his own work) restored and reinvigorated the cathedral. Nôtre-Dame became a valued symbol of civic unity after its renovation. In 1870 and again in 1940 thousands of Parisians attended masses to pray for deliverance from the invading Germans. On August 26, 1944, Charles de Gaulle braved Nazi sniper fire to come here and give thanks for the imminent liberation of Paris. All of these upheavals seem to have left the cathedral unmarked, as have the hordes of tourists who invade its sacred portals every day. In the words of e. e. cummings, "The Cathedral of Nôtre-Dame does not budge an inch for all the idiocies of this world."

EXTERIOR. "Few architectural pages," Hugo proclaimed, "are as beautiful as this facade...a vast symphony in stone." Though begun in the 12th century, work on the **facade** continued into the 17th century, when artists were still adding Baroque statues. The carvings, designed to instill piety in a largely illiterate medieval population, were recently restored. The oldest work is found above the **Porte de St-Anne** (right), mostly dating from 1165-1175. The **Porte de la Vierge** (left), relating the life of Virgin Mary, dates from the 13th century. The central **Porte du Jugement** was almost entirely redone in the 19th century; the figure of Christ dates from 1885. Revolutionaries wreaked havoc on the facade during the ecstasies of the 1790s. Not content to decapitate Louis XVI, they attacked the stone images of the Kings of Judah above the doors, which they thought were his royal predecessors. The heads were found in the basement of the Banque Française du Commerce in 1977 and were installed in the Musée de Cluny (see **Museums**, p. 254).

The two towers—home to the cathedral's most famous fictional resident, Quasimodo the Hunchback—stare with grey solemnity across the square below. There's usually a line to make the climb, but it's well worth it. The perilous and claustrophobia-inducing staircase emerges onto a spectacular perch, where rows of gargoyles survey a rewarding view over the heart of the city, particularly of the Left Bank's *quartier latin* (in the 5*ème*) and the Marais on the Right Bank (in the 3*ème* and 4*ème*). The climb generally deters the tour bus set; you may even have the towers to yourself if you come early. In the south tower, a tiny door opens onto the 13-ton bell that even Quasimodo couldn't ring: it requires the force of eight people to move. For a striking view of the cathedral, cross Pont St-Louis (behind the cathedral) to Ile St-Louis and turn right on quai d'Orléans. At night, the buttresses are lit up, and the view from here is beautiful. The Pont de Sully, at the far side of Ile St-Louis, also affords an impressive view of the cathedral.

INTERIOR. From the inside, the cathedral seems to be constructed of soaring, and seemingly weightless walls. This effect is achieved by the spidery **flying buttresses** that support the vaults of the ceiling from outside, allowing for the construction of delicate stained glass walls. The transept's **rose windows,** nearly 75% 13th-century glass, are the most spectacular feature of the interior. At the center of the 21m north window is the Virgin, depicted as the descendent of the Old Testament kings and judges which surround her. The base of the south window shows Matthew, Mark, Luke, and John on the shoulders of Old Testament prophets, while in the central window Christ is surrounded by the 12 apostles, virgins, and saints of the New Testament. The cathedral's **treasury,** south of the choir, contains an assortment of glittering robes, sacramental cutlery, and other gilded artifacts from the cathedral's past. Far below the cathedral towers, in a cool excavation beneath the pavement of the square in front of the cathedral, the **Crypte Archéologique,** pl. du Parvis du Nôtre-Dame, houses artifacts unearthed in the construction of a parking garage. Essentially an archeological dig, the *crypte* offers a self-guided tour through the history of Ile de la Cité, allowing you to wander among architectural fragments from Roman Lutèce up through the 19th-century sewers. *(Tel. 01 43 29 83 51.)*

THE REST OF THE ISLAND

PALAIS DE JUSTICE. The Palais de Justice harbors the infamous Conciergerie, a Revolutionary prison, and the Ste-Chapelle, the private chapel of St-Louis. Since the 13th century, the buildings between the Conciergerie and the Ste-Chapelle have housed the **district courts** of Paris. After WWII, Pétain was convicted in Chambre 1 of the Cour d'Appel. All trials are open to the public, but don't expect a *France v. Dreyfus* every day. Even if your French is not up to legalese, the theatrical sobriety of the interior, with lawyers dressed in archaic black robes, makes a quick visit worthwhile. *(Spans the western side of the island. M: Cité. Tel. 01 44 32 51 51. Courtrooms open M-F 9am-noon and 1:30-5pm. Free.)*

STE-CHAPELLE. The Ste-Chapelle remains one of the foremost examples of flamboyant Gothic architecture and a triumph of medieval stained glass. Construction on the church began in 1241 to house the most precious of King Louis IX's possessions: the crown of thorns from Christ's Passion. Bought along with a section of the Cross by the Emperor of Constantinople in 1239 for the ungodly sum of 135,000 livres, the crown required an equally princely chapel. Although the crown—minus a few thorns that St-Louis gave away in exchange for political favors—has been moved to Nôtre-Dame, Ste-Chapelle still remains a masterpiece. Crowded into an inner courtyard of the *palais*, the church appears plain and unassuming from the outside, a simple structure topped with a 33m cedar steeple built in the 19th century. The Lower Chapel echoes this architectural modesty with a low ceiling and walls of peeling gold paint. The climb to the Upper Chapel, formerly reserved for royalty and their court, gives entrance to some of the most sublime stained glass in the world. The windows are large but close to the visitor and unobstructed by columns, creating an impression more intense than that of cathedrals. Their blues and reds combine to produce a claret-colored light, giving rise to the saying "wine the color of Ste-Chapelle's windows." Read from bottom to top, left to right, the windows narrate the Bible from Genesis to the Apocalypse. The glass you see is for the most part the same under which St-Louis prayed to his own personal holy relic. Check weekly publications for occasional concerts held in the Upper Chapel mid-March through October, or ask at the information booth. *(M: Cité. At the heart of the Palais de Justice. Tel. 01 53 73 78 50. Open daily Apr.-Sept. 9:30am-6:30pm; Oct.-Mar. 10am-5pm. Last admission 30min. before closing. Admission 35F, twin ticket with Conciergerie 50F, seniors and ages 12-25 23F, under 12 free.)*

MÉMORIAL DE LA DÉPORTATION. A simple but moving memorial erected for the French victims of Nazi concentration camps; two hundred thousand flickering lights represent the dead, and an eternal flame burns close to the tomb of an unknown deportee. The names of all the concentration camps glow in gold triangles that recall the Stars of David that French and European Jews were forced to wear on their clothing. A series of quotations is engraved into the stone walls—most striking of which is the injunction, *"Pardonne. N'Oublie Pas"* (Forgive. Do

Not Forget) engraved over the exit. Old men frequent the memorial and chant the *kaddish*, the Jewish prayer for the dead. (*M: Cité. At the very tip of the island on pl. de l'Île de France, behind the cathedral, and down a narrow flight of steps. Open daily Apr.-Sept. 10am-noon, 2-7pm; Oct.-Mar. 10am-noon, 2-5pm. Free.*)

CONCIERGERIE. Around the corner of the Palais de Justice from the entrance to the Ste-Chapelle, a dark but fascinating monument to the Revolution lurks ominously over the Seine. The northern facade, blackened by auto exhaust, is an appropriately gloomy introduction to the prison. At the farthest corner on the right, a stepped parapet marks the oldest tower, the **Tour Bonbec,** which once housed the prison's torture chambers. The modern entrance lies between the **Tour d'Argent,** stronghold of the royal treasury, and the **Tour de César,** which housed the Revolutionary tribunal.

Follow the "rue de Paris," the corridor leading from the entrance, named for "Monsieur de Paris," the executioner during the Revolution. These same stones were once trod by Queen Marie-Antoinette and the 2700 people sentenced to death between 1792 and 1794 who spent their final days in the Conciergerie. Past the hall, stairs lead to replicas of cells which give an impression of daily life in the cell block. Farther down the hall is the cell where Maximilien de Robespierre, the mastermind behind the Reign of Terror, awaited his death. The cell has been converted into a display of his letters, and engraved on the wall are Robespierre's famous last words: *"Je vous laisse ma Mémoire. Elle vous sera chère, et vous la défendrez"* ("I leave you my memory. It will be dear to you, and you will defend it"). Brought back to Paris from Vincennes while trying to escape with her husband and her hairdresser Léonard, Marie-Antoinette was imprisoned in the Conciergerie for five weeks before her head was ignobly shaven and severed from her body by the guillotine on October 16, 1793. Other exhibits tell the story of the Revolutionary factions which battled each other for power (see **History**, p. 5). Concerts and wine tastings are occasionally held in the Salle des Gens d'Armes. (*1, quai de l'Horloge. M: Cité. Tel. 01 53 73 78 50. Open daily Apr.-Sept. 9:30am-6:30pm; Oct.-Mar. 10am-5pm. Last ticket 30min. before closing. Admission 35F, students 23F. Guided tour in French at 11am and 3pm included. For English tours, call in advance.*)

PONT NEUF. You can leave Ile de la Cité from here by the oldest bridge in Paris, ironically named the **Pont Neuf** (New Bridge). Completed in 1607, the bridge broke tradition by not having its sides lined by houses. Before the construction of the Champs-Elysées, the bridge was Paris's most popular thoroughfare, attracting peddlers, performers, thieves, and street physicians. More recently, Christo, the Bulgarian performance artist, wrapped the entire bridge in 44,000 square meters of nylon. Unfortunately, the bridge itself is not of particular architectural interest, although it does have individual gargoyle capitals on its supports that can be viewed by craning your neck over the side or, better yet, from a bâteau-mouche. Alternatively, you can follow the directions below to **Ile St-Louis.**

SIGHTS

THE BEST PLACES TO KISS IN PARIS

■ In the garden to the west of the Pont Neuf (p. 166).
■ The 9th-floor terrace of Samaritaine (p. 303).
■ Under Pont Marie, also known as "Pont des Amoureux" (Lovers' Bridge; p. 166).
■ Below the C in Café de l'Hôtel de Ville, site of a famous Robert Doisneau shot of lovers embracing (p. 180).
■ The stairs of Montmartre, particularly between 30 and 32 rue des Trois Frères (p. 228).
■ The garden of the Musée Rodin, preferably near "Le Baiser" (p. 251).
■ Trocadéro esplanade, under the Eiffel Tower (p. 222).
■ From cinema: *Diva*, outside the Théatre du Châtelet, in Pl. du Châtelet (p. 168); *Last Tango in Paris*, on the métro quai at Bir-Hakeim (p. 191).

OTHER SIGHTS. The nearby **Hôtel Dieu** was a hospital built in the Middle Ages to provide aid to foundlings. It became more a place to confine the sick than to cure them—guards were posted at the doors to keep the patients from getting out and infecting the city. More recently, Pasteur did much of his pioneering research inside. In 1871, the hospital's proximity to Nôtre-Dame saved the cathedral—*communards* were dissuaded from burning the cathedral for fear that the flames would engulf their hospitalized wounded. The hospital's serene gardens lie within the inner courtyard. Across the street is the **Préfecture de Police,** where at 7am on August 19, 1944, members of the Paris police force began an insurrection against the Germans that lasted until the Allies liberated the city six days later. *(Open daily 6:30am-8pm.)*

ÎLE ST-LOUIS

From Ile de la Cité, a short walk across the Pont St-Louis will take you to the elegant enclave of **Ile St-Louis.** Originally two small islands—the Ile aux Vâches (Cow Island) and the Ile de Nôtre-Dame—it was considered suitable for duels, cows, and little else throughout the Middle Ages. In 1267, Louis IX departed for the Tunisian Crusade from the Ile aux Vâches, never to return, and the island was later named *in memoriam.* It became residential in the 17th century due to a contractual arrangement between Henri IV and the bridge entrepreneur Christophe Marie, after whom the Pont Marie is named. Virtually all of the construction on the island happened within a few short decades in the mid-17th century. Thanks to architect Louis Le Vau, this gave the Ile St-Louis an architectural unity, lacking in most Parisian neighborhoods. For an overview of this area, refer to the color map of the **Fifth and Sixth Arrondissements** in the front of this book.

Today, the island looks much as it did 300 years ago, still full of cows, dueling 11th-century Frenchmen, and ice cream eating tourists. Its *hôtels particuliers* and townhouses have attracted an elite that now includes Guy de Rothschild, the Aga Khan, and Pompidou's widow—what block parties they must have. Voltaire, Mme de Châtelet, Daumier, Ingrès, Baudelaire, and Cézanne number among its past residents. Floating somewhere between a small village and an exclusive *quartier,* the island retains a certain remoteness from the rest of Paris. Older residents say *"Je vais à Paris"* ("I'm going to Paris") when leaving by one of the four bridges linking Ile St-Louis and the mainland. In a rare burst of vigor, inhabitants even declared the island an independent republic in the 1930s.

QUAI DE BOURBON. Sculptor Camille Claudel lived and worked at no. 19 from 1899 until 1913, when her brother, the poet Paul Claudel, had her incarcerated in an asylum. Because she was the protegé and lover of sculptor Auguste Rodin, Claudel's most striking work is displayed in the Musée Rodin (see **Museums,** p. 251). At the intersection of the quai and rue des Deux Ponts sits the café **Au Franc-Pinot,** whose wrought-iron and grilled facade is almost as old as the island itself. The grapes that punctuate the ironwork gave the café its name; the *pinot* is a grape from Burgundy. Closed in 1716 after authorities found a basement stash of antigovernment tracts, the café-cabaret reemerged as a treasonous address during the Revolution. Cécile Renault, daughter of the proprietor, mounted an unsuccessful attempt on Robespierre's life in 1794. A young admirer of Charlotte Corday, she was guillotined the following year. Today it houses a mediocre jazz club, something which can no longer be denounced by the government. *(The quai wraps around the northwest edge of the island; it is to the left immediately after crossing the Pont St-Louis.)*

QUAI D'ANJOU. The island's most beautiful old *hôtels* line the quai d'Anjou, between Pont Marie and Pont de Sully. No. 29 once housed Ford Madox Ford's *Transatlantic Review,* the expatriate lit rag to which Hemingway frequently contributed. No. 9, quai d'Anjou, was the address of Honoré Daumier, realist painter and caricaturist, from 1846 to 1863.

LITERARY BAD BOYS OF THE ISLAND

■ Many a literary personage has watched the passage of the *bateaux-mouches* down this stretch of the Seine and past the Ile St-Louis, notably Jake Barnes in *The Sun Also Rises*. However, what has been truly of interest to the islands creative denizens has not been its view. At no. 17, the **Hôtel Lauzun,** built in 1657 by Le Vau (and currently under construction for the next few years), features gold filigree on the iron balcony and on the fish-shaped drainpipes. In the 1840s, the *hôtel* became the clubhouse for the *Hachis-chiens,* a bohemian literary salon with a hookah-heavy bent. **Baudelaire** and Théophile Gautier reclined with the magical pipes at its evening gatherings. Baudelaire lived here for a while, writing *Fleurs du Mal* in his attic apartment. Proust fans should remember that Swann lived nearby on **quai d'Orléans.** And, although Proust's Aunt Léonie found the island "a neighborhood most degrading," naughty Marcel found its streets, *bordels,* and beautiful boys amusing enough.

RUE ST-LOUIS-EN-L'ÎLE. The main thoroughfare of Ile St-Louis harbors shops, art galleries, and traditional French restaurants as well as the famous Berthillon *glacerie* (see **Ice Cream,** p. 160). The Hôtel Lambert, at no. 2, was designed by Le Vau in 1640 for Lambert le Riche and was home to Voltaire and Mme de Châtelet, his mathematician mistress. On either side of rue St-Louis-en-l'Ile, residential streets lead to the quais. *(To get there, loop around the end of the quai d'Anjou and walk down rue St-Louis-en-l'Ile.)*

Follow rue Budé to the **Musée Adam Mickiewicz,** 6, quai d'Orléans, the former home of the Polish poet, which now displays exhibits on his circle of exiled Polish artists, including Chopin and Chopin's death mask (see **Museums,** p. 263). Marie Curie lived on the other side of rue des Deux Ponts at 36, quai de Béthune, until she died of radiation-induced cancer in 1934.

EGLISE ST-LOUIS-EN-L'ÎLE. This church is more than just another Le Vau creation built between 1664 and 1726. If you get beyond the sooty, humdrum facade, you'll find a blazing Rococo interior decorated with gold leaf, marble, and statuettes and lit by more windows than seemed to exist on the outside. Legendary for its acoustics, the church hosts concerts throughout the year and every night in July and August (check with FNAC for details or call the church). *(3, rue Poulletier. Tel. 01 46 34 11 60. Open Tu-Su 9am-noon and 3-7pm.)*

FIRST ARRONDISSEMENT

In the shadow of the Louvre, home to kings and queens, stretches the first arrondissement. Today, the bed-chambers and dining rooms of innumerable rulers house the world's treasures. The Sun King's well-tended gardens are now filled with sunbathers, cafés, and carnival rides. While the Ritz stands in the regal pl. Vendôme, less-ritzy souvenir shops crowd rue du Louvre and Les Halles. Farther west, smoky jazz clubs pulse on bd. Sebastopol, while hopping gay bars crowd rue des Lombards. Just blocks from the Louvre, the Queens still hold court. For a map of this area, refer to the color map of the First and Second Arrondissements in the front of this book.

JARDIN DES TUILERIES

*M: Tuileries. Tel. 01 40 20 90 43. **Open** daily Apr.-Sept. 7am-9pm; Oct.-Mar. 7:30am-7:30pm. Free **tours** in English at varying times from the Arc de Triomphe du Carrousel. Call for details. Amusement park open late June to mid-Aug. and Dec. to early Jan. Rides 20F, under 12 15F.*

Sweeping down from the **Louvre** to the **place de la Concorde,** the Jardin des Tuileries celebrates the victory of geometry over nature. Missing the public promenades of her native Italy, Catherine de Medicis had the gardens built in 1564. In 1649, André Le Nôtre (designer of the gardens at Versailles) imposed his preference for straight lines and sculpted trees upon the landscape of the Tuileries. It is fitting that Louis XIV's mistress was responsible for the completion of the park, now a major pick-up area when the sun goes down. During the day the pleasures are more subdued. The elevated terrace by the Seine offers remarkable views of the Louvre, the gardens, the Eiffel Tower, and the Musée d'Orsay (across the river). From the central path, you can see the Obélisque de Luxor (in pl. de la Concorde), the Arc de Triomphe, and, on a clear day, the Grande Arche de La Défense. Turn around to face the **Arc de Triomphe du Carrousel** and the glass **pyramid** of the Louvre's Cour Napoléon. Sculptures by Rodin and others stand amid the gardens' cafés and *pétanque* courts. In the summer, the rue de Rivoli terrace becomes an **amusement park** with children's rides, food stands, and a huge ferris wheel.

JEU DE PAUME AND L'ORANGERIE. Flanking the pathway at the Concorde end of the Tuileries are the **Galérie National du Jeu de Paume** and the **Musée de l'Orangerie** (see **Museums,** p. 259 and p. 259). If the Orangerie is swamped in Monet's Water Lilies and the people who come to see them, the Jeu de Paume is a breath of fresh air. Constructed as a *jeu de paume* (an ancestor of tennis) court for Napoleon III, the building now serves as a space for contemporary art. When the Nazis took over Paris, they sent plundered art here, where much of it was labeled "degenerate" and burned.

PALAIS DES TUILERIES. At the other end of the gardens once stood the Palais des Tuileries, which stretched along the Jardin du Carrousel, forming the western wall of the Louvre. In 1791, Louis XVI and Marie-Antoinette attempted, unsuccessfully, to flee this palace, where they had been kept after a mob of Parisian housewives dragged them back from Versailles. Napoleon lived here before his exile. Louis XVIII was chased out upon Napoleon's return in 1814. Louis-Philippe fled in similar haste during the Revolution of 1848, and in 1870, the Empress Eugénie scrambled out as the mob crashed in the main entrance. Nine months later, as forces streamed into the city to crush the Commune, a *communard* packed the palace with gunpowder, tar, and oil, and set it on fire. The ruins survived until 1882 when the Municipal Council had them flattened.

PLACE VENDÔME

Stately Place Vendôme, three blocks north along rue de Castiglione from the Tuileries, was begun in 1687 by Louis XIV. Designed by Jules Hardouin-Mansart, the *place* was built to house embassies, but bankers created lavish private homes for themselves within the elegant facades. Today, the smell of money is still in the air: bankers, perfumers, and jewelers, including Cartier (at no. 7), line the square.

In the center of pl. Vendôme, Napoleon stands atop a large **column,** dressed as Caesar. In 1805, Napoleon erected the work, modeled after Trajan's column in Rome, and surrounded it with reliefs of military exploits. After Napoleon's exile, the Royalist government arrested the sculptor and forced him, on penalty of execution, to get rid of it. For all his pains, the return of Napoleon from Elba soon brought the original statue back to its perch. Over the next 60 years it would be replaced by the white flag of the ancient monarchy, a renewed Napoleon in military garb, and a classical Napoleon modeled after the original. Dur-

PUTTIN' ON THE... Founded by César Ritz at the turn of the century, the unaffordably opulent Ritz hotel (no. 15 Place Vendôme) stands as a monument to both wealth and misery. It was here where Princess Diana had her last meal, where American Ambassador Pamela Harriman died in 1997 while swimming in the pool, and where Hemingway escaped the grind of the Left Bank to drink (and drink, and drink some more). After riding into Paris with the U.S. Army in 1944, Hemingway gathered Resistance troops and went off to liberate the Ritz. Greeted by his old chum, the assistant manager, Hemingway proceeded to order 73 dry martinis.

ing the Commune, a group led by Gustave Courbet toppled the entire column, planning to replace it with a monument to the "Federation of Nations and the Universal Republic." The original column was recreated with new bronze reliefs, at Courbet's expense.

PALAIS-ROYAL AND SURROUNDINGS

PALAIS-ROYAL. The once regal and racy Palais-Royal lies farther down rue de Rivoli, across from the Louvre. Constructed in 1632 by Jacques Lemercier as Cardinal Richelieu's Palais Cardinal, it became a Palais Royal when Richelieu gave it to Louis XIII, a few years before both of them died. Louis's widow moved in after his death, preferring the palace to the Louvre, and gave the home its current name. Louis XIV was the first king to inhabit the palace, and it was from here that, as a child, he fled when the Fronde uprising broke out. In 1784, the broke Duc de Chartres rented out the elegant buildings that enclose the palace's formal garden, turning the complex into an 18th-century shopping mall with boutiques, restaurants, theaters, wax museums, and gambling joints. Its covered arcades were a favorite for prostitutes and lewd encounters, a reputation it unfortunately no longer holds. 18th-century malls, however, do seem to fan the flames of revolution. On July 12, 1789, 26-year-old Camille Desmoulins leaped onto a café table here and urged his fellow citizens to arm themselves, shouting, "I would rather die than submit to servitude." The crowd filed out and was soon skirmishing with cavalry in the Tuileries garden. The Revolutions of 1830 and 1848 also began with angry crowds in these gardens. In the second half of the 19th century, Haussmann's boulevards regentrified the area and moneyed aristocrats moved back in.

Today, the 1*er*'s galleries contain shops and cafés with splendid views of the palace fountain, flower beds, and **gardens.** In summer, the fountain becomes a mecca for tourists in need of a foot bath. (*Fountain open daily June-Aug. 7am-11pm; Sept. 7am-9:30pm; Oct.-Mar. 7am-8:30pm; Apr.-May 7am-10:15pm.*) The floors above the cafés and shops are occupied by the Ministry of Culture and the Conseil d'État. In the central courtyard, the **colonnes de Buren**—a set of black and white striped pillars—are as controversial today as they were when installed by artist Daniel Buren in 1986.

COMÉDIE FRANÇAISE. On the southwestern corner of the Palais-Royal, facing the Louvre, the Comédie Française is home to France's leading dramatic troupe (see **National Theaters,** p. 269). Built in 1790 by architect Victor Louis, the theater became the first permanent home for the Comedie Française troupe, which was created by Louis XIV in 1680. The entrance displays busts of famous actors by celebrated sculptors, including Mirabeau by Rodin, Talma by David, and Voltaire by Houdon. Ironically, Molière, the company's founder, took ill here on stage while playing the role of the Imaginary Invalid. The chair onto which he collapsed can still be seen. At the corner of rue Molière and rue Richelieu, Visconti's **Fontaine de Molière** is only a few steps from where Molière died at no. 40.

BURN, BABY, BURN

■ Parisians love to spend their days, especially during outbreaks of revolution, burning their beautiful buildings. The sights of these former landmarks, or their reconstructed versions, are an excellent, if not invisible, addition to any Parisian itinerary. Formerly closing off the quadrangle of the Louvre, and the sight of many an unsuccessful royal attempt to flee an angry mob, the **Palais des Tuileries** (below) was finally torched by the *communards* in 1870. In the next year of Communard frenzy, they set the **Hôtel de Ville** (p. 180) ablaze, and for eight days burned it down to the frame. It has since been rebuilt, but only a horde of pissed-off shopkeepers or foreign heads of state can enter without joining a group tour. During the May 1968 riots, students broke into the **Théâtre de l'Odéon** (p. 187) and destroyed much of the interior, before police found them and quelled the party. Perhaps the most famous of no-longer-with-us sights is the king's former prison, the **Bastille** (p. 209). The anniversary of the storming is accompanied with life-threatening fireworks, pomp, and Jaques Chirac in person (p. 277).

STATUE OF JOAN OF ARC. When the Burgundians and the English occupied Paris in 1429, Joan of Arc was hit by an arrow while attempting to liberate the city at what is now 163, rue St-Honoré. Her troops carried her back to pl. André-Malraux, but the wound was serious and the attack was called off. A shining **statue of Joan of Arc** commemorates the saint on pl. des Pyramides.

LES HALLES AND SURROUNDINGS

ÉGLISE DE ST-EUSTACHE. The Eglise de St-Eustache towers over Les Halles. Eustache (Eustatius) was a Roman general who adopted Christianity upon seeing the sign of a cross between the antlers of a deer, although why he was looking there has never been settled. As punishment (for converting, not antler weirdness), the Romans locked him and his family into a brass bull that was placed over a fire until it became white-hot. Construction of the church in his honor began in 1532 and dragged on for over a century. In 1754, the unfinished facade was demolished and replaced with the Romanesque one that stands today—incongruous with the rest of the Gothic building but appropriate for its Roman namesake. Richelieu, Molière, and Mme de Pompadour were all baptized here. Louis XIV received communion in its sanctuary, and Mozart chose to have his mother's funeral here. The chapels contain paintings by Rubens, American artist Keith Haring's glittering triptych, *Life of Christ*, and British artist Raymond Mason's *Departure of the Fruits and Vegetables from the Heart of Paris*, commemorating the closing of the market at Les Halles in February, 1969. Summer concerts are played on the exquisite organ, commemorating St-Eustache's premiers of Berlioz's *Te Deum* and Liszt's *Messiah* in 1886. In front of the church, Henri de Miller's 1986 sculpture *The Listener* features a huge human head and hand in front of the church. *(M: Les Halles. Tel. 01 42 36 31 05. Open June-Aug. M-F 10am-8pm, Sa 9am-12:30pm and 2:30-8pm; Sept.-May M-F 9am-7pm. High Mass with choir and organ, Su 11am. Organ tickets 80-150F.)*

LES HALLES. Emile Zola called Les Halles "*le ventre de Paris*" ("the belly of Paris"). A sprawling food market since 1135, Les Halles received a much-needed face-lift in the 1850s with the construction of large iron-and-glass pavilions to shelter the vendors' stalls. Designed by Victor Baltard, the pavilions resembled the one that still stands over the small market at the Carreau du Temple in the 3*ème*. In 1970, authorities moved the old market to a suburb near Orly. Politicians and city planners debated how to fill "*le trou des Halles*" ("the hole of Les Halles"), 106 open acres that presented Paris with the largest urban redesign opportunity since Haussmannization. Most of the city adored the elegant pavilions and wanted to see them preserved. But transport-happy planners destroyed the pavilions to build a subterranean transfer-point between the métro and the new commuter rail, the RER. The city retained architects Claude Vasconti and Georges Penreach to replace the pavilions with a subterranean shopping mall, the **Forum des Halles.** If the markets of Les Halles were once Paris's belly, then this underground maze is surely its bowels. Descend on one of the four main entrances to discover over 200 boutiques and three movie theaters. Putting the mall underground allowed its designers to landscape the vast Les Halles quadrangle with greenery, statues, and fountains. Striking a delicate balance between hypermodernity and *verdure*, the gardens avoid some of the aesthetic pitfalls of the forum beneath them. Both forum and gardens, however, present the danger of pickpockets. Hold onto your wallet and stay above ground at night.

BOURSE DU COMMERCE. Between rue du Louvre and the Forum des Halles, the large round Bourse du Commerce brokers commodities trading. Exciting as that may sound, it is absolutely true. The Bourse du Commerce's recently restored iron-and-glass cupola is surrounded by paintings and frescoes. In the Middle Ages, a convent of repentant sinners occupied the site. Catherine de Médici threw out the penitent women in 1572, when a horoscope convinced her that she should abandon construction of the Tuileries, build her palace here instead, and that

"August is a good month for meeting someone new." Catherine's palace was demolished in 1748, leaving only the observation tower of her personal astrologer as a memorial to her superstition. Louis XV replaced the structure with a grain market. It was transformed into a commodities market in 1889. *(M: Louvre-Rivoli. Tel. 01 55 65 55 65; www.ccip.fr. Open M-F 9am-6pm. Tours in French and English.)*

RUE DE LA FERRONNERIE. Southeast of the forum along rue St-Honoré is rue de la Ferronnerie. In 1610, as Henri IV passed no. 11 in his carriage, he was assassinated by François Ravaillac, who leaped into the coach and stabbed the king who tolerated French Protestants. Bad move for Ravaillac, who was seared by red-hot pincers, scalded with boiling lead, and then torn to pieces by an angry mob.

FONTAINE DES INNOCENTS. Built in 1548 and designed by Pierre Lescot, the nearby Fontaine des Innocents is the last trace of the Eglise and Cimetière des St-Innocents, which once bordered and overlapped Les Halles. Until its demolition in the 1780s, the edges of the cemetery were crowded by tombstones, the smell of rotting corpses, and vegetable merchants selling their produce. The cemetery was closed during the Enlightenment's hygienic reforms, and the corpses were relocated to the city's catacombs (see **Sights**, p. 217). Once attached to the church, the fountain is now a huge rendezvous for punks with spiked hair and the overflow crowd from McDonald's.

ÉGLISE ST-GERMAIN L'AUXERROIS. Tucked behind the Louvre near the Pont Neuf is the Gothic Eglise St-Germain l'Auxerrois. On August 24, 1572, the church's bell functioned as the signal for the St. Bartholomew's Day Massacre (see **History**, p. 4). Thousands of Huguenots were rounded up by the troops of the Duc de Guise and slaughtered in the streets, while King Charles IX shot at the survivors from the palace window. Today, visitors are allowed a quiet visit inside to view the lovely violet stained-glass windows or listen to the Sunday evening vespers. *(Vespers nightly 5pm. Mass with organ Su 11am.)*

OTHER SIGHTS. The **Pont Neuf,** the oldest and most famous of the Seine bridges, connects the 1er to the Ile de la Cité, and is currently undergoing much-needed renovation. On its left and spanning three blocks along rue de Rivoli, **Samaritaine** is one of the oldest department stores in Paris. Founded in 1869, it ushered in the modern age of consumption. The building began as a delicate iron and steel construction in 1906 and was revamped in the Art Deco style of 1928. The roof has one of the best free views of Paris in the city (see **Department Stores**, p. 303).

SECOND ARRONDISSEMENT

Since the 19th century, the 2*ème* has been a commercial district. From stocks and bonds trading at the Bourse des Valeurs to 19th-century shopping in the arrondissement's numerous glass-covered *passages* to prostitution on rue St-Denis and rue d'Aboukir, the 2*ème* has a long history of trade and commerce. Abundant fabric shops and cheap women's clothing stores hover between rue du Sentier and rue St-Denis, while way-upscale boutiques crowd the streets in the arrondissement's western half. For more of a laugh, the Opéra Comique is found in between boulevard des Italiens and rue de Richelieu. For an overview of the area, refer to the color **map** of the **First and Second Arrondissements** in the front of this book.

GALERIES, PASSAGES, AND THE BIBLIOTHÈQUE NATIONALE

In the early 19th century, speculators profiting from the confiscation of property from the church and the aristocracy in the Revolution began to build numerous glass-housed *galeries* or *passages* between the Grands Boulevards. Under these structures, pedestrians could be safe from the cold, rain, and mud of Paris' streets before Haussmannization (see p. 29). Designed in the same glass and steel atrium-style of Paris's main train stations, over 100 of these *galeries* existed in the early 1800s, whereas fewer than 20 survive today.

GALERIE COLBERT AND GALERIE VIVIENNE. These were the most fashionable *galeries* of the 1820s. Within these marbled pedestrian walkways, built within city blocks, shops, cafés, and *flâneurs* (strollers) mingled. Today, the *galeries* continue to house shops, boutiques, and antique stores. Enter **Galerie Vivienne** and you'll encounter a showcase of pastel luxury, tiny shops, and *trompe l'oeil* faux-marble columns. *(4, rue des Petits Champs, or 2, rue Vivienne. Near the Palais Royal.)*

Galerie Colbert is notable for its bronze sculptures and rotunda. The space used by the Bibliothèque Nationale as a storage annex and exhibition space features temporary exhibits, with at least one dedicated to contemporary photography. *(At the end of the corridor of Galerie Vivienne. Call 01 47 03 85 71 for exhibit info. Exhibitions open M-Sa noon-8pm. Free.)*

BIBLIOTHÈQUE NATIONALE SITE RICHELIEU. With a 12 million volume collection that includes Gutenberg Bibles and other first editions dating from the 15th century to the present, the Richelieu was previously the largest library in Continental Europe. Since 1642, every book published in France has been legally required to enter the national archives, which evolved out of the Bibliothèque du Roi, the royal book depository, and sizeable donations from noted bibliophiles and authors such as Victor Hugo and Emile Zola. To accommodate the ever-increasing volume of books, annexes were purchased near the library (see above). In the late 1980s, the French government eschewed annexes as a short-term solution and resolved to build the mammoth Bibliothèque de France in the 13*ème* (see Sights, p. 216), where the collections from the Richelieu branch were relocated between 1996 and 1998. Scholars must pass through a strict screening process to gain access to the main reading room; plan to bring a letter from your university, research advisor, or editor stating the nature of your research and two pieces of photo ID. *(58, rue de Richelieu. Just north of the Galeries Vivienne and Colbert, across Rue Vivienne. Main office tel. 01 47 03 81 26; info line 01 53 79 59 59. Open M-Sa 9am-4:30pm only to researchers who prove they need access to the collection.)*

For the public, however, the library's **Galerie Mazarin** and **Galerie Mansart**, host excellent temporary exhibitions of books, prints, and lithographs from the Bibliothèque Nationale archives. *(Tel. 01 47 03 81 10 for info. Galerie Mansart open Tu-Su 10am-7pm. Admission 35F, students, 24F.)*

Upstairs, the **Cabinet des Médailles** that displays coins and medallions rests in the Hôtel Tubeuf, a building that once belonged to both Mazarin and Duchess Hortense Mancini. Across from the library's main entrance, pl. Louvois's sculpted fountain personifies the four great rivers of France—the Seine, the Saône, the Loire, and the Garonne—as heroic women. Completed by Visconti in 1839, cherubs ride sea creatures that spout water through their nostrils, true to French custom. *(Open M-F 1-5:45pm, Sa 1-4:45pm, Su noon-6pm. Admission 22F, reduced 15F.)*

OTHER PASSAGES. West of the library, off rue des Petits Champs and after rue Ste-Anne, the **Passage Choiseul** features down-market clothing shops. To the north, between bd. Montmartre and rue St-Marc, the less conspicuously posh **Passage des Panoramas** is the oldest of Paris's remaining *galeries*. Built in 1799, it contains a fully intact 19th-century glass-and-tile roof and a more recently installed collection of ethnic restaurants. Probably the most beautiful of the remaining passages, and in the worst area, is the **Passage du Grand Cerf** off of Rue St-Denis. Its stained glass portal windows are worth the walk past the strip clubs.

BOURSE DES VALEURS AND THE OPÉRA COMIQUE

BOURSE DES VALEURS. The Neoclassical exterior belies the frenetic activities that once took place inside. Founded in 1724, Paris's stock exchange opened well after those of Lyon, Toulouse, and Rouen. Bourbon kings soon began issuing

S I G H T S

> **UNIONIZE!** In the mid-1970s Paris's prostitutes demonstrated in churches, monuments, and public squares demanding unionization. They marched down rue St-Denis, the central artery of the city's prostitution district, to picket for equal rights and protection under the law. Their campaign was successful and prostitution is now legal in France. Officially, sex workers are still not allowed to work the streets and only the prostitutes themselves can use the money they earn on the job. Even if a woman uses her earnings to help support her family, her husband can be prosecuted as a procurer. Despite its legalization, however, prostitution in France is far less visible and common than in countries like the Netherlands and Thailand.

worthless bonds there, which helped finance their expensive taste in palaces and warfare. Jacobins closed the exchange during the Revolution in order to fend off war profiteers, but it reopened under Napoleon. Construction of the present building began in 1808, proceeded slowly, and halted between 1814 and 1821 for lack of funds. The wings of the building were added from 1902 to 1907. Today's traders' pit is tame compared to those of London, Tokyo, and New York, as the entire process of trades has been computerized since 1986. *(Rue Nôtre-Dame des Victoires. M: Bourse. Tel. 01 40 41 62 20. Admission 30F, students 15F. 45min. English tours M-F 1:15-4pm on the ¼hr. English audioguide translations available during the French tour with 50F deposit.)*

Even so, the Bourse has its detractors: **Galerie Junk Bond,** an artist/squatters settlement across from the Bourse on Rue Vivienne offers interactive weirdness, which may or may not protest anything in particular, in its ground floor windows and graffitied facade. The lengthy tour of the Bourse opens windows onto the world, daring to ask questions like "How exactly does one issue a bond in a regulated market?" all to a somewhat ominous Philip Glass soundtrack.

OPÉRA COMIQUE. Laughs and sobs have resonated at the Opéra Comique for two centuries; originally built as the Comédie Italienne, it burned down twice in the 1840s and was finally rebuilt in 1898. It was here that Bizet's *Carmen* first hitched up her skirts, cast a sweltering sidelong glance at the audience, and seduced Don José with the trilled declaration *"Si tu m'aimes pas, je t'aime. Et si je t'aime prends garde à toi"* ("If you don't love me, I love you. And if I love you watch out"). *(M: Richelieu Drouot. To the west of the Bourse, between rue Favart and rue Marivaux. For performance information, see **Classical Music, Opera, and Dance,** p. 272)*

OTHER SIGHTS. A center of food commerce and gastronomy since the 13th century, the marble-cobbled **Marché Montorgueil** (Mount Pride Market) is composed of a number of wine, cheese, meat, and produce shops. To the left of rue Montorgueil stand the well-preserved remnants of the 15th-century **Tour de Jean Sans Peur** (Tower of Fearless John), built next to the former city wall and is now rue Etienne Marcel. Soon after ordering the successful assassination of the king's brother, Louis d'Orléans, in 1408, M. Sans Peur erected a tower in his house, the Hôtel de Bourgogne. To crown this mountain of pride he named it in his own honor.

THIRD ARRONDISSEMENT

THE UPPER MARAIS

The 3ème and 4ème arrondissements comprise the area known as the Marais. Drained by monks in the 13th century, the Marais ("swamp") was land-filled to provide building space for the Right Bank. With Henri IV's construction of the Place des Vosges (see **Sights,** p. 181) at the beginning of the 17th century, the area became the city's center of fashionable living. Leading architects and sculptors of the period designed elegant mansions and *hôtels particuliers* with large courtyards and rear gardens. Under Louis XV, the center of Parisian life moved to the *faubourgs* (then considered suburbs) St-Honoré and St-Germain, and construction in the Marais ceased. Many *hôtels* fell into ruin or disrepair, but in the 1960s the Marais was declared an historic neighborhood and a thirty-year period of gentrification attracted trendy boutiques, cafés, and museums. The area's narrow streets nevertheless retain the stamp of a medieval village.

THE NORTH AND RUE DU TEMPLE

Place Émile-Chautemps lies between **boulevard Sébastopol,** Haussmann's great thoroughfare, and the **Conservatoire National des Arts et Métiers,** 292, rue St-Martin (tel. 01 40 27 22 20), a technical institute whose immense **Foucault Pendulum** swings against the earth's axis. The medieval **rue Volta** boasts some of Paris's oldest residential buildings, including the stooping house at no. 3, which dates from 1300.

Place de la République (M: République), the meeting point of the 3*ème*, 10*ème*, and 11*ème*, centers around Morice's monument to the Republic of France and its revolutionary history. Brasseries and cafés offer lunch by day; prostitutes and swindlers carouse by night. A kitschier symbol of the Republic, **Tati** is Paris's cheapest, campiest department store (see **Shopping,** p. 303). For cheaper options, the **Carreau du Temple** market at rue du Petit Thouars and rue de Picardie (see **Markets,** p. 312) and the **garment district** on rue du Temple offer frenetic bargaining.

Built by Mansart in the 17th century, the **Hôtel Guénégaud,** 60, rue des Archives, houses the **Musée de la Chasse** (see **Museums,** p. 261). The beautiful 18th-century **Fontaine des Haudriettes** on rue des Archives features a water-spouting lion.

THE OLD MARAIS

RUE VIEILLE-DU-TEMPLE. This street is lined with stately residences including the 18th-century **Hôtel de la Tour du Pin** (no. 75) and the more famous **Hôtel de Rohan** (no. 87). Built between 1705 and 1708 for Armand-Gaston de Rohan, Bishop of Strasbourg and alleged love-child of Louis XIV, the *hôtel* has housed many of his descendants. Frequent temporary exhibits allow access to the interior *Cabinet des Singes* and its original decorations. The Hôtel de Rohan, part of the National Archives, also boasts an impressive courtyard and rose garden. *(Tel. 01 40 27 60 09 01 40 27 60 00 for exhibit info. Open M-F 9am-6pm. Free.)* Equally engaging are the numerous art galleries that have taken root on the street. (See **Galleries,** p. 265.)

Across rue Vieille-du-Temple, the **alleyway** at 38, rue Francs-Bourgeois, gives a sense of what Henri IV's dark and claustrophobic Paris felt like. At the corner of rue des Francs-Bourgeois and rue Vieille-du-Temple, the flamboyant Gothic **Hôtel Hérouët** and its turrets were built in 1528 for Louis XII's treasurer, Hérouët.

ARCHIVES NATIONALES. Housed in the 18th-century Hôtel de Soubise, the **Musée de l'Histoire de France** (see **Museums,** p. 262) is the main exhibition space of the National Archives. The Treaty of Westphalia, the Edict of Nantes, the Declaration of the Rights of Man, Marie-Antoinette's last letter, Louis XVI's diary, letters between Benjamin Franklin and George Washington, and Napoleon's will are all preserved here. Like George III's diary entry for July 4, 1776 (the American Declaration of Independence), Louis XVI's entry for July 14, 1789 (Bastille

S I G H T S

ONE DAY IN THE THIRD ARRONDISSEMENT

■ Peruse the **Musée Carnavalet** (p. 258), **Archives Nationale** (p. 175), **Musée de l'Art et du l'Histoire du Judaisme** (p. 258), and **Musée Picasso** (p. 253). Expand your definition of art at some of the Paris's most interesting **galleries** (p. 265). Press your nose up against the windows of rue des Francs-Bourgeois's fun and funky boutiques. Stop at **Apparemment Café** for a quick lunch (p. 134) and save **Le Réconfort** for a delicious dinner (p. 134).

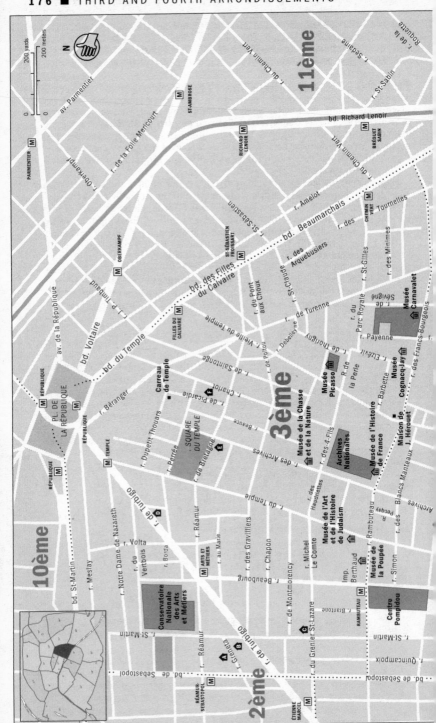

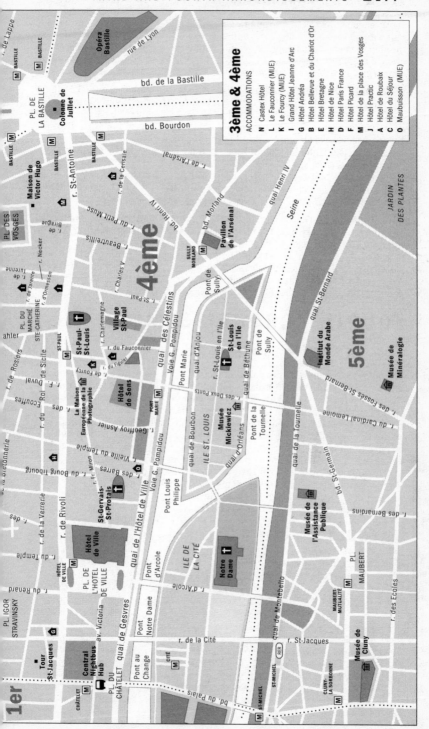

3ème & 4ème

ACCOMMODATIONS

N Castex Hôtel
L Le Fauconnier (MIJE)
K Le Fourcy (MIJE)
I Grand Hôtel Jeanne d'Arc
G Hôtel Andréa
B Hôtel Bellevue et du Chariot d'Or
E Hôtel Bretagne
H Hôtel de Nice
D Hôtel Paris France
F Hôtel Picard
M Hôtel de la place des Vosges
J Hôtel Practic
A Hôtel de Roubaix
C Hôtel du Séjour
O Maubuisson (MIJE)

Day) reads simply *Rien* (Nothing). Out at Versailles, far from the uprising in Paris, it had been a bad day for hunting. The only documents on display are featured in the museum's temporary exhibits. Call for upcoming events. *(60, rue des Francs Bourgeois. M: Rambuteau. Tel. 01 40 27 64 19 or 01 40 27 64 20. Scholars should apply to the Centre d'Accueil et de Recherche des Archives Nationales, 11, rue des Quatre-Fils.)*

HÔTEL SALÉ. This *hôtel* houses the **Musée Picasso** (see **Museums,** p. 253). Built for a salt merchant, the Hôtel Salé (salted *hôtel*) became the Dépôt Nationale Littéraire in 1793. By the 19th century, it had become a boarding-house for poor students and artists, including Honoré de Balzac, who based his portrait of the Maison Vauquer pension in his novel *Père Goriot* on the damp old place. Today, the museum is brighter and full of Picasso prints, paintings, and sculptures. *(5, rue de Thorigny. M: Chemin-Vert.)*

The nearby **Hôtel Libéral-Bruant,** 1, rue de la Perle, was built in the 17th century by Bruant, the architect of the Invalides. It now hosts a small lock museum, **Musée de la Serrurie.** *(Tel. 01 42 77 79 62. Open Tu-F 10am-noon and 2-5pm, M 2-5pm.)*

HÔTEL CARNAVALET. This former *hôtel particulier* of Mme de Sévigné, houses the museum of the history of Paris, the **Musée Carnavalet** (see **Museums,** p. 258). The exquisite *hôtel* was originally built in the 16th century for Jacques des Ligneris, the president of the Parlement de Paris. The statue of Louis XIV in the courtyard once stood in front of the Hôtel de Ville (see Sights, p. 180). *(23, rue de Sévigné. M: Chemin-Vert.)* From the Musée Carnavalet, continue your tour of the Marais by proceeding down rue des Francs-Bourgeois to pl. des Vosges in the 4ème.

FOURTH ARRONDISSEMENT

THE LOWER MARAIS

The Marais is a supremely fun neighborhood. It's accessible. It's soft-core hip. It's red wine. It's just-barely-affordable, sort-of-designer shops. It's amateur dance-theater. It's falafels—and knishes. It's gay men out for an afternoon snack. It's family-run goodness. Let the festivities begin. (Open on Sunday.)

But the Marais wasn't always this way. Until 1600, when Henri IV chose the area as the new location for his courtly residences, the area was an uninhabitable marshland (*marais* is French for swamp). When the court and the king opted for better digs at Versailles, the merchants moved in. During the Revolution, the former haunts of the sovereign gave way to slumlords and their tenements. The Marais remained in this run-down state until the 1960's, when Charles de Gaulle declared it an historical monument and the area began a period of renewal and renovation, the results of which are visible today.

MERDE! The French have a love affair with their dogs, and nearly 500,000 pooches call Paris home. According to official figures, the dogs of Paris leave over 11 tons of *déjections canines* on Paris's streets per day. Sidewalks are veritable mine fields; experienced Parisians keep one eye on the ground. Since 1977, the Paris government has been campaigning—under the title *"La lutte contre les polutions canines"* (The Fight Against Canine Pollution)—to encourage people to have their best friends defecate in street gutters. Inspiring slogans include: "Teach him the gutter" and "If you love Paris, don't let him do that!" Clean-up efforts are now aided by a technological triumph called the *Caninette*, or more informally the *Motocrotte* (crap mobile). You may see these hybrid motorcyle/vacuum cleaners sucking up *excreta* all around town. If you have the misfortune of stepping into some *crotte de chien*, hope it's with your left foot; according to Parisian superstition, it's good luck. For those who'd rather wring their little necks, take pleasure in the 17ème's **Cimetière des Chiens** (see **Sights,** p. 225).

THE NORTH: BEAUBOURG

CENTRE POMPIDOU. One of the most visible examples of renovation in the 4*ème* is the Centre Pompidou, the ultra-modern exhibition, performance, and research space considered alternately as either an innovation or an eyesore (see **Museums,** p. 251). Dominating Beaubourg, a former slum *quartier* whose high rate of tuber-culosis earned it the classification of an *îlot insalubre* (unhealthy block) in the 1930s, the Pompidou shocked Parisians when it opened in 1977. Its architects, Richard Rogers, Gianfranco Franchini, and Renzo Piano designed a building whose color-coded electrical tubes (yellow), water pipes (green), and ventilation ducts (blue) highlight the exterior of the building. Some claim that its industrial look resembles an oil refinery or an auto plant. Still, more people visit the Pompi-dou every year than visit the Louvre. Home of the **Musée Nationale de l'Art Moderne** (see **Museums,** p. 251), the Pompidou is undergoing massive renovations for the year 2000, when it will reopen as Paris's symbol of modernity and culture for the new Millennium. The cobblestone square in front gathers a mixture of artists, musicians, rebels, and passersby. Exercise caution: pickpockets frequent the area by day and rougher types hang out there by night. *(M: Rambuteau or Hôtel-de-Ville.)*

The **Fontaine Stravinsky,** dedicated to composer Igor Stravinsky, complements the Beaubourg's crowd of tourists and eccentrics with its cartoon-like kinetic sculptures. Its dancing g-clef, spinning bowlers, and multi-colored elephants spit water on passing crowds. *(Next to the Centre Pompidou.)*

RUE DES ROSIERS. At the heart of the Jewish community of the Marais, kosher shops, butchers, bakeries, and falafel counters are abundant. Until the 13th cen-tury, Paris's Jewish community was concentrated in front of Nôtre-Dame. When Philippe-Auguste expelled the Jewish population from the city limits, many fami-lies moved to the Marais, just outside the walls. Since then, this quarter has been Paris's Jewish center, witnessing the influx of Russian Jews in the 19th century and new waves of North African Sephardim fleeing Algeria in the 1960s. This mix of Mediterranean and Eastern European Jewish cultures gives the area a unique flavor, with *kugel* and falafel served side-by-side. During WWII, many who had fled to France to escape the pogroms of Eastern Europe were murdered by the Nazis. Assisted by French police, Nazi soldiers stormed the Marais and hauled Jewish families to the Vélodrome d'Hiver (Vél d'Hiv), an indoor sports stadium. Here, French Jews awaited deportation to work camps like Drancy, in a northeast sub-urb of Paris, or to camps farther east in Poland and Germany. The Mémorial de la Déportation on the Ile de la Cité commemorates these victims (see **Sights,** p. 165). Despite these atrocities, the Jewish community thrives in the Marais, as its two synagogues (at 25, rue des Rosiers, and at 10, rue Pavée, designed by Art Nouveau architect Hector Guimard in 1913). *(Four blocks east of Beaubourg, parallel to rue des Francs-Bourgeois. M: St-Paul.)*

MÉMORIAL DU MARTYR JUIF INCONNU. The Memorial to the Unknown Jewish Martyr commemorates European Jews who died at the hands of the Nazis and their French collaborators. Due to a 1980 terrorist attack, visitors must now pass through a metal detector. The crypt and monument contain ashes brought back from concentration camps and from the Warsaw ghetto. *(17, rue Geoffroy de l'Asnier. M: St-Paul. Open Su-Th 10am-1pm and 2-6pm, F 10am-1pm and 2-5pm. Admission 15F. Entrance to the left of the gates.)*

Upstairs, the **Centre de Documentation Juive Contemporaine** (Jewish Contempo-rary Documentation Center) organizes two permanent exhibitions, The Intern-ment of the Jews under Vichy and Letters from Internment Camps in France, as well as frequent temporary exhibits. The center's library holds more than 50,000 documents in its archives and more than one million items relating to the Nazi era. *(Tel. 01 42 77 44 72; fax 01 48 87 12 50; email memcdjc@calva.net; www.calvacom.fr/cal-vaweb/memorial/cdjchome.html. Open M-Th 2-6pm. Admission 15F.)*

RUE VIEILLE-DU-TEMPLE AND RUE STE-CROIX DE LA BRETTONERIE. Alongside the Jewish *quartier*, these streets form the heart of Paris's vibrant gay community. This is where the boys are. Paris's chic-est gay restaurants, shops, and bars rub elbows with bakeries in this *quartier*. Although many establishments fly the international, rainbow-colored freedom flag, both gay and straight convene here to window shop and brunch on the cobbled streets.

HÔTEL DE VILLE AND SURROUNDINGS

29, rue de Rivoli. M: Hôtel-de-Ville. Tel. 01 42 76 43 43, tours tel. 01 42 76 50 49. **Open** *M-Sa 9am-6:30pm.* **Free tours** *offered the first Monday of each month at 10:30am; call in advance to reserve a place.*

The Hôtel de Ville, Paris's grandiose city hall, dominates a large square with fountains and Belle Epoque lampposts. The present edifice is a 19th-century creation, which replaced the medieval structure built originally as a meeting hall for the cartel that controlled traffic on the Seine. In 1533, under King François I, the old building was destroyed. A new building was designed by Boccadoro in the Renaissance style of the Loire châteaux. The elegant building witnessed municipal executions on place Hôtel de Ville. In 1610, Henri IV's assassin Ravaillac was quartered alive by four horses bolting in opposite directions.

On May 24, 1871, the *communards* doused the building with petrol and set it afire. Lasting a full eight days, the blaze spared nothing but the frame. The Third Republic built a virtually identical structure on the ruins, with a few significant changes. The Republicans integrated statues of their own heroes into the facade: historian Michelet flanks the right side of the building while author Eugène Sue surveys the rue de Rivoli. The Third Republic installed brilliant crystal chandeliers, gilded every interior surface, and created a Hall of Mirrors in emulation of Versailles. When Manet, Monet, Renoir, and Cézanne offered their services, they were all turned down in favor of ponderous, didactic artists whose work decorates the Salon des Lettres, the Salon des Arts, the Salon des Sciences, and the Salon Laurens. The Information Office holds exhibits on Paris in the lobby.

Originally called pl. de Grève, the **place Hôtel de Ville** made a vital contribution to the French language. Poised on a marshy embankment *(grève)* of the Seine, the medieval square served as a meeting ground for angry workers, giving France the useful phrase *en grève* (on strike). Strikers still gather here amid riot police. During the 1998 World Cup, fans watched the French victory on huge screens erected on the square.

TOUR ST-JACQUES. The Tour St-Jacques stands alone in the center of its own park. This flamboyant Gothic tower is the only remnant of the 16th-century Eglise St-Jacques-la-Boucherie. The 52m tower's meteorological station and the statue of Pascal at its base commemorate Pascal's experiments on the weight of air, performed here in 1648. The tower marks Haussmann's *grande croisée* (great crossing) of rue de Rivoli and the bd. Sébastopol, the intersection of his east-west and north-south axes for the city, only meters from where the earliest Roman roads crossed two thousand years ago. *(39-41, rue de Rivoli. M: Hôtel-de-Ville. Two blocks west of the Hôtel de Ville.)*

SOUTH OF RUE ST-ANTOINE AND RUE DE RIVOLI

ÉGLISE ST-GERVAIS-ST-PROTAIS. The Eglise St-Gervais-St-Protais was named after Gervase and Protase, two Romans martyred under Nero. The church's classical facade, flamboyant Gothic vaulting, stained glass, and Baroque wooden Christ by Préault are part of a working monastery. The public is welcome to matins (Tu-Sa 7am), vespers (Tu-Sa 6pm), and high mass (Su 11am) to hear the nave filled with Gregorian chant. *(rue François-Miron. M: Hôtel-de-Ville.)*

The **Hôtel de Beauvais** at 68, rue François-Miron, was built in 1655 for Pierre de Beauvais and his wife Catherine Bellier. Bellier, Anne d'Autriche's chambermaid, had an adolescent tryst with the Queen's son, 15-year-old Louis XIV. As the story goes, Anne was overjoyed to learn that her son would please his future wife more

than Anne's impotent husband Louis XIII had pleased her. From the balcony of the *hôtel*, Anne d'Autriche and Cardinal Mazarin watched the entry of Louis XIV and his bride, Marie-Thérèse, into Paris. A century later, as a guest of the Bavarian ambassador, Mozart played his first piano recital here. Restored in 1967, the half-timbered 14th-century **Maison à l'Enseigne du Faucheur** (no. 11) and **Maison à l'Enseigne du Mouton** (no. 13) illustrate what this medieval quarter of Paris once looked like.

HÔTEL DE SENS. The Hôtel de Sens is one of the city's few surviving examples of medieval residential architecture. Built in 1474 for Tristan de Salazar, the Archbishop of Sens, its military features reflect the violence of the day. The turrets were designed to survey the streets outside, while the square tower served as a dungeon. An enormous Gothic arch entrance—complete with chutes for pouring boiling water on invaders—contributes to the mansion's intimidating air. The former residence of Queen Margot, Henri IV's first wife, the Hôtel de Sens has witnessed some of Paris's most daring romantic escapades. In 1606, the 55-year-old queen drove up to the door of her home, in front of which her two current lovers were arguing. One opened the lady's carriage door, and the other shot him dead. Unfazed, the queen demanded the execution of the other, which she watched from a window the next day. The *hôtel* now houses the **Bibliothèque Forney,** a fine arts library that hosts some temporary exhibits (see **Libraries,** p. 86). *(1, rue du Figuier. M: Pont Marie.)*

LA MAISON EUROPÉENNE DE LA PHOTOGRAPHIE. The galleries, library, and *videothèque* are housed in the Hôtel Henault de Cantobre, a farmer's home built in 1706. They host temporary exhibits of international photographers. The interesting permanent display *Les Plus Beaux Plans du Monde*, displayed on 40 screens, presents photography and film from the late 1950s to the present, and includes shots of events such as post-war Berlin, a Christmas in 1950s London, and Parisian fashion shows in the 60s. *(5-7, rue de Fourcy. M: St-Paul. Tel. 01 44 78 75 00; fax 01 44 78 75 15; www.mep-fr.org. Open W-Su 11am-8pm. Admission 30F, students 15F. Wheelchair accessible.)*

ÉGLISE ST-PAUL-ST-LOUIS. This church dates from 1627 when Louis XIII placed its first stone. Its large dome—a trademark of Jesuit architecture—is visible from afar but hidden by ornamentation on the facade. Paintings inside the dome depict four French kings: Clovis, Charlemagne, Robert the Pious, and St-Louis. The embalmed hearts of Louis XIII and Louis XIV were kept in vermeil boxes carried by silver angels before they were destroyed during the Revolution. The church's Baroque interior is graced with three 17th-century paintings of the life of St-Louis and Eugène Delacroix's dramatic *Christ in the Garden of Olives* (1826). The holy-water vessels were gifts from Victor Hugo. *(99, rue St-Antoine. M: St-Paul. Tel. 01 42 72 30 32. Open daily 9am-8pm. Free tours at 2:30pm, every 2nd Su of the month. Mass Sa 6pm, Su 10, 11:15am, and 7pm.)*

OTHER SIGHTS. Further west, **rue du Petit Muse** takes its name (*"Pute y muse,"* the prostitute idles here) from the prostitutes who worked here. Jim Morrison died (allegedly of a heart attack) in his bathtub on the third floor of 17, **rue Beautreillis**. His grave can be found at Cimetière Père Lachaise (see **Sights,** p. 231).

PLACE DES VOSGES AND SURROUNDINGS

PLACE DES VOSGES. At the end of rue des Francs Bourgeois sits the magnificent pl. des Vosges, Paris's oldest public square. The central park, lined with immaculately manicured trees centered around a splendid fountain, is surrounded by 17th-century Renaissance townhouses. Kings built several mansions on this site, including the Palais de Tournelles, which Catherine de Medicis ordered destroyed after her husband Henri II died there in a jousting tournament in 1563. Henri IV later ordered the construction of a new public square, to be known as pl. Royale.

Each of the 36 buildings has arcades on the street level, two stories of pink brick, and a slate-covered roof. The largest townhouse, forming the square's main entrance, was the king's pavilion; opposite, the pavilion of the queen is smaller but gracious. The marriage of Louis XIII's sister to the crown prince of Spain drew a crowd of 10,000 here in 1612. Originally intended for merchants, the pl. Royale attracted the wealthy, including Mme de Sévigné and Cardinal Richelieu. Molière, Racine, and Voltaire filled the grand parlors with their bon mots. Mozart played a concert here at the age of seven. Even when the city's nobility moved across the river to the Faubourg St-Germain, pl. Royale remained among the most elegant spots in Paris. During the Revolution, however, the 1639 Louis XIII statue in the center of the park was destroyed (the statue there now is a copy), and the park was renamed pl. des Vosges after the first department in France to pay its taxes (in 1800). Follow the arcades around the edge of pl. des Vosges for an elegant promenade, window-shopping, and a glimpse of plaques that mark the homes of famous residents. Théophile Gautier and Alphonse Daudet lived at no. 8. Victor Hugo lived at no. 6, which is now a museum of his life and work (see **Museums**, p. 262). During the summer, the arcades fill with classical musicians. Leave pl. des Vosges through the corner door at the right of the south face (near no. 5), which leads into the garden of the Hôtel de Sully. *(M: Chemin Vert or St-Paul.)*

HÔTEL DE SULLY. Built in 1624, the Hôtel de Sully, was acquired by the Duc de Sully, minister to Henri IV. Often cuckolded by his young wife, Sully would say when giving her money, *"voici tant pour la maison, tant pour vous, et tant pour vos amants"* (here's some for the house, some for you, and some for your lovers), asking only that she keep her paramours off the staircase. The small inner courtyard offers the fatigued tourist several stone benches and an elegant formal garden. *(62, rue St-Antoine. M: St-Paul.)*

On the side of the *hôtel* along St-Antoine is the **Caisse Nationale des Monuments Historiques,** which distributes free maps and brochures on monuments and museums. *(Tel. 01 44 61 21 50. Open M-F 9am-6pm, Sa 10am-1:15pm and 2-5pm.)*

HÔTEL DE LAMOIGNON. The Hôtel de Lamoignon is one of the finest *hôtels particuliers* in the Marais. Built in 1584 for Henri II's daughter, Diane de France, the facade is in the Colossal style, later used in the Louvre.

The Lamoignan and the modern buildings adjacent now house the **Bibliothèque Historique de la Ville de Paris,** a non-circulating library of Parisian history with 800,000 volumes (see **Libraries**, p. 86). An exhibition hall located next door focuses on the history of the *quartier*. *(24, rue Pavée. M: St-Paul. Tel. 01 44 59 29 60. Open Tu-Sa 10am-6pm, Su noon-7pm. Admission 20F, students and seniors 10F.)*

FIFTH ARRONDISSEMENT

THE LATIN QUARTER

Even as wave after wave of tourists break on the Rive Gauche, the 5*ème* maintains its reputation as the nerve center of young Paris. The autumn influx of Parisian students is undoubtedly the prime cultural preservative of the *Quartier Latin*, which takes its name from the language of scholarship used in its prestigious *lycées* and universities prior to 1798. Compared to the now opulent café scene of St-Germain-des-Prés, the Latin Quarter is relatively relaxed and more genuinely intellectual. Some say the quarter has fallen into a state of malaise since the upheaval of May 1968 (see **History**, p. 12), symbolized by the dull gray slabs which replaced the cobblestones used as missiles in the '68 protests. Indeed, in the 30 years since, many artists and intellectuals have migrated to the less expensive outer arrondissements, such as the 11*ème* and 13*ème*, as the *haute bourgeoisie* moved in. Yet the student population remains, and thus the arrondissement still holds the most diverse selection of bookstores, cinemas, bars, and jazz clubs in the city. A map of the Fifth and Sixth Arrondissements can be found in the front of this book.

BOULEVARD ST-MICHEL AND THE SORBONNE

PLACE ST-MICHEL. The busiest spot in the Latin Quarter, pl. St-Michel holds much of its political history as well: the Paris Commune began here in 1871, as did the student uprising of 1968. The 1860 fountain features a WWII memorial commemorating the students who fell here during the Liberation of Paris in August 1944. Ice cream shops and *crêpe* stands line rue St-Severin, while Greek *gyro* counters and restaurants crowd the pedestrian streets of rue de la Huchette.

The nearby **Eglise St-Julien-le-Pauvre,** built 1170-1230, is the oldest in Paris. At the intersection of bd. St-Germain and bd. St-Michel, the **Hôtel de Cluny,** 6, pl. Paul-Painlevé was once a medieval monastery, built on the ruins of a first-century Roman bath house. Today, the building houses the **Musée de Cluny's** collection of medieval art, tapestries, and illuminated manuscripts (see **Museums,** p. 254). As a major tourist thoroughfare, **boulevard St-Michel** (or the *Boul' Mich'*) won't give you much of an impression of the local life; however, many of the traditional bistros of the quarter hold their ground on the nearby streets. *(M: St-Michel.)*

LA SORBONNE. Place de la Sorbonne's cafés, students, and bookstores face out from the Sorbonne itself, one of Europe's oldest universities. Founded in 1253 by Robert de Sorbon as a dormitory for 17 theology students, the Sorbonne soon became the administrative base for the University of Paris. Its scholars were treated as nobility. In 1469, Louis XI established France's first printing house here. As it grew in power and size, the Sorbonne often contradicted the authority of the French throne, siding with England over France during the Hundred Years War. Not always on the liberal vanguard, the Sorbonne opposed the rationalist Philosophes resulting in its own suppression during the Revolution, only to be revived by Napoléon. Today, the Sorbonne is officially known as Paris IV, one of the University of Paris's 13 campuses. Among the centuries of illustrious students who have taken degrees from the Sorbonne are the existentialist philosopher Jean-Paul Sartre and the feminist writer Simone de Beauvoir. *(45-7, rue des Ecoles. M: Cluny-La Sorbonne or RER: Luxembourg.)*

Commissioned in 1642 by Cardinal Richelieu, the university's main building, **Ste-Ursule de la Sorbonne** on rue des Ecoles is open to the public. The cardinal lies buried inside the **chapel,** his hat suspended above him by a few threads hanging from the ceiling. Legend has it that when Richelieu is freed from purgatory, the threads will snap and the hat will tumble down. *(Open M-F 9am-5pm.)*

COLLÈGE DE FRANCE. Created by François I in 1530 to contest the university's authority, the Collège de France stands behind the Sorbonne. The outstanding courses at the *Collège*, given by such luminaries as Henri Bergson, Paul Valéry, and Milan Kundera are free and open to all. Check the schedules that appear by the door in September. *(Courses run Sept.-May. For more information, call 01 43 29 12 11 or 01 44 27 12 11.)*

OTHER SCHOLARLY SIGHTS. Just south of the *Collège* lies the Lycée Louis-le-Grand, where Molière, Robespierre, Victor Hugo, Baudelaire, and Pompidou spent part of their pre-university years. Sartre taught there as well.

France's premier university, the **Ecole Normale Supérieure,** is located southeast of the Sorbonne on rue d'Ulm. Part of the Grands Ecoles, a sort of Ivy-League of France's best universities including **HEC** (Hautes Etudes Commerciales) and **ENA** (Ecole Nationale d'Administration), Normale Sup' (as its students, the *normaliens* call their alma mater) accepts only the most gifted students to enroll in its programs in literature, philosophy, and the natural sciences. Some of the more famous alumni of the Grands Ecoles include philosophers Jacques Derrida and Michel Foucault, and President Jacques Chirac.

SIGHTS

THE PANTHÉON

Pl. du Panthéon. M: Cardinal Lemoine. Tel. 01 44 32 18 01. **Open** *daily 10am-6:30pm; last admission 5:45pm.* **Admission** *35F, students 23F.*

Built on the **Montagne Ste-Geneviève,** the dome of the Panthéon towers over the Latin Quarter and the Left Bank. Originally the site of a Roman temple to Mercury and Clovis's shrine to Saints Peter and Paul, the hilly region was renamed in honor of Paris's patron saint Geneviève whose prayers deflected Atilla's invading hordes in 450 CE (see **Nuns,** p. 2). In gratitude to Ste-Geneviève after surviving a grave illness in 1744, Louis XV commissioned the current neoclassical structure. Jacques-Germain Soufflot's design launched a Greek revival in France.

The Revolution converted the church into a mausoleum of heroes, designed to rival the royal crypt at the Basilique de St-Denis (see **Daytripping, p. 338**). On April 4, 1791, Mirabeau was interred, only to have his ashes expelled the next year when his correspondence with Louis XVI was revealed. Voltaire's body was moved here with great ceremony. The Panthéon is a national necropolis: in the crypt you will find Voltaire, Rousseau, Hugo, Zola, Jean Jaurès, and Louis Braille. At Hugo's interment in 1885, two million mourners and Chopin's *Marche Funèbre* followed the coffin to its resting place.

The Panthéon's other attraction is a monstrous **Foucault's Pendulum** mounted under the dome, whose plane of oscillation stays fixed as the Earth rotates around it. The pendulum's apparent rotation demonstrates the rotation of the earth to any non-believers, including President Louis Napoleon III and a large crowd in 1851. While everyone's dying to get in, not all of France's luminaries are buried in the Panthéon. Pascal and Racine are buried next door in the **Eglise St-Etienne du Mont.** Built from 1492 to 1626, the flamboyant Gothic interior features rose windows and relics of Ste-Geneviève.

PLACE DE LA CONTRESCARPE

South on rue Descartes, past the prestigious Lycée Henri IV, **place de la Contrescarpe** is the geographical center of the 5*ème*. Like those of a tiny medieval village, the area's streets were built on Roman causeways. South of pl. de la Contrescarpe, **rue Mouffetard**, the ancient road to Rome, plays host to the liveliest street market in Paris (see **Food Markets,** p. 157). Hemingway lived here at 74, rue du Cardinal Lemoine, during his first years in Paris. Next door once stood the Bal du Printemps, a dance hall Hemingway describes in *A Moveable Feast* and *The Sun Also Rises*. John Dos Passos and Samuel Beckett were also residents. Today, rue Mouffetard and rue Monge bind much of the tourist and student social life. At the intersection of rue de Navarre and rue des Arènes, the **Arènes de Lutèce** were built by the Romans to accommodate 15,000 spectators. Similar to oval amphitheaters in Rome and southern France, the ruins were unearthed and restored in 1910; all the seats are reconstructions.

LE MOUFF' Rue Mouffetard wasn't always the snaking alley of gourmet shops and touristy jazz clubs you'll find there today. The most storied street of the Latin Quarter, running down the backside of Mt. St-Geneviève, was the main thoroughfare of a wealthy villa from the 2nd century Roman state until the 13th century. Records from 1260 show that the residents of the seven large estates in the southeast quarter of the 5*ème* included the president of the courts and Charles V's architect. The nearby river Bièvre, now relegated to the sewer system, was shortly thereafter found excellent for cloth dyeing, and this discovery brought in factories and taverns to the once bucolic district. Pl. de la Contrescarpe soon became one of the most dangerous parts of the city; in the 16th century police estimated finding 15 murder victims there each morning. And so it remained until the late 19th century; the now wealthy spillover from the 6*ème*, including the homes of the mayor and president of the National Assembly, have only sprung up in the past 15 years.

JARDIN DES PLANTES

In the eastern corner of the 5ème, the **Jardin des Plantes** offers 45,000 square meters of flowers and greenery. Opened in 1640 by Louis XIII's doctor, Guy de la Brosse, the gardens were intended for growing medicinal plants to promote His Majesty's health. In the 18th century, the American Ambassador Thomas Jefferson spent much time here admiring the flora and fauna. *(M: Jussieu. Tel. 01 40 79 30 00.)*

Today, the gardens include the **Musée d'Histoire Naturelle** (see **Museums**, p. 258), the Ménagerie zoo (see below), and two botanical theme parks, the **Jardin Alpin** and **Serres Tropicales**. *(Jardin Alpin open M-F 8-11am and 1:30-5pm. Free. Serres Tropicales open W-M 1-6pm Apr.-Oct., 1-5pm Nov.-Mar. Admission 15F, students 10F.)*

Although no match for the Parc Zoologique in the Bois de Vincennes (see **Sights**, p. 238), the **Ménagerie Zoo** will lighten up anyone's day with its stimulating collection of primates, large game, birds, and reptiles. During the siege of Paris in 1871, the zoo was raided for meat and elephants were served to starving Parisians. *(Tel. 01 40 79 37 94. Open Apr.-Sept. 9am-6pm; Oct.-Mar. 9am-5pm. Last admission 30min. before closing. Admission 30F, students and ages 4-16 20F.)*

MOSQUÉE DE PARIS AND INSTITUT DU MONDE ARABE

MOSQUÉE DE PARIS. The Institut Musulman houses the beautiful Mosquée de Paris, a Muslim place of worship constructed in 1922 by French architects to honor the role played by the countries of North Africa in World War I. Green-tiled arcades and cool courtyards, sometimes quiet enough to hear the water of the fountains, provide a soothing setting for prayer, mint tea in the café, or an afternoon in the exquisite *hammam* (see **Cafés**, p. 137). *(Behind the Jardin des Plantes at pl. du Puits de l'Ermite. M: Jussieu. Tel. 01 45 35 97 33. Open June-Aug. Sa-Th 9am-noon and 2-6pm. Guided tour 15F, students 10F.)*

INSTITUT DU MONDE ARABE (IMA). Closer to the Seine, the breathtaking Institut du Monde Arabe (IMA) is housed in one of the city's most striking buildings. Facing the Seine, the *Institut* resembles a ship, representing the boats on which Algerian, Moroccan, and Tunisian immigrants sailed to France. The south facade is made up of thousands of Arabesque portals that, like camera lenses, open and close to admit the shifting rays of the sun. Inside, the *Institut* houses permanent and rotating exhibitions on Maghrebian, Near Eastern, and Middle Eastern Arab cultures as well as a library, research facilities, lecture series, film festivals, and a gorgeous rooftop terrace, where you don't have to eat in the expensive restaurant to see the views of the Seine, Montmartre, and the Île de la Cité. (For more on the IMA, see **Museums**, p. 259.) *(23, quai St-Bernard. M: Jussieu. Tel. 01 40 51 38 38. Open Tu-Su 10am-6pm. Admission 25F, ages 12-18 20F, under 12 free.)*

OTHER SIGHTS. Next door, **La Tour d'Argent**, 15, quai de la Tournelle, is one of Paris's most expensive restaurants. *(M: Maubert-Mutualité.)* The beautiful **Jardin des Sculptures en Plein Air**, quai St-Bernard, boasts a collection of modern sculpture on a long stretch of green along the Seine, with works by Zadkine and Brancusi. A nice place to read and sunbathe by day, but exercise caution at night. Farther west along the Seine, pl. René Viviani affords one of the best views of Nôtre-Dame. *(M: St-Michel.)*

SIXTH ARRONDISSEMENT

Sartre. Hemingway. Pound. Picasso. Nin. Camus. Apollinaire. Miller. These are all names. They are names that you will hear over and over when spending any span of time in the 6ème. It seems that these intellectual giants ate, slept, lived, loved, and spat in every cute little bohemian and intellectual corner of this arrondissement, and its residents and restaurateurs can't wait to remind you. Even so, the 6ème still has a genuine art scene kept alive by its excellent galleries and the Ecole des Beaux Arts, and an intellectual flavor not killed by the tourists clogging its celebrated cafés. For a map of this area, refer to the color map of the Fifth and Sixth Arrondissements in the front of this book.

S I G H T S

BOULEVARD DU MONTPARNASSE

The southernmost flank of the 6*ème* is peppered with schools and artsy haunts. At cafés like the **La Closerie des Lilas,** 171, bd. du Montparnasse, which Hemingway described as "one of the best cafés in Paris," such Parisian artists as Baudelaire, Verlaine, Breton, and Picasso came to listen to poetry and discuss their latest works. Farther down the boulevard, other expatriate watering holes are found: **Le Séléct** at no. 99, to which Jake Barnes and Brett Ashley taxied in Hemingway's *The Sun Also Rises*, and **La Coupole** at no. 102-104. (For info on these cafés, see **Cafés,** p. 139). But alas, an artist cannot live on coffee alone, as Gertrude Stein and her brother Leo well understood. They welcomed the century's greatest artists at 27, rue de Fleurus (off bd. Raspail), giving encouragement and financial support to broke characters by the name of Picasso, Matisse, and Hemingway. Curving down from bd. Raspail toward Montparnasse is 86, rue Nôtre-Dame-des-Champs, where the American artist James MacNeill Whistler had a studio steps from Ezra Pound's rear garden apartment at no. 70.

The horses of the **Fontaine de l'Observatoire** (1875) mark the halfway point between the Jardin du Luxembourg and the 17th-century **Observatoire de Paris,** an astrological observatory that, though difficult to visit today, used to be the French benchmark for 0° longitude, like its northern neighbor in Greenwich, England.

JARDIN DU LUXEMBOURG AND ODÉON

JARDIN DE LUXEMBOURG. "There is nothing more charming, which invites one more enticingly to idleness, reverie, and young love, than a soft spring morning or a beautiful summer dusk at the Jardin du Luxembourg," wrote Léon Daudet in an absolute fit of sentimentality and mushiness in 1928. Parisians flock to these formal gardens to sunbathe, write, stroll, read, and gaze at the rose gardens, central pool, and each other. A residential area in Roman Paris, then the site of a medieval monastery, and later the home of naughty 17th-century French royalty, the gardens were liberated during the Revolution and are now free to all. Children can sail toy boats in the fountain, ride ponies, and see the *grand guignol* (a puppet show; see **Guignols,** p. 271) while their parents and grandparents pitch *boules*. Feel free to saunter through the park's paths, past sculptures of France's queens, poets, and heroes and the Fontaine Medici in the northeast corner of the gardens. A mammoth task-force of gardeners tends to this most beloved of Parisian gardens; each spring they plant or transplant 350,000 flowers and move the 150 palm and orange trees out of winter storage. *(M: Odéon and RER: Luxembourg. Open daily Apr.-Oct. 7:30am-9:30pm; Nov.-Mar. 8:15am-5pm. The wrought-iron gates of the main entrance are on bd. St-Michel. Guided tours of the gardens given in French the first Wednesday of every month Apr.-Oct. at 9:30am; depart from pl. André Honorat behind the observatory.)*

PALAIS DU LUXEMBOURG. The Palais du Luxembourg, located within the park and now serving as the home of the French Senate, was built in 1615 at Marie de Medicis's request. Homesick for her native Tuscany, she tried to re-create its architecture and gardens in central Paris. Her builders finished the Italianate palace in a mere five years and Marie moved in 1625. But a feud with the powerful Cardinal Richelieu made her time there brief. Marie's son, Louis XIII, promised that he would dismiss the cardinal but he revoked his promise the following day. Wielding great power, Richelieu banished the Queen Mother in 1630 to Cologne, where she died penniless. The palace later housed members of the nobility, including the Duchesse de Montpensier (known as *la Grande Mademoiselle* because of her girth). Robert le Pieux made it the site of his pleasure dome, the Chateau de Vauvert: for years after its demolition, locals referred to *le diable de Vauvert,* due to rumors of the goings-on there. During the Terror, the palace was first a prison for nobles on deck for the guillotine and then for Revolutionary Jacobin perpetrators.

The Luxembourg again took center stage during the First and Second Empires. Imprisoned in the palace during the Revolution with her republican husband, Beau-

FOR ALL THE LITTLE PEOPLE OUT THERE

■ Paris is often seen as a city for grown-ups only, with its grown-up food (snails and sweetbreads do not a happy five-year-old make); grown-up fashion; and grown-up romance (enough to make any self-respecting adolescent nauseous). Little known to most non-residents, however, is that a world of parks awaits all those too young to be interested in Beaujolais and Chanel. Give the following a whirl: the **Jardin du Luxembourg** (see p. 186) offers ponies, mini sail boats, and enough cotton candy to make a dentist see dollar signs; the **Parc Monceau** (see p. 202), among whose architectural follies half of France's ruling elite was wheeled about as babies; the **Parc Buttes-Chaumont** (see p. 231), whose cliffs and waterfalls will impress pre-teens, and whose *guignols* and explorable creeks are the favorites of many of muddy local child; the expansive **Parc de la Villette** (see p. 238), whose Cité des Science et de l'Industrie is fun and educational (don't say the second word in front of the children), and whose other gardens are the best in the city for romping about; the **Jardin d'Acclimatation** (see p. 235), which contains a plethora of sure hits, including pony rides, mini-golf, a zoo, bumper cars, and carousels.

harnais, the future Empress Josephine returned five years later to take up official residence with her second husband, the new Consul Napoleon Bonaparte. After the Emperor's exile to Elba, his young nephew was tried in the palace for leading several abortive rebellions against the July Monarchy. Sentenced to life imprisonment, he escaped and prepared his return to France, where in 1851 he declared the Second Empire and became Emperor Napoleon III. During World War II, the palace was occupied by the Nazis who made it the headquarters of the Luftwaffe.

In 1852 the palace first served its current function as the meeting place for the *Sénat*, the upper house of the French parliament. Despite (or perhaps because of) its large and increasing membership, the Senate is a fairly ineffectual body that may be overruled by the Parliament. The president of the Senate lives in Petit Luxembourg, originally a conciliatory gift from Marie de Medicis to her nemesis Richelieu. The **Musée du Luxembourg**, next to the palace on rue de Vaugirard, shows free exhibitions of contemporary art. *(Tel. 01 42 34 25 95. Open M-Sa 11am-6:30pm.)*

THÉÂTRE DE L'ODÉON. The Théâtre Odéon is Paris's oldest and largest theater (see **National Theaters**, p. 269). Completed in 1782, the Odéon was purchased by Louis XVI and Marie-Antoinette for the Comédie Française. Founded by Molière in the 17th century, the celebrated theater troupe did not have a theater of its own. Beaumarchais's *Marriage of Figaro*, nearly banned by Louis XVI for its attacks on the nobility, premiered here in 1784 before delighted aristocratic audiences. In 1789 the actor Talma staged a performance of Voltaire's *Brutus* in which he imitated the pose of the hero in David's painting. As the Revolution approached, the Comédie Française splintered over the issue of political loyalties. Republican members followed Talma to the Right Bank, settling into the company's current location near the Louvre (see **National Theaters,** p. 269). Those actors who remained behind were jailed under the Terror and the theater was closed. It was later known as the *théâtre maudit* (cursed theater) after two fires and a chain of failures left it nearly bankrupt. Its present Greco-Roman incarnation dates from an 1818 renovation overseen by David. The Odéon's fortunes changed after World War II, when it became a venue for contemporary, experimental theater. On May 17, 1968, student protesters seized the building and destroyed much of its interior before police quelled the rebellion. *(M: Odéon. Across from the Jardin du Luxembourg.)*

ÉGLISE ST-SULPICE. the Eglise St-Sulpice was designed by Servadoni in 1733, but it remains unfinished. The church contains Delacroix frescoes in the first chapel on the right (his famous *Jacob Wrestling with the Angel* and *Heliodorus Driven from the Temple*), a *Virgin and Child* by Jean-Baptiste Pigalle in one of the rear chapels, and an enormous Chalgrin organ. In the transept of the church, an inlaid copper band runs along the floor from north to south, connecting a plaque in the south to an obelisk in the north. A ray of sunshine passes through a hole in the upper window of the south transept during the winter solstice, striking marked points on the obelisk at exactly mid-day. A beam of sunlight falls on the copper plaque during the summer solstice and behind the communion table during the spring and autumn equinox. *(M: St-Sulpice. Two blocks west of the theater. Tel. 01 46 33 21 78. Open daily 7:30am-7:30pm. Guided visit in French daily at 3pm.)*

SHAKESPEARE AND CO. From 1921-1940, Sylvia Beach's bookstore, Shakespeare and Co., stood at 12, rue de l'Odéon. Here, Beach published James Joyce's *Ulysses* and harbored British and American expatriate writers such as F. Scott Fitzgerald, T.S. Eliot, Ezra Pound, and Ernest Hemingway, whose collection of essays, *A Moveable Feast*, chronicles those expatriate years and F. Scott Fitzgerald's drinking habits. What Gertrude Stein was for Paris's struggling artists, Sylvia Beach was for its struggling writers. During WWII, Beach hid from the Nazis for over two years in an attic space on bd. St-Michel. Shakespeare, et al. have relocated to the *5ème* (see **Bookstores**, p. 307). Thomas Paine, pampleteer and hero of the French, lived at #10 and never had his apartment ransacked, as that would have been a violation of his right to property.

ST-GERMAIN-DES-PRÉS

Known as *le village de Saint-Germain-des-Prés*, the area around **boulevard St-Germain** between St-Sulpice and the Seine pocketed with cafés, restaurants, cinemas, and expensive boutiques, is always crowded and noisy.

CAFÉS. The bd. St-Germain's cafés have long been gathering places for literary and artistic notables. **Aux Deux Magots,** 6, pl. St-Germain-des-Prés, is named for two porcelain figures that adorned a Chinese silk and imports store at this spot in the 19th century. It quickly became a favorite hangout of Verlaine, Rimbaud, and Mallarmé (see **Cafés,** p. 139). Forty years later, it attracted Surrealists Breton and Artaud as well as Picasso, Léger, and Gide. Established in 1890, the **Café de Flore,** 172, bd. St-Germain, was made famous in the 1940s and 50s by literati Sartre, Camus, and Prévert who favored the warmth of its wood-burning stoves over their cold apartments (see **Cafés,** p. 139).

ÉGLISE DE ST-GERMAIN-DES-PRÉS. The nearby Eglise de St-Germain-des-Prés, is the oldest standing church in Paris. King Childebert I commissioned the first church on this site to hold relics he had looted from the Holy Land. Completed in 558, it was consecrated by St-Germain, Bishop of Paris, on the very day of King Childebert's death—and not a moment too soon: the king had to be buried inside the church's walls.

The rest of the church's history reads like an architectural Book of Job. Sacked by the Normans and rebuilt three times, the present-day church dates from the 11th century. On June 30, 1789, the Revolution seized the prison in a sort of dress rehearsal for the storming of the Bastille. The church then did a brief stint as a saltpeter mill and in 1794, 15 tons of gunpowder that had been stored in the abbey exploded. The ensuing fire devastated the church artwork and treasures, including much of its renowned monastic library. Baron Haussmann destroyed the last remains of the deteriorating abbey walls and gates when he extended rue de Rennes to the front of the church and created place St-Germain-des-Prés.

The magnificent interior, painted in shades of terra-cotta and deep green with gold, was restored in the 19th century. In the second chapel on the right inside the church you'll find a stone marking the interred heart of 17th-century philosopher René Descartes (see **Literature,** p. 15), who died of pneumonia at the frigid court of Queen Christina of Sweden, and an altar dedicated to the victims of the September 1793 massacre, in which 186 Parisians were slaughtered in the courtyard. Pick up one of the free maps of the church with information in English on St-Germain's history, artifacts, and frequent concerts. As in most medieval churches, built to accommodate an age without microphones, the acoustics are awesome. (See **Classical Music, Opera, and Dance,** p. 272). *(3, pl. St-Germain-des-Prés. M: St-Germain-des-Prés. Tel. 01 43 25 41 71. Open daily 8am-7:45pm. Information office open Tu-Sa 10:30am-noon and 2:30-7pm.)*

PARLEZ-VOUS FRANGLAIS? One of the branches of the Institut de France is the prestigious **Académie Française,** which, since its founding by Richelieu in 1635 (see **Literature,** p. 15), has assumed the tasks of compiling the official French dictionary and serving as guardian of the French language. Having already registered its disapproval of *le weekend (la fin de semaine), le parking (le stationnement), le walkman (le balladeur), l'air bag, le snack bar* and other "Franglais" nonsense, the Academy recently triumphed with the passage of a constitutional amendment affirming French as the country's official language. It is so difficult to become elected to this arcane society, limited to 40 members, that Molière, Balzac, and Proust never made it. In 1981 the first woman, novelist Marguerite Yourcenar, gained membership. Influenced by the presence of more women, the Academy decided in 1998 to allow the use of feminine forms of normally masculine nouns, such as *avocate (avocat,* lawyer), reflecting the role of women in professions from which they were once *barred.*

GALLERIES. Moving north from bd. St-Germain toward the Seine, you'll come upon some of the most tangled streets in central Paris. Haussmann retired before he could figure out a way to extend rue de Rennes across the Seine to meet up with rue de Louvre. Today the maze of streets on the rue de Seine, rue Mazarine, rue Bonaparte, and rue Dauphine is home to art gallery after art gallery, all providing an amazing glimpse at contemporary art that is on its way into the annals of art and often can't be seen anywhere else.

ÉCOLE NATIONALE SUPÉRIEURE DES BEAUX ARTS. France's most acclaimed art school, the Ecole Nationale Supérieure des Beaux Arts was founded by Napoleon in 1811 and soon became the stronghold of French academic painting and sculpture. The current building, the Palais des Etudes, was finished in 1838 and is a mishmash of styles and monuments to the Old Masters. The public is not permitted to tour the building itself nor to prowl around its gated courtyard, but you can get a look at the next Léger or Delacroix at the changing public shows in the Exhibition Hall at 13, quai Malaquais. If you have the talent to be the one on display, the school admits foreign students. *(14, rue Bonaparte, at quai Malaquais. M: St-Germain-des-Prés. Tel. 01 47 03 50 00; www.ensba.fr. For application information call 01 47 03 50 65.)*

PALAIS DE L'INSTITUT DE FRANCE. The Palais de l'Institut de France broods over the Seine beneath its famous black and gold-topped dome. Designed by Le Vau to lodge a college established in Cardinal Mazarin's will, it has served as a school (1688-1793), a prison (1793-1805), and is now a mix of the two, housing the humorless Académie Française. The glorious building has housed the *Institut de France* since 1806. Founded in 1795, the institute was intended to be a storehouse for the nation's knowledge and a meeting place for France's greatest scholars. During the Restoration, appointment to the institute depended more on political position than talent, but since 1830 the process has been slightly more meritocratic. Positively egalitarian is the way the public can waltz into the courtyard and take a right to see Mazarin's enormous funereal scultpure. *(Pl. de l'Institut. M: Pont-Neuf. One block to the east of the ENSB-A on quai Malaquai.)*

ODÉON. After the arch of the **Cour du Commerce St-André,** a pedestrian passageway off bd. St-Germain, stands the **Relais Odéon,** a Belle Epoque bistro whose stylishly painted exterior, decked with floral mosaics and a hanging sign, is a fine example of Art Nouveau (see **Fine Arts,** p. 25), as is the doorway of #7, rue Mazarine, several blocks north. Farther down this passageway, on the top floor of the building on your left, was the site of the Revolutionary-era clandestine press that published Marat's *L'Ami du Peuple.* Marat was assassinated by Charlotte Corday in the bathtub of his home, which once stood where the courtyard meets rue de l'Ancienne Comédie. The poet Baudelaire was born at 15, rue Hautefeuille, just off pl. St-André-des-Arts. *(M: Odéon.)*

SIGHTS

OTHER SIGHTS. Once the mint for all French coins, **Hôtel des Monnaies** next door proudly displays its austere 17th-century facade to the heart of the Left Bank. The footbridge across from the *Institut*, appropriately called the **Pont des Arts**, is celebrated by poets and artists for its delicate ironwork, its beautiful views of the Seine, and its spiritual locus at the heart of France's most prestigious Academy of Arts and Letters. Built as a toll bridge in 1803, the *pont* was first bridge to be made of iron and was built for pedestrians only. On the day it opened, 65,000 Parisians paid to walk across it; today, it is less crowded, absolutely free, and still lovely.

SEVENTH ARRONDISSEMENT

Since the 18th century, the *7ème* has stood its ground as the city's most elegant residential district. Home to the National Assembly, countless foreign embassies, the Invalides, the Musée d'Orsay, and the Eiffel Tower, this section of the Left Bank is a medley of France's diplomatic, architectural, and military achievements. You might be the only one without a uniform, gun, or cellular phone on some streets in the *7ème*, where policemen and soldiers guard the area's consulates and ministries.

TO THE WEST: THE EIFFEL TOWER

M: Bir Hakeim. Tel. 01 44 11 23 45; www.eiffel-tower.com. **Open** *daily June-Aug. 9am-midnight; Sept.-May 9:30am-11pm. Last lift at 10:30pm.* **Elevator** *to 1st floor 21F, under 12 12F; 2nd floor 43F, under 12 22F; 3rd floor 60F, under 12 31F.* **Stairs** *to 1st and 2nd floors 15F. Under 4 free.*

Of the Eiffel Tower, its engineer Gustave Eiffel wrote: "France is the only country in the world with a 300m flagpole." Designed in 1889 as the tallest structure in the world, the Eiffel Tower was conceived as a monument to engineering and industry, to surpass the Egyptian pyramids in size and notoriety. Yet before construction had even begun, shockwaves of dismay reverberated through the city. In February of 1887, one month after builders broke ground on the Champ de Mars, French writers and artists, such as Guy de Maupassant, Dumas *fils*, Charles Garnier (architect of the Opéra), and the composer Gounod, published a scathing letter of protest in *Le Temps* condemning the "useless and monstrous Eiffel Tower." After the building's completion, Maupassant ate lunch every day at its ground-floor restaurant—the only place in Paris, he claimed, from which he couldn't see the offensive thing.

Nevertheless, when it was inaugurated in March, 1889, as the centerpiece of the Universal Exposition, it brought popular, if not critical, acclaim; nearly 2,000,000 people ascended the tower during the event. Numbers dwindled by comparison during the following decades. As time wore on and the 20-year property lease approached expiration, Eiffel faced the imminent destruction of his masterpiece. It survived because of its importance as a communications tower, a function Eiffel had helped cultivate in the 1890s. The radio-telegraphic center on the top of the tower worked during WWI to intercept enemy messages, including the one that led to the arrest and execution of Mata Hari, the Danish dancer accused of being a German spy.

GHOSTS OF PARIS'S PAST It may surprise some that the staid *7ème* has been a favorite address of some of Paris' most famous intellectuals. Quai Voltaire, known for its lovely views of Seine bridges, also has an artistic heritage as distinguished as any block in the city. At No. 27 Voltaire himself spent his last days. No. 19 housed Baudelaire in 1856-58 while he wrote *Les Fleurs du Mal*, as well as Wagner as he composed Die Meistersinger in 1861-62; Oscar Wilde also spent some time here. Delacroix lived at No. 13 from 1829-1836, as well as Corot somewhat later. At No. 11, Ingres died in 1867.

With the 1937 World Exposition, the Eiffel Tower again became a showpiece. Eiffel himself walked humbly before it, remarking: "I ought to be jealous of that tower. She is more famous than I am." Since then, Parisians and tourists alike have reclaimed the monument in over 150,000,000 visits.

On everything from postcards to neckties and umbrellas, Eiffel's wonder still takes the heat from some who see it as Maupassant did: an "excruciating nightmare" overrun with tourists and their trinkets. Don't believe the anti-hype, though. The tower is a wonder of design, and all those kitschy replicas are nothing like the tower in the lattice-iron flesh. It is a soft brown, not the metallic steel gray that most visitors anticipate. And despite the 18,000 pieces of iron, 2,500,000 rivets, and 9,100,000 kilograms of sheer weight that compose it, the girders appear light and elegant, especially at night, when artfully placed spotlights turn the tower into a lacy hologram.

The cheapest way to ascend the tower is by walking up the first two floors (15F). The Cinemax, a relaxing stop midway through the climb on the first floor, shows films about the tower. Posters chronicling its history are a good excuse to catch your breath and rest your legs. Visitors must take an elevator to get to the third story. Tickets can be bought from the caisse or from the coin-operated dispenser (18F). The top floor offers the obvious reward of an unparalleled view of the city, and captioned aerial photographs (in English) help you locate landmarks.

Across the river (and the **Pont d'Iéna**) from the Eiffel Tower are the **Trocadéro** and the **Palais de Chaillot.** Built for the 1937 World's Fair, the Palais de Chaillot's elegant, expansive terrace and gardens provide the city's best views of the tower. Save your pictures for here.

NEAR THE TOWER

CHAMP DE MARS. Though close to the 7ème's military monuments and museums, the Champ de Mars (Field of Mars) celebrates the god of war in name alone. The park's name comes from its previous function as a drill ground for the adjacent Ecole Militaire. This flower-embroidered carpet stretching from the Ecole Militaire to the Eiffel Tower is a great place to view the tower. You'll find many groups of backpackers sprawled on the grass with bottles of wine in their hands. Travelers don't get a full night's sleep here, regardless of what you've heard; *gardiens* kick them off the grass at 3am. In 1780, Charles Montgolfier launched the first hydrogen balloon (with no basket attached) from here. During the Revolution, the park witnessed infamous civilian massacres and political demonstrations. At the Champ's 1793 Festival of the Supreme Being, Robespierre proclaimed Reason the new Revolutionary religion. During the 1889, 1900, and 1937 expositions, the space was used for fairgrounds. After the 1900 Exhibition, the municipal council considered parceling off the Champ de Mars for development. They concluded that Paris needed all the open space it could get.

ECOLE MILITAIRE. Louis XV created the Ecole Militaire at the urging of his mistress, Mme de Pompadour, who hoped to make educated officers of "poor gentlemen." In 1784, the 15-year-old Napoleon Bonaparte arrived from Corsica to enroll. A few weeks later he presented administrators with a comprehensive plan for the school's reorganization. The building still belongs to the army today, and no tours are available to the public.

UNESCO. As the Ecole Militaire's architectural and spiritual antithesis, UNESCO (United Nations Educational, Scientific, and Cultural Organization), occupies the Y-shaped building across the road. Established to foster science and culture throughout the world, the agency developed a reputation for waste, cronyism, and manufacturing Marxist propaganda, prompting the U.S., the U.K., and Singapore to withdraw in 1984 (the U.K. rejoined in 1997). Among the building's decorations are a painting by Picasso, a Japanese garden, a meditation area, and an angel from the facade of a Nagasaki church destroyed by nuclear bomb during WWII. UNESCO

16ème

8ème

Musée Guimet

Palais Galliera

PLACE D'IÉNA

Wilson

IÉNA

Palais de Tokyo

Musée d' Art Moderne

av. du Président

av. George V

avenue Montaigne

rue Jean Goujon

r. François 1er

PLACE DE l'ALMA

Cours Albert 1er

ALMA MARCEAU

Pont de l'Alma

Pont des Invalides

Palais de Chaillot

avenue de New York

Seine

PONT DE L'ALMA

PLACE DE LA RÉSISTANCE

Musée dèmes Egouts de Paris

quai d'Orsay

St-Thomas d'Aquin

PLACE DE VARSOVIE

quai Branly

Museé-Galerie S.E.I.T.A.

Pont de d'Iéna

rue de l'Université

rue Jean Nicot

rue Malar

boulevard de la Tour Maubourg

avenue Rapp

rue E. Valentin

avenue Bosquet

rue St-Dominique

Tour Eiffel

avenue Gustave Eiffel

avenue de la Bourdonnais

7ème

rue de Grenelle

rue Cler

LATOUR MAUBOURG

RER CHAMP DE MARS/ TOUR EIFFEL

quai Branly

Bouvard

PLACE JACQUES RUEFF

A B C

D

rue du Champs Mars

E

rue de la Motte Picquet

Musée de l'Ordre de la Libération

rue Jean Ray

CHAMPS DE MARS

avenue de Suffren

avenue Charles Risler

F

ECOLE MILITAIRE

PLACE DE L'ÉCOLE MILITAIRE

JARDIN DE L'INTENDAN

BIR HAKEIM

rue de la Fédération

rue Desaix

Statue de Maréchal Joffre

G

H

Ecole Militaire

boulevard de Grenelle

rue de Lourmel

PLACE DUPLEIX

DUPLEIX

avenue de la Motte Picquet

de Lowendal

COUR D'HONNEUR

PLACE DE FONTENOY

avenue Duquesne

av. de Ségur

rue Foundary

rue Violet

boulevard de Grenelle

LA MOTTE PICQUET GRENELLE

U.N.E.S.C.O.

avenue de Saxe

15ème

r. du Commerce

rue Frémicourt

AV. ÉMILE ZOLA

PLACE CAMBRONNE

CAMBRONNE

rue Pérignon

SÉGUR

av. de Suffren

rue de la Croix Nivert

rue de l'Admiral Roussin

rue Cambroni

boulevard Garibaldi

rue François Bonvin

SÈVRES LECOURBE

rue Jean Daudin

rue Lecourbe

7ème

ACCOMMODATIONS

A Hôtel Kensington
B Hôtel Malar
C Hôtel de la Paix
D Grand Hôtel Lévèque
E Hôtel du Champs de Mars
F Royal Phare Hôtel
G Hôtel Eiffel Rive Gauche
H Hôtel de France

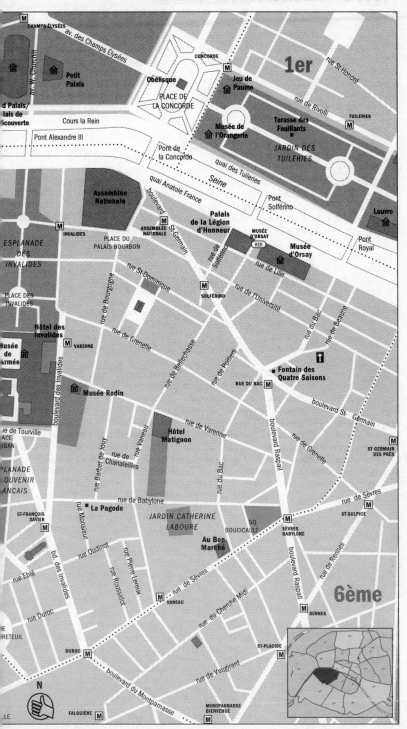

often mounts small but free exhibitions of photography as well as exhibits on art, science, and culture. For information on internships with UNESCO, see **Alternatives to Tourism,** p. 69. *(7, pl. de Fontenoy. M: Ségur. Tel. 01 45 68 10 00; www.unesco.org. Bookstore open M-F 9am-1pm and 2-6pm. Exhibition hours vary.)*

OTHER SIGHTS. From the Ecole Militaire, av. Bosquet takes you to rue St-Dominique's myriad restaurants and *pâtisseries*, while rue Cler features a colorful street market. At the end of av. Bosquet, by the Seine, is the **Musée des Egouts de Paris** (Sewer Museum; see **Museums,** p. 262).

INVALIDES AND THE EAST

INVALIDES. The gold-leafed dome of the Hôtel des Invalides shines at the center of the 7*ème*. The green, tree-lined **Esplanade des Invalides** runs from the *hôtel* to the **Pont Alexandre III,** a bridge with gilded lampposts from which you can catch a great view of the Invalides and the Seine. **Napoleon's tomb,** as well as the **Musée de l'Armée, Musée d'Histoire Contemporaine,** and **Musée de l'Ordre de Liberation,** are housed within the Invalides museum complex (see **Museums,** p. 252). Enter from either pl. des Invalides to the north or pl. Vauban and av. de Tourville to the south. To the left of the Tourville entrance, the **Jardin de l'Intendant** provides a shady place to rest on a bench when you've had your fill of guns and emperors. Lined with foreign cannons, the ditch used to be a moat and still makes it impossible to leave by any but the official entrance. *(2, av. de Tourville. M: Invalides.)*

ASSEMBLÉE NATIONALE. East of the Esplanade, the **Palais Bourbon** would probably not be recognized by its original occupants. Built in 1722 for the Duchesse de Bourbon, daughter of Louis XIV, today the palace is the well-guarded home of the French parliament, the Assemblée Nationale. Machine-gun-toting police stationed every few yards are ostensibly there to prevent a replay of the unsuccessful 1934 Fascist coup, during which rioters stormed the building. *(33, quai d'Orsay. M: Assemblée Nationale. Tel. 01 40 63 63 08; www.assemblée-nat.fr. Open Oct.-June while the Assembly is in session. Tours Sa 10am, 2, and 3pm. Free.)*

Free guided tours (in French, with pamphlet in English) of the Assembly's chambers, which includes a visit to the **Salon Delacroix** and the library (both spectacularly painted by Eugène Delacroix) are available. The library's holdings include the original transcripts of Joan of Arc's trial. The tour continues in the Assembly chamber, the **Salle de Séances,** where the Président du Conseil presides. Behind him, a framed tapestry of Raphael's *School of Athens* depicts the republic of philosopher-kings. Members of the political right and left sit to the right and left of the president's seat. The **Kiosque de l'Assemblée Nationale** provides more information as well as the standard line-up of souvenirs. *(4, rue Aristide-Briand. Tel. 01 40 63 61 21. Open Sept.-July M-F 9:30am-7pm, Sa 9:30am-1pm; Aug. M-F 10am-noon and 2-5pm. AmEx, MC, V.)*

PALAIS DE LA LEGION D'HONNEUR. Once the elegant **Hôtel de Salm,** the Palais de la Legion d'Honneur was built in 1786 by the architect Rousseau for the Prince de Salm-Kyrbourg. Unable to make payment, the prince later returned it to Rousseau but continued to live there as a tenant until he was decapitated in 1794. The state raffled the *hôtel* the following year to a wealthy wig maker named Lieuthraud who presented himself as Count Beauregard until 1797, when he was jailed as a forger. The mansion was then purchased by the Swedish ambassador and his wife, *salonnière* Mme de Staël. Purchased by Napoleon in 1804, the *hôtel*'s current name bears the mark of its most recent owner. Now it houses the **Musée National de la Legion d'Honneur** (see **Museums,** p. 263). Although the museum's display of medals and military honoraria may not spark the interest of many tourists, admission allows a look at the 18th- and 19th-century interiors. Across the street stands the world-famous **Musée d'Orsay,** a former train station now known for its glass-and-steel elegance and immense collection of Impressionist works (see **Museums,** p. 247). *(At the corner of rue de Lille and rue de Bellechasse. M: Solférino.)*

MUSÉE RODIN. At 77, rue Varenne, you'll find the beautiful Musée Rodin (see **Museums,** p. 251). Housed in the **Hôtel Biron,** built by Gabriel in 1728, it became an artists' pension in 1904. The French sculptor Auguste Rodin rented a studio on its ground floor in 1908. When the Ministry of Fine Arts evicted all tenants in 1910, Rodin offered to donate his works to make the *hôtel* an art museum, on the condition that he be permitted to spend his last years there. Nearby at 57, rue Varenne stands **Hôtel Matignon,** once owned by Talleyrand and now the official residence of the prime minister.

LA PAGODE. A Japanese pagoda built in 1895 by the Bon Marché department store magnate M. Morin as a gift to his wife, La Pagode endures as a testament to the 19th-century Orientalist craze in France. Incidentally, the marriage lasted as long as the orientalist fad: Mme Morin left her husband for his colleague's son just prior to WWI. The building then became the scene of Sino-Japanese soirées, although these years saw a period of tension between the two countries (which deepened with Japan's conquest of Manchuria). In 1931, La Pagode opened its doors to the public, becoming a cinema and swank café where the likes of silent screen star Gloria Swanson were known to raise a glass. The theater closed during the Nazi occupation, despite the Axis allegiance. Although it reopened in 1945, it was again closed in 1998 due to a lack of funds to maintain it. A campaign to save la Pagode is underway, but for now visitors must content themselves with the pagoda's exteriors. *(South of the Musée Rodin, at the intersection of rue de Babylone and rue Monsieur.)*

   South of rue Monsieur, along the southern edge of the 7*ème*, the **Bon Marché** department store that inspired the pagoda (see **Shopping,** p. 302) has no fear of closing its doors.

OTHER SIGHTS. The 17th-century **Eglise St-Thomas d'Aquin,** stands on rue de Gribeauval, off rue du Bac. Originally dedicated to St-Dominique, it was reconsecrated by Revolutionaries as the Temple of Peace. *(Tel. 01 42 22 59 74. Open M-F 9am-7pm, Su 9am-noon.)*

   Farther south, at 55-57, rue de Grenelle, the **Fontaine des Quatre Saisons** (Fountain of Four Seasons) features a personified, seated version of the city of Paris near reclining figures of the Seine and the Marne. Bouchardon built the fountain in 1739-45 to provide water to this part of the city. Nearby at 202, bd. St-Germain, the poet Guillaume Apollinaire lived and died. *(M: Rue du Bac.)*

EIGHTH ARRONDISSEMENT

THE CHAMPS-ELYSÉES

Full of expansive mansions, expensive shops and restaurants, grand Haussmann boulevards like the Champs-Elysées, and grandiose monuments like the Arc de Triomphe, the 8*ème* is probably the most glamorous arrondissement of the twenty. Crazily upscale salons and boutiques of *haute couture* line fashionable streets such as the rue du Faubourg St-Honoré. Embassies crowd around the Palais de l'Elysée, the state residence of the French president. The neighborhood took off in the early 19th century with the construction of boulevards Haussmann, Malesherbes, Victor Hugo, Foch, Kléber, and the others that shoot out from the Arc de Triomphe in a radiating formation known as l'Étoile (the star). The grand symmetry of the **Axe Historique,** the line that stretches from the Arc de Triomphe du Carrousel in front of the Louvre, down the Champs-Élysées to the Arc de Triomphe, and down av. de la Grande Armée to La Défense, reflects the largesse of the 8*ème*'s big streets, big money, and big attitude.

16ème

7ème

MONCEAU

PARC DE
MONCEA

PLACE DE
DE JANE

Musée Jacquemart
André

St-Philippe
du Roule

FRANKLIN D.
ROOSEVELT

ROND
POINT DES
CHAMPS
ELYSÉES

CHAMPS ÉLYSÉ
CLEMENCE

Palais de la
Découverte

Grand
Palais

boulevard de Courcelles

avenue Mac Mahon

avenue Carnot

CHARLES DE
GAULLE-ETOILE

RER

TERNES

r. Daru

COURCELLES

avenue de Wagram

avenue Hoche

rue Beaujon

r. de Courcelles

Monceau

r. de

CHARLES DE
GAULLE-ETOILE

Arc de
Triomphe

PLACE
CHARLES
DE GAULLE

avenue Friedland

rue A. Houssaye

rue Balzac

KLÉBER

avenue Marceau

rue Galilée

rue Vernet

rue de Bassano

GEORGE V

rue Washington

rue de Berri

rue d'Artois

ST-PHILIPPE
DU ROULE

B

rue de Ponthieu

avenue des Champs-Elysées

rue du Colisée

rue J. Mermoz

avenue d'Iéna

rue Quentin

Serbie

avenue Pierre 1er de

avenue George V

r. Pierre Charron

rue Bauchart

rue François 1er

rue de Marignan

avenue Franklin D. Roosevelt

Roosevelt

av

American
Cathedral

A

rue Marbeuf

rue de la Trémoille

avenue Montaigne

rue Bayard

PLACE
FRANÇOIS 1ER

IENA

Palais
Galliera

avenue du Président Wilson

Palais
de Tokyo

Musée
d'Art Moderne

Crazy Horse
Saloon

Théâtre de
Champs Elysées

rue Jean Goujon

ALMA
MARCEAU

PLACE DE
L'ALMA

Cours Albert 1er

Cours La Rein

Pt. de l'Alma

RER

PONT DE
L'ALMA

PLACE DE LA
RÉSISTANCE

Pt. des Invalides

Pl. Alexandre III

quai d'Orsay

rue de l'Université

INVALI

avenue du Pré

0   200 yards
0   200 meters

N

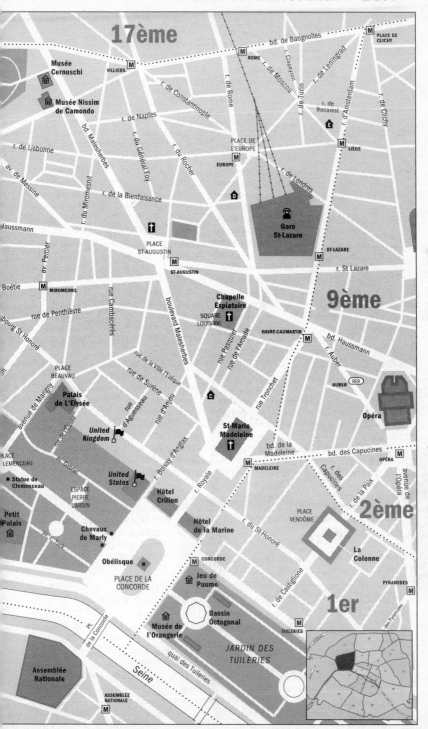

AVENUE DES CHAMPS-ELYSÉES

Here there was a strange little exhibitionist who thought that if he could walk unclothed and unmolested from the Etoile to the Place de la Concorde he could solve many things—and, perhaps, Dick thought, he was quite right.

—F. Scott Fitzgerald, *Tender is the Night*

ARC DE TRIOMPHE

M: Charles-de-Gaulle-Etoile. Tel. 01 55 37 73 77. **Open** *daily Apr.-Sept. 9:30am-10:30pm; Oct.-Mar. 10am-6pm. Last entry 30min. before closing.* **Admission** *40F, ages 12-25, 25F, under 12 free. Expect lines even on weekdays. Buy your ticket in the pedestrian underpasses before going up to the ground level.*

Looming gloriously above the Champs-Elysées at pl. Charles de Gaulle-Etoile, the Arc de Triomphe commemorates France's military history and victories. The world's largest triumphal arch and an internationally recognized symbol of France, this grand arch was commissioned by Napoleon in 1805. When construction began, the Etoile marked the western entrance to the city. Napoleon was exiled before the monument was completed, but Louis XVIII ordered the completion of the work in 1823 and dedicated the arch to the war in Spain and to its commander, the Duc d'Angoulême. Designed by Chalgrin, the Arc de Triomphe was consecrated in 1836, 21 years after the defeat of the Napoleon's great army. There was no consensus on what symbolic figures could cap the monument, as its original theme of "Napoleon the Grand" seemed a bit retro at the time, and so it has retained its simple unfinished form. The names of Napoleon's generals and battles are engraved inside; those generals underlined died in battle. The most famous of the Arc's allegorical sculpture groups depicting the military history of France is François Rude's *Departure of the Volunteers of 1792*, commonly known as *La Marseillaise*, to the right facing the arch from the Champs-Elysées.

The Arc is primarily a military symbol. As such, the horseshoe-shaped colossus has proved a magnet to various triumphal armies. The victorious Prussians marched through in 1871, inspiring the mortified Parisians to purify the ground with fire. On July 14, 1919, however, the Arc provided the backdrop for an Allied celebration parade headed by Maréchal Foch. His memory is now honored by the boulevard, the widest street in the city, that bears his name and stretches out from the west side of the Arc into the 16ème.

The **Tomb of the Unknown Soldier** has been under the Arc since November 11, 1920. It is the eternal resting place of an unknown soldier killed in World War I. The **eternal flame** is rekindled every evening at 6:30pm, when veterans lay wreaths decorated with blue, white, and red. In 1940, Parisians shed tears of defeat as the Nazis goose-stepped through the Arc and down the Champs-Elysées. De Gaulle's famous cry for *Résistance*, broadcast over the BBC from his WWII exile in London in 1940, is inscribed on a brass plaque in the pavement below the Arc. After four years of Nazi occupation, France was liberated by British, American, Canadian, Québecois, and French troops who marched through the Arc de Triomphe on August 26, 1944, to the roaring cheers of thousands of grateful Parisians.

THINGS ARE NOT WHAT THEY SEEM In 1805,
Napoleon told his troops, newly victorious at Austerlitz, that they would "go home beneath triumphal arches." The first stone of said arch was placed the following year, but events conspired to necessitate a little *trompe l'oeil*. In1810, Napoleon was set to marry Marie-Louise, the daughter of the Austrian emperor, so that he could have an heir. The only hitch in his plan was the still incomplete triumphal arch, through which he desired to process on the way to his wedding at the Louvre. Always one to have his way, the emperor had his architect Chalgrin build a full-scale mock-up of the arch for the couple to parade through on their way to the altar.

SIGHTS

The Arc de Triomphe sits in the center of the Étoile, which in 1907 became the world's first traffic circle. Rather than risk an early and painful death by crossing the street to reach the Arc, use the underpasses on the even-numbered sides of both the Champs-Elysées and avenue de la Grande-Armée. Inside the Arc, climb 205 steps up a winding staircase to the *entresol* between the Arc's two supports, and then 29 more to the *musée*, or tackle the lines at the elevator for a lift. Motion impaired visitors should be aware that the elevator is often not running, so that access to the top of the Arc is by stairs only: call in advance to check. The museum explains (in French) the Arc's architecture and history. Just 46 steps beyond, the **terrasse observation deck** at the top of the Arc provides an brilliant view of the Champs-Elysées, the tree-lined avenue Foch (see **Sights**, p. 221), and the Axe Historique from the Arc de Triomphe du Carrousel and the Louvre Pyramid at one end to the Grande Arche de la Défense at the other.

AVENUE DES CHAMPS-ELYSÉES. The avenue des Champs-Élysées is the most famous of the 12 symmetrical avenues radiating from the huge rotary of pl. Charles de Gaulle-Étoile. The Champs-Elysées, though quite beautiful in parts, can be disappointing upon first sight, as it is increasingly becoming a tourist runway packed with mini-malls, burger bars, and famous cafés that hold on by reputation alone. Nonetheless, glimmers of its former glamour can be seen in the area around the Rond-Poin, and the gardens leading up to the Pl. de la Concorde. Le Nôtre planted trees here in 1667 to extend the Tuileries vista, completing the work begun under Marie de Médici in 1616. In 1709, the area was renamed the "Elysian Fields" because of the shade provided by the trees. During the 19th century, the Champs (as many Parisians call it) developed into a fashionable residential district. Mansions sprang up along its sides, then apartments and smart boutiques, making this strip of pavement the place to see and be seen in Paris. Balls, café-concerts, restaurants, and circuses drew enormous crowds. The infamous *Bal Mabille* opened in 1840 at no. 51, and, at no. 25, in a somewhat more subdued setting. There, Marquise de Païva, the most famous courtesan of the 19th century, a charming hostess, and a spy, entertained her famous guests.

OTHER SIGHTS. Today, you can watch others cling desperately to the Champs glorious past at **Fouquet's,** a famous and outrageously expensive café-restaurant where French film stars ostensibly hang out. The red-awninged eatery still hosts the French answer to the Oscars, the annual César awards (see p. 141 for the full listing). At night, Paris's hottest dance club, **Le Queen,** 102 Champs-Élysées, features the fattest house music on the Right Bank and the most beautiful and best-dressed people in the city (and their straight friends). (See p. 294 for full listing.)

FASHION HOUSES AND
THE GRAND AND PETIT PALAIS

Six big avenues radiate from the Rond Point des Champs-Elysées. Avenue Montaigne runs southwest and shelters the houses of *haute couture*.

PALAIS DE L'ÉLYSÉE. The guards pacing around the house at the corner of avenue de Marigny and rue du Faubourg St-Honoré are protecting the Palais de l'Elysée. Built in 1718, the *palais* was later home to the Marquis de Marigny, brother of Madame de Pompadour. During the Restoration, July Monarchy, and Second Empire, the Elysée was used to house royal guests. Since 1870, it has served as state residence of the French president, now Jacques Chirac. Although entrance requires a personal invitation, the persistent visitor can catch a glimpse of the gardens. *(M: Champs-Elysées-Clemenceau.)*

The Union Jack flying overhead at no. 35, rue du Faubourg-St-Honoré, marks the **British Embassy.** At 2, av. Gabriel, the **American Embassy** flies the Stars and Stripes.

GRAND PALAIS AND THE PETIT PALAIS. At the foot of the Champs-Elysées, the Grand Palais and the Petit Palais face one another on avenue Winston

Churchill. Built for the 1900 World's Fair, both *palais* are examples of Art Nouveau architecture; the glass over steel and stone composition of the Grand Palais makes the top look like a giant greenhouse. The Petit and Grand Palais host exhibitions on architecture, painting, sculpture, and French history. The Grand Palais also houses the **Palais de la Découverte** (see **Museums**, p. 264). Most beautiful at night, the glass dome of the Grand Palais glows greenly from within, and its statues are backlit. Around the time that the palaces were built, the first stone of Pont Alexandre III was placed by the czar's son, Nicholas II. It made a stir as the first bridge to cross the Seine in a single span. At the time of its building, stringent restrictions were placed on the bridge, so that it would not block the view of any of the other beautiful buildings on the Seine. Today it is considered the most beautiful bridge across the Seine, providing a noble axis with the still-visible Invalides (see **Sights**, p. 194).

OTHER SIGHTS. Built by the Perret brothers in 1912 with bas-reliefs by Bourdelle, the **Théâtre des Champs-Élysées** is best known for staging the controversial premiere of Stravinsky's *Le Sacre du Printemps*, where Nijinksy humped the stage in mock imitation of carnal eroticism, and a riot ensued. The three large *salles* still host performances. (*15, av. Montaigne. M: Alma-Marceau. See p. 274 for full listing.*)

Around the corner from the theater, the **Crazy Horse Saloon**, long famous for its cabaret, still entertains fans of the "Art du Nu" (art of the nude). **Pershing Hall**, 49, rue Pierre Charron, is a 113-year-old, five-story piece of America. Given to the U.S. government, the building has allegedly been used as a brothel, a brawling bar, a casino, a black-market exchange, and a Council Travel office. Now closed, it awaits its next incarnation.

PLACE DE LA CONCORDE

PLACE DE LA CONCORDE. Paris's largest and most infamous public square forms the eastern terminus of the Champs-Elysées. With your back to avenue Gabriel, the Tuileries Gardens are to your left, while across the river lie the gold-domed Invalides and the Greek-styled columns of the Assemblée Nationale. Behind you stands the Madeleine. Constructed between 1757 and 1777 to provide a home for a monument to Louis XV, this vast area soon became pl. de la Révolution, the site of the guillotine that severed 1,343 necks. On Sunday, January 21, 1793, Louis XVI was beheaded by guillotine on a site near where the Brest statue now stands. The celebrated heads of Louis XVI, Marie-Antoinette, Charlotte Corday (Marat's assassin), Lavoisier, Danton, Robespierre, and others rolled into baskets here and were held up to the cheering crowds who packed the pavement. In 1993, hundreds of French (and the American ambassador) honored this event with flowers placed on the very spot. After the Reign of Terror, the square was optimistically renamed pl. de la Concorde (place of Harmony).

Much favored by film crews for its views of Paris's monuments (and especially for the view of the Eiffel Tower in relief against the Paris sky), this square has been featured in many films, such as the dream sequence in Gene

Kelly and Stanley Donen's *An American in Paris*. On Bastille Day (July 14) a military parade marches through pl. de la Concorde (usually around 10am) and down the Champs-Elysées to the Arc de Triomphe led by the President of the Republic (see **Festivals,** p. 282). In the evening, an impressive fireworks display lights up the sky over pl. de la Concorde. Asking the French about "Bastille Day," may garner blank stares, as July 14 is known in France as La Fête Nationale. At the end of August, the Tour de France finalists pull into the home stretch on the Champs-Élysées and the pl. de la Concorde. Get there early for a view of the cyclists. *(M: Concorde.)*

OBÉLISQUE DE LUXOR. At the center of pl. de la Concorde, the Obélisque de Luxor was offered by Mehemet Ali, Viceroy of Egypt, to Charles X in 1829. Getting the obelisk from Egypt to the center of Paris was no simple task; a canal to the Nile had to be dug, the monolith had to be transported by sea, and a special boat built to transport it up the Seine. Erected in 1836, Paris's oldest monument dates back to the 13th century BCE and recalls the deeds of Ramses II. At night the obelisk, fountains, and turn-of-the-century cast-iron lamps are illuminated, creating a romantic glow, somewhat mitigated by the scaffolding covered state of one of the fountains and the base of the obelisk until spring 2000.

CHEVEAUX DE MARLY. Flanking the Champs-Elysées at pl. de la Concorde stand the Guillaume Coustou 18th-century Cheveaux de Marly, which were originally designed for Marly, Louis XIV's château near Versailles. Also known as *Africans Mastering the Numidian Horses*, the original sculptures are now in the Louvre to protect them from the effects of city pollution. Perfect replicas graciously hold their places on the Concorde. Eight large statues representing France's major cities also grace the *place*. Juliette Drouet, Victor Hugo's mistress, allegedly posed for the town of Strasbourg, with Victor Hugo posing as the horse.

THE MADELEINE. Mirrored by the Assemblée Nationale across the Seine, the **Madeleine,** formally called Église Ste-Marie-Madeleine (Mary Magdalene), was begun in 1764 by Louis XV and modeled after a Greek temple. Construction was halted during the Revolution, when the Cult of Reason proposed transforming the building into a bank, a theater, or a courthouse. Completed in 1842, the structure stands alone in the medley of Parisian churches, distinguished by its four ceiling domes that light the interior in lieu of windows, 52 exterior Corinthian columns, and a curious altarpiece. An immense sculpture of the ascension of Mary Magdalene, the church's namesake, adorns the altar. Marcel Proust spent most of his childhood nearby at 9, bd. Malesherbes, which might explain his penchant for his aunt Léonie's *madeleines* with tea. *(Pl. de la Madeleine. M: Madeleine. Tel. 01 44 51 69 00. Open daily 7:30am-7:15pm. Regular organ and chamber concerts. Contact the church for a schedule, and Virgin or FNAC for tickets.)*

You can stop and eat a few *madeleines* or pick up some chocolate *macarons* at the world-famous food shop, **Fauchon,** 24-30, pl. de la Madeleine, just behind the church (see **Specialty Stores,** p. 155). Do not mistake the Madeleine with Ludwig Bemelman's 1939 children's classic, *Madeline*, who lived in Paris with Miss Clavel and twelve girls, all in a line.

OTHER SIGHTS. Directly north of pl. de la Concorde, like two sentries guarding the gate to the Madeleine, stand the **Hôtel de Crillon** (on the left) and the **Hôtel de la Marine** (on the right). Architect Jacques-Ange Gabriel built the impressive colonnaded facades between 1757 and 1770. On February 16, 1778, the Franco-American treaties were signed here, making France the first European nation to recognize the independence of the United States of America. Chateaubriand lived in the Hôtel de Crillon between 1805 and 1807. Today it is one of the most expensive, elegant hotels in Paris (single 2600-3200F; suite with shower 29,800F). World-renowned **Maxim's** restaurant, 3, rue Royale, won't even allow you a peek into what was once Richelieu's home.

S I G H T S

YOU SAY YOU WANT A REVOLUTION The organizers of the French Revolution believed the world was starting afresh, made clean by the ensuing bloodbath. In a typical burst of zeal, they abolished the existing Julian calendar, and took the day the Republic was declared, September 22, 1792, as the inception-date of their brave new world. The system of twelve months remained, although each month was renamed with pleasant-sounding and nature-loving names like Ventôse (wind) or Guillotine. Each month was three periods of ten-days long, with the remaining five days devoted to public holidays.

CHAPELLE EXPIATOIRE AND PARC MONCEAU

CHAPELLE EXPIATOIRE. Place Louis XVI includes the improbably large Chapelle Expiatoire, its monuments to Marie-Antoinette and Louis XVI, and a lovely park with benches. Once affiliated with the Madeleine, a cemetery was opened on the site in 1722. During the Revolution, victims of the guillotine, including the King and Queen, were dumped here. Although Louis XVIII had his brother and sister-in-law's remains removed to St-Denis in 1815, Marat's assassin Charlotte Corday and Louis XVI's cousin Philippe-Égalité (who voted for the king's death only to be beheaded himself) are buried on either side of the staircase. Statues of the expiatory King and Queen, with their crowns at their feet, stand inside the Chapelle. Their last letters are engraved in French on the base of the sculptures. *(29, rue Pasquier, just below bd. Haussmann. M: Madeleine. Open Tu, F, Sa 1-4pm. 15F.)*

GARE ST-LAZARE. The Gare St-Lazare's platforms and iron-vaulted canopy are not to be missed by train riders and fans of Monet's impressionist painting *La Gare St-Lazare* (at the Musée d'Orsay) and Émile Zola's novel about the station and its trains, *La Bête Humaine*. To the north of the train station is pl. de Dublin, the setting for Gustave Caillebotte's famous urban impressionist painting, *A Rainy Day in Paris* (now at the Art Institute of Chicago). *(M: St-Lazare.)*

PARC MONCEAU. The Parc Monceau, an expansive natural urban refuge guarded by gold-tipped, wrought-iron gates, borders the elegant bd. de Courcelles. The Parc Monceau is a pastoral setting for kids to play and parents to unwind or read in the shade. This park is also popular with joggers (see **Sports**, p. 277). The painter Carmontelle designed the park for the Duc d'Orléans, and it was completed by Haussmann in 1862. The *Rotonde de Monceau* is a remnant of the *fermiers généraux* wall of the 1780s. A tollhouse designed to enforce customs duties rather than to keep out invaders, the wall and its fortifications reflected their creator's penchant for ornament. An array of architectural follies—a pyramid, a covered bridge, an East Asian pagoda, Dutch windmills, and Roman ruins—make this formal garden *cum* romping ground for kids (complete with roller rink) a Kodak commercial waiting to happen. As in other Parisian parks, frolicking, lying, or playing on the grass is forbidden and you are likely to be told to move *tout de suite* by the strangely clairvoyant park police. *(M: Monceau or Courcelles. Open Apr.-Oct. 7am-10pm; Nov.-Mar. 7am-8pm. Gates close 15min. earlier.)*

CATHÉDRALE ALEXANDRE-NEVSKI. Thanks primarily to Catherine the Great, French culture became a staple in the diet of Russian aristocrats for centuries. Almost all of the young upper class Russians came to Paris to seek cultivation, and many families owned vacation homes in the area. As the pogroms intensified in the late 19th century, France opened its doors. Again, after the 1917 revolution, Russian culture streamed into Paris. Built in 1860, the onion-domed Eglise Russe, also known as Cathédrale Alexandre-Nevski, is a Russian Eastern Orthodox church. The gold domes, spectacular from the outside, are equally beautiful on the inside. They were intricately painted by artists from St. Petersburg, and are currently undergoing restoration. *(12, rue Daru. M: Ternes. Tel. 01 42 27 37 34. Open Tu and F 3-5pm. Services Su at 10am.)*

NINTH ARRONDISSEMENT

OPÉRA

The boulevards and *quartier* surrounding the Opéra Garnier are simply called *l'Opéra*. On the southernmost border of the 9*ème*, the Opéra is the arrondissement's most prosperous and visited area. For those less interested in the high art offerings of the Garnier's ballets, concerts, and opera, the 9*ème* is filled with cinemas and is home to the legendary Olympia, one of Paris's most famous concert stages for American, European, and Brazilian pop, jazz, and rock performances. Perhaps the busiest sites of the 9*ème*, however, are the arrondissement's department stores, Au Printemps and Galeries Lafayette, where thousands of Parisians and tourists seek out the fairest of the(m)all (see **Department Stores,** p. 302).

OPÉRA GARNIER AND SURROUNDINGS

M: Opéra. Tel. 01 44 73 13 99, for recorded information 08 36 69 78 68, for reservations 08 44 73 13 00. **Open** *daily 10am-5pm, last entry 4:30pm; in summer 10am-6pm, last entry 5:30pm.* **Admission** *30F, ages 10-16, students and 60 and over 20F.* **Tours** *in English at noon daily in summer, varying otherwise, 60F; students, ages 10-16, or above 60 45F; under 10 25F. For info on tours, call 01 40 01 22 63. For concert info, see* **Classical Music, Opera, and Dance,** *p. 274.*

Emerging from the Opéra métro station, your eyes will quickly be drawn to the grandiose and grand Opéra Garnier, or at least to the enormous scaffolding covering its front for much-needed renovations in the middle of pl. de l'Opéra. Designed by Charles Garnier under Napoleon III in the showy eclecticism of the Second Empire, the Opéra is perhaps most famous as home to the legend of the Phantom of the Opéra. Towering high above the *grands boulevards* of the southern 9*ème*, the building epitomizes both the Second Empire's ostentation and its rootlessness; a mix of styles and odd details ties it to no formal tradition. Queried as to whether his building was in the style of Louis XIV, Louis XV, or Louis XVI, Garnier responded that his creation belonged to Napoleon III, who financed the project. The interior of the Opéra, with its grand staircase, golden foyer, and five-tiered auditorium, was designed as a stage for not only opera performance but also for 19th-century bourgeois social life, with balconies designed for the audience members to watch one another as well as the show.

Garnier's design outshined hundreds of competing plans in an 1861 competition, including the entry of the "Pope of Architects" Viollet-le-Duc, who restored Nôtre-Dame. Garnier was virtually unknown at the time, and the commission made him famous. Opened in 1875, the magnificent interiors are adorned with Gobelin tapestries (see p. 214), gilded mosaics, and a six-ton chandelier that fell on the audience in 1896. In 1964, Chagall was commissioned to paint the ceiling. Since 1989, when the new Opéra de la Bastille was inaugurated, most operas have been performed

SIGHTS

THE RITES OF SCANDAL

■ Everyone's favorite Igor, Igor Stravinsky, left his mark upon Paris, its theaters and monuments. The **Théâtre des Champs-Elysées** (see p. 200), in the 8*ème*, is best known for staging the first production of *Le Sacre du Printemps* (The Rite of Spring), where dancer Nijinsky and co.'s erotic interpretation caused a riot to break out on opening night. The home theater of this innovative dance troupe, led by Diaghilev, was the **Opéra Garnier** (see p. 203). It now holds a museum tracing the roots of the group's definite break from fluffy Romanticism. Commemorating the controversial composer is the **Stravinsky Fountain,** in the Beaubourg (see p. 179), whose primary-colored musical figures are controversial only when they spurt water onto the wrong passer-by.

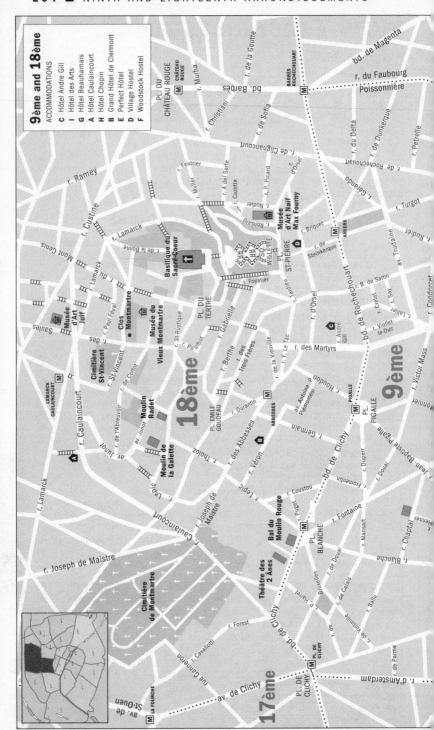

9ème and 18ème

ACCOMMODATIONS

C Hôtel Andre Gill
I Hôtel des Arts
G Hôtel Beauharnais
A Hôtel Caulaincourt
H Hôtel Chopin
B Grand Hôtel de Clermont
E Perfect Hôtel
D Village Hostel
F Woodstock Hostel

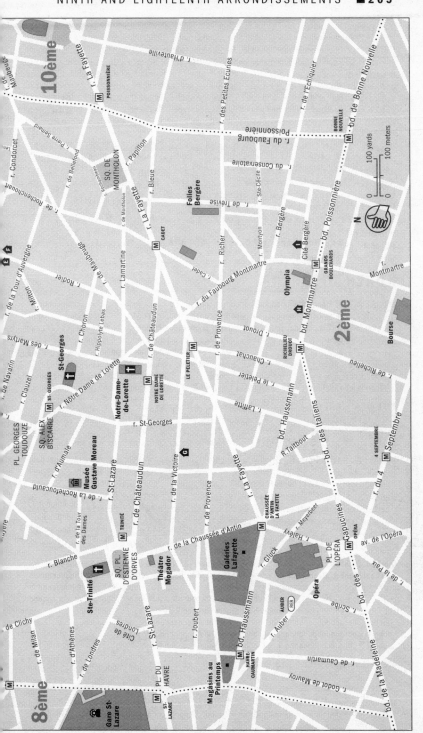

at the Bastille, while the Opera Garnier has been used mainly for ballets. In 1992, Rudolf Nureyev made his last public appearance here, his home since his defection from the Soviet Union, shortly before his death.

Guided tours are available in several languages, but they are in high demand during the summer months. Ask about availability at the entrance when you arrive. The Opéra also houses a **library** and **museum** on the history of opera and dance that focus particularly on Nijinksy and the Ballet Russe, Diaghilev's innovative troupe that liberated classical dance from fluffy Romanticism with such controversial, erotic 20th-century works as Stravinsky's *Firebird* and *Rite of Spring*. *(Open daily 10am-noon and 2-5pm.)*

To the right of the Opéra, the **Café de la Paix,** 12, bd. des Capucines, is the quintessential 19th-century-café. Like the Opéra, it was designed by Garnier and today caters to the after-theater crowd and anyone else who doesn't mind paying 30F for coffee (see **Cafés,** p. 142). Farther down bd. des Capucines, the giant red glowing letters of the **Olympia** music hall signal the place where Edith Piaf achieved fame. Popular artists still perform here. *(Tel. 01 47 42 25 49.)* The carnivalesque **Musée Grévin** is a French wax museum (see **Museums,** p. 262), with figures from Royalty and the Revolution. West of the Opéra, the department stores **Au Printemps** and **Galeries Lafayette** stand on the bd. Haussmann (see **Department Stores,** p. 302).

NORTH OF OPÉRA

EGLISE NÔTRE-DAME-DE-LORETTE. Farther east, on pl. Kossuth, Eglise Nôtre-Dame-de-Lorette was built in 1836 to "the glory of the Virgin Mary." This Neoclassical church is filled with statues of saints and frescoes of scenes from the life of Mary. Built in 1840, rue Nôtre-Dame-de-Lorette was less saintly than its name. A thoroughfare of ill-repute in the late 1960s, this street became the debauched hang-out of Émile Zola's *Nana* (whose name is now slang for chick or babe). The term *lorette* came to refer to the quarter's young prostitutes. The mere mention of Nôtre-Dame-de-Lorette made men look away and good girls blush. *(M: Nôtre-Dame-de-Lorette.)*

RUE DES MARTYRS. Rue des Martyrs, once home to bars and restaurants for the kind of crowd that rents hotel rooms by the hour, revelled in an equally bad reputation. Now filled with pornographic fruit stands, naughty cheese shops, and debauched *épiceries*, the street has barely mended its sordid ways. *(M: Pigalle.)*

PIGALLE. Farther north, at the border of the 18*ème*, is the infamous area called Pigalle, the so-called un-chastity belt of Paris. During World War II, American servicemen aptly called Pigalle "Pig-alley." Stretching along the bd. de Clichy from pl. Pigalle to pl. Blanche is a salacious, voracious neighborhood. Sex-shops, brothels, porn stores, lace, leather, and latex boutiques line the streets. As a result, the area swarms with police. Although Pigalle is undergoing a slow gentrification, tourists (especially women) should be wary of walking alone here at night. The areas to the north of bd. Clichy and south of pl. Blanche are comparatively calmer. *(M: Pigalle.)*

OTHER SIGHTS. Built at the end of the 19th century in Italian Renaissance style, **Eglise de la Sainte-Trinité** on rue de la Chaussée has beautiful, painted vaults and is surrounded by a fountained park with tree-shaded benches. *(M: Trinité. Open daily 4:30-6:30pm.)* The **Musée Gustave Moreau,** 14, rue de La Rochefoucauld, is housed in the painter's house and studio (see **Museums,** p. 264).

TENTH ARRONDISSEMENT

Far from most tourist itineraries, the 10*ème*'s working-class neighborhoods offer a few hidden sights and many marvels of urban planning designed to keep the working-class in line. The tree-lined Canal St-Martin is a refreshing break from the city while the Faubourg St-Denis features North and West African markets, restaurants, and shops. Europe's train lines converge at the Gare de l'Est and the Gare du Nord, and the 3*ème*, 10*ème*, and 11*ème* converge at pl. de la République. One word of caution: bd. Magenta and bd. Faubourg tend to be risky at night. Beware of pickpockets.

GARE DU NORD AND GARE DE L'EST. Designed by Jacques-Ignace Hittorf in 1863, the Gare du Nord's grandiose, beige neoclassical exterior is topped by statues representing the cities of France. Inside, the platforms are covered by a vast vault of glass and steel, which Napoleon III called the station's *parapluie* (umbrella).

Similarly, the Gare de l'Est's 19th-century glass and ironwork spins a fan-like facade and latticed roof. Surrounding the station on pl. du 11 Nov. 1918 and bd. de Strasbourg, Alsatian restaurants serve Franco-Germanic specialties brought to this quartier by WWI refugees from Alsace-Lorraine. Shops on **rue de Paradis** display china and crystal produced at the famous **Cristalleries Baccarat,** 30bis, rue de Paradis, suppliers of fine crystal for Europe's royal houses since 1764 (see **Museums,** p. 262).

PORTE ST-DENIS AND PORTE ST-MARTIN. At the end of rue Faubourg St-Denis, the grand **Porte St-Denis** looms triumphantly. Built in 1672 to celebrate the victories of Louis XIV in Flanders and the Rhineland, the gate imitates the Arch of Titus in Rome. Once the site of a medieval entrance to the city, the present arch serves only as a rotary for traffic. In the words of André Breton, *c'est très belle et très inutile* (it's very beautiful and very useless). On July 28, 1830, it was the scene of intense fighting as revolutionaries scrambled to the top and rained cobblestones on the monarchist troops below. Two blocks down bd. St-Denis, the 1674 **Porte St-Martin** is a smaller copy with a silly Herculean Louis XIV on the facade in nothing but a wig and a smile. Built in 1866, the **Marché St-Quentin,** 85bis, bd. de Magenta, houses a flower, butcher, and produce market in its cavernous iron and glass spaces (see **Food Markets,** p. 157). *(M: Strasbourg/St-Denis.)*

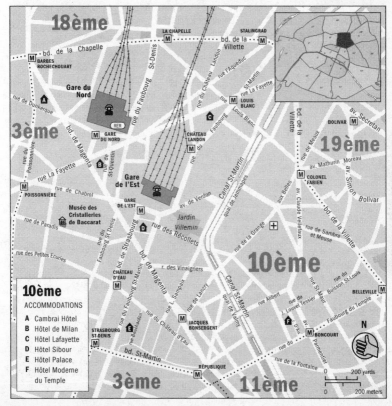

RÉPUBLIQUE. The stretch from Porte St-Martin to pl. de la République along rue René Boulanger and bd. St-Martin served as a lively theater district in the 19th century and has recently begun to retrieve some of its former sparkle. A shining example is the **Théâtre de la Renaissance,** with its sculpted facade of griffins and arabesques by Carrier-Belleuse. Newly refurbished, it has breathed new life into the neighborhood. **Pl. de la République** is the meeting point of the *3ème, 10ème,* and *11ème* arrondissements. At its center, Morice's sculpture of *La République* glorifies France's many revolutionary struggles. Ironically, it was created by Haussman, who had to demolish several theaters for its expanse, to divide and conquer the rather-revolutionary arrondissements that border it. Buzzing with crowds during the day, the area can be dangerous at night. (See **Sights**, p. 175, for more on the *place.*) *(M: République.)*

CANAL ST-MARTIN. The most pleasant area of the *10ème* is the tree-lined Canal St-Martin. Measuring 4.5km, the canal connects to the Seine and has several locks, which can be traveled by boat on one of the **canauxrama** trips (see p. 162). It was made in 1825 as a shortcut for river traffic on the Seine. It was also a natural defense again the upstart eastern arrondissements at the time. East of the canal, follow rue Bichat to the **Hôpital St-Louis.** Built in 1607 by Henri IV as a sanctuary/prison for victims of the plague, it was located across a marsh and downwind of the rotting Buttes-Chaumont (see **Sights**, p. 230). Its distance from any water-source suggests that it was intended more to protect the city from contamination than to help the unfortunates inside. Today, the hospital boasts the lovely **Quadrilatère Historique de St-Louis,** a flowered courtyard. At 53, rue de la Grange-aux-Belles, there used to be a path uphill to the **Montfaucon Gallows.** Famous for its hanging capacity of 60, this system of pillars and chains once executed medieval prisoners with an efficiency unrivaled until the invention of the guillotine. The unfortunates were hung in clusters and left to rot, the smell of which could poison the city on a windy day. In the 14th century, the gallows were replaced with a more efficient design by Pierre Rémy, treasurer to Charles IV, who in 1328 was hung by his own creation.

ELEVENTH ARRONDISSEMENT

The 11*ème* is most famous for hosting the Revolutionary kick-off at the Bastille prison on July 14, 1789 (see **History**, p. 5). Although nothing remains of the famous debtors' prison, pl. de la Bastille's opera house has inspired new revolts by architects and citizens alike. But like the *sans-culottes,* who came up empty when they

SIGHTS OF THE REVOLUTION

■ Begin your tour at **pl. de la Bastille** (p. 209) where the storming of the Bastille prison occurred on July 1789. The only remnants of the prison are some of its stones which can be found in **Pont de la Concorde** as well as in a commemorative pile in **pl. Henri Galli** (p. 209). Interestingly, a number of the revolution's profiteers lived around the Bastille; visit **Maison de Retraite et de Santé,** a sham sanitorium where Dr. Belhomme hid condemned aristocrats (p. 209). Wander through the 12ème, an area once known as the 'red belt' for its participation in the 1830 and 1848 revolutions to **pl. de la Nation** (p. 214), where 1300 nobles were executed during the revolution of 1789. The Revolution converted **the Pantheon** into a mausoleum of heroes (p. 184). Café **Au Franc-Pinot** on Ile St-Louis was a treasonous address during the Revolution, and the proprietor's daughter attempted to assassinate Robespierre in 1794. This same year, Robespierre took refuge in what is now the **Hôtel de Ville** (p. 180). In this location, where Paris' 300 regional electors met to discuss matters in 1789, his jaw was smashed by a bullet, and he was brought to the Conciergerie. Finally, visit the **Musée de Cluny** where you can see 13th-century stone heads of Judean and Israelite kings which were severed from Nôtre-Dame's portals by Revolutionaries who mistook them for ancestors of Louis XVI. The **Musée Carnavalet** has weapons, intriguing plates, games, toys, and documents from all revolutions (p. 258).

CLOUDY, WITH A CHANCE OF RAIN Although the storming of the Bastille, prison of Voltaire and the Marquis de Sade, has come to symbolize the Revolution of 1789, the actual event was less significant than might be expected. The Bastille prison was hardly used toward the end of the monarchy. Louis XVI himself was considering tearing it down, since it hindered his plans for the development of the city. In fact, in 1789, only 7 prisoners were being held at the Bastille. Their liberation was only fleeting—the excitement was too much for them to handle and they were quickly re-imprisoned for their insanity. In Louis XVI's journal entry for July 14, 1789, he states *"Aujourd'hui, rien"* ("Today, nothing"). The storming was a political symbol, and pl. de la Bastille is still used as a political market. Marches, celebrations, and demonstrations for all sorts of ideals and causes can be viewed there.

crashed the prison (see **History,** p. 5) those looking for the opéra in the 11*ème* will also be disappointed—it's in the 12*ème* (see p. 212). Cutting-edge-hip a few years ago, the eleventh is largely a polluted cesspool of once-too-cool bars and cafés. It still has some hips areas, but overall it is laid back, cheap, and crowded.

BASTILLE

THE BASTILLE PRISON. The Bastille prison was originally commissioned by Charles V to safeguard the eastern entrance to Paris. A royal treasury under Henri IV, the fortress became a state prison under his successor Louis XIII. Internment there, generally reserved for religious heretics and political undesirables, followed specific orders from the king. The man in the iron mask languished here at Louis XIV's request. Despite imprisonment, many titled inmates furnished their suites, brought their servants, and received guests. The Cardinal de Rohan held a dinner party for 20 in his cell. The prison itself provided fresh linens. Notable prisoners included Mirabeau, Voltaire, and the Marquis de Sade, one of the last seven prisoners to be held there. Seldom one to miss a party, he left July 7, 1789, just a week before the prison's liberation.

When Revolutionary militants stormed the Bastille, they came for its supply of gunpowder. Having sacked the Invalides for weapons, they needed munitions. Surrounded by an armed rabble, too short on food to entertain a siege, and unsure of the loyalty of the Swiss mercenaries who defended the prison, the Bastille's governor surrendered. While he was under armed escort to the Hôtel de Ville, the mob hacked off his head with a pocketknife and paraded it around on a pike. Despite the gruesome details, the storming of the Bastille has come to symbolize the triumph of liberty over despotism. Its first anniversary was the cause for great celebration in Revolutionary Paris. Since the late 19th century, July 14 has been the official state holiday of the French Republic (see **Festivals,** p. 282). Demolition of the prison began the day after its capture and concluded in October 1792. Some of its stones were incorporated into the **Pont de la Concorde.** *(M: Bastille.)*

PLACE HENRI GALLI. A commemorative pile of stones from the Bastille can also be found in pl. Henri Galli. A certain Citizen Palloy, the demolition contractor, used the stones to construct 83 models of the prison that he sent to the provinces as reminders of "the horror of despotism." In 1831 King Louis-Philippe laid the cornerstone for the July Column at the center of pl. de la Bastille to commemorate the Republicans who died in the Revolutions of 1789 and 1830. The column's vault contains the bodies of 504 martyrs of 1830 along with two mummified Egyptian pharaohs that were moved from the Louvre when they began to rot. *(M: Bastille. Down bd. Henri IV from pl. de la Bastille.)*

MAISON DE RETRAITE ET DE SANTÉ. Many of the Revolution's profiteers lived along the streets radiating from pl. de la Bastille. The *hôtel* at 157-161, rue de Charonne, housed the infamous Dr. Belhomme, whose Maison de Retraite et de

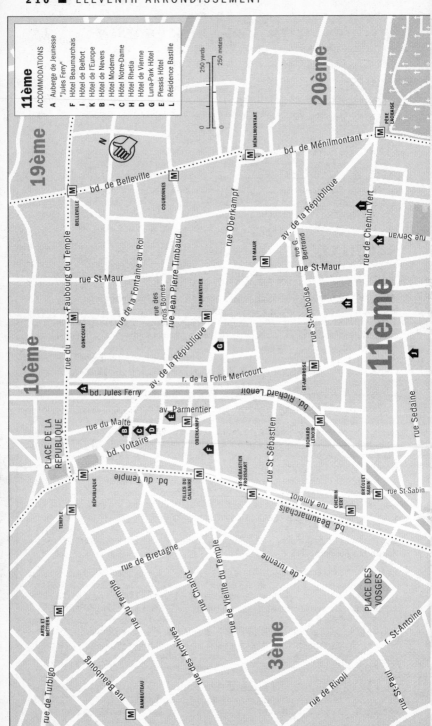

11ème
ACCOMMODATIONS
A Auberge de Jeunesse "Jules Ferry"
F Hôtel Beaumarchais
I Hôtel de Belfort
K Hôtel de l'Europe
B Hôtel de Nevers
J Hôtel Moderne
C Hôtel Notre-Dame
H Hôtel Rhetia
D Hôtel de Vienne
G Luna-Park Hôtel
E Plessis Hôtel
L Résidence Bastille

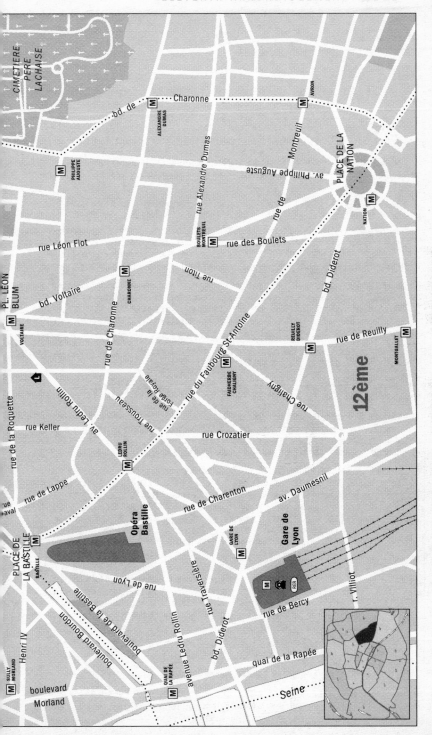

Santé sheltered condemned aristocrats with ready cash during the Terror (1792-1795). For 1000 *livres* a month, Dr. Belhomme would let a room in his sham sanatorium and certify his clients as too ill to brave the scaffold. Arrested himself after word got out, the savvy Dr. Belhomme holed up in a similar establishment on rue de Picpusin in the 12*ème*. *(M: Alexandre Dumas.)*

RUE DE LA ROQUETTE. Some residues of the Bastille's spurt of chicness can be found along the curvy rue de la Roquette, a 17th-century byway that was home to Verlaine (at no. 17), and is now lined with cafés, bars, elegant boutiques, and an intriguing avant-garde church. Off rue de la Roquette, the narrow rue de Lappe is crammed with bars and tapas joints. *(M: Bastille/Voltaire.)*

OTHER SIGHTS. **Rue de Charonne** features some contemporary art galleries and funky boutiques, while **rue Keller** has a number of alternative CD and DJ-oriented record shops. *(M: Bastille/Charonne.)*

OBERKAMPF, MÉNILMONTANT

In the early 1990s, the neighborhood near the Opéra Bastille was touted as the next Montmartre, the next Montparnasse, and the next Latin Quarter: the city's latest Bohemia. But the Bastille's 15 minutes are over. In the scramble to find the next new "in" place, crowds have surged north toward Oberkampf and Ménilmontant.

OBERKAMPF. Glassbox, 113 bis rue Oberkampf, attracts politically engaged artists. Plans are also being laid to build a **Centre de Danse Africaine et Culture du Monde.** Rue Oberkampf and the surrounding streets ooze with bars, cafés and ethnic restaurants, most of which are reasonably priced. *(M: Oberkampf.)*

ATELIERS DE MÉNILMONTANT. To preserve the area's older buildings, the Ateliers de Ménilmontant holds open studios and brings artists together to paint outdoor frescoes. *(42, rue Alexandre Dumas. M: Alexandre Dumas.)*

TWELFTH ARRONDISSEMENT

One-third of the three corners of pl. de la Bastille, the 12*ème* draws youthful momentum from the neighboring 4*ème* and 11*ème*. But while its northwestern fringes are decidedly funky, its core is solid working class with a large immigrant population. The Opéra Bastille is but one of the 12*ème*'s recent architectural additions.

OPÉRA BASTILLE. Once known as the "Red Belt" around Paris because of its participation in both the 1830 and 1848 Revolutions, the 12*ème* also saw its residents make up large sectors of the Parisian Resistance during WWII. The only rebellions staged these days are over the Opéra Bastille, one of Mitterrand's *grands projets*. Presiding over the **pl. de la Bastille** and designed by Carlos Ott, a Canadian mall architect, the Opéra opened in 1989 to protests over its unattractive and questionable design (nets still surround parts of the building to catch falling tiles). The building is second only to Disneyland Paris in the minds of Parisians as an example of architectural Chernobyl. The "People's Opera" has further been described as a huge toilet because of its resemblance to the coin-operated facilities in the streets of Paris. Many complain that the acoustics of the hall are defective. Worse yet, "the people," for whom the opera was supposedly designed, often can't afford to go there; as a result, the Opéra costs in taxes a lot more than it returns. On Bastille day, all performances are free, but the queues are long. Your best shot is to join the line very early in the morning. The Opéra has not struck a completely sour note, though, and has helped renew local interest in the arts. *(130, rue de Lyon. M: Bastille. Tel. 01 40 01 19 70; www.opera-de-paris.fr. Tours daily at 1pm. 50F, students, under 16, and over 60 30F. For concert info, see* **Classical Music, Opera, and Dance,** *p. 272.)*

AROUND BASTILLE. Opened in 1995 in a renovated railway viaduct, the **Viaduc des Arts,** 9-121, av. Daumesmil provides workspace and showrooms for potters, painters, weavers, glass blowers, opera paraphernalia designers, and furniture manufactur-

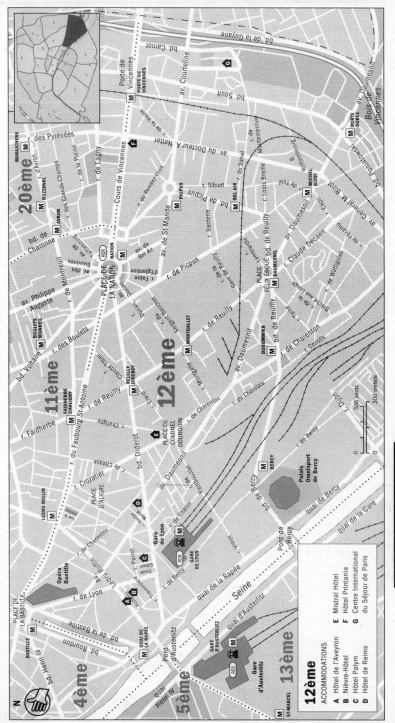

SIGHTS

12ème

ACCOMMODATIONS

A Hôtel de l'Aveyron
B Nièvre-Hôtel
C Hôtel Palym
D Hôtel de Reims

E Mistral Hôtel
F Hôtel Printania
G Centre International
   du Séjour de Paris

ers. Above the viaduct runs the **Promenade Plantée,** Paris's longest and skinniest park and probably the only one in the world accessible solely by train, elevator, or stairs. Trees, roses, and shrubs line an old railroad track high above the avenue, the traffic, and the stores below. *(M: Bastille.)* **Jean-Paul Gaultier's gallery** is at 30, rue Faubourg-St-Antoine. *(M: Bastille/Ledru-Rollin.)* Farther down the promenade and to the north is **pl. Aligre,** where the busy North African street market takes place. *(M: Ledru-Rollin.)*

PLACE DE LA NATION. Pl. de la Nation's current reputation as a red-light district belies the fact that it was once the site of a royal wedding between Louis XIV and Marie-Thérèse in 1660. During the Revolution, 1300 nobles were executed on this spot. It became pl. de la Nation on July 14, 1880. *(M: Nation.)*

BOIS DE VINCENNES AND CHÂTEAU DE VINCENNES. At the eastern edge of the 12ème stands the beautifully green **Bois de Vincennes** (see **Sights,** p. 238). Once a royal hunting ground, the Bois now contains the premier zoo in France, the **Parc Zoologique** and the royal **Château de Vincennes.**

THE BERCY QUARTER. East of the **Gare de Lyon,** the Bercy quarter has seen the rapid construction of Mitterand's new **Ministère des Finances** building, the mammoth grass-and-glass facaded **Palais Omnisports** concert and sports complex, and Frank Ghery's brilliant 1994 **American Center,** which offers cultural programs and events on American culture. *(M: Bercy.)*

THIRTEENTH ARRONDISSEMENT

With the central arrondissements losing artistic momentum due to high prices and numbing gentrification, the periphery has established itself as the seat of French intellectual and cultural life. The heart of Paris now rests in its lower right corner. A vast urban sprawl in the midst of an architectural face-lift, the 13ème is also in the fetal stages of a hip rebirth. Largely a working-class immigrant neighborhood, the 13ème—bordering the 14ème's Cité Universitaire and scholastic 5ème—affordably houses a growing number of students in its northern and western areas, and is conveniently also the site of the new **Bibliothèque de France.** At the center of this large arrondissement is the modern **pl. d'Italie** and the young and bouncing **Butte aux Cailles;** below it **Chinatown** bustles. Most recently, a slew of restaurant-, club-, and bar-boats have docked on **Port de la Gare Quai Francois Mauriac,** along the Seine. This trendy nightlife spot is crowded enough to be a safe place in which to stroll along the Seine by night, but is still quiet enough to still be romantic. Kissy, kissy.

Until the 20th century, the 13ème was one of Paris's poorest neighborhoods. Victor Hugo used parts of the 13ème as a setting for *Les Misérables.* Traversed by the **Bièvre,** a stagnant stream clogged with industrial refuse, it was notoriously the city's worst-smelling district. Environmentalists eventually won their campaign to close its tanneries and paper factories, and in 1910 the Bièvre was filled in.

MANUFACTURE DES GOBELINS. The Manufacture des Gobelins, a tapestry workshop over 300 years old, is all that is left of the 13ème's industrial past. In the mid-17th century the Gobelins produced some of the priceless tapestries now displayed in the **Musée de Cluny** (see **Museums,** p. 254). Still an adjunct of the state, the factory receives commissions from French ministries and foreign embassies. Extensive and interesting guided tours (the only way inside) explain the intricacies of the weaving process. *(42, av. des Gobelins. M: Gobelins. Tel. 01 44 61 21 69. Tours in French with free English-language handout, 1½hr., Tu-Th 2 and 2:45pm; 45F, ages 7-24 25F, under 7 free.)*

BUTTE AUX CAILLES. Farther southwest, the Butte aux Cailles (Quail Knoll) district features cobblestone streets, tree-shaded sidewalks, and street lamps. One of the first areas to fight during the Revolution of 1848, the area around rue des Cinq Diamants was the unofficial headquarters of the *soixante-huitards,* the student and intellectual activists of the 1968 riots. Today the fight continues in the Butte's cooperative bar, **La Folie en Tête** (see **Nightlife,** p. 296) and intellectual

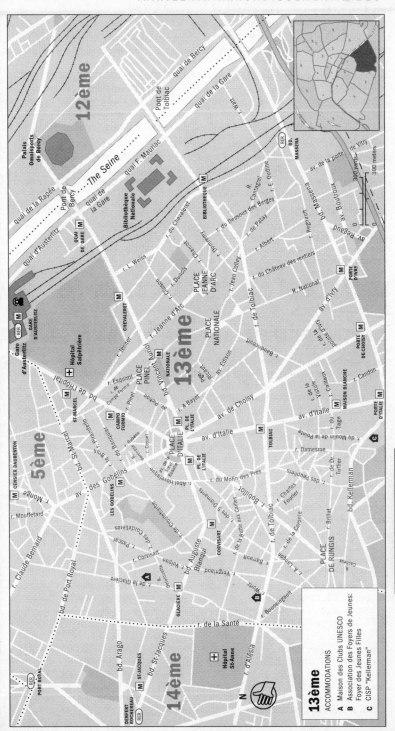

13ème

ACCOMMODATIONS

A Maison des Clubs UNESCO
B Association des Foyers de Jeunes:
   Foyer des Jeunes Filles
C CISP "Kellerman"

SIGHTS

hang-out, **Le Temps des Cérises** (see **Restaurants,** p. 145). The nascent gentrification of the 13ème has attracted trend-setters, artists, and intellectuals, but residents are worried that once-affordable real estate may go the way of the now unaffordable Marais. *(M: Corvisart or Place d'Italie.)*

ÉGLISE SAINTE-ANNE DE LA MAISON BLANCHE. The Byzantine Eglise Sainte-Anne de la Maison Blanche on rue Tolbiac owes its completion to the Lombard family who in 1898 donated funds from their chocolate store on av. de Choisy to complete the construction. The front of the church is nicknamed *la facade chocolat* in their honor. *(M: Tolbiac.)*

CHINATOWN. East of Ste-Anne on av. de Choisy and av. d'Ivry lies Paris's Chinatown, home to large Chinese, Vietnamese, and Cambodian communities. Asian restaurants, shops, and markets like **Tang Frères** (see **Specialty Stores,** p. 156) on rue d'Ivry offer embroidered slippers, exotic fruits, fresh vegetables, and Asian specialties. *(M: Porte d'Ivry, Tolbiac, or Maison Blanche.)*

BIBLIOTHÈQUE DE FRANCE. Opened in 1996, the Bibliothèque de France is the last and most expensive of Mitterrand's *grand projets*. Replacing the old Bibliothèque Nationale in the 2ème (still open to scholars), the new library is open to the public and houses 10 million volumes. Designed by Dominique Perrault, the four L-shaped towers are designed to look like open books from above. (See **Libraries,** p. 86.) The library is just one piece of the 13ème's urban renewal. A new project called ZAC (Zone d'Aménagement Concerte) plans to build a new university, five schools, a sports complex, a public garden, numerous office blocks, exhibitions spaces, cinemas, and a new métro. *(M: Quai de la Gare or Bibliothèque Francois-Mitterrand.)*

FOURTEENTH ARRONDISSEMENT

Like Montmartre and the *quartier latin*, the 14ème has long been a haven for 20th-century artists and writers like Man Ray, Modigliani, and Henry Miller. While gentrification has forced struggling artists out of those *quartiers*, the 14ème's affordability and café culture still attract some young artists and student writers who debate at the Cité Universitaire. However, the arrondissement is largely an amalgam of cultures and styles, and emits more a sense of serene fatigue than it does a charged artistic vigor. There is no one street which best characterizes the varied area; discrete streets, restaurants, galleries, cafés, and the Montparnasse cemetery offer some intrigue.

MONTPARNASSE

AROUND THE STATION. Generations of newly arrived immigrants have called Montparnasse home. The first to arrive were Bretons, who left Brittany in the 19th century after failed harvests. Arriving en masse at the **Gare de Montparnasse,** they settled in the neighborhood around the station, now known as Petite Bretange. Breton *crêperies*, handicraft shops, and cultural associations line **rue du Montparnasse.** *(M: Montparnasse-Bienvenüe.)*

BOULEVARD DE MONTPARNASSE. In the early 20th century, Montparnasse became a center for avant-garde artists including Modigliani, Utrillo, Chagall, and Montmartre ex-pat Léger. Political exiles like Lenin and Trotsky talked strategy over cognac in the cafés along boulevard Montparnasse. After WWI, Montparnasse attracted American expatriates. Man Ray transformed an apartment into a photo lab; Calder worked on his first sculptures; Hemingway did some serious writing (and drinking); and Henry Miller produced the steamy *Tropic of Cancer* at Seurat's villa with the amorous help of Anaïs Nin. The Spanish Civil War and WWII ended this golden age of bohemia. To see where Lenin, Hemingway, and Sartre sat and racked their brains, check out the café **La Coupole** (see **Cafés,** p. 147). *(M: Montparnasse-Bienvenüe or Vavin.)*

CIMETIÈRE MONTPARNASSE. In the shadow of the modern Tour Montparnasse, (see **Fifteenth Arrondissement,** p. 220) hides the beautiful Cimetière Montparnasse. This serene cemetery brings repose to writers Guy de Maupassant (p. 18), Samuel Beckett (p. 19), Simone de Beauvoir (p. 20), Jean-Paul Sartre (p. 19), and Charles Baudelaire (p. 24). Filmmaker François Truffaut and his favorite actress Jean Seberg (p. 34) are also buried here, along with artists Man Ray (p. 9), Brancusi, and Frédéric Bartholdi, the sculptor of the Statue of Liberty. Ironically, the accused traitor Alfred Dreyfus and the anti-Semitic WWII traitor Maréchal Pétain lie just feet away from each other (p. 9 and p. 10). Composer Camille Saint-Saëns is buried not far from 70s pop singer, Serge Gainsbourg, whose graffitied grave resembles Jim Morrison's across town at Père Lachaise (see **Sights,** p. 231). With a free *Index des Célébrités* (available to the left of the entrance), you can pay your respects. *(3, bd. Edgar Quinet. M: Edgar Quinet. Tel. 01 44 10 86 50. Open mid-Mar. to Oct. M-F 8am-6pm, Sa 8:30am-6pm, Su 9am-6pm; Nov.-Mar. M-F 8am-5:30pm, Sa 8:30am-5:30pm, Su 9am-5:30pm. Free.)*

RESIDENTIAL SOUTH. Surrounding Montparnasse's residential neighborhoods are rue d'Alésia's clothing stores (between rue des Plantes and av. du Général Leclerc), and rue de la Gaité's porn shops. *(M: Alésia.)* The pedestrian rue Daguerre and its surrounding streets are lined with restaurants, specialty food shops, and galleries (see p. 267). The architecture in this area is as diverse as its inhabitants, and ranges from colorful Art Nouveau tiled facades scattered along the small streets that come off bd. Raspail to classical Greek-columned housing projects at rue de l'Ouest and rue du Château. *(M: Gaîté or Denfert-Rochereau.)* Artists sell their work in an **open air market** at the foot of the tower on bd. Edgar Quinet every Sunday from 10am-7pm. *(M: Edgar Quinet.)*

THE CATACOMBS

*1, pl. Denfert-Rochereau. M: Denfert-Rochereau. Tel. 01 43 22 47 63. **Open** Tu-F 2-4pm, Sa-Su 9-11am and 2-4pm. **Admission** 33F, under 25 22F, under 7 free. **Tour** lasts 45 minutes.*

At the intersection of six avenues, a lion sculpted by Bartholdi (who created the Statue of Liberty) and commemorating *La Défense Nationale de 1870-1871* dominates **Pl. Denfert-Rochereau.** Most visitors observe Bartholdi's Leo from their place in the line to visit the **Catacombs,** a series of tunnels 20m below ground and 1.7km in length. They were originally excavated to provide stone for building the city. By the 1770s, much of the Left Bank was in danger of caving in and digging promptly stopped. The former quarry was then used as a mass grave to relieve the stench emanating from Paris's overcrowded cemeteries. The entrance warns "Stop! Beyond Here Is the Empire of Death." In 1793, a Parisian got lost and became a permanent resident, so stick to the tour. During WWII, the Empire of Death was full of life when the Resistance set up headquarters among the departed. The catacombs are like an underground city, with street names on walls lined with femurs and craniums. The ghoulish arrangement features rooms with cheery proverbs—*"Pensez le matin que vous n'irez peut être pas jusques au soir et au soir que vous n'irez pas jusques au matin"* ("Think each morning that you may not be live 'til evening, and each evening that you may not be live 'til morning"). Beware the low ceilings and bring a sweater (and a flashlight if you have one). The catacombs are not recommended for the faint of heart or leg; there are 85 steep steps to climb on the way out.

PARC MONTSOURIS AND CITÉ UNIVERSITAIRE

Begun in 1867 by Haussmann, the **Parc Montsouris** features hundreds of rare and freakish trees, a gaggle of ducks and snow geese, and bright flowers in the summer. Sunbathers and children stretch out on the grass. (Open M-F 7:30am-10pm, Sa-Su 9am-10pm.) Across bd. Jourdan, thousands of students from 122 countries study, argue, and drink themselves silly in the **Cité Universitaire,** a 40-hectare residential campus with 30 dorms, two of them designed by Le Corbusier (see p. 30).

SIGHTS

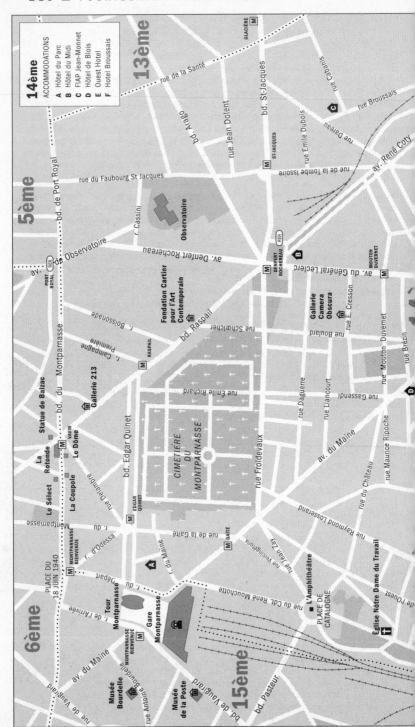

14ème
ACCOMMODATIONS
A Hôtel du Parc
B Hôtel du Midi
C FIAP Jean-Monnet
D Hôtel de Blois
E Ouest Hotel
F Hotel Broussais

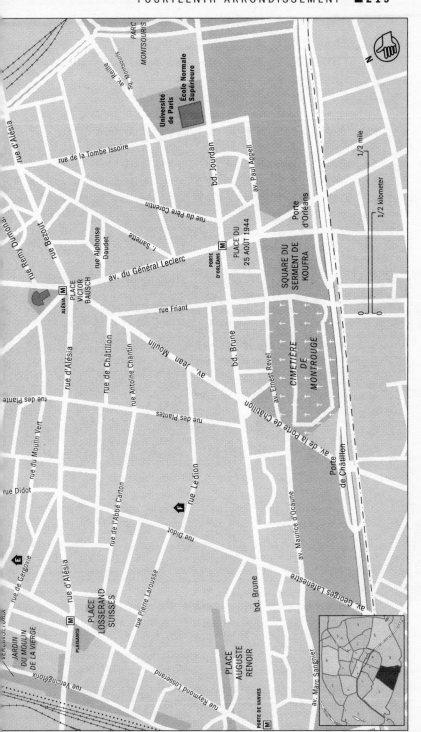

The **Pavilion Suisse** (1932) reflects the architect's dream of a vertical city, although its roof garden housed anti-aircraft guns during WWII. In 1959, Le Corbusier returned to build the **Maison du Brasil.** While the **Maison des Etats-Unis** houses Americans in prison-like squalor, the **Maison Suédoise** and **Maison Japonaise** offer delightful accommodations. The swankiest addition is the luxurious **Maison d'Espagne.** (For long-term housing, see **Student Accommodations,** p. 102). Surrounding the Cité Universitaire, joggers, bikers, and frisbee ultimaters occupy the lawns.

FIFTEENTH ARRONDISSEMENT

As the most populous arrondissement, middling in incomes and politics, the 15ème is the picture of bourgeois Parisian life, but has few designated sites. You'll probably only explore here if your stay extends beyond a week. Its varied neighborhoods, generally calm and safe at night, are similar to those of smaller French cities like Nantes or Rouen. The locals all have their favorites among the grocers on rue du Commerce, the cafés at the corner of rue de la Convention and rue de Vaugirard, and the specialty shops along avenue Emile Zola. The 15ème is a place of subtle pleasures, like the lovely view of the Seine and the Eiffel Tower on the métro ride between M: Trocadéro and M: La Motte-Picquet-Grenelle.

AN AFTERNOON IN THE FIFTEENTH ARRONDISSEMENT

■ The three top attractions are close together and can be visited in a single afternoon. Ride to the top of the **Tour Montparnasse** for one of the best views of the city, day or night. Next, explore the artistic heritage of the quarter at the **Musée Bourdelle** and the **Musée de Montparnasse.** Refresh at the **Café Aux Artistes,** and then head down the street to the **Institute Pasteur** for a look at France's proud scientific tradition.

TOUR MAINE-MONTPARNASSE. The modern tower dominates the *quartier*'s northeast corner. Standing 59 stories tall and completed in 1973, the controversial building looks out of place amid Montparnasse's 19th-century architecture. Shortly after it was erected, the city forbid further skyscraping, designating La Défense (see **Sights,** p. 240) the sole home for future *gratte-ciels*. For an open-air all-encompassing view of the city, bypass the 52 floors of office space and ride the elevator to the 56th floor, then climb three flights to the rooftop terrace. The Tour is a good way to orient yourself as you explore the city. *(33 av. du Maine. M: Montparnasse-Bienvenüe. Tel. 01 45 38 52 56. Open daily May-Sept. 9:30am-11:30pm; Oct.-April M-F 9:30am-10:30pm. Admission 46F, students 35F, seniors 38F, under 14 30F.)*

PLACE DU 18 JUIN. This *place* commemorates two important events from WWII. On June 18, 1940, General de Gaulle broadcast his first BBC radio address from London, urging France to resist the Nazi occupiers and the collaborationist Vichy regime of Maréchal Pétain (the entire speech is engraved by the Tomb of the Unknown Soldier under the Arc de Triomphe; see **Sights,** p. 198). It was also here that General Leclerc, the leader of the French forces, accepted the surrender of General von Choltitz, the Nazi commander of the Paris occupation, on August 25, 1944. Despite orders from Hitler to destroy Paris and retreat, von Choltitz disobeyed and saved the city (see **Paris Is(n't) Burning,** p. 10). *(At the intersection of rue de l'Arrivé and bd. Montparnasse. M: Montparnasse-Bienvenüe.)*

LA RUCHE. In the early twentieth century, the 15ème was a locus of the Parisian art scene. Designed by Gustave Eiffel, this brick compound (the Beehive) used to house struggling artists like Chagall and Soutine. Today the Fondation La Ruche offers grants, studios, and housing to young artists. Sculptures by La Ruche residents line the garden. *(52, rue Dantzig. M: Convention.)*

INSTITUT PASTEUR. Founded by the French scientist Louis Pasteur in 1887, the institute is now a center for biochemical research, development, and treatment. It was here that Pasteur, a champion of 19th-century germ theory, developed pas-

15ème

ACCOMMODATIONS

I Aloha Hostel
H Hôtel Camélia
G Hôtel de la Paix
E Hôtel Printemps
J La Maison Hostel
F Mondial Hôtel
B Nainville Hôtel
D Pacific Hôtel
A Practic Hôtel
C 3 Ducks Hostel

teurization, his technique for purifying milk products and beer. It was also here in 1983 that Dr. Luc Montaigner (in conjunction with Robert Gallo) first isolated HIV, the virus that causes AIDS. The institute's small museum houses Pasteur's projects, lab, awards, and living quarters. Don't miss his tomb, an ornate marble and tile construction dedicated to the four virtues of faith, hope, charity, and science. (25, rue du Dr. Roux. M: Pasteur. Tel. 01 45 68 82 82 or 01 45 68 82 83. Open Sept.-July M-F 2-5:30pm. Admission 15F, students 8F.)

OTHER SIGHTS. The most impressive museum here is the **Musée Bourdelle,** which houses the towering works of French sculptor Émile-Antoine Bourdelle in his long-time studio (see p. 260). Near M: Félix Faure, many buildings sport **Art Nouveau facades,** such as 24, pl. Étienne Pernet, and 31 & 40, av. Félix Faure, whose front depicts Aesop's *The Crow and the Fox.* The quiet Jardin Atlantique contains two other WWII-related museums, The **Musée de la Liberation de Paris** and the **Musée Jean Moulin** (see p. 263).

SIXTEENTH ARRONDISSEMENT

On January 1, 1860, the wealthy villages of Auteuil, Passy, and Chaillot banded together and joined Paris, forming what is now the 16ème arrondissement. More than a century later, the area's original aristocratic families continue to hold their ground, making the 16ème a stronghold of conservative politics, fashion, and culture. It is rumored that some members of the local nobility forbid their children to sing *La Marseillaise,* the anthem of the Revolutionaries who beheaded their

SIGHTS

ancestors. In this lavish residential neighborhood, *hôtels particuliers* (mansions and gardened townhouses) retire graciously from wide, quiet streets. Businesses, storefronts, and tackiness are at a minimum. Instead, this quarter has over 60 embassies, about half of Paris's museums, the Trocadéro, and the Bois de Boulogne (see **Bois de Boulogne**, p. 234). Métro stops are few and far between, and as inexpensive restaurants are difficult to find, do some grocery shopping lest you wander from museum to museum feeling overheated and hungry. The steps of the Trocadéro provides a spectacular view of the Eiffel Tower.

TROCADÉRO AND SURROUNDINGS

PLACE D'IÉNA. The Pl. d'Iéna positions you for a sweep of the most popular museums, including Henri Bouchard's impressive facade for the **Eglise St-Pierre de Chaillot** (1937), between rue de Chaillot and av. Pierre I de Serbie. *(Open M-Sa 9:30am-12:30pm and 3-7pm, Su 9:30am-12:30pm.)* The **Musée Henri Bouchard** is also in the 16*éme* (see **Museums**, p. 260). *(M: Iéna.)*

To the east, Pl. de l'Alma carries a replica of the torch of Bartholdi's Statue of Liberty, one of several tributes in the 16*ème* to France's most famous gift to the United States, and a memorial to Lady Diana near the site of her fatal auto crash.

PALAIS DE TOKYO. The Palais de Tokyo houses the **Musée d'Art Moderne de la Ville de Paris** (see **Museums**, p. 258) and its world-class collection of 20th-century art. Built for the 1937 World Expo, the palace took its name from the adjacent quai de Tokyo. After WWII, in which Japan fought as an Axis power, it was renamed the quai de New York. *(11, av. du Président Wilson. M: Iéna.)*

PALAIS GALLIERA. The gardens of the Palais Galliera draw young children and sculpture enthusiasts to contemplate the three allegorical figures representing painting, architecture, and sculpture. The Palais Galliera was built for the Duchess of Galliera by Louis Ginain as a repository for her collection of Italian Baroque art, but the collection was sent to Genoa instead. The Italianate structure, completed in 1892, now houses the more contemporary and international **Musée de la Mode et du Costume** (see **Museums**, p. 263). To enter the museum, follow either of the streets next to the garden to av. Pierre I de Serbie. Farther down the avenue at pl. d'Iéna, the **Musée Guimet** (see **Museums**, p. 260) contains a spectacular collection of Asian art. *(M: Iéna. Across from the Palais de Tokyo.)*

PALAIS DE CHAILLOT. A museum and cinema temple, the Palais de Chaillot houses the **Musée de l'Homme** (see p. 262), the **Musée de la Marine** (see p. 263), the **Musée National des Monuments Français** (see p. 264), the **Théâtre National de Chaillot** (see p. 270) and the **Cinémathèque Française** (see p. 272). Built for the 1937 World Exposition, Jacques Carlu's design features two curved wings cradling a gorgeous Art Deco courtyard and terrace overlooking spectacular cannon-fountains. Surveyed by the 7.5m tall bronze Henri Bouchard *Apollo*, the terrace attracts tourists, vendors, skateboarders, and in-line skaters and offers brilliant **views** of the Eiffel Tower and Champs de Mars, particularly at night. This spot is where most postcards of the tower are taken, so bring your camera. From this angle, the Eiffel Tower looks deceptively close—the walk down the Trocadéro steps, by the fountains, and across the Pont d'Iéna takes about 15 minutes. Be aware of pickpockets and traffic as you gaze upwards. As parts of the Jardins du Trocadéro are not well-lit at night, be careful and don't go alone.

The Palais de Chaillot is actually the last of a series of buildings built on this site. Catherine de Medicis had a château here, which was later transformed into a convent by Queen Henrietta of England. Napoleon razed the old château and planned to build a more lavish one on the same site for his son until his rotten luck at Waterloo brought construction to a screeching halt. In the 1820s, the Duc d'Angoulême built a fortress-like memorial to his Spanish victory at Trocadéro—hence the present name. That in turn was replaced in 1878 by the pavilion on Islamic architecture for the World Exposition, also since demolished. Below the

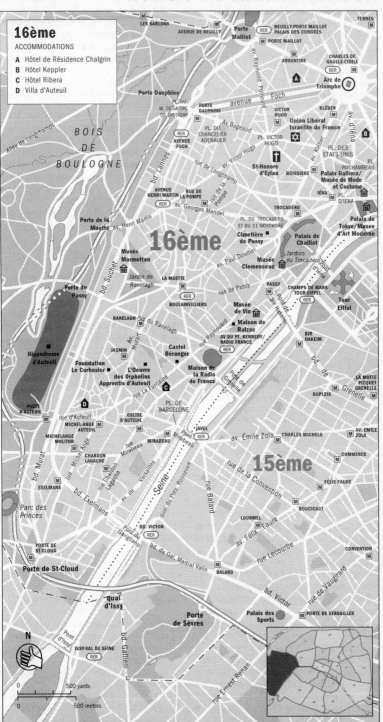

16ème

ACCOMMODATIONS

A Hôtel de Résidence Chalgrin
B Hôtel Keppler
C Hôtel Ribera
D Villa d'Auteuil

SIGHTS

palace, the **Jardins du Trocadéro** extend to the Seine. The **fountains** lining the central av. Gustave V de Suède and Albert I de Monaco are particularly striking when lit at night. After a day of sight-seeing, children of all ages might enjoy the carousel (10F) in pl. de Varsovie in front of the Eiffel Tower or a crêpe from one of the many outdoor stands.

PASSY AND AUTEUIL

Located south and southwest of Trocadéro, **Passy** was once famous for its restorative waters, although it's more recently known as the set for *Last Tango in Paris*, as well as for its expensive shopping. Running along the northern walls and shaded by a chestnut bower, the small **Cimetière de Passy** contains the tombs of Debussy, Fauré, and Manet. Ask the concierge at the entrance for directions to the grave sites. *(2, rue de Commandant Schloesing. M: Trocadéro. Open M-F 8am-6pm, Sa 8:30am-6pm, Su 9am-6pm, Nov. 6-Mar. 15 closes at 5:30pm.)*

PASSY. Rue Benjamin Franklin commemorates the elder statesmen's one-time residence in Passy. Franklin lived at 66, rue Raynouard, from 1777 to 1785 while negotiating a treaty between the new United States and the old Louis XVI; the present building was built long after his stay. Located in former Prime Minister Clemenceau's own home (see **Museums**, p. 261), the **Musée Clemenceau** at 8, rue Benjamin Franklin, chronicles the life and times of France's hardline negotiator of the WWI Treaty of Versailles. While completing the last volumes of *La Comédie Humaine*, Honoré de Balzac lived at what is now the **Maison de Balzac**, 47, rue Raynouard (see **Museums,** p. 260). The large, white, round building at the end of rue Raynouard is the **Maison de Radio France** (see **Museums**, p. 264). Just past it, rue de Boulainvilliers will take you down to the miniature Bartholdi **Statue of Liberty** near the pont de Grenelle. Donated by a group of American expatriates in 1885, it was moved to this spot for the 1889 World Exposition. *(M: Trocadéro.)*

AUTEUIL. The end of rue Raynouard marks the boundary of Passy and Auteuil, a 17th-century meeting-place for men of letters such as Racine, Molière, and Boileau and home to beautiful *hôtels particuliers* with Art Nouveau and Modernist architecture. A number of Hector Guimard buildings line rue La Fontaine (an extension of rue Raynouard). The award-winning **Castel Béranger** (1898), at no. 14, flaunts its Art Nouveau flourishes, swooping arabesque balconies, staircases, and rooftops. Guimard himself lived here briefly before moving to his building at 122, av. Mozart. Other Guimard buildings cluster on rue La Fontaine, including no. 17 (1911) and 9-10, rue Agar, an odd, T-shaped street that is Art Nouveau down to its street sign. **L'Oeuvre des Orphelins Apprentis d'Auteuil** (Society of Apprenticed Orphans), 40, rue la Fontaine, was founded in 1866 to provide a home and future for local orphans, who now perform apprenticeships in 30 occupations throughout France (the Auteuil campus does printing). Apprentice gardeners tend the beautiful grounds. **Proust** fans might want to visit 96, rue Fontaine, where the writer was born on July 10, 1871. *(M: Jasmin or Michel-Ange Auteuil.)*

Seventeenth-century *hôtels particuliers* line rue d'Auteuil. John Adams and his son John Quincy Adams lived at no. 43-47. On rue Raffe, pink stucco, black marble, and mosaic-covered townhouses adjoin more familiar-looking gray facades and iron grillwork. *(M: Michel-Ange Auteuil.)*

Around the corner and set back behind 55, rue du Docteur-Blanche, stand two **Le Corbusier** villas, completed in 1925. **Villa La Roche** and **Villa Jeanneret** are stark, white structures that now house the **Fondation Le Corbusier.** Villa La Roche contains a small collection of 20th-century paintings, sculpture, and furniture, although the masterpiece of the collection is the building itself (see **Museums,** p. 261). *(M: Jasmin.)*

Boulevard de Beauséjour is the continuation of bd. Montmorency as it approaches the La Muette métro stop. Northwest of the métro once stood the Château de la Muette, where Louis XV entertained his mistresses. In 1783 Pilâtre de Rozier and the Marquis d'Arlandes became the first two humans to defy gravity, lifting off from the castle's lawn in a Montgolfier balloon and landing 20 minutes later in what is now the 13*ème*. West of M: La Muette, past the playgrounds, *carrousel*, and *guignol* (puppet show) of the **Jardin de Ranelagh,** the **Musée Marmottan,** displays exquisite Impressionist paintings (see **Museums,** p. 259).

SEVENTEENTH ARRONDISSEMENT

Hugging the northwestern edge of the city and sandwiched in between more luxurious and famous arrondissements, the 17*ème* suffers from a bit of multiple personality disorder. Like its aristocrat neighbors in the 8*ème*, 16*ème*, and Neuilly, the arrondissement's southern border looks like old money. Like its more tawdry eastern neighbors, Pigalle and the 18*ème*, the arrondissement's eastern border can be seedy, especially around pl. de Clichy. In between these two extremes, the 17*ème* is a predominantly working-class residential neighborhood.

While barricades were erected, nobles beheaded, and novels written in the heart of the city, **les Batignolles** was little more than farmers' fields until the mid-19th century. If you happen to be staying in the center of the 17*ème*, though, the **Musée Jean-Jacques Henner,** 43, av. de Villiers, might be worth a look (see **Museums,** p. 262). Nearby, the **Banque de France,** 1, pl. Général Catroux, features a small garden, mosaic brickwork, and a facade with leering gargoyles and serpentine iron drainpipes that slither down the walls, spiralled with gold paint and capped with spitting-fish spouts. Inside, the lobby's vaulted ceilings rise to impossible heights.

BATIGNOLLES

Rue des Batignolles is considered the center of the **Village Batignolles,** a quiet village of shops and residences starting at av. des Batignolles and extending to pl. du Dr. Felix Lobligeois. To the west, restaurants and cafés line rue des Dames, while shops stand on rue des Lévis (M: Villiers). On the other side of rue des Batignolles, rue Lemercier (M: Brochant) has a daily covered market filled with meat, cheese, flowers, produce, and old women who have shopped here since WWII. Farther down, at no. 45, is yet another of Verlaine's Parisian addresses. Several blocks north, rue de la Jonquière (M: Guy Môquet) is lined with Moroccan, Tunisian, and Algerian shops and restaurants. **La Cité des Fleurs,** 59-61, rue de la Jonquière, boasts a row of exquisite private homes and gardens straight out of a Balzac novel. Created in 1847, this prototypical condominium required each owner to plant at least three trees in the gardens. Don't miss the elegantly sculpted facades at no. 29 and no. 33.

The **Cimetière des Batignolles,** 8, rue St-Just (tel. 01 46 27 03 18), sandwiched between a noisy *lycée* and the car horns of the Périphérique in the northwest corner of the 17*ème*, contains the graves of André Breton, Paul Verlaine, and Benjamin Peret. The guards at the entrance give out maps and can refer you to other sources of information on the resident stars. To get to the cemetery from the métro, follow av. de Porte de Clichy toward the highway, then turn right onto av. du Cimetière des Batignolles. (M: Porte de Clichy. Open M-F 8am-6pm, Sa 8:30am-5:30pm, Su 9am-5:30pm. Free.) Across the Seine, the less famous **Cimetière des Chiens,** 4, Pont de Clichy (tel. 01 40 86 21 11) in Asnières, is the final resting spot for countless Parisian pets. (M: Gabriel Péri Asnières-Gennevilliers. Open W-M 10am-6pm; Oct. 15-March 15 W-M 10am-noon and 2-5pm. Free.) Names like Fifi, Jean-Pierre, Jack, and Chérie mark small stones and tiny graves. From the métro, take rue Gabriel Péri to bd. Voltaire to the *cimetière*.

NEAR PLACE DES TERNES

Back within the city limits, the enormous and ultra-modern **Palais des Congrès** stands at the western end of the 17*ème* (M: Porte Maillot). The glass tower's upper-crust restaurants, shopping galleries, and conference halls house a year-round convention center, keeping guests entertained with the Palais's in-house disco and cinema. When not welcoming a variety of business groups, the conference hall hosts music, theater, and dance performances by the likes of Ray Charles and the Red Army Chorus. (For show info call 01 40 68 00 05.) The open-air terrace on the seventh floor offers a free view of the sprawling Bois de Boulogne to the south and La Défense to the west. Nearby, the lovely **pl. des Ternes** (M: Ternes), on the border of the *8ème*, hosts a number of cafés and a daily flower market. From pl. des Ternes, it's a quick walk down bd. des Courcelles to the **Parc Monceau** (M: Monceau; see **Sights,** p. 202).

EIGHTEENTH ARRONDISSEMENT

MONTMARTRE

Built high above the rest of Paris on a steep hill, Montmartre gets its name from a history of Roman occupation and Christian martyrdom and a series of etymological coincidences. A site of worship since before the arrival of the Druids, the hilltop was once home to an altar dedicated to Mercury and a shrine in honor of Mars. At different points in the Roman era, it was referred to as *Mons Mercurii* or *Mons Martis*. The mini-mountain suffered from this confused identity until a bishop named Dionysus, now known as St-Denis, came to introduce Christianity to the Gauls in the late 3rd century. Unimpressed, the Romans eschewed constructive criticism and cut off his head. St-Denis then picked up his head and carried it north, until he collapsed 7km away in St-Denis on the spot that is now the Basilique de St-Denis (see **Daytripping,** p. 338). To honor his gumption, the hill's name was changed to *Mont Martyrum* (Hill of Martyrs), which then became **Montmartre.** During the Revolution, the hill was renamed *Montmarat* after the Revolutionary martyr Marat, but the change was so subtle that the name Montmartre stuck and has been used ever since.

Along with the Montagne Ste-Geneviève in the *5ème* (see **Sights,** p. 184), Montmartre is one of the two Parisian hills and few Parisian neighborhoods Baron

---

PICASSO IN PARIS

From his first visits as an impoverished Catalonian upstart to his last years of self-satisfied international acclaim, Paris was the main setting for Picasso's long and turbulent life. Though most of his studio-residences have been converted back to apartments, the buildings and neighborhoods have changed relatively little during this century. Starting from his earliest installment among the down-and-out in Montmartre, his changing residences in the city show his transformation from a painter at the fringes to the *ne plus ultra* of modern art.

■ 1900-01. 49, rue Gabrielle (p. 229) and 130ter, bd. de Clichy, 18ème (p. 229).

■ 1902. Hôtel des Ecoles, rue Champollion, 5ème (p. 183).

■ 1903. Hôtel du Maroc, 57, rue de Seine, 6ème (p. 189).

■ 1904-09. Bateau-Lavoir, pl. Emile Goudeau, 18ème. Although Picasso's Blue Period was inspired by characters and experiences from Montmartre, most of the works were painted in Spain. Picasso entered his Rose period and introduced Cubism along with Braque here. The studio was a frequent meeting place for Apollinaire, Max Jacob, Matisse and Picasso's ardent supporter Gertrude Stein.

■ 1909-12. 11, bd. de Clichy, 18ème (p. 229).

■ 1912-13. 242, bd. Raspail, 14ème (p. 216).

■ 1913-16. 5bis, rue Schoelcher, 14ème. This Montparnasse studio saw his experiments with collage and sculpture-painting assemblages (p. 216).

■ 1916-18. 22, rue Victor Hugo, Montrouge. Picasso moved outside Paris for the remainder of the First World War.

■ 1918-40. 23bis, rue La Boétie, 8ème. Financially secure, Picasso settled into this large studio near the Champs-Elysées (p. 195).

■ 1937-67. 7, rue des Grands-Augustins, 6ème (p. 189). His last prodigious years saw his war canvases and the monumental *Women of Algiers* series.

17ème

ACCOMMODATIONS

A Hôtel Belidor
B Hôtel Camperret Héliopolis
C Hôtel Riviera
D Hôtel Jouffrey

18ème

9ème

8ème

17ème

16ème

PLACE DE CLICHY

av. de Clichy

r. d'Amsterdam

r. St. Pétersbourg

LIÈGE

r. de Moscow

r. Biot

r. Darcy

LA FOURCHE

av. de Clichy

av. de St-Ouen

GUY MÔQUET

Guy Môquet

r. Jean Leclaire

r. de la fonderie

r. Sauffroy

r. de Moines

r. Davy

L. Lacroix

L. Legendre

Cité des Fleurs

r. Pouchet

r. Pouchet

r. Berzélius

BROCHANT

r. Brochant

r. Lemercier

r. Nollet

r. Truffaut

r. des Dames

r. des Batignolles

r. Boursault

PL. DU DR LOBLIGEOIS

r. de Rome

bd. de Batignolles

ROME

r. Constantinople

r. du Rocher

r. de Madrid

r. de Naples

EUROPE

ST-AUGUSTIN

M

MIROMESNIL

bd. Malesherbes

r. de Lisbonne

r. de Messine

bd. Haussmann

r. de Lévis

r. de Tocqueville

r. Cardinet

r. de Saussure

PÉREIRE-LEVALLOIS

PORTE DE CLICHY

av. de la porte de Clichy

r. Cardinet

r. Jouffroy

r. Jouffroy

MALESHERBES

r. Legendre

r. Pouncq

r. de Prony

r. Médéric

r. de Courcelles

MONCEAU

COURCELLES

r. de Courcelles

bd. de Courcelles

av. Hoche

av. de Friedland

WAGRAM

av. Ampère

av. de Villiers

VILLIERS

av. Gourgaud

PÉREIRE-LEVALLOIS

PÉREIRE

av. de Wagram

r. Fourcroy

r. Laugier

r. Bayen

r. Jouffroy

r. Gouvion St-Cyr

av. de la Grande Armée

av. Niel

av. Carnot

av. de la Grande Armée

TERNES

CHARLES DE GAULLE ÉTOILE

C

av. Macmahon

Arc de Triomphe

PTE CHAMPERRET

B Héliopolis

r. Stéphane Mallarmé

PORTE DE CHAMPERRET

av. de la Somme

bd. du Lyser

av. de Villiers

av. des Ternes

r. d'Armaillé

r. de Colonel Moll

ARGENTINE

LEVALLOIS PERRET

LOUIS MICHEL

ANATOLE FRANCE

av. de la Porte d'Asnières

bd. Berthier

bd. Bineau

av. de Malakoff

bd. de Lannes/Bruix

bd. de Gaulle

av. du Roule

av. de Malakoff

bd. Victor Hugo

bd. Bineau

r. de Dunkerque

Dhrumude

A Air France Terminal

NEUILLY-PORTE MAILLOT PALAIS DES CONGRÈS

PORTE MAILLOT

Porte Maillot

r. St-Sénégambie

av. de Malakoff

500 yards

500 meters

N

SIGHTS

Haussmann left intact when he redesigned the city and its environs. A rural area outside the city limits until the 20th century, the *butte* (hill) used to be covered with vineyards, wheat fields, windmills, and gypsum mines. Its picturesque beauty and low rents attracted bohemians like Toulouse-Lautrec and Eric Satie as well as performers and impresarios like Aristide Bruant. Toulouse-Lautrec, in particular, immortalized Montmartre through his paintings of life in disreputable nightspots like the Bal du Moulin Rouge (see below). A generation later, just before WWI smashed its spotlights and destroyed its crops, the *butte* welcomed Picasso, Modigliani, Utrillo, and Apollinaire into its artistic circle. Nowadays Montmartre is a mix of upscale bohemia above rue des Abbesses and sleaze along bd. de Clichy—not to mention the legions of panting tourists near Sacré Coeur, the front of which provides a dramatic panorama of the city. The northwest part of the *butte* retains some village charm, with breezy streets speckled with interesting shops and cafés. At dusk, gas lamps trace the stairways up the hillside to the basilica.

MOUNTING MONTMARTRE

One does not merely visit Montmartre; one climbs it. The standard approach is from the south, via M: Anvers or M: Abbesses, though other directions provide interesting, less-crowded climbs. From M: Anvers, the walk up rue Steinkerque to the ornate switchbacked stairway is short and pretty but sometimes overcrowded with tourists and associated commerce. The longer climb from M: Abbesses, also the safest at night, leads one through more worthwhile cafés and shops: follow rue de la Vieuville to rue Drevet, turning right on rue Gabrielle and left up the stairs to rue du Cardinal Dubois.

For a less difficult ascent, use the glass-covered **funicular** from the base of rue Tardieu (from M: Anvers, walk up rue Steinkerque and take a left on rue Tardieu). Reminiscent of a ski lift, it is operated by the RATP and can be used with a normal métro ticket. In 45 seconds, you are miraculously whisked 100m up an impressive 45-degree gradient while the city below comes almost immediately and spectacularly into sight. (Open 6am-12:45am. 8F.)

BASILIQUE DU SACRÉ-COEUR

*35, rue du Chevalier de la Barre. M: Anvers, Abbesses, or Château-Rouge. Tel. 01 42 51 17 02. **Open** daily 7am-11pm. **Free. Dome and crypt** open daily 9am-6pm. **Admission** to each 15F, students 8F.*

The Basilica of the Sacred Heart is like an exotic headdress or a white meringue floating above Paris. In 1873, the Assemblée Nationale selected the birthplace of the Commune as the location for the Sacré-Coeur, "in witness of repentance and as a symbol of hope," although politician Eugène Spuller called it "a monument to civil war." It was hoped by the Catholic establishment that the Sacré-Coeur would "expiate the sins" of France after the bloody civil war in which thousands of *communards* (leftists who proclaimed a new populist government, known as the Commune of Paris) were massacred by the Thiers government troops sent from Versailles. After a massive fund-raising effort, the basilica was completed in 1914 and consecrated in 1919. Both its Romanesque-cum-Byzantine styles (a hybrid of onion domes and arches) and its white color sets it apart from the gray, smoky grunge of most Parisian buildings. The church's bleached look is a quirk of its stone, which secretes white lime when wet. As a result, the parts of the building sheltered from rain are noticeably darker than more exposed ones. Most striking inside the basilica are the mosaics, especially the depiction of Christ on the ceiling and the mural of the Passion at the back of the altar. The narrow climb up the dome offers the highest vantage point in Paris and a view that stretches as far as 50km on clear days. Farther down, the crypt contains a relic of what many believe to be a piece of the sacred heart of Christ.

NEAR SACRÉ-COEUR

Place du Tertre teems with tourist cafés, restaurants, and portrait and silhouette artists. At no. 21, the **tourist office** gives out annotated maps (5F) and information. (Tel. 01 42 62 21 21. Open daily Apr.-Sept. 10am-10pm; Oct.-Mar. 10am-7pm.) Around the corner, the **Musée Salvador Dalí**, 11, rue Poulbot, displays some lesser-known lithographs and sculptures by the mustachioed artist (see **Museums**, p. 261).

Still going strong among quaint shuttered houses at 22, rue des Saules, is the **Lapin Agile** cabaret. Frequented by Verlaine, Renoir, Modigliani, and Max Jacob, the establishment was first known as the "Cabaret des Assassins" until André Gill decorated its facade with a *lapin* (rabbit) striking a pose as it leaps out of a pot while balancing a hat on its head and a bottle on its paw. The cabaret immediately gained renown as the "Lapin à Gill," (Gill's rabbit). By the time Picasso began to frequent the establishment, walking over from his first studio at 49, rue Gabrielle, the name had contracted to "Lapin Agile." In a zany satire of Picasso's work, other regulars at the café borrowed the owner's donkey, tied a canvas to its back and a paintbrush to its tail, and exhibited the resulting mess as the work of an unknown Italian artist (the painting received favorable reviews and fetched a respectable sum when sold).

Overlooking the vineyard at 12, rue Cortot, the **Musée du Vieux Montmartre** presents a history of the neighborhood and has one of the few zinc bars to have escaped metal rationing during WWI (see **Museums**, p. 264). To the east of Pl. Willette, the **Musée d'Art Naïf Max Fourny** houses neoprimitivist art in a 19th-century iron and glass market-pavilion (see **Museums**, p. 260).

DOWNHILL

ABBESSES. These days tasty restaurants, trendy cafés, and *boulangeries* crowd this corner of Montmartre around rue des Abbesses and rue Lepic. Tall iron gates hide the beautiful gardens of 18th-century townhouses. Walking down rue Lepic will carry you past the **Moulin Radet,** one of the last remaining windmills on Montmartre. Farther down is the site of the **Moulin de la Galette,** depicted by Renoir during one of the frequent dances held there, and one of Van Gogh's former homes at 54, rue Lepic. Parallel to rue Lepic, rue Caulaincourt leads downhill to the landscaped, secluded **Cimetière Montmartre,** where writers Alexandre Dumas and Stendhal, painter Édgar Degas, physicists André Ampère and Leon Foucault, composer Hector Berlioz, and filmmaker François Truffault are buried. Emile Zola also reposed here until his corpse joined the Panthéon in 1908. In 1871, this cemetery became the site of huge mass graves after the siege of the Commune. *(20, av. Rachel. M: Pl. de Clichy or Blanche. Tel. 01 43 87 64 24. Open daily 8am-5:30pm.)*

PLACE PIGALLE AND LE MOULIN ROUGE. Along the bd. de Clichy and bd. de Rochechouart, you'll find many of the cabarets and nightclubs that were the definitive hangouts of the Belle Epoque, including the infamous cabaret **Bal du Moulin Rouge** immortalized by the paintings of Toulouse-Lautrec and the music of Offenbach. At the turn of the century, Paris's upper bourgeoisie came to the Moulin Rouge to play at being bohemian. After WWI, Parisian bohemians relocated to the Left Bank and the area around pl. Pigalle became a world-renowned seedy red-light district (see **Sights,** p. 206). Today, the crowd consists of tourists out for an evening of sequins, tassels, and skin. The revues are still risqué, but the admission is prohibitively expensive. *(M: Blanche. Tel. 01 53 09 82 82.)*

Place Pigalle hosts several discos and trendy nightspots for Parisian and foreign youth. Other than that, it offers a seedy selection of peep-shows, prostitutes, and XXX movie theaters. Farther down bd. de Clichy, at the edge of the 17*ème*, **pl. de Clichy** is resplendent in the glowing neon of restaurants and cinemas. Busy during the day, it can (like Pigalle) be dangerous at night.

SIGHTS

LA GOUTTE D'OR

Further east, the 18ème becomes an immigrant ghetto in the midst of urban renewal. Still filled with crumbling buildings, the quarter takes its name, "drop of gold," from the medieval vineyard that stood here. During the Algerian war for independence in the early 1960s, the presence of the Algerian National Liberation Front (FLN) kept the area relatively segregated. Nowadays ambitious plans augur a change from its status as one of the few refuges of cheap housing in the city. Along bd. Barbès you'll find numerous discount clothing shops, as well as African cloth, food, and gift shops around rue Doudeauville and rue des Poissonniers. Square Léon is interesting as a crossroads of the community. Those unfamiliar with the area should avoid it at night.

NINETEENTH ARRONDISSEMENT

Like Paris's other periphery arrondissements, the 19ème is a predominantly working-class, residential quarter. However, near the Parc des Buttes, wealthy Parisians pay handsomely for houses with small gardens, or views of one of Paris' finer parks. The 19ème is also home to a large part of Paris's Asian community, making it full of wonderful, inexpensive restaurants. At night, avoid rue David d'Angiers, bd. Indochine, and av. Corentin Cariou.

PARC DE LA VILLETTE. The only major sight in the 19ème is the amazing Parc de la Villette (see **Museums**, p. 255), which features huge grassy areas for frisbee and soccer, paths for jogging and biking, wacky sculpture gardens, and the futur-

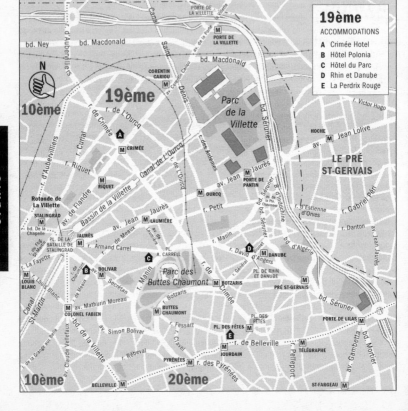

19ème

ACCOMMODATIONS

A Crimée Hotel
B Hôtel Polonia
C Hôtel du Parc
D Rhin et Danube
E La Perdrix Rouge

istic **Cité des Sciences et de l'Industrie** complex that includes the Géode Omnimax theater, the Explora and Technocité science museums, the Argonaute oceanic museum, and the Cinaxe film complex.

PARC DES BUTTES-CHAUMONT. To the south, Parc des Buttes-Chaumont is a mix of man-made topography and transplanted vegetation. Nostalgic for London's Hyde Park, where he spent much of his time in exile, Napoleon III added four public parks to Paris: the Bois de Boulogne, the Bois de Vincennes, the Parc Montsouris, and the Parc des Buttes-Chaumont. All English gardens, they are filled with artificial lakes and grass you can actually lounge on, instead of the immaculately trimmed, rigidly geometrical forms of traditional French gardens like the Jardin du Luxembourg, the Tuileries, and Versailles.

Before the construction of the Buttes-Chaumont, the *quartier* had been (since the 13th century) the host to a gibbet (an iron cage filled with the rotting corpses of criminals), a dumping-ground for dead horses, a breeding-ground for worms (sold as bait), and a gypsum quarry (the source of "plaster of Paris"). Making a park out of this mess took four years and 1000 workers. Designer Adolphe Alphand had all of the soil replaced and the quarried remains built up with new rock to create enormous fake cliffs surrounding a lake, waterfalls, caves with stalactites, all crowned with a Roman temple, from which there is a great view of the *quartier*. (M: Buttes-Chaumont. Open daily May-Sep. 7am-11pm; Oct.-Apr. 7am-9pm. Gates close 15 minutes before.)

BELLEVILLE. Just east of the park, on the western and southern sides of pl. de Rhin et Danube, pleasant villas line the cobbled rue Miguel Hidalgo and rue de l'Egalité of Belleville, one of Paris's new "in" neighborhoods, especially the part bordering the 11*ème* near rue Oberkampf.

TWENTIETH ARRONDISSEMENT

As Haussmannization expelled many of Paris's workers from the central city, thousands migrated east to **Belleville** (the northern part of the 20*ème*), **Ménilmontant** (the southern), and **Charonne** (the southeastern). By the late Second Republic, the 20*ème* had come to be known as a "red" arrondissement, solidly proletarian and radical. In January 1871, just before the lifting of the Prussian siege, members of Belleville's National Guard stormed a prison to demand the release of leftist political leaders—an omen of the civil war to come. Some of the heaviest fighting during the suppression of the Commune took place in these streets, where the communards made desperate last stands on their home turf. Caught between the Versaillais troops to the west and the Prussian lines outside the city walls, the Commune fortified the Parc des Buttes-Chaumont (see **19ème** above) and the **Cimetière Père-Lachaise** but soon ran out of ammunition. On May 28, 1871, the communards abandoned their last barricade and surrendered (see **History,** p. 8).

After the Commune, the 20*ème* kept on as the fairly isolated home of those workers who survived the massacres. "Many a workman's child," historian Eugene Weber has observed, "grew to adolescence before World War I without getting out of Ménilmontant or Belleville." Today, the arrondissement has a similar feel, with busy residential areas and markets that cater not to visitors but to locals. The area is also the home to sizable Greek, North African, Russian, and Asian communities.

PÈRE LACHAISE CEMETERY

*16, rue du Repos. M: Père-Lachaise. Tel. 01 43 70 70 33; www.cemetary.org/lachaise/lachaise.intro.html. **Open** Mar.-Oct. M-F 8am-6pm, Sa 8:30am-6pm, Su and holidays 9am-6pm; Nov.-Feb. M-F 8am-5:30pm, Sa 8:30am-5:30pm, Su and holidays 9am-5:30pm. Last entrance 15min. before closing. **Free.** Free maps supposedly available at guard booths by main entrances, but they're usually out; it may be worth the 10F or so to buy a detailed map from a nearby tabac before entering. 2hr. guided tour in English June-Sept. Sa 3pm; in French Sa at 2:30pm, occasionally Tu at 2:30pm and Su at 3pm as well as numerous theme-tours; 37F, students 26F; meet at the bd. de Ménilmontant entrance* *(tel. 01 40 71 75 23 for info)With its winding paths and elaborate sarcophagi, Cimetière Père Lachaise has become the final resting place of French and foreign giants. Balzac, Colette, David, Delacroix, La Fontaine, Haussmann, Molière, and Proust are buried here, as are Chopin, Jim Morrison (see below), Gertrude Stein, and Oscar Wilde. With so many tourists, they're hardly resting in peace. The land for Père Lachaise was bought by Napoleon's government in 1803 from Père de la Chaise, Louis XIV's confessor, to create a "modern and hygienic necropolis" that would relieve the overcrowding of city cemeteries. At first, Parisians were reluctant to bury their dead so far from the city. To increase the cemetery's popularity, Napoleon ordered that the remains of a few famous figures be dug up and reburied in Père Lachaise. Thus abruptly arrived the remains of Molière, La Fontaine, those sexy medieval lovers Abélard and Héloïse, and several other luminaries.*

The antithesis of the church cemetery, Père Lachaise is like a 19th-century garden party for the dead. Many of the tombs in this landscaped grove strive to remind visitors of the dead's many worldly accomplishments: the tomb of French Romantic painter Géricault wears a reproduction of his *Raft of the Medusa;* on Chopin's tomb sits his muse Calliope with a lyre in her hand. Oscar Wilde's grave is marked by a life-sized streaking Egyptian figure. The well-endowed likeness of journalist Victor Noir that stands atop his tomb is said to have magical fertility powers. Haussmann, the man of the boulevards, wanted to destroy the cemetery as part of his urban-renewal project, but obviously relented; he occupies a mausoleum in Père Lachaise. Remembered by plaques here are dancer Isadora Duncan, author Richard Wright, opera diva Maria Callas, and artist Max Ernst. The most-visited grave is that of Jim Morrison, the former lead singer of The Doors. His graffiti-covered bust was removed from the tomb, leaving his fans to fill the rest of the cemetery with their messages. In summer, dozens of young people bring flowers, joints, beer, poetry, and Doors paraphernalia to leave on his tomb; the sandbox in front of the stone is now the sanctioned site for the creative expression of those pensive mourners. At least one guard polices the spot at all times.

Over one million people are buried in the cemetery. Curiously, there are only 100,000 tombs. The discrepancy is due to the old practice of burying the poor in mass graves. Corpses are removed from these unmarked plots at regular intervals to make room for new generations of the dead. This grisly process is necessary in a densely populated city like Paris. Even with such purges, the 44 hectares of Père Lachaise are filled to bursting, so the government makes room by digging up any grave that has not been visited in a certain number of years. To avoid this fate, some hire an official "mourner," much as wealthy patrons used to hire choirs to sing their funeral masses.

Perhaps the most moving sites in Pére Lachaise are those that mark the tragic deaths of collective groups. The **Mur des Fédérés** (Wall of the Federals) has become a site of pilgrimage for left-wing sympathizers. In May 1871, a group of *communards* murdered the Archbishop of Paris, who had been taken hostage at the beginning of the Commune. They dragged his mutilated corpse to their stronghold in Père Lachaise and tossed it in a ditch. Four days later, the victorious *Versaillais* found the body. In retaliation, they lined up 147 Fédérés against the eastern wall of the cemetery, shot them, and buried them on the spot. Since 1871, the Mur des Fédérés has been a rallying point for the French Left, which recalls the massacre's anniversary every Pentecost. Ironically, Republican Adolphe

DYING TO GET IN How did Jim Morrison and Oscar Wilde end up here? Simply by dying in Paris (that is, if Jim is really dead and not hiding out in South America). Anybody who was born in or who died in Paris has the right to burial in a Parisian cemetery. Because of overcrowding, however, city policy now requires a family to pay a hefty fee for a departed member to be inhumed in a popular cemetery like Père Lachaise. Still, if you're looking for a unique gift for that special someone, a gravesite near a path is 38,395F and one away from a path is only 23,595F. If these prices are beyond your reach, you can rent shelf space for your cremated ashes in the columbarium: 50 years 9000F, 30 years 6000F, 10 years 2000F. *Pax vobiscum.*

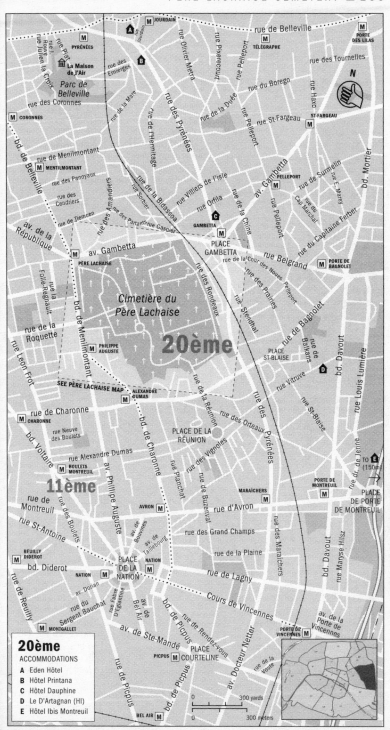

20ème

ACCOMMODATIONS

A Eden Hôtel
B Hôtel Printana
C Hôtel Dauphine
D Le D'Artagnan (HI)
E Hôtel Ibis Montreuil

Thiers, who ordered their execution, shares the cemetery with them; he died of natural causes in 1877. Near the wall, a number of moving monuments containing human remains commemorate both Resistance fighters from WWII as well as Nazi concentration camp victims.

CHARONNE, MÉNILMONTANT, AND BELLEVILLE

CHARONNE. Of all the old neighborhoods in the 20ème, **Charonne** has been swallowed up least by the concrete and metal of urbanization. *(M: Alexandre Dumas.)* The best-preserved vestige of Charonne is the **Eglise de St-Germain-de-Charonne,** a 13th-century church ravaged by fire in 1737 and restored in the 18th century. The church cemetery is the burial site of the murdered *communards*, who were accidently dug up in 1897 during the building of a reservoir. Directly opposite, the cobbled rue St-Blaise gives a taste of what Charonne used to be. *(4, pl. St-Blaise. M: Porte de Bagnolet. Tel. 01 43 71 42 04. Open M-F 9am-noon and 2-7pm, Sa 10am-noon. Cemetery open daily Mar. 15-Nov. 5 9am-7pm; Nov. 6-Mar. 15 9am-5:30pm.)*

MÉNILMONTANT. Along the western edge of Pére Lachaise, rue de Ménilmontant's busy ethnic markets, cafés, alleyways, housing projects, and small parks reveal little of the flavor of the old Ménilmontant quartier. *(M: Philippe Auguste or Père Lachaise.)*

BELLEVILLE. The same is true of the old village and quartier Belleville, which is now home to one of Paris's largest Asian communities, and is in its natal stages of gentrification. Just south of rue de Belleville, is 72, rue des Pyrénées, where the legendary crooner Edith Piaf was abandoned as a child (see **Music,** p. 32).

PARC DE BELLEVILLE. The Parc de Belleville is the best-kept secret of the arrondissement. A good example of urban renewal gone right, the terraced park is a green oasis nestled in among the stark grey of the surrounding housing projects. Squeaky clean and constantly patrolled by authorities, the park is replete with waterfalls, fountains, gorgeous views of Paris, and the fascinating **Maison de l'Air** (see **Museums,** p. 259). *(At the corner of rue de Piaf and rue des Envierges. M: Pyrénées.)*

BOIS DE BOULOGNE

The **Bois de Boulogne** (M: Porte Maillot, Sablons, Pont de Neuilly, Porte Dauphine, or Porte d'Auteuil) is an 846-hectare green canopy at the western edge of Paris and a popular place for walks, jogs, and picnics. Formerly a royal hunting ground, the *bois* was given to the city of Paris by Napoleon III in 1852. The Emperor had become a dilettante landscape-architect during his exile in England and wanted Paris to have something comparable to Hyde Park. Acting on these instructions, Baron Haussmann filled in sand-pits, dug artificial lakes, and cut winding paths through thickly wooded areas. This attempt to copy nature marked a break with the tradition of French formal gardens, rectilinear hedges, and flower beds established by Le Nôtre.

When Paris annexed Auteuil in 1860, the park, though outside the city walls, became part of the 16ème. In 1871, it was the site of a massacre of *communards*. General Gallifet shot the most politically and socially undesirable people he could discern among the prisoners bound for Versailles—men with gray hair, watches, glasses, or with "intelligent faces." At the turn of the century, the park became fashionable for carriage rides. Aristocratic families rode weekly to the park to spend a Sunday afternoon "in the country." Balzac's *Nana*, Colette's *Gigi*, and Vincente Minnelli's film *Gigi* feature Belle Epoque carriage rides through the Bois.

Until a couple of years ago, the *bois* by night was a bazaar of sex and drugs, where transvestite prostitutes would stand along the roads and violent crime was quite common. In 1991, a flood of newly liberated Eastern Europeans visiting Paris camped out in the park, in odd imitation of the Cossacks who bivouacked here after Waterloo. All lawn-crashers have been nudged out (for better or for worse) and police are now especially attentive to the *bois*, closing the

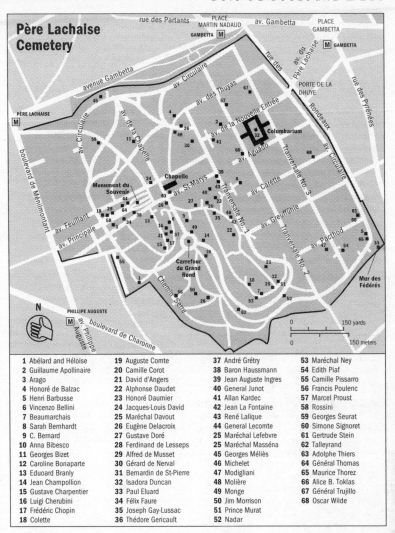

Père Lachaise Cemetery

1 Abélard and Héloïse	19 Auguste Comte	37 André Grétry	53 Maréchal Ney
2 Guillaume Apollinaire	20 Camille Corot	38 Baron Haussmann	54 Edith Piaf
3 Arago	21 David d'Angers	39 Jean Auguste Ingres	55 Camille Pissarro
4 Honoré de Balzac	22 Alphonse Daudet	40 General Junot	56 Francis Poulenc
5 Henri Barbusse	23 Honoré Daumier	41 Allan Kardec	57 Marcel Proust
6 Vincenzo Bellini	24 Jacques-Louis David	42 Jean La Fontaine	58 Rossini
7 Beaumarchais	25 Maréchal Davout	43 René Lalique	59 Georges Seurat
8 Sarah Bernhardt	26 Eugène Delacroix	44 General Lecomte	60 Simone Signoret
9 C. Bernard	27 Gustave Doré	25 Maréchal Lefebvre	61 Gertrude Stein
10 Anna Bibesco	28 Ferdinand de Lesseps	25 Maréchal Masséna	62 Talleyrand
11 Georges Bizet	29 Alfred de Musset	45 Georges Méliès	63 Adolphe Thiers
12 Caroline Bonaparte	30 Gérard de Nerval	46 Michelet	64 Général Thomas
13 Eduoard Branly	31 Bernardin de St-Pierre	47 Modigliani	65 Maurice Thorez
14 Jean Champollion	32 Isadora Duncan	48 Molière	66 Alice B. Toklas
15 Gustave Charpentier	33 Paul Eluard	49 Monge	67 Général Trujillo
16 Luigi Cherubini	34 Félix Faure	50 Jim Morrison	68 Oscar Wilde
17 Frédéric Chopin	35 Joseph Gay-Lussac	51 Prince Murat	
18 Colette	36 Thédore Gericault	52 Nadar	

roads at night and stepping up patrols. Nonetheless, the boulevards around the periphery of the *bois* continue to be lined with prostitutes at night. It is a bad idea to come here for a moonlight stroll.

STADIUMS. The Bois de Boulogne contains several stadiums, the most famous of which are the **Hippodromes de Longchamp** and **d'Auteuil.** During the Belle Epoque, the Grand Prix at Longchamp in June was one of the premier events of the social calendar. Also within the *bois*, the **Parc des Princes** hosts football (soccer) matches. The **Stade Roland Garros** is home of the **French Open** tennis tournament (see **Sports,** p. 279). The *bois*'s boathouses rent rowboats (see below).

JARDIN D'ACCLIMATATION. The **Jardin d'Acclimation** offers a small zoo, mini-golf course, carousels, kiddie motorcycle racetrack, bumper cars, pony rides, and outdoor jazz concerts. *(M: Sablons. At the northern end of the bois. Tel. 01 40 67 90 82. Open daily 10am-6pm. Ticket office closes 5:45pm. Admission 12F, under 3 free. No dogs allowed.)*

IT'S NOT EASY BEING GREEN London has Hyde Park, New York has Central Park, but Paris has Woods *(Bois)* and Gardens *(Jardins)*. While Haussmann and Napoleon III's 19th-century **Bois de Boulogne** and **Bois de Vincennes** keep politely on the western and eastern edges of town, the 18th-century **Jardin des Tuileries** and **Jardins du Luxembourg's** formal geometric French gardens offer relief in the center of Paris. In truth, Paris also has its **Parcs:** Haussmann and Napoleon III's **Buttes-Chaumont, Monceau,** and **Montsouris** green the city-scene. Since the 1980s, Mitterrand and Chirac have lobbied for even more flowers, grass, and trees. Opened in 1985, **La Villette's** exquisite urban park mixes nature and technology. The **Jardin de l'Atlantique** (M: Montparnasse-Bienvenüe) is an engineering feat of trees and bamboos suspended 18m over the busy railway tracks of Montparnasse. The **Promenade Plantée** (M: Bastille) features roses and shrubs amid the railway tracks above the Viaduc des Arts. Opened in 1993, the **Parc André Citroën** (M: Citroën) sprawls on the site of the former car factory. And the latest project for Paris 2000 is the proposed **Tour de la Terre** (Tower of Earth), a 200m high, 3000 square-meter mountain of earth, topped by cafés, restaurants, and Millennium exhibitions, which will symbolize Paris's commitment to the environment. Critics argue that it will take thousands of felled trees to build this millennial monument. So much for the future.

MUSÉE EN HERBE. Within the park, the Musée en Herbe is a modern art museum designed for children ages 4 to 11. Previous shows have featured Chagall and Picasso. The museum also offers a studio workshop. A participatory theater company for children stages plays (Oct.-July W and Sa-Su) and puppet shows (W, Sa-Su, and daily during school vacations) at 3:15 and 4:15pm; free). *(M: Porte Maillot. From the métro, go to the big house marked l'Orée du Bois and follow the brown signs that point to the right of the building, or take the little train to the left of the building. Tel. 01 40 67 97 66. Open Su-F 10am-6pm, Sa 2-6pm. Admission 16F. Studio sessions July-Aug. daily at 2 and 4pm; Sept.-June W, Sa, and Su at 2 and 4pm. Call to make reservations. Participation 25F. Trains W, Sa-Su, and public holidays every 10min. 1:30-6:30pm, 5F, under 3 free.)*

PRÉ CATELAN. The Pré Catelan is a neatly manicured meadow supposedly named for a troubadour who died in these woods. Arnault Catelan, who rode from Provence to Paris in order to deliver gifts to Philippe le Bel, hired a group of men to protect him on his journey. The men robbed and murdered him in the dead of night, believing that Arnault carried valuable parcels. In fact, Arnault carried only rare perfumes and essences. Authorities later captured the marauders, who, doused in scent, were easily identified. The huge purple beech on the central lawn is almost 200 years old. You can sit on the grass, except where there are *pelouse interdite* signs. *(Take the métro to Porte Maillot then take bus #244 to Bagatelle-Pré-Catelan. Tel. 01 40 19 95 33. Open daily 8:30am-7:30pm.)*

Inside the Pré Catelan, the **Jardin de Shakespeare** features plants mentioned by the bard, grouped by play—there is a collection of Scottish highland vegetation in the **Macbeth** area, a Mediterranean section for **The Tempest,** etc. In the center, a lovely 300-person open-air **Théâtre de Verdure du Jardin Shakespeare** gives popular summer performances of Shakespeare's and others' plays in French. *(Tel. 01 46 47 73 20. Jardin de Shakespeare open daily 3-3:30pm and 4:30-5pm. Admission 5F, students 3F, under 10 2F.)*

PARC DE LA BAGATELLE. The Parc de la Bagatelle was once a private estate within the *bois*, which became a public park in 1905. In 1777, the future Charles X employed 900 workers to toil night and day to build the little **Château de la Bagatelle** when Marie Antoinette, his sister-in-law, bet him that he could not have it ready to receive her in 60 days. The Anglo-Chinese garden is famous for its stunning June rose exhibition (35F, seniors 25F, plus 10F park admission; call for specific dates) and for its water lilies, which the gardener added in tribute to Monet. Do not walk on the grass (they really care about this—enough to put up signs in English). *(Same bus stop as Pré Catelan. Tel. 01 40 67 97 00. Open daily Jan. 1-15 9am-4:30pm; Jan. 16-Feb. 15 and Oct. 16-Nov. 30 9am-5:30pm; Feb. 16-28 and Oct. 1-15 9am-*

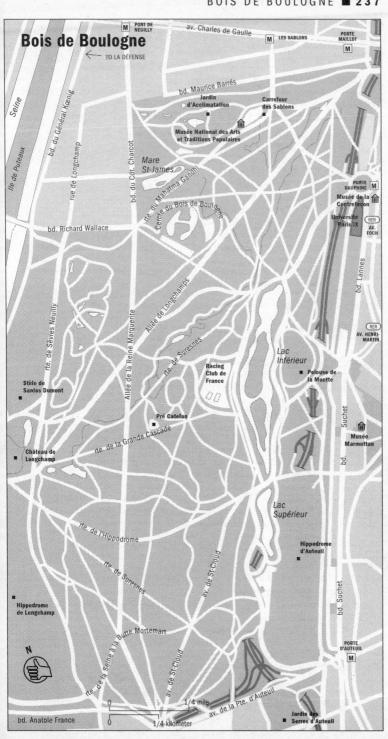

Bois de Boulogne

← TO LA DÉFENSE

M PONT DE NEUILLY

av. Charles de Gaulle

M LES SABLONS

PORTE MAILLOT M

bd. Maurice Barrés

Jardin d'Acclimatation

Carrefour des Sablons

Musée National des Arts et Traditions Populaires

Seine

Île de Puteaux

bd. du Général Koenig

rue de Longchamp

bd. du Cdt. Charcot

Mare St-James

rte. du Mahatma Gandhi

Cercle du Bois de Boulogne

PORTE DAUPHINE M

Musée de la Contrefaçon

Université Paris IX

RER AV. FOCH

bd. Richard Wallace

bd. Lannes

Allée de Longchamps

rte. de Sèvres Neuilly

Allée de la Reine Marguerite

rte. de Suresnes

RER AV. HENRI-MARTIN

Lac Inférieur

Racing Club de France

Pelouse de la Muette

Stèle de Santos Dumont

Pré Catelan

Suchet

Musée Marmottan

Château de Longchamp

rte. de la Grande Cascade

bd.

Lac Supérieur

rte. de l'Hippodrome

rte. de Suresnes

Hippodrome d'Auteuil

av. de St-Cloud

bd. Suchet

Hippodrome de Longchamp

rte. de la Seine à la Butte Mortemart

N

PORTE D'AUTEUIL M

0   1/4 mile
0   1/4 kilometer

av. de St-Cloud

av. de la Pte. d'Auteuil

bd. Anatole France

Jardin des Serres d'Auteuil

SIGHTS

6pm; March 1-15 8:30am-6:30pm; March 16-April 30 and Sept. 8:30am-7pm; June-July 8:30am-8pm. Ticket office closes 30min. earlier. Admission to park 10F, ages 6-10 5F. Why they made it this complicated, we don't know.)

LAKES. The two artificial **lakes** stretching down the eastern edge of the Bois feature the manicured islands of **Lac Inférieur**, which can be reached by rented rowboat only. Lake Superior, on the other hand, requires an airplane. *(M: Porte Dauphine. Boathouses open late Feb. to early Nov. daily 10am-7pm, weather permitting. Rentals 45F per hr., 400F deposit; with insurance against damage to boat 52F per hr., 200F deposit.)*

JARDIN DES SERRES D'AUTEUIL AND JARDIN DES POÈTES. The **Jardin des Serres d'Auteuil** (Greenhouse Garden) is full of hothouse flowers and trees. (Enter at 1, av. Gordon-Bennett, off bd. d'Auteuil. *(M: Porte d'Auteuil or Michel-Ange Molitor. Open daily May-Aug. 10am-6pm; Sept.-Apr. 10am-5pm. Admission 3F.)*

Free and prettier, if something of a make-out spot, is the neighboring **Jardin des Poètes**. Poems are attached to each flower bed: scan Ronsard, Corneille, Racine, Baudelaire, and Apollinaire. Rodin's sculpture of Victor Hugo is partially obscured by a thicket. Rent bicycles from the boathouse at the northern end of the Lac Inférieur and in front of the entrance to the Jardin d'Acclimatation. *(Tel. 06 07 35 40 17. Both open from Apr. 16-Oct. 15 daily 10am-7pm; Oct. 16-Apr. 15 W and Sa-Su 10am-7pm. Organized rides through the park 3-5pm, 100F. To rent a bicycle without a guide 130F, half day 70F; deposit for rides limited to the bois 1000F, for rides outside 1500F. Call for reservations.)*

OTHER SIGHTS. Hear pins drop at the **Bowling de Paris,** near the route Mahatma Gandhi entrance of the Jardin d'Acclimatation (see **Sports,** p. 276).

BOIS DE VINCENNES

BOIS DE VINCENNES. Like the Bois de Boulogne, the Bois de Vincennes was once a royal hunting forest. Today it is the largest expanse of greenery in Paris. Since it lay outside the city limits and beyond the reach of Parisian authorities, it was also a favorite ground for dueling. The elder Alexandre Dumas dueled a literary collaborator here who claimed to have written the *Tour de Nesle.* Dumas's pistol misfired and the author had to content himself with using the experience as the basis for a scene in *The Corsican Brothers.* Like the Bois de Boulogne, the Vincennes forest was given to Paris by Napoleon III, to be transformed into an English-style garden. Not surprisingly, Haussmann oversaw the planning of lakes and pathways. Annexed to a much poorer section of Paris than the Bois de Boulogne, Vincennes was never quite as fashionable or as formal. As one *fin-de-siècle* observer wrote, "At Vincennes, excursionists do not stand on ceremony, and if the weather is sultry, men may be seen lounging in their shirt sleeves, and taking, in other respects, an ease which the inhabitants of the boulevards, who resort to the Bois de Boulogne, would contemplate with horror." Today, the Bois de Vincennes's bikepaths, horsetrails, zoo, and Buddhist Temple are wonderful escapes from the grind of the city. *(M: Château de Vincennes or Porte Dorée.)*

PARC ZOOLOGIQUE DE PARIS. In a country not known for its zoos, the Parc Zoologique de Paris is considered the best of the bunch. It is the Bois de Vincennes's most popular attraction and recently has been working hard to improve the animals' environment. The *phoques* (the French word for *seal* that is pronounced just as you think it is) are fed daily at 4:30pm. And, oh, those crazy baboons! *(53, av. de St-Maurice. M: Porte Dorée. Tel. 01 44 75 20 10. Open May-Sept. M-Sa 9am-6pm, Su 9am-6:30pm; Oct.-Apr. M-Sa 9am-5pm, Su 9am-5:30pm. Ticket office closes 30min. before zoo. Admission 40; ages 4-16, students 16-27, and over 60 30F; under 4 free. Kiddie train tour leaves from restaurant; 12F, under 10 10F. Guidebook to the zoo 30F.)*

The park is also home to the privately owned **Grand Rocher,** an observatory. The 20F fee is a bit exorbitant, but the view is lovely.

Bois de Vincennes

N

ST-MANDÉ TOURELLE M

M CHÂTEAU DE VINCENNES

M FONTENAY-SOUS-BOIS

NOGENT SUR MARINE M

M JOINVILLE LE PORT

PORTE DORÉE M

LIBERTÉ M

av. de la Dame Blanche

av. de Nogent

av. de Paris

av. Foch

av. Victor Hugo

av. des Minimes

rte. de la Tourelle

rue de la République

bd. Soult

bd. Périphérique

av. Daumesnil

av. de Gravelle

rue de Paris

Château de Vincennes

Fort de Vincennes

Esplanade St-Louis

Caserne

Entrance, Parc Floral de Paris ■

PARC FLORAL DE PARIS

Stade Municipal de Vincennes

Institut National des Sports

Stade Pershing

Lac des Minimes

Jardin Tropical

av. de la Belle Gabrielle

Ecole d'Horticulture

rte. de la Ferme

av. du Tremblay

rte. du Montreuil

Hippodrome

ARBORÉTUM

rte. du Pesage

rte. St-Hubert

rte. de Pyramide

rte. de la Faluère

rte. Dauphine

rte. Bourbon

Allée Royale

rte. de la Demi Lune

rte. de la Tourelle

Lac de St-Mandé

PARC ZOOLOGIQUE

Entrances, Parc Zoologique ■

Boats ■

Temple Bouddhique

Cimitière de Charenton

Lac Daumesnil

Musée des Arts Africains et Océaniens 🏛

Vélodrome J. Anquetil ■

0 1/4 mile
0 1/4 kilometer

CHÂTEAU DE VINCENNES. Called "the Versailles of the Middle Ages," the French kings held court here as early as the 13th century, and although the Louvre was royalty's principal home, every French monarch from Charles V to Henri IV spent at least part of his time at Vincennes. On the spot that Philippe-Auguste chose for a royal hunting residence, Charles V built up a medieval fortress. Henri III found it a useful refuge during the Wars of Religion, and Mazarin and the court found its defenses useful in the wake of the Fronde. In the 18th century, Vincennes became a country-club prison for well-known enemies of the state. Mirabeau spent 3½ years here, killing time by writing lecherous letters to his (married) mistress. When Diderot was imprisoned in the château, Rousseau walked through the forest to visit. In the 19th century, the complex resumed its military functions, serving as fortress, arsenal, and artillery park. In 1917, the infamous Mata Hari, convicted of spying for the Germans, faced a firing squad within its walls. In 1940, the château was headquarters for General Maurice Gamelin, Supreme Commander of French Land Forces. De Gaulle criticized Gamelin for holing up in Vincennes, without even a radio to connect him with the front. *(M: Château de Vincennes. On the northern edge of the park. Open daily May-Sept. 10am-noon and 1:15-6pm; Oct.-Apr. 10am-noon and 1:15–5pm. Admission by guided tour only; long tour 32F, students 21F; short tour 25F, students 15F; under 12 free.)*

PARC FLORAL DE PARIS. One of the gems of the Bois de Vincennes is the Parc Floral de Paris, which can be reached by walking down rue de la Pyramide from the castle. The park has a library, a butterfly garden, miniature golf, and assorted games for kids. Picnic areas, restaurants, and open-air concerts make it a metropolis of summer entertainment. *(Esplanade du Château. M: Château de Vincennes. Tel. 01 43 43 92 95. Open daily Apr.-Sept. 9:30am-8pm; Oct.-Mar. 9:30am-5pm. Admission 10F, ages 6-18 5F, under 6 free.)*

LAC DAUMESNIL. Joggers, cyclists, and people-watchers share the turf around Lac Daumesnil. Others row boats. *(Boat rental daily Mar.-Nov. 10:30am-5:30pm. 1-2 people 54F per hr., 3-4 people 60F per hr., 50F deposit plus recommended tip.)* Penetrate farther into the park for running and cycling paths. The **Vélodrome Jacques Anquetil,** the **Hippodrome de Vincennes,** and other sports facilities await you (see **Participatory Sports,** p. 276).

FERME DE PARIS. If you're with the kids, or just feel the need for some heavy petting, head to the Paris Farm. Full of barnyard animals and fields of produce, the farm encourages kids and adults with some hands-on learning. *(Tel. 01 43 28 47 63. Open Sa-Su and holidays in summer 1:30-7pm; in winter 1:30-5:15pm. Admission 22F, under 18 11F.)*

SAINTE-CHAPELLE AND DONJON. Built between 1360 and 1370, the 52m-high donjon (big square tower) is a striking example of medieval architecture. It has been closed for restoration for the past five years, however, and unfortunately will probably not be open until early in the next millennium. The Ste-Chapelle was founded as a church in 1379, but the building was not inaugurated until 1552. Dainty in its decor and especially beautiful in late afternoon, the Ste-Chapelle is looking even better these days after restoration of the exterior. Guided tours are the only way to get in, but the church, stripped down to its bare bones over the centuries, is more impressive from the outside. There are archaeological digs to survey in the main courtyard, and the ramparts offer a pleasant, if unexciting, view of the area.

LA DÉFENSE

M/RER: La Défense, or the #73 bus. The RER is faster, but the métro is cheaper. If you take the RER, buy the RER ticket before going through the turnstile. A normal métro ticket may get you into the RER station in Paris, but won't get you out without a fine at La Défense. Grande Arche open daily 10am-7pm; roof closes 1hr. after ticket office, which closes at 6pm. Admission 43F; under 18, students, and seniors 33F. Beyond the small lawn, the Info Défense booth offers free maps, guides, and a permanent exhibit on the architectural history and *future of La Défense. Tel. 01 47 74 84 24. Open M-F 10am-1pm and 2-5pm. For **French tours** call Défense-Evenement or take the petit train. Tel. 01 46 92 17 50. 35F, students 25F. **French petit train tours** every 40min. Apr.-Oct. daily 10am-6:30pm from under the Grande Arche; 27F, under 10 15F.*

Just outside Paris's most exclusive suburbs lies a gleaming, teeming space crammed with eye-popping contemporary architecture, enormous office buildings, and one very geometric triumphal arch. Great efforts have been made since La Défense's initial development in 1958, especially by Mitterrand and his *grands projets* program, to inject social spaces, monuments, and art into La Défense's commercial landscape. Shops, galleries, gardens, and sculptures by **Miró, Calder,** and **César** cluster around the **Grande Arche de la Défense,** a breathtaking 35-story building in the shape of a white hollow cube.

After the construction of the Tour Montparnasse in 1973 (see **Sights,** p. 220), Parisian authorities restricted the further construction of skyscrapers *(gratte-ciels)* within the 20 arrondissements for fear that new highrises would alter the Paris skyline. As a result, new building projects moved to La Défense, and modern Paris was born. To maintain the symmetry of the **Axe Historique** (the line that stretches from the Arc de Triomphe du Carrousel in front of the Louvre, down the Champs-Élysées to the Arc de Triomphe, and down the av. de la Grande Armée to La Défense), I.M. Pei suggested a plan for a monument to anchor the Défense end of the axis. Ultimately, Pei was asked instead to design the eastern terminus in the courtyard of the Louvre. French Presidents Pompidou, Giscard d'Estaing, and Mitterrand sponsored international contests for a monument. Of 424 projects, four were presented anonymously to the president, who chose Danish architect Otto von Spreckelsen's Grande Arche for its "purity and strength." Spreckelsen backed out of the project before its completion, disheartened by red tape and by his own design, which he deemed a "monument without a soul." British engineer Peter Rice finished the work and designed the canvas tent "clouds" suspended to soften the arch's austere angles.

The Arche was inaugurated on the French Republic's bicentennial, July 14, 1989, when it hosted a G7 summit. The roof of this unconventional office building covers 2.5 acres—Nôtre-Dame could nestle in its hollow core. The arch's walls are covered with white marble and mirrors so that it shines brilliantly in sunlight. Ride the outdoor glass elevators for an unparalleled view at the top and a redux of the end of *Charlie and the Chocolate Factory.*

Despite La Défense's 20th-century architecture and modernist look, the area dates from the 19th century. In 1871, Louis-Ernest Barrias's design beat 100 other proposals (including one by Auguste Rodin) in a contest to commemorate the defense of Paris against the Prussians. The name has caused some confusion: the Managing Director of La Défense was once refused entry to Egypt when he was mistaken for a military official.

Other Défense buildings include the **Bull Tower,** the tent-like **Palais Défense,** and the Star-Trek influenced **CNIT building,** a center for congresses, exhibitions, and conferences that, at 37 years old, is La Défense's oldest building. The **Musée de l'Automobile,** 1, pl. du Dôme, features car-related accessories, exhibits on the history of the automobile, and 110 vintage *voitures. (Open daily 12:15-7:30pm. Admission 30F, students, seniors, and under 16 25F.)* The globe-shaped **Dôme IMAX** houses a huge-screen omnimax theater (see **Cinema,** p. 272). To the right of the booth, the **Galerie de l'Esplanade** features temporary art exhibits. *(Open daily noon-7pm.)*

The huge **Quatre Temps** shopping center—one of the largest shopping malls in Europe—contains cafés, supermarkets, and 30 restaurants. Enter from the Grande Arche métro stop, or from doors behind the Miró sculpture. The info desk on the first floor near the escalator to the métro distributes maps of the complex. *(Shops open M-Sa 10am-8pm. Supermarkets open M-Sa 9am-10pm.)* The CNIT building contains six restaurants, including a café and sandwich shop with outdoor seating and views of the Grande Arche.

MUSEUMS AND GALLERIES

Since Charles de Gaulle appointed France's first Minister of Culture in 1956, thousands of hours and millions of francs have been spent shaking the dust off the reputation of the Parisian museum. Paris's national museums are multi-purpose, user-friendly institutions shaped by public interest and state funds. Serving as forums for lectures, art films, concerts, and the occasional play, the museums here—most prominently the Louvre, Orsay, and Pompidou—broadcast Paris, past and present.

Paris's *grands musées* cater to an international public and are mobbed, particularly in summer. Take advantage of evening hours, avoid weekends and reduced admission days where possible, and be forewarned: the *Mona Lisa* will be obscured by raised cameras and clamoring schoolchildren. If you tire of dangling from chandeliers for a better view, look for Paris's smaller museums, which display specialized collections often comparable in content to wings of their larger cousins. For temporary exhibits, consult the bimonthly *Paris Museums and Monuments*, available at the tourist office, 127, av. des Champs-Elysées (tel. 08 36 68 31 12; 2.23F per min.). *Pariscope* and *l'Officiel des Spectacles* contain weekly updates of hours and temporary exhibits (see **Newspapers and Listings,** p. 85).

If you are in Paris for a short period of time or are generally hoping to do a sight-seeing blitz, you may want to invest in a **Carte Musées et Monuments,** which offers admission to 65 museums in the Paris area. This card will probably save you money if you are planning to visit more than 3 museums/sights every day and will enable you to sail past all of the frustrated tourists standing in line. In summer, lines can be more than half an hour long. You may want to coordinate your purchase of this card with a visit to Versailles, where the card is indispensable: you will skip the hour and a half line in the summer heat. The card is available at major museums and in almost all métro stations. Ask for a brochure listing participating museums and monuments, though almost every major sight participates. A pass for one day is 80F; for three consecutive days 160F; for five consecutive days 240F. For more information, call **Association InterMusées,** 25, rue du Renard, 4*ème* (tel. 01 44 78 45 81; fax 44 78 12 23; www.intermusees.com).

Larger museums often offer group tours in various languages. Prices are typically around 500F for a group of adults, 250F for students and visitors 60 years and older. Smaller museums with major exhibits are generally annotated in French only. Relatively inexpensive English pamphlets can usually be found at bookstores within these museums. Paris's **art galleries** feature contemporary art in a more intimate setting. see **Galleries,** p. 265.

MAJOR MUSEUMS

MUSÉE DU LOUVRE

M: Palais-Royal/Musée du Louvre. Tel. 01 40 20 50 50; www.louvre.fr. **Open** M and W 9am-9:45pm, Th-Su 9am-6pm. Last entry 45min. before closing, but people are asked to leave 15-30min. before closing. **Admission** W-Sa 9am-3pm 45F, 3pm-close and all day Su 26F, under 18 and first Su of the month free. **Temporary exhibitions** in the Cour Napoléon: Open at 10am; additional admission 30F, under 18 free. **Ticket to both** regular and temporary expositions 60F before 3pm, 40F after 3pm and on Su. **English Tours** M and W-Sa 17F; call 01 40 20 53 17 or check the special events board behind the info desk to the left for exact times. **Bookstore** open same hours as the museum.

Built on the foundations of a medieval castle in order to house French kings for four centuries, restructured by a 20th-century Socialist politician and a Chinese-American architect, and filled with priceless objects from the tombs of Egyptian pharaohs, the halls of Roman emperors, the studios of French painters, and the walls of Italian churches, the Louvre is an intersection of time, space, and national boundaries. Explore the endless exhibition halls, witness new generations of artists at work on easels in the galleries, and see the Louvre's most famous residents: the *Mona Lisa*, the *Venus de Milo*, and the *Winged Victory of Samothrace*.

PRACTICAL INFORMATION

The **surface entrance** to the Louvre is through I.M. Pei's center glass pyramid, where an escalator descends into the Cour Napoléon. From the métro, you can reduce your wait in lines and enter directly by following signs through the Carrousel du Louvre, a new subterranean mall under the museum, whose food court, gift shops, and inverted pyramid reflect the architecture on the surface. **Tickets** for the museums are sold in the Cour Napoléon. If you are buying full-priced tickets, save time by using coins or a credit card in one of the automatic ticket machines. You can also buy your tickets before you leave home and save yourself the hassle once in Paris. Simply go to the Louvre's website, order by credit card, and the tickets will be mailed to you. Website tickets are valid through the end of the calendar year in which they are purchased. Holders of a *Carte Musée et Monuments* (see **Museums,** p. 242) can skip the line by entering the Louvre from the Richelieu entrance (in the passage connecting the Cour Napoléon to the rue de Rivoli). To avoid heat and crowds, visit on weekday afternoons or on Monday and Wednesday evenings, when the museum stays open until 9:45pm.

Due to constant renovations and conservation efforts, accelerated by millennial celebrations, no guidebook can give you a completely accurate walking tour of the museum. To find out which rooms will be open on your visit check the home page, ask the information desk, or call museum information (tel. 01 40 20 51 51). Be sure to pick up an updated map at the circular information desk in the center of the Cour Napoléon. Whatever your visiting pace, consider purchasing *The Guide for the Visitor in a Hurry* (20F), an English-language brochure available in the bookstore of the Cour Napoléon. **Audioguides,** available at the top of both the Denon and Sully escalators (rental 30F; deposit of driver's license, passport, or credit card), describe over 350 of the museum's highlights. **Tours** fill up quickly. The free plastic info cards *(feuillets)* found in gallery corners, provide detailed commentary and historical context on art work in each gallery.

There are three **places to eat** in the Cour Napoléon. Two cafés are located on the upper and main floors (sandwiches 20-29F). A pricier restaurant is on the main floor. Better than these two establishments is the Universal Resto food court on the second floor of the Carrousel du Louvre mall, on the other side of the inverted pyramid. Here, you can get coffee for 8F or eat a decent, fast meal for 35-60F.

The Louvre is fully **wheelchair-accessible.** You may borrow a wheelchair for free at the central information desk (passport deposit). Call information for disabled visitors (tel. 01 40 20 59 90). The Louvre has begun a series of workshops for children in English (see the information desk in the Cour Napoléon for info). The auditorium in the Cour Napoléon hosts concerts (65-130F), films, lectures, and colloquia (all 25F). For more information, call 01 40 20 51 86. There is also a small theater in the hall with free one-hour films relating to the museum (M-F 10am, Sa-Su every 1½hr. from 11am).

If you're under 26 years old or a teacher and plan to visit the Louvre more than twice in the next twelve months, consider buying the *Carte Louvre Jeunes*. An amazing deal at 100F, it entitles its holder to one year's unlimited entrance (without waiting in line) to the permanent collection and temporary exhibits, visits with a guest on Monday nights from 6 to 9:45pm, and discounts on all books, tours, concerts, movies, and classes offered at the Louvre. For more information call 01 40 20 51 04 or inquire at the information desk for an application.

THE LAYOUT

When visiting the Louvre, strategy is everything. Think like a four-star general; the goal is to come and see without being conquered. The reality is that you can't *do* the Louvre, not all of it anyway. Pick a few areas you'd like to see, and take the time to see them well. A fine place to start is at **CyberLouvre,** a free computer library where you can access the Louvre's for-sale CD-Roms, web sites, and other databases, all for free. If you're a first-time visitor, it will help you figure out what you want to see, and where it is (tel. 01 40 20 67 30; open W-M 9am-6pm).

The Louvre is organized into three different wings—Sully, Richelieu, and Denon—each leading off of the center of the Cour Napoléon. Each wing is divided into different sections according to the artwork's date, national origin, and medium (for example, "18th-century French Painting"). The color-coding and room numbers on the Louvre's free maps correspond to the colors and numbers on the plaques at the entrances to every room within the wing. Getting lost is an inevitable part of the Louvre experience, but there are plenty of blue-jacketed docents (many who speak English) who can point you in the right direction. The collection itself is divided into seven departments that spread out over the three wings: Oriental Antiquities; Egyptian Antiquities; Greek, Etruscan, and Roman Antiquities; Painting; Sculpture; Decorative Arts; and Graphic Arts.

THE BUILDING

Construction of the Louvre began in 1190 and isn't finished yet. King Philippe-Auguste built the original structure to protect Paris while he was away on a crusade. In the 14th century, Charles V extended the city walls beyond what is now the Jardin des Tuileries (see **Sights,** p. 168), thus stripping the Louvre of its defensive utility. Not one to let a good castle go to waste, Charles converted the austere fortress into a residential château. Later monarchs avoided the narrow, dank, and rat-infested building. In 1527, however, François I returned to the Louvre in an attempt to flatter the Parisian bourgeoisie, whom he hoped to distract from their raised taxes. François razed Charles's palace and commissioned Pierre Lescot to build a new royal palace in the open style of the Renaissance. All that remains of the old Louvre are its foundations, unearthed in the early stages of Mitterrand's renovations and displayed in an underground exhibit called Medieval Louvre (admission included in museum ticket).

François I started work on the **Cour Carrée** (Square Courtyard) in 1546. Most of the Cour owes its classicism to Louis XIV, who hired a trio of architects—Le Vau, Le Brun, and Perrault—to transform the Louvre into the grandest palace in Europe. Louis XIV eventually abandoned the Louvre in favor of Versailles, and construction did not get past the Cour Carrée. The main courtyard is the **Cour Napoléon,** begun by Catherine de Medici 200 years before it was completed by Napoleon III. The two wings stretching into the distance were once connected by the Palais des Tuileries, a royal residence begun in 1563 to grant Catherine privacy (it was burned by the *communards* in 1871; see **History,** p. 8). Henri IV completed the Tuileries and embarked on what he called the Grand Design—a project to link the Louvre and the Tuileries with the two large wings you see today. He only built a fraction of the project before his death in 1610.

In 1725, after years of relative abandonment, the Academy of Painting inaugurated annual salons in the halls to show the work of its members. For over a century, French painting would revolve around the salons, and, in 1793, the Revolution made the exhibit permanent, thus creating the Musée du Louvre. Napoleon filled the Louvre with plundered art from continental Europe and Egypt. With his defeat at Waterloo, however, most of this art had to be returned to the countries from which it had been "borrowed." More durably, Napoleon built the **Arc de Triomphe du Carrousel,** a copy of Rome's Arch of Septimus Severus, to commemorate his victories.

In 1857, Napoleon III continued work on Henri IV's Grand Design, extending the Louvre's two wings to the Tuileries palace and remodeling the facades of the older buildings. The François I wing gained a new face on its west side but retained its original design on the Cour Carrée side. 14 years after the completion of the Grand Design, the Tuileries palace was burned to the ground by the Paris Commune.

For most of the 20th century, the Louvre was a confusing maze of government offices and inaccessible galleries. Until 1989, the Finance Ministry occupied the Richelieu wing of the Louvre. Mitterrand's *Grands Projets* campaign transformed the Louvre into an accessible, well-organized museum. Internationally renowned American architect I.M. Pei came up with the idea of moving the museum's entrance to the center of the Cour Napoléon, on an underground level surmounted by his stunning and controversial **glass pyramid.** At first, Pei's proposal met with intense disapproval. Others consider Pei's pyramid a stroke of genius. The Cour Napoléon glows in the sun streaming through the glass pyramid. There are 666 panes of glass on the pyramid, each one seeming to contribute one more degree of intense heat while waiting inside on a summer's day.

PAINTINGS

The Louvre's painting collection begins with the Middle Ages and includes works dating up to the mid-19th century. The **Flemish Gallery** (second floor, Richelieu) houses such masterworks as **Van Hemessen's** *Young Tobias Gives Sight to His Father*, **Hieronymous Bosch's** *Ship of Fools*, and **Jan Van Eyck's** *Madonna of Chancellor Rolin*, remarkable for the minute detail of the countryside that can be seen beyond the window of the foreground and thought to be one of the first oil paintings. **Peter Paul Rubens's** 24-paneled *Médicis Cycle* (1621-25) occupies its own room. Returning from an exile imposed by her son Louis XIII, Marie de Medici hired Rubens to retell her personal history to the world (or at least to the treacherous French court). These wall-sized Baroque canvases show a mythical Marie de Medici as well as Rubens's famous buxom maidens, nymphs, and goddesses.

French works, which stretch from the Richelieu wing through the entire Sully wing and part of the Denon wing, include paintings from the Neoclassical, Rococo, and Romantic schools of 16th-century through 1848, after which time the Musée d'Orsay takes over. The Rococo works of **Antoine Watteau, Jean-Honoré Fragonard,** and **François Boucher** showcase aristocratic styles of architecture and dress that culminated in the reign of Louis XIV, the Sun King. Watteau's unsettling *Gilles* (also called *Pierrot*) illustrates an awkward boy in a clown suit staring uncomfortably out at the observer while other characters mock him. **Jacques-Louis David's** 1785 work, *Le serment de Horaces (The Oath of the Horatii)*, was politically controversial, focusing on three brothers swearing allegiance to their country before going off to battle, an ominous theme for Paris on the eve of the Revolution. One of the largest paintings in the Louvre, and similarly political, his *Sacre de Napoleon 1er à Notre Dame de Paris (The Coronation of Napoleon)* rests across from *Mona Lisa*, who finds the whole thing rather amusing (see p. 246). David's other paintings, the *Les Sabines (Rape of the Sabine Women)* and the *Léonidas aux Thermopyles* also hang in the Denon wing (for more on David, see **Fine Arts,** p. 23). **Jean-Auguste-Dominique Ingres,** one of David's students, abandoned his mentor's hard, sculptural physiques in favor of the fleshy roundness of the Italian Renaissance master Raphael. Ingres's *Le Bain turc* gives you an idea what an afternoon at a *hammam* is like. **Théodore Géricault's** *Le Radeau de la Méduse (Raft of the Medusa)* tells the true story of the survivors of the sunken ship Medusa, who were forced to resort to cannibalism to make it through two weeks on the open sea. Salon-goers were horrified by the portrayal of half-eaten corpses (Géricault studied real ones in preparation for this work). **Delacroix's** *La Liberté guidant le peuple (Liberty Leading the People)* personifies Liberty as a woman on the barricades of the French Revolution. Louis-Philippe thought it so dangerous that he bought the painting and hid it from the public. Delacroix's *La Mort de*

MUSEUMS

Sardanapale depicts the final scene of a play by Byron in which King Sardana-palus slaughters his horses and concubines as the enemy surrounds his palace.

The **Italian Renaissance** collection (on the first floor of the Denon wing) is rivaled only by that of the Uffizi museum in Florence. For the best in Renaissance portraiture, look to **Raphael's** *Portrait of Balthazar Castiglione* and **Titian's** *Man with a Glove.* Titian's *Fête Champêtre* inspired Manet's *Déjeuner sur l'Herbe* (see **Musée d'Orsay**, p. 249). **Veronese's** gigantic *Wedding Feast at Cana* occupies an entire wall. A few years ago it was accidentally dropped while being restored; the fall caused a meter-long tear in the canvas, since then repaired. The models for the apostles were 16th-century aristocratic Venetians, with Veronese himself playing the cello. Bought by François I during the artists's visit to Paris, **Leonardo da Vinci's** *Mona Lisa* (or *La Joconde, The Smiling One*) smiles mysteriously at millions of guests each year. In the struggle to elbow your way to a close-up view, don't forget to look at her remarkable neighbors. Da Vinci's *Virgin of the Rocks* displays the *sfumato* (smoky) technique for which he is famous.

MS. MONA'S WILD RIDE The lovely Mona is fortunate to be here at all. Louvre curators discovered her missing one morning in 1911. Guillaume Apollinaire warned his friend Pablo Picasso, who owned two statues stolen from the Louvre, that a search for the *Mona Lisa* might uncover the contraband sculptures. The pair panicked, and at midnight struck out into the darkness with the statues packed into a suitcase, intending to dump them in the Seine. Near the *quais*, they suspected they were being followed and decided to leave the statues anonymously with a local newspaper. But the police soon tracked down and jailed Apollinaire as a suspect in the *Mona Lisa* heist. After two days of intense questioning, Apollinaire's resolve broke and he accused Picasso of stealing the painting. In spite of this treachery, Picasso cleared his name with a convincing plea. Only through the efforts of local artists, who attested to the fine quality of Apollinaire's character, was the poet released. The *Mona Lisa* turned up two years later in the possession of a former Louvre employee who had snuck it out under his overcoat, leaving only the frame and a fine impression of his left thumb. Unfortunately, the museum had recorded employees' right thumb prints only. The joyful, albeit embarrassed, museum directors returned the smiling lady to her proper place, where she now resides securely within a glass enclosure.

GREEK, ETRUSCAN, AND ROMAN ANTIQUITIES

Although most visitors stumble into this section looking for two of the museum's most famous pieces, the **Venus de Milo** and the **Winged Victory of Samothrace,** the rest of the Louvre's collection of ancient sculpture is extraordinary. Despite polite yearly requests from the Greek Minister of Culture to return its collection of antiquities, the Louvre maintains that these sculptures are better off in Paris. The Louvre's collection of **Greek vases** is one of the finest in the world. Beautiful black and red *kylix's* and *kraters* (used to mix wine and water) depict nymphs and satyrs doing things for which you could be arrested in some southern American states. The collection, acquired in 1861 by Napoleon III, includes the **Melos Amphora** with its painting of Hercules and Athena, surrounded by the Olympian bratpack.

Greek and Roman sculpture at the Louvre covers too many floors and periods to be tackled by all but the classics junkies, but there are some standouts. The **Winged Victory of Samothrace** dominates the landing between the Denon and Sully wings. Despite the thousand pictures you've seen of her (most notably with Audrey Hepburn in *Funny Face*), she is still breathtaking, especially from the staircase below. Originally situated on a rocky precipice overlooking the sea, the *Winged Victory* was excavated in 1863 on the Greek island of Samothrace by a French archaeologist. The statue commemorates a Rhodian naval victory and is one of the most important examples of Hellenistic sculpture. The recently restored **Borghe-sian Gladiator** pulses with ripples of Roman musculature and was imitated widely in works of the 17th and 18th century. Found in 1820 on the Greek island of Milos, the **Venus de Milo** (on the ground floor of the Sully wing) depicts the goddess of love wrapped in sculpted folds of cloth. The 8th century BC Etruscan **Sarcophagus of a Married Couple** (in the Denon wing) depicts a couple reclining at a banquet, the husband's arm wrapped around his wife's shoulder. Resting atop their coffin, this funerary sculpture illustrates their love for each other, together in life as in death.

OTHER COLLECTIONS

The **Oriental Antiquities** department houses an impressive collection of pre-Christian antiques and sculpture from the Fertile Crescent region. This collection includes the world's oldest legal document, a basalt slab from the 18th century BC on which is inscribed the **Code of King Hammurabi.** Room 4 presents the reliefs from the Palace of Khorsabad built by Sargon II in the 7th century BC and five winged bulls, which guarded the palace doors. The **Islamic Art** collection (in Richelieu and Sully) features rugs, tapestries, armor, and scientific instruments. Half of the first floor stands as a showcase for **Objets d'Art**—the jewelry, tapestries, furniture, dishes, and decorations belonging to centuries of ruling classes. The **Sculpture** department includes everything after the Roman period until the 19th century. The stars of the collection are **Michelangelo's** *Les Esclaves (The Slaves).*

SPECIAL EXHIBITIONS

In addition to its regular collections, the Louvre features rotating exhibits in the Cour Napoléon and the three main wings. Though the Louvre will not have an official celebration to ring in 2000, the museum is staging an exhibition called **The Invention of Time** to begin in January of the new **millennium.** There will also be an exhibition entitled "Vivant Denon" about the work of the museum's first curator.

MUSÉE D'ORSAY

*62, rue de Lille, 7ème. M: Solférino or RER: Musée d'Orsay. Tel. 01 40 49 48 48; recorded information 01 45 49 11 11; www.musee-orsay.fr. **Open** June 20-Sept. 20 Tu-W and F-Su 9am-5:45pm, Th 9am-9:30pm; Sept. 21-June 19 Tu-W and F-Su 10am-5:45pm, Th 10am-9:45pm. Last ticket sales 30min. before closing. **Admission** 40F, ages 18-25 and all on Su 30F, under 18 free. **Tours** in English Tu-Sa, 90min., 36F. **Bookstore and Boutique:** open Tu-W and F-Su 9:30am-6:30pm, Th 9:30am-9:30pm.*

While the Musée d'Orsay has established itself as *the* Impressionist museum, those who come only to see the soft strokes of Monet, Degas, Manet, and Pissarro will miss the breadth and excitement of its full collection. Paintings, sculpture, decorative arts, architecture, photography, and cinema are presented in this former Beaux Arts railway station, with works spanning the period from 1848 until the First World War. Beneath the great steel roof-beams and ornate clocks that took the city's breath away during the Universal Exposition, the Impressionists' and their descendants' work is displayed in elegant galleries.

PRACTICAL INFORMATION

The museum is least crowded on Sunday mornings and on Thursday evenings when it is open late. Avoid visiting on a Tuesday if at all possible, since this is the day the Louvre closes. The *Guide to the Musée d'Orsay* by Caroline Mathieu, the museum's curator, is excellent (95F), or you can buy the practical condensed *Guide for the Visitor in a Hurry* (20F). Hand-held **audioguides,** available in English and other languages, provide anecdotal histories and analyses of 60 masterpieces throughout the museum. The recording lasts two hours, but you should set aside at least three to visit all the rooms. (30F; driver's license, passport, credit card, or 500F deposit required.) **Tours** leave regularly from the group reception. In addition to the permanent collection, seven **temporary exhibition** spaces, called *dossiers*, are dispersed throughout the building. Call or pick up a free copy of *Nouvelles du Musée d'Orsay* to find out which temporary exhibitions are currently installed. The museum also hosts conferences, special tours, and concerts. (Museum tel. 01 40 49 48 48 or for recorded information 01 45 49 11 11.)

The **Café des Hauteurs** is situated on the upper level behind one of the train station's huge iron clocks. There is also a self-serve food stand directly above the café. The **Restaurant du Palais d'Orsay** on the middle floor is worth a peek, even if you don't plan on lunching. A Belle Epoque artifact designed by Gabriel Ferrier, the restaurant offers a view of the Seine and magnificent chandeliers, on top of pricey dining options.The **bookstore** downstairs offers reproductions, postcards, art books, and historical and architectural guides to Paris. The museum's **boutique** offers jewelry, scarves, and sculptures inspired by the museum's collection.

THE BUILDING

Built for the 1900 Universal Exposition, the Gare d'Orsay's industrial function was carefully masked by architect Victor Laloux behind glass, stucco, and a 370-room luxury hotel, so as to remain faithful to the station's elegant surroundings in the prestigious 7*ème*. For several decades, it was the main departure point for southwest-bound trains, but newer trains were too long for its platforms, and it closed in 1939. After WWII, the station served as the main French repatriation center, receiving thousands of concentration camp survivors and refugees. Orson Welles filmed *The Trial* here in 1962. The Musée d'Orsay opened in 1986 as one of the grands projets of President Valéry Giscard d'Estaing, taking works from the Louvre, Jeu de Paume, Palais de Tokyo, Musée de Luxembourg, provincial museums, and private collections.

For all its size and bustle, the Orsay delights art lovers as one of the friendliest museums in Paris. A specially marked escalator at the far end of the building ascends directly to the Impressionist level, and maps and English-language information are available. The museum's visit begins on the ground floor, then goes to the top floor and ends on the middle floor, as signs and maps clearly indicate.

GROUND FLOOR: CLASSICISM TO PROTO-IMPRESSIONISM

Triumphant Napoleons and toga-clad figures line the central aisle's collection of sculpture from 1850 to 1870. **Jean-Baptiste Carpeaux's** massive *Ugolin* depicts the punishment of the condemned count and his four children in Dante's *Inferno*. Carpeaux's *La Danse* illustrates five female figures dancing around a leaping male spirit, a work which attracted outrage as "ignoble saturnalia," but brought him fame. Academic paintings and portraiture from the Second Empire fill the galleries along the right side of the ground floor. **Jean-Auguste-Dominique Ingres's** *La Source* features the soft, rounded curves that defined Classical style. The feverish brushwork of **Eugène Delacroix's** preliminary sketch of *La Chasse aux Lions* heralded the dawn of Fauvism (see **Fine Arts,** p. 26). In the rooms to the left of the aisle, **Jean-François Millet, Jean-Baptiste-Camille Corot,** and **Théodore Rousseau** are delegates of the Barbizon school of painting, known for its nostalgic depiction of rural life. While they shared a common subject matter, Realists like **Gustave Courbet** did not depict as idyllic a version of humanity as did the Barbizon painters. "How can it be possible to paint such awful people?" one critic demanded upon viewing the tired, imperfect faces of the funeral-goers in Courbet's *Un Enterrement à Ornans (A Burial at Ornans)* in 1850.

Edouard Manet's *Olympia* caused a scandal at the 1865 salon. Inspired by Titian's *Venus of Urbino*, a standard for female nudes in Western art, Manet asked a famous courtesan to pose for this painting. The classical reference to Titian mixed with the vulgar subject of the Paris *demi-monde* drew great contro-

IMPRESSIONIST PARIS As the Île-de-France was the birthplace of Impressionism, it isn't surprising that Paris should be the subject matter of many of its greatest works. Among the most painted bridges, boulevards, and parks:

The Pont Neuf. Monet and Renoir both painted the bridge looking from the southeast corner in 1872. Renoir's captures the bustle of carriages on a sun-drenched day, while Monet's depicts a crowd of grey and purple umbrellas on a misty, dreary one. Pissarro's 1901 view, more colorful and energetic, includes the newly-erected Samaritaine department store.

Luxembourg Gardens. Van Gogh's *Terrace of the Luxembourg Gardens* (1886) experiments with the bright colors of the grove of trees west of Pl. Edmond Rostrand. William Singer Sargent's more restrained *Luxembourg Gardens at Twilight* (1879) evokes the tranquility of the central fountain in the setting sun.

Grands Boulevards. Pissaro's *Boulevard Montmartre* (1897) and Van Gogh's *Boulevard de Clichy* (1887) used the immense open spaces of the new boulevards to create more distant, abstract views of street life.

versy. Caricatures of the painting covered the pages of Paris's newspapers and art journals, while Manet himself was accused of creating pornography and insulted in the streets. Baudelaire and Zola, on the other hand, were enthusiastic supporters. Manet's *Portrait de Zola* can be seen to the right of *Olympia*. The **decorative arts** and **architecture** galleries focus on industrial design from 1850 to 1900. Here you can stand above the Paris Opéra thanks to scale models and drawings.

UPPER LEVEL:
IMPRESSIONISM AND POST-IMPRESSIONISM

Chosen for its soft, natural light, the upper level of the d'Orsay features a series of rooms devoted to **Impressionists** and their heirs, such as **Van Gogh, Gauguin,** and **Seurat.** Though considered mainstream today, Impressionism was an upheaval of artistic standards and the beginning of abstract modern art. When a group of radicals lead by **Claude Monet** exhibited this new style in 1874, they were derided as *"Impressionistes."* Artists like **Renoir, Bazille, Manet, Pissarro, Dégas,** and **Caillebotte** adopted the name and a new era in Art History was born (see **Fine Arts,** p. 24).

The first room of the upper level features **Manet's** *Déjeuner sur l'Herbe,* in which two bourgeois gentleman picnic with a nude lady. Denied entrance to the 1863 Salon, it showed the provocative nature of what was to come while paying tribute to Titian and Raphael's nudes. **Monet's** *La Gare St-Lazare* and **Renoir's** *Le bal du Moulin de la Galette* capture the iron train stations, crowded boulevards, and society balls of the industrialized Paris of the 1870s. Monet's experiments with light and atmospheric effects culminated in his *Cathédral de Rouen* series. Paintings by **Alfred Sisley, Camille Pissarro,** and **Berthe Morisot** probe the allegorical beauty of the simple country life. **Edgar Dégas's** dancers in *La classe de danse* scratch their backs, massage their tense necks, and cross their arms while listening to their teacher. Such scenes are further developed in his electric **pastels,** a few rooms ahead. The *Petite danseuse de quatorze ans (Little fourteen-year-old dancer)* was the only one of Dégas's sculptures exhibited before his death. At the time of the exhibition, the public was scandalized by its realism; she had doll hair, real ballet slippers, a real tutu, and polychrome skin. Dégas's *Absinthe* (see **The Green Party,** below) highlights the loneliness and isolation of life in the city.

James Whistler, the American artist associated with French Realism, is represented by his *Portrait of the Artist's Mother,* a painting of a seated old woman in a black dress and white bonnet staring blankly, hands folded. More than a dozen of diverse works by **Vincent Van Gogh** follow, including his tormented *Portrait de l'Artiste.* **Paul Cézanne's** still lifes, portraits, and landscapes experiment with the soft colors and geometric planes that would open the door to Cubism.

MUSEUMS

The north wing focuses on the late 19th-century avant-garde. **Pointillists** like **Paul Signac** and **Georges Seurat** strayed from the blur of Impressionism to the dot-matrix precision of Pointillism. Like photography and film, their paintings are made up of thousands of tiny dots of color (see **Fine Arts,** p. 25). **Henri de Toulouse-Lautrec** left his aristocratic family behind to paint dancers and prostitutes. **Paul Gauguin** left his family and job as a stockbroker to join the School of Pont Aven, an artists colony in Brittany. His *Belle Angèle* sets a Breton wife against a background reminiscent of Japanese art.

THE GREEN PARTY Dégas's *L'absinthe* (1875) features the green concoction being downed at a café in Pigalle. Van Gogh, some think, owed much of his inspiration (and madness) to it. Like Baudelaire and Verlaine, Hemingway wrote about absinthe, calling it "that opaque, bitter, tongue-numbing, brain-warming, stomach-warming, idea-changing liquid alchemy." Picasso, Toulouse-Lautrec, and hoards of Parisians loved and drank it fanatically. Much romanticized, the liquor absinthe made a big emerald splash on the Paris scene in the 19th century. First distilled in 1792 from the wormwood plant *(Artemisia absinthium)* and chlorophyll that makes it green, the 120-proof, licorice-like drink was initially used by French soldiers in Algeria to foil dysentery. They came back to France in the 1830s with a taste for the stuff, and soon it seemed that all of Paris was riding the green wave. Bars had *l'heure vert* (green hour), where water was poured onto a sugar cube and into the clear green liquor, turning it a darker, cloudy hue. Drinkers talked about the *fée verte* (green fairy—she's all over Art Nouveau posters) that stole the drinker's soul, while others warned of *le peril vert,* and in 1915 absinthe was outlawed in France. Most countries followed suit, although it's still available in Spain and the Czech Republic. *Pernod* tastes similar, but for the real thing most of us will probably have to settle for anecdotes. "After the first glass," wrote Oscar Wilde, "you see things as you wish they were. After the second, you see things as they are not. Finally you see things as they really are, and that is the most horrible thing in the world." (See the **Musée d'Absinthe** in **Auvers-sur-Oise,** p. 338.)

MIDDLE LEVEL:
BELLE ÉPOQUE & ART NOUVEAU

Once the elegant ballroom of the Hôtel d'Orsay, the neo-Rococo *Salle des Fêtes* on the middle level displays late 19th-century salon sculpture, painting, and decorative arts. These salon works show what was going on in the sanctioned art world, while Impressionists were rebelling against the Academy. Nearly one-third of the middle level's terrace is devoted to **Auguste Rodin.** Commissioned in 1880 to be the main doors to the new Ecole des Arts Décoratifs, the unfinished *Porte de l'Enfer (Gates of Hell)* is encrusted with figures from Dante's *Inferno;* Rodin recast many of these in larger bronzes such as *Le Penseur (The Thinker),* who sits atop the gates, surveying the hell below, and *Ugolino,* whose starvation in hell tempts him to eat his own sons. On the terrace stands *l'Age Mûr,* a sculpture by Rodin's lover, Camille Claudel. (For more Rodin, see the **Musée Rodin,** p. 251.)

Most of the western half of the middle level is devoted to the works of **Art Nouveau.** Modeled after the English Arts and Crafts movement, Art Nouveau's mantra was "unity in design:" Art Nouveau techniques and styles sought a marriage of function and form. Doing away with heavy ornamentation, the pieces were now animated by the grain of the wood or the play of light on metal. Artists from various disciplines—carpenters, glassblowers, and painters—joined together in close collaboration. One example of this joint effort can be seen in the Belle Epoque Dining Room of **Charpentier, Bigot,** and **Fontaine,** which was commissioned by the banker who financed much of the Paris métro. Art Nouveau had an often tortured relationship with the general public. Concerned with the accessibility of artisanal works and committed to the fair distribution of its creations to the underprivileged classes, Art Nouveau eventually became the domain of private patrons and bankers. Objects like **René Lalique's** delicately wrought *Flacon à odeurs* (scent bottle, 1900), with a gold-leafed stopper, was a thing of beauty, but not an affordable one. Walk forward into the 20th century with the large-scale works by the **Nabis** artists (a name meaning "prophets" in Hebrew), which combine elements of theater decor and Japanese art. The visit ends with the **Birth of Cinematography** display.

CENTRE POMPIDOU

IT'S 23. BUT WHO'S COUNTING? After two years of renovations, the Centre Pompidou will reopen on December 31, 1999. While the **Atelier Brancusi** is open during renovations, you should head to the **Musée d'Art Moderne de la Ville de Paris** (see **Museums**, p. 258) and the **Musée Picasso** (see **Museums**, p. 253) to satisfy your cravings for the 20th century's greatest hits.

Often called the Beaubourg, the **Centre National d'Art et de Culture Georges Pompidou** has inspired architectural controversy ever since its inauguration in 1977. Named after French president Georges Pompidou, it fulfills his desire for Paris to have a cultural center embracing music, cinema, books, and the graphic arts. Chosen from 681 competing designs, Richard Rogers and Renzo Piano's building-turned-inside-out bares its circulatory system to all. Piping and ventilation ducts in various colors run up, down, and sideways along the outside (blue for air, green for water, yellow for electricity, red for heating). Framing the building like a cage, huge steel bars support its weight. The Centre Pompidou attracts more visitors per year than any other museum or monument in France—eight million annually compared to the Louvre's three million. *(Rue Beaubourg, 4ème. M: Rambuteau. Tel. 01 44 78 12 33 or 01 44 78 14 63.)*

The **Musée National d'Art Moderne,** the Pompidou's main attraction, houses a rich selection of 20th-century art, from the Fauves and Cubists to Pop and Conceptual Art. Most of the works were contributed by the artists themselves or by their estates; Joan Miró and Wassily Kandinsky's wife number among the museum's founding members. The **Salle Garance** hosts adventurous film series, and the **Bibliothèque Publique d'Information** is a free, non-circulating library. The **Institut de la Recherche et de la Coordination Acoustique/Musique (IRCAM)** is a musical institute where the public can research using a database of 20th-century music (see p. 273).

MUSÉE RODIN

*77, rue de Varenne, 7ème. M: Varenne. Tel. 01 44 18 61 10; www.musee-rodin.fr. **Open** Apr.-Sept. Tu-Su 9:30am-5:45pm; Oct.-Mar. Tu-Su 9:30am-4:45pm. Last admission 30min. before closing. **Admission** 28F, students, seniors, under 18, and all on Su 18F. **Park** alone 5F. Audio tour 25F. Temporary exhibits housed in the chapel, to your right as you enter. Entrance included in the price of museum admission. Persons who are blind or vision-impaired may obtain advanced permission to touch the sculptures.*

Located in the elegant 18th-century **Hôtel Biron,** in which the artist lived and worked at the end of his life, the Musée Rodin highlights the work of one of France's greatest sculptors. During his lifetime, Auguste Rodin (1840-1917) was among the country's most controversial artists, classified by many as Impressionism's sculptor (Monet, incidentally, was a close friend and admirer). Today, almost all acknowledge him as the father of modern sculpture. Born in a working-class district of Paris, Rodin began study at the Petite Ecole, a trade school for technical drawing. He tried three times to get into the famous Ecole des Beaux-Arts (see **Sights,** p. 189) and failed each time. Frequenting the Louvre to study Classical sculpture, he later worked as an ornamental carver, setting up a small studio of his own. His travels away from Paris allowed him to articulate a definitive, powerful style, completely unlike the flowery academic style then in vogue. He refused the standard of "ideal beauty" for a more expressive style of realism, which incorporated raw textures and tense, dynamic poses. Nonetheless, his technical skill was unequalled: one of his first major pieces, *The Age of Bronze*, was so anatomically perfect that he was accused of molding it directly from the body.

The museum houses many of Rodin's better known sculptures in plaster, bronze, and marble, such as *Le Main de Dieu (The Hand of God)* and *Le Baiser (The Kiss)*, along with nearly 500 other works. *Le Cathédral* shows two hands twisted around each other, palms facing and fingertips touching; look twice and you'll notice that both of the hands are right hands, one a man's and one a woman's. Rodin's training in drawing is evident everywhere; as he said, "my sculpture is but drawing in three dimensions." One room is dedicated to a rotating display of drawings and studies. In addition, the museum has several works by **Camille Claudel,** Rodin's muse, collaborator, and lover. Claudel's *L'Age Mûr* has been read as her response to Rodin's decision to leave her for Beuret, here depicted as an angel of death; Claudel, on her knees, begs the aging Rodin to stay.

The *hôtel*'s expansive garden is a museum unto itself. Flowers, trees, and fountains frame outdoor sculptures. If you're short on time or money, consider paying the smaller admission fee for the grounds only. You won't miss the collection's star; just inside the gates sits Rodin's most famous work, *Le Penseur (The Thinker)*. *Balzac*, to the right of *Le Penseur*, was commissioned in 1891 by the Société des Gens de Lettres. A battle over Rodin's design and his inability to meet deadlines raged for years. Unlike the flattering portrait the Société expected, the finished product shows a dramatic, haunted artist with hollow eyes. The plasticity of the body and the distortion of the author's well-known face enraged artists and non-artists alike. Rodin canceled the commission and kept the statue himself. Later in his life, he noted, "Nothing that I made satisfied me as much, because nothing had cost me as much; nothing else sums up so profoundly that which I believe to be the secret law of my art." On the other side of the garden, a cast of the stunning *Burghers of Calais* (1884-95) somberly recreates a moment in the Hundred Years War. Beyond stands one version of Rodin's largest and most intricate sculpture, the unfinished *Porte de l'Enfer (The Gates of Hell)*. Inspired by Dante's *Inferno*, the figures emerge from and disappear back into an endless whirlwind. Presiding above it all is the small *Thinker*, representing the author (and protagonist) as he sits and contemplates man's fate. Originally commissioned as the entrance doors for the new Ecole des Arts Décoratifs, the sculpture was never finished. Rodin replied to his critics, "Were the cathedrals ever finished?"

The small, upscale **cafeteria** is a superb place for lunch, it offers salads (40F) and sandwiches (25-30F). (Open Apr.-Sept. 10am-6pm; Mar. 10am-4:30pm.)

THE INVALIDES MUSEUMS

Esplanades des Invalides, 7ème. M: Invalides. Tel. 01 44 42 37 72; www.invalides.org. **Open** *daily Apr.-Sept. 10am-7pm; Oct.-Mar. 10am-5pm. Last ticket sales 30min. before closing.* **Admission** *38F, students under 26 and ages 12-17 28F, under 12 free. Accepts MC, V for sales of 50F or more. Ticket also permits entry to the Musée de l'Armée, Musée des Plans-Relief, and the Musée de l'Ordre de la Libération.*

The glorious Hôtel des Invalides, framed by neo-classical facades and topped by the massive gilded cupola of the **Eglise du Dôme,** sets the monumental scale of the *7ème* and guards France's military museums. In 1670, Louis XIV decided to "construct a royal home, grand and spacious enough to receive all old or wounded officers and soldiers." Architect Liberal Bruand's building accepted its first wounded in 1674, and veterans still live in the Invalides today. Jules Hardouin-Mansart provided the final design for the chapel within the Invalides complex. This church received Napoleon's body for funeral services in 1840, 19 years after the former emperor died in exile. His body was said to be perfectly preserved when exhumed from its original coffin before the service. Completed in 1861, **Napoleon's tomb** consists of six concentric coffins, made of materials ranging from mahogany to lead—perhaps to make sure he doesn't escape again, like he did from Elba (see **History**, p. 7). The tomb is placed on the lower level and viewed first from a round balcony above, forcing everyone who visits to bow down to the emperor even in his death (this delighted Adolf Hitler on his visit to Paris in 1940). Names of significant battles are engraved in the marble surrounding the coffins; oddly enough, Waterloo isn't there. Ten bas-reliefs recall Napoleon's institutional reforms of law and education. Bonaparte himself is depicted as a Roman emperor in toga and laurels. Six chapels dedicated to different saints lie off the main room, sheltering the tombs of famous French Marshals. Bring a 10F coin to the tomb for a five-minute recorded explanation in English.

MUSÉE DE L'ARMÉE. More war trophies are housed in the Musée de l'Armée which celebrates French military history. The museum is housed in two wings on opposite sides of the Invalides' cobblestone main courtyard, the Cour d'Honneur. The East Wing *(Aile Orient)* houses war paraphernalia from the 17th, 18th, and 19th centuries and culminates in the First Empire exhibit on the second floor, with a special focus on Napoleon. The West Wing *(Aile Occident)* holds 20th-century exhibits revolving around Charles de Gaulle and the two World Wars. Be prepared for more detail than you ever wanted to know. *(Tel. 01 44 42 37 72. Open daily Apr.-Sept. 10am-6pm; Oct.-Mar. 10am-5pm. Admission included in ticket for Napoleon's tomb.)*

MUSÉE DES PLANS-RELIEFS. The Musée des Plans-Reliefs on the fourth floor is a collection of about 100 models of fortified cities. Spanning the period from 1668 to 1870, the exhibit is of special interest to architects, urban planners, and historians. A free English brochure is available at the museum's entrance. *(Tel. 01 45 51 95 05. Open daily Apr.-Sept. 10am-6pm; Oct.-Mar. 10am-5pm. Admission included in price for Napoleon's tomb. No wheelchair access.)*

MUSÉE DE L'ORDRE DE LA LIBÉRATION. The Musée de l'Ordre de la Libération tells the story of those who fought for the liberation of France. A diverse collection of de Gaulle-related paraphernalia is complemented by tributes to the Resistance fighters of Free France. The exhibit juxtaposes journals and prisoners' drawings with camp uniforms and instruments of Nazi torture in an attempt to document the mental and physical horror endured by POWs and Holocaust victims. *(51bis, bd. de Latour-Maubourg. In the west wing and accessible both from the street and from the Cour d'Honneur. Tel. 01 47 05 04 10. Open daily Apr.-Sept. 10am-6pm; Oct.-Mar. 10am-5pm. Free.)*

MUSÉE D'HISTOIRE CONTEMPORAINE. Independent from the above museums, the Musée d'Histoire Contemporaine mounts two temporary exhibits per year Originally constructed in 1914 to hold documents about the history of the unfolding World War, the three-room museum probes recent history, propaganda, and popular culture. The exhibits are in French, but the visual nature of the exhibits helps transcend the language barrier. *(Housed in a gallery off the Invalides' Cour d'Honneur. Tel. 01 44 42 54 91 or 01 44 42 38 39. Call for information regarding temporary exits and hours. Admission 30F, students and ages 12-17 20F, under 12 free.)*

MUSÉE PICASSO

*5, rue de Thorigny, 3ème. M: Chemin-Vert. Tel. 01 42 71 63 15 or 01 42 71 70 84. **Open** Apr.-Sept. W-M 9:30am-6pm, last entrance 5:15pm; Oct.-Mar. 9:30am-5:30pm, last entrance 4:45pm. **Admission** 30F, ages 18-25 and Su 20F, under 18 free. **Tours** Sa and Su in French 36F, ages 7-18 25F.*

The Musée Picasso catalogues (in French only) the life, work, and 70-year career of one of the most prolific and inventive artists of the 20th century. The museum leads the viewer chronologically through Picasso's earliest work in Barcelona to his Cubist and Surrealist years in Paris and his Neoclassical work on the French Riviera. In order to provide viewers with a clear understanding of the evolution of the artist's career, each room in the museum covers one period of Picasso's life, detailing the progression of both his technique and his personal life, from his many mistresses to his reactions to the two World Wars.

Born in Málaga, Spain in 1881, Picasso loved Paris and moved to the studios of the Bateau-Lavoir in Montmartre (see **Sights,** p. 226), where he painted the *Demoi-*

selles d'Avignon in 1907. In the late 20s, Picasso moved to Montparnasse (see **Sights,** p. 216), where he frequented the Café Sélect and La Closerie des Lilas (see **Cafés,** p. 139) along with Cocteau and Breton. Unable to return to Spain during the Franco régime, Picasso adopted France as his permanent home in 1934. Later, he moved to the French Riviera, where he died in Cannes in 1973.

The collection begins with Picasso's arrival in Paris from Spain, when he experimented with various styles including Impressionism. The first floor shows work from his Blue and Pink periods, including a haunting blue *Autoportrait*. Picasso initially gained attention and fame due to his collage and Cubist work. His guitar and musician collages, such as *Le violin et la musique (Violin with Sheet Music)*, moved his art toward abstraction. In his post-Cubist painting *Deux femmes courant sur la plage (Two Women Running on the Beach)*, Picasso painted thick-limbed, Neoclassical figurative bodies reminiscent of Roman statues but whose movement and color celebrates vitality. Picasso's dear friend, poet Paul Eluard, wrote in 1926 that "Picasso loves intensely, but he kills what he loves." A collection of Picasso's sculptures in the 1930s demonstrate his experiments in rearranging bodily organs and human morphology; soon after, his disconcerted and somber paintings reflect the gloom he felt about the Spanish Civil War. His paintings at the time of the Second World War are restrained and less energetic than his earlier work. The museum displays a selection of Picasso's last works, which include many flamboyant 'Rennaisance' pieces that incorporate an amalgam of Picasso's styles as well as those of other painters.

Many works highlight both Picasso's experiments with abstraction and his many love affairs, including *La femme qui lire (Woman Reading)*, a portrait of his lover Marie-Thérèse Walter, *La femme qui pleure (Woman Crying)*, inspired by the surrealist photographer Dora Maar, and *The Kiss*, painted later in his life while he was married to Jacqueline Roque. By their wedding, Clouzot's film *Le Mystère Picasso* and retrospectives at the Petit Palais were already celebrating his life's work.

When Picasso died in 1973, his family paid the French inheritance tax in artwork. The French government opened the Musée Picasso in 1986 to display the collection. Housed in the 17th-century *Hôtel Salé* (see **Sights,** p. 178), the museum's large and breezy rooms and Giacometti light fixtures display Picasso's large, turbulent works, while the courtyard and fountain below provide a quiet spot for rest and reflection. Behind the *hôtel*, through the central courtyard, a sculpture garden features Picasso's abstract series of *Bathers*.

MUSÉE DE CLUNY

*6, pl. Paul Painlevé, 5ème. M: Cluny-Sorbonne. Tel. 01 43 25 62 00. **Open** W-M 9:15am-5:45pm. **Admission** 30F; students, under 25, over 60, and Su 20F; under 18 free. **Tours** in English W 12:30pm; 36F; under 18 25F. **Concerts** F 12:30pm, Sa 5pm, and summer evenings; 60F, students and seniors 50F, under 18 20F. For information, call 01 53 73 78 00.*

The **Hôtel de Cluny** houses the **Musée National du Moyen Âge,** one of the world's finest collections of medieval art, jewelry, sculpture, and tapestries. The *hôtel* itself is a flamboyant 14th-century medieval manor built on top of first-century Roman ruins. One of three ancient *thermae* (public baths) in Roman Lutèce, the baths were purchased in 1330 by the Abbot of Cluny, who built his residence upon them. In the 15th century, the *hôtel* became home to the monastic Order of Cluny, led by the powerful Amboise family. In 1843 the state converted the *hôtel* into the medieval museum; excavations after WWII unearthed the baths. Roman bathing was an important social ritual. After working out in the *palestre*, bathers would take a hot bath in the *caldarium*, then dip in the lukewarm *tepidarium*, before plunging into the cold *frigidarium*. Only the *frigidarium* and swimming pool remain intact and open to visitors.

The medieval museum's collection includes art from Paris's most important medieval structures: the Ste-Chapelle, Nôtre Dame, and St-Denis. Panels of brilliant stained glass in ruby reds and royal blues from the Ste-Chapelle line the

MUSEUMS

ground floor. The brightly lit *galerie des rois* contains sculptures from Nôtre Dame. Discovered in 1977, these 13th-century stone heads of Judean and Israelite kings were severed from Nôtre-Dame's portals in 1793 when the Revolution mistook them for ancestors of Louis XVI. A collection of medieval jewelry includes royal crowns, courtly brooches, and jewelled daggers.

The museum's collection of 15th- and 16th-century tapestries includes the famous series entitled *La Dame et la Licorne* (The Lady and the Unicorn). The first five panels represent the five senses. The sixth panel, emblazoned with the dedication *À mon seul désir*, depicts a lady holding a necklace from a jewelry box. Some hold that the lady is removing her necklace, locking it away, and rejecting the material, sensual world of the first five tapestries. In this way, *À mon seul désir* could mean "by my own volition," a wish to abandon the body and retreat to the spiritual. Others argue that the lady is donning the necklace and accepting the pleasures of the next five tapestries. In this way, the dedication is to "my only desire." One also wonders why m'lady strokes the unicorn's horn, but it's certainly not worth a dissertation. The museum sponsors chamber music concerts in its Roman and medieval spaces.

LA VILLETTE

La Villette, in the 19ème, is a gorgeous, highly successful urban renewal project in the northeastern corner of Paris. Its 55 hectares enclose an incredibly landscaped park, science museum, Omnimax cinema, conservatory, exhibition hall, jazz club, concert and theater space, and a high-tech music museum surrounded by sparkling canals. A former meat-packing district, the area used to contain slaughterhouses that provided Paris with most of its pork and beef. With the advent of refrigerated transport in 1969, it became more economical to kill cattle in the countryside and deliver the meat directly to butchers. It also became cheaper to have a park for children instead of a neighborood slaughterhouse where kids could play. The government closed down the 19ème's meat industry in 1974. Work began on La Villette in 1979, and in 1985, President Mitterrand inaugurated the complex with the motto, "The place of intelligent leisure." Oddly enough, he used the same line when referring to his house, while trying to lure those fashion models (see **History**, p. 13). Appropriately, La Villette has an extensive program of millennium activities planned for 2000 (see **The Millennium**, p. 284). *(M: Porte de la Villette.)*

CITÉ DES SCIENCES ET DE L'INDUSTRIE

The **Cité des Sciences et de l'Industrie** perches on the northern end of La Villette, next to the Porte de la Villette métro station. (Info. 01 40 05 80 00, in French; www.cite-sciences.fr.)

EXPLORA SCIENCE MUSEUM. Dedicated to bringing science to the young layperson, the star attraction is the Explora science museum. The architecture of the buildings alone is worth a visit, but the exhibits can only be described as absolutely fabulous: kids will love them. Close to 300 separate exhibits, ranging from astronomy and mathematics to computer science and sound. Dare to ask "what is a hunter-killer submarine used for?" and "when will the sun burn out?" The museum also features a **planetarium** (Floor 2), the Cinéma Louis Lumière with 3D movies, a modest **aquarium** (Floor S2), and the Médiathèque, a multimedia scientific and technical library that has over 4000 films (open daily noon-8pm; free). *(Open M-Sa 10am-6pm, Su 10am-7pm. A one-day Cité-Pass covers entrance to Explora, the planetarium, the Louis Lumière 3-D cinema, and the Argonaute submarine, 50F.)*

If you're traveling with children, the Explora's **Cité des Enfants** offers one set of programs for kids ages 3-5 and another for ages 5-12. Both require adult accompaniment, but no more than two adults per family are admitted. Although programs are in French, the interactive exhibits are just as fun for English-speaking explorers. The *vestiare* on the ground floor rents strollers and wheelchairs. *(Children's programs on Tu, Th, and F 9:30, 11:30am, 1:30, and 3:30pm; W, Sa, and Su 10:30am, 12:30, 2:30, and 4:30pm. 1½hr. long, 25F.)*

Also located on the ground floor, **Technocité** (for those age 12 and older) challenges visitors to program their own computer games, design a custom bicycle, work with computer animation, and experiment with industrial art. *(Hours vary; inquire at the front desk or call 01 40 05 12 12 for scheduling; visits 1½hr. Admission 25F.)*

GÉODE. Outside the Cité, the enormous Géode is a huge mirrored sphere mounted on a water basin, like a disco ball in a birdbath. The exterior is coated with 6,433 polished, stainless-steel triangles that reflect every detail of their surroundings. Inside, **Omnimax movies** on volcanoes, glaciers, and other natural phenomena are shown on a 1000-square-meter hemispheric screen (see **Cinema,** p. 271 for more info). *(Tel. 01 40 05 12 12. Tickets 57F.)*

To the right of the Géode, the **Argonaute** submarine details the history of submersibles from Jules Verne to present-day nuclear-powered subs. This 400-ton, 50m-long fighter submarine was designed in 1950 as part of the French national fleet. *(Open Tu-F 10:30am-5:30pm, Sa-Su 11am-6:30pm. Admission 25F, under 7 free. An audioguide tour of the submarine, in English or French, is included.)*

Between the Canal St-Denis and the Cité, **Cinaxe** (tel. 01 40 05 12 12) features inventive movies filmed in first-person perspective from vehicles like Formula One cars, low-flying planes, and Mars land-rovers, while hydraulic pumps simulate every curve and bump. Lunch beforehand is not recommended. *(Open Tu-Su 11am-6pm; shows every 15min; tickets 34F, 29F if bought with another exhibition ticket).*

CITÉ DE LA MUSIQUE

M: Porte de Pantin. Tel. 01 44 84 44 84; info. 01 44 84 45 45; www.cite-musique.fr. **Open** *Tu-Th noon-6pm, F-Sa noon-7:30pm, Su 10am-6pm.* **Admission** *35F, reduced 25F, children 6-18 10F, under 6 free. 10F more for temporary exhibits.* **Guided tours in French** *Sa at 2:30pm, thematic tours F at 7pm, kiddie tour Su at 11am; 60F, reduced 45F, children 6-18 20F, under 6 free.*

At the opposite end of La Villette from the Cité des Sciences is the Cité de la Musique. Designed by Franck Hammoutène and completed in 1990, it has been an overwhelming success. The complex of buildings is visually stunning, full of curves and glass ceilings. The highlight is the **Musée de la Musique,** a collection of paintings, sculptures, and 900 instruments. Visitors don a pair of headphones that tune into musical excerpts and explanations of each instrument.

The Cité de la Musique's two performance spaces—the enormous 1200-seat **Salle des Concerts** and the smaller 230-seat **Amphithéâtre**—host an eclectic range of shows and concerts year round (see **Music,** p. 273). The Cité de la Musique also contains a **music and dance information center** (open M-Sa noon-6pm, Su 10am-6pm) and the **Médiathèque Hector-Berlioz** (tel. 01 40 40 45 40) with 90,000 books, documents, music journals, and photographs *(open M-F 12:30-5:30pm; all free).*

PARC DE LA VILLETTE

Cut in the middle by the **Canal de l'Ourcq** and the **Canal St-Denis,** the **Parc de la Villette** separates the Cité des Sciences from the Cité de la Musique. Rejecting the 19th-century notion of the park as natural oasis, Bernard Tschumi designed a 20th-century urban park, which feels like a step into the future.

Constructed in 1867 as the La Villette beef building, the steel-and-glass **Grande Halle** (tel. 08 03 30 63 06 or 08 03 07 50 75; 2.23F/min) features frequent plays, concerts, temporary exhibitions, and films. Unifying the park is a set of red cubical structures that form a grid of squares, known as **Folies.** One houses that questionable fast-food restaurant, Le Quick, day-care centers, coffee shops, education centers, and one, at the entrance near M: Pte. de Pantin, is an **information office** (tel. 01 40 03 75 10 or 01 40 03 75 64; open daily 10am-7pm). Every summer there is a free open-air **film festival** that shows foreign, art, and generally funky movies from July to August next to the Grande Salle. The **Zénith** concert hall (tel. 01 42 08 60 00) hosts major rock bands. Nirvana played one of their last concerts here in February

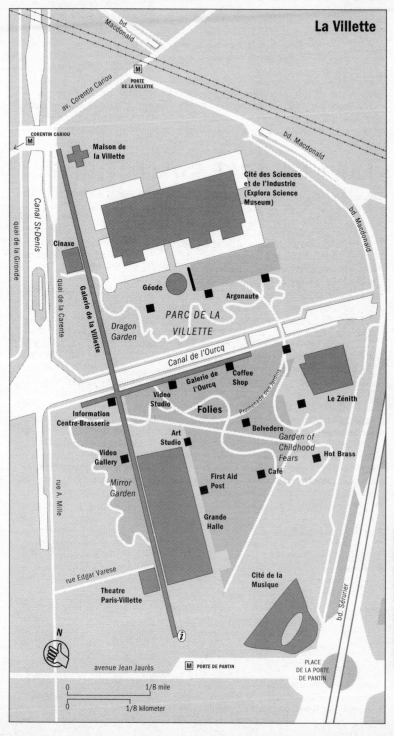

La Villette

bd. Macdonald

av. Corentin Cariou

M PORTE DE LA VILLETTE

bd. Macdonald

CORENTIN CARIOU
M

Canal St-Denis

quai de la Gironde

Maison de la Villette

Cité des Sciences et de l'Industrie (Explora Science Museum)

bd. Macdonald

Cinaxe

quai de la Carente

Galerie de la Villette

Géode

Argonaute

Dragon Garden

PARC DE LA VILLETTE

Canal de l'Ourcq

Galerie de l'Ourcq

Coffee Shop

Promenade des Jardins

Le Zénith

Video Studio

Folies

Information Centre-Brasserie

Belvedere

Garden of Childhood Fears

Hot Brass

Art Studio

Video Gallery

Mirror Garden

First Aid Post

Café

rue A. Mille

Grande Halle

rue Edgar Varese

Cité de la Musique

Theatre Paris-Villette

bd. Sérurier

N

avenue Jean Jaurès

M PORTE DE PANTIN

PLACE DE LA PORTE DE PANTIN

0   1/8 mile
0   1/8 kilometer

MUSEUMS

1994. Directly behind Zénith is the **Hot Brass** jazz club (tel. 01 42 00 14 14). The park's great yearly jazz festival is extraordinarily popular (see **Festivals,** p. 281).

Finally, the **Promenade des Jardins** links several thematic gardens, such as the **Mirror Garden,** which uses an array of mirrors to create optical illusions, the **Garden of Childhood Fears,** which winds through a wooded grove resonant with spooky sounds, and the rollercoaster **Dragon Garden.** The promenade ends at Jardin des Dunes and the Jardins des Vents, a playground for kids 12 and under (with parental accompaniment, lest the fun get out of control). Join a gaggle of moppets leaping on trampolines, running on rolling hills, and flying on a zip line in what will probably be the highlight of a kid's trip to Paris. *(Open May-Sept. 10am-8pm, Oct.-Feb. 10am-dusk. Free.)*

OTHER NOTABLE COLLECTIONS

Musée d'Art Moderne de la Ville de Paris, 11, av. du Président Wilson, 16è*me* (tel. 01 53 67 40 00). M: Iéna. Housed in magnificent galleries of the Palais de Tokyo (see **Sights,** p. 222), this museum contains one of the world's foremost collections of 20th-century art, on a smaller scale than that of the Centre Pompidou. Two stand-outs: Matisse's *The Dance* and Raoul Dufy's epic of electricity, *La Fée Électricité.* Picasso, Braque, Léger, and Chagall are also represented, as are current artists using a variety of media to create stimulating experiences. Open Tu-F 10am-5:30pm, Sa-Su 10am-6:45pm. Admission 30-45F, students and seniors 20-35F.

Musée de l'Art et d'Histoire du Judaism, 71, rue de Temple, 3è*me* (tel. 01 53 01 86 53). M: Hôtel de Ville. This newly renovated museum, housed in a grand *hôtel* which was once used as a tenement house for Jews fleeing Eastern Europe, displays a history of Jews in Europe, France, and North Africa through religious objects and artwork dating from the Middle Ages. Not to be missed: an ornate 15th-century Italian ark, letters written to Dreyfus, a small collection of Chagall and Modigliani paintings, Lissitzky lithographs illustrating a Passover nursery rhyme, and modern art collections looted from Jewish homes by the Nazis. Temporary exhibits of contemporary Jewish art and photography, as well as films and music events. Open M-F 11am-6pm, Su 10am-6pm. Admission 40F, students 25F, includes excellent English audioguide. Wheelchair accessible.

Musée Carnavalet, 23, rue de Sévigné, 3è*me* (tel. 01 42 72 21 13). M: Chemin-Vert. Housed in Mme. de Sévigné's 16th-century *hôtel particulier* (see **Sights,** p. 178), this museum traces Paris's history from its origins to the present, with exhibits on the city from prehistory, and Roman conquest, to Medieval politics, 18th-century splendor and Revolution, 19th-century Haussmannization, and Mitterrand's *grands projets.* The philosopher's chamber guards Voltaire's and Rousseau's writing supplies. Open Tu-Su 10am-5:40pm. Admission 30F, students 20F, seniors and under 18 free.

Musée Cernuschi, 7, av. Velasquez, 8è*me* (tel. 01 45 63 50 75). M: Villiers or Monceau. A magnificent collection of Asian art housed in a villa that belonged to financier Henri Cernuschi (1820-96), it contains the collection he started in 1871 that is still being expanded today. Second only to the Musée Guimet (see p. 260) in Asian art, the Cernuschi contains a rich collection of ancient to 18th-century Chinese and Japanese pieces such as a three-ton Buddha and an impressive array of funereal pottery. Open Tu-Su 10am-5:40pm. Admission 18F (30F during exhibits), students 9F (18F), seniors and under 18 free.

Grand Palais, 3, av. du Général Eisenhower, 8è*me* (tel. 01 44 13 17 30 or 01 44 13 17 17). M: Champs-Élysées-Clemenceau. Designed for the 1900 Universal Exposition. Most of the building houses the **Palais de la Découverte** (see below), but the *palais* also hosts enormous temporary exhibits or retrospectives. Open Th-M 10am-8pm, W 10am-10pm. Last entry 45min. before closing. Admission varies by exhibit, and some require reservations. Anticipate something like 50F, students and M 35F, under 13 free.

Musée d'Histoire Naturelle, in the Jardin des Plantes, 5è*me* (tel. 01 40 79 39 39). M: Gare d'Austerlitz. Three science museums in one, scattered through the jardin. The star is the 4-floor **Grand Galerie d'Evolution,** a taxonomist's dream which tells the story of evolution creatively. Next door the **Musée de Minéralogie,** surrounded by luscious rose trellises, contains some lovely diamonds, rubies, and sapphires, along with an exhibit on volcanos. At the other end of the garden, the **Gallery of Comparative Anatomy and Paleontology** houses a dinosaur exhibit, whose triumph is the 7m skeleton of an iguanodon, with other large skeletons (like those of elephants and whales) as well as some fossils. All museums open M and W-F 10am-5pm, Sa-Su 10am-6pm, last admission 30min. before closing. Grand Galerie open until 10pm Thursday, admission 40F, students 30F. Admission to others 30F, students 20F.

Galérie Nationale du Jeu de Paume, 1er (tel. 01 47 03 12 50; recorded info at 01 42 60 69 69). M: Concorde. Huge windows bathe this spectacular exhibition space in afternoon sunlight. Connoisseurs and tourists alike come to appreciate the changing contemporary art exhibitions. There is a café with sandwiches (25F). Open Tu noon-9:30pm, W-F noon-7pm, Sa-Su 10am-7pm. Admission 38F, students under 26, seniors, and ages 13-18 28F, under 13 free. Tours in French W, Sa 3pm and Su 11am.

Musée Marmottan Monet, 2, rue Louis-Boilly, 16ème (tel. 01 44 96 50 33). M: La Muette. Follow Chaussée de la Muette, which becomes av. Ranelagh, through the Jardin du Ranelagh park. As Monet equals tourist money, the name has changed to reflect his over 100 top-rate paintings on view in the sparkling basement gallery, plus a smattering of works by Renoir, Pissarro, et al. Housed in a stately mansion near the Bois de Boulogne, the museum holds several rooms of Napoleonic furniture and art, a few Renaissance tapestries, gorgeous medieval illuminations, and Morisot paintings on its upper floors. Open Tu-Su 10am-5pm. Admission 40F, students and seniors 25F, under 8 free.

Institut du Monde Arabe, 23, quai St-Bernard, 5ème (tel. 01 40 51 38 38). M: Jussieu. The museum assembles 3rd- to 18th-century art from 3 Arab regions: the Maghreb, the Near East, and the Middle East. Level 4 is devoted entirely to contemporary Arab artists. Extensive public library. From Sept.-June the auditorium hosts Arab movies (subtitled in English and French; 25F, students 20F) and theater (80-100F). The rooftop terrace has a fabulous and free view of Montmartre, the Sacré Coeur, the Seine, and Ile de la Cité. Museum and library open Tu-Su 10am-6pm. Museum admission 25F, ages 12-18 20F, under 12 free. 90min. tours Tu-F at 3pm, Sa-Su at 2 and 4pm; 50F.

Musée de l'Orangerie, southwest corner of the Jardin des Tuileries, 1er (tel. 01 42 97 48 16). M: Concorde. Opened in 1927, the museum is home to works by Renoir, Cézanne, Rousseau, Matisse, Picasso, and Monet's *Les Nymphéas* (Water Lilies). Finished before his death in 1926, these 8 murals of Monet's Giverny lilies were the artist's gift to France on the day of the Armistice, *"comme un bouquet des fleurs."* Unfortunately, the museum is closed until Spring 2001 for renovations, including turning some of the walls into glass, per Monet's wishes, so the lilies get as much light as possible.

Petit Palais, av. Winston Churchill, 8ème (tel. 01 42 65 12 73). M: Champs-Elysées-Clemenceau or FDR. Also called the **Palais des Beaux-Arts de la Ville de Paris.** Built for the 1900 Universal Exposition, the palais houses 17th- to 20th-century Flemish, French, and Dutch painting and sculpture, including Carpeaux's *Young Fisher with the Shell,* Camille Claudel's *Bust of Rodin,* and Monet's *Sunset at Lavacourt* as well as works by Rubens, Rembrandt, Cézanne, Pisarro, and Renoir. The Palais also houses a collection of medieval French crafts. Call ahead for wheelchair access. Sign language visits can also be arranged. Open Tu-Su 10am-5:40pm, last entry 5pm. Admission to temporary collection 30F, students 25F, seniors and under 18 free. Regular admission includes both permanent and temporary exhibits: 55F, 45F, free.

THE BEST OF THE REST

La Maison de l'Air, 27, rue Piat, 20ème (tel. 01 43 28 47 63). This brand-new municipal museum allows you to touch, hear, and smell your way into a broader understanding of the air around you. Exhibits investigate the wonders of flight, the atmosphere, meteorology, and the evils of air pollution (a growing problem in Paris). One memorable exhibit allows you to sniff different samples of Parisian air: flowers, traffic, and the métro! Open

MUSEUMS

Apr.-Sept. Tu-F 1:30-5:30pm, Sa-Su 1:30-6:30pm; Oct.-Mar. Tu-Su 1:30-5pm. Admission 22F, ages 11-18 and over 60 11F, ages 6-10 5F.

Musée des Arts Africains et Océaniens, 293, av. Daumesnil, 12ème (tel. 01 43 46 51 61). M: Porte Dorée. On the western edge of the Bois de Vincennes. A stunning collection of several millennia of African and Pacific art. Impressive display of African statues, masks, jewelry, and wedding dresses from the Maghreb. Built for the 1931 Colonial Exposition, the building is still decorated with its original Eurocentric murals and friezes. Downstairs, families and schoolchildren crowd the tropical fish aquarium and crocodile room. Open W-M 10am-5:30pm, Sa-Su 12:30-6pm. Last entry 30min. before closing. Admission 30F, students and children 20F; temporary exhibits 38F, 28F, Su 28F.

Musée National des Arts Asiatiques (Musée Guimet), 6, pl. d'Iéna, 16ème (tel. 01 45 05 00 98). M: Iéna. A large collection of Asian art representing 17 different countries. Closed until spring 2000 for renovations, much of the museum's collection has been placed in storage. Some pieces, however, have been moved to the Musée Guimet's annex, the **Musée du Panthéon Bouddhique** (below).

Musée du Panthéon Bouddhique, 19, av. d'Iéna, 16ème (tel. 01 45 05 00 98). M: Iéna. Located just a few steps away in the Hôtel Heidelbach. Small museum tracing the religious history of Japan and China through sculpture, painting, and sacred figures dating from the 4th-19th centuries. Tranquil Japanese garden in the back. Open W-M 9:45am-5:45pm. Admission 16F, students and seniors 12F, under 18 free.

Musée d'Art Naïf Max Fourny, 2, rue Ronsard, 18ème (tel. 01 42 58 72 89). M: Anvers. Walk up rue de Steinkerque, turn right at pl. St-Pierre, then left onto rue Ronsard. Installed within the impressive iron and glass structure of what used to be a Parisian marketplace, the museum contains neoprimitivist and folk art ranging from child-like scrawls to raw, moving tableaux. Participatory games for visitors ages 3-12. The Halle St-Pierre also contains a quiet café open the same hours as the museum. Open Sept.-July daily 10am-6pm. Admission 40F, students 30F.

Cristalleries Baccarat, 30bis, rue de Paradis, 10ème (tel. 01 47 70 64 30). M: Gare de l'Est. Walk against traffic on bd. Strasbourg and turn right on rue de la Fidelité, which becomes rue de Paradis. Since its founding in 1764 by Louis XV, Baccarat has become one of the most prestigious of crystal makers, patronized by kings, czars, and shahs. The glittering display of every imaginable crystal object looks like a magic ice palace, or a scene from Balzac's *La Peau de Chagrin*. Open M-Sa 10am-6pm. Admission 15F, students and groups 8F, under 12 free.

Maison de Balzac, 47, rue Raynouard, 16ème (tel. 01 55 74 41 80). M: Passy. Home of Honoré de Balzac from 1840-47. Balzac is among the world's greatest novelists and author of keen, sweeping commentaries on 19th century Parisian society. Here he sought refuge from bill collectors, writing *La Comédie Humaine* for 17 hours a day. Several rooms of famous portraits, memorabilia, manuscripts, a plaster cast of Balzac's hand, and great temporary exhibits. The museum is more fun if you've read a Balzac novel or two. Open Tu-Su 10am-5:40pm. Admission 22F, students 15F, over 60 free.

Musée Henri Bouchard, 25, rue de l'Yvette, 16ème (tel. 01 46 47 63 46). M: Jasmin. Housed in the workshop of Henri Bouchard (1875-1960), sculptor of the Palais de Chaillot's *Apollo,* this museum illustrates his dexterity with bronze, tin, plaster, clay, and stone. Bouchard's son and daughter-in-law are the friendly curators, available to explain his style and technique. The first Saturday of the month, Mme Bouchard guides a free tour at 3pm. Call about lectures on sculpting technique.Open July-Sept. 15, Oct.-Dec. 15, Jan. 2-Mar. 15, and Apr.-June 15 W and Sa 2-7pm. Admission 25F, students 15F.

Musée Bourdelle, 18, rue Antoine Bourdelle, 15ème (tel. 01 49 54 73 73). M: Montparnasse-Bienvenüe. From av. du Maine, turn left onto rue Antoine Bourdelle. A pupil of Rodin and mentor of Giacometti, Richier, and da Silva, Émile-Antoine Bourdelle (1861-1929) sculpted the reliefs that adorn the Théâtre des Champs-Élysées (see **Music,** p. 274) and the Opera House in Marseilles. The museum presents 500 works in marble, plaster, and bronze, including Bourdelle's masterpiece, *Heracles as Archer,* and an impressive series of 40 busts of Beethoven. Visit the 3 intimate sculpture gardens, the

The MCI WorldCom Card.

The easy way to call when traveling worldwide.

The MCI WorldCom Card gives you...

- Access to the US and other countries worldwide.
- Customer Service 24 hours a day
- Operators who speak your language
- Great MCI WorldCom rates and no sign-up fees

For more information or to apply for a Card call:

1-800-955-0925

Outside the U.S., call MCI WorldCom collect (reverse charge) at:

1-712-943-6839

COUNTRY	WORLDPHONE TOLL-FREE ACCESS #
Argentina (CC)	
To call using Telefonica ■	0800-222-6249
To call using Telecom ■	0800-555-1002
Australia (CC) ♦	
To call using AAPT ■	1-800-730-014
To call using OPTUS ■	1-800-551-111
To call using TELSTRA ■	1-800-881-100
Austria (CC) ♦	0800-200-235
Bahamas	1-800-888-8000
Belgium (CC) ♦	0800-10012
Bermuda ❖	1-800-888-8000
Bolivia (CC) ♦	0-800-2222
Brazil (CC)	000-8012
British Virgin Islands ❖	1-800-888-8000
Canada (CC)	1-800-888-8000
Cayman Islands	1-800-888-8000
Chile (CC)	
To call using CTC ■	800-207-300
To call using ENTEL ■	800-360-180
China ❖	108-12
For a Mandarin-speaking Operator	108-17
Colombia (CC) ♦	980-9-16-0001
Collect Access in Spanish	980-9-16-1111
Costa Rica ♦	0800-012-2222
Czech Republic (CC) ♦	00-42-000112
Denmark (CC) ♦	8001-0022
Dominican Republic	
Collect Access	1-800-888-8000
Collect Access in Spanish	1121
Ecuador (CC) ❖	999-170
El Salvador	800-1767

COUNTRY	WORLDPHONE TOLL-FREE ACCESS #
Finland (CC) ♦	08001-102-80
France (CC) ♦	0800-99-0019
French Guiana (CC)	0-800-99-0019
Guatemala (CC) ♦	99-99-189
Germany (CC)	0-800-888-8000
Greece (CC) ♦	00-800-1211
Guam (CC)	1-800-888-8000
Haiti ❖	193
Collect Access in French/Creole	190
Honduras ❖	8000-122
Hong Kong (CC)	800-96-1121
Hungary (CC) ♦	00▼800-01411
India (CC) ❖	000-127
Collect Access	000-126
Ireland (CC)	1-800-55-1001
Israel (CC)	
BEZEQ International	1-800-940-2727
BARAK	1-800-930-2727
Italy (CC) ♦	172-1022
Jamaica ❖	Collect Access 1-800-888-8000
(From Special Hotels only)	873
(From public phones)	#2
Japan (CC) ♦	To call using KDD ■ 00539-121▶
To call using IDC ■	0066-55-121
To call using JT ■	0044-11-121
Korea (CC) ♦	To call using KT ■ 00729-14
To call using DACOM ■	00309-12
To call using ONSE	00369-14
Phone Booth❖	Press red button, 03, then *
Military Bases	550-2255
Lebanon	Collect Access 600-MCI (600-624)

COUNTRY	WORLDPHONE TOLL-FREE ACCESS #
Luxembourg (CC)	0800-0112
Malaysia (CC) ♦	1-800-80-0012
To call using Time Telekom	1-800-18-0012
Mexico (CC)	Avantel 01-800-021-8000
Telmex ▲	001-800-674-7000
Collect Access in Spanish	01-800-021-1000
Monaco (CC) ♦	800-90-019
Netherlands (CC) ♦	0800-022-9122
New Zealand (CC)	000-912
Nicaragua (CC)	Collect Access in Spanish 166
(Outside of Managua, dial 02 first)	
Norway (CC) ♦	800-19912
Panama	108
Military Bases	2810-108
Philippines (CC) ♦	To call using PLDT ■ 105-14
To call using PHILCOM ■	1026-14
To call using Bayantel	1237-14
To call using ETPI	1066-14
Poland (CC) ❖	00-800-111-21-22
Portugal (CC) ❖	800-800-123
Puerto Rico (CC)	1-800-888-8000
Romania (CC) ❖	01-800-1800
Russia (CC) ♦ ❖	
To call using ROSTELCOM ■	747-3322
(For Russian speaking operator)	747-3320
To call using SOVINTEL ■	960-2222
Saudi Arabia (CC) ❖	1-800-11
Singapore	8000-112-112
Slovak Republic	(CC) 00421-00112
South Africa (CC)	0800-99-0011
Spain (CC)	900-99-0014

Worldwide Calling Made Easy

The MCI WorldCom Card, designed specifically to keep you in touch with the people that matter the most to you.

www.wcom.com/worldphone

Please cut out and save this reference guide for convenient U.S. and worldwide calling with the MCI WorldCom Card.

And, it's simple to call home or to other countires.

1. Dial the WorldPhone toll-free access number of the country you're calling from (listed inside).

2. Follow the easy voice instructions or hold for a WorldPhone operator. Enter or give the operator your MCI WorldCom Card number or call collect.

3. Enter or give the WorldPhone operator your home number.

4. Share your adventures with your family!

COUNTRY		WORLDPHONE TOLL-FREE ACCESS #
St. Lucia ÷		1-800-888-8000
Sweden (CC) ◆		020-795-922
Switzerland (CC) ◆		0800-89-0222
Taiwan (CC) ◆		0080-13-4567
Thailand ★		001-999-1-2001
Turkey (CC) ◆		00-8001-1177
United Kingdom	(CC) To call using BT ■	0800-89-0222
	To call using CWC ■	0500-89-0222
United States (CC)		1-800-888-8000
U.S. Virgin Islands (CC)		1-800-888-8000
Vatican City (CC)		172-1022
Venezuela (CC) ÷ ◆		800-1114-0
Vietnam ●		1201-1022

(CC) Country-to-country calling available to/from most international locations.
÷ Limited availability.
▼ Wait for second dial tone.
▲ When calling from public phones, use phones marked LADATEL.
■ International communications carrier.
★ Not available from public pay phones.
◆ Public phones may require deposit of coin or phone card for dial tone.
● Local service fee in U.S. currency required to complete call.
► Regulation does not permit intra-Japan calls.
❖ Available from most major cities

MCI WorldCom Worldphone Access Number

MCI WORLDCOM.

artist's studio, and Bourdelle's private collection of paintings. Open Tu-Su 10am-5:40pm. Last entry 5:15pm. Admission 18F, students 9F.

Fondation Cartier pour l'Art Contemporain, 261, bd. Raspail, 14ème (tel. 01 42 18 56 51; www.fondation.cartier.fr). M: Raspail or Denfert-Rochereau. Standard modern glass facade deceives from afar–this is not a building, but a mammoth bubble of glass sheets surrounding a crafted botanical garden and outdoor theater. Nestled in this flora, the fondation hosts exhibitions on subjects ranging from Warhol to the history of birds. The *Soirées Nomades* series offers films, lectures, music, dance, and art performances linked to the current exhibition. Open Tu-Su noon-8pm. Admission 30F, students and seniors 20F, under 10 free. *Soirées Nomades* Sept.-June Th at 8:30pm.

Musée de la Chasse, 60, rue des Archives, 3ème (tel. 01 53 01 92 40). M: Rambuteau. Housed in the grand 17th-century Hôtel Guénégaud, the eerie hunting museum is packed with stuffed glassy-eyed animals. Open Tu-Su 11am-6pm. Admission 30F, students and seniors 15F, ages 5-16 5F.

Musée du Cinéma Henri Langlois, (tel. 01 45 53 74 39). Formerly in the 16ème, the museum will be reopening in spring 2000 in the Parc de Bercy (12ème); call for prices and hours. Features over 3000 versions of projectors and cameras as well as demonstrations of how they work. Exhibits trace the history of film from its beginnings in 1895.

Musée Clemenceau, 8, rue Benjamin Franklin, 16ème (tel. 01 45 20 53 41). M: Passy. Through a small courtyard. The museum thoroughly documents the life of revered and vilified journalist and statesman Georges Clemenceau (1841-1929): publisher of Emile Zola's *J'accuse*, Prime Minister of France, and much-criticized negotiator of the Treaty of Versailles. On the ground floor, Clemenceau's apartment has been left as it was when he died, including a portrait of Clemenceau by his friend Monet. Open Tu, Th, and Sa-Su 2-5pm. Admission 20F, students and seniors 15F.

Musée Cognacq-Jay, 8, rue Elzévir, 3ème (tel. 01 40 27 07 21). M: St-Paul. Walk up rue Pavée and take a left on rue des Francs-Bourgeois and a right on rue Elzévir. The 16th-century Hôtel Donon houses a collection of Enlightenment art, including minor works by Rembrandt, Ingres, Rubens, Canaletto, and Fragonard. Occasional plays and concerts. Open Tu-Su 10am-5:40pm, last admission 5:10pm. Admission 22F, students and under 25 15F, seniors and under 18 free. Gardens open May-Sept. 10am-5:40pm.

Fondation le Corbusier, 10, sq. du Docteur-Blanche, 16ème (tel. 01 42 88 41 53). M: Jasmin. Walk up rue de l'Yvette and turn left on rue du Docteur-Blanche and left again at no. 55 into pl. du Docteur-Blanche. The foundation is located in Villas La Roche and Jeanneret, both designed and furnished by Le Corbusier. Le Corbusier trademarks include his use of light, nature, curved forms, and ramps. Literature on Le Corbusier and maps locating his other Parisian creations available. The Villa Jeanneret next door holds the library and offices. Open Sept.-July M-Th 10am-12:30pm and 1:30-6pm, F 10am-12:30pm and 1:30-5pm (library open after 1:30pm). Admission 15F, students 10F.

Musée de la Curiosité et de la Magie, 11, rue St-Paul, 4ème (tel. 01 42 72 13 26). M: St-Paul. A wacky collection of holograms, robots, trinkets, illusions of all kinds and magic paraphernalia relating the history of magic. Magic shows on the half-hour. Admission 45F, children 30F. Open W, Sa-Su 2-7pm.

Musée Salvador Dalí (Espace Montmartre), 11, rue Poulbot, 18ème (tel. 01 42 64 40 10). M: Anvers or Abbesses. From pl. du Tertre follow rue du Calvaire toward the view, then turn right onto rue Poulbot. Something of a tourist trap, the museum is full of lesser-known lithographs and sculptures by the Spanish surrealist. Laid out in "Surrealist surroundings," which amounts to interesting lighting, erotic artwork, and space-music in the background. Open daily Nov.-Mar. 10am-6pm, Oct.-Apr. 10am-9pm, last entrance 30min. before closing. Admission 40F, students 25F.

Musée Delacroix, 6, pl. Furstenberg, 6ème (tel. 01 44 41 86 50). M: St-Germain-des-Prés. Behind the Eglise St-Germain off rue de l'Abbaye. At the courtyard, follow the sign to the atelier Delacroix. Located in the 3-room apartment in which he lived until his death in 1863. One of the leaders of French Romanticism, Delacroix is most famous for his painting *Liberty Leading the People* (see **Musée du Louvre**, p. 242). Sketches, watercolors, engravings, and letters to Théophile Gautier and George Sand belie a gen-

MUSEUMS

tler artist than a visitor to the Louvre might expect. Also hosts temporary exhibits of some of the artist's works. Open W-M 9:30am-5pm, last entry 4:30pm. Admission 30F, ages 18-25 and over 60 23F, under 18 free.

Musée des Egouts de Paris (The Sewers of Paris), (tel. 01 53 68 27 81) across from 93 quai d'Orsay, 7ème. M: Pont de l'Alma. A tour through the sewers illustrating the struggle for drinkable water and a clean Seine through the ages. Don't breath deep—the smell can be overwhelming. Tours and brochures in English. Open May-Sept. Sa-W 11am-4pm; Oct.-Apr. Sa-W 11am-5pm. Last tickets sold 1 hr. before close. Closed last 3 weeks of January. Admission 25F, students and under 10 20F, under 5 free.

Musée d'Ennery, 59, av. Foch, 16ème (tel. 01 45 53 57 96). M: Porte Dauphine. Like the Musée Guimet (see above), the Musée d'Ennery features treasures of East Asian art. The museum houses the collection of Clémence d'Ennery (wife of author Adolphe d'Ennery), who scavenged the city's flea markets and antique shops for Orientalist art during the 19th century. Open Sept.-July Th and Su 2-5:45pm. Free. On the ground floor, the **Musée Arménien** (tel. 01 45 56 15 88) displays Armenian jewelry, paintings, and religious decoration. Closed for renovations until spring 2000.

Musée Grévin, 10, bd. Montmartre, 9ème (tel. 01 42 46 13 26). M: Rue Montmartre. This wax museum's ornate halls feature Marie-Antoinette awaiting her execution in the Conciergerie, the cannibals from Géricault's *Raft of the Medusa,* and the King of Pop (the photos of him visiting are worth the price of admission). Open daily Apr.-Aug. 10am-7pm, Sept.-Mar. 1-7pm, last entry 6pm. Admission 58F, ages 6-14 38F. Who's who guide booklet, 10F. AmEx, V, MC (130F minimum). The smaller branch at level "-1" of the Forum des Halles, near the Porte Berger, 1er (tel. 01 40 26 28 50; M: Châtelet-Les-Halles), presents figures from Paris's Belle Epoque.

Musée Jean-Jacques Henner, 43, av. Villiers, 17ème (tel. 01 47 63 42 73). M: Malsherbes. Three floors of the works of Jean-Jacques Henner (1829-1905), on the periphery of Realism with his soft-focus subjects with haunting, luminous, bone-white skin. Open Tu-Su 10am-noon and 2-5pm. Admission 20F, students and seniors 15F, under 18 free.

Musée de l'Histoire de France, 60, rue des Francs-Bourgeois, 3ème (tel. 01 40 27 60 96). M: Rambuteau. Walk up rue Rambuteau, which becomes rue des Francs-Bourgeois. Housed in the Hôtel de Soubise, this museum is the main exhibition space of the Archives Nationales, featuring important documents, such as an edict drafted by Richard the Lionheart, an extract from Louis XVI's diary the day he was arrested by Revolutionaries, and a letter from Napoleon to Josephine. For more about the Hôtel Soubise and the Archives Nationales, see **Sights,** p. 175. Open M and W-F noon-5:45pm, Sa-Su 1:45-5:45pm. Admission 15F, students, seniors, and Su 10F, under 18 free.

Musée de l'Homme (Museum of Man), pl. du Trocadéro, 16ème (tel. 01 44 05 72 00 or 01 44 05 72 72). M: Trocadéro. In the Palais de Chaillot. Anthropology museum illustrating world cultures through the ages via a painted cart from Sicily, a Turkish store, Eskimo fishing boats, and hats from Cameroon, among other artifacts. Dioramas and glass cases abound. Open W-M 9:45am-5:15pm. Admission 30F, under 27 and seniors 20F, under 4 free. Films Sept.-July W and Sa at 3 and 4pm.

Maison de Victor Hugo, 6, pl. des Vosges, 4ème (tel. 01 42 72 10 16). M: Chemin-Vert or Bastille. Dedicated to the father of the French Romantics and housed in the building where he lived from 1832 to 1848, the museum displays Hugo memorabilia. One room is devoted to paintings of scenes from *Les Misérables,* another to *Nôtre-Dame de Paris.* A desk displays the inkwells of Lamartine, Dumas, Sand, and Hugo. Open Tu-Su 10am-5:40pm. Admission 22F, students 15F, under 18 free.

Musée Jacquemart-André, 158, bd. Haussmann, 8ème (tel. 01 42 89 04 91). M: Miromesnil. As you wander through the music room, smoking room, reception area, and boudoir of this opulent mansion, you will surely ask yourself, "How did two people (Nélie Jacquemart and her husband) have so much time and money?" The building dates from the 19th century, while the works of art are mostly French and Italian Renaissance and Baroque pieces: Rembrandt, Botticelli, Bellini, and others. Well-done audio guide included with admission. Open daily 10am-6pm; last visitors admitted at 5:30pm. Admission 47F, students and ages 7-17 35F, under 7 free.

Musée National de la Légion d'Honneur et des Ordres de Chevalerie (Legion of Honor and Chivalry), 2, rue de Bellechasse, 7ème (tel. 01 40 62 84 25). M: Solférino. Housed in an 18th-century mansion, this museum displays medals and uniforms of the French Legion of Honor, created by Napoleon in 1802. Open Tu-Su 11am-5pm. Admission 25F, students and seniors 15F.

Mémorial de la Libération de Paris, 23, allée de la D-B, Jardin Atlantique, 15ème (tel. 01 40 64 39 44). M: Montparnasse-Bienvenüe. Above the tracks of the Gare Montparnasse. Follow signs to the Jardin Atlantique from the train station, pl. du Pont des Cinq Martyrs du Lycée Buffon, or rue Commandant René Mouchotte. Officially the Mémorial du Maréchal Leclerc de Hauteclocque, and next to the Musée Jean Moulin (primary figure in the Resistance). From Africa to the beaches of Normandy and from a liberated Paris to the capture of Berchtesgaden, this museum traces the military maneuvers of Leclerc and the liberation of Paris with a wealth of rare film footage, posters, and photographs. Open Tu-Su 10am-5:40pm, last ticket 5:15pm. Admission 27F, students and seniors 19F.

Musée de la Marine (Museum of the Navy), pl. du Trocadéro, 16ème (tel. 01 53 65 69 69). M: Trocadéro. In the Palais de Chaillot. Model ships of incredible detail, and a couple of real boats from the 17th-19th centuries are anchored here, including the golden dinghy built for Napoleon in 1810. Sailing equipment and oil paintings of stormy sea battles round out the collection. Open W-M 10am-6pm. Last entry at 5:30pm. Admission 38F, under 25 and seniors 25F.

Centre de la Mer et des Eaux, 195, rue St-Jacques, 5ème (tel. 01 44 32 10 90). RER: Luxembourg. More than just the requisite tanks of colorful fish—a multimedia marine experience. Interactive exhibits on fish disguises and algae life cycles. Films and exhibitions change, but most come from the adventures of late sea czar Jacques Cousteau. Open Tu-F 10am-12:30pm and 1:15-5:30pm, Sa-Su 10am-5:30pm. Admission 30F, students 18F, children 4-12 12F.

Musée Adam Mickiewicz, 6, quai d'Orléans, 4ème (tel. 01 55 42 83 83), on the Ile-St-Louis. M: Pont Marie. Ring the doorbell and enter to your left in the courtyard. Located in the **Bibliothèque Polonaise de Paris,** the museum is dedicated to the Polish poet Adam Mickiewicz (1798-1835), and includes letters from Goethe and Hugo and a sketch by Delacroix on George Sand's letter-head. In the same building are the **Musée Boleslas Bregas,** with work by the sculptor and the **Salon Chopin,** with manuscripts, letters, and his death mask. Library open Tu-F 2-6pm and Sa 10am-1pm. Museums open Th 2-6 and can only be visited with a guided tour at 2, 3:30, or 5pm. Admission 30F, students 15F, children free.

Musée de la Monnaie, 11, Quai de Conti, 6ème (tel. 01 40 46 56 66; www.monnaide-paris.fr). M. Odéon. Entrance on rue Guénégaud. See more money than you'll ever make honestly. Located in the Hôtel des Monnaies, where coins were minted until 1973, the museum displays coins, medals, and documents on the history of money-making in France. Call 01 40 46 55 35 for information on tours. Open Tu-Su 1-6pm. Admission 20F, free on Sundays and always to those under 16.

Musée de la Mode et du Costume (Museum of Fashion and Clothing), in the Palais Galliera, 10, av. Pierre I-de-Serbie, 16ème (tel. 01 47 20 85 23). M: Iéna. With 30,000 outfits and 70,000 accessories, the museum has no choice but to rotate temporary exhibitions showcasing fashions of the past 3 centuries. A fabulous place to visit to see the history of Paris fashion, haute couture, and society. Visit and get ideas before you head off to the vintage stores (see **Shopping,** p. 305). Open Tu-Su 10am-6pm. Last entry at 5:30pm. Admission 45F, students and seniors 35F.

Musée de la Mode et du Textile, 107, rue de Rivoli, Palais du Louvre, 1er (tel. 01 44 55 57 50). M: Palais-Royal. Housed in the Louvre with the Musée des Arts Décoratifs, the Musée de la Mode et du Textile is a huge collection of all that has been *en vogue* since the 18th century. Exhibits rotate annually and tell changing stories of the history of costume, from 17th century brocade evening dresses to pointy latex bras by Jean-Paul Gaultier. A research center is available by appointment. Open Tu, Th, F 11am-6pm, W 11am-9pm, Sa-Su 10am-6pm. Admission 30F, students 20F. Wheelchair accessible.

Musée National des Monuments Français, pl. du Trocadéro, 16ème (tel. 01 44 05 39 05). M: Trocadéro. In the Palais de Chaillot: but **closed until 2001.** A scholarly museum appealing to artists, architects, and medievalists, the collection features models of facades and tombs from medieval churches around France.

Musée Gustave Moreau, 14, rue de La Rochefoucauld, 9ème (tel. 01 48 74 38 50). M: Trinité. Housed in the 19th-century home of symbolist painter Gustave Moreau, the museum contains thousands of his drawings and paintings, including the celebrated painting of Salomé dancing before the severed head of John the Baptist. Open M and W 11am-5:15pm, Th-Su 10am-12:45pm and 2-5:15pm. Admission 22F, students and over 60 15F, under 18 free.

Musée Nissim de Camondo, 63, rue de Monceau, 8ème (tel. 01 53 89 06 40). M: Villiers or Monceau. Just next to the Musée Cernuschi is another private collection gone public. Named after the son of a Turkish Count who died in the Great War, this palatial home houses the family's collection of aristocratic bric-a-brac, including tapestries, silverware, and furniture. Open W-Su 10am-5pm. Admission 27F, age 18-25, 18F, and free for those under 18. Guided tours Sunday at 11:30am.

Palais de la Découverte, 8ème (tel. 01 01 40 74 80 00 or 01 40 74 81 82). M: FDR or Champs-Elysées-Clemenceau. In the Grand Palais, entrance on av. Franklin D. Roosevelt. Less flashy than the Cité des Sciences, this Palace of Discovery, housed in the Grand Palais, features interactive science exhibits. Kids tear around pressing buttons that start comets on celestial trajectories, spinning on seats to investigate angular motion, and glaring at all kinds of cleverly camouflaged creepy-crawlies. Planetarium (tel. 01 40 74 81 73) shows 4 times per day. Call for info on lectures and movies. Open Tu-Sa 9:30am-6pm, Su 10am-7pm. Admission 30F, students, seniors, and under 18 20F. Family entrance 80F for two adults, and two children over 5, then 15F for each additional child over 5.

Musée de la Poupée, Impasse Berthaud, 3ème (tel. 01 42 72 73 11). M: Rambuteau. Follow signs for rue Beaubourg near the Centre Pompidou. 300 Parisian dolls from 1860-1960 are displayed by era in 4 rooms. Interesting analysis. Open Tu-Su 10am-6pm. Admission 35F, students, under 26, and over 60 25F, ages 3-18 20F.

Maison de Radio France, 116, av. du Président Kennedy, 16ème (tel. 01 42 30 15 16). M: Passy or RER: Av. du Pt. Kennedy/Maison de Radio France. Head for the Seine and enter through Door A of the big, white, cylindrical building. The museum, accessible only by guided tour, presents the history of communications compressed into one hour, at the headquarters of France's public radio stations (programs broadcast live at www.radio-france.fr). Attractions range from ancient radio specimens to studios and concert hall. Inquire about attending free tapings of TV programs. Season tickets to concerts with the resident Orchestre National de France are also available. Free English-language brochure at the information desk. Open M-Sa; tours at 10:30, 11:30am, 2:30, 3:30, and 4:30pm. English tours at 3pm Tu-F during the summer (check by phone). Admission 20F, students and seniors 15F.

Musée-Galerie de la SEITA (Société d'Exploitation Industrielle des Tabacs et Allumettes), 12, rue Surcouf, 7ème (tel. 01 45 56 60 17). M: Invalides. On the corner of rue de l'Université and rue Surcouf. Holy smokes! While non-smoking grows in other countries, France celebrates its love affair with tobacco. Stages impressive temporary exhibits of photography and paintings by artists such as Klimt and Kokoschka. Permanent exhibit on the story of tobacco includes pipe and cigarette holders depicting everything from nudes to nuns. Learn smoker trivia like the fact that "nicotine" is named after Jean Nicot, who introduced tobacco to France in 1561. Open M-Sa 11am-7pm. Permanent exhibit free, Temporary exhibits 15F, students 10F.

Musée du Vieux Montmartre, 12, rue Cortot, 18ème (tel. 01 46 06 61 11). M: Lamarck-Caulaincourt. Turn right on rue Lamarck, right again up steep rue des Saules, then left onto rue Cortot. Dedicated to the political, artistic, cultural, and religious past of the butte, the museum occupies a 17th-century house overlooking Paris's only vineyard. Once home to artists like Renoir and Utrillo, the museum features maps, paintings, photographs, and a wooden model of the quartier, as well as a re-created turn-of-the-century café, complete with one of the few zinc bar counters left after the metal rationing during WWI. Open Tu-Su 11am-6pm. Admission 25F, students and seniors 20F.

Musée du Vin, rue des Eaux, or 5-7, sq. Charles Dickens, 16ème (tel. 01 45 25 63 26). M: Passy. Go down the stairs, turn right on pl. Alboni, and then turn right on rue des Eaux. This mildly amusing cave is peopled with strange wax models engaged in the process of wine-making, including one of Honoré de Balzac fleeing his creditors. You may have to remind the receptionist to give you your free tasting of red, rosé, or white. Open Tu-Su 10am-6pm. Admission 35F, seniors 30F, students 29F.

Musée Zadkine, 100bis, rue d'Assas, 6ème (tel. 01 43 26 91 90). M: Vavin or Port-Royal. Just south of the Jardin du Luxembourg. Installed in 1982 in the house and studio where he worked, the museum highlights the work of Russian sculptor Ossip Zadkine (1890-1967), whose work spans from the extremes of Cubism to neo-Classicism. Lovely gardens feature the artist's works, including his two-faced *Woman with the Bird.* Open Tu-Su 10am-5:30pm. Admission 27F, students 19F.

GALLERIES

Visiting Paris's galleries is the best way to see what's new in contemporary art. Most of the city's 200 galleries specialize in one type of art. The 8ème is loaded with Old Master galleries. Those near M: Franklin Roosevelt on the Champs-Elysées, av. Matignon, rue du Faubourg St-Honoré, and rue de Miromesnil focus on Impressionism and post-Impressionism. Thanks to the new opera house, the Bastille area has become a haven for artists and galleries with an *épater-les-bourgeois* (shock-the-bourgeoisie) spin. The highest concentration of galleries is in the Marais, especially on rue Quincampoix and rue des Blancs-Manteaux. In St-Germain-des-Prés, rue Mazarine, rue de Seine, rue des Beaux-Arts, and rue Bonaparte also contain an assembly of small galleries focusing on 20th-century art. These galleries have an *épater-votre-portefeuille* (shock-your-wallet) spin. The *Portes Ouvertes* festival in May or October allows visitors to witness artists in action in their studios (see **Festivals,** p. 283).

You're not usually expected to buy; however, the galleries that require appointments are not appropriate for casual browsing. Most galleries are closed Sunday and Monday and are open until 7pm on other days, often with a break at lunch. Almost all galleries close in August. Our listings cover some of the best galleries from all over the city, although in some areas that are wall-to-wall art space, notably the 6ème, we've merely tried to point you in the right direction.

ÎLE ST-LOUIS

Galerie Félix, 54, rue St-Louis-en-l'Ile (tel. 01 40 46 05 58). M: Pont Marie. For those who didn't get to stand close enough to Impressionist paintings at the Musée d'Orsay. Open daily 11:30am-7:30pm.

Galerie Clorinde Martin, 77, rue St-Louis-en-l'Ile (tel. 01 43 29 08 09). M: Pont Marie. A less pretentious gallery than is the norm on the Île St-Louis, shows more postmodern paintings than anything else, but nothing too over the top. Open M-Sa noon-7pm.

THIRD ARRONDISSEMENT

The swank galleries in the Marais display some of Paris's most exciting and avant-garde art, and the 3ème is saturated with them. Paintings, sculptures, photographs, and installations peek out of store-front windows along **rue de Perche, rue Debellyme, rue Vieille-du-Temple, rue de Poitou,** and **rue Beaubourg.** The area around the Picasso Museum houses a number of more mainstream painting galleries.

Galerie Askéo, 19, rue Debellyme (tel. 01 42 77 17 77). M: Filles de Calvaire. This three-story metallic gallery displays large, engaging installation art. Open Tu-Sa 2:30-7pm.

Galerie Sanguine, 26, rue Beaubourg (tel. 01 53 65 12 44). M: Rambuteau. This two-floor gallery specializes in post-1960 painting, photography and graphics, and regularly includes works by Lichtenstein, Cesar, Christo, Goldin, and Klasen. Open M-Sa 2-7pm.

Galerie Eterso, 108, rue Vieille-du-Temple (tel. 01 42 72 65 20). M: Filles de Calvaire. Suave leather couches and glass-topped tables, contemporary sculpture and small installations. Open Tu-Sa 11am-1pm and 2-6pm.

Fall Galerie, 127, rue Vieille-du-Temple (tel. 01 44 78 07 64). M: Filles de Calvaire. A small room which hosts some intriguing installations. Open Tu-Sa 2:30-6:30pm.

Bzzznet, 10, rue Brantome (tel. 01 44 54 05 05; www.bzzznet.com). M: Rambuteau. This new gallery displays fun contemporary paintings. With 8 computers, it also serves as an internet stop (1F per minute). Open M-F 9am-midnight, Sa-Su 9am-10pm.

FOURTH ARRONDISSEMENT

A little wandering through the Lower Marais, especially through alleys and back streets, is likely to reveal obscure and intriguing display spaces. Centre Pompidou-fever has spawned a community of nearby galleries.

Galerie Rachlin Lemaire, 23, rue de Renard (tel. 01 44 59 27 27). M: Rambuteau or Châtelet. Adventurous contemporary drawings, paintings, and sculpture. Open M-Sa 10:30am-1pm and 2:30pm-7pm.

Fiesta Galerie, 45, rue Vieille-du-Temple (tel. 01 42 71 53 34). M: St-Paul. Retro-pop fun. Giant stuffed M&Ms and miniature Yodas. Open Tu-Sa noon-7pm, Su-M 2-7pm.

Galerie Gana Beaubourg, 3, rue Pierre au Lard (tel. 01 42 71 00 45). M: Rambuteau. Capacious international contemporary art space. Open Tu-Sa 10am-7pm.

EIGHTH ARRONDISSEMENT

Galerie Lelong, 13, rue de Téhéran (tel. 01 45 63 13 19). M: Miromesnil. A standard display of quite famous (Miró, Koons) 20th-century art. Open Tu-F 10:30am-6pm.

Galerie Louis Carré et Cie, 10 av. de Messine (tel. 01 45 62 57 07). M: Miromesnil. Three solid meals a day of modern French painting and sculpture, and a regular snack of the greats (Delaunay, Calder, and the gang) equals complete gallery nutrition. Mmmm. Open M-Sa 10am-12:30pm and 1:30-6:30pm.

ELEVENTH ARRONDISSEMENT

Galerie Jousse Séguin, 34, rue de Charonne (tel. 01 47 00 32 35). M: Ledru-Rollin. Popular, large, and photo-philic. Open M-F 10–noon and 2:30-7pm, Sa 11-7pm.

Galerie J. et J. Donguy, 57, rue de la Roquette (tel. 01 47 00 10 94). M: Bastille. At the back of a courtyard, features performance pieces and installations. Open daily 1-7pm.

Bo Plastic, 31, rue de Charonne (tel. 01 53 36 73 16). M: Ledru-Rollin. Plastic plus. Sells retro 60s-70s furniture and accessories. Open M-Sa 11am-8pm.

Espace d'Art Yvonamor Palix, 13, rue Keller (tel. 01 48 06 36 70). M: Ledru-Rollin. Small gallery displays international art. Open M-F by appointment, Sa 2-7pm.

TWELFTH ARRONDISSEMENT

The 12*ème* has a few galleries; most of them are located among workshops and studios in the **Viaduc des Arts** (see **Sights,** p. 212). They showcase design, contemporary art, leather, glass, furniture, and architectural models. And fabulous, fabulous **Jean Paul Gaultier** has a gallery at 30, Faubourg St-Antoine.

Galerie Claude Samuel, 69, av. Daumesnil (tel. 01 53 17 01 11). M: Bastille. One of the only contemporary art spaces in the Viaduc. Opening hours variable.

Fireworks, 101, av. Daumesnil (tel. 01 46 28 46 46). M: Bastille. Intriguing colored glass; some are even affordable. Open M 2-6pm, Tu-F 9:30am-6:30pm, Sa 2-7pm.

THIRTEENTH ARRONDISSEMENT

The 13ème's art scene is cutting edge. Galleries are lodged into a building of the Minister of Finance complex along **rue Louise-Weisse** (M: Chevarelet). Many of the displayed artists still use the Site de Frigos warehouse across the railway.

Galerie Emmanuel Perrotin, 30, rue Louise-Weiss (tel. 01 42 16 79 79). M: Chevarelet. Radical European and Japanese multimedia art. Open Tu-F 2-7pm, Sa 11am-7pm.

Galerie Kreo, 11, rue Louise-Weiss (tel. 01 53 60 18 42). M: Chevarelet. Bizarre furniture, unusual light fixtures. Open Tu-F 2-7pm, Sa 11am-9pm.

FOURTEENTH ARRONDISSEMENT

Gallerie 213, 213, bd. Raspail (tel. 01 43 22 83 23.) M: Vavin or Raspail. This spacious two-story gallery is dedicated to displaying the works of young photographers. The gallery's trendy book shop—a decorative amalgam of wood, mirrors, and blue mermaids— stocks a selection of contemporary photography books. Open Tu-Sa 11am-7pm.

Gallerie Camera Obscura, 12, rue Ernest Cresson (tel. 01 45 45 67 08; email camera-obscura@claranet.fr). M: Denfert-Rochereau. A simple and elegant gallery which exhibits the works of international photographers. Open Tu-Sa 2-7pm.

MUSEUMS

ENTERTAINMENT

Alors, something groovy, you know?

—French man, quoted by Maya Angelou

Les temps changent, mec.

—MC Solaar

Paris can satisfy all tastes and desires. When looking for something to do, consult the bibles of Paris entertainment, the weekly bulletins **Pariscope** (3F) and **Officiel des Spectacles** (2F), both on sale at any newsstand. Even if you don't understand French, you should be able to decipher the listings of times and locations. Contact **Info-Loisirs,** a recording that keeps tabs on what's on in Paris (English tel. 01 49 52 53 56; French tel. 01 49 52 53 55).

You don't need to speak fluent French to enjoy the theater scene. Paris's theaters present productions whose music, physical comedy, and experimental abstraction lend themselves to any audience. The comedy-oriented **café-théâtres** and the music-oriented **cabarets** perpetuate the ambiance of 1930s Paris. Paris's ballet and modern dance companies often host performances by visiting companies, including the Kirov Ballet, the Alvin Ailey Dance Company, and the Dance Theater of Harlem. Paris's new **Stade de France** and other athletic venues offer **spectator** and participant sports galore.

Among Paris's many treasures, film and music top the list. Recently, Paris has witnessed the fusion of West African music, Caribbean calypso and reggae, Latin American salsa, North African raï, European house, techno, and rap. Classical concerts are staged in both expensive concert halls and churches, particularly during the summer. To get more information and to buy tickets for rock, rap, jazz, or classical concerts, head to **FNAC Spectacles** (see below, p. 269). Parisians are inveterate film-goers, greedy for film from all over the world. Frequent English-language film series and festivals make Parisian cinema accessible, inventive, challenging, and entertaining.

THEATER

Thankfully for the non-fluent, Parisian theater is still highly accessible, thanks in part to its dependence on French and international classics, and also thanks to its love of a grand spectacle. In general, the private theaters of the Right Bank and Montparnasse play a variety of classics to an affluent crowd. The state-funded national theaters typically give space to more experimental works in order to appease their "more Left Bank than thou" audiences. Intimate performance spaces like *café-théâtres* and *chansonniers* book anything from Vaudevillian comics to accordionists. Many theaters do not offer performances on Mondays, and many

---

CIRCUS MAXIMUS Circus is not just for children. Circus is high art. If you're sick of pretentious Parisian theater, try these cutting-edge establishments for a bit of techno music and a bit of somersaulting: **Zingaro** in the Fort d'Aubervilliers (tel. 01 49 87 59 59) is an equestrian circus whose mega-artsy shows are like ballet on horseback; **Espace Chapiteaux,** (tel. 08 03 07 50 75, 2,23F/min) in La Vilette (see p. 230) holds circuses of all varieties year-round in its giant tent, with tickets ranging from 60-110F, depending upon your age and willingness to put your head in a lion's mouth; **Archaos** (tel. 01 46 40 77 78) in suburb Neuilly-sur-Seine is pantomime and house music, dealing with modern issues.

more close in July and August. *Pariscope* and *l'Officiel des Spectacles* provide complete listings of current shows, as well as listing one of the best ways to see theater in Paris: **half-price previews**. Another cheap theater event not to miss is the three-day *fête* in late April or early May where the mayor buys you a free second ticket for every theater ticket purchased. Unfortunately, you do not get to sit next to him. Partial 2000 schedules for national theaters are listed below.

TICKET SERVICES

Kiosque-Théâtre, 15, pl. de la Madeleine, 8è*me*. M: Madeleine. To the left of the church. Also in the 15ème in front of the Gare Montparnasse. M: Montparnasse-Bienvenüe. *The* best discount box office, selling discount tickets the day of the show. 16F per seat commission. Open Tu-Sa 12:30-7:45pm, Su 12:30-3:45pm. No credit cards.

Kiosque Info Jeune, 25, bd. Bourdon, 4è*me* (tel. 01 42 76 22 60). M: Bastille. Also at 101, quai Branly, 5è*me* (tel. 01 43 06 15 28). M: Bir Hakeim. A youth information service provided by the *Mairie*. Sells theater tickets at half-price and distributes free passes to concerts, plays, and exhibits. You must be under 26 for discounts. Bastille branch open M-F 10am-7pm; quai Branly branch open M-F 9:30-6pm.

Alpha FNAC: Spectacles, 136, rue de Rennes, 6è*me* (tel. 01 49 54 30 00). M: Montparnasse-Bienvenüe. Also at Forum des Halles, 1-7, rue Pierre Lescot, 1*er* (tel. 01 40 41 40 00), M: Châtelet-Les-Halles; 26, av. des Ternes, 17è*me* (tel. 01 44 09 18 00), M: Ternes; and 71, bd. St-Germain, 5è*me* (automated tel. 01 44 41 31 50). Tickets for theater, concerts, and festivals. Easy pickup, but no discounts. Open M-Sa 10am-7:30pm. AmEx, MC, V.

NATIONAL THEATERS

Four of France's five national theaters, those bastions of traditional French drama, are located in Paris (the fifth is in Strasbourg). With the advantages of giant auditoriums, great acoustics, veteran acting troupes, and centuries of prestige, they stage popular and polished productions of Molière, Racine, Goethe, and Shakespeare (all in French). Unless you're banking on last-minute rush tickets, make reservations 14 days in advance.

La Comédie Française, 2, rue de Richelieu, 1*er* (tel. 01 44 58 15 15; www.comedie-francaise.fr). M: Palais-Royal. Founded by Molière, now the granddaddy of all French theaters. Much pomp and prestige, with red velvet and chandeliers. Expect wildly gesticulated slapstick farce. You don't need to speak French to understand the jokes. Performances take place in the 892-seat Salle Richelieu. 2000 will feature a boatload of Molière (*L'Avare, Les Fourberies de Scapin*) and Goethe's *Faust,* among others. Box office open daily 11am-6pm. Tickets 70-190F, under 27 60-70F (remainders). Rush tickets (30F) available 45 min. before show; line up an hour in advance. They also have special package deals, often for students under a certain age, with reduced prices for tickets to three plays or more. Call for details. The *comédiens français* also mount plays in the 330-seat **Théâtre du Vieux Colombier,** 21, rue des Vieux Colombiers, 6è*me* (tel. 01 44 39 87 00 or 01 44 39 87 01). M: St-Sulpice. 2000 will feature *The Misanthrope* by Molière and George Feydeau's *Chat en Poche.* Tickets 160F, over 60 110F, under 27 85F; rush tickets 65F sold 45min. before performances, available to students under 27 and anyone under 25.

Odéon Théâtre de l'Europe, 1, pl. Odéon, 6è*me* (tel. 01 44 41 36 36; www.theatre-odeon.fr). M: Odéon. Programs in this elegant neoclassical building range from classics to avant-garde, but the Odéon specializes in foreign plays in their original language. 1042 seats. Also Petit Odéon, an affiliate with 82 seats. 2000 will give host to *fanfares* by Georges Lavaudant and Molière's *Don Juan.* Open Sept.-July. Box office open M-Sa 11am-6:30pm. Tickets 30-180F for most shows; student rush tickets 60F, available 45min. before performance. Petit Odéon 70F, students 50F. MC, V. Call ahead for wheelchair access.

Théâtre National de Chaillot, pl. du Trocadéro, 16ème (tel. 01 53 65 30 00). M: Trocadéro. In the Palais de Chaillot. Plays, music, and dance concerts take place in 2 rooms, one with 1000 and the other with 400 seats. 2000 season includes: August Strindberg's *Le Songe* presented by Robert Wilson, and Blanca Li's *Zap! Zap! Zap!* Can arrange spiffy translation into English for non-francophones. Call to arrange wheelchair access. Box office open M-Sa 11am-7pm, Su 11am-5pm. Tickets 160F, under 25 and seniors 120F, same-day student rush 80F. MC, V.

Théâtre Nationale de la Colline, 15, rue Malte-Brun, 20ème (tel. 01 44 62 52 00, for reservations tel. 01 44 62 52 52). M: Gambetta. The Grand Théâtre has 754 seats, the Petit Théâtre 240 seats. Founded in 1988, this fledgling national theater features French and foreign contemporary plays. 2000 boasts Brecht's *The Life of Galilee* and Edward Bond's *Café*. Call ahead for wheelchair access or braille plot summaries. Open Sept.-June. Informal talk/soirée Wednesday before show in lounge. Box office open M-Sa 11am-7pm, Su 2-5pm. Call to reserve tickets M-Sa 11am-7pm, until 9pm on show days. Tickets 160F, over 60 130F, students and under 30 180F; Tu shows 110F.

PRIVATE THEATERS

Paris's private theaters, though less celebrated than their state-run counterparts, often stage outstanding productions. In this realm of the weird and wonderful, risky performances sometimes misfire. Check the reviews in newspapers and entertainment weeklies before investing in a seat.

Bouffes du Nord, 37bis, bd. de la Chapelle, 10ème (tel. 01 46 07 34 50). M: La Chapelle. This experimental theater, headed by the British director Peter Brook, produces cutting-edge performances and occasional productions in English. Closed July and Aug. Box office open M-Sa 11am-6pm. Tickets 70-140F. Handicapped accessible.

Théâtre de la Huchette, 23, rue de la Huchette, 5ème (tel. 01 43 26 38 99). M: St-Michel. 100-seat theater where Ionesco's *La cantatrice chauve (The Bald Soprano)* and *La leçon (The Lesson)* premiered and continue to play today, 43 years later. A bastion of Left Bank intellectualism, but still a good choice for people with functional high school French. Shows M-Sa. *La cantatrice chauve* starts at 7pm, *La leçon* at 8pm. No one admitted after curtain. Box office open M-Sa 5-7pm. Tickets 100F, students under 25 M-F 80F; both shows 160F, students M-F 120F. Handicapped accessible.

Théâtre de la Ville, 2, pl. du Châtelet, 4ème (tel. 01 42 74 22 77). M: Châtelet. 1000 seats. Excellent productions, including classical music concerts and ballets. Box office open M 11am-6pm, Tu-Sa 11am-8pm; open for telephone sales M 9am-7pm, Tu-Sa 9am-8pm. Tickets 95-190F, students/under 25 same-day rush tickets half-price. MC, V.

CAFÉ-THÉÂTRES

Visit one of Paris's *café-théâtres* for an evening of word play and social satire in mostly black-box theater settings. Expect low-budget skits filled with political puns and double-entendres. Do not expect a café or a theater (this is not a joke). In general, knowledge of French slang and politics is a must for audience members. One person shows are the staple of the genre.

Au Bec Fin, 6, rue Thérèse, 1er (tel. 01 42 96 29 35). M: Palais-Royal or Pyramides. A tiny, 60-seat theater featuring 2-3 shows per night. Shows at 7, 8:30, and 10:15pm. Tickets 80F, students 65F (except Sa). Seats for auditions open to the public every M at 9:30pm, 50F. The auditions are like a French Gong Show, with often questionable production values (sometimes it's awful). MC, V.

Café de la Gare, 41, rue du Temple, 4ème (tel. 01 42 78 52 51; reservations 01 40 09 64 06). M: Hôtel-de-Ville. Couched in the Centre de Danse du Marais, where its line-up includes solo comics and Addams Family Goth seances. Box office open daily 3-7pm and 30min. before the show. Shows W-Sa at 8 and 10pm, Su 6:30pm. Tickets 100F, 25 and under 80F. MC, V.

Point Virgule, 7, rue Ste-Croix-de-la-Bretonnerie, 4ème (tel. 01 42 78 67 03). M: Hôtel-de-Ville. Built by the actors and comedians themselves, Le Point Virgule is as immediate and interactive as theater can be, with crowds of 130 sitting shoulder-to-shoulder on benches. Frequent slapstick acts ideal for non-French speakers. Reservations suggested. 3 shows daily at 8, 9:15, and 10:15pm. Tickets to 1 show 80F, students 65F; 2 shows 130F; 3 shows 150F. Open daily 5pm-midnight.

CABARET

The following are the Cinderellas to the nauseating stepsister cabarets, **Lido** and the **Moulin Rouge,** which never tire of stripping tourists of their wads of cash to see a girlie show. The *cabaret*, the musical cousin of the *café-théâtre*, is popular music in the best sense of the word, a mix of nostalgia, biting commentary, and tunes everyone knows. The better your French, the better the time you'll have. Admission usually includes one drink, to loosen the vocal chords and encourage a full-out sing-along.

Au Lapin Agile, 22, rue des Saules, 18ème (tel. 01 46 06 85 87). M: Lamarck-Coulain-court. Turn right on rue Lamarck, then right again up rue des Saules. Picasso, Verlaine, Renoir, and Apollinaire hung out here during the heyday of Montmartre; now a mainly tourist audience crowds in for comical poems and songs. Originally called the *Cabaret des Assassins*, this *chansonnier* inspired Steve Martin's 1996 hit play *Picasso at the Lapin Agile*. In 1875, when the artist André Gill painted a rabbit on the theater's facade, it came to be known as *le lapin à Gill* (Gill's Rabbit), a name that eventually morphed into *Le lapin agile* (the nimble rabbit). Shows Tu-Su at 9:15pm. Admission and first drink 130F, students 90F. Subsequent drinks 30-45F.

Caveau de la République, 1, bd. St-Martin, 3ème (tel. 01 42 78 44 45). M: République. A Parisian crowd fills the 482 seats of this 96 year-old venue for political satire. Shows consist of 6 separate comedy and song acts; the sequence is called the *tour de champs* (tour of the field). Good French skills and knowledge of French politics needed to get the gags. Tickets sold up to 6 days in advance, daily 11am-6pm. Shows mid-Sept. to June Tu-Sa 9pm, Su 3:30pm. Admission M-Th 145F, F-Sa 180F, Tu-Th students 85F and over 60 110F. MC, V.

CINEMA

With a tradition that goes back to the very birth of cinema, Paris is a cinophile's silver-screened heaven. Invented by the Frenchmen Auguste and Louis Lumière, cinema had its world debut in Paris. When the first movie about a train pulling up into a station premiered at the **Grand Café**, 14, bd. des Capucines, in 1895 the audience ran screaming, terrified of being run over. At the time, Louis belittled his innovation as "an invention without a future." For more on French cinema, see **Film,** p. 33.

The French love affair with cinema is reflected in the fact that there are probably more films shown in Paris—over 300 a week—than in any other city in the world. You'll find scores of cinemas throughout the city, particularly in the *quartier latin* and on the Champs-Elysées. Many theaters in Paris specialize in programs featuring classic European film, current independent film, Asian classics, American classics, and current Hollywood blockbusters. The two big theater chains—**Gaumont** and **UGC**—offer *cartes privilèges*, discounts for five visits or more. In late June, the wonderful two-day **Fête du Cinéma** offers great discounts and interesting films (see **Festivals**, p. 281).

Check *Pariscope* or *l'Officiel des Spectacles* (available at any kiosk or newsstand, 3F) for weekly film schedules, prices, and reviews. The notation V.O. *(version originale)* after a non-French movie listing means that the film is being shown in its original language with French subtitles; watching an English-language film with French subtitles is a great way to pick up new vocabulary. V.F. *(version française)* means that the film has been dubbed—an increasingly rare phenomenon. Paris's cinemas offer student, senior, and family discounts. On Monday and Wednesday, prices drop about 10F for everyone. Many theaters show a series of commercials and previews *(séance)* that roll for as long as half an hour. The *séance* is often as entertaining as the film itself, and French ads are creative and witty. However, the film begins at the listed time.

Musée du Louvre, 1er (tel. 01 40 20 51 86 for info; 01 40 20 52 99 for schedules and reservations). M: Musée du Louvre. Art films, films on art, and silent movies with live musical accompaniment. Admission 25-70F, students 15-50F. Open Sept.-June.

Les Trois Luxembourg, 67, rue Monsieur-le-Prince, 6ème (tel. 01 46 33 97 77). M: Odéon. High-quality independent, classic, and foreign films, all in V.O. Popular. Purchase tickets early for a good seat. Admission 40F, students 30F.

Action Christine, 4, rue Christine, 6ème (tel. 01 43 29 11 30). M: Odéon. Off rue Dauphine. Plays an eclectic, international selection of art and cult films from the 40s and 50s. Always V.O. Admission 40F, early show (usually 6 or 7pm) 25F; M and students 30F. For 180F, buy a 1-year pass for 6 movies. One of the 2 rooms is wheelchair accessible; descend a steep staircase to reach the other.

L'Arlequin, 76, rue de Rennes, 6ème (tel. 01 45 44 28 80). M: St-Sulpice. A revival cinema with occasional visits from European directors and first-run preview showings. Some films in V.O., others are dubbed. Buy tickets in advance. Admission 46F, students M-F 36F, W all tickets 36F. Su matinée 30F. MC, V.

Cinémathèque Française, pl. du Trocadéro, 16ème (tel. 01 45 53 21 86). M: Trocadéro. At the Musée du Cinéma in the Palais de Chaillot; enter through the Jardins du Trocadéro. Also 18, rue du Faubourg-du-Temple, 11ème. M: République. Recording (tel. 01 47 04 24 24) lists all shows. A must for film buffs. 2-3 classics, near-classics, or soon-to-be classics per day. Foreign films usually in V.O. Buy tickets 15-20 min. early. Open W-Su 5-9:45pm. Admission 28F, students 17F.

La Géode, 26, av. Corentin Cariou, 19ème (tel. 01 40 05 12 12; recorded schedule 08 36 68 29 30, 2.23F per min.). M: Porte de la Villette. In La Villette (see **Museums,** p. 272). Science and nature movies on a huge spherical screen in a building that looks like a giant silver alien ship. Shows Tu-Su on the hour 10am-9pm. Admission 57F, students M-F 44F. Reserve well in advance.

Dôme IMAX, pl. de la Défense (tel. 08 36 67 06 06; 2.23F/min.). M: Grande Arche de la Défense. The big dome to the right with your back to the Grand Arche. An IMAX cinema with huge-screen documentary films like *The Fires of Kuwait* and *Antarctica*. Documentaries are in French, but what you see is more important. Admission 55F, students, seniors, and under 16 40F. For 2 shows 75F, students, seniors, and under 16 65F.

MUSIC

CLASSICAL MUSIC, OPERA, AND DANCE

Paris toasts the classics under lamppost, spire, and chandelier. The city's squares, churches, and concert halls feature world-class performers from home and abroad. Acclaimed foreign and provincial dance companies visit Paris frequently; watch for posters and read *Pariscope*. Connoisseurs will find the thick and indexed *Programme des Festivals* (free at *mairies* and at tourist offices) an indispensable guide to seasonal music and, to a lesser extent, dance series and celebrations in and around Paris. The monthly publication *Paris Selection*, free at tourist offices throughout the city, also keeps track of concerts in churches and museums, many of which are free or reasonably priced. In general, Paris offers cheap tickets to high culture in great quantities, thanks to a decade of socialism that offered arts to the masses. Beware, however, of rock-bottom prices. The **Opéra Bastille** allegedly suffers from poor acoustics. And while Balanchine may have said "see the music, hear the dance," you may not be able to do either from the upper eaves of the **Opéra Garnier.** Try to check a theater floor plan and ask about the obstructed views whenever possible before purchasing a ticket. **Alpha FNAC** is the most popular booking agent (see **Theater,** p. 269). For more information about seasonal events, consult **Festivals and other Seasonal Events,** p. 279.

Free concerts are often held in churches and parks, especially during summer festivals. These concerts are extremely popular, so get there early. Check *Pariscope* and *L'Officiel des Spectacles* and the Alpha FNAC offices for concert notices. The **American Church in Paris,** 65, quai d'Orsay, 7*ème* (tel. 01 40 62 05 00; M: Invalides or Alma Marceau), sponsors free concerts (Sept.-June Su at 5pm). **Eglise St-Merri,** 78, rue St-Martin, 4*ème* (M: Hôtel-de-Ville), is also known for its free concerts (Sept.-July Sa at 9pm and Su at 4pm); contact Accueil Musical St-Merri, 76, rue de la Verrerie, 4*ème* (tel. 01 42 71 40 75 or 01 42 71 93 93; M: Châtelet). Concerts take place W-Su in the **Jardin du Luxembourg** band shell, 6*ème* (tel. 01 42 34 20 23); show up early for a seat or prepare to stand. Infrequent concerts in the **Musée d'Orsay,** 1, rue Bellechasse, 7*ème* (tel. 01 40 49 49 66; M: Solferino), are occasionally free with a museum ticket but usually cost 20-130F. The **Maison de Radio France** (see **Museums,** p. 264) hosts a wide range of concerts, some free; pick up their extensive program list at the studio.

Many churches stage frequent concerts that are somewhat expensive but feature fantastic acoustics and atmosphere. Check schedules at **Eglise St-Germain-des-Prés,** 3, pl. St-Germain-des-Prés, 6*ème* (tel. 01 44 62 70 90; M: St-Germain-des-Prés); **Eglise St-Eustache,** 2 rue du Jour, 1*er* (tel. 01 42 36 31 05; M: Les Halles); **Eglise de la Trinité,** pl. Estienne d'Orves, 9*ème* (tel. 01 48 74 12 77; M: Trinité); **Eglise St-Louis-en-l'Ile,** 19bis, rue St-Louis-en-l'Ile, 4*ème* (tel. 01 46 34 11 60; M: Pont Marie); and **Eglise St-Julien-le-Pauvre,** 23, quai de Mortebello, 5*ème* (tel. 01 43 54 52 16). Arrive 30-45min. ahead for good seats. Ste-Chapelle also hosts fabulous concerts a few times per week in the summer. Contact the box office at 4, bd. du Palais, 1*er* (tel. 01 53 73 78 50; M: Cité).

Centre Nationale de La Danse, 9, rue Geoffroy-l'Asnier, 4*ème* (tel. 01 42 74 44 22; fax 01 40 29 06 46). is a new organization which will promote choreography and dance in France and will bring international companies to Paris. They don't have a specific venue but will host events in various theaters. The 2000 program includes the Paul Taylor Dance Company.

Cité de la Musique, at La Villette, 19*ème* (tel. 01 44 84 44 84; www.cite-musique.fr). M: Porte-de-Pantin. Hosts everything from lute concerts to American gospel year-round in its enormous *salle des concerts* and smaller *amphithéâtre.* Tickets run 65-200F. One particularly good deal offered by the Cité is a *carnet* of 4 tickets for 160F. There are free concerts throughout the year in both spaces; call for information. Shows at 8pm, box office opens 30min. prior.

L'Etoile du Nord, 16, rue Georgette Agutte, 18*ème* (tel. 01 42 26 47 47; fax 01 42 26 63 98). M: Guy-Môquet. An independent dance space with a core group of impressive modern choreographers. Tickets 50-120F.

IRCAM, Institut de Recherche et Coordination Acoustique/Musique, Centre Pompidou, 1, pl. Igor-Stravinsky, 4*ème* (tel. 01 44 78 48 43; mediatheque.ircam.fr). M: Rambuteau. This institute, which invites scholars, composers, and interpreters to come together in the study of music, often holds concerts. Contemporary works sometimes accompanied by film or theater. Stop by the office at the Stravinsky fountain or at the Centre Pompidou for schedules. There are 2 computers in the lobby that allow you to "visit" IRCAM and play musical games. The institute houses a music library for scholars. The music library, or médiathèque, is open mid-Aug. to mid-July M and W-F 10am-7pm, Th noon-7pm, Sa 1pm-7pm. 20F per afternoon; 300F per year, students 150F.

Musée du Louvre, 1*er* (tel. 01 40 20 51 86 for information, 01 40 20 52 99 for schedule, 01 40 20 84 00 for reservations; www.louvre.fr). M: Palais-Royal-Musée du Louvre. Classical music in the classy Louvre auditorium. Concerts 100-135F; student-rush 30min. before show 50F. Open Sept.-June.

Opéra de la Bastille, pl. de la Bastille, 11ème (tel. 08 36 69 78 68; 2,23F/min.; fax 01 44 73 13 74; www.opera-de-paris.fr). M: Bastille. The Opéra de la Bastille staged its first performance on July 14, 1989, during the bicentennial jubilee. Hailed by some as the hall to bring opera to the masses, decried by others as offensive to every aesthetic sensibility, this huge theater features elaborate opera and ballet, often with a modern spin. The Bastille Opera is said to have acoustical problems spread democratically throughout the theater, so it's not the place to go all-out for front row seats. Subtitles in French. The year 2000 will feature *Don Giovanni, Carmen, La Traviata, Rigoletto,* and more. Tickets 60-670F. Call, write, or stop by for a free brochure of the season's events. Tickets can be purchased by internet, mail, fax, phone (M-Sa 9am-7pm), or in person (M-Sa 11am-6:30pm). Tickets on sale 14 days in advance of performance. Reduced rush tickets for students under 25, and anyone over 65 often available 15min. before show; 120F for operas, 70F for ballets, and 50F for concerts. Wheelchair access: call at least 15 days in advance. MC, V.

Opéra Comique, 14, rue Favart, 2ème (tel. 01 42 44 45 46; fax 01 49 26 05 93). M: Richelieu-Drouot. Operas on a lighter scale—from Rossini to Offenbach. It was here that Bizet's *Carmen* first scandalized the Parisian public. The '00-'01 season will include Mozart's *Don Giovanni* in Feb. and Boeldieu's *La Dame Blanche* in Apr., as well as works by Puccini and Debussy. Buy tickets at the box office M-Sa 11am-7pm or reserve by phone. Tickets 35-550F, student cut-rates available 15min. before show starts, 50F.

Opéra Garnier, pl. de l'Opéra, 9ème (tel. 08 36 69 78 68; 2.23F/min.; fax 01 44 73 13 74; www.opera-de-paris.fr). M: Opéra. Although the renovations of this historic Opéra will not be finished until 2002, it will be open for the 2000 season. The Garnier hosts the Ballet de l'Opéra de Paris, symphonies and chamber music. Tickets available at the box office 2 weeks before each performance M-Sa 11am-6pm. The year 2000 will feature *Cendrillon, Giselle,* and more. Ballet tickets 30-420F; opera tickets up to 670F. Lowest-end tickets often have obstructed views. Show up an hour before to buy leftover tickets at remarkable discounts (especially in summer). MC, V.

Orchestre de Paris, 252, rue du Faubourg St-Honoré, 8ème (tel. 01 45 61 65 60; www.orchestredeparis.com). M: Ternes. The internationally renowned orchestra delivers first-class performances under Semyon Bychkov. 2000 season includes Dvorák, Berlioz, Lizst, Ravel, Beethoven, and more. Season runs Oct.-June; call or stop by for concert calendar. 2-4 concerts per week, W-Sa. Box office open M-Sa 11am-6pm and until 8pm shownights. Shows at 7:30. Tickets 60-320F. Student rush tickets 30min. before show for 50F. MC, V.

Théâtre des Champs-Elysées, 15, av. Montaigne, 8ème (tel. 01 49 52 50 50, reservations 01 49 52 50 50). M: Alma Marceau. Top international dance companies and orchestras, from world music to chamber music, as well as opera. To play here is to "arrive" on the highbrow music scene. When asked by a passerby, "How do I get to the Théâtre des Champs-Elysées?", Horowitz replied, "Practice. Lots and lots of practice." Season runs Sept.-June. Buy tickets 3 weeks in advance. Reserve by telephone M-F 10am-noon and 2-6pm; box office open M-Sa 1-7pm. Tickets 40-750F.

Théâtre Musical de Paris, pl. du Châtelet, 1er (tel. 01 40 28 28 40). M: Châtelet. A superb 2300-seat theater featuring orchestras, ballet companies, opera, and dance. Magnificent acoustics. Season Oct.-June; 2000 will feature 8 operas including *Alceste, Daphne,* and *Hamlet,* and 3 ballets. Tickets usually 60-775F. Last-minute reduced rate tickets sold 15min. before performance (opera 100F, all others 50F). AmEx, MC, V.

Théâtre de la Ville, 2 pl. du Châtelet, 4ème (tel. 01 42 74 22 77). M: Châtelet. Primarily known for its innovative theatrical and dance productions, this venue also offers a selection of classical and world music concerts. The 2000 season will feature performers from Iran, China, and Brazil, as well as Vivaldi, Strauss, and Schumann. Shows 95-190F, students 70-80F. Call for program and series discounts. Second venue in Montmartre: **Les Abbesses,** 31, rue des Abbesses, 18ème. Tickets sold by phone (M-Sa 11am-7pm) and at the theaters (open M 11am-7pm, Tu-Sa 11am-8pm. Abbesses open Tu-Sa 5-8pm). Shows begin 5pm and 8:30pm. AmEx, MC, V.

KIDS

First off, younger kids tend to love the big monoliths of touristy Paris. Get ready to do the Eiffel Tower, climb up Nôtre-Dame, and cruise in the *bateaux mouches*. Beyond the obvious, the following attractions will most likely be trip favorites for the little people.

Parks, gardens, and zoos are plentiful and often have a children's area. For a superlative suggested itinerary of green spots, see p. 187. The **Jardin du Luxembourg** (p. 186) is famous for its *guignol* (see below), pony rides, go-carts, carousel, boats (to rent and sail on the ponds), and swings. In summer, the carnival at the **Tuileries** gardens (p. 168) and **La Foire du Trône** has rides suitable for all ages. The **Jardin d'Acclimatation** (tel. 01 40 67 90 82), in the **Bois de Boulogne,** offers a children's zoo, a hall of mirrors, and miniature golf for only 15F. Donkey rides, remote-control speed boats, and remote-control speed donkeys cost extra (7-10F). The newest addition is the explor@dome, an interactive science museum in which kids can try out virtual reality and science demonstrations. In the summer there are numerous arts and crafts workshops in the Musée en Herbe, within the Jardin. The **Jardin des Plantes** (p. 185) is good for a pleasant stroll and a trip to its insect museum, turtle- and bird-filled tropical greenhouse and tiny menagerie, including lions, monkeys, and ostriches (don't tell your kids the story of the Parisians eating all the animals during a siege by the Prussians). The **Parc Zoologique** (p. 238) in the Bois de Vincennes is great for animal-lovers. On the other side of the Bois is the **Parc Floral** (p. 240) which has one of the best playgrounds in Paris, including ping-pong, mini-golf, a tiny choo-choo touring the park, and a butterfly garden. The **Parc Monceau** is the romping ground of many little Pierres. Less bucolic and more convenient is the **merry go-round** at M: St-Paul.

If your goal is to trick your kids into learning something while on this trip, Paris has its fair share of clever ruses to that end. **Parc de la Villette** (p. 255), boasting a huge science museum, aquarium, and Omnimax theater complex, offers an entire day's worth of entertainment, and will have fun-loving youngsters contemplating when the sun will explode and the nature of the hole in the ozone layer. The **Palais de la Decouverte** (p. 264) in the Grand Palais offers a more central and smaller version of the La Villette's Cité des Sciences et de l'Industrie. The **Musée de la Curiosité** is just that, turning kids into mini-magicians and psychics (p. 261). The **Muséum National d'Histoire Naturelle** (p. 258) is good for kids who want an up-close look at blue whales, elephants, and giraffes, with a place for games and a kickin' gift store. The 8*ème* offers the ultimate gory site of the Revolution, **Place de la Concorde** (p. 200), for kids who can't get enough of historical drama.

In case of emergency, do not be afraid to break the glass, pull down the red handle, and launch the tactical strike that is **Disneyland Paris** (p. 327). Kids go gaga for it, and it is a blessed bargaining chip in getting them to accompany you to the Musée d'Orsay and the like.

Kids who generally subsist on pizza, burgers, and chicken nuggets will not gleefully join you on a trip to the Tour d'Argent. Nevertheless, it is possible for them to eat happily in Paris, without your bringing a suitcase of mac and cheese or living at McDo's (as McDonald's calls itself in France). *Crêperies* are a good bet with kids, as choosing their own fillings gives a flexibility most restaurant menus lack, not to mention the preponderance of dessert crêpes. Sunday brunch, especially in the bustling Marais, is also a good way to feed the moppets for the day, with most menus offering classics like pancakes, and scrambled eggs (p. 134). Kids also tend to dig the Parisian café and *brasserie* aesthetic, with glitzy (although somewhat pricey) intelligentsia-faves, like **La Coupole** (p. 147) or **Café de Flore** (p. 139), offering a fun people-watching experience. If all else fails, most restaurants are willing to fix something simple for kids, like pasta, or a *croque monsieur*. Remember: we all scream for ice cream (p. 160).

If your kids aren't avant-garde French theater buffs, do not worry, as there are plenty of other spectacles to amuse them. The **Cirque de Paris** (tel. 01 47 99 40 40) gives little ones the chance to be an animal and meet the clowns. They offer day-long programs where the under-12s train with the clowns, visit the animals, walk the tightrope, and then see the show (caution: do not let your children run away with a French circus). The **Théâtre de Champs-Elysées** (p. 274) also hosts a kids the-ater program intermittently; call for details. The **American Library** (p. 87) holds a weekly story-telling session, and lends books, tapes, and books on tape. Teens might want to give **Bowling International Stadium** (p. 296), **Bowling de Paris** (p. 297), and the roller-rink **La Main Jeune** (p. 298) a whirl. Then there are the crossover mar-ionnette hits, the *guignols* (below). As Crosby, Stills, and Nash once said, every-one does Punch and Judy in the same language.

GUIGNOLS

Grand guignol is a traditional Parisian marionette theater featuring the *guignol*, its classic stock character, like *Punch and Judy*, but without the domestic vio-lence. Although the puppets speak French, they're very cosmopolitan puppets, and you'll have no trouble understanding the slapstick, child-geared humor. Nearly all parks, including the popular Jardin du Luxembourg (see **Sights,** p. 186) have *guignols;* check *Pariscope* for more information.

Marionettes du Luxembourg, Jardin du Luxembourg, 6ème (tel. 01 43 26 46 47). M: Odéon or Vavin, or RER: Luxembourg. The best *guignol* in Paris. This theater plays the same classics it has since it opened in 1933: *Little Red Riding Hood, The Three Little Pigs,* etc. It's all very Grimm. Running time is about 45min. Arrive 30min. early for good seats. Shows generally M, W, F, and Sa, at differing times, depending on the season. Call for schedules. Admission 25F.

Marionettes Marcel Lebul, 164, rue Faubourg-St-Honoré, 8ème (tel. 01 42 56 18 22). M: St-Philipe du Roule. The classic adventures of the *guignol* character. Shows Sept. to mid-July W and Sa-Su at 3pm. Admission 25F.

Théâtre Guignol du Parc des Buttes Chaumont, 19ème (tel. 01 43 98 10 95). M: Laumière or buses #60 or 75. Puppets interact with excitable children in a park setting ripe for romping. 7 different 40min. shows. W at 3pm and 5:30pm, Sa, Su and holidays at 3, 4, and 5pm. Call before going; shows are often added or cut. Admission 15F.

SPORTS

You might find it hard to believe while pounding the city's pavement, but Paris and its surroundings teem with indoor and outdoor sports opportunities. For more info call the Mairie de Paris's sports hotline, **Allô-Sports** (tel. 01 42 76 54 54; open M-Th 10:30am-5pm, F 10:30am-4:30pm). Many of the courses offered by the city are for residents only. *Pariscope* has a *Sports et Détente* section with pages of facili-ties, hours, and prices for a variety of sports locations. Also see *Paris Pas Cher* for lists of affordable gyms geared toward the long-term visitor. The tourist office on the Champs-Elysées provides booklets, maps, and information concerning sports and leisure in and around Paris, as well as the free *Guide de sport à Paris* which is an extensive list of all sports activities and venues.

BOWLING. Bowling de Paris (tel. 01 53 64 93 00), in the Bois de Boulogne near the route Mahatma Gandhi entrance of the Jardin d'Acclimatation. After the park closes, this entrance remains open. Games M-F 9am-noon 13F, noon-8pm 26F, 8pm-2am 36F; Sa-Su 9am-noon 19F, noon-8pm 35F, 8pm-2am 36F. Obligatory bowling shoe rental 12F. Because the Bowling de Paris is inside the garden, you must also pay the garden's admission fee (13F). **Bowling International Stadium**, 66, av. d'Ivry, 13ème (tel. 01 45 86 55 52; M: Tolbiac), is a joint bowling alley and bil-liard hall. American billiards require a 100F deposit, a 5F supplementary fee, and cost 50F per hr. Bowling in any of the 12 lanes costs 16-33F depending on the time of day, the day of the week, and who you are (reduced prices for students and seniors); shoe rental 10F. Open daily 2pm-2am.

CYCLING. The city is not a good place for a leisurely afternoon pedal, although the highway along the Seine near Châtelet is closed to cars on Sundays. The tourist office on the Champs-Elysées has maps and information about cycling in and around Paris. Cyclists peddle away the hours in the **Bois de Vincennes,** 12ème (M: Porte Dorée), around Lac Daumesnil or deeper into the woods. The **Bois de Boulogne,** 16ème, officially boasts 8km of bike paths, but any cyclist can make up an original route among the innumerable trees. The Canal de l'Ourcq passes through the **Parc de la Villette,** 30, av. Corentin Cariou, 19ème (M: Porte de la Villette), and has a bicycle path alongside. For information about bike rentals and organizations, consult **Two Wheelers,** p. 82, or see **Sights,** p. 234, for info on the Bois de Boulogne. Hard-core cyclists may want to try the 109km ride out to **Ferté Milon** in the province of Aisne. Also consider the **Forêt de Fontainebleau** (see **Fontainebleau,** p. 321).

DANCE. The bustling **Centre de Danse du Marais,** 41, rue de Temple, 4ème (tel. 01 42 72 15 42; M: Hôtel de Ville) is housed in a lovely Marais building around a courtyard café. It offers classes ranging from classical bar to Argentinian tango. Registration fee 40F, 1 class 90F, 4 classes 320F, 8 560F, 12 750F. Open daily 9am-10:30pm. **Le Centre International Danse Jazz,** 54a, rue de Clichy, 9ème (tel. 01 53 32 75 00; M: Place de Clichy) is another dance megaplex. It is not limited to jazz, and boasts a number of superstar teachers. 1 class 78F, 10 classes 640F (for 10 or more classes, you must pay an annual registration fee of 200F).

GYMS AND FITNESS. **Alésia Club,** 143, rue d'Alésia, 14ème (tel. 01 45 42 91 05; M: Alésia), has a gym, sauna, and other facilities and sell memberships for the day (150F, students 100F) or longer. Students 450F for 1 month, 1200F for 6 months, 1700F for 1 year; 100F for required insurance. Open M-F 11:30am-9pm, Sa 11:30am-8pm, Su 2-8pm. Or try the **Espace Vit'Halles,** 48, rue Rambuteau, 3ème (tel. 01 42 77 21 71; M: Rambuteau), near Les Halles in pl. Beaubourg. With a weight room, sauna, and aerobics and step classes, Vit'Halles offers both long- and short-term memberships. Students 720F per month. Open M-F 8am-10pm, Sa 10am-7pm, Su 10am-4pm. **Gymnase Club,** 149, rue de Rennes, 6ème (tel. 01 45 44 24 35). There are at least 20 in Paris. Each one has different classes and equipment. Most have pools, aerobics, weights, and sauna. Some have martial arts and tennis.

JOGGING. Running is difficult in the city, where both traffic and pollution can be dangerous. Many joggers head to one of Paris's many public parks. Remember that running in deserted or unknown areas is dangerous, especially after dark. In Central Paris: the **Champs de Mars,** 7ème (M: Bir Hakeim), is a popular spot, with a 2.5km path around the outside, and with gardens that are broken up into 200m lengths; the leafy **Jardin du Luxembourg,** 6ème (M: Cluny-La Sorbonne), offers a 1.6km circuit and a huge crowd; the **Parc Monceau,** 8ème (M: Monceau), crawls with kids but remains serenely green; 1km loop. **On the Periphery:** the **Parc des Buttes-Chaumont,** 19ème (M: Buttes Chaumont). Labyrinthine paths great for hillwork. A swooping path (1.6km) rings the park; the **Bois de Boulogne,** 16ème, has 35km of trails. Maps are to be found at regular intervals on the periphery of the park; less renowned, but no less winnable, is the **Boys de Valenciennes,** 12ème; begin at the northwest corner of the park at the medieval **Chateau de Valenciennes** (M: Chateau de Valenciennes). Peripheral path, marked in red and yellow on park maps, is 11km; inside path (marked in blue and white) is 8km. Avoid the southwest corner of the park, especially if you're alone.

ROLLER SKATING. In-line skates are catching on in Paris streets. The **Jardins du Trocadéro,** in front of the Palais de Chaillot, fill with motorless Evil Knievals. Rent in-line skates at **FranScoop,** 47, rue Servan, 11ème (tel. 01 47 00 68 43; M: St-Maur),

CITYOFLIGHT EXPRESS If you have ever been witness to the Friday night "Roller Rally" that leaves Place d'Italie at about quarter of ten and winds throughout the city with about 5000 skaters in tow, then you know what mayhem is. Fear no more, though, as the Paris police force has responded with a swift-footed fleet of about thirty policemen on in-line skates. Yes, that's right, cops on wheels, in full regalia, plus elbow and knee pads, helmet, *and a gun.*

45-90F per day, 120F per weekend, 240F per week. Open M-Sa 9:30am-1pm and 2-7:30pm. Or check out **La Main Jaune,** pl. de la Porte-de-Champerret, 17*ème* (tel. 01 47 63 26 47; M: Porte de Champerret). It's a roller disco, popular with the high school crowd. Open W and Sa-Su 2:30-7pm, F-Sa and holidays 10pm-dawn. Admission W and Sa-Su 50F (includes a drink), skate rental 10F; F-Sa night it beats with Portuguese music and non-skating clientele

SWIMMING AND WATER-SPORTS. The Mairie de Paris has created a network of public-access pools. Opening hours vary, but all are open in summer (hours at pools are variable, so call ahead). Call Allô-Sports to have a copy of *Les Piscines à Paris* sent to you, or pick one up at a *mairie*. It lists hours and services available at each pool. Entry to any **municipal pool** 16F; under 17, over 64, or those accompanying children but not swimming 9F. Possible charge for lockers (2F). Ask about 1-year passes and discounts. Under 8 must be accompanied. Last entry 30min. before closing; pools are cleared 15min. before closing. Some pools have a *"nocturne"* 1-2 nights a week, when they're open past 8pm. Some central pools are **Piscine Suzanne-Berlioux** at Forum des Halles, 10 pl. de la Rotunde, 1*er* (tel. 01 42 36 98 44), and **Piscine Jaen Taris,** 16 rue Thouin, 5*ème* (tel. 01 43 25 54 03). If you feel the need for a beach, perhaps a jacuzzi, wavepool, and waterslide will do at **Aquaboulevard,** 4, rue Louis Armand, 15*ème* (tel. 01 40 60 10 00; M: Balard). Come early to avoid the crowds. Admission 68F for 4hr., 58F for under 12; 600F for Sept.-June; 1300F for 1 year. Open M-Th 9am-11pm, F 9am-midnight, Sa 8am-midnight, Su 8am-11pm, last admission 9pm. Associated fitness club gives access to sauna, gym, tennis and squash courts, aerobic classes, and a golf course, as well as water park. Open M-F 8am-10pm, Sa-Su 8am-8pm. 160F per day, 3528F per year.

OTHER SPORTS. Paris boasts 170 municipal **tennis courts** in 45 "tennis centers," each open to the individual player. You must have your own equipment for municipal courts. Free intro lessons for children. To use municipal courts, apply for a free **Carte Paris Tennis,** which enables you to reserve space through Minitel. Reservation is crucial, especially in summer. Pick up an application at tennis centers throughout the city. Cards take 5 weeks to process. Municipal courts 38F per hr. To get a handle on **angling** in the Bois de Boulogne, contact the Annicale des Pêcheurs de Neuilly, Levallois, et environs, Base Halientique de la Jatte, 19, bd. de Levallois Prolongé, 92000 Levallois-Perret (tel. 01 43 48 36 34).

SPECTATOR SPORTS

Parisians follow sports with fierce interest, reading between the lines of their own sports daily, *l'Equipe* (6F). The **Palais Omnisports Paris Bercy,** 8, bd. de Bercy, 12*ème* (tel. 01 44 68 44 68; M: Bercy), hosts everything from beach volleyball to figure skating, horse jumping, and surfing beneath its radical, sod-covered roof.

CYCLING. Call the **Fédération Française de Cyclisme** (tel. 01 49 35 69 00) for information about cycling events. The women's **Tour de France** leaves Paris in mid-Aug. near the Eiffel Tower. Held in July, the men's **Tour de France** pits 200 of the world's best male cyclists against the Alps, the elements, and each other for 21 grueling stages. Call *l'Equipe* (tel. 01 41 33 15 00), one of the tour's sponsors, for information about the race's itinerary. Spectators turn out in droves along the way, stationed at bends in highways to cheer their favorites to victory. Parisians and tourists alike line the Champs-Elysées for the triumphal last stage, usually between noon and 6pm. Show up early and be prepared for a mob scene. The **Grand Prix Cycliste de Paris** is an annual time trial competition held in June in the Bois de Vincennes, 12*ème* (tel. 01 43 68 01 27).

FOOTBALL/SOCCER. Unless you're American (and even then), you would have to have been in a coma for the past two years not to realize that France hosted and won the **1998 World Cup** in the final match over Brazil in Paris's new **Stade de France** in St-Denis (see p. 334). Called *le football*, France's hands-down national sport consumes Paris, especially during the World Cup *(La Coupe du Monde)*. The **Club de Football Paris St-Germain** is Paris's own professional football team, splitting its time between road games and matches at the enormous **Parc des Princes,** the city's premier outdoor stadium venue. Tickets to all events can be purchased at the Parc des Princes box office, 24, rue du Commandant-Guibaud, 16*ème* (tel. 01 49 87 29 29; M: Porte d'Auteuil), and go on sale anywhere from 2 days to 2 weeks in advance. Games on weekends and some weekday evenings. Tickets 50-300F. Box office open M-F 9am-8pm, Sa 10am-5pm. MC, V.

HORSE RACING. The numerous hippodromes in and around town host races of all kinds throughout the year. Far from seedy, an afternoon at the track is a family outing. The level of classiness climbs a notch or two for the season's championship races. **Hippodrome de Vincennes,** 2, route de la Ferme, in the Bois de Vincennes, 12*ème* (tel. 01 49 77 17 17; M: Château de Vincennes). A hike through the woods from the métro stop takes you to the home of Parisian harness racing since 1906. Prix d'Amérique (late Jan.), Prix de France (early Feb.), and Prix du Président de la République (late June). Tickets 15-30F, even for the big races. **Hippodrome d'Auteuil,** in the Bois de Boulogne, 16*ème* (tel. 01 44 10 20 30). M: Porte d'Auteuil. Steeplechases since 1873; the stands date from 1921. For big races in June and July, shuttles run from the métro and RER stations. Open Sept.-Nov. and Feb.-June. Tickets M-F 25F, Su 40F, major events 50F. No reservations.

TENNIS. The *terre battue* (red clay) of the **Stade Roland Garros,** 2, av. Gordon Bennett, 16*ème* (M: Porte d'Auteuil), has ended more than one champion's quest for a Grand Slam. Two weeks each year during May and June, **Les Internationaux de France de Tennis (the French Open)** welcomes the world's top players to Paris. Write to the Fédération Française de Tennis (tel. 01 47 43 48 00), located at the stadium, in February for information on tickets for the next spring's tournament. Call in March for prices; seats generally range 45-295F. Also, write or call your national tennis association; they sometimes have an extra supply of tickets.

FESTIVALS AND SEASONAL EVENTS

Paris is a city where nearly every art form, historical moment, or celebrity has a corresponding festival or cultural event, offering year-round opportunities to celebrate with various degrees of pomp and libation. While the city-wide Fête de la Musique and the Bastille Day are difficult to miss—even if you want to—some of the smaller festivities require some explanation. The Office de Tourisme (see p. 86) has a home page (www.paris-touristoffice.com) and a pricey information line (tel. 08 36 68 31 12; 2.23F/min.) with information on all the festivals. Another good source of information, closer to the date of the event, is *Pariscope*, and its English-language insert, *Time Out*, both of which come out on Wednesdays. You can also get a listing of festivals before you leave home by writing the French Government Tourist Office.

NATIONAL HOLIDAYS

When a holiday falls on a Tuesday or Thursday, the French often take off the Monday or Friday, a practice known as *faire le pont* (to make a bridge). Banks and public offices close at noon on the nearest working day before a public holiday.

DATE	FESTIVAL	ENGLISH
January 1	Le Jour de l'An	New Year's Day
April 13	Le Lundi de Pâques	Easter Monday
May 1	La Fête du Travail	Labor Day
May 8	L'Anniversaire de la Libération	Victory in Europe Day
May 21	L'Ascension	Ascension Day
June 1	Le Lundi de Pentecôte	Whit Monday
July 14	La Fête Nationale	Bastille Day
August 15	L'Assomption	Feast of the Assumption
November 1	La Toussaint	All Saints' Day
November 11	L'Armistice 1918	Armistice Day
December 25	Le Noël	Christmas

FESTIVALS

JUNE, JULY, AND AUGUST

Gay Pride (Fierté), June. Gay Paree celebrates its annual Pride celebration with parties, special events, film festivals, demonstrations, art exhibitions, concerts, and a huge Pride Parade through the Marais and the streets of Paris. For specific dates and events, call the Centre Gai et Lesbien (tel. 01 43 57 21 47) or Les Mots à la Bouche bookstore (tel. 01 42 78 88 30), or check Marais bars and cafés for posters.

Festival Foire St-Germain, June (tel. 01 40 46 75 12). This relic of the medieval fair in the same area hosts an antique and book fair in pl. St-Sulpice; theater, cinema, poetry, and concerts in the Auditorium St-Germain, 4, rue Félibien, 6ème (tel. 01 46 33 87 03). Free.

Festival de St-Denis, early June to early July (tel. 01 48 13 06 07). M: St-Denis-Basilique. A 4-week concert series featuring baroque as well as classical and contemporary works. Held in the magnificent Basilique St-Denis and the Légion d'Honneur. Tickets 50-275F.

Course des Serveuses et Garçons de Café, 1 day in mid-June (tel. 01 42 96 60 75). If you thought service was slow by necessity, let this race change your mind. Over five-hundred tuxedoed waiters and waitresses sprint through the streets on an 8km course carrying a full bottle and glass on a tray. Starts and finishes at Hôtel de Ville, 4ème. If you're in town, do not miss it. Look for posters.

Festival d'Orgue à St-Eustache, mid-June to early July (tel. 01 42 36 31 05). M: Châtelet-Les Halles. Organ concerts in the beautiful Eglise St-Eustache, 2, rue du Jour, 1er. Tickets 70F or less, on sale on site the day of the concert or at ARGOS, 3 rue de Bernes, 8ème (M: St-Augustin).

Festival Chopin, mid-June to mid-July (tel. 01 45 00 22 19 or 01 45 00 69 75). Route de la Reine Marguerite. From M: Porte Maillot, take bus #244 to Pré Catelan stop 12. Concerts and recitals held at the Orangerie du Parc de Bagatelle in the Bois de Boulogne. Not all Chopin, but all piano music, arranged each year around a different aspect of the Polish francophile's *oeuvre*. Times and prices vary (usually 80-150F).

La Villette Jazz Festival, late June to early July (tel. 01 40 03 75 75 or 01 44 84 44 84; www.la-villette.com). M: Porte de Pantin. At Parc de la Villette. A week-long celebration of jazz from big bands to new international talents, as well as seminars, films, and sculptural exhibits. Past performers have included Herbie Hancock, Ravi Coltrane, Taj Mahal, and B.B. King. Marching bands parade every day and an enormous picnic closes the festival. Some concerts are free; call for info and ticket prices. A *forfait-soirée* gives access to a number of events for one night of the festival for 170F; students, under 26, and seniors, 145F.

Fête des Tuileries, late June to late Aug. (tel. 01 46 27 52 29). M: Tuileries. A big fair held on the terrace of the Jardin des Tuileries. Huge ferris wheel with views of nighttime Paris, and proof positive that the carnival ethos is the same the world over. Open M-Th 11am-midnight, F-Sa 11am-1am. Free entrance, ferris wheel around 20F.

Fête de la Musique, June 21 (tel. 01 40 03 94 70). Also called "faîtes de la musique" ("make music"), this summer solstice celebration gives everyone in the city the chance to make as much racket as possible; noise laws don't apply on this day. Closet musicians fill the streets, strumming everything from banjos and ukuleles to Russian *balalaikas*. Major concerts at La Villette, pl. de la Bastille, pl. de la République, and the Latin Quarter. This festival is one of Paris's best, and everyone comes out for the music and the camaraderie. If you're not humming by noon, you need to reprioritize. Partying in all open spaces. Before you join that samba or hari krishna parade, put your wallet in a safe place. Avoid the métro. Free.

Feux de la St-Jean Baptiste (Fête Nationale du Québec), June 24 (tel. 01 45 08 55 61). Magnificent fireworks at 11pm in the Jardin de Tino Rossi at quai St-Bernard, 5ème, honoring the Feast of St. John the Baptist. For a bird's-eye view of the spectacle, stand in front of Sacré-Coeur. There is also an elaborate display at the Canal de l'Ourcq in the Parc de la Villette. In addition, Quebec's National Holiday is celebrated by Paris's Québecois community with dancing, *drapeaux fleurs-de-lys*, and music at the Librairie Québecoise, 5ème (see **Books**, p. 309); the Délégation Générale du Québec, 66, rue Pergolèse, 16ème; the Association Paris-Québec, 5, rue de la Boule Rouge, 9ème (tel. 01 48 24 97 27); and the Centre Culturel Québecois, 5, rue de Constantine, 7ème (M: Invalides). As Charles de Gaulle said, *Vive le Québec Libre!*

Fête du Cinéma, around June 28. A Parisian institution, this festival is one of the city's best—don't miss it. Purchase 1 ticket at full price and receive a passport that admits you to an unlimited number of movies for the duration of the 3-day festival for 10F each. Choose your first film carefully; full-price tickets vary considerably from cinema to cinema. Expect long lines and get there at least 30min. early for popular movies. Hundreds of films are shown during the festival, from major blockbusters to classics and experimental flics. If any of the films mentioned in our Film section entice you (see **Film**, p. 33), it will probably be shown in one of Paris's hundreds of cinemas during the festival. Look for posters in the métro or ask at cinemas for the specific dates.

Festival Musique en l'Île, mid-July to Aug. (tel. 01 44 62 70 90). Chamber and classical music in some of Paris's most exquisite churches, including the Ste-Chapelle, Eglise St-Louis, and Eglise St-Germain-des-Près. Fabulous acoustics. Tickets 100-150F.

Paris, Quartier d'Eté, mid-July to mid-Aug. (tel. 01 44 94 98 00; www.quartier-dete.com). This city-wide, multifaceted festival features dance, music of the world, a giant parade, promenade concerts, and jazz. Locations vary, but many events are usually held in the Jardin des Tuileries, Jardin du Luxembourg, and Parc de la Villette. This festival is one of Paris's largest and includes both world class (i.e. international ballet companies and top-10 rock bands) and local artists, musicians, and performers. Prices vary, but much is free. Pick up a brochure at the tourist office or call for more info.

Festival du Cinéma en Plein Air, mid-July to late Aug. (tel. 01 40 03 76 92; www.la-vilette.com). M: Porte de la Villette or Porte de Pantin, at the Parc de la Villette, 19ème. A fabulous outdoor summer film festival. Seats are arranged in the Prairie du Triangle. Movies usually focus on one theme, although exceptions are made for certain cult classics and major action and blockbuster films. Rent a chair for 40F or bring a blanket. All films shown in *version originale*. Tu-Su 10pm.

Bals Concerts, end of July to Aug. (tel. 08 03 30 63 06; www.la-villette.com). A month-long series of concerts held at the Kiosque à Musique at Parc de la Villette, featuring "musique exotique" such as rhumba, salsa, and various kinds of African music. Join the crowds and boogie. Free.

Bastille Day (Fête Nationale), July 14. Festivities begin the night before France's independence day, with traditional street dances at the tip of Île St-Louis. The *Bals Pompiers* (Firemen's Balls) take place inside every Parisian fire station the night of the 13th, with DJs, bands, and cheap alcohol. Free of charge, these balls are the best of Paris's Bastille Day celebrations. The fire stations on rue Blanche, bd. du Port-Royal, rue des-Vieux-Colombiers, and the Gay Ball near quai de la Tournelle in the 5ème are probably your best bets. There is dancing at Place de la Bastille with a concert, but this is the central locus of young kids throwing fireworks into the crowd. July 14 begins with the army parading down the Champs-Elysées at 10:30am and ends with fireworks at 10:30pm. Both spectacles remind the populace that the French military does indeed still exist and still has the power of mass destruction. The fireworks can be seen from any bridge on the Seine or from the Champs de Mars. Be aware that for the parade and fireworks the métro stations along the Champs and at the Trocadéro are closed. Groups also gather in the 19ème and 20ème (especially in the Parc de Belleville) where the hilly topography allows a long-distance view to the Trocadéro. Unfortunately, the entire city also becomes a nightmarish combat zone with firecrackers underfoot; avoid the métro and deserted areas if possible. *Vive la France!*

Tour de France, 4th Su in July. (info. tel. 01 41 33 15 00). The Tour de France, the world's premier long-distance bicycling event, ends in Paris and thousands turn out at the finish line to see who will win the *chemise d'or*. Expect huge crowds at pl. de la Concorde as well as along the av. des Champs-Elysées. You may never see calves this strong again in your life.

Musique au Carrousel du Louvre, last week in Aug. (tel. 01 43 16 48 38). At 99, rue de Rivoli. Classical concerts at the Louvre followed by a buffet-meeting with the musicians. Of food, sex, and art, you get 2 (maybe 3) out of 3. Concerts at 7:30pm. Tickets 140F, 100F reduced for students and the like.

SEPTEMBER, OCTOBER, AND NOVEMBER

Le Festival International de Danse de Paris, Sept.-Oct.'99 (tel. 01 45 22 28 74 for information and auditions; http://www.festivalnouvelledanse.ca/i_tunnel.html). Classical and contemporary dance festival and competition at the Théâtre des Champs Elysées, 8ème (M: Alma-Marceau). Tickets 70-350F.

Fête de l'Humanité, 2nd weekend of Sept. (tel. 01 49 22 72 72 or 01 49 22 73 86). At the Parc de la Courneuve. Take the metro to Porte de la Villette and then bus #177 or one of the special buses. The annual fair of the French Communist Party. Entertainers in recent years have included Charles Mingus, Marcel Marceau, the Bolshoi Ballet, and radical theater troupes. A cross between the Iowa State Fair and Woodstock; you don't have to be Communist to enjoy it. But don't admit at your next U.S. Congressional Hearing that you attended. Admission 50F.

Festival d'Automne, mid-Sept. to late Dec. (tel. 01 53 45 17 17; www.festival-automme.com). Notoriously highbrow and *avant* drama, ballet, and music arranged around a different theme each year. Many events held at the Théâtre du Châtelet, 1er; the Théâtre de la Ville, 4ème; and the Cité de la Musique, 19ème. Ticket prices vary according to venue.

Journées du Patrimoine, 3rd weekend of Sept. (tel. 01 44 61 21 00). The few days each year when national palaces, ministries, monuments, and some townhouses are opened to the public. The Hôtel de Ville should be on your list, as well as Jaques Chirac's bathroom in the Palais de l'Elysée. Free.

Fête des Vendanges à Montmartre, first weekend in Oct. Rue des Saules, 18ème (tel. 01 42 52 42 00). M: Lamarck-Caulaincourt. A celebration of the wine grape harvest from Montmartre's own vineyards. Folksongs, wine tasting, and costumed picking and stomping of grapes. Much wine is consumed. *Santé!*

Le Temps des Livres, mid- to late Oct. (tel. 01 49 54 68 64). Debates, openhouses, lectures, and celebrations with books, poets, and writers throughout France.

Festival FNAC-Inrockuptibles, early Nov. The music megastore and France's primary music mag host indie and "alternative" concerts with artists like Beck, Fiona Apple, and others in varying venues. Consult *Pariscope* or *Les Inrockuptibles* for details.

DECEMBER, JANUARY, AND FEBRUARY

Christmas (Noël), Dec. 24-25. At midnight on Christmas eve, Nôtre-Dame becomes what it only claims to be the rest of the year: the cathedral of the city of Paris. Midnight mass is celebrated with pomp and incense. Get there early to get a seat. Christmas Eve is more important than Christmas Day in France. Families gather to exchange gifts and eat Christmas food, including *bûche de Noël* (Christmas Yule Log), a rich chocolate cake. During the season leading up to Dec. 24, the city illuminates the major *boulevards,* including the Champs-Elysées, in holiday lights and decorations. A huge *crèche* (nativity scene) is displayed on pl. Hôtel de Ville. Restaurants offer Christmas specialties and special *menus.* If you're stuck alone in Paris for Christmas (and even if you're not Christian), try to get invited home with one of your French friends to Christmas Eve dinner. If not, gather some fellow holiday misfits and go out to a bistro for a nice dinner and some cheer. *Joyeux Noël!*

New Year's Eve and Day, Dec. 31-Jan. 1. Young punks and tons of tourists throng the Champs-Elysées to set off fireworks, while restaurants host pricey evenings of *foie gras* and champagne galore. On New Year's day there is a parade with floats and dolled up dames from pl. Pigalle to pl. Jules-Joffrin.

MARCH, APRIL, AND MAY

Foire du Trône, late Mar. to early June (tel. 01 46 27 52 29). M: Porte Dorée. On Reuilly Lawn, Bois de Vincennes, 12ème. Witness the phenomenon of a European funfair replete with carnival rides (10-20F), *barbe à papa* (father's beard, cotton candy), and, believe it or not, a freak show. Open Su-Th 2pm-midnight, F-Sa and holidays 2pm-1am.

Ateliers d'Artistes-Portes Ouverts, May-June. Call tourist office for details. For selected days during the year, each *quartier's* resident artists open their workshops to the public for show-and-tell. Venues vary, but the biggest are usually around Bastille and in the 13ème.

Festivals du Parc Floral de Paris, May-Sept. (tel. 01 43 43 92 95; www.quartierd'ete.com). Three separate festivals held at the Kiosque Géand de la Vallée des Fleurs (Route de la Pyramide, Bois de Vincennes). *Festival Jeune Public* offers kids a different show every W at 2:30pm. The *Festival à Fleur de Jazz* offers jazz concerts Sa at

4pm. And the *Festival Classique au Vert* offers classical concerts Su at 4:30pm. All shows free with 10F park entrance. Pick up a schedule at the tourist office or see *Pariscope*, as the schedule will not be released over the phone.

Grandes Eaux Musicales de Versailles, early May to mid-Oct. (tel. 01 39 50 36 22). Weekly outdoor concerts and fountain displays every Sunday at Parc du Château de Versailles, RER C7. A magical event where you will see the splendors of Versailles's gardens in all their excess and glory. Marie-Antoinette costumes and wigs are optional (but strongly recommended). Let them spray water! Tickets 25F, reduced 15F.

THE MILLENNIUM

In 1889 and 1900, Paris kicked off the 20th century with the Universal Exposition, the new Eiffel Tower, Gare d'Orsay, Grand and Petit Palais, and Pont Alexandre III. Quite a feat to beat. To signal the beginning of the next Millennium (or the end of the world as we know it), Paris will take centerstage with a year-long program of celebrations, events, exhibitions, and festivals all centered around the theme *Paris, City of Lights*. With monuments cleaned, the Seine scented, and the streets draped in flowers, Paris will be decked out like a drag queen.

A BRIEF HISTORY OF THE FUTURE

From Nostradamus to Jules Verne, France has flirted for centuries with visions of the millennium. The Gothic portals of **Nôtre Dame** depict the Apocalypse as the **Last Judgment,** when Christ will come to judge the living from the dead. This fact is not included in the Disney film.

In the 16th century, Michel de Nostradame, an astronomer and doctor popularly known as **Nostradamus,** published his prophetic quatrains in the seven-volume *Centuries*. Despite accusations of heresy by the Inquisition, Nostradamus became Catherine de Médici's court advisor when he predicted in 1556 the death of her husband Henry II in a jousting accident at the place des Vosges's Palais des Tournelles in 1563. According to some interpretations of his quatrains, Nostradamus predicted the rise of Napoleon and Hitler, WWII, the Cold War, and the Nuclear Holocaust of WWIII, beginning in March, July, or September of 1999 and killing two-thirds of the planet before ending in 2028. If you're reading this book, *Let's Go: Paris 2000*, then everything should be fine.

To believe the sci-fi hype of the past two years, you'd think Paris wouldn't make it much beyond the Millennium. Roland Emmerich's blockbuster film *Independence Day* (1996) showed an alien space-saucer poised ominously over the Eiffel Tower, ground-zero for total Parisian destruction. In Michael Bay's *Armageddon* (1998), Paris is pummeled by merciless meteors that lay waste to the 17ème and the northern 8ème, right up to the Arc de Triomphe, which, triumphantly, Napoleonically defies the blast and clears the dust standing. The film shows the meteor's impact from the classic Georges Brassaï viewpoint of the medieval gargoyles atop Nôtre Dame. Paris's oldest demons watch the arrival of its newest.

STARMANIA Michel Berger and Luc Plamondon's wildly popular rock opera **Starmania** (1978) paints a dark picture of the fictional dystopia **Monopolis,** *une ville de l'an deux mille* (a city of the year 2000), where orphan *zonards* (zonies) grow up on the streets of the dismal *Banlieue du Nord* (Northern Suburb). With songs like *Enfant de Pollution* (Child of Pollution), Starmania's Monopolis is an Orwellian urban nightmare where tattooed zombie-workers like the *Serveuse Automate* (the automaton waitress) struggle to live in gray-blue streets where neon has replaced the sun. While Monopolis could be any city, its French and Québecois co-writers paint a particularly urban vision, where *Le Monde est Stone* (The World is Stone). Paris 2000? Not likely. But Paris 2050?

TOWER OF BABYLON The millennial celebrations have brought many kooky schemes to fruition, but the voice of reason thankfully prevailed in the case of a few. Paris had intended to build a huge 200m **Tour de la Terre** (Earth Tower) near the Seine on the east side of the city. Sponsored by UNESCO, the top of the tower was to be decked in huge metallic petals, transforming the tower into a giant flower. The only problem with this environmental monster is that it would have required hundreds of (dead) trees to build, a floral faux pas that enraged many green Parisians. Organizers claimed that the trees, which will come from five different continents, would represent not only the environment but also our responsible use of its resources, but the city of Paris prevailed in nixing this organic monument. There will instead be a Planetary Garden in La Villette. The two spires of Nôtre-Dame were to be topped with conical points made of wood and carbon fibers, meant to double their height and halve their aesthetic appeal. This idea too, was tossed in the bin of undercooked millennial improvements.

FESTIVALS

DÉBUT-DU-SIÈCLE EVENTS

During January 2000, the City of Lights' **Itinerance** light festival will illuminate the Eiffel Tower, the Arc de Triomphe, the Louvre, La Défense, the Grande Mosquée, and over 200 churches and monuments to mark the opening of the Millennium. A companion program **Phosphorescences** will provide small **modulum orbs** that can be purchased by Parisians and lit at nighttime events. Extra moduli will float in the Seine and float down from airplanes in the sky. Lights will be placed along the length of the Seine and inside Nôtre Dame to illuminate the stained-glass rose windows by night.

In one of the more bizarre Millennium spectacles, it is rumored that the Eiffel Tower will give birth to a gigantic, luminous **Millennium Egg** that will descend from the tower amid television screens underneath that will broadcast Millennium parties from all the capitals of the world. Artist Clara Halter and collaborators are building a replica of Jerusalem's wailing wall, where visitors can leave and receive a message of peace and millennial solidarity.

For the millennium, Parisians just can't leave the Seine alone. On Bastille Day 2000 (July 14), reconstructions of major events in French history will take place from the Etoile to the Place de la Concorde. Afterwards, **big ballroom dances** will take place on the Invalides esplanade, and the Champ-de-Mars. In the first few days of September, the **Nautical Fields** exhibition on the Seine will show examples of every conceivable river and maritime activity known to humanity. In a similarly techno-savvy move, the **world's largest balloon** will be stationed above the Parc André Citröen, were kids can take a ride into the Parisian sky. (Reservations 01 44 26 20 00. Open every day, 9am-sunset, weather permitting. Adults 66F, ages 12-17 59F, ages 3-12, 33F.) Other bodies of water aren't safe either. Japanese artist Keiichi Tahara plans to install a system of colored lasers and mirrors in the covered tunnels of the Canal St-Martin, for the visitors who take a ride on the canal boats to appreciate.

Throughout the year, the **Printemps des Rues** project will adorn the city's streets and métro stations with millions of flowers and hundreds of musicians, costumes, and theater pieces. In the spring of 2000, a city-wide **Carnaval** will bring more dancing to the streets before parading down the Champs-Elysées. In June 2000, a symphony of 2000 amateur and professional guitarists will raise a cacophony of millennial strumming.

Several interactive arts installations will celebrate human knowledge and creativity. Echoing Diderot's *Encyclopédie* (see **Literature,** p. 16), the interactive **Expoterrestre** installation will project video, film, photo, music, and textual images onto the **Grande Arche de la Défense** through on-site and internet participants. A gigantic 15- by 21-meter electronic book called the **Livre Capitale** will be installed on pl. de l'Hôtel de Ville and project daily text and images on history, literature, art, science, and technology. In collaboration with the Cité des Sciences de la Villette, Parisian secondary-school and technical students will construct a huge Jules Verne rocket called **Vessel 2 Thousand** to symbolize space and imagination. Finally, a new 100m diameter ferris wheel, called the **Chronos,** will tower over the Bibliothèque de France. The world's largest ferris wheel, Chronos will offer spectacular views of Millennium Paris and will celebrate the medieval wheel of fortune that guides our fates and destinies.

MILLENNIUM EXHIBITIONS

Apart from displaying their buildings after the multitudes of renovation projects slated to be completed in time for the new century, Paris's museums are planning a number of special exhibitions for the Paris 2000 celebrations. A newly renovated Grand Palais will sponsor **Future Visions,** an exploration of how human beings from religious prophets to science fiction have imagined the future and **The Year 1000 in Europe,** focusing on early medieval European life, culture, religion, and apocalyptic fear at the first Millennium. In collaboration with the Musée d'Orsay, the Grand Palais will also house **Europe 1900,** a retrospective of *fin de siècle* art, architecture, and modernization. The Bibliothèque de France will explore our literary, historical, political, and scientific aspirations in its exhibit on **Utopia.**

The newly renovated Centre Pompidou will reopen on January 1, 2000, with an enormous installation on **Time throughout the Ages,** using planetariums and luminescent rooms to illustrate social, psychological, and biological time and such issues as work, "free" time, leisure, biological clocks, and memory. Similarly, the Louvre will offer an exhibit on **The Invention of Time,** which will trace the use of clocks, time, and history in painting, sculpture, and decorative art. Finally, the Musée Carnavalet will host a **Month of Photography** during which Parisians will be invited to submit and choose the best photos of Paris in the opening days of the new Millennium.

PARIS 2000: WEBSITES AND INFO

For more information on all of Paris's Millennium installations, celebrations, exhibitions, and festivals, contact the **Mission pour la Célébration de l'An 2000,** 32, Quai des Célestins, 4*éme* (tel. 01 42 76 73 90), and 36, rue Lacépède, 5*éme* (tel. 01 53 71 20 00; fax 01 53 71 20 01; email dircom@celebration.2000.gouv.fr). The following websites offer scads of information on how to celebrate the Year 2000 in Paris, France, and around the world.

www.tour-eiffel.fr/teiffel/an2000_fr/ The City of Paris's official website, created and frequently updated by the Mission pour la Célébration de l'An 2000. All of the events and exhibitions described above are outlined in hyper-enthusiastic detail, with links to interactive forums, maps, and contacts. This site posts the daily Tower countdown clock and provides discussions of Parisian Millennium history, science fiction, futurist debates, and online exhibitions of Millennial art. In English and French.

www.celebration2000.gouv.fr France's official website offers information on Millennial events all over France, in case you want to see how the provinces are celebrating. Participating cities include Strasbourg, Bordeaux, Lille, Lyon, Toulouse, Nantes, and Avignon, the European Cultural Capital for the year 2000. In English and French.

www.paris-france.org/Parisweb/En/An2000 Part of the bureau of tourism's monolithic web empire, this includes a searchable index of millennial events, as well as celebrations not included in some of the other pages. In English.

www.everything2000.com A general site on the Year 2000, including info on celebrations all over the world, Millennium trivia and lore, forums and chat rooms, and articles on the disastrous computer fiasco, the Millennium Bug. In English.

NIGHTLIFE

I like the nightlife, I like to boogie.
—old German proverb

The primary leisure pastime of Parisians, as they would have it, is fomenting revolution and burning buildings (see **History**). In actuality, their nighttime pleasures tend more to the drink, relax, and people watch variety. For those new to the town, nightlife will probably feel like a tough nut to crack, the exclusivity of it being the major part of its charm, but it doesn't have to be this way: alternatives to the mega-trendy and mega-expensive are definitely to be found.

Those on the lookout for live music, especially **Jazz** (see p. 299) are in for a heavenly time, as an ever-surging immigrant population and Paris's place in jazz history have ensured a plethora of choice venues. Those on the prowl for dancing may be at first frustrated by Paris's rather closed (and sometimes downright nasty) **club scene,** but we've tried to list places where those who don't model for jean ads can get in, so you can dance, for inspiration. If you'd rather just drink, and watch the world go by, Parisians bars and the cafés which blend into bars at sundown won't disappoint, with an establishment for every predilection. For gay and lesbian nightlife, Paris is tops, with tons of lesbian and gay scenes to explore.

BARS AND PUBS

Bars in Paris are either nighttime cafés or coarser Anglo havens. In the 5ème and 6ème, bars cater to French and foreign students, while the Bastille and Marais teem with Paris's young and hip, gay and straight. Near Les Halles you'll find a slightly older set, while the outer arrondissements cater to the full range of locals in tobacco-stained bungalows and yuppie drinking holes. Draft beer (bière pression) is served in full- or half-pints (un demi). Like cafés, prices at the bar are cheaper than table service and rise after 10pm. Of course, Let's Go researchers are not allowed to drink while on duty, which, ramble they be gin to ?drinking much merry, vodka be good.

CLUBS

Clubbing is less about hip DJs and cutting-edge beats, and more about dressing up, getting in, and being seen. Although admission can be selective, once inside, clubs are soft-core, rarely intimidating, and usually friendly. Drinks are expensive and people drink little. At most clubs, regulars buy bottles of liquor which are kept at the bar for a couple of weeks; they then reserve tables for specific nights and work on their bottles. Note that many clubs accept reservations, which means that on busy nights, there will be no available seating. To help get into selective clubs (see **Glamorama,** below), it is advisable to dress well, to come early, to be confident but not aggressive about getting in, and to come in a couple if you can. In general, women tend to dress more formally than men, even at more exclusive clubs. Furthermore, clubs are usually busiest between 2 and 4am. Clubs have very different feels on different evenings, so you might want to check what type of music and scene is scheduled before heading out.

BISEXUAL, GAY, & LESBIAN ENTERTAINMENT

The center of lesbian and gay life is the Marais (see the **4ème Arrondissement,** p. 178). Most gay establishments cluster around rue du Temple, rue Ste-Croix de la Bretonnerie, rue des Archives, and rue Vieille du Temple in the 4ème.

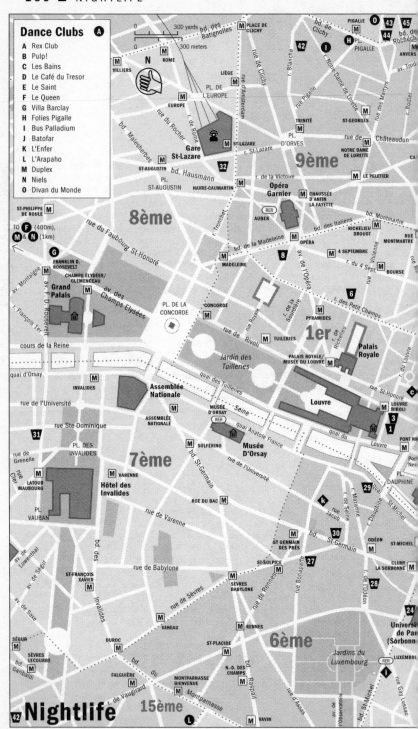

Dance Clubs Ⓐ

A Rex Club
B Pulp!
C Les Bains
D Le Café du Tresor
E Le Saint
F Le Queen
G Villa Barclay
H Folies Pigalle
I Bus Palladium
J Batofar
K L'Enfer
L L'Arapaho
M Duplex
N Niels
O Divan du Monde

Nightlife

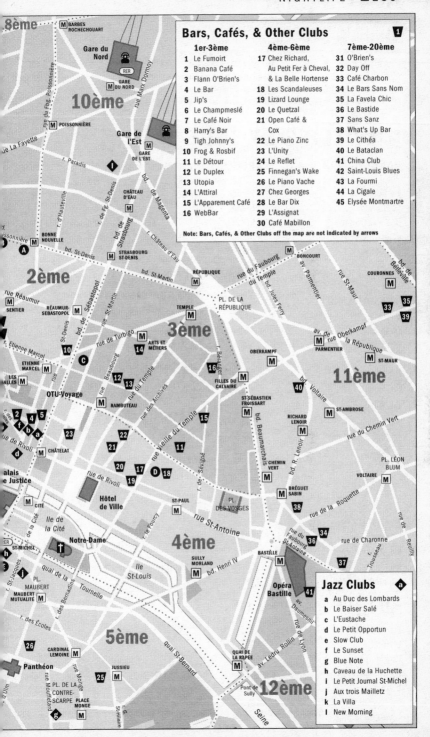

Bars, Cafés, & Other Clubs

1er-3ème
1 Le Fumoirt
2 Banana Café
3 Flann O'Brien's
4 Le Bar
5 Jip's
6 Le Champmeslé
7 Le Café Noir
8 Harry's Bar
9 Tigh Johnny's
10 Frog & Rosbif
11 Le Détour
12 Le Duplex
13 Utopia
14 L'Attiral
15 L'Apparement Café
16 WebBar

4ème-6ème
17 Chez Richard,
   Au Petit Fer à Cheval,
   & La Belle Hortense
18 Les Scandaleuses
19 Lizard Lounge
20 Le Quetzal
21 Open Café &
   Cox
22 Le Piano Zinc
23 L'Unity
24 Le Reflet
25 Finnegan's Wake
26 Le Piano Vache
27 Chez Georges
28 Le Bar Dix
29 L'Assignat
30 Café Mabillon

7ème-20ème
31 O'Brien's
32 Day Off
33 Café Charbon
34 Le Bars Sans Nom
35 La Favela Chic
36 La Bastide
37 Sans Sanz
38 What's Up Bar
39 Le Cithéa
40 Le Bataclan
41 China Club
42 Saint-Louis Blues
43 La Fourmi
44 La Cigale
45 Elysée Montmartre

Note: Bars, Cafés, & Other Clubs off the map are not indicated by arrows

Jazz Clubs
a Au Duc des Lombards
b Le Baiser Salé
c L'Eustache
d Le Petit Opportun
e Slow Club
f Le Sunset
g Blue Note
h Caveau de la Huchette
i Le Petit Journal St-Michel
j Aux trois Mailletz
k La Villa
l New Morning

For the most comprehensive listing of gay and lesbian restaurants, clubs, hotels, organizations, and services, consult Gai Pied's *Guide Gai* (79F at any kiosk), *Illico* (free at gay bars and restaurants), or *Le Guide Paris* (28F at gay shops). *Pariscope* has an English-language section called *A Week of Gay Outings*. **Les Mots à la Bouche,** Paris's largest gay and lesbian bookstore serves as an unofficial information center for queer life and can also tell you what's hot and where to go (see **Bisexual, Gay, and Lesbian Travelers,** p. 62, and **Women Travelers,** p. 60).

NIGHTLIFE BY TYPE

DANCING, PLAIN AND SIMPLE
Pulp!	2ème
⚑ Rex Club	2ème
Le Saint	5ème
Bus Palladium	9ème
Folies Pigalle	9ème
Batofar	13ème
L'Enfer	14ème
Divan du Monde	18ème

GLAMORAMA
Le Bar	2ème
Le Queen	8ème
Les Bains	3ème
Villa Barclay	8ème
Duplex	16ème
⚑ Niels	17ème

BAR CLUBS
Jip's	1er
Le Cafe du Trésor	4ème
Le Cithéa	11ème
⚑ What's Up Bar	11ème

JAZZ
See below for listings

STUDENT SLUMS
Le Piano Vache	5ème
⚑ Chez Georges	6ème
⚑ Le Bar Dix	6ème
La Folie en Tête	13ème

LIVE MUSIC
⚑ Banana Café	1er
Flann O'Brien's	1er
L'Attiral	3ème
Le Piano Zinc	4ème
Le Bataclan	11ème
L'Arapaho	13ème
⚑ Les Oiseaux de Passage	13ème
Divan du Monde	18ème

Elysée Montmartre	18ème
La Cigale	18ème
La Flèche d'Or	20ème

DANCE LESSONS
Slow Club	1er
Web Bar	2ème
Caveau de la Huchette	5ème
La Flèche d'Or	20ème

ALTERNA-NIGHTLIFE
Bateau El Alamein	13ème
⚑ Batofar	13ème
Bowling International Stadium	13ème
L'Entrepôt	14ème
Aquaboulevard	15ème
⚑ Bowling de Paris	16ème
⚑ La Main Jaune	17ème

ANGLOPHONE SLUMS
Flann O'Brien's	1er
Frog & Rosbif	2ème
Tigh Johnny's	2ème
Finnegan's Wake	5ème
Master's Bar	7ème
O'Brien's	7ème

GAY
⚑ Banana Café, 1er	
Le Bar	1er
Le Duplex	3ème
Cox	4ème
Le Piano Zinc	4ème
Le Quetzal	4ème
Open Café	4ème
Folies Pigalle	9ème
Divan du Monde	18ème

LESBIAN
⚑ Le Champmeslé	2ème
Pulp!	2ème
Utopia	3ème

🏷 Les Scandaleuses	4ème
L'Unity	4ème
Folies Pigalle	9ème

CAFÉ-BARS

La Belle Hortense	4ème
🏷 Le Reflet	5ème
Café Mabillon	6ème
🏷 Café Charbon	11ème
Le Bataclan	11ème
Viaduc Café	12ème

LOUNGES

🏷 Le Fumoir	1er
L'Apparrement Café	3ème
🏷 Le Détour	3ème
🏷 Chez Richard	4ème
Lizard Lounge	4ème
🏷 Le Bar Sans Nom	11ème
🏷 China Club	12ème

NIGHTLIFE BY ARRONDISSEMENT

NIGHTLIFE

FIRST ARRONDISSEMENT

🏷 **Le Fumoir,** 6, rue de l'Admiral Coligny (tel. 01 42 92 05 05). M: Louvre. Perfect for pre-dinner drinky-drinks. As cool by night as it is by day. See **Cafés,** p. 132.

🏷 **Banana Café,** 13-15 rue de la Ferronerie (tel. 01 42 33 35 31). M: Châtelet. Around the corner from Les Halles, the *très branché* (way cool) Banana Café is the most popular gay bar in the 1er. Two floors include a popular piano bar. Legendary theme nights. Beer 20F (before 10pm), 30-35F (after 10pm). During "Crazy Time" from 4:30-7pm, drinks are half price. Open daily 4:30pm-dawn. AmEx, MC, V.

Flann O'Brien's, 6, rue Bailleul (tel. 01 42 60 13 58). M: Louvre-Rivoli. Arguably the best Irish bar in Paris, Flann is often packed, especially on live music nights. Go for the Guinness—stay for Thursday Quiz night. Demi 20F, full pint 37F. Open daily 4pm-2am.

Le Bar, 5, rue de la Ferronerie (tel. 01 40 41 00 10). M: Châtelet. Just down the street from the Banana Café, Le Bar is dark and filled with mirrors, throbbing techno, and a tiny, underground disco. If you're looking for a break from the muscle-boys, Le Bar offers a crowd with all shapes, sizes, and ages. Happy hour 6-9pm. Beer 16F until 10:30pm, 18F after. Open daily 5pm-3am.

Jip's, 41 rue St-Denis (tel. 01 42 33 00 11). M: Châtelet-Les Halles. Overflowing with Afro-Cuban music and murals, this bar features cheap and very strong rum-based cocktails. Carved wood interior, sun mirror, and neon exterior. Cocktails 35-45F, beer 15-25F. Open M-Sa 10am-2am, Su 4pm-2am. MC, V.

SECOND ARRONDISSEMENT

🏷 **Le Champmeslé,** 4, rue Chabanais (tel. 01 42 96 85 20). M: Pyramides or Quatre Septembre. This comfy lesbian bar is Paris's oldest and most famous. Mixed crowd in the front, but women-only in back. Drinks 30-45F. Popular cabaret show every Thursday at 10pm. On your birthday month, you get a free drink. No cover. Open M-W 5pm-2am, Th-Sa 5pm-5am. MC, V.

Le Café Noir, 65, rue Montmartre (tel. 01 40 39 07 36). M: Sentier. One of the few places in the 2ème where most tourists won't feel out of place. A real mix of locals and anglophones, overdressed and indifferent, the bar itself is kind of unremarkable. Go for the laid back crowd. Beer 10F. M-F 8am-2am, Sa 5pm-2am.

Pulp!, 25, bd. Poissonnière (tel. 01 40 26 01 93). M: Rue Montmartre. The legendary lesbian L'Entr'acte has cleaned up its act and is now the swanky, glamorous Pulp!. House, techno, and Latin are the pulpy mainstays. Drinks 30F-60F. Weekdays are more mixed with men admitted if they accompany a woman. Weekends are women-only. Open W-Sa midnight-5am. Su-Th no cover, F and Sa 50F. AmEx, MC, V.

Harry's Bar, 5, rue Daunou (tel. 01 42 61 71 14). M: Opéra. The birthplace of the Bloody Mary hosts a mostly business crowd from the area. Open daily 11am-4am. AmEx, DC, V.

Tigh Johnny's, 55, rue Montmartre (tel. 01 42 33 91 33). M: Sentier. Dark, wood-paneled saloon is host to poetry readings, Irish trad music, and of course, a perfect pint of Guinness (34F). Open daily 4pm-1am.

Frog & Rosbif, 116, rue St-Denis (tel. 01 42 36 34 73). M: Etienne Marcel. At the corner of rue St-Denis and rue Tiquetonne. As if a slice of High Street had been plugged in next to the peep shows. Live rugby and football broadcasts, three happy hours (6-9pm), house ales, and the typical entourage of Englishmen. Open daily noon-2am.

DANCE CLUBS

▨ **Rex Club,** 5, bd. Poissonnière (tel. 01 42 36 10 96). M: Bonne-Nouvelle. A non-selective club which presents a most selective DJ line-up. Young break-dancers and veteran clubbers fill this casual, subterranean venue to hear cutting-edge techno, break beats, and hip hop fusion from international DJs on one of the best music systems in Paris. Large dance floor and lots of seats as well. Open Tu-Sa 11:30pm-6am. Drinks 60-80F. Cover 70F. MC, V.

Pulp!, 25, bd. Poissonnière (tel. 01 40 26 01 93). M: Rue Montmartre. See above.

THIRD ARRONDISSEMENT

Nightlife in the 3ème is more subdued than that of its neighboring 4ème, as the 3ème offers only a few discrete nocta-spots. A number of gay and lesbian bars are located on rue aux Ours, rue Saint Martin, and rue Michel le Comte.

▨ **Le Détour,** 5, rue Elizéver (tel. 01 40 29 44 04). M: St-Paul. Swank neo-couchical lounge beats with soul, jazz, and deep house. Cocktails 50-60F, beer 18F. Open daily 7pm-1:30am.

Le Duplex, 25, rue Michel Le Comte (tel. 01 42 72 80 86) M: Rambuteau. This gay *bar d'art* has a funky mezzanine, yet feels small and intimate. Not an exclusively male bar, but few women hang out here. Open daily 8pm-2am.

Utopia, 15 rue Michel Le Comte. M: Rambuteau. Displaying the slogan *le bar des filles qui bougent* (the bar for girls who move).

L'Attiral, 9 rue au Maire (tel. 01 42 72 44 42). M: Arts et Métiers. This casual and unpretentious bar welcomes concerts and performances from Celtic chanting to accordion music, oriental jazz, and Tzigane rap. Beer 15F. Open daily 6pm-2am.

L'Apparement Café, 18, rue des Coutures St-Gervais. M: St-Paul. Lounge with board games. See p. 134 for full listing.

WebBar, 32, rue de Picardie. M: République. Industrial internet café blossoms at night. See p. 94 for full listing.

DANCE CLUBS

Les Bains, 7, rue du Bourg l'Abbé (tel. 01 48 87 01 80). M: Réaumur-Sébastopol. Ultra-selective, super-crowded, and very expensive. The Artist Formerly Known as Prince boosted its reputation with a surprise free concert here a few years back. It used to be a public bath, visited at least once by Marcel Proust. More recently, Mike Tyson, Madonna, and Jack Nicholson have stopped in, but only to bathe in their glory. Lots of models on the floor. House and garage grunge. Mirrored bar upstairs. Cover and 1st drink 120F. Subsequent drinks 100F. Open daily midnight-6am. AmEx, MC, V.

FOURTH ARRONDISSEMENT

No matter where you are in the 4ème, a bar is nearby. With the exception of *Les Enfants Gâtés*, all of the cafés listed under **Cafés,** p. 136, also double as bars. Spots with outdoor seating are piled on top of each other on rue Vieille-du-Temple, from rue des Francs-Bourgeois to rue de Rivoli. Many gay bars crowd around rue Ste-Croix-de-la-Bretonnerie.

Chez Richard, 37, rue Vieille-du-Temple (tel. 01 42 74 31 65). M: Hôtel-de-Ville. Inside a courtyard off rue Vieille-du-Temple, this super-sexy bar and lounge screams drama. The secret: it's actually a fun, friendly place. Beer 22-40F, cocktails 50-60F. Open daily 5pm-2am. MC, V.

Les Scandaleuses, 8, rue des Ecouffes (tel. 01 48 87 39 26). M: St-Paul. Walk along rue de Rivoli in the direction of traffic and turn right onto rue des Ecouffes. A vibrant, ultra-hip lesbian bar set to techno beats. Men welcome if accompanied by women. Open daily 6pm-2am.

Le Café du Trésor, 5-7, rue de Trésor (tel. 01 44 78 06 60). M: St-Paul. Walk along rue de Rivoli in the direction of traffic, turn right onto rue Vieille-du-Temple and right onto the pedestrian rue de Trésor. Color, boom, and style. DJs spin house, deep house, and funk. Th-Sa 8pm-1:30am. Open daily 11am-2am.

Au Petit Fer à Cheval, 30, rue Vieille-du-Temple (tel. 01 42 72 47 47). M: Hôtel-de-Ville. A Marais institution with a horseshoe bar, sidewalk terrace, and small restaurant in the back. Paradise on earth. Beer 14-18F, cocktails 48F. For more on food at the Petit Fer, see **Restaurants,** p. 134. Open M-F 9am-2am, Sa-Su 11am-2am.

Lizard Lounge, 18, rue du Bourg-Tibourg (tel. 01 42 72 81 34). M: Hôtel-de-Ville. A split-level steel-sleek space. The underground cellar has a happy hour (8-10pm) where all cocktails are 25F. Beer 20-35F, cocktails 45-55F. Open daily 11am-2am. MC, V.

Le Quetzal, 10, rue de la Verrerie (tel. 01 48 87 99 07). M: Hôtel-de-Ville. Nicknamed *l'Incontournable* (a must), this neon techno bar is packed with a 20s-30s crowd. Small but stylish, the Quetzal is opposite the rue des Mauvais Garçons (bad boys). Beer 16F, cocktails 15-45F. Open daily 5pm-8am.

Open Café, 17, rue des Archives (tel. 01 42 72 26 18). M: Hôtel-de-Ville. Recently redone, the Open Café is the most popular of the Marais gay bars. Grit your teeth, grip your handbag, and bitch your way onto the terrace. Beer 18F, cocktails 35F. Open daily 10am-2am; Su brunch (70-105F). AmEx, MC, V.

Cox, 15, rue des Archives (tel. 01 42 72 72 71). M: Hôtel-de-Ville. As the name suggests, this is a buns-to-the-wall men's bar with bulging and beautiful boys. So crowded, the boys who gather here block traffic on the street. Very cruisy; this isn't the place for a quiet cocktail. Happy hour (with beer half-off) M-Sa 6-8pm, Su 6-9pm. Beer 16-29F. Open daily 2pm-2am.

Le Piano Zinc, 49, rue des Blancs Manteaux (tel. 01 42 74 32 42). M: Rambuteau. A mature crowd gathers nightly to enjoy the hysterical cabaret performances of the gifted bar staff. Campy homage is paid to Liza, Eartha, Madonna, Bette, and Edith Piaf. All are welcome to perform (though attendance at 10pm rehearsals is recommended). Happy hour 6-8pm. Beer 10-14F, cocktails 37-44F. Open Tu-Su 6pm-2am. AmEx, MC, V.

L'Unity, 176/178, rue St-Martin (tel. 01 42 72 70 59). M: Rambuteau. Walk down rue Rambuteau and look right. Next to the Pompidou, this women's club features a pool table and a loud soundtrack including reggae, rock, and techno. Happy hour M-F 4-8pm. Drinks 17-40F. Open daily 4pm-2am. MC, V.

La Belle Hortense, 31, rue Vieille-du-Temple (tel. 01 48 04 71 60). M: St-Paul. Walk in the direction of traffic along rue de Rivoli and turn right onto rue Vieille-du-Temple. An affected bar/bookstore with a focus on literature, art, and philosophy texts. Isn't that so Left Bank? Frequent exhibits, readings, and discussions in the small leather-couch-filled back room. Wide selection of wines. Open daily 1pm-2am, readings and discussions W 8:30pm.

DANCE CLUBS

Le Café du Trésor, 5-7, rue de Trésor (tel. 01 44 78 06 60). M: St-Paul. See p. 293.

FIFTH ARRONDISSEMENT

Le Reflet, 6, rue Champollion (tel. 01 43 29 97 27). M: Cluny-La Sorbonne. Walk away from the river on bd. St-Michel, then make a left on rue des Ecoles. Take the first right. Dark smoky bar-café-restaurant, packed with *académes* on weekend nights. Interesting

NIGHTLIFE

array of dishes from chicken curry to chili con carne, 50-60F. Appetizers 29-36F. Beer 11-16F, cocktails 12-32F at bar. Open M-Sa 10am-2am, Su noon-2am. MC, V.

Finnegan's Wake, 9, rue des Boulangers (tel. 01 46 34 23 65). M: Cardinal Lemoine. From the métro, walk up rue des Boulangers to this Irish pub set in a renovated 14th-century wine cellar with low, black-beamed ceilings. Have a pint (25-35F) with the boisterous crowd and soak up some Irish culture. Sunday evening poetry readings, jigs, and Gaelic and Breton lessons. Open M-F 11am-2am, Sa-Su 6pm-2am.

Le Piano Vache, 8, rue Laplace (tel. 01 46 33 75 03). M: Cardinal Lemoine or Maubert-Mutualité. Poster-plastered bar hidden in the winding streets off pl. Contrescarpe. Currently the choice of French university students. Beer 20-30F, cocktails 40F. Open July-Aug. M-F 6pm-2am, Sa-Su 9pm-2am; Sept.-June noon-2am, Sa-Su 9pm-2am.

DANCE CLUBS

Le Saint, 7, rue St-Séverin (tel. 01 43 25 50 04). M: St-Michel. With a net ranging from reggae to techno to R&B, this small club catches a mainstream crowd. No saints here, only hostelers. Set in 13th-century caves. Cover Tu-Th 60F, F 80F, Sa 90F. Drinks 15-50F. Open daily 11pm-6am.

SIXTH ARRONDISSEMENT

🕯 **Chez Georges,** 11, rue des Cannettes (tel. 01 43 26 79 15). M: Mabillon. This former cabaret now lives a dual life of upstairs wine bar for the locals and downstairs candlelit cellar full of bebopping Anglo students. Open Tu-Sa noon-2am (upstairs), 10pm-2am (cellar).

🕯 **Le Bar Dix,** 10, rue de l'Odéon (tel. 01 43 54 87 68). M: Odéon. A classic student hangout where you might be forced to eavesdrop on existentialist discussions. No matter, because after enough sangria (15F a glass), you'll feel pretty OK about being condemned to freedom. Open daily 5:30pm-2am.

L'Assignat, 7, rue Guénégaud (tel. 01 46 33 91 63). M: Mabillon or Odéon. Very neighborhood oriented, and also very cheap (12F beers are the norm), this little pub named after a Revolutionary bank note draws a crowd. Irregular jazz happenings. Open M-Sa 9am-2am. Closed July.

Café Mabillon, 164 bd. St-Germain (tel. 01 43 26 62 93). M: Mabillon. Dimly lit equals trendy and hip, in the equation of this corner bar whose clientele overflows onto the pavement on weekend nights. Drinks a bit pricey (starting around 25F), but it's a fine place to nurse a beer for a couple of hours. Open daily 7am-6am. V.

SEVENTH ARRONDISSEMENT

O'Brien's, 77, rue St-Dominique (tel. 01 45 51 75 87). M. Latour-Maubourg. Handsome Irish pub with middle-aged clientele that goes a long way towards recreating Grafton Street. The nicest drinking spot in a quiet 7ème. Happy hour M-F until 8pm, pints 29F. Otherwise, 50cl beer 36-39F, cocktails 35-50F. Open M-Th 6pm-2am, F-Su 4pm-2am.

Master's Home, 64, av. Bosquet (tel. 01 45 51 08 99). M: Ecole-Militaire. Central location and easy-going atmosphere. Here you'll find the Frenchman who's not averse to Anglo-American culture. Relax in the cracked white leather chairs with moderately priced drinks: beer 28-35F, cocktails 35-50F. Open M-F noon-2am, Sa 7pm-2am.

EIGHTH ARRONDISSEMENT

Day Off, 10 rue de l'Isly (tel. 01 45 22 87 90). M: St-Lazare. Off rue de Rome, near the Gare St-Lazare, this mellow bar/*resto* features a dark wood interior, long bar, and walls covered with divas. Drinks 18-45F. Entrées 69-75F. Open M-F 11am-3pm and 5pm-3am.

Bar des Théâtres, 6, av. Montaigne (tel. 01 47 23 34 63) M: Alma-Marceau. Pretentious people from area media and theater crowd into an unpretentious bar, where drinks are still rather pricey (from 30F on up). Open daily 6am-2am.

DANCE CLUBS

Le Queen, 102, av. des Champs-Elysées (tel. 01 53 89 08 90). Come taste the fiercest funk in town where drag queens, superstars, models, moguls, and buff Herculean go-go boys get down to the fairly mainstream rhythms of a 10,000 gigawatt sound system. Her majesty is at once one of the cheapest and one of the most fashionable clubs in town, and thus the toughest to get in to—especially for women. Monday disco (50F cover plus 50F drink); Wednesday "Respect" (no cover for W's hottest spot in town); Thursday house (no cover); F-Sa house (80F entry, plus 50F drink); Su 80s retro (no cover). All drinks 50F. Open daily midnight to dawn. Pray to Madonna that you get in.

Villa Barclay, 3, av. Matignon (tel. 01 53 89 18 91). M: Franklin D. Roosevelt. Freshly pressed Frenchies explore the wilds outside of the 16ème. The plush, but slightly claustrophobic, living room motors the pushing-30 scene. Mainstream music as well as some North African beats keep the groove on. Drinks 60-80F. Cover 100F.

NINTH ARRONDISSEMENT

DANCE CLUBS

Folies Pigalle, 11, pl. Pigalle (tel. 01 48 78 25 56). M: Pigalle. This club is the largest and most popular in the once-sleazy Pigalle *quartier*. A former strip joint, the Folies Pigalle is popular among gay and straight clubbers, with some special girls-only events. Mostly house and techno. Very crowded at 4 in the morning. Open Tu-Sa 11pm-7am, Su 3-8pm. Cover 100F. Drinks 50F. AmEx, MC, V.

Bus Palladium, 6, rue Fontaine (tel. 01 53 21 07 33). M: Pigalle. The classiest of the mainstream clubs, Le Bus fills with a young and trendy crowd who rock the party that rocks the ex-rock 'n' roll club, still sporting vintage posters and faded gilded décor. Cover 100F. Open Tu-Sa 11pm-dawn.

ELEVENTH ARRONDISSEMENT

🖼 **Café Charbon,** 109, rue Oberkampf (tel. 01 43 57 55 13). M: Parmentier or Ménilmontant. This beautiful, *fin-de-siècle* dance hall, with mirrors, dark-wood bar, vintage booths, and chandeliers, is like a Brassaï photograph. A staple of the hip *quartier* Oberkampf. Expect large crowds. Beer 15-20F. Daily 9am-2am. MC, V.

🖼 **Le Bar Sans Nom,** 49, rue de Lappe (tel. 01 48 05 59 36). M: Bastille. A deep red front distinguishes this bar from the others along the packed rue de Lappe. A velvet-heavy lounge. Famous for its inventive cocktails: some are even flambé. Beer 30-40F, cocktails 50F. Open M-Sa 7pm-2am.

La Favela Chic, 131, rue Oberkampf (tel. 01 43 57 15 47). M: Parmentier. Scorching-hot tapas bar. Come early, or have your drinks while standing out on the sidewalk. Open daily 8pm-2am.

Le Bastide, 18, rue de Lappe. M: Bastille. A tiny bar stuffed between more flamboyant neighbors on rue de Lappe, but remarkable for its eclectic tunes and relaxed atmosphere. Great place to stop for an early-evening drink and a real conversation. Beer 12F. Drink prices go up after 10pm. Open M-Sa 5pm-2am, Su 3pm-2am.

Sans Sanz, 49, Faubourg St-Antoine (tel. 01 44 75 78 78). M: Bastille. The only industry still here is the pick-up. Red velvet drapes, lead pipes, and a large baroque-framed screen playing scenes from other areas of the bar. Outdoor seating, and indoor air conditioning! Beer 10F, drink prices go up after 9pm. Open daily 9:30am-2am.

CLUBS

🖼 **What's Up Bar,** 15, rue Daval (tel. 01 48 05 88 33). M: Bastille. One of those rare Paris miracles: a place that is (almost always) free and funky. Set up in a concrete bunker, this bar/club has DJ competitions and its own magazine. Still a good place to chill/chat. M drum and bass, W Electronic, F Garage, Sa Freestyle. Open M-F 10pm-2:30am, Sa-Su 10pm-5am. No cover M-Th; F-Sa 50F. Drinks 25F and up. MC, V.

NIGHTLIFE

Le Cithéa, 114, rue Oberkampf (tel. 01 40 21 70 95). M: Parmentier. More of a bar with live music than a pulsing, flash-dancing club. In the very hip Oberkampf *quartier* and full of young, artsy folk, Le Cithéa features a wide variety of jazz, hip hop, and free jack fusion bands, as well as occasional DJs spinning drum 'n' bass. Drinks 25F-60F. Open daily 9:30pm-5:30am. Cover F-Sa 50F with 1 or 2 drinks. MC, V.

Le Bataclan, 50, bd. Voltaire (tel. 01 47 00 39 12). M: Oberkampf. A concert space and café-bar that hosts indie rock bands like Guided By Voices and Beck. Funky sliding toward trendy. Tickets start at 100F and vary with show. Th (free) is low-key. F (80F) is gay night, and Sa (80F) is house. Open Sept.-July Th-Sa 11pm-dawn.

TWELFTH ARRONDISSEMENT

🌊 **China Club,** 50, rue de Charenton (tel. 01 43 43 82 02). M: Ledru-Rollin or Bastille. Swank Hong Kong gentlemen's club with a speakeasy-style cellar and lacquered *fumoir chinois* look. High-class prices, but a Chinatown (gin fizz with mint) is hard to resist. Cocktails (70-90F) and jazz. Open M-Th 7pm-2am, F-Sa 7pm-3am. AmEx, MC, V.

Viaduc Café, 43, Daumesnil (tel. 01 44 74 70 70). A large late-night spot built into the Viaduc des Arts (see **Sights,** p. 212). Only a couple of palm trees and a canvas or two complement the cement viaduc support. Et voila! Industrial charm. Outdoor seating. Coffee 12F. Open daily noon-4am, food served until 3am.

THIRTEENTH ARRONDISSEMENT

🌊 **Les Oiseaux de Passage,** 7, passage Barrault (tel. 01 45 89 72 42). M: Corvisart. From rue de la Butte aux Cailles, turn right on rue des Cinq Diamants then left on passage Barrault. Young, hip, and laid-back. Art openings, live music, multiple board games, and theme evenings, including silent discussion night. Very laid-back. Beer and *kir* 12F; most food under 55F. Open Tu-Su 10am-2am.

Bateau El Alamein, Port de la Gare Quai Francois Mauriac (tel. 01 45 86 41 60). M: Quai de la Gare. This calm, plant-filled boat lodged on the Seine is the perfect spot for a nightcap. Beer 20F. During the summer open 6pm-2am.

La Folie en Tête, 33, rue de la Butte aux Cailles (tel. 01 45 80 65 99). M: Corvisart. "The" artsy axis mundi of the 13ème. Magazines, writing workshops, and musical instruments. Crowded concerts on Saturday nights. A/C. Beer 10F, coffee 7F, selection of 10F cocktails before 8pm, all prices increase by 2F after 10pm. Open M-Sa 5pm-2am.

Le Merle Moqueur, 11, rue de la Butte aux Cailles (tel. 01 45 65 12 43). M: Corvisart. Take rue Bobillot south until rue de la Butte aux Cailles branches right. Bamboo walls, African music, and a shabby-cool ambiance. Cheap beer (14F) and food (nothing over 50F). No frills and few tourists. Most customers head for the terrace but the back room is cooler. Happy hour 5-8pm. Open daily 3pm-2am. MC, V.

Bowling International Stadium, 66, av. d'Ivry (tel. 01 45 86 55 52). M: Tolbiac. A joint bowling alley and billiard hall. American billiards require a 100F deposit, a 5F supplementary fee, and 50F per hr. Bowling in any of the 12 lanes costs 16-33F depending on the time of day, the day of the week, and who you are (reduced prices for students and seniors); shoe rental 10F. Open daily 2pm-2am.

DANCE CLUBS

🌊 **Batofar,** facing 11, Quai François-Mauriac (tel. 01 56 29 10 00). M: Quai de la Gare. A club on a light-boat! Only the light has been replaced and the boat's innards have been transformed into cavernous bar areas and a sizeable dance floor. Friendly industrial environment. Jungle, Dub, Drum 'n Bass, eccentric Electronic and Su "blue note groove" live jazz. Open in the summer daily 10pm-3am. Tapas 20F. Cover 40-60F.

L'Arapaho, 30, av. d'Italie, Centre Commercial Italie 2 (tel. 01 45 89 65 05). M: Pl. d'Italie. It's the gray door on the right, just past Au Printemps. Since 1983, this place has built up a reputation for hosting some of the best hard-core, rap, pop, and metal bands to come through Paris. A pitstop on most indie rock bands' tour itineraries. Past acts have included Pavement, Sebadoh, Shellac, Bim Skala Bim, and Soul Asylum. Tickets usually around 60-130F. Beer 20F, cocktails 50F. Open F-Sa 11pm-dawn; F Asian Folly night with splashy costumes and decor, Sa Cuban. Cover 80F.

FOURTEENTH ARRONDISSEMENT

L'Entrepôt, 7-9, rue Francis de Pressensé (tel. 01 45 40 78 38; film schedule 08 36 68 05 87; restaurant reservations 01 45 40 60 70). M: Pernety. Walk down rue Raymond Losserand and turn right onto rue Francis de Pressensé. An alternative cinema coupled with a plush, trendy bar that features live music and a garden patio. *Ciné-Philo,* a screening and discussion café, is held on Sunday at 2:30pm and occasional other days (42F, students 32F). Open daily 11am-1:30am.

Smoke Bar, 29, rue Delambre (tel. 43 20 61 73). M: Vavin. Unpretentious yet stylish. Dark wood, red ceilings, blue lights, jazz posters, blues music. A perfect place to hang out with a drink for a while. Cocktails 30-45F, beer 22-26F. Open M-Sa noon-2am.

Le Troupeau, 11, rue Francis de Pressensé. M: Pernety. Walk down rue Raymond Losserand and turn right onto rue Francis de Pressensé. Although the café's name does not appear on its outside, its bright yellow and orange walls and reggae tunes make it hard to miss. The name does appear on the inside on a poster for the film *Le Troupeau* that was signed by the filmmaker Yilmaz Guney upon a visit to the café after his escape from a Turkish prison. Buzzing, but not packed, Le Troupeau is a relaxed place to come for a pleasantly cheap drink. Coffee 5F, cocktails 20F. Open daily 6pm-1:30am.

DANCE CLUBS

L'Enfer, 34, rue de Départ (tel. 01 42 79 94 94). M: Montparnasse-Bienvenüe. Pretty, pretty young clubbers get down with their bad selves to mainstream hip hop. More mature crowd on Saturdays. Open F-Sa 11:30pm-dawn. Cover 100F with drink.

FIFTEENTH ARRONDISSEMENT

Saint-Louis Blues, 33, rue Blomet (tel. 01 47 34 30 97). M: Sèvres Lecourbe. Make a right on rue Lecourbe, then a left on Blomet. Original French blues, with some American influence in the nostalgic decor. Mainly locals, average age in the low 30s. Cover 35F. Concerts Th-Sa 10pm-1am.

Aquaboulevard, 4, rue Louis Armand (tel. 01 40 60 10 00). M: Balard. Waterpark open F and Sa until midnight. See **Sports,** p. 278 for full listing.

SIXTEENTH ARRONDISSEMENT AND BOIS DE BOULOGNE

■ **Bowling de Paris** (tel. 01 53 64 93 00), in the Bois de Boulogne near the route Mahatma Gandhi entrance of the Jardin d'Acclimatation. After the park closes, you have to enter through the park's Mahatma Gandhi entrance, which remains open. Games M-F 9am-noon 13F, noon-8pm 26F, 8pm-2am 36F; Sa-Su 9am-noon 19F, noon-8pm 35F, 8pm-2am 36F. Obligatory bowling shoe rental 12F. Because the Bowling de Paris is inside the garden, you must also pay the garden's admission fee (13F).

DANCE CLUBS

Duplex, 2bis, av. Foch (tel. 01 45 00 45 00). M: Charles-de-Gaulle-Etoile. Walk around the Arc to this glitzy nightclub where the jet set parties on two floors to international techno. Dress smartly and carry your nose high, lest the bouncer turn you away. Also houses expensive restaurant open Tu-Su 9pm-1am. Club open Tu-Su midnight-dawn. Admission and first drink 100F.

SEVENTEENTH ARRONDISSEMENT

L'Endroit, 67, pl. du Dr-Félix-Lobligeois (tel. 01 42 29 50 00). M: Rome. Follow rue Boursault to rue Legendre, and make a right. The purveyor of cool in work-a-day Batignolles, it's the most happening place around, day or night. On a homey square facing the church, beer (22-30F), wine (20-25F), and liquor (45F) are just the start. Open daily noon-2am. MC, V.

La Main Jaune, pl. de la Porte-de-Champerret (tel. 01 47 63 26 47). M: Porte de Champerret. A roller disco with regular dancing as well, it's popular with the high school crowd. Open W and Sa-Su 2:30-7pm, F-Sa and holidays 10pm-dawn. Admission W and Sa-Su 50F (includes a drink), skate rental 10F; F-Sa night it becomes a disco with Portuguese music and non-skating clientele.

DANCE CLUBS

Niels, 27, av. des Ternes (tel. 01 47 66 45 00). M: Ternes. Equal parts swank and soul, Niels is all-around fun. Music is mainstream but the dance floor is packed. Open daily 11:30pm-dawn. Drinks 95F. Cover Th-Sa 100F with drink.

EIGHTEENTH ARRONDISSEMENT

Chez Camille, 8, rue Ravignan (tel. 01 46 06 05 78). M: Abbesses. Small and trendy bar with a pretty terrace looking down the *butte* to the Invalides dome. Cheap coffee and tea. Beer 23-30F, wine 22-28F, and cocktails 30-50F. Open M-Sa noon-2am.

La Fourmi, 74, rue des Martyrs (tel. 01 42 64 70 35). M: Pigalle. Popular stop-off before clubbing at Divan du Monde, this bar has character. More spacious than other bars, and more energetic as well. Crowd is young and scrappy. Beer 25-35F, wine 25-40F, cocktails 30-60F. Open M-Sa 8:30am-2am, Su 10:30am-2am. MC, V.

LIVE MUSIC CLUBS

La Cigale, 120, bd. Rochechouart (tel. 01 49 25 89 99). M: Pigalle. One of the two large rock clubs in Pigalle, seating 2000 for international indie, punk, hard-core bands. Concerts 100-180F. The converted theater also brings in modern dance shows. Music starts 8:30pm, box office open M-Sa noon-showtime. MC, V.

Elysée Montmartre, 72, bd. Rochechouart (tel. 01 44 92 45 42). M: Anvers. The biggest-name rock, reggae, and rap venue in a neighborhood fixture. Featuring well-known British and American groups in addition to home-grown talent, and a large dance floor for disco and salsa nights. Drinks 30-50F, shows 80-150F. AmEx, MC, V.

DANCE CLUBS

Divan du Monde, 75, rue des Martyrs (tel. 01 44 92 77 66). M: Pigalle. Not quite global, but this grungy den does try with Brazilian music, live bands, English DJs, and funk evenings. Youngish crowd varies depending on the nightly program; frequent week-long festivals. Su is gay tea dance. Open daily 7:30pm-dawn. Cover 40F-100F. Drinks from 20F. MC, V.

TWENTIETH ARRONDISSEMENT

La Flèche d'Or, 102bis, rue de Bagnolet (see **Restaurants,** p. 151). Live music from ragga hip hop to Celtic rock every night, art videos, dance classes, Sunday *bals*, and crazy theater on the tracks below the terrace. Open daily 10pm-2am.

Lou Pascalou, 14, rue des Panoyaux (tel. 01 46 36 78 10). M: Ménilmontant. Follow bd. de Ménilmontant; make a left on rue des Panayaux. A bit out of the way, Lou Pascalou features open-air terrace seating, a pool table, occasional concerts, and art displays. Beer 14, cocktails 22-45F, add 2F after 10pm. Open daily 10am-2am.

JAZZ

Jazz began to trickle into Paris with U.S. servicemen during WWI. By the 1940s Paris had emerged as a jazz hot spot. Jazz is commonly recognized by Parisian intellectuals as one of America's few totally unique and worthy cultural contributions. American jazz musicians flocked to Paris, as they were accorded great respect and appreciation by the French (see **Music,** p. 32). Since then, French jazz musicians, including pianist and native Parisian Michel Petrucciani, have themselves become fixtures of the international scene. In Paris, pianist Laurent de Wilde won France's Django Prize in 1993. Funk leader and guitarist Hervé Krief is well loved by French crowds, as is the old-guard blues organist Eddy Louis. From the American scene, Herbie Hancock, McCoy Tyner, Benny Baily, Duffy Jackson, and Kenny Garrett frequent the Paris circuit. Nearly every type of jazz is represented, from New Orleans to cool jazz, from acid jazz to hip hop and fusion. Brazilian samba and bossa nova are steadily growing in popularity together with music from the West Indies and Francophone Africa. Paris jazz clubs charge either through inflated drink prices or a cover charge. Once you have paid your cover, you are not required to drink and will likely not be disturbed should you choose to nurse one drink for the rest of the night.

Frequent summer festivals sponsor free or nearly free jazz concerts. The **Fête du Marais** often features free Big Band jazz, while the **La Villette Jazz Festival** offers very big names and a few free shows (see **Festivals,** p. 281). In the fall, the **Jazz Festival of Paris** comes to town as venues high and low open their doors to celebrity and up-and-coming artists. French mags *Jazz Hot* (45F) and *Jazz Magazine* (35F) are great sources, as is the bimonthly *LYLO* (*Les Yeux, Les Oreilles;* free). If you can't find them in bars or FNACs, try the main office, 55, rue des Vinaigriers, 10*ème*. *Pariscope* and *l'Officiel des Spectacles* also have jazz listings.

🎵 **Au Duc des Lombards,** 42, rue des Lombards, 1*er* (tel. 01 42 33 22 88). M: Châtelet. Murals of Ellington and Coltrane swathe the exterior of this premier jazz joint. Still the best in French jazz, with occasional American soloists, and hot items in world music. Excellent acoustics, dark and smoky atmosphere, and the hippest crowd for its league. Cover 80-100F, music students 50-80F. Beer 28-48F, cocktails 55F. Music starts at either 8:30pm or 10pm and wails on until 3am (4am on weekends). Open daily 7:30pm-4am. V.

🎵 **Le Baiser Salé,** 58, rue des Lombards, 1*er* (tel. 01 42 33 37 71). M: Châtelet. Lower-key than Lombards. Cuban, African, Antillean music featured together with modern jazz and funk upstairs in the basic first floor room. Month-long African music festival Oct.-Nov.; bass festival June. Concerts start at 10pm, music until 3am (typically 3 sets). Cover 40-80F, depending on performers; mainly new talent. Free Monday jam sessions with 1 drink min. Beer 26F, cocktails 46F. Bar open daily 4pm-dawn.

L'Eustache, 37 rue Berger, 1*er* (tel. 01 40 26 23 20). M: Châtelet-Les Halles. Fun and relaxed bar near Les Halles featuring good, free jazz on the weekend Sept.-June. Open daily 11am-4am, music starts at 10:30pm. AmEx, MC, V.

🎵 **Le Petit Opportun,** 15, rue des Lavandières-Ste-Opportune, 1*er* (tel. 01 42 36 01 36). M: Châtelet. Basement cave venue in three rooms; to see the band, show up early for a spot in the front room. Younger crowd, and some of the best modern jazz around, including many American performers. Nice pub upstairs. Cover 50-80F depending on act. Drinks 30-60F. Open Sept.-July Tu-Sa 9pm-5am; music begins at 10:30pm.

Slow Club, 130, rue de Rivoli, 1*er* (tel. 01 42 33 84 30). M: Châtelet. In a cellar that used to be a banana-ripening warehouse. An old favorite of Miles Davis hosts Big Band, Dixieland, and rock 'n' roll in a rock-around-the-clock vein. Playful but painfully tacky old-time setting. Older crowd than la Huchette. Lessons offered (tel. 01 42 53 14 49). Expect dancing and a crowd in their 30s. Weekday cover 60F, students 55F; weekend cover from 75F. Drinks from 25F. Open Tu-Th 10pm-3am, F-Sa 10pm-4am.

NIGHTLIFE

Le Sunset, 60, rue des Lombards, 1er (tel. 01 40 26 46 60). M: Châtelet. An easy-going club with an old and widespread reputation, Le Sunset is where musicians come to unwind and jam into the wee hours after their gigs around Paris. The room resembles the métro in shape but also in its acoustics, so sit close. Mostly French and European acts. W-Sa international jazz, Sunday jazz vocalists, Monday jam sessions, Tuesday new generation jazz. Cover 50-100F, with a 20% discount for Let's Go readers; drinks 30-65F. Open daily 10pm-dawn; hang around past 2am to catch the jam scene.

Blue Note, 38, rue Mouffetard, 5ème (tel. 01 45 87 36 09). M: Monge. Take rue Monge north and turn left on rue Lacépède then left on rue Mouffetard at pl. de la Contrescarpe. Brazilian music, jazz, and blues in a small, laid-back, albeit warm, setting. Excellent samba guitarists and new groups. Play along yourself with the makeshift percussion implements on each table. Try the house drink caipirinha (caçhaça and lime 50F). No cover. Drinks 25-55F. Music starts F-Sa 11pm, Su and Tu-Th 10pm. Open daily from 6:30pm.

Caveau de la Huchette, 5, rue de la Huchette, 5ème (tel. 01 43 26 65 05). M: St-Michel. Come prepared to listen, watch, and dance the jitterbug, bebop, swing, and jive in this extremely popular jazz club. Be-bop dance lessons offered M-F evenings before club opens; call 01 42 71 09 09. Lots of tourists, good music, and an atmosphere which is both lively and strange. Varied age-group (ages 20-60). The caves served as tribunal, prison, and execution rooms for Danton, Marat, St-Just, and Robespierre during the Revolution. When the club moved into this space in the late 40s, they found 2 skeletons chained together, dancing. Crowded on weekends. Cover Su-Th 60F, F-Sa 75F. Students 55F. Drinks 26-35F. Open daily 9:30pm-2:30am, F till 3:30am, Sa till 4am.

Le Petit Journal St-Michel, 71, bd. St-Michel, 5ème (tel. 01 43 26 28 59). M: Luxembourg. Another of the early strongholds, though more traditional and with an older crowd (40s-50s). First-class New Orleans and Big Band performers play in this Parisian center of the "Old Style." Open M-Th 8:30pm-12:30am, F-Sa till 1:30am. Obligatory 1st drink 100F, subsequent drinks 40F.

Aux Trois Mailletz, 56, rue Galande, 5ème (tel. 01 43 54 00 79). M: St-Michel. The basement houses a fun and crowded café featuring world music and jazz vocals. Leans toward Latin and Afro-Cuban, but also has jazz, blues, and gospel musicians from Europe and the U.S. 80-100F admission to club, admission to bar is free. Beer 36-50F, cocktails 65F. Bar open daily 5pm-dawn; cave 8:30pm to dawn.

La Villa, 29, rue Jacob, 6ème (tel. 01 43 26 60 00). M: St-Germain-des-Prés. Downstairs from 4-star Hôtel La Villa, this exclusive and expensive club can afford to fly American artists here for week-long engagements. Stars that have appeared include Shirley Horn and Joshua Redman. The sort of place with drinks like "Night and Day" and "So What." First drink M-F 120F, Sa-Su 150F. Special musician price 60F. Open M-Sa 10pm-2am. AmEx, MC, V.

New Morning, 7-9, rue des Petites-Ecuries, 10ème (tel. 01 45 23 51 41). M: Château d'Eau. 400-seat former printing plant with the biggest American headliners in the city. Dark, smoky, and crowded, it's everything a jazz club should be. Sit in the lower front section or near the wings for the best acoustics. All the greats have played here—from Chet Baker to Stan Getz and Miles Davis—and the club still attracts big names like Wynton Marsalis, Betty Carter, John Scofield, and Archie Shepp. Open Sept.-July from 8pm; times vary; concerts usually at 9pm. Tickets available at box office, the FNAC, or Virgin Megastore; 110-140F. Drinks 35-65F. MC, V.

SHOPPING

Attention shoppers: you have reached Mecca, and its name is Paris. The City of Lights is an endless parade of all that is extravagant, form-fitting, and flattering. Even if your *franc* flow doesn't match your fabulousness, it is possible find good deals. Stylish clothes and accessories are spread democratically throughout a variety of price ranges. And, although it can be intimidating to enter a designer's lair, act like you belong there and have a little fun. You may not be welcomed with open arms, but remember: that salesclerk may *look* well dressed, but he's only earning 25F an hour. Think *Pretty Woman*.

While it is nearly impossible to procure a ticket to the ready-to-wear fashion shows held in October (for Spring/Summer collections) and March (Autumn/Winter collections), fashion-oriented exhibits and festivals that are open to the public are generally held at the same time as the shows. Galeries Lafayette, for example, often holds free fashion shows displaying ready-to-wear clothing by top designers.

Budget shoppers should keep a keen eye out for the Paris **sales.** Last-season sales in Paris are outstanding, especially during **January** and **July** when most stores offer too-good-to-be-true discounts of 30-50%. Non-EU residents who have made purchases worth over 1200F in one store should ask about getting a refund on the 20.6% value-added tax (TVA; see **Reclaiming Value-added Tax,** p. 42).

SHOPPING BY ARRONDISSEMENT

ÉTIENNE-MARCEL AND LES HALLES (1ER AND 2ÈME). As sweet as Baby, and as spicy as Ginger, the area around M: Etienne-Marcel pairs nice with naughty. At the Agnés B. empire on rue du Jour, the black classics sun never sets, and Claude Pierlot at 3, rue de Turbigo does button-up cardigans with a well-bred touch. The stores on rue Etienne Marcel and rue Tiquetonne are best for technicolor clubwear. *(M: Etienne-Marcel.)* Forum Les Halles, a subterranean shopping mall (see p. 302) located just south of the Etienne Marcel area, and the streets that surround it contain a large range for a full urban warrior aesthetic.

MARAIS (4ÈME AND THE LOWER 3ÈME). The Marais gives less lip than the Etienne Marcel area, trading street wise edge for a consistent line-up of affordable, trendy boutiques. While its siren song is of-the-moment techno, what the Marais does best is the mid-priced clothing chains, independent designer shops, as well as vintage stores that line **rue Vieille-du-Temple, rue de Sévigne, rue Roi de Sicile** and **rue des Rosiers.** Lifestyle and tchatchke shops line **rue de Bourg-Tibourg** and **rue des Francs-Bourgeois.** The best selection of affordable-chic men's wear in Paris can be found here, especially along rue **Ste-Croix-de-la-Bretonnerie.** Most stores are open late on weekdays, and are open and hopping on Sundays. *(M: St-Paul or Hôtel-de-Ville.)*

ST-GERMAIN-DES-PRÉS (6ÈME AND EASTERN BORDER OF 7ÈME). Post-intellectual, materialistic St-Germain-des-Prés, particularly the triangle bordered by bd. St-Germain, rue St-Sulpice and rue des Saints-Pères, is super saturated with high-budget names. But don't just settle for *lécher les vitrines (window shopping,* lit. licking the windows); rue du Four hosts fun and affordable designers such as Paul and Joe (no. 40, tel. 01 45 44 97 70; open M 2-7:30pm, Tu-Sa 11am-7:30pm) and Sinéquanone (no. 16, tel 01 56 24 27 74). *(M: Odéon and M: Sèvres-Babylone.)* Closer to the Jardin du Luxembourg, calm rue de Fleurus hosts A.P.C. (see p. 304) as well as the interesting designs of t*** at no. 7. *(M: St-Placide.)* In the *7ème*, visit rue de Pré-aux-Clercs and rue de Grenelle to witness avant-garde jewelry at Stella Cadente no. 22. In general, the *7ème* is very expensive. *(M: Rue du Bac.)*

BASTILLE (11ÈME). Rue de la Roquette is the shopping hub with numerous trendy clothing and accessories shops. **Rue de Keller** and its surrounding streets are lined with record shops, while rue de Faubourg-St-Antoine is the epicenter of furniture and design.

5ÈME. St-Michel, which borders the 5*ème* and 6*ème*, is lined with chain mid-priced shops, as well as stationary and book stores. There are a few vintage clothing shops on **rue de Mouffetard.**

MONTMARTRE (18ÈME). Boutiques and vintage clothing stores clutter around **rue des Abesses.** A few can be found on **rue des Trois-Frères.**

MONTPARNASSE (14ÈME). Stock stores line **rue d'Alesia** between rue Didot and Place Victor Basch. Crowded on weekends, they offer some real steals.

AVENUE MONTAIGNE, FAUBOURG ST-HONORÉ. See **Sights,** p. 162.

DEPARTMENT STORES

It's strange that a country where one must go to a thousand speciality shops to assemble one complete meal would be the birthplace of the *grand magasin*, those meccas of one-stop shopping. Designed as glamorous showplaces for affordable, ready-to-wear goods, Paris's department stores were the first in the world. When visiting the city's grand old stores like Samaritaine and Bon Marché, check out their turn-of-the-century ornamented ceilings and decorative metal work. Many *grands magasins* contain *coiffeurs* (beauty salons), post offices, grocery stores, cafés, and other conveniences that would allow one to live an entire life within their confines. Department stores tend to have more conventional clothing, though Printemps and the Galeries Lafayette have high-quality clothes for high prices. Lower on each, Tati and Monoprix are nevertheless budget fantasies. Pay where it says *caisse* and if a salesperson is hassling you, always remember two magic words: *je regarde* (I'm looking).

Au Bon Marché, 22, 38 rue de Sèvres, 7ème (tel. 01 44 39 80 00). M: Sèvres-Babylone. Paris's oldest department store (supposedly Eiffel advised on its ironwork), Bon Marché has it all, from scarves to smoking accessories, designer clothes to a wonderful back-to-school children's section. Across the street is *La Grande Epicerie de Paris,* Bon Marché's celebrated gourmet food annex (see **Specialty Stores,** p. 155) and across rue du Babylone is the Conran housewares hut. Open M-Sa 9:30am-7pm. MC, V.

Au Printemps, 64, bd. Haussmann, 9ème (tel. 01 42 82 50 00). M: Chaussée d'Antin-Lafayette or Havre-Caumartin. Also at 30, pl. d'Italie, 13ème (tel. 01 40 78 17 17), M: pl. d'Italie; 21-25, cours de Vincennes, 20ème (tel. 01 43 71 12 41), M: Porte de Vincennes. One of the two biggies in the Parisian department store scene, containing mostly goods far beyond the budget category. Caters more to women's fashion than men's. Obscenely large accessories department. Most hotels have 10% discounts for use in the store. Haussmann open M-W, F, Sa 9:30am-7pm, Th 9:30am-10pm. MC, V.

BHV, 52-64, rue de Rivoli, 4ème (tel. 01 42 74 90 00). M: Hôtel-de-Ville. The initials stand for Bazar de l'Hôtel de Ville. *Comment dit-on* Do it Yourself? BHV has a basement full of tools, paint, housewares and electronic equipment to show you how. Lovely building, especially so for a glorified hardware store. Open M-Tu and Th-Sa 9:30am-7pm, W 9:30am-10pm. AmEx, MC, V.

Forum des Halles, M: Les Halles or RER: Châtelet-Les Halles, 2ème (tel. 01 44 76 96 56). An immense and somewhat shabby underground shopping mall. Descend from one of the 4 main entrances to discover over 200 boutiques. There is a branch of the FNAC music and CD store, a branch of the cosmetics wonderland, Sephora, a movie theater complex, and a swimming pool. Usually safe during the day, but chancy at night. All stores open M-Sa 10am-7:30pm.

Galeries Lafayette, 40, bd. Haussmann, 9ème (tel. 01 42 82 34 56). M: Chaussée d'Antin. Also at 22, rue du Départ, 14ème (tel. 01 45 38 52 87), M: Montparnasse. Chaotic (the equivalent of Paris's entire population visits here each month), but carries it all, including mini-boutiques of Kookaï, Agnès B., Gap, and Benetton. Worth a visit for the toy department, and the beautiful stained glass ceiling in the main gallery. So many American tourists come here that it was considered unsafe during the terrorist attacks of the mid-80s. Most hotels offer 10% discount coupons for the store. Open M-W, F, Sa 9:30am-7pm, Th 9:30-8pm. AmEx, MC, V.

Monoprix, branches all over Paris. Standard hours 9:30am-7:30pm, but some location open until 10pm. Good value for groceries, fashion, and housewares. MC, V.

Samaritaine, 67, rue de Rivoli, 1er (tel. 01 40 41 20 20). M: Pont-Neuf, Châtelet-Les-Halles, or Louvre. 4 large buildings between rue de Rivoli and the Seine, connected by tunnels and bridges. Not as chic as Galeries Lafayettes or Bon Marché, as it dares to sell souvenirs (gasp!) and merchandise at down-to-earth prices (the horror!). Big toy and sporting goods departments. The rooftop observation deck provides one of the best views of the city; take the elevator to the 9th floor and climb the short, spiral staircase. Open M-W and F-Sa 9:30am-7pm, Th 9:30am-10pm. AmEx, MC, V.

Tati, 11, pl. de la République, 3ème (tel. 01 48 87 72 81). M: République. Also at 106, rue Faubourg du Temple, 11ème (tel. 01 43 57 92 80), M: Belleville; 140, rue de Rennes, 6ème (tel. 01 45 48 68 31), M: Montparnasse; and 4, bd. de Rochechouart, 18ème (tel. 01 42 55 13 09), M: Barbès-Rochechouart. Rub elbows with Parisian parents buying t-shirts for François to take to camp. A fabulously kitschy, chaotic, crowded, and cheap department store. Tati recently commissioned designers to create cheaper, hipper clothes. Generally low-end, but worth rummaging. Get your sales slip made out by one of the clerks (who stand around for just that purpose) before heading to the cashier. All branches open M-Sa 10am-7pm. MC, V.

CLOTHES

No more wire hangers!
—Joan Crawford

OUTLET STORES

Stock is French for an outlet store, with big names for less—often because they have small imperfections or are last season's remainders. Widen your stock portfolio and invest! Many are on rue d'Alésia in the 14ème (M: Alésia), including **Cacharel Stock** (no. 114; tel. 01 45 42 53 04; open M-Sa 10am-7pm; AmEx, MC, V), **Stock Chevignon** (no. 122; tel. 01 45 43 40 25; open M-Sa 10am-7pm; MC, V), **Stock Daniel Hechter** (no. 92; tel. 01 47 07 88 44; open M-Sa 10am-7:30pm; MC, V), and a small **Stock Kookaï** (no. 111; open M 1-7pm and Tu-Sa 10am-7pm). A much larger **Stock Kookaï** bustles at 82 rue Réamur, 2ème (tel. 01 45 08 93 69; open M-Sa 10:30am-7:30pm).

MID-PRICED

Prêt-à-porter is not just a Robert Altman film; it is ready-to-wear clothing by designer names. Often, big-name labels still mean big price tags. Although the last few years have witnessed a Gap invasion in Paris (look for the signature blue shopping bags), you may want affordable French style that your neighbors won't be wearing at home. There's a good chance of finding it at these mid-priced *magasins* and *boutiques.*

MEN'S AND WOMEN'S

A.P.C., 3-4 rue de Fleurus, 6ème (tel. 01 42 22 12 77; www.apc.fr). M: St-Placide. A resource for wardrobe staples, A.P.C. is hip without being outrageous, specializing in cigarette pants, rib-knit tops, and the fundamentals of wardrobe, in anti-colors like black and beige. Open M-Sa 10:30am-7pm. AmEx, MC, V.

Agnès B., 2, 3, 6, 10, and 19 rue du Jour, 1er (tel. 01 45 08 56 56 or 01 42 33 04 13). M: Etienne-Marcel. Upscale but affordable, these pieces are the kind of well-made clothes that are classic but stylishly French. All of the *BCBG* basics, along with accessories and even a line of cosmetics. Open M-Sa 10am-7pm. MC, V.

Junk, 54, rue Etienne-Marcel, 2ème (tel. 01 42 36 36 97). M: Etienne-Marcel. The bubble-gum Japanese designs of Junko Shimada are young, funky, and innovative. Most clothing is casual and clubby, but some is more elegant. A selection of wild and colorful bags. Junky cold medina. Open Tu-Sa 10am-7pm, M 11am-7pm.

Kiliwatch, 64, rue Tiquetonne, 1er (tel. 01 42 21 17 37). M: Etienne-Marcel. Kiliwatch is an enormous store with a surprisingly affordable collection of casual and club wear. Open M 2-7pm, Tu-Sa 11am-7pm.

▨ **MKDM,** 24 rue de Sévigne, 4ème (tel. 01 42 77 00 74). M: St-Paul. 20% 'Independent Japanese designers', 30% 'chic-casual' and unisex, and 50% 'Paris-Tokyo tendencies.' Innovation doesn't come cheap: creations range from 180-700F. Open daily 2-8pm.

Mosquitos, 25, rue du Four, 6ème (tel. 01 43 25 25 16). M: Mabillon. Funky and chunky shoes in all colors and for all occasions. Open M-Sa 11am-7pm.

▨ **Le Shop,** 3, rue d'Argout, 2ème (tel. 01 40 28 95 94). M: Etienne-Marcel. Two levels, 1200 square meters and 24 corners of club wear. Plus, a live DJ. Open M 1-7pm, Tu-Sa 11am-7pm.

▨ **Zadig & Voltaire,** 15, rue du Jour, 1er (tel. 01 42 21 88 70). M: Etienne-Marcel. Also at 1, rue des Vieux Colombiers, 6ème (tel. 01 43 29 18 29), M: Odéon and 4, 12 rue Ste-Croix-de-la-Bretonnerie (tel. 01 42 72 09 55), M: St-Paul. Men's and women's designs by T. Gillier as well as items from Helmut Lang, etc. A wonderful selection of handbags. Opening hours change per branch. Main branch open M-Sa 11am-7pm.

WOMEN'S

Kookaï, 12, rue Gustave-Gourbet, 16ème (tel. 01 47 55 18 00). M: Victor Hugo. With sexed-up runway knock-offs and a hip young staff, Kookaï is the place to find women's slip dresses, minis and sheer, shimmery shirts at affordable prices. Although Kookaï is located throughout Paris, this location is their flagship store, with the largest selection. Open M-Sa 10:30am-7:30pm. AmEx, MC, V.

Abou d'Abi Bazar, 10, rue des Francs-Bourgeois, 4ème (tel. 01 42 77 96 98). M: St-Paul. Paul and Joe, Diabless, French Connection and other designers at reasonable prices. Many items under 200F. Open Su-M 2-7pm and Tu-Sa 10:30am-7pm.

Spleen, 3bis, rue des Rosiers, 4ème (tel. 01 42 74 65 66). M: St-Paul. Featuring avant-garde cuts and fabrics as well as a number of Italian designers, this boutique is pricey, but worth a splurge. Open M 3-7pm, Tu-Sa 10am-9pm, Su 2-7pm.

MEN'S

Boy'z Bazaar, 5, rue Ste-Croix-de-la-Bretonnerie, 4ème (tel. 01 42 71 94 00). M: St-Paul. A large selection of all that's trendy-casual in men's wear from Energie to Paul Smith. Caters largely to a gay clientele. Open daily noon-midnight.

Loft Design By Paris, 12, rue du Faubourg-St-Honoré, 8ème (tel. 01 42 65 59 65). M: Concorde or Madeleine. Mostly for men, Loft sells well-tailored men's shirts and casual sweaters and pants. A French version of The Gap. There is also a branch in the Marais, at 12, rue de Sévigné. Open M-Sa 10am-7pm. AmEx, MC, V.

SECONDHAND AND VINTAGE

Snazzy *magasins de troc* (secondhand stores) resell clothes bought and returned at more expensive stores. Prices may still be high, but they're usually a good deal if you want a designer find. Their stock often includes lots of basics as well as some pretty wild finds. Paris's vintage clothing scene is marginal. A number of stylish vintage clothes shops can be found in the Marais, on rue de Mouffetard in the 5*ème*, in the 1*er* and 2*ème* around Les Halles, and in the 17*ème* around av. de Clichy and rue des Dames. If you don't find what you're looking for here, you may have better luck at one of Paris's many flea markets (see p. 311).

SECOND HAND

Mouton à Cinq Pattes, 8-10-18, rue St-Placide, 6*ème* (tel. 01 45 48 86 26). M: Sèvres-Babylone. Also at 19, rue Grégoire de Tours, 6*ème* (tel. 01 43 29 73 56), M: Odéon; 15, rue Vieille de Temple, 4*ème* (tel. 01 42 71 86 30), M: St-Paul; and 130 av. Victor Hugo (tel. 01 47 55 42 25; M: Victor Hugo). A huge selection of designer clothing, as well as some accessories, at lower prices. Little costs less than 200F here, but if you're willing to dig through the rainbow piles, you might find a pot of gold. Open M-F 10:30am-7:30pm, Sa 10:30am-8pm. AmEx, MC, V.

Réciproque, 16*ème* (tel. 01 47 04 30 28). M: Pompe. Discounted designer clothing. Different branches, all on rue de la Pompe, have different specialties: women's cocktail and evening dresses at no. 93; women's casual wear and shoes at no. 95; menswear at no. 101; women's coats at no. 123; leather goods and handbags at no. 89. Great pieces, but not-so-great prices. All branches open Tu-Sa 11:15am-7pm. AmEx, MC, V.

La Clef des Marque, 20, pl. du Marché St-Honoré, 1*er* (tel. 01 47 03 90 40). M: Pyramides. 2 stories of designer merchandise, including lingerie, swimwear, basic cotton tops, and shoes. You may stumble upon Prada pumps or Gaultier jeans for less than your hotel room. Open M-Sa 12:30am-7pm. MC, V.

Alternatives, 18, rue de Roi-de-Sicile, 4*ème* (tel. 01 42 78 31 50). M: St-Paul. A small collection of exclusive second-hand designer wear which looks new. Stylish, as well as pricey. Open Sept.-July M 11am-1pm and Tu-Su 12:30am-7pm.

VINTAGE

Son et Image, 8, rue Ste-Croix-de-la-Bretonnerie, 4*ème* (tel. 01 42 76 03 36). M: St-Paul. A large selection of funky menswear as well as some colorful remade skirts and dresses. Most items over 200F. Branch near Les Halles at 85-87 rue St-Denis, 1*ère* (tel. 01 40 41 90 61). Open daily 10:30am-8pm.

Antiquités New-Puces, 43, rue Mouffetard, 5*ème* (tel. 01 43 36 15 75). M: Monge. Some camp and some class. Clothes upstairs for 100-300F; downstairs for real bargains (50-150F). Open M-F 11:30am-11:30pm, Sa 10am-9pm.

Nadivine, 16, rue des Dames, 17*ème* (tel. 01 43 87 98 04). M: Pl. de Clichy. Some interesting concoctions by Laroche, Dior, and the lesser known. Open M-Sa 11am-7pm.

Guerrisol, 19-29-31 and 33, av. de Clichy, 17*ème* (tel. 01 42 94 13 21). M: La Fourche. Also at 9, 21, and 21bis, bd. Barbès, 18*ème* (tel. 01 42 52 19 73), M: Barbès-Rochechouart; 45, bd. de la Chapelle, 10*ème* (tel. 01 45 26 80 85), M: La Chapelle; 116-118, rue Jean-Pierre Timbaud, 11*ème* (tel. 01 43 38 69 05), M: Courconnes; and 22, bd. Poissonière, 9*ème* (tel. 01 47 70 35 02), M: Bonne Nouvelle. This popular chain has racks upon racks for men and women. Silk shirts and leather coats, jeans (40-60F), and more (10-120F). Most branches open M-Sa 9:30am-7pm.

Tandem, 20, rue Houdron, 18*ème* (tel. 01 44 92 97 60). M: Abbesses. From the métro, go left on rue Abbesses and take a right on rue Houdron. This small store has racks of 60s and 70s polyester and glitter squeezed next to retro-wear from the 40s and 50s. Baubly jewelry 40-70F. Big selection of men's pants and jackets. Dresses and pants 120-200F. Open Tu-Sa 11am-2:30pm and 3:30-8pm.

SHOPPING

SPECIALTY SHOPS

Colette, 213, rue St-Honoré (tel. 01 55 35 33 90; www.colette.tm.fr; M: Concorde), is an ultra-minimalist "anti-department store" whose bare display tables feature an eclectic selection of scuba watches, Japanese vases, and mineral water. Their Scandinavianesque water-bar offers over 50 different kinds of sparkling aqua. Colette's sense of Calvin Klein classicism, oh-so-bored minimalism, and California clean living project a late-90s aesthetic where less is more and attitude is everything. Some cutesey designer items are affordable and make for interesting souvenirs, but the best way to shop minimalist is to buy nothing at all. Open M-Sa 10:30am-7:30pm.

Sephora, 70-72, av. des Champs-Elysées, 8ème (tel. 01 53 93 22 50). M: Charles-de-Gaulle-Etoile. An overwhelming array of cosmetic products carefully designed to elicit your secret vanity. The tantalizing rainbow arrangements and the sheer magnitude of perfumes, powders, pungents, and exfoliaters at Sephora could convince even Snow White that she needed Shiseido's help. Everything from MAC to Mabelline, as well as Bourgois, a discount brand available only in Europe and made in the same factory as the pricier Chanel. Prices run the gamut from very reasonable to quite absurd. Open M-Sa 10-midnight, Su noon-midnight. AmEx, V, MC.

■ **Muji,** 27 rue St-Sulpice, 6ème (tel. 01 46 34 01 10). M: Odéon. Made in Japan: this bric-a-brac is affordable, modern, and gently minimalist. Could be the place for next year's It pen. Tons for under 30F. Furniture and clothing as well. Open M-Sa 10am-8pm.

Octée, 18, rue des Quatre-Vents, 6ème (tel. 01 46 33 18 77). M: Odéon. A unique selection of scents, candles, and soaps. Open Tu-Sa 11am-7pm.

Totale Eclipse, 40, rue de la Roquette, 4ème (tel. 01 48 07 88 04). A small boutique with a wonderful collection of funky jewelry and handbags. Open M-Sa 11am-7:30pm.

Marais Plus, 20, rue des Francs-Bourgeois, 4ème (tel. 01 48 87 01 40). From novelty books to fluorescent cutlery, this *tchatchkerie* sells high quality fun stuff and is a wonderful place to buy gifts. Open daily 10am-7:30pm.

Au Vieux Campeur, 48-50, rue des Ecoles (main branch), 5ème (tel. 01 53 10 48 48). M: Maubert-Mutualité. One of the largest outdoors shops in France, with 18 separate boutiques in a one-block radius, outfitting for everything from ice-climbing to beach-combing. Oodles of high quality sleeping bags, tents, packs, boots, sporting equipment, and supplies. Open M-F 9am-6pm, Sa 9am-1pm.

BOOKS AND MAGAZINES

As a proud bearer of the literary vanguard and a well-read city, Paris overflows with high-quality bookstores. Large and small, they fall into two categories: the efficient shop, with large windows and black paneling, bearing sleek new editions with nary a place to sit as you browse through them; or the gallery of curiosities, crooked shelves crammed with equal parts moth-fodder and lost treasures, more a lifestyle than a business for the owner and his loyal clients.

The 5ème and 6ème are particularly bookish: interesting shops line every large street in the Latin Quarter, not to mention the endless stalls along the quais of the Seine. English-language editions tend to be expensive, but you can save money at the myriad vendors of used books *(livres d'occasion)*. Some specialty bookshops

IT IS BETTER TO GIVE THAN TO RECEIVE

■ A little *quelquechose* from Paris will go far to put a smile on your mom's face and may guarantee future happiness with the one you love. Keeping in mind your limited wallet, luggage space, and time, here are some groovy gift spots for mementos that they're guaranteed to adore.

■ Food and wine: **Nicolas** (p. 156), **Fauchon** (p. 155), **Hédiard** (p. 155) **La Maison du Chocolat** (p. 160).

■ Tchatchkes: **Colette** (p. 306), **Marais Plus** (p. 306), and **Muji** (p. 306).

serve as informal community centers for students, intellectuals, and travelers with special concerns. English bookshops like **The Village Voice** have bulletin boards where you can post and read events and housing notices. **Les Mots à la Bouche** offers gay, bi, and lesbian information. **Présence Africaine** can direct you to Caribbean, Maghrebin, and West African resources.

If you are in Paris for a semester or a year, apply for a Paris library card at the **Centre Pompidou** branch, or for a fee, at the **American Library in Paris** (see **Libraries,** p. 86). If you are continuing your French studies after you leave Paris, buy your books here at a fraction of the price back home, and ship them via the very cheap, very slow surface-mail book-rate (see **Mail,** p. 92).

Note that in French *librairie* means bookstore; the word for library is *bibliothèque. Journal* refers to a newspaper; a magazine is called *une revue.* A *papeterie* is a stationers, selling paper supplies, gift cards, pens, and so on.

ENGLISH-LANGUAGE

Galignani, 224, rue de Rivoli, 1er (tel. 01 42 60 76 07). M: Tuileries. The first English bookstore on the continent, Galignani was founded in 1804 and has inhabited its current location since 1856. Frequented by Thackeray and Garibaldi in the 19th century and occupied by the German general staff during WWII. Wood paneling, *belles lettres,* coffee table art books, paperbacks, and travel guides. Open M-Sa 10am-7pm. MC, V.

W.H. Smith, 248, rue de Rivoli, 1er (tel. 01 44 77 88 99). M: Concorde. Large general selection including the latest publications from Britain and America and many scholarly works. Large selection of magazines. Sunday *New York Times* available by Tuesday. Open M-Sa 9am-7:30pm, Su 1pm-7:30pm. AmEx, MC, V.

Brentano's, 37, av. de l'Opéra, 2ème (tel. 01 42 61 52 50). M: Opéra. An American and French bookstore with an extensive selection of English literature, guidebooks, and greeting cards in English. Paperbacks 40-75F. Open M-Sa 10am-7:30pm. AmEx, MC, V.

Shakespeare and Co., 37, rue de la Bûcherie, 5ème. M: St-Michel. Across the Seine from Nôtre-Dame. Run by *bon vivant* George Whitman (who claims to be the great-grandson of Walt), this shop seeks to reproduce the atmosphere of Sylvia Beach's establishment at 8, rue Dupuytren (later at 12, rue de l'Odéon), a gathering-place for expatriates in the 20s. Beach published James Joyce's *Ulysses* in 1922. The current location has no official link to any Lost Generation notables. It has, however, accumulated a quirky and wide selection of new and used books. Bargain bins outside include French classics in English (30F). Profits support impoverished writers who live and work in this literary cooperative—former residents include beatniks Allen Ginsberg and Lawrence Ferlinghetti. If you're interested in living here and serious about writing, the Sunday evening tea party is a good way to introduce yourself. Live poetry M nights. Open daily noon-midnight.

Tea and Tattered Pages, 24, rue Mayet, 6ème (tel. 01 40 65 94 35). M: Duroc. The place to go for second-hand English-language books. The crazy-quilt, mostly pulp fiction selection is subject to barter and trade. Sell books at 3-5F a paperback and get a 10% discount on your next purchase. Books cost 25-45F. If they don't have what you want, sign the wish list and you'll be called if it comes in. Tea room serves root beer floats, brownies, lunch, and American coffee with free refills. Regular poetry readings and photo exhibits. Open daily 11am-7pm.

The Village Voice, 6, rue Princesse, 6ème (tel. 01 46 33 36 47). M: Mabillon. Takes its name less from the Manhattan paper than from the Parisian neighborhood that 15 years ago was known as "le village de St-Germain-des-Prés." An excellent Anglophone bookstore, not to mention the locus of the city's English literary life, featuring 3-4 readings, lectures, and discussions every month (always at 7pm) with Paris luminaries like Edmund White. Paperbacks 48-90F. Many American and British newspapers and magazines. Open M 2-8pm, Tu-Sa 11am-8pm. AmEx, MC, V.

The American Library, 10, rue Général Camou, 7ème (tel. 01 53 59 12 60; email: 100142.1066@compuserve.com). M: Ecole-Militaire. The largest English library in Paris hosts a 5-10F book sale every spring—call in March for the exact dates. For full listing, see **Libraries,** p. 87.

GENERAL FRENCH

Gibert Jeune, 5, pl. St-Michel, 5ème (tel. 01 43 25 70 07). M: St-Michel. Near the Seine, it's the biggest in town. Main branch plus 6 specialized branches clustered around the Fontaine St-Michel. The main location for books in all languages including lots of reduced-price books. Extensive stationery department downstairs; used books bought down here, too. The branch at 27, quai St-Michel (tel. 01 43 54 57 32), M: St-Michel, sells university texts. Additional branch at 15bis, bd. St-Denis, 2ème (tel. 01 55 34 75 75) sells general books and texts, open 10am-7pm. Main branch open M-Sa 9:30am-7:30pm. AmEx, MC, V.

Gibert Joseph, 26-30-32-34, bd. St-Michel, 6ème (tel. 01 44 41 88 88). M: Odéon or Cluny-Sorbonne. A gigantic *librairie* and music store all rolled into one with both new and used selections. Frequent sidewalk sales with crates of books, notebooks, and old records starting at 10F. Good selection of used dictionaries and guidebooks. *Papeterie* at 32, bd. St-Michel, open M-Sa 9:30am-7pm; all other departments M-Sa 9:30am-7:30pm. MC, V.

Librairie Gallimard, 15, bd. Raspail, 7ème (tel. 01 45 48 24 84). M: Rue du Bac. The main store of this famed publisher of French classics features a huge selection of pricey Gallimard books. Basement is filled with Folio paperbacks. Open M-Sa 10am-7pm. AmEx, MC, V.

FNAC (Fédération Nationale des Achats de Cadres): St-Lazare branch: 109, rue St-Lazare, 9ème (tel. 01 55 31 20 00), M: St-Lazare. Open M-Sa 10am-7:30pm; Th until 9:30pm. See also **Forum des Halles** (1er, the largest), **Montparnasse** (6ème), and **Etoile** (17ème) branches listed under **Music,** p. 310. Large bookstores carrying most subjects with particularly large travel and maps selections. MC, V.

SPECIAL INTEREST

Alias, 21, rue Boulard, 14ème (tel. 01 43 21 29 82). M: Denfert-Rochereau. Turn right off av. du Général Leclerc onto rue Daguerre, then turn left onto rue Boulard. Sloping, floor-to-ceiling stacks of books stop many visitors at the door to this bookstore specializing in new and used art books and magazines. If you know what you're looking for, the proprietor will usually squeeze through the narrow passageways and find it. Open Tu-Sa 11am-8pm, Su 11am-2pm. MC, V.

Les Archives de la Presse, 51, rue des Archives, 3ème (tel. 01 42 72 63 93). M: Rambuteau. Huge collection of vintage magazines—especially politics, fashion, photography, music, sports, and cinema. Some precious 50s finds, including fabulous *Vogue* issues (French and foreign). A magazine from a friend's birthday makes a great gift (about 50F). Open M-Sa 10:30am-7pm.

Chantelivre, 13, rue de Sèvres, 6ème (tel. 01 45 48 87 90). M: Sèvres-Babylone. A pricey children's bookstore with a play area for the kids. Classics for the young *(Puss in Boots)* and not so young (Dumas, Jack London). Small English-language section. Open M 1-7pm, Tu-Sa 10am-7pm. MC, V (100F min.).

CineReflet, 3, rue Champollion, 5ème (tel. 01 40 46 02 72). M: Cluny-La Sorbonne. Surrounded by art-and-classics cinemas, with an intriguing selection of actor and director biographies, film analysis, old film press packages, scripts, and photographs. Open W-M 1-8pm. MC, V.

Eyrolles, 61, bd. St-Germain, 5ème (tel. 01 44 41 11 73; www.eyrolles.com). M: Maubert-Mutualité. Large collection of computer resources for the novice to network administrator. Strong selection of all scientific fields, architecture, and travel. Open M-F 10am-7pm, Sa 10am-7:30pm. MC, V.

Le Funambule, 48, rue Jean-Pierre Timbaud, 11ème (tel. 01 48 06 74 94). M: Parmentier. Small, artsy bookstore with (among other things) a good selection of gay- and lesbian-interest books, from literature to fine arts. Most books used, out of print, or rare; some in English. Carries *Spartacus* and *Gay Pied.* Open W-Sa 4-8pm.

Institut Géographique National, 107, rue La-Boétie, 8ème (tel. 01 43 98 85 00). M: Miromesnil. Exhaustive collection of travel books in French and maps for every country in the world, including souvenir antique maps and travel paraphernalia. Upstairs you'll find recreation books and an archive of satellite maps. Some titles in English. Open M-F 9:30am-7pm, Sa 11am-12:30pm, 2-6:30pm. MC, V.

La Hune, 170, bd. St-Germain, 6ème (tel. 01 45 48 35 85). M: St-Germain-des-Prés. Next door to one of surrealist André Breton's favorite cafés, this well-stocked, crisp bookstore is a hot-spot for literati and art-lovers. Upper level is devoted to *beaux arts* and has a very good collection of critical works. Open M-Sa 10am-midnight. MC, V.

Librairie Gourmande, 4, rue Dante, 5ème (tel. 01 43 54 37 27; fax 01 43 54 31 16). M: Maubert-Mutualité. Bookstore on the art of cooking and dining par excellence. New and old volumes chronicle food and drink from the Middle Ages to the New Age. Some English titles. Remainders around 30F. Open daily 10am-7pm. MC, V.

La Librairie des Gourmets, 98, rue Monge, 5ème (tel. 01 43 31 16 42). M: Monge. A smaller, neater collection of books on French cuisine than that of the Librairie Gourmande (see above), and exclusively new editions. Open M-Sa 10:30am-7pm. MC, V.

L'Harmattan, 21bis, rue des Ecoles, 5ème (tel. 01 46 34 13 71). M: Maubert-Mutualité. A tremendous resource within a center of world studies research. Enormous collection of history, art, culture, politics, economics, and literature from nearly every nation. Call for the catalogue of the 200,000 book collection. Open M-Sa 10am-7pm. MC, V.

Librairie du Québec, 30, rue Gay Lussac (tel. 01 43 54 49 02) RER: Luxembourg. *Un coin du Québec au coeur de Paris,* this wonderful bookshop supplies thousands of titles on Québecois literature, history, politics, culture, film, music, and Québec sovereignty. A great resource for the Québecois community in Paris with listings of upcoming poetry readings, performances, and festivals, including the *Fête Nationale* (June 24th, see **Festivals,** p. 280). M-Sa 9:30am-7pm.

Librairie Ulysse, 26, rue St-Louis-en-l'Ile, 4ème (tel. 01 43 25 17 35; email ulysse@ulysse.fr). M: Pont Marie. Anyone with a passion for travel should head to this magical, 1-room bookstore filled floor-to-ceiling with books about every place you've ever dreamed of visiting. Impressive stock of maps. 4000 copies of *National Geographic* since the 20s. There is a section on Paris and plenty of used books outside. English spoken. Open Tu-Sa 2-8pm. MC, V (over 500F).

Librairie Un Regard Moderne, 10, rue Git-le-Coeur, 6ème (tel. 01 43 29 13 93). M: St-Michel. A wild combo of high and low, kitsch and *kunst*. Racy comix, glossy art and photo books, high and low-brow, porn, and gen-X literature pile up in a cramped, smoky room. Small gallery features young artists. Open M-Sa 11:30am-8pm. MC, V.

Le Monde Libertaire, 145, rue Amelot, 11ème (tel. 01 48 05 36 08). M: République. Walk up bd. Voltaire and turn right on rue Amelot. One of the only anarchist and Marxist bookstores in Paris. Books and magazines on human rights, revolutions, and social change. Sale items 10-50F. Open M-F 2-7:30pm, Sa 10am-7:30pm.

Les Mots à la Bouche, 6, rue Ste-Croix-de-la-Bretonnerie, 4ème (tel. 01 42 78 88 30). M: St-Paul or Hôtel-de-Ville. Extensive collection of gay and lesbian literature, including novels, essays, poetry, history, art criticism, and magazines in French and English. Also a small selection of videos. A must-visit for those in search of an inside line on gay and lesbian nightlife and political and cultural events. Open M-Th 11am-11pm, F-Sa 11am-midnight, Su 2-8pm. MC, V.

Presence Africaine, 25bis, rue des Ecoles, 5ème (tel. 01 43 54 15 88). M: Maubert-Mutualité. French-language texts from Antilles and Africa put out by the famous publishing house of the same name, which first published Césaire and Fanon. Children's books, scholarly texts, poetry, and more. Paperbacks 30-70F. A resource for travelers seeking businesses that cater to black clientele. Open M-Sa 9:30am-7pm. MC, V.

MUSIC

Highly taxed in France, CDs are considered luxury goods. In addition to expensive imported American and British pop, grunge, rock, rap, alternative, R&B, and classical, you'll find great selections of French pop, rap, rock, techno, house, punk, and cabaret as well as huge supplies of classic jazz, acid jazz, jungle, raï, African,

Arabic, and fusion. *Disques d'occasion* (used CDs), at 20-60F, are generally no more expensive than in the U.S. and U.K. and can often be found at flea markets (see **Markets,** p. 310), and at a growing number of second-hand music stores. Many independent music vendors can be found in the 11*ème*, on rue de Charonne and side streets, and in the 5*ème* between rue des Ecoles and rue Mouffetard. For a list of what's hot in French music, from classical to pop to rap, see **Music,** p. 33. In addition to **Gibert Joseph's** many tables of CDs (see **Books,** p. 308), the following stores stock most of what's available.

B.P.M. (Bastille Paris Musique), 1, rue Keller, 11*ème* (tel. 01 40 21 02 88). M: Bastille. Catering to your rave needs, this address is a clubhouse, information point, and music store for house and techno fans. From groovy French House to jungle. Record players so you can listen before buying. Check posters and fliers for upcoming parties. Open M-Sa noon-8pm. MC, V.

FNAC (Fédération Nationale des Achats de Cadres). Several branches. **Forum des Halles:** 1-7, rue Porte Lescot, 1*er* (tel. 01 40 41 40 00), M: Les Halles. **Montparnasse:** 136, rue des Rennes, 6*ème* (tel. 01 49 54 30 00), M: Rennes. **Champs-Elysées:** 74, av. des Champs-Elysées, 8*ème* (tel. 01 53 53 64 64), M: Franklin D. Roosevelt. **Italiens:** 24, bd. des Italiens, 9*ème* (tel. 01 48 01 02 03); M: Opéra. **Bastille:** 4, pl. de la Bastille, 12*ème* (tel. 01 43 42 04 04), M: Bastille. **Etoile:** 26-30, av. des Ternes, 17*ème* (tel. 01 44 09 18 00), M: Ternes. Huge selection of tapes, CDs, and stereo equipment. The branch at Les Halles contains a well-stocked shelf of books about music. The Champs-Elysées, Bastille and Italiens branches have particularly large selections. Box office sells concert and theater tickets. **Montparnasse, Etoile,** and **Forum des Halles** branches open M-Sa 10am-7:30pm. **Italiens** branch open M-Sa 10am-midnight. **Bastille** branch open M-Sa 10am-8pm, W and F until 10pm. **Champs-Elysées** branch open M-Sa 10am-midnight, Su noon-midnight. MC, V.

Rough Trade, 30, rue Charonne, 11*ème* (tel. 01 40 21 61 62). M: Bastille. Parisian branch of the British record label that brought you the Smiths, Stiff Little Fingers, Wire, Père Ubu, and countless other pop and punk bands. Techno, hip-hop, and house downstairs; rock, pop, noise, and CDs upstairs. They also sell tickets to concerts around town as well as to all the major European music festivals. Open June-Aug. M-W 1-7pm, Th-Sa noon-8pm; Sept.-May M noon-8pm, Tu-W noon-8pm, Th-Sa 11am-8pm. MC, V.

Crocodisc, 40-42, rue des Ecoles, 5*ème* (tel. 01 43 54 47 95 or 01 43 54 33 22). M: Maubert-Mutualité. Browse through 2 rooms of used CDs, tapes, and records under the sweet sound of their big yellow speakers. Mainly stocks rock, pop, techno, reggae, classical. Buys CDs for 10-30F. Nearby **Crocojazz,** 64 rue de la Montagne-Ste-Geneviève (tel. 01 46 34 78 38) stocks jazz and blues. Both stores open Tu-Sa 11am-7pm. MC, V.

La Chaumière à Musique, 5, rue de Vaugirard, 6*ème* (tel. 01 43 54 07 25). M: Odéon. Classical music superstore with a knowledgeable staff. User-friendly listening stations let you try before you buy. Open M-Sa 11am-8pm, Su 2-8pm. MC, V.

MARKETS

Looking for that special something? From silver serving platters to Stevie Wonder 45s, Balzac to blue jeans, Paris's covered and uncovered markets are an affordable way to discover the charm and chintz of daily life in the neighborhood. Paris's many flea markets *(marchés aux puces)* are great options if you are decorating an apartment or university room and need cheap furniture, appliances, and cooking utensils. You'll also find vintage clothing, used bicycles, old televisions, stereos, telephones, and answering machines. Feel free to haggle and bargain. Wherever you are, watch your wallet. The bustle of market day brings out the pickpockets in hordes. For info on market food, see **Food and Drink,** p. 154.

MARCHÉS AUX PUCES (FLEA MARKETS)

PUCES DE ST-OUEN

Located in St-Ouen, a town just north of the 18ème. M: Porte de Clignancourt. Open Sa-M 7am-7:30pm; many of the official stalls close earlier, but renegade vendors may open at 5am and stay open until 9pm.

The granddaddy of all flea markets, the **Puces de St-Ouen** is an overwhelming smorgasbord of stuff. It opens early and shuts late, and serious hunters should allow themselves the better part of a day in order to cover significant ground; the market tends to be least crowded before noon.

From antique armoires and fine silverware to LPs and vintage 60s hippie gear, you'll find everything you need (and don't) in the many acres of criss-crossing pedestrian alleys of the Puces St-Ouen. Prices and quality vary as widely as the merchandise, from dirt-cheap, low-quality bargains found among renegade stalls and tables to antique-dealers who use buzzers to ring in their preferred customers while keeping out the riff-raff. The market began during the Middle Ages, when merchants resold the cast-off clothing of aristocrats (crawling with the market's namesake insects) to peasant-folk on the edge of the city. Today, it is a highly structured, regular market alongside a wild, anything-goes street bazaar.

The market is officially divided into a number of sub-markets, each specializing in a certain type of item. The structure of the market is terribly confusing, however, as stalls and vendors bleed from one square into the next. Ask around for directions to the particular market you seek; otherwise, wander aimlessly and enjoy the pandemonium.

The 10-minute walk along av. de la Porte de Clignancourt, under the highway, and left on rue Jean Henri Fabre to the official market is jammed with tiny **unofficial stalls.** Most of these stalls sell flimsy new clothes, T-shirts, African masks, and teenage jewelry at exorbitant prices. If this renegade bazaar turns you off, continue to the official market where you'll be able to browse leisurely in a much more pleasant setting.

The **official market** comprises many sales forums, located on rue des Rosiers and rue Jules Vallès. From rue Jean Henri Fabre, slip into the **Marché Malik,** a warehouse-type space filled with new and used clothing, shoes, music booths, and a tattoo parlor. Exiting onto rue Jules Vallès, and walking away from the bongo drums and hard-sell banter of rue Fabre, you'll encounter the indoor **Marché Jules Vallès** with its overwhelming collection of old trinkets and antique miscellany. **Marché Paul Bert,** on rue Paul Bert, has more antique bric-a-brac as well as a large collection of wooden furniture. Next door at the **Marché Serpette,** more specialized furniture stores reign side-by-side with shops dealing in antique firearms. **Marché Biron** on rue des Rosiers and **Marché Dauphine** on rue Fabre will help you plan what

 COMMENT DIT-ON "RIP-OFF"? First-time visitors should note some important tips. First, there are no five-franc diamond rings here. If you find the Hope Diamond in a pile of schlock jewelry, the vendor planted it there. Second, be prepared to bargain; sellers don't expect to get their starting price. Third, pickpockets love crowded areas, especially the one around the unofficial stalls. Fourth, the Three Card Monte con artists proliferate. Don't be pulled into the game by seeing someone win lots of money: he's part of the con, planted to attract suckers. Finally, if you are a savvy rock-and-roll connoisseur with a cultivated sense of patience, this is the place to find rare records. Record peddlers seem not to know what they have, and if you look long enough, you might just find a priceless LP for next to nothing.

to buy for your home when you're rich and famous. **Marché Vernaison,** located between rue des Rosiers and av. Michelet, has more upper-class tchatchkes, prints, beads, buttons, and musical instruments.

The **Marché des Rosiers,** rue Paul Bert (lamps, vases, and 20th-century art), and the **Marché Autica,** rue des Rosiers (paintings, furniture), are small, paler shadows of the large markets and deal mainly in new or fairly modern goods. The **Marché Malassie** is as new as any of this stuff gets; more a mall than a market, it specializes in "antiques" from the 60s and uninteresting furniture and artwork. Leaving the markets via av. Michelet takes you past a herd of leather coats, boots, and bags.

If you want to stop for lunch at the flea market, try a steaming bowl of *moules marinière* with *frites*, the uncontested specialty of restaurants in the area. The restaurant **Chez Louisette,** 130, av. Michelet (tel. 01 40 12 10 14), inside the Marché Vernaison, allée no. 10, all the way at the back, stands out. Here, campy singers, including Claude the Pompier chantant, liven up this eclectically decorated restaurant—dominated by large gold drapes—with classic French café *chansons,* a French version of American show tunes. Unfortunately, the secret is out, and you'll hear as much English and German as French. (*Moules* 60F. Open Sa-M 8am-7pm.)

OTHER FLEA MARKETS

Puces de Vanves, along rue Marc Sanguier between av. de la Porte de Vanves and av. Georges La Fenestre, 14ème. M: Porte de Vanves. Less crowded, much smaller, and more manageable than Ouen, Vanves carries a fairly good assortment of antique cameras, jewelry, furniture, lace, spoons, dishes, 19th-century books, and 20th-century comic books. Open Sa-Su 8am-7pm.

Puces de Montreuil, extends from pl. de la Porte de Montreuil along av. du Professeur André Lemierre and av. Galliéni, 20ème. M: Porte de Montreuil. Cheap in every sense. Auto parts, stereos, and tools (look for the amazing shower-head stall) abound, but the market's heart is in its piles of used clothes and eccentric hats, most priced between 5F and 50F. Bargain freely and watch your wallet. Open Sa-M 7:30am-7:30pm.

OTHER MARKETS

Carreau du Temple, 2-8, rue Perrée, at the corner of rue Dupetit Thouars and rue de Picardie, 3ème. M: Temple. Follow rue du Temple away from the métro and turn left on rue Dupetit Thouars. This structure of blue steel and glass is a neighborhood sports center in the afternoon and a clothes market in the morning. Good especially for leather, new clothes, and fabrics. You can usually get the already low price down at least 25% by haggling. More crowded on weekends. Open Tu-F 9am-noon, Sa-Su 9am-1pm.

Marché aux Fleurs, on pl. Louis-Lépine just across from the M: Cité staircase, 4ème. This permanent flower market fills the plaza near the Palais de Justice with color and fragrance and makes for a romantic walk down the Seine. Open M-Sa 9am-7pm. On Sunday an animal market appears instead, featuring rabbits, gerbils, and bird cages. Parakeets 95-800F. Rabbits 100F. Hamsters 20F. Goldfish 10F. Open Su 9am-6pm.

Marché aux Timbres, from the Rond-Point des Champs-Elysées to the corner of av. Matignon and av. Gabriel, 8ème. M: Franklin D. Roosevelt. A world of stamps for the philatelists in us all. Open Th and Sa-Su 10am-7pm.

Quai de Mégisserie, 1er. M: Pont-Neuf or Châtelet. Creatures lovable and lunchable squawk, purr, yelp, and gobble in this 300-year-old animal bazaar. Cages spill from the stores onto the street, and fauna mingles with flora. Open daily 8am-7pm.

DAYTRIPPING

These miraculous escapes from the toils of a great city give one a clearer impression of the breadth with which it is planned, and of the civic order and elegance pervading its whole system.
—Edith Wharton, *A Motor-Flight Through France*, 1908

TRIP	TRAVEL TIME
Versailles	30-40 minutes
Fontainebleau	55-65 minutes
Chartres	65-75 minutes
Giverny	60-70 minutes
Disneyland Paris	45-50 minutes
Chantilly	40-50 minutes
Châteaux de Malmaison	45-55 minutes
Vaux-le-Vicomte	75-120 minutes
Provins	75-85 minutes
Saint-Denis	15-20 minutes
Saint-Germain-en-Laye	30-35 minutes
Auvers-sur-Oise	60-90 minutes

VERSAILLES

The RER has direct and frequent train service between Paris and Versailles. Trains run from M: Invalides on RER Line C5 to the Versailles Rive Gauche station (30-40min., departs every 15min., 28F round-trip). From the Invalides métro stop, take trains with labels beginning with "V" (Vick, Vora, and so on). Buy your RER ticket before going through the turnstile to the platform; although a métro ticket will get you through these turnstiles, it will not get you through RER turnstiles at Versailles and could get you in trouble with the controlleurs. Tel. 01 30 84 74 00; www.chateauversailles.com. **Open** *May-Sept. Tu-Su 9am-6:30pm; Oct.-Apr. Tu-Su 9am-5:30pm. Last admission 30min. before closing. Admission to* **palace and self-guided tour, entrance A:** *45F; ages 18-25, over 60, and after 3:30pm 35F. Supplement for* **audio tour, entrance C:** *1hr., 25F, ages 7 and up, under 7 free. Supplement for* **guided tour, entrance D:** *1hr., 25F, ages 7-17 17F; 1½hr., 37F, ages 7-17 26F; 2hr., 50F, ages 7-17 34F; under 7 free (see* **Audio and Lecture Tours,** *p. 318).* **Gardens** *open daily sunrise-sundown. Free.* **Fountains** *turned on for special displays mid-Apr. to mid-Oct. Sa-Su 3:30-5:30pm. 28F.*

By sheer force of ego, the Sun King converted a hunting lodge into the world's most famous palace. The sprawling château, with its Hall of Mirrors, royal suites, guest rooms, antechambers, and portrait galleries, stands as a testament to the despotic playboy-king who lived, entertained, and governed on the grandest of scales. A century later, while Louis XVI and Marie-Antoinette entertained in lavish style, the peasants of Paris starved. The opulence of Versailles makes clear why it is they lost their heads (see **History,** p. 4).

HISTORY

A child during the aristocratic insurgency called the Fronde, Louis XIV is said to have entered his father's bedchamber one night only to find (and frighten away) an assassin. Fearing noble conspiracy the rest of his life, Louis chose to move the center of royal power out of Paris and away from potential aristocratic insubordination. In 1682 the Sun King decided on Versailles, the hunting lodge-cum-palace built and decorated by Le Vau, Le Brun, and Le Nôtre (see **Vaux-le-Vicomte,** p. 326).

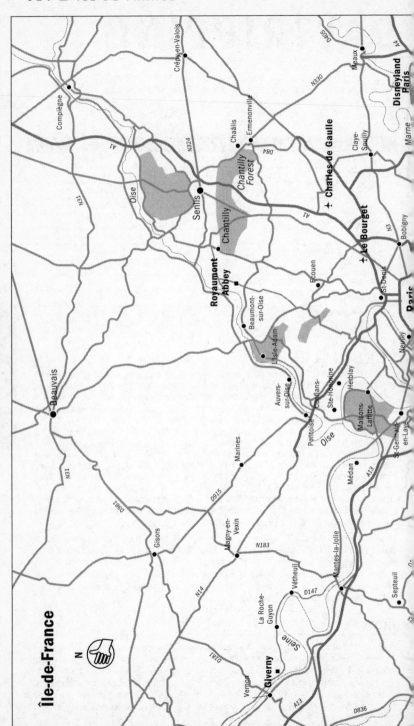

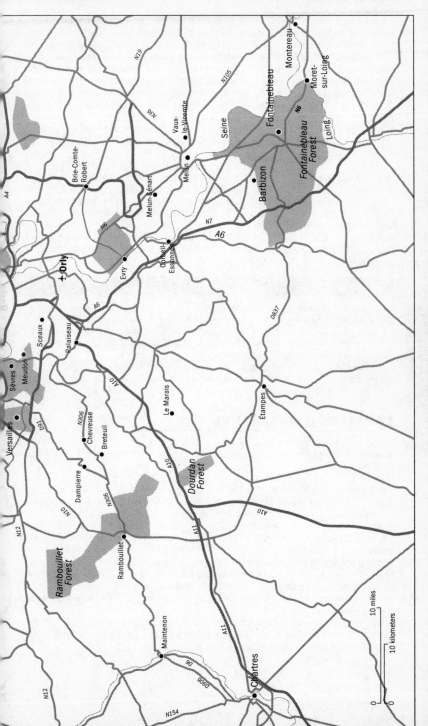

By Louis's decree, the court became the mandatory nucleus of noble life, where more than 1000 of France's aristocrats vied for the king's favor (see **History**, p. 4).

The château itself is a gilded lily of classical Baroque style. No one knows just how much it cost to build Versailles; Louis XIV burned the accounts to keep the price a mystery. At the same time, life there was less luxurious than one might imagine: courtiers wore rented swords and urinated behind statues in the parlors, wine froze in the drafty dining rooms, and dressmakers invented the color *puce* (literally, "flea") to camouflage the insects crawling on the noblewomen. Still, the mass extortion that Versailles represents would spark the French Revolution a century later. On October 5, 1789, 15,000 Parisian fishwives and National Guardsmen marched out to the palace and brought the royal family back to Paris, where they were later guillotined in 1793.

During the 19th century, King Louis-Philippe established a museum to preserve the château, against the wishes of most French people, who wanted Versailles demolished just as the Bastille had been. In 1871, the château took the limelight once again, when Wilhelm of Prussia became Kaiser Wilhelm I of Germany in the Hall of Mirrors. That same year, as headquarters of the Thiers regime, Versailles sent an army against the Parisian Commune. The *Versaillais* pierced the city walls and crushed the *communards*. At the end of WWI, a vengeful France forced Germany to sign the ruinous Treaty of Versailles in the Hall of Mirrors, the very room of modern Germany's birth.

WHAT TO SEE

■ Visiting Versailles is a mammoth undertaking. One day will allow thorough visits of all of the major attractions. At least two days are needed to see everything. A standard day-long visit: The first **3 hours** should be spent in the **Château,** on the tours commencing at entrances A and C, with an option to substitute some of that time with one of the **1 to 2-hour guided tours** (in French and English) leaving from Entrance D. After lunch, spend **an hour or two** in the **gardens,** either walking through the Hameau, or on one of the daily guided walks. Finally, spend **1 hour** in the **Grand Trianon,** the best furnished of the royal quarters, and if time permits, **30 minutes** in the **Petit Trianon.**

🛈 PRACTICAL INFORMATION

Arrive early in the morning to avoid the crowds, which are worse on Sunday from May to September (when the fountains are turned on) and in late June (when French schoolchildren are on field trips). When you arrive at the Versailles Rive Gauche RER train stop, exit the station and take a right. Proceed 200m, and the gilt-fenced outer courtyard of the Château is on your left, at the end of a long driveway. An equestrian statue of a crimped, turned-out Louis XIV stands at the courtyard's center. Overlooking the courtyard is the terrace on which Molière's *Tartuffe* debuted. The clock on the pediment, flanked by Hercules and Mars, was traditionally set to the time of death of the previous king. The balcony of the **King's Bedroom** is visible at the center of the east-west axis along which the château and gardens are laid out. Signs in the courtyard point you to Entrance A, B, C, D, or H. Most of Versailles's visitors enter at **Entrance A,** located on the right-hand side in the north wing, or **Entrance C,** located in the archway to the left. (**Entrance B** is for groups, **Entrance D** is where tours with a living, breathing guide begin, and **Entrance H** is for visitors in wheelchairs.)

For more on Versailles château events, sights, lodging, and food, call the **Office de Tourisme de Versailles,** 7, rue des Reservoirs (tel. 01 39 50 36 22; fax 01 39 50 68 07), down the street from the château on the Opéra side.

DAYTRIPPING

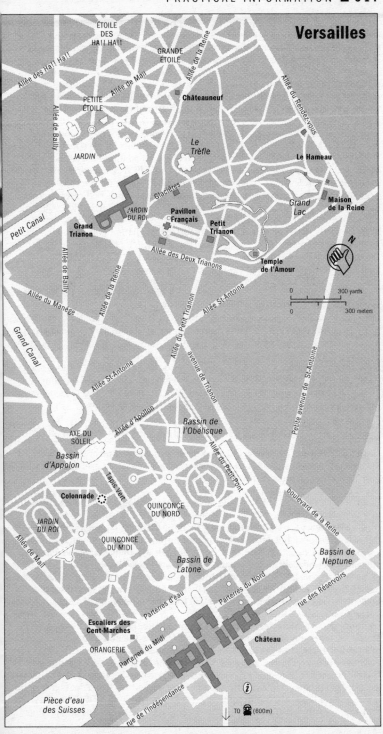

Versailles

ÉTOILE DES HA!! HA!!
GRANDE ÉTOILE
Allée des Ha!! Ha!!
Allée de Mail
Allée de la Reine
PETITE ÉTOILE
Allée de Bailly
Châteauneuf
Allée du Rendez-vous
JARDIN
Le Trèfle
Le Hameau
Glacières
Pavillon Français
Grand Lac
Maison de la Reine
JARDIN DU ROI
Petit Trianon
Petit Canal
Grand Trianon
Allée des Deux Trianons
Temple de l'Amour
Allée de Bailly
Allée de la Reine
Allée St-Antoine
Allée du Manège
Allée St-Antoine
Allée du Petit Trianon
avenue de Trianon
Grand Canal
Allée St-Antoine
Petite avenue de St-Antoine
Allée d'Apollon
Bassin de l'Obélisque
AXE DU SOLEIL
Bassin d'Appolon
Allée du Petit-Pont
Colonnade
Tapis Vert
QUINCONCE DU NORD
boulevard de la Reine
JARDIN DU ROI
QUINCONCE DU MIDI
Bassin de Neptune
Allée de Mail
Bassin de Latone
Parterres du Nord
rue des Réservoirs
Parterres d'eau
Escaliers des Cent-Marches
ORANGERIE
Parterres du Midi
Château
Pièce d'eau des Suisses
rue de l'Indépendance
TO 🏠 (600m)

0 — 300 yards
0 — 300 meters

N

ⓘ

DAYTRIPPING

👁 THE SELF-GUIDED TOUR: ENTRANCE A

General admission allows entrance to the following rooms: the *grands appartements*, where the king and queen received the public; the War and Peace Drawing Rooms; and the *Galerie des Glaces* (Hall of Mirrors). The King's and Queen's apartments may be seen only by guided tour. If you intend to take one, proceed directly to either Entrance C or D (see **Audio and Lecture Tours,** below), purchase the regular admission ticket, and inquire about guided visits.

The general admission ticket starts your visit in the **Musée de l'Histoire de France,** created in 1837 by Louis-Philippe to celebrate his country's glory. Along its textured walls hang portraits of men and women who shaped the course of French history. The face of Louis XIV is everywhere. Of particular interest are portraits by Philippe de Champaigne, a court artist under Louis XIII. The 21 rooms (arranged in chronological order) seek to construct a historical context for the château.

Each of the gilded **drawing rooms** in the **State Apartments** is dedicated to a mythological god: Hercules, Mars, and the ever-present Apollo (the Sun King identified with the sun god). The ornate **Salon d'Apothon** was Louis XIV's throne room. Framed by the **War and Peace Drawing Rooms** is the **Hall of Mirrors,** which was a gloomy hallway until Mansart added a series of mirrored panels in order to double the light in the room. These mirrors were the largest that 17th-century technology could produce and were an unbelievable extravagance. Le Brun's ceiling paintings tell the history of Louis XIV's heroism, culminating in the central piece, entitled *The King Governs Alone.* It was here in this vast room that the Treaty of Versailles was ratified, effectively ending the First World War.

The **Queen's Bedchamber,** where royal births were packed, public events, is now furnished year-round in its floral summer decor—not the darker plush red and black velvet used during 18th-century winters. A version of the David painting depicting Napoleon's self-coronation (the original is in the Louvre) dominates the **Salle du Sacré** (also known as the Coronation Room). In this room, the king used to wash the feet of a lucky 13 poor children every Holy Thursday. The sometimes-open **Hall of Battles** rounds out the non-guided visit. Dominated by huge paintings, the hall is a monument to 14 centuries of France's military battles.

👁 THE AUDIO AND LECTURE TOURS: ENTRANCES C & D

Head for Entrance C to purchase an **audioguide** to the **Apartment of Louis XIV,** the **Hall of Mirrors,** and the **Apartments of the Dauphin and Dauphine.** The **King's Bedroom,** which affords a blinding look at the monarch's gold bed and balustrade, also features Nocret's beautiful family portrait, depicting Louis XIV as Apollo and his brother, Philippe d'Orléans, as holder of the morning star. Philippe was the first after the morning chaplain to see the Sun King—he was also kept in skirts until he was 18.

All **guided tours** depart from Entrance D, at the left-hand corner as you approach the palace. Choose between seven tours of different parts of the château. Three are offered in English: **Private apartments of Louis XV, Louis XVI, Marie-Antoinette, Madame de Pompadour,** and **Madame Du Barry;** the **Opéra** and the **Chapel;** and a **Day in the Life of Louis XIV.** Sign-language tours are available for the King's State Apartments, the Hall of Mirrors, and the Apartment of the Queen. Reservations must be made in advance with the Bureau d'Action Culturelle (tel. 01 30 83 77 88).

The **Opéra,** which took architect Jacques-Ange Gabriel 20 years to design, was completed at breakneck speed by 20,000 workmen in time for the wedding of Marie-Antoinette and the future Louis XVI. Often considered the world's most beautiful theater, the pink and blue oval room is a marvelous fake. It looks like marble or bronze, but the hall is actually made of wood because the meticulous Gabriel wanted it to resound like a violin. The mirrored galleries reflect chandeliers and gilt archways, making the theater seem larger than it is. The room's splendor brought Marie-Antoinette to breach royal etiquette on her wedding day; she took her eyes off the stage and ogled the decor. Many of Molière's plays premiered here, accompanied by the music of court composer Jean-Baptiste Lully. Today, performances are rare because of the cost of lighting the many chandeliers.

The tour of **Louis XV's apartments** showcases a small collection of furnishings, instruments, and tapestries. Mozart played in one of these rooms on his youthful visits to Versailles (at ages 7 and 22). The visit to **Marie-Antoinette's apartments** does not trail through as many lavish rooms as you might hope; on October 6, 1789, a crowd of bloodthirsty Parisians stormed the Queen's bedroom, demanding the head of the "Austrian whore." The palace was never the same.

THE GARDENS

Versailles's gardens are massive, perfectly scaled to the palace. Numerous artists—Le Brun, Mansart, Coysevox—executed statues and fountains here, but master gardener André Le Nôtre provided the overall plan. Louis XIV, landscape enthusiast, wrote the first guidebook to the gardens, entitled the *Manner of Presenting the Gardens at Versailles*. Tours should begin, as the Sun King commanded, on the terrace and admire the wide paths and tall trees. To the left, the **Parterre du Midi** graces the area in front of Mansart's **Orangerie**, once home to 2000 orange trees; the temperature inside still never drops below 6°C (43°F). In the center of the terrace lies the **Parterre d'Eau,** while the **Bassin de Latone** fountain below features Latona, mother of Diana and Apollo, shielding her children as Jupiter turns villains into frogs.

Past the fountain and to the left is the **Rockwork Grove,** built between 1681 and 1683. Once a marble dance floor, the grove shows off fetid water cascading over shell-encrusted steps. The south gate of the grove leads to the magnificent **Bassin de Bacchus,** one of four seasonal fountains. The **Bassin du Miroir d'Eau** spurts near the peaceful **Jardin du Roi** and the **Bassin de Saturne.** The king used to take light meals amid the **Colonnade's** 32 columns, sculptures, and white marble basins. The north gate to the Colonnade exits onto the **Tapis Vert** (Green Carpet), the central mall linking the château to the **Char d'Apollon** (Chariot of Apollo). Pulled by four prancing horses, the Sun God rises out of dark water to enlighten the world.

On the north side of the garden is Marsy's incredible **Bassin d'Encelade.** One of the giants who tried to unseat Jupiter from Mount Olympus, Enceladus cries in agony under the weight of rocks that Jupiter hurled to bury him. When the fountains are turned on, a 25m jet bursts from Enceladus's mouth. Flora reclines on a bed of flowers in the **Bassin de Flore,** while Ceres luxuriates in sheaves of wheat in the **Bassin de Cérès.** The **Parterre du Nord,** full of flowers, lawns, and trees, overlooks some of the garden's most spectacular fountains. The **Allée d'Eau,** a fountain-lined walkway, provides the best view of the **Bassin des Nymphes de Diane.** The path slopes toward the sculpted **Bassin du Dragon,** where a dying beast spurts water 27m into the air. Ninety-nine jets of water attached to urns and seahorns surround a menacing Neptune in the **Bassin de Neptune,** the gardens' largest fountain.

Beyond Le Nôtre's classical gardens stretch wilder woods and farmland. Check out the **Grand Canal,** a sharp-edged pond beyond the Bassin d'Apollon. To explore further, rent a bike to the right of the canal, just outside the garden gates (30F per hr.). If you're with friends, rent a boat for four people at the boathouse to the right of the canal (open Tu-F noon-5:30pm, Sa-Su 11am-6pm; 72F per hr., 50F refundable deposit). The two-hour "Discovering Groves Tour" provides the history of Le Nôtre's gardens and their fountains (June-Oct.; call tel. 01 30 83 77 88; 1hr.; 15F).

> # MIRROR, MIRROR
> The Hall of Mirrors, perhaps the centerpiece of the visit to Versailles, united the best of available artistic talent. 73 meters long and 10.5 meters wide, it was begun by Jules Hardouin Mansart in 1678 and worked in turn by Le Brun, Le Comte, Caffieri, and Coysevox until its completion eight years later. 17 mirrors, each an incredible expense at the time, face 17 windows which look out onto the gardens. The ceiling paintings, elevating the military triumphs of Louis XIV to biblical significance, were conceived by Le Brun.

THE TRIANONS AND MARIE-ANTOINETTE'S HAMEAU

*Shuttle trams from the palace to the Trianons and the Hameau leave from behind the palace: round-trip 32F, ages 3-12 20F. The walk takes about 25min. **Both Trianons: Open** May-Sept. Tu-Sa 10am-6:30pm; Oct.-Apr. Tu-F 10am-12:30pm and 2-5:30pm, Sa-Su 10am-5:30pm; last entrance 30min. before closing. **Admission** to Grand Trianon 25F, reduced tariff 15F; Petit Trianon 15F, reduced tariff 10F. Combined ticket to the Trianons 30F, reduced tariff 20F.*

Although it may be difficult after visiting the château to muster the energy, the Trianons and Hameau provide a racier counterpoint to the stuffy formality of the château. It was here that kings trysted with lovers and where Marie-Antoinette lived like the peasant she wasn't.

PETIT TRIANON

Down the wooded path from the château, the Petit Trianon appears on the right, a neoclassical gem built between 1762-68 by the architect Gabriel to be the lovenest for Louis XV and his mistress Madame de Pompadour. By the time it was completed, Pompadour was dead and Louis's new lover was the Countess du Barry. Marie-Antoinette took control of the Petit Trianon in 1774 and claimed it as her new favorite spot, thus earning it the nickname "Little Vienna." Upon giving it to his queen, Louis XVI is said to have remarked, "Since you love flowers, I am offering you a bouquet that is the Petit Trianon." She had the formal gardens ripped up, sent them to the Jardin des Plantes in Paris, and installed a trendy English garden. The Petit Trianon was later inhabited by Napoleon's sister and the Empress Marie-Louise. In 1867, the Empress Eugénie, who worshipped Marie-Antoinette, turned it into a museum. Today the lower level of the Petit Trianon is under restoration, but visitors can still tour the main level with its large portrait of Marie-Antoinette.

Exit the Petit Trianon, turn left, and follow the marked path to the libidinous **Temple of Love,** a domed rotunda with columns rising out of a small island. The temple shelters a copy of Bouchardon's famous statue of Cupid shooting his arrow. Marie-Antoinette held many intimate nighttime parties in the small space, during which thousands of torches would be illuminated in the surrounding ditch. The Queen was perhaps at her happiest and most ludicrous when spending time at the **Hameau,** her Norman-style cottage hamlet down the path from the Temple of Love. Inspired by Jean-Jacques Rousseau's theories on the goodness of nature so in vogue in the second half of the 18th century, the Queen aspired to a more simple life, peasant-style. She commissioned Richard Mique to build a compound of 12 buildings in which she could play at country life, including a mill, a dairy, and gardener's house, all surrounding a quaint artificial lake. At the center is the Queen's Cottage. Any illusions of her slumming it with the farmhands disappear after crossing through her cottage doors. The rooms contained ornate furniture, marble fireplaces, chambers designated for Marie-Antoinette's silver, monogrammed linens, and footmen.

GRAND TRIANON

The single-story, stone and pink marble Grand Trianon was intended as a château-away-from-château for Louis XIV, who longed to escape the demands of court life and spend a little quality time with his mistress, Madame de Maintenon. Here the King could be reached only by boat along the Grand Canal, eliminating all of those pesky issues of everyday rule. The palace, which consists of two wings joined together by a central peristyle porch, was designed by Mansart and erected in 1687-88. Formal gardens are located behind the colonnaded porch. The mini-château was stripped of its furniture during the Revolution but was later restored and inhabited by Napoleon and his second wife. Charles de Gaulle installed presidential apartments and rooms for visiting heads of state in the Grand Trianon, and the constitutional amendment for Maastricht was written here.

🎵 SPECIAL EVENTS

On Sundays from mid-April through mid-October and Saturdays in July and August, when the fountains are in full operation, the **Grandes Eaux Musicales** play. A slightly diminished version called the **Grande Perspective** runs 11am to noon. Tour the 24 activated, musically accompanied fountains 3:30 to 5:15pm. A free pamphlet lays out a suggested walking path; don't bother with the expensive fountain guide (25F). (Admission to park during Grandes Eaux 28F; under 10 free.)

As Voltaire urged, "Pleasure is the object, the duty, and aim of all reasonable beings." So by all means attend one of the stunning **Fêtes de Nuit,** musical and fireworks extravaganzas that imitate the huge fêtes of Louis XIV. The garden at Versailles had to be finished in 1664 in time for one such party, the Fête of the Enchanted Isle, for which Molière wrote a *masque.* (Fêtes held 7 times in July and late Aug.-early Sept.; Sa at 10pm, 1½hr., 70-250F, under 10 free. Tickets at the tourist office, box offices within Paris, or at www.fnac.com. Enter at 2, bd. de la Reine. Info tel. 01 30 83 78 88. Doors open 1½hr. before the show.) The **Nouveaux Plaisirs de Versailles** is a foundation that coordinates musical, dance, and theater events at the château, from Mozart to Molière. (Tickets 70-320F, call 01 30 83 78 88 for info.)

Versailles offers two ongoing **lecture** series. The first, **Histoire du Château,** provides an in-depth historical look at the palace. The second, **Visites Approfondies,** offers lectures like "Court Costumes under the Old Regime." (Oct.-May Sa or Su at 2pm; 40F; call 01 39 50 36 22 for topics and dates.)

FONTAINEBLEAU

More digestible than Versailles, the Château de Fontainebleau acheives nearly the same grandeur, with a charm unique among the great châteaux. Two men stand out among the parade of post-Renaissance kings and their corresponding apartments, galleries, and terraces: François I, responsible for dazzling ballrooms lined with work of Michelangelo's school, and Napoleon, who restored the post-Revolution dilapidation to a home befitting an emperor. Together with the lush surrounding gardens, the beautiful estate harbors many peaceful corners even during peak hours, and ranks among the best day-trips from Paris.

🚉 PRACTICAL INFORMATION

Across from the château, the **Fontainebleau Tourist Office,** 4, rue Royal (tel. 01 60 74 99 99; fax. 01 60 74 80 22), organizes tours of the village, helps find accommodations, and has maps of Fontainebleau and Barbizon (open M-Sa 9:30am-6:30pm, Su 10am-4pm). From Paris, hourly **trains** run to Fontainebleau from the Gare de Lyon, banlieue level (45min., 94F round-trip). The château is a 30-minute walk or 10-minute bus ride away. From the station, **Car Vert A** (tel. 01 64 22 23 88) runs buses (9.50F) after each train arrival from Paris; take the bus in direction "Château-Lilas" and get off at the Château stop. You can also rent a bike from **MBK** (tel. 01 64 22 36 14; fax 01 60 72 64 89) at the train station. (60F per day; mountain bikes 120F per day. Helmets 10F. Open daily 9am-7pm. MC, V.)

HISTORY

Kings of France have hunted on these grounds since the 12th century, when the exiled Thomas à Becket consecrated Louis VII's manor chapel. In 1528, François I rebuilt the castle to bring himself closer to the game he so loved to hunt. Italian artists designed and decorated the palace, and their paintings, including the *Mona Lisa,* filled François's private collections. Subsequent kings commissioned their favorite designers to add magnificent rooms and new wings. Louis XIII was born here in 1601, Louis XIV revoked the Edict of Nantes here in 1685, and Louis XV was married here in 1725. Napoleon, who visited Fontainebleau frequently, called it "La Maison des Siècles" (the House of Centuries). In 1814, Napoleon bid goodbye to the Empire from the central courtyard, now called the **Cour des Adieux** in his honor. Also known as the **White Horse Court,** it is the main entry to the château. The entrance was redecorated during the Third Empire under Napoleon III.

▨ CHÂTEAU DE FONTAINEBLEAU

Tel. 01 60 71 50 70. **Open** *July-Aug. W-M 9:30am-6pm; May-June and Sept.-Oct. W-M 9:30am-5pm; Nov.-Apr. W-M 9:30am-12:30pm and 2-5pm. Last entry 45min. before closing.* **Admission** *35F; students, seniors, and Sundays 23F, under 18 free.*

The pamphlet handed out with your admission is of little use: you may want to invest in a small printed guide (20F) available down the hall from the ticket booth. Audio tours (30F, 90min.) are sold in town at the Fontainebleau Tourist Office (see below). Most rooms feature information placards with a few sentences in English, and about three times as many in French.

GRANDS APPARTEMENTS. The Grands Appartements provide a lesson in the history of French architecture and decoration. Dubreuil's **Gallery of Plates** tells the history of Fontainebleau on a remarkable series of 128 porcelain plates, fashioned in Sèvres between 1838 and 1844. In the long **Galerie de François I,** the most famous room at Fontainebleau, muscular figures by Il Rosso (known in French as Maître Roux) tell mythological tales of heroism, brilliantly illuminated by light flooding in from windows that look out onto the **Fountain Courtyard.** Similarly, the **Ball Room's** magnificent octagonal ceiling, heavy wood paneling, and bay windows look out onto the **Oval Courtyard.** Decorated under Henri IV, the **King's Cabinet** (also known as the **Louis XIII Salon** because Louis XIII was born there) was the site of *le débotter*, the king's post-hunt boot removal. Gobelin tapestries and Savonnerie carpets line walls and floors throughout the palace. Napoleon pored over the volumes of the long, lofty, sunlit **Bibliothèque Diana.** Since the 17th century, every queen and empress of France has slept in the gold and green **Queen's Bed Chamber;** the gilded wood bed was built for Marie-Antoinette. The N on the red and gold velvet throne of the **Throne Room** is a testament to Napoleon's humility in what is today the only existing throne room in France. Sandwiched between two mirrors, **Napoleon's Bed Chamber** is a monument to either narcissism or eroticism, while the Emperor's austere **Small Bed Chamber** contains a small military bed. In the **Emperor's Private Room,** known today as the **Abdication Chamber,** Napoleon signed off his empire in 1814. The tour ends with the 16th-century, Italian-frescoed **Trinity Chapel.**

MUSÉE CHINOIS DE L'IMPÉRATRICE EUGÉNIE. This museum was created in 1863 by the Empress to house her collection of Chinese decorative art, porcelain, jade, and crystal, which she had received as gifts during the 1860 Franco-English campaign in China and from the Siamese ambassador in 1861. *(Admission is included in price of the château.)*

PETITS APPARTEMENTS. Parts of the château can be seen only by guided tour. The tour of the **Petits Appartements** features the private rooms of Napoleon and the Empress Josephine, as well as the impressive map room and Galerie des Cerfs *(4 tours daily, call for hours).*

MUSÉE NAPOLÉON. The Musée Napoléon features a collection of the Emperor's personal toothbrush, his tiny shoes, his field tent, his son's toys, and state gifts from European monarchs such as Carlos IV of Spain. *(2 tours per morning, M, Th, Sa.)* Other tours feature Napoléon III's influence on the château *(2 tours per morning, W, F, Su). (Admission 16F, under 26 and over 60 12F, under 18 free.)*

THE GARDENS. Fontainebleau's serene **Jardin Anglais** and **Jardin de Diane** feature quiet grottoes guarded by statues of the Greek huntress and the **Etang des Carpes,** a carp-filled pond that can be explored by rowboat. *(Boat rental June-Aug. daily 10am-12:30pm and 2-7pm; Sept. Sa-Su 2-6pm. 50F per 30min., 80F per hr.)* The **Forêt de Fontainebleau** is a thickly wooded 20,000-hectare preserve with hiking trails, bike paths, and sandstone rock-climbing. The tourist office provides maps. Fans of 19th-century art will recognize the thick hardwoods and sandstones made famous by Rousseau and Millet, painters of the Barbizon school (see **Museums**, p. 247).

IN THE TOWN

The **Musée Napoléonien d'Art et d'Histoire Militaire** (tel. 01 64 22 49 80, ext. 424) displays more of Napoleon's military paraphernalia. (88, rue St-Honoré. Open Tu-Sa 2-5pm. Last entrance 4:45pm. Admission 10F, under 12 free.)

CHARTRES

Were it not for a piece of fabric, the cathedral of Chartres and the town that surrounds it might only be a sleepy hamlet southwest of Paris. Because of this sacred relic—the cloth that the Virgin Mary supposedly wore when she gave birth to Jesus—Chartres became a major medieval pilgrimage center. The spectacular cathedral that towers above the surrounding rooftops and wheat fields is not the only reason to visit the city. Like the cathedral, the *vieille ville* (old town) is a masterpiece of medieval architecture with cobblestone staircases, gabled roofs, half-timbered houses, and iron lamps of a village forgotten by little else but time.

⚡ PRACTICAL INFORMATION

Trains: Chartres is accessible by frequent trains from Gare Montparnasse, Grandes Lignes (tel. 08 36 35 35 35). Roughly 1 train per hr. during the summer; call ahead for winter schedule (slightly over 1hr.; round-trip 142F, under 26 and over 60 108F). To reach the cathedral from the train station, walk straight along rue Jehan de Beauce to pl. de Châtelet and turn left into the place, right onto rue Ste-Même, and left onto rue Jean Moulin. Alternatively, just head toward the massive gothic spires.

Tourist Office: (tel. 02 37 21 50 00; fax 02 37 21 51 91). In front of the cathedral's main entrance at pl. de la Cathédrale. Helps find accommodations (10F fee) and supplies visitors with a list of restaurants, brochures, and two good maps, one with a walking tour and the other with hotels and other sites. Open Apr.-Sept. M-Sa 9am-7pm, Su 9:30am-5:30pm; Oct.-Mar. M-Sa 10am-6pm, Su 10am-1pm and 2:30-4:30pm.

▌ACCOMMODATIONS

Accommodations in Chartres are generally cheaper than their Parisian counterparts, and an overnight stay here can be an affordable and enjoyable escape.

Le Boeuf Couronné, 15, pl. Châtelet (tel. 02 37 18 06 06; fax 02 37 21 72 13). From the SNCF station, walk up av. Jehan de Beauce; hotel is on the right-hand side of the *place*. Small, clean, and airy rooms with TV and phone. Elevator. Breakfast 30F. Showers 20F. Dog 20F. Singles 158F, with shower and toilet 230F, with bath and toilet 247F; doubles 167F, with shower and toilet 288F, with bath and toilet 310F; triples 340F. AmEx, MC, V.

Hôtel Jehan de Beauce, 19, av. Jehan de Beauce (tel. 02 37 21 01 41; fax 02 37 21 59 10), across from the SNCF station. The colorful rooms (with phone and TV) may be small, but you can't beat the location. Elevator. Breakfast 30F. Singles 150F, with shower and toilet 200-230F; doubles 170F, with shower and toilet 230-250F; triples and quads with shower and toilet 300F. AmEx, MC, V.

◖ FOOD

There are lots of restaurants in Chartres but they are all expensive. Sandwiches are the most economical solution. An especially good and cheap bakery is **Au Bon Croissant de Chartres,** 1 rue de Bois Merrain (tel. 02 37 21 36 28), at the corner of rue de Bois Merrain and rue de la Tonnellerie. Sandwiches run 10F, *tartes* 11F.

👁 THE CATHEDRAL

*Tel. 02 37 21 75 02 or 02 37 28 15 58. **Open** M-Sa 7:30am-7:15pm, Su and holidays 8:30pm-7:15pm. No casual visits during mass. **Masses** M, W, Th, and Sa at 8 and 11:45am, T and F at 9am, M-Sa 6pm, Su 9:30 (Latin), 11am and 6pm. Call the tourist office for info on concerts in the cathedral, the annual student pilgrimage in late May, and other pilgrimages and festivals throughout the year. **Treasury** open Apr.-Oct. Tu-Sa 10am-noon and 2-6pm, Su and holidays 2-6pm; Nov.-Mar. Tu-Sa10am-11:40pm and 2:30-4:30pm, Su and holidays 2-5pm. Free. **Tower** open May-Aug. M-Sa 9am-6pm, Su 2-6pm; Sept.-Mar. M-Sa 9:30-11:30am and 2-5pm, Su 2-5pm. Admission 25F, ages 12-25 15F, under 12 free. Leave a piece of iden-tification in order to rent English audioguides from the gift shop (15-30F for various tours). **English tours of the cathedral** begin at the rear of the church nave and last 1¼hr.; Apr.-Jan. M-Sa noon and 2:45pm; 30F, students 20F. **French tours of the crypt** leave from La Crypte, 18, Cloître Nôtre-Dame. Tel. 02 37 21 56 33. Tours 30min., Apr.-Oct. M-Sa 11am, 2:15, 3:30, 4:30, and 5:15pm; Nov.-Mar. 11am and 4:15pm. Admission 11F, students 8F.*

The Cathédrale de Chartres survives today as one of the most sublime creations of the Middle Ages. It is the best-preserved medieval church in Europe, miraculously escaping major damage during the Revolution and WWII. A patchwork master-piece of Romanesque and Gothic design, the cathedral was constructed by gener-ations of unknown masons, architects, and artisans who labored for centuries.

SANCTA CAMISIA. The year after he became emperor in 875, Charlemagne's grand-son, Charles the Bald, donated to Chartres the Sancta Camisia, the cloth believed to be worn by the Virgin Mary when she gave birth to Christ. Although a church dedi-cated to Mary had existed on the site as early as the mid-700's, the emperor's bequest required a new cathedral to accommodate the growing number of pilgrims. In the hope that the sacred relic would bring healing and answer prayers, thousands flocked to the church on their knees. Just as at Lourdes, the sick were nursed in the crypt below the sanctuary, usually for a period of nine days. The powers of the relic were confirmed in AD 911 when the cloth saved the city; under attack from invading Goths and Vikings, converted the viking leader Rollon to Christianity. He became the first duke of Normandy and proved that cloths ruin Goths (see **Nuns,** p. 2).

Beginning in the 10th century with the arrival of the scholar Fulbert, the Acad-emy at Chartres became one of the great institutions of learning in medieval Europe. The founding of the rival Sorbonne contributed to the academy's decline. In 1194, a fire destroyed the town of Chartres and severely damaged the cathedral. Only the western tower, one of the entryways, and the crypt containing the Sancta Camisia were spared. Taking this damage as a sign from Mary, the Cardinal marched the relic out to the public and called on them to rebuild a more grand and fitting church. Because there were few hotels, pilgrims bunked and took their meals in the cathedral itself. All this communal living came at an olfactory price, particularly during the warmer months; the floor of the nave was deliberately sloped to allow for washing the floors after the pilgrims left, and panels of the win-dows could be removed to air out the sanctuary.

No visit to Chartres would be complete without seeing the Sancta Camisia, which is in a chapel to the left of the entrance of the cathedral's **treasury,** where other significant garments and objects from the building's history are preserved.

STAINED GLASS. Few cathedrals rival Chartres in size and majesty. Sculpture and stained glass depict Christian history from creation to the last judgement. At a time when books were rare and the vast majority of people illiterate, the cathedral was a multimedia teaching tool. Most of the stained glass dates from the 13th cen-tury and was preserved through both World Wars by heroic town authorities, who dismantled over 2000 square meters and stored the windows pane by pane in Dor-dogne. The medieval merchants who paid for each window are shown in the lower panels, providing a record of daily life in the 13th century. The famous Blue Virgin, Tree of Jesse, and Passion and Resurrection of Christ windows are among the sur-viving 12th-century stained glass. The center window of the Incarnation shows the story of Christ from the Annunciation to the ride into Jerusalem. Bring binoculars if you can (or rent them for 10F per hr plus ID or 300F deposit). As with all medieval stained glass, the stories should be "read" from bottom to top, left to right.

LABYRINTH. The windows of Chartres often distract visitors from the treasures below their feet. Though often covered with chairs, a winding labyrinth is carved into the floor in the rear of the nave. Designed in the 13th century, the labyrinth was laid out for pilgrims as a means of penitence, or as a substitute for a journey to the Holy Land. By following this symbolic journey on their hands and knees, the devout would act out a voyage to heavenly Jerusalem. A brass medallion, emblazoned with satanic minotaurs and a Virginesque Ariadne, stood in the center.

TOUR JEHAN-DE-BEAUCE. The adventurous can climb the cathedral's north tower, Tour Jehan-de-Beauce (named after its architect and completed in 1513) for a stellar view of the cathedral roof, the flying buttresses, and the city below. The tower is a wonderful example of flamboyant Gothic, a late medieval style. Built to replace a wooden steeple that repeatedly burned down, it provides a striking counterpart to its more sedate partner, the **octagonal steeple,** built just before the 1194 fire.

CRYPT. Parts of Chartres's **crypt,** such as a well down which Vikings tossed the bodies of their victims during raids, date back to the 9th century. You can enter the subterranean crypt only as part of a tour that leaves from La Crypte, the store opposite the cathedral's south entrance. The tour is in French, but information sheets are available in English.

OTHER SIGHTS. The Gothic and Romanesque exterior of the church is marked by three entrances. The 12th-century statues of the **Portale Royale** present an assembly of Old Testament figures. The 13th-century **Porche du Nord** depicts the life of Mary while the **Porche du Sud** shows the life of Christ. Inside the church, the Renaissance choir screen, begun by Jehan de Beauce in 1514, depicts the Virgin Mary's life from the birth of Christ to her assumption into heaven.

The only English-language **tours** of the cathedral are given by campy British tour-guide Malcolm Miller, an authority on Gothic architecture who has been leading visitors through the church for the past 40 years. His presentations on the cathedral's history and symbolism are intelligent, witty, and enjoyable for all ages. If you can, take both his morning and afternoon tours—no two are alike. He will doubtless hawk his book, *Chartres, the Cathedral, and Old Town* (30F), which is helpful to cover the information you've missed.

THE TOWN

Founded as the Roman city *Autricum*, Chartres is a medieval village at heart. Clustered peacefully around its mammoth house of God, the town's oldest streets are named for the trades once practiced there. Although the town is surrounded by flat fields, Chartres is built on a hill, and some of the best views of the cathedral are found by walking down the well-marked tourist circuit. Chartres's typically medieval tangle of streets can be maddening; free maps are available from the tourist office. For those with difficulty walking or who want a more relaxed tour of the town, a *petit train* runs from April to October with half-hour narrated tours (in French only) of the old city. *(Tel. 02 37 21 87 60. Tours begin in front of the tourist office. Adults 30F, kids under 12 18F.)*

MUSÉE DES BEAUX-ARTS. The Musée des Beaux-Arts, resides in the former Bishop's Palace. Built mainly in the 17th and 18th centuries (on a site occupied by bishops since the 11th century), the palace houses an eclectic collection of painting, sculpture, and furniture. Zurbarán and Vlaminck figure prominently, as do medieval wood polychrome statues from the 13th century. *(29, rue du Cloître Nôtre-Dame. Next to the cathedral. Tel. 02 37 36 41 39. Open May-Oct. M and W-Sa 10am-noon and 2-6pm, Su 2-6pm, Nov.-Apr. M and W-Sa 10am-noon and 2-5pm, Su 2-5pm. Admission 15F, students and seniors 7.5F.)*

DAYTRIPPING

MONUMENT TO JEAN MOULIN. A monument to Jean Moulin, the famous WWII Resistance hero who worked closely with de Gaulle, stands on rue Jean Moulin, off rue Cheval Blanc. Prefect of Chartres before the war, Moulin attempted suicide rather than sign a Nazi document accusing French troops of atrocities. Tortured and killed by the Gestapo in 1943, he was eventually buried in the Panthéon.

OTHER SIGHTS. The **Centre International du Vitrail** hosts temporary exhibitions on stained glass. The 13th-century barn in which it is housed was once used to store wine and grains for the clergy. *(5, rue du Cardinal Pie. Tel. 02 37 21 65 72. Open M-F 9:30am-12:30pm and 1:30-6pm, Sa-Su 10am-12:30pm and 2:30-6pm. Admission 20F, students 12F.)*

Rebuilt in the 16th century, the feudal **Eglise St-Aignan,** on rue des Greniers, offers summer concerts. *(Open daily 8am-6:30pm.)* The 12th-century Romanesque **Eglise St-André** sits on a rue St-André on the banks of the Eure River. *(Open daily 10am-noon and 2-6pm.)* Once part of the Benedictine monastery of St-Père-en-Vallée, the **Eglise St-Pierre,** on pl. St-Pierre, is a 13th-century Gothic masterpiece. Its western bell tower dates from 1000 and was used as a refuge for monks during attacks on the cathedral. *(Open daily 9am-5pm.)*

GIVERNY

Drawn by the verdant hills, haystacks, and lily pads on the Epte river, Impressionist Claude Monet and his eight children settled in Giverny in 1883. By 1887, John Singer Sargent, Paul Cézanne, and Mary Cassatt had placed their easels beside Monet's and turned the village into an artists' colony. (For more on Impressionism, see **Fine Arts,** p. 24.) When he was not painting flowers and water lilies, Monet devoted much time to his garden, explaining *"Mon jardin est mon plus beau chef d'oeuvre"* ("My garden is my most beautiful masterpiece").

ⓘ PRACTICAL INFORMATION

Getting to Giverny requires some patience and planning. **Trains** run erratically from Paris to Vernon, the nearest station. (Check the fickle timetables posted in the Grandes Lignes reservation rooms at Gare St-Lazare or call SNCF at 08 36 35 35 35. 132F round-trip.) To get to Giverny, rent a **bike** from the Vernon station (tel. 02 32 51 01 72; 55F per day; deposit of 1000F or credit card; MC, V) or take a **bus** (tel. 02 32 71 06 39) from the station. (10min.; M-Sa 6 per day each way, Su and holidays 4 per day each way; 12F, round-trip 20F.) Make sure you coordinate train and bus schedules before you start your trip to avoid three-hour delays. **Taxis** in front of the train station are another option. (One-way 65F weekdays, 80F weekends.) The 6km, hour-long **hike** from the Vernon station to Giverny along a pedestrian and cyclist path is long and lacks shade but is beautiful. The path is unmarked, but begins as the dirt road that intersects rue de la Ravine above the highway. Get a free map at the Vernon tourist office.

ⓢ SIGHTS

FONDATION CLAUDE MONET. Today, Monet's house and gardens are maintained by the Fondation Claude Monet. From April to July, Giverny overflows with roses, hollyhocks, poppies, and the heady scent of honeysuckle. The water lilies, the Japanese bridge, and the weeping willows look like—well, like Monets. An army of gardeners work year-long to create the lush floral colors that Monet once painted. The serenity is broken only by the crowds of tourists and schoolchildren. The only way to avoid the rush is to go early in the morning and, if possible, early in the season. In Monet's thatched-roof house, big windows, solid furniture, and pale blue walls house his collection of 18th- and 19th-century Japanese prints. Like his studio and the blue and white tiled kitchen, each room is bathed in light and flooded by garden scents. The second-floor windows offer lovely views of the Japanese garden. *(84, rue Claude Monet. Tel. 02 32 51 28 21. Open Apr.-Oct. Tu-Su 10am-6pm. Admission 35F, students and ages 12-18 25F, ages 7-12 20F. Gardens only 25F.)*

MUSÉE D'ART AMÉRICAIN. Near the foundation, the new and spacious Musée d'Art Américain is the sister institution to the Museum of American Art in Chicago and houses a small number of works by American expatriates James Whistler, John Singer Sargent, and Mary Cassatt. *(99, rue Claude Monet. Tel. 02 32 51 94 65. Open Apr.-Oct. Tu-Su 10am-6pm. Admission 35F, students, seniors, teachers, and ages 12-18 20F, under 12 15F.)*

NEAR GIVERNY: VERNON

A healthy walk or bike-ride away, Giverny's **Forêt de Vernon** sits amid hay fields and poppies. The Vernon **tourist office,** 36, rue Carnot, distributes free maps and hiking trails. To reach the tourist office from the Vernon station, turn right onto rue Émile Loubet, left on rue d'Albuféra, and right on rue Carnot. (Tel. 02 32 51 39 60. Open Apr.-Oct. Tu-Sa 9:30-12:15am and 2:30-6:30pm, Su 10-12:15am; Nov.-Mar. Tu-Sa 10-12:15am and 2-5pm.) If you remain on rue d'Albuféra, pont Clémenceau will carry you across the Seine; to the left on the far side of the river there's a **picnic spot** beside an old mill and a singing bird named Pokey; to the right, signs lead to Giverny. Amid Vernon's half-timbered houses, the **Musée de Vernon,** 12, rue du Pont, exhibits an eclectic collection including one work by Monet. From rue d'Albuféra as you face the bridge, turn left on rue Carnot and right on rue du Pont. (Tel. 02 32 21 28 09. Open Apr.-Oct. Tu-F 11am-1pm and 2-6pm, Sa-Su 2-6pm; Nov.-Mar. Tu-Su 2-5:30pm. Admission 15F, students and under 18 free.)

DISNEYLAND PARIS

It's a small, small world and Disney is hell-bent on making it even smaller. When Euro-Disney opened on April 12, 1992, Mickey Mouse, Cinderella, and Snow White were met by the jeers of French intellectuals and the popular press, who called the Disney theme park a "cultural Chernobyl." Resistance seems to have subsided since Walt & Co. renamed it Disneyland Paris and started serving wine. A touch of class can go a long way. If you've been to other Disney parks, you'll likely notice the way this one has been Frenchified. For example, Disney had to change its policy of squeaky-clean, tattoo- and earring-less employees, because that just didn't fly with the unions.

Disneyland Paris's designers (called "Imagineers") and staff (referred to as "Cast Members") have created a resort that ostensibly celebrates imagination, childhood, fantasy, creativity, technology, and fun. Pre-construction press touted the complex as a vast entertainment and resort center covering an area one fifth the size of Paris. In truth, Disney owns (and may eventually develop) 600 hectares, but the current theme park doesn't even rank the size of an arrondissement. From the gate it takes only 10 minutes to walk to the farthest point inside the park, a fact disguised by the park's maze-like design. Despite its dimensions, this Disney park is the most technologically advanced yet, and the special effects on some rides will knock your socks off.

Despite a slow start, Disneyland Paris has been a hit, and Disney has had to close the ticket windows repeatedly for hours at a time to keep ride lines down during the summer. Try to get there on a weekday. Discreetly posted signs at the entrances of the more popular rides alert you to how long you can expect to wait for your allotted two- to 10-minute rush. The crowds thin out toward 5pm, when parents start crying to go home, reducing waits to as little as 15 minutes. Saving the bigger rides for the evening is probably the best way to go, considering that the park closes at 11pm during the summer.

⑦ PRACTICAL INFORMATION

Everything in Disneyland Paris is in English and French. The staff is extremely helpful, and the detailed guide called the *Park Guide Book* has a map and information on everything from restaurants and attractions to bathrooms and first aid. The *Guests Special Services Guide* has all the dirt on handicapped accessibility throughout the park. For more helpful information on Disneyland Paris, visit their website at www.disneylandparis.com.

Transportation: The easiest way to get to Disneyland Paris is by taking **RER** A4 from Paris. Get on at either M: Gare de Lyon or Châtelet-Les-Halles and take the train (direction: "Marne-la-Vallée") to the last stop, "Marne-la-Vallée/Chessy." Before boarding the train, check the illuminated electric boards hanging above the platform to make sure there's a light next to the Marne-la-Vallée stop; otherwise the train won't end up there (45min., departs every 30min., round-trip 76F children 38F). The last train to Paris leaves Disney at 12:22am, but you may have trouble getting the métro at the other end. **By car,** take the A4 highway from Paris and get off at exit 14, marked "Parc Disneyland Paris," about a 30min. drive from the city. You can park for 40F per day in any one of the 11,000 spaces in the parking lot. **Disneyland Paris Buses** make the rounds between the terminals of both Orly and Roissy/Charles de Gaulle airports and the bus station near the Marne-la-Vallée RER (40min.; departs every 45-60 min. 8:30am-7:45pm, 8:30am-10pm at CDG on weekends; round-trip 85F). **TGV** service from Roissy/Charles de Gaulle reaches the park in a mere 15min., making Disneyland Paris fantastically accessible for travelers with Eurail passes. Certain **Eurostar** trains now run directly between Waterloo Station in London and Disneyland, in addition to a daily service (departure for Disney is usually around 9:15pm returning at 7:30pm; prices vary between 750 and 2090F; reserve as far in advance as possible to take advantage of discounts; call Eurostar for exact info at 08 36 35 35 39).

Admission and Hours: Instead of selling tickets, Disneyland Paris issues *passeports,* available at the 50 windows located on the ground floor of the Disneyland Hotel. You can also buy *passeports* at the Paris tourist office on the Champs-Elysées (see **Tourist Offices,** p. 85) or at any of the major stations on RER line A, such as Châtelet-Les-Halles, Gare de Lyon, or Charles-de-Gaulle-Etoile. Pursue either of these options if you plan on coming out on a weekend, so you won't risk wasting a couple of hours while the windows remain closed due to the crowds. The *passeport* is valid for 1 day; be sure to have your hand stamped if you plan to leave the park and return later. Admission Apr.-Sept. and Dec. 23-Jan. 7 220F, ages 3-11 170F; Jan. 8-Mar. and Oct.-Dec. 22 175F, ages 3-11 145F. 2- and 3-day *passeports* are also available. Park open daily July 11-Aug. 31 9am-11pm; Apr.-May and Sept.-June hours vary but are generally M-F 10am-8pm, Sa-Su 10am-8pm. Hours also subject to change during the winter when snow and sleet make the experience less magical.

⑥ FOOD AND DRINK

Most importantly, the no-alcohol policy of other Disney parks has been ditched for something a little more Euro: wine and beer flow freely throughout the park, and there's nothing like Space Mountain half-crocked, eh? Consult the guidebook for full restaurant listings: there are over 50. Restaurants are marked on the map and classified by the type of service: sit-down, cafeteria, or snack bars. For a sit-down, 3-course *menu,* expect to pay 100-200F. Cafeteria meals run 45-55F for simpler menus (i.e. burger, fries, and a drink). Snack stands located throughout the park offer hot dogs, ice cream, and the like for 9-20F. The least expensive options are the fish and chips at **Toad Hall Restaurant,** the frontier grub and saloon show at **Lucky Nugget Saloon,** the Italian staples of pasta and pizza at **Pizzeria Bella Notte,** the burgers at Discoveryland's **Café Hyperion,** and pizza at the Toy Story-themed **Buzz Lightyear's Pizza Planet Restaurant.** The Lucky Nugget offers what is perhaps the best value in the whole park: 85F at lunch and 150F at dinner buys a 4-course meal with buffalo wings, a bowl of chili, a hot beef sandwich, and a brownie. You're not supposed to bring picnic food into the park (bags are usually searched), but the French seem to do it anyway. Most restaurants are open 11am-10pm during the summer and 11am until the park's closing the rest of the year.

■ SIGHTS AND ACTIVITIES

For the wildest rides, look for those with the most dire warnings. While "may frighten certain young children" might sound promising, it only means that the ride is dark and things pop out at you. Warnings directed at pregnant women and people with chronic heart problems, or offering exit routes once already in line, are the hallmarks of the real thing.

The park is divided into five areas. **Main Street USA,** a storybook depiction of a turn-of-the-century town, is more American than apple pie and the first area you'll pass through after the gate. It funnels you through a consumer's paradise of shops and restaurants before depositing you at the center of the park. At the heart of the Magical Kingdom, **Sleeping Beauty's Castle** contains a high-tech, smoke-breathing dragon in the dungeon. Behind the château lies **Fantasyland.** Although the rides are tame, the spinning **Mad Hatter's Teacups** offer a trippy experience if you lean your head back and merit a whirl. **Alice's Curious Labyrinth** is a hedge maze, replete with squirting fountains, a hookah-smoking caterpillar, and a palace with a view; it's best visited at night when you just might get lost. Drift through a world of laughter, a world of tears, a world of hopes, and a world of fears on **It's a Small World,** where tiny automated dolls from around the world sing you into submission.

Adventureland awaits both the explorer and the weary parent with a mix of themes from so-called adventurous regions: the Middle East, West Africa, and the Caribbean. **Pirates of the Caribbean** presents 10 minutes of frighteningly life-like corsairs and a fantastic water-dungeon set. Be warned: the line outside is only a fraction of the total wait. Also be warned: one look at the crusty old pirates, and most children will scream. **Indiana Jones and the Temple of Doom** features the first 360° loop ever on a Disney ride. More demanding thrill-seekers might want to mosey on over to rough and ready **Frontierland,** where **Thunder Mesa,** a towering sunset-colored reproduction of a New Mexican desert mesa, hosts the park's best ride: **Big Thunder Mountain.** At high noon, the line is almost as deadly as the ride, but the ride is fun. Set apart on a scraggly hill, the creaky **Phantom Manor** is the park's classic haunted house. While the Haunted Mansion at Disney World in Florida is a huge scary fortress, the architecture had to be changed in Europe, where fortresses and châteaux are common; this haunted manor is based instead on the Victorian mansion in the film *Psycho.*

Light-years away on the other side of the park, **Discoveryland** flaunts the park's latest technological wizardry. **Star Tours** invites you to fly the not-so-friendly skies around the Death Star. Michael Jackson's **Captain Eo** is a bit too close for comfort in 3-D at nearby **Cinémagique,** and the **Visionarium's** 360° time-travel film is a good break. One of the newest rides at Disneyland Paris, **Space Mountain** is touted as "the crowning achievement of forty years of innovation by Disney Imagineers." It puts the Florida, Tokyo, and California versions of this ride to shame: you'll travel at speeds of 70km per hour through three loops in pitch blackness—a 360° loop, a corkscrew, and a 180° horseshoe—while a synchronized eight-speaker soundtrack deafens you with the illusion that you're being shot all the way to the moon, with a victory chant awaiting you once you're safe on earth. Not for the weak of stomach. The newest spectacle in the park is its virtual reality version of the hit film, *Honey I Shrunk the Audience,* where you'll squeal when a giant dog tries to lick you.

In addition to the rides, Disney puts on a variety of special daily events including a **Disney Character Parade** with myriad elaborate floats; the **Main Street Electrical Parade** (for the best view of the parades stand to the left at the top of Main St. near the pseudo-rotary—that's where the special effects on the floats are timed to go off); and a fantastic **son et lumières** show, set against the background of the château. Musical extravaganzas based on the latest Disney movies and other special events are listed in the brochure *Programmes: Spectacles & Restaurants.*

D A Y T R I P P I N G

NIGHTLIFE

Disney Village is separate from Disneyland Paris and free to enter. The village is a street filled with bars and game rooms where people roam about wearing cowboy hats and clutching beers at the **Sports Bar, Billy Bob's Country and Western Saloon, Rock'n Roll America,** or **Hurricanes** (25-42F per bottle or glass). For 20F, you can even try your hand on top of a mechanical bucking bronco while clutching onto a saddle-horn. To complete the American cultural invasion, **Planet Hollywood** recently landed in the Village. **Buffalo Bill's Wild West Show** provides western entertainment with Buffalo Bill, Chief Sitting Bull, Annie Oakley, and a host of other cowboys, together with horses and shooting acrobatics, presented with all the authenticity and cultural sensitivity that has made Disney what it is today.

CHANTILLY

You'd think this place would have whipped-cream-capped spires, like the Dairy Queen's palace. The small and picturesque 14th- to 19th-century **Chateau de Chantilly** is surrounded by a moat, Le Nôtre gardens, lakes, and canals. A Roman citizen named Cantilius built his villa here and a succession of medieval lords constructed elaborate fortifications. In the 17th century, Louis XIV's cousin, the Grand Condé, commissioned a château and asked Le Nôtre to create the gardens. The Grand Château was razed during the Revolution. In the 1870s, the Duc d'Aumale, fifth son of King Louis-Philippe, commissioned the château you see today, complete with neo-Renaissance facade, lush greenery, and extravagant entrance hall.

PRACTICAL INFORMATION. To get to Chantilly from Paris, take the **train** from the Gare du Nord (Grandes Lignes) to Chantilly Gouvieux (35min.; approximately every hour from 5am-midnight; round-trip 82F). You can catch a free and frequent **navette** (shuttle) to the château from the Gare Routière, which is just to the left as you exit the train station. Otherwise, the chateau is a pleasant half-hour walk from the station. The **tourist office,** 60 av. du Mal Joffre, offers brochures, maps, and a schedule of the free shuttle buses running to and from the château. To get there, walk out the front door of the station and go straight ahead up rue des Otages. The office is 50m up on the right. (Tel. 03 44 57 08 58. Open daily May-Sept. 9am-6pm, Oct.-Apr. M-Sa 9-12:30am and 2-6pm.) To continue to the stables and castle, leave the office and turn left on av. Mal Joffe, and then right on rue de Connetable, the town's main street (2km). The tourist office can also call a taxi (38F).

SIGHTS. The **gardens** are the château's main attraction. Maps of the gardens (6F) offer a suggested walking tour, but wandering is just as effective. A bike can help you explore the château's 115 hectares of parks and grounds on wheels. Directly in front of the château, the gardens' central expanse is designed in French formal style, with neat rows of carefully pruned trees and calm statues overlooking geometric pools. To the right, hidden within a forest, the rambling English garden attempts to re-create untamed nature. Here, paths meander around pools where lone swans float. Windows carved into the foliage allow you to see fountains in the formal garden as you stroll. The gardens also hide a play village

DAYTRIPPING

AND A PRETTY FACE The Chantilly area, famous for its castle and horse racing, is probably just as likely associated with its lace. A lace-making school was established in Chantilly by Catherine d'Orléans in 1620, and the region's cottage lace-making industry expanded until the First World War. The town started producing its famous, delicate black lace, known as Chantilly Lace, when Napoleon III's Spanish wife Eugénie declared it stylish. The creation of a triangular piece of Chantilly Lace of 8x6x6 feet requires 10 workers working full-time for one year. See Chantilly Lace in Chantilly at the **Musée du Patrimonie et de la Dentelle,** 34, rue d'Aumale. (Tel. 03 44 58 28 44. Open W and Sa 10-11:30am and 3-5:3-pm. Admission 10F.)

Hameau, the inspiration for Marie-Antoinette's hamlet at Versailles. Elsewhere, a statue of Cupid reigns over the "Island of Love." If you want to see the château and grounds all at once, levitate for 10 minutes in the world's largest **hot air balloon.** Located on the park grounds, the balloon (attached to the ground, alas, by a cable) rises 150m, providing a view as far as the Eiffel Tower in clear weather. (Tel. 03 44 62 62 62. Castle and park open Mar.-Oct. W-M 10am-6pm; Nov.-Feb. M and W-F 10:30am-12:45am and 2-5pm, Sa-Su 10:30am-5pm. Admission to castle and park is 39F, students 34F, children 12F. Admission to park only 17F, students 17F, children 10F. For castle, park and a boat tour 69F, students, 64F, children 32F. For a balloon tour 49F, students 43F, children 28F.)

Inside, the château's **Musée Condé** houses the duke's private collection of premodern paintings, which is the second largest in France, only superseded by the Louvre. The picture galleries contain 700 paintings, among them works by Raphael, Titian, Corot, Delacroix, and Ingres. Per the Duke of Aumale's will, the paintings and furniture are arranged as they were over a century ago. Unfortunately, the castle's remaining treasures can be visited only via a dry (though free) guided tour in French which is focused more on the furniture and artifacts than on the juicy history of the castle. Still, the tour's highlights, a Gutenberg Bible and a facsimile of the museum's most famous possession, the Très Riches Heures du Duc de Berry, a 15th-century manuscript showing the French peasantry and aristocracy in seasonal labors, are impressive. (Frequent daily tours, 45min., free.)

The approach to the castle passes the Grandes Ecuries, immense stables that housed 240 horses and hundreds of hunting dogs from 1719 until the Revolution. The stables were originally ordained by Louis-Henri Bourbon, who hoped to live in them when he was reincarnated as a horse. They now house the Musée Vivant du Cheval, a run-down museum dealing with all things equine. In addition to thirty live horses, donkeys, and ponies, saddles, horseshoes, international merry-go-rounds, and a horse statue featured in a James Bond film are displayed. During the first weekend of every month and Christmas, holiday-themed equestrian shows, such as "Horse and Gospel" are a highlight. Two of France's premier horse races are held here in June. In mid-September, Polo at the Hippodrome is free to the public (matches daily at 11am, 12:30, 2, 3:15, and 4:30pm). (Tel. 03 44 57 13 13. Open Apr.-Oct. M and W-F 10:30am-6:30pm, Sa-Su 10:30am-7pm; May-Aug. also open Tu 10:30am-5:30pm. Call for schedule of horse shows. Admission to museum and show 50F, students and seniors 45F.)

CHÂTEAUX DE MALMAISON AND BOIS-PREAU

To get to the château, do not take the bus or metro to Rueil-Malmaison, which is very far from the museum; instead, take the RER or metro to La Défense, and then take Exit A to change to bus #258, dir: St-Germain-en-Laye (30min., 8F). The RER stop is in zone 3 while the métro stop is in zone 2, so you need an extra ticket if you take the RER. The bus stop "Bois-Preau" goes to Bois-Preau; the stop "Château" takes you to Malmaison. Tel. 01 41 29 05 55. **Open** May-July W-M 10am-5:45pm, Sa-Su 10am-6:15pm; Apr. and Aug.-Sept. W-M 10-12:30am and 1:30-5:45pm, Sa-Su 10am-6:15pm; Oct.-Mar. 10-12:30am and 1:30-5:15pm, Sa-Su 10am-5:45pm. **Admission** 30F, students and Su 20F. Free guided tours in French throughout the day. **Museum** open Apr.-Sept. Th-Su 12:30am-6:30pm; Oct.-Mar. Th-Su 12:30am-6pm. **Admission** 30F; students, seniors, and Su 20F; under 18 free.)

Bought in 1799 on the eve of Napoleon's rise to power, the Château de Malmaison was Napoleon and Josephine's newlywed home and Josephine's own Elba after their marriage was annulled in 1809. It is unknown why the house is called "Malmaison" or "bad/sick house." Constructed in 1622 for the Counselor to the Parliament of Paris, the original building was enlarged in 1690 and again in 1770, when the grounds were landscaped. Bonaparte had Fontaine and Percier modernize the château, adding the military-tent veranda and renovating the interiors.

Malmaison is a mix of his and hers. The restored Empire interiors mix *trompe l'oeil* marble and neoclassical armchairs with Romantic landscape paintings. The public apartments feature paintings of the emperor by David, Greuze, and Gros.

Josephine furnished the private apartments in the Empire style with Egyptian-motif chairs, square tables, and tentlike beds. The château museum houses Empress memorabilia: jewels, shoes, colossal dress bills, harp, and perfumes. Josephine preferred the modest, sunny bedroom, whose large windows look out onto her garden, to the lavish bedroom in which she eventually passed away.

In one of history's most famous and tragic love stories, Napoleon divorced Josephine when she failed to give him an heir, and he then married Marie Louise d'Autriche. Josephine lived out her remaining years at Malmaison, cultivating the grounds in plush seclusion. A devotee of the natural sciences, she consulted botanists worldwide about her gardens and collected exotic animals, including camels, zebras, and kangaroos, which once walked the grounds. Josephine, née Rose, changed her name to please her husband but devoted much attention to the rose gardens that now surround the château. The **Roseraie Ancienne,** to the right as you enter the château features hundreds of varieties of roses that bloom in May and June. Pierre-Joseph Redouté's roses were painted from the flowers in Josephine's gardens, and some of his drawings are now in the museum's collection.

Those unfamiliar with Napoleon's empire should visit the **Château de Bois-Preau,** a museum-cum-shrine to the emperor. The ground floor summarizes Napoleon's life. The second floor is devoted to Napoleon's final days on St. Helena, complete with models and sketches of the his house, grounds, and death-chamber, articles of his clothing, and items form his *toilette,* including the emperor's toothbrush, tweezers, and the handkerchief he carried at Toulon.

VAUX-LE-VICOMTE

Nicolas Fouquet, Louis XIV's Minister of Finance, assembled the famous triumvirate of Le Vau, Le Brun, and Le Nôtre (architect, artist, and landscaper) to build Vaux in 1641. The result was a new standard for country châteaux and fame for the talented trio. Though smaller and less opulent than Versailles, Vaux impresses with architectural coherence and *trompe l'oeil.* Be attentive to optical tricks in both the château and the gardens.

On August 17, 1661, upon the completion of what was then France's most beautiful château, Fouquet threw an audacious and extravagant 6,000-guest party in honor of Louis XIV. The King and Anne d'Autriche were but two of the witnesses to a regal bacchanalia that premiered poetry by La Fontaine and a comedy-ballet, *Les Facheux,* by Molière. The evening concluded in a fireworks extravaganza featuring the King and Queen's coat of arms and pyrotechnic squirrels (Fouquet's family symbol). The housewarming bash, however, was the beginning of the end for Fouquet. Shortly thereafter, young Louis XIV—supposedly furious at having been upstaged—ordered Fouquet arrested. Hidden causes lay behind Fouquet's downfall. Colbert, another minister, had been turning the monarch against Fouquet for years. Fouquet's affection for the king's mistress Mme. de Lavallière didn't help matters either. Despite having kept the French treasury solvent by raising funds against his own fortune, Fouquet was the fall guy for the state's abysmal financial condition. In a trial that lasted three years, the judges in Fouquet's case voted narrowly for banishment over death. Louis XIV overturned the judgment in favor of life imprisonment—the only time in French history that the head of state overruled the court's decision in favor of a more severe sentence. Despite entreaties by Mme de Sévigné and La Fontaine, Fouquet was to remain imprisoned at Pignerol, a dreary citadel in the French Alps, until his death in 1680. Many suspected that Fouquet was the famous man in the iron mask, including Alexandre Dumas who fictionalized the story in *Le Vicomte de Bragelonne.*

In addition to being a savvy financier—one who certainly lived up to his motto, *Quo non ascendet* (What heights will he not scale)—Fouquet was also an aesthete and patron. Louis XIV himself held Fouquet's tastes in high esteem. Soon after the minister's arrest, the King confiscated many of Vaux's finest objects, including trees from the garden. Louis then hired the same trio—Le Vau, Le Brun, and Le Nôtre—to work their magic at Versailles.

⁊ PRACTICAL INFORMATION

Vaux is exquisite and much less crowded than Versailles, but getting there is an exquisite pain, especially if money is dear, as there is no shuttle service from the train station in Melun to the château 7km away. The best option is to visit Vaux with several other people so that you can split the cab fare from the train station to the castle, or the cost of renting a car. The castle is 50km out of Paris. Take Autoroute A4 or A6 from Paris and exit at Val-Maubué or Melun, respectively. Head toward Meaux on N36 and follow the signs. Or, take the **RER** to Melun from Châtelet-Les-Halles or Gare du Nord (45min., round-trip 90F). The **taxi ride** (tel. 01 64 52 51 50) will cost 100-150F each way. The walk takes 1½-2 hours on a busy highway.

The **tourist office**, 2, av. Gallieni (tel. 01 64 37 11 31), by the train station in Melun, can help you with accommodations and sight-seeing opportunities and give you a free map (open Tu-Sa 10am-noon and 2-6pm). If the tourist office is closed, do not fear. While the traffic on the highway is perilous, the directions are relatively simple: just follow av. de Thiers through its many name-changes to highway 36 (direction: "Meaux") and follow signs to Vaux-Le-Vicomte.

👁 CHÂTEAU AND GARDENS

Tel. 01 64 14 41 90; www.vaux-le-vicomte.com; email chateau@vaux-le-vicomte.com. **Open** *daily Mar. 11-Nov. 11, 10am-6pm. Visits by appointment for groups of 20 or more the rest of the year.* **Admission** *to château and gardens 62F, students, seniors, and ages 6-16 49F, under 6 free.* **Admission** *to gardens and équipages 30F, students, seniors, and ages 6-16 27F. On Saturday evenings from May to the end of September, the château is candle-lit for night-time visits. 8pm-midnight. 80F, 70F for ages 6-16, students, and seniors.*

CHÂTEAU. The château unites the grandeur of a Roman past and the utility of a French fort, complete with Neoclassical columns, squat walls, and moat. Note that the moat is completely invisible from the road. Another optical trick is the appearance of three entries where only one exists. The château is covered with ornate scripted "F"s, squirrels (Fouquet's symbol), and the tower with three battlements, his second wife's crest. **Madame Fouquet's Closet** once had walls lined with small mirrors, the decorative forerunner of Versailles's Hall of Mirrors. Over the fireplace of the **Square Room** hangs Le Brun's portrait of Fouquet. Le Brun's **Room of the Muses** is one of his most famous decorative schemes. Le Brun had planned to crown the **Oval Room** (or **Grand Salon**) with a fresco entitled *The Palace of the Sun*, but Fouquet's arrest halted all activity. The tapestries once bore Fouquet's squirrel, but Colbert seized them and replaced the rodents with his own adders. The ornate **King's Bedchamber** boasts an orgy of cherubs and lions fluttering around the centerpiece, Le Brun's *Time Bearing Truth Heavenward*.

GARDENS. Vaux-le-Vicomte presented André Le Nôtre with his first opportunity to create an entire formal garden. Three villages (including Vaux), a small château, and 70 acres of trees were destroyed to open up the required space. With Vaux, Le Nôtre gave birth to a truly French style of garden—shrubs were trimmed, lawns shaved, bushes sculpted, and pools strategically placed. Starting with Versailles, and for a century thereafter, Vaux would serve as the model for gardens all over Europe. Vaux owes its most impressive *trompe l'oeil* to Le Nôtre's adroit use of the laws of perspective. From the back steps of the château, it looks as if you can see the entire landscape at a glance. The grottoes at the far end of the garden appear directly behind the large pool of water. Yet as you approach the other end, the grottoes seem to recede, revealing a sunken canal known as **La Poêle** (the Frying Pan), which is invisible from the château. The right-hand *parterre* (literally "on the ground," referring to the arabesques and patterns created with low, clipped box plants) was originally a flowerbed, but today it is dominated by a statue of Diana. The **Round Pool** and its surrounding 17th-century statues mark an important intersection; to the left, down the east walkway, are the Water Gates, likely the backdrop for Molière's performance of *Les Facheux*. The **Water Mirror,**

farther down the central walkway, was designed to reflect the château perfectly, but you may have some trouble positioning yourself to enjoy the effect. A climb to the **Farnese Hercules,** a 19th-century addition to the gardens, is the vanishing point when you look out from the castle. Today, the old stables house a fantastic carriage museum, **Les Equipages.** The fountains in Le Nôtre's gardens are turned on from 3 to 6pm every second and last Saturday of the month from April to October.

PROVINS

Amid brilliant corn fields and green woods, on top of a ridge and above the rest of the world, Provins is one of the best preserved medieval towns in France. The oldest parts date from the 12th century, when it was France's third-largest city after Paris and Rouen. Unlike those two cities, which changed and grew, Provins's ancient walls covered with ivy. The town's *ville haute* is thus more like a gleaming, historical film set, at times even complete with knights, maidens, and monks (see **Entertainment,** below). The lower, newer *ville basse,* historically the town's center of trade, remains populated by pedestrian shopping streets.

⑦ PRACTICAL INFORMATION. To get to Provins, take the SNCF **train** marked Provins from Gare de l'Est (1¼hr., 6 trains per day, buy a ticket from the *Banlieues* counter or machines, round-trip 122F.). To get from the train station *(ville basse)* to the tourist office *(ville haute),* take the bus from in front of the station to Porte St-Jean. The tourist office is just outside the walls of the *ville haute.* (Tel. 01 64 60 26 26. Open daily 9am-5:30pm.)

◎ SIGHTS. Enter the settlement in style through the **Porte St-Jean,** one of the main gates in the town's stellar ramparts, built between the 11th and 13th centuries. This fortified gate protected Provins's route to Paris. Beyond the gate on rue St-Jean is the 12th-century **Grange aux Dîmes** (tithe barn), which originally served as a market for cloth, dye, and wine merchants and a storehouse for merchandise and church tithes. Past the Grange, **place du Châtel** features the gothic **Croix des Changes,** the cross of changes (also the name of Enigma's first album), where the Counts of Provins posted edicts and other unpopular declarations.

Above the *place,* the **Tou César** is Provins's town symbol. Legend says that Caesar built the tower himself; reality says that the tower dates from 1137. Narrow stairwells spiral to the top of the tower were you'll find a 16th-century 6000-pound bell from St-Quiriace. (Open Apr.-Sept. daily 10am-6pm; Jan.-Mar. and Nov.-Dec. M-F 2-5pm, Sa-Su 11am-5pm. Admission 17F, children 10F.)

Nearby, Provins's **Souterrains,** a system of underground catacombs, dug over 1000 years ago, were used as a war-time refuge and a wine cellar. (Open Apr.-Sept. Sa-Su 10:30am-6pm; Nov.-Mar. guided visits Sa-Su 2, 3, and 4pm. Admission 22F, children 14F.) The striking slate-domed 12th-century **Eglise de Saint-Quiriace** was built on the ruins of a Merovingian church (AD 500-750), when the first dynasty of Frankish kings ruled Gaul.

⎘ ENTERTAINMENT. Provins boasts three **medieval festivals:** *A l'assault des remparts* (The Assault of the Ramparts; July-Aug. Tu-Sa 4pm; May-June M-Tu and Th-F 2:30pm, Sa-Su 4pm; admission 40F, children 25F) in which the Provinois siege their own town (*"Attention aux projectiles!"*); *Les Aigles de Remparts* (The Eagles of the Ramparts; Apr.-Oct, daily at 2:30pm at minimum; admission 45F, children 30F) a slick bird show; and *Le jugement de Dieu* (The Judgement of God; June 26-Aug. Su 4pm; admission 80F, children 50F), which features battles, falconry, jousting, and, for the kids, monastic flagellation.

SAINT-DENIS

Fifteen minutes from the center of Paris, and in a suburban *banlieue* whose names is now synonymous with soccer, St-Denis is home to the Basilique de St-Denis, the burial crypt of France's royal families for centuries. The royal tombs of almost every French king (save three) remain the town's main attraction. But this working-class suburb also has a large multicultural immigrant community, a growing annual arts festivals, and the new Stade de France, where host-country France won the World Cup in 1998 over Brazil. With a flying-saucer-like roof and 80,000 seats, the stadium was built expressly for World Cup '98 and continues to pack 'em in with stadium rock and Celine Dion (For info, see **Spectator Sports,** p. 279).

7 PRACTICAL INFORMATION

To get to Saint-Denis, take the métro or RER to M: St-Denis-Basilique or RER: St-Denis. The helpful **tourist office,** 1, rue de la République, has information on the basilica and the town of St-Denis, including maps, suggested walks, and restaurant guides. (Tel. 01 55 87 08 70. Open Apr.-Oct. M-Sa 9:30am-7pm, Su 10am-1pm and 2-6pm; Nov.-Mar. M-Sa 9:30am-6pm, Su 10am-1pm and 2-4:30pm.)

SIGHTS

BASILIQUE DE ST-DENIS

1, rue de la Légion d'Honneur. From the métro/RER walk towards the town square, then take a left at the tourist office. Tel. 01 48 09 83 54. **Open** *Apr.-Sept. M-Sa 10am-6:30pm, Su noon-6:30pm; Oct.-Mar. M-Sa 10am-4:30pm, Su noon-4:30pm.* **Admission** *to nave, side aisles and chapels free.* **Admission** *to transept, ambulatory, and crypt 32F, seniors and students 12-25 21F, under 12 free.* **Audioguide,** *25F for one person, 35F for two. Ticket booth closes 30min. before the church.* **Tours** *in French daily at 11:15am and 3pm.*

Surrounded by modern buildings, markets, and non-Christian communities, the Basilique de St-Denis stands as an odd, archaic symbol of the long-dead French monarchy. The first church on this site was built on top of an existing Gallo-Roman cemetery, in honor of the missionary bishop Denis (see **History,** p. 1 for his tragic tale). His story is told in stained glass on the northern side of the nave. In 475, a small church was built to mark St-Denis's grave. King Pepin the Short built a larger basilica to accommodate the many pilgrimages and was buried here in 768. Of the more famous monarchs, Clovis, François I, Anne d'Autriche, Louis XIV, Louis XVI, and Marie-Antoinette also lie here. Their funerary monuments range from medieval simplicity to Renaissance extravagance. Dogs at the feet of the queens mark their fidelity; the kings have lions as symbols of their virility and courage. Inexplicably, Henri II and Catherine de Medici are the only monarchs whose monuments depict them marching into the hereafter in the nude. Marie-Antoinette, always one for a scandal, looks like she is losing her top in her funerary monument. A room on the left side of the church contains funerary garments.

The basilica's 12th-century ambulatory is the oldest example of Gothic architecture in Europe. In 1136, Abbot Suger began rebuilding the basilica in a style that would open it to the "light of the divine." Suger was dissatisfied with dark Romanesque interiors, with their small windows and forests of thick columns. Instead, he brought together known architectural elements to create an unprecedented openness in the nave. The vaulted arches funnel the weight of the roof into a few points, supported with long, narrow columns inside and flying buttresses outside. Freed from the burden of supporting the roof, the walls gave way to the huge stained-glass windows that became the trademark of Gothic style. Suger's shocked contemporaries worked to outdo him, building ever more intricate interiors, larger stained-glass windows, and loftier vaults. The Gothic age was ignited.

Suger died in 1151, well before the basilica was finished, having made the basilica synonymous with the crown, as keeper of the coronation paraphernalia and *Oriflamme* (royal banner). His successors created an unusually wide transept, complete with gigantic rose windows. Extra space was needed to accommodate the royal crypts. In 1593, underneath the spacious nave, Henri IV converted to Catholicism with his famous statement (see **History,** p. 4).

St-Denis was a prime target for the wrath of the Revolution. Most of the tombs were desecrated or destroyed, and the remains of the Bourbon family were thrown into a ditch. Most of the basilica's stained glass was shattered. With the restoration of the monarchy in 1815, Louis XVIII ordered that the necropolis be reestablished, and Louis XVI and Marie-Antoinette were buried here with great pomp in 1819. The remains of the Bourbons were dug out of their ditch and placed in a small ossuary inside the crypt, and tombs and funerary monuments were relocated and replaced. The result of this anti-monarch revelry can be seen in the pieced-together stone headstones in the necropolis.

Virtually all of St-Denis's original stained glass was replaced during the 19th century, but some of the original 12th-century windows can be seen in the center of the ambulatory. Look closely and you can discern something other than biblical tales: the Abbot Suger ensured his immortality by having his likeness —a small monk prostrate before the Virgin Mother—added to the design.

MUSÉE D'ART ET D'HISTOIRE. The Musée d'Art et d'Histoire features exhibits on daily life in medieval St-Denis and on the convent's most famous resident, Madame Louise, beloved daughter of Louis XV, who spent her life here in quiet devotion. To reach the museum from the basilica, walk down rue de la Légion d'Honneur, and turn right on rue Franciade and then left on rue Gabriel Péri. Another big draw of the museum is an exhibit covering the life of poet Paul Eluard, born in the town, and the Surrealist movement. *(22bis, rue Gabriel Péri. Tel. 01 42 43 05 10. Open M and W-Sa 10am-5:30pm, Su 2-6:30pm. Admission 20F, students and seniors 10F, under 16 free.)*

🗑️ 🎵 FOOD AND ENTERTAINMENT

Reasonably priced Turkish, Indian, and Greek restaurants cluster around the park in front of the church, and numerous sandwich shops and *salons de thé* line rue Gabriel Péri between rue de la République and pl. de la Résistance. There is also a large enclosed **market** in the place Victor Hugo, next to the Hôtel de Ville, teeming with all kinds of stands selling produce, meats (alive and dead), and cheeses. (Open Tu-F and Su 9am-1pm.) The **Banlieues Bleues** jazz and blues festival and the **Festival de St-Denis** bring world-class orchestras and musicians, such as opera diva Barbara Hendricks, conductor Charles Dutoit, and the Orchestre National de France, to the basilica every June. (Call 01 48 13 06 07.)

SAINT-GERMAIN-EN-LAYE

More of a wealthy Parisian suburb than a provincial town, St-Germain-en-Laye offers a break from the intensity of Paris: people are friendlier, life is slower, and the air is cleaner. The winding streets of the town center are packed with restaurants, cafés, and shops. Home to François I's 16th-century château and Claude Debussy's birthplace, this chic little hamlet is worth a visit, especially in the summer during the **Fête des Loges** (see Entertainment, p. 338).

🚹 PRACTICAL INFORMATION

St-Germain is 25 minutes from M: Charles-de-Gaulle on RER Line A1 (trains leave every 10-25 min., round-trip 39F). **Office Municipal de Tourisme,** Maison Claude Debussy, 38, rue au Pain, provides all that you need to know about the festival as well as lists of restaurants and hotels, a free detailed map, and information about the town in English. To reach the tourist office from the RER station, exit at *Eglise,* turn right onto the pedestrian rue de la Salle, and then left onto rue au Pain. (Tel. 01 34 51 05 12; fax 01 34 51 36 01; email Saint.Germain.en.Laye.Tourisme@wanadoo.fr. Open Mar.-Oct. Tu-F 9:15am-12:30pm and 2-6:30pm, Sa 9:15am-6:30pm, Su 10am-1pm; Nov.-Feb. closed Su.)

SIGHTS

CHÂTEAU DE ST-GERMAIN-EN-LAYE

Museum tel. 01 39 10 13 00. Open W-M 9am-5:15pm. Admission 25F, students 17F; temporary exhibits 25F/17F; combined ticket 38F, 28F. 1hr. tour in French 24F, 17F. Under 18 all is free. *Garden* open daily May-July 8am-9:30pm; Aug.-Apr. 8am-5pm.

Louis VI "Le Gros" built the first castle here in the 12th century, near the site on which his ancestor Robert the Pious had constructed a monastery dedicated to St-Germain. Rebuilt by Charles V after its destruction during the Hundred Years' War, the castle took on its present appearance in 1548 under François I. Lover of all things Italian, François I ordered his architects Chabiges and Delormé to construct a Renaissance palace (the current **château vieux**) on the foundations of the old church and castle. The castle's mix of brick and stone is typical of the Renaissance. Henri II added the **château neuf,** home to Louis XIII and birthplace in 1638 of the future Louis XIV. Quite a list of names graced these two châteaux—among them Colbert, Mme. de Sévigné, Molière, Voltaire, and Rousseau. Molière and Lully collaborated on festivals at the châteaux. James II of England died here in exile in 1701, kicking off what was to be a rough century for the estate. During the period from the Revolution to the July Monarchy, St-Germain was used as a civilian prison, a cavalry school, and a military prison. In the 19th century it became a popular weekend outing, and the first railroad in France was built between here and Paris in 1837. In 1919, St-Germain-en-Laye served as the site of the official dismantling of the Austro-Hungarian Empire.

In 1862 Napoleon III decided to make the castle into a museum of antiquity. Today, the **Musée des Antiquités Nationales** claims to have the richest collection of its kind in the world, tracing the history of early man in France to the Middle Ages. Unfortunately, a stroll through the museum does not provide a particularly intriguing window into the castle. At first, the display looks a bit like someone's pet rock collection, but the work gets more sophisticated. Especially interesting is the museum's collection of Gallic artifacts and a Neanderthal skull, which belonged to a man who voted for Jean-Marie LePen.

The château's garden terrace, probably the town's greatest asset, was designed by Le Nôtre. The current gardens and nearby forest provide a panoramic view of western Paris, the Grande Arche de la Défense, and the banlieues. A map of forest trails (50F) is available from the tourist office. Numerous cafés with lounge chairs are scattered throughout the park.

EGLISE ST-GERMAIN. The Eglise St-Germain was consecrated in 1827 on the site of the 11th-century priory that gave St-Germain its name. Large and stately pillars support the Romanesque structure, the fourth church to be built on this site since 1028. Louis XV laid the first stone 60 years before the church was completed. The church's 14th-century stone statue of Nôtre-Dame-de-Bon-Retour (Our Lady of Safe Return) was found when they dug the foundations for the church in 1775. James II's tomb is at the front. *(Across from the château. Tel. 01 34 51 99 11. Open daily 8:30am-noon and 2-7pm. Mass M-F 7:15pm, Sa 6:30pm, Su 10:15am, 11:30am and 6:30pm.)*

MAISON CLAUDE DEBUSSY. The Maison Claude Debussy is the Impressionist composer's birthplace. An autographed copy of *Il pleut doucement sur la ville* is among the eclectic array of documents and pictures about the man who said, "I want to dare to be myself and to suffer for my truth." The museum's auditorium hosts two concerts per month (tickets 30-70F). *(38, rue au Pain. Follow rue de la Salle to rue au Pain and turn left. Tel. 01 34 51 05 12. Open Tu-Sa 2-6pm. Free.)*

MUSÉE DÉPARTEMENTAL MAURICE DENIS LE PRIEURÉ. The Musée Départemental Maurice Denis le Prieuré is dedicated to the works of Maurice Denis (1870-1943), the Symbolists, the Nabis, the Post-Impressionists, and the Pont-Aven group. The museum has no permanent exhibition, but instead displays thematic temporary expositions. Built in 1678 for the Marquise de Montespand and used as an almshouse, a hospital, and a retirement home for Jesuits, Le Prieuré (The Priory) was purchased by Denis in 1914. With long windows overlooking the priory's gardens, the museum features a chapel decorated by Denis's own interpretation of the Beatitudes and works by Vuillard and Moret. *(2 bis, rue Maurice-Denis. Tel. 01 39 73 77 87. Open W-F 10am-5:30pm, Sa-Su 10am-6:30pm. Tours Su at 3:30pm 10F. Admission 25F, students 15F, under 12 free.)*

🎵 ENTERTAINMENT

From the first Sunday of July to August 15th, St-Germain is the home to the **Fête des Loges.** The "loges" refer back to the huts built by the woodsmen of the nearby forest. St-Louis (King Louis IX) constructed a chapel here dedicated to St-Fiacre, and in 1652, after Pope Innocent X was sainted, the area became the sight of an annual pilgrimage. With hordes of pilgrims, a festival was inevitable. After the Revolution, the pilgrimage lost its religious significance but continued to offer annual music, song, drink, and dancing. By 1830, about 15,000 of the Paris area's most elegant would attend, with 10 balls, 50 restaurants, and 180 merchants from which to choose. Today, the festival sees 3.5 million visitors, who annually consume half a million chickens, 30,000 pigs, 75 tons of mussels, and 1.5 million liters of beer. *(Tel. 01 53 80 07 67; www.fetedesloges.com. Open Su-Th 2pm-1:30am, F-Sa 2pm-2:30am.)*

AUVERS-SUR-OISE

I am entirely absorbed by these plains of wheat on a vast expanse of hills like an ocean of tender yellow, pale green, and soft mauve, with a piece of cultivated land dotted with clusters of potato vines in bloom, and all this under a blue sky tinted with shades of white, pink, and violet.

—Vincent Van Gogh, 1890

Relatively little has changed in Auver-sur-Oise since Van Gogh's arrival in 1890. Located 30km northwest of Paris, this little village attracted the Impressionists Pissarro, Daubigny, and Gachet to its lush green fields, winding paths, and stone houses. Ironically, the artist who stayed the shortest period of time in Auvers—a mere 70 days—has become its most honored son. Fleeing Provence where he had been so unhappy, Van Gogh arrived at Auvers-sur-Oise in May 1890 and immediately began to paint and sketch. In a scant ten weeks he produced over 70 drawings, studies, and canvases. This intense productivity did not bring with it peace of mind. On the afternoon of July 27, the 37-year-old Van Gogh shot himself in the chest while standing in the wheat fields he had painted only days before. He died two days later in his room at the Auberge Ravaux, with his friend Dr. Gachet and his beloved brother Théo at his side.

🗺 **PRACTICAL INFORMATION.** To get to Auvers, take the **train** from Gare St-Lazare or Gare du Nord to Pontoise (this may involve intermediate changes; consult the station's information desk), then switch to the Persau Creil line and get off at Gare d'Auvers-sur-Oise (1-1½hr., depart every hr., 58F roundtrip). Should you hit the afternoon lull in return train service, catch the **bus** to Pontoise running along the road next to the train station. Housed in the Manoir des Colombières, rue de la Sansonne, the **Office de Tourisme d'Auvers-sur-Oise** (tel. 01 30 36 10 06) offers helpful walking maps (1-3F) and souvenirs. 90-minute guided tours of the village depart from here. (Open daily 10am-12:30pm and 2-5pm. Tours Apr.-Oct. Su 3pm; 25F, under 14 10F.)

📷 **SIGHTS.** While the **Maison de Van Gogh,** 8, rue de la Sansonne (tel. 01 34 48 05 47), has little to offer beyond a glimpse of Van Gogh's bare room and a pretty slideshow, the cost of admission includes an elegant, souvenir "passport" to Auvers-sur-Oise that details the history of the *auberge* and Van Gogh's sojourn there. The booklet also gives information on the town's other museums and self-guided walking tours, as well as discounts to four of the museums. (Open Tu-Su 10am-6pm. Admission 30F.) The 10-minute walk from the *maison* to the **Cimetière d'Auvers** is well worth the rural beauty; on the way you'll pass **Nôtre-Dame d'Auvers,** the 12th-century subject of Van Gogh's *Eglise d'Auvers* (1890), which hangs in the Musée d'Orsay (see **Museums,** p. 247).

The **chemin du cimetière** leads through the fields where Van Gogh painted his *Champ de blé aux corbeaux* (*Wheatfields with Crows,* 1890) and emerges near the **Atelier de Daubigny,** 61, rue Daubigny (tel. 01 34 48 03 03), once the home and studio of pre-Impressionist painter Charles-François Daubigny. (Open Easter-Oct. Tu-Su 2-6:30pm. Admission 20F, under 12 10F.) Near the *atelier,* on a side street off rue de Léry, the **Musée de l'Absinthe,** 44, rue Callé (tel. 01 30 36 83 26), is yet another memorial to the Impressionists, this one devoted to the mythical drink that Manet and Degas immortalized in art (see **The Green Party,** p. 250). (Open June-Sept. W-Su 11am-6pm; Oct.-May Sa-Su 11am-6pm. Admission 25F, students 20F.)

APPENDIX

TEMPERATURE CONVERSION

The average rainfall varies slightly throughout the year: 4.3 mm (Jan), a constant 5.3 mm in April and July, peaking at 5.5 mm in October. For a rough approximation from °C to °F, double the Celsius and add 25. To go the other way, subtract 25 and cut it in half.

°CELSIUS	-5	0	5	10	15	20	25	30	35	40
°FAHRENHEIT	23	32	41	50	59	68	77	86	95	104

MEASUREMENTS

MEASUREMENT CONVERSIONS

1 inch (in.) = 25.4 millimeters (mm)	1 millimeter (mm) = 0.039 in.
1 foot (ft.) = 0.30m	1 meter (m) = 3.28 ft.
1 yard (yd.) = 0.914m	1 meter (m) = 1.09 yd.
1 mile = 1.61km	1 kilometer (km) = 0.62 mi.
1 ounce (oz.) = 28.35g	1 gram (g) = 0.035 oz.
1 pound (lb.) = 0.454kg	1 kilogram (kg) = 2.202 lb.
1 fluid ounce (fl. oz.) = 29.57ml	1 milliliter (ml) = 0.034 fl. oz.
1 gallon (gal.) = 3.785L	1 liter (L) = 0.264 gal.
1 acre (ac.) = 0.405ha	1 hectare (ha) = 2.47 ac.
1 square mile (sq. mi.) = 2.59km^2	1 square kilometer (km^2) = 0.386 sq. mi.

TIME ZONES

GMT -9	GMT -8	GMT -6	GMT	GMT +1	GMT +2	GMT +5	GMT +8	GMT +10
Vancouver Los Angeles	Calgary Denver	New York Toronto	London Dublin	Paris Madrid Rome Berlin Stockholm Zurich	Athens Istanbul Johannesburg	New Delhi	Hong Kong Perth	Sydney

PHRASEBOOK

GENERAL		
Hello/Good day.	Bonjour.	bohn-ZHOOR.
Good evening.	Bonsoir.	bohn-SWAHR.
Goodbye.	Au revoir.	oh rev-WAHR.
Good night.	Bonne nuit.	bun NWEE.
Please.	S'il vous plaît.	see voo PLAY.
Thank you.	Merci.	mehr-SEE.
You're welcome.	De rien.	duh rhee-EHN.
Pardon me.	Excusez-moi.	ex-koo-zay MWAH.

GREETINGS AND SALUTATIONS		
How are you?	Ça va?	Come-on SAH VAH?
No thanks.	Non, merci.	NOHN, mehr-SEE.
No problem.	C'est pas grave.	say PAH grahv.
What is it?	Qu'est-ce que c'est?	kess-KUH say?
Why?	Pourquoi?	poor-KWAH?
Excuse me?	Pardon?	pahr-DOHN?

Please repeat.	Répétez, s'il vous plait.	ray-pey-tay, see voo PLAY.
Help!	Au secours!/Aidez-moi!	oh suc-KOR!/Ay-day-MWAH!
Do you speak English?	Parlez-vous anglais?	PAR-lay voo ahn-GLAY?
I would like ...	Je voudrais ...	ZHUH voo-DRAY ...
the bill	l'addition	lad-ees-SYOHN
the hospital	l'hôpital	LOH-pee-tahl
breakfast	petit déjeuner	puh-TEE day-JOON-ay
lunch, dinner	déjeuner, dîner	day-JOON-ay, dee-NAY
subway, airport	métro, aeroport	meh-TROH, air-oh-POOR
train station	la gare	lah GAIR
ATM	guichet automatique	ghee-SHAY aw-toh-MAT-eek
I would like to make a reservation ...	Je voudrais réserver ...	ZHUH voo-DRAY ray-zer-VAY ...
How do you say ... in French?	Comment dit-on ... en français?	Come-on deet-ON ahn frahn-SAY?
What are your hours?	Quelles sont vos horaires d'ouverture?	kell SOHN vohz or-AIRZ douv-air-TYUR?
I don't know.	Je ne sais pas.	ZHUH nuh say PAH.

DIRECTIONS

(to the) left	à gauche	ah GOH-shh	(to the) right	à droite	ah DWOT
far	loin	luh-WAHN	near	près de	pray DUH
east	est	eh-ST	north	nord	NOHR-d
west	ouest	west	south	sud	sood
beyond	au-delà de	oh duh-LAH duh	follow	suivre	swee-vruh

NUMBERS

one	un	uhn	fourteen	quatorze	catorze
two	deux	duh	fifteen	quinze	can-zz
three	trois	twah	sixteen	seize	sez
four	quatre	cat-ruh	seventeen	dis-sept	deese-set
five	cinq	saynk	eighteen	dix-huit	deese-wheat
six	six	see-ss	nineteen	dix-neuf	deese-neuf
seven	sept	set	twenty	vingt	van
eight	huit	hweet	twenty-five	vingt-cinq	van-saynk
nine	neuf	nuh-f	thirty	trente	trahn-t
ten	dix	dee-ss	forty	quarante	care-ahnt
eleven	onze	ohn-zz	fifty	cinquante	saynk-ahnt
twelve	douze	do-zz	one hundred	cent	sahn
thirteen	treize	trezz	one thousand	mille	meel

TIME

open	ouvert	oo-VAIRT	What time is it?	Quelle heure est-il?	kell UHR ay-TILL?
closed	fermé	fair-MAY	until	jusqu'à	zhuh-SKUH
morning	le matin	luh MAH-tan	except	sauf	soh-FF
afternoon	l'après-midi	lap-PRAY mid-ee	holidays	jours fériés, congés	ZHOOR fair-ee-AY, cohn-JAY
evening	le soir	luh SWAHR	January	janvier	jan-vee-AY
night	la nuit	lah NWEE	February	février	fehv-ree-AY
today	aujourd'hui	oh-johr-DWEE	March	mars	mahr
yesterday	hier	ee-AIR	April	avril	av-REEL
tomorrow	demain	duh-MAN	May	mai	may
Monday	lundi	loon-DEE	June	juin	joo-ANN
Tuesday	mardi	mar-DEE	July	juillet	joo-ee-AY
Wednesday	mercredi	mair-cruh-DEE	August	août	oot

Thursday	jeudi	zhuh-DEE	September	septembre	sep-tahm-BRUH
Friday	vendredi	vahn-druh-DEE	October	octobre	awk-toh-BRUH
Saturday	samedi	sam-uh-DEE	November	novembre	noh-vahm-BRUH
Sunday	dimanche	dee-mahn-SH	December	décembre	day-sahm-BRUH

MENU READER

l'agneau (m)	lamb	la crème fraîche	fresh heavy cream
l'ail (m)	garlic	la crêpe	thin pancake
l'andouillette (f)	tripe sausage	les crêpes Suzette (f)	warm dessert of crêpe flamed in orange liqueur
l'apéritif (m)	pre-dinner drink	la crevette	shrimp
l'asperge (f)	asparagus	la croque-madame	croque-monsieur with fried egg
l'assiette (f)	plate	la croque-monsieur	toasted ham and cheese sandwich
l'aubergine (f)	eggplant	les crudités (f)	raw vegetables
la bavette	flank	eau de robinet	tap water
le beurre	butter	l'échalote (f)	shallot
bien cuit	well done	l'entrecôte (m)	chop (cut of meat)
la bière	beer	l'escalope (f)	thin slice of meat
le bifteck	steak	l'escargot (m)	snail
le blanc de volaille	chicken breast	farci	stuffed
bleu/saignant	rare	le faux-filet	sirloin steak
le boeuf	beef	le feuilleté	puff pastry
la boisson	drink	le flan	custard
la bouillebaisse	fish soup of Provence	le foie gras d'oie/de canard	liver of fattened goose/duck
la brioche	pastry-like bread	forestière	with mushrooms
la brochette	shish-ka-bab	frais	fresh
le canard	duck	la fraise	strawberry
la carafe d'eau	pitcher of tap water	la framboise	raspberry
le cassoulet	meat and bean stew	les frites	French fries
les cervelles	brain	le fromage	cheese
le champignon	mushroom	le gâteau	cake
chaud	hot	le gésier	gizzard
la chèvre	goat cheese	le gibier	game
choix	choice	la glace	ice cream
la choucroute	sauerkraut	le granité	icy sorbet
le chou-fleur	cauliflower	la grenouille	frog (legs)
la ciboulette	chive	l'haricot vert (m)	green bean
le citron	lemon	l'huitre (f)	oyster
le citron vert	lime	le jambon	ham
le civet	stew	le kir	white wine and cassis
la compote	stewed fruit	le lait	milk
le confit	preserve	le lapin	rabbit
le confit de canard	duck cooked and preserved in its own fat	le légume	vegetable
coq au vin	rooster stewed in wine	le légume	vegetable
la côte	rib or chop	le magret de canard	duck breast
la courgette	zucchini/courgette	maison	home-made
la crème brulée	custard dessert with carmelized sugar	le marron	chestnut
la crème Chantilly	whipped cream	le miel	honey

la moule	mussel	les rillettes	pork hash cooked in fat
la moutarde	mustard	du riz	rice
nature	plain	la salade verte	green salad
les noix (f)	nuts	le sanglier	wild boar
l'oeuf	egg	le saucisson	sausage
l'oie	goose	le saumon	salmon
l'oignon	onion	le sel	salt
le pain	bread	la steak hachette	ground beef cooked like steak
les pâtes (f)	pasta	le steak tartare	raw meat w/ raw egg
la pâtisserie	pastry, pastry shop	le sucre	sugar
le plat	main course	la tarte	pie
le pétoncle	scallop	tête	head
poêlé	pan-fried	le thé	tea
à point	medium	le thon	tuna
le poisson	fish	le tournedos	beef filet
le poivre	pepper	la truffe	truffle (mushroom)
la pomme	apple	la viande	meat
la pomme/la pomme de terre	potato	la vichyssoise	leek and potato soup
le potage	soup	le vin	wine
le poulet	chicken	yaourt (f)	yogurt

FRENCH - ENGLISH GLOSSARY

abbaye: abbey
allée: lane, avenue
abri: shelter
aller-retour: round-trip
arc: arch
arène: arena
arrondissement: neighborhood
auberge: inn, hostel
banlieue: suburb
baroque: real ornate style
basse ville: lower town
BCBG: yuppie (bon chic bon genre)
beffroi: belfry
bibliothèque: library
billet: ticket
bois: forest, wood
boulangerie: bakery
car: bus
carte orange: metro pass
cathédrale: cathedral
cave: cellar
centre ville: downtown
chambre: room
chambre d'hôtel: B&B
chandaille: sweater
charcuterie: butcher
château: mansion, castle
chaussures: shoes
chemin: path
cimetière: cemetery
cloitre: cloister
collabo: collaborator

côte: coast
coupon vert: metro pass
couvent: convent
CPCH: yuppie (collier de perles, carré Hermès)
cravatte: tie
cru: vineyard, vintage
défense de ...: it is forbidden to ...
dégustation: tasting
dégeulasse: disgusting
donjon: keep (of a castle)
douane: customs
école: school
église: church
entrée: appetizer
fabuleux: fabulous!
faubourg : quarter, street
fermeture: closing time
fête: celebration, festival
ferme: farm
foire: fair
fontaine: fountain
forêt: forest
formule: daily special
gare: train station
gare routière: bus station
gite d'étape: rural b&b
halles: covered market
haute ville: upper town
HLM: public housing
horloge: clock
hors: out of order
hors-saison: off-season
hôtel particulier: mansion, town house
hôtel de ville : city hall
hôtel-Dieu: old hospital
ile: island
jours fériés: holidays
jupe: skirt

kir: white wine & cassis
mairie: town hall
manteau: coat
marché: market
mec: a guy
mef: a chick
menu: daily special
montagne: mountain
mur: wall
omelette: omelette
palais: palace
pantalons: pants
parc: park
place: square
plât principale: entrée
pont: bridge
poste: post office
pression: draft beer
Québecois: not Canadian
quartier: district of a town
quiche: quiche
randonnée: hike
RER: commuter train
robe: dress
routière: bus station
rue: street
salaud: jerk!
salon: drawing room
sentier: path, lane
soldes: sales
sortie: exit
téléphérique: cable car
thermes: hot springs
tour: tower
truc: a thing
vallée: valley
va chier!: piss off!
vendange: grape harvest
veste: sport coat, blazer
vieille ville: old town
vitraux: stained glass

INDEX

A

A.P.C. 304
Abdication Chamber 322
abortion 49
Abou d'Abi Bazar 304
Absinthe 250, 339
Academic style 23
Académie Française 189
Académie Royale 23
Accommodations 98–123
  general info 59
Action Christine 272
ACT-UP PARIS 89
Adams, John 224
Adams, John Quincy 224
Adjani, Isabelle 35
Adventureland 329
Agence pour le
  développement des
  relations interculturelles 90
Agnès B 304
AIDS 48, 49, 85
Air 33
airplane travel
  charter flights 57
  courier flights 56
  fares 53
  standby 57
airports
  Orly 75
  Roissy-Charles de Gaulle 74
alcohol 50
Alcoholics Anonymous 85
Alcools 19
aleatory music 32
Alésia Club 277
Algerian Cuisine 149, 151
Alias 308
Alice's Curious Labyrinth 329
Alléosse 155
allergies 48
Allô Logement Temporaire 103
Allô-Sports 276
Aloha Hostel 120
Alternatives 305
alternatives to tourism 65
Alvin Ailey Dance Company 268
AMAC 95
Ambulance 83
American Express 45, 46, 47, 94, 97
American Library 307
Amnésia Café 136
Androuet 155
Angelina's 152
Angelou, Maya 268
angling 278
années folles 32
Annicale des Pêcheurs de
  Neuilly, Levallois, et
  environs 278
Antiquités New-Puces 305
Anti-Theatre 20
Apocalypse 284
Apollinaire 228, 238

Apollinaire, Guillaume 32
Apostrophe, l' 137, 293
Apparement Café 134, 292
Aquaboulevard 278, 297
Aquarius 136
Aquarius Café 146
Aragon, Louis 19
Arapaho, l' 296
Arc de Triomphe 7, 198
Arc de Triomphe du
  Carrousel 244
Arc du Carrousel 7
Archives de la Presse 308
Arènes de Lutèce 184
Argonaute 231, 256
Arlequin, l' 272
Armageddon 284
Art Deco 222
Art Galleries 265
Art Nouveau 221, 224, 250
ARTE 95
Arts and Entertainment 268–279
As du Falafel, l' 135
Assemblée Nationale 194
Association des Etudiants
  Protestants de Paris 111
Association des Foyers de
  Jeunes 117
Association des Trois
  Mondes 90
Association InterMusées 242
asthma 48
Atelier Brancusi 251
Atelier de Daubigny 339
Ateliers d'Artistes-Portes
  Ouverts 283
Ateliers de Ménilmontant 212
Atlantide, L' 151
ATM cards 47
Au Bec Fin 270
Au Bon Croissant de
  Chartres 323
Au Bon Marché 302
Au Franc-Pinot 167
Au Gamin de Paris 135
Au Gourmet de l'Isle 131
Au Lapin Agile 271
Au Pair 68
Au Panetier 159
Au Pied de Fouet 140
Au Printemps 206, 302
Au Produits Du Sud-Ouest 147
Au Rendez-Vous Des
  Camionneurs 146
Au Revoir les Enfants 35
Au Sauvignon 152
Au Vide Gousset 133
Au Vieux Campeur 306
Auberge de Jeunesse "Jules
  Ferry" (HI) 116
Auberge de Jeunesse "Le
  D'Artagnan" (HI) 123
Auberge Ravaux 338
Auteuil 221, 224
Auvers-sur-Oise 338
Aux Iles des Princes 149

Aux Quatre Saisons 156
Avenue des Champs Elysées 199
Avenue Gustave V de Suède 224
Axe Historique 195, 241
Ay, Caramba! 151
Aznavour, Charles 32

B

B.P.M. (Bastille Paris
  Musique) 310
Babylone Bis 133
baguette 154
Bains, Les 292
bakeries 158
Bal du Moulin Rouge 229
Ballets Russes 32
Bals Concerts 282
Balzac, Honoré de 17, 162, 224, 225, 234
Banana Café 291
Banane Ivoirienne, À la 143
Banlieues Bleues Festival 336
Banque de France 225
Bar des Théâtres 141, 294
Bar Sans Nom 295, 296
Bar, Le 291
Barbizon 24
Baron Haussmann 8
Baroque 28, 164
bars 159
Bartholdi 224
Basilique de St-Denis 184, 226, 335
Basilique du Sacré-Coeur 228
Bastille 6, 27, 208
Bastille Day 201, 280, 282
Bastille prison 209
Bataclan, Le 296
bâtard 154
Bateau El Alamein 296
Bateaux-Mouches 162
Batignolles, les 225
Battle of Algiers 35
Baudelaire, Charles 18, 167, 168, 183, 238
Bazile, Frédéric 249
Beaubourg 179
Beauvais 327
Beauvoir, Simone de 20, 183
Beckett, Samuel 19, 20, 217
Beethoven 27
Belhomme 209
Belle Époque 234
Belleville 231, 234
Bemelman, Ludwig 201
Berger, Michel 284
Bergson, Henri 183
Berlioz, Hector 31
Berthillon 160
Bête Humaine, La 202
Betty Blue 35
Beurre et Cacao 158
BHV 302
Bibliothèque de France 86,

173, 216
Bibliothèque du Roi 173
Bibliothèque Forney 181
Bibliothèque Historique de la
  Ville de Paris 182
Bibliothèque Nationale site
  Richelieu 173
Bibliothèque Polonaise de
  Paris 263
Bibliothèque Publique
  d'Information 251
bicycles 277, 278
Bièvre 214
Big Thunder Mountain 329
Billy Bob's Country and
  Western Saloon 330
Binoche, Juliette 35
birth control 49, 84
Bisexual, Gay, and Lesbian
  Entertainment 287
Bismarck 8
Bistros 124, 149
Bistrot du Peintre 143
Bizet, Georges 31, 174
blind travelers 63
Blois 28
Blue (film) 35
Blue Note 300
Bo Plastic 266
Boeuf Couronné, Le 323
Bohemia 24
Boileau, Louis-Auguste 29
Bois de Boulogne 222, 234, 236, 275, 277
Bois de Vincennes 214, 236, 238, 277
Bois-Preau 331
Bon Marché 195, 302
Bonaparte, Napoleon 7, 28, 198, 262, 284, 321, 331
bookstores 306
booze 152
Borghesian Gladiator 246
Bosch, Hieronymus 245
Bouchard, Henri 222
Boucher, François 24, 245
Bouffes du Nord 270
boulangeries 154
Boulevard Beaumarchais 27
Boulevard Sébastopo 175
Boulevard St-Martin 27
Boulevard St-Michel 183
Boulez, Pierre 32
Boulle, Pierre 284
Bourbon dynasty 4
Bourdelle, Emile-Antoine 260
Bourse des Valeurs 172, 173
Bourse du Commerce 171
bowling 276
Bowling de Paris 238, 276, 297
Bowling International
  Stadium 276, 296
Braque, Georges 26, 27
Brassaï, Georges 26, 284
brasseries 128
Brentano's 307
Breton, André 19, 225
Brigitte Bardot 34

ABOUT LET'S GO

FORTY YEARS OF WISDOM

As a new millennium arrives, *Let's Go: Europe*, now in its 40th edition and translated into seven languages, reigns as the world's bestselling international travel guide. For four decades, travelers criss-crossing the Continent have relied on *Let's Go* for inside information on the hippest backstreet cafes, the most pristine secluded beaches, and the best routes from border to border. In the last 20 years, our rugged researchers have stretched the frontiers of backpacking and expanded our coverage into Asia, Africa, Australia, and the Americas. We're celebrating our 40th birthday with the release of *Let's Go: China*, blazing the traveler's trail from the Forbidden City to the Tibetan frontier; *Let's Go: Perú & Ecuador*, spanning the lands of the ancient Inca Empire; *Let's Go: Middle East*, with coverage from Istanbul to the Persian Gulf; and the maiden edition of *Let's Go: Israel*.

It all started in 1960 when a handful of well-traveled students at Harvard University handed out a 20-page mimeographed pamphlet offering a collection of their tips on budget travel to passengers on student charter flights to Europe. The following year, in response to the instant popularity of the first volume, students traveling to Europe researched the first full-fledged edition of *Let's Go: Europe*, a pocket-sized book featuring honest, practical advice, witty writing, and a decidedly youthful slant on the world. Throughout the 60s and 70s, our guides reflected the times. In 1969 we taught travelers how to get from Paris to Prague on "no dollars a day" by singing in the street. In the 80s and 90s, we looked beyond Europe and North America and set off to all corners of the earth. Meanwhile, we focused in on the world's most exciting urban areas to produce in-depth, fold-out map guides. Our new guides bring the total number of titles to 48, each infused with the spirit of adventure and voice of opinion that travelers around the world have come to count on. But some things never change: our guides are still researched, written, and produced entirely by students who know first-hand how to see the world on the cheap.

HOW WE DO IT

Each guide is completely revised and thoroughly updated every year by a well-traveled set of over 250 students. Every spring, we recruit over 180 researchers and 70 editors to overhaul every book. After several months of training, researcher-writers hit the road for seven weeks of exploration, from Anchorage to Adelaide, Estonia to El Salvador, Iceland to Indonesia. Hired for their rare combination of budget travel sense, writing ability, stamina, and courage, these adventurous travelers know that train strikes, stolen luggage, food poisoning, and marriage proposals are all part of a day's work. Back at our offices, editors work from spring to fall, massaging copy written on Himalayan bus rides into witty, informative prose. A student staff of typesetters, cartographers, publicists, and managers keeps our lively team together. In September, the collected efforts of the summer are delivered to our printer, which turns them into books in record time, so that you have the most up-to-date information available for your vacation. Even as you read this, work on next year's editions is well underway.

WHY WE DO IT

We don't think of budget travel as the last recourse of the destitute; we believe that it's the only way to travel. Living cheaply and simply brings you closer to the people and places you've been saving up to visit. Our books will ease your anxieties and answer your questions about the basics—so you can get off the beaten track and explore. Once you learn the ropes, we encourage you to put *Let's Go* down now and then to strike out on your own. You know as well as we that the best discoveries are often those you make yourself. When you find something worth sharing, please drop us a line. We're Let's Go Publications, 67 Mount Auburn St., Cambridge, MA 02138, USA (email: feedback@letsgo.com). For more info, visit our website, http://www.letsgo.com.

READER QUESTIONNAIRE

Name: _____

Address: _____

City: _____ State: _____ Country: _____

ZIP/Postal Code: _____ E-mail: _____ How old are you?____

And you're...?   in high school   in college   in graduate school
                 employed   retired   between jobs

Which book(s) have you used? _____

Where have you gone with Let's Go? _____

Have you traveled extensively before?   yes   no

Had you used Let's Go before?   yes   no   **Would you use it again?**   yes   no

How did you hear about Let's Go? friend   store clerk   television
                                 review   bookstore display
                                 ad/promotion   internet   other: _____

Why did you choose Let's Go?   reputation   budget focus   annual updating
                               wit & incision   price   other: _____

Which guides have you used?   Fodor's   Footprint Handbooks   Frommer's $-a-day
                              Lonely Planet   Moon Guides   Rick Steve's
                              Rough Guides   UpClose   other: _____

Which guide do you prefer? Why? _____

Please rank the following in your Let's Go guide: (1=needs improvement, 5=perfect)

packaging/cover	1 2 3 4 5	food	1 2 3 4 5	maps		1 2 3 4 5
cultural introduction	1 2 3 4 5	sights	1 2 3 4 5	directions		1 2 3 4 5
"Essentials"	1 2 3 4 5	entertainment	1 2 3 4 5	writing style		1 2 3 4 5
practical info	1 2 3 4 5	gay/lesbian info	1 2 3 4 5	budget resources	1 2 3 4 5	
accommodations	1 2 3 4 5	up-to-date info	1 2 3 4 5	other: _____	1 2 3 4 5	

How long was your trip?   one week   two wks.   three wks.   a month   2+ months

Why did you go?   sightseeing   adventure travel   study abroad   other: _____

What was your average daily budget, not including flights? _____

Do you buy a separate map when you visit a foreign city?   yes   no

Have you used a Let's Go Map Guide?   yes   no   **If you have, which one?** _____

Would you recommend them to others?   yes   no

Have you visited Let's Go's website?   yes   no

What would you like to see included on Let's Go's website? _____

What percentage of your trip planning did you do on the web? _____

What kind of Let's Go guide would you like to see? recreation (e.g., skiing)   phrasebook
              spring break   adventure/trekking   first-time travel info   Europe altas

Which of the following destinations would you like to see Let's Go cover?

     Argentina   Brazil   Canada   Caribbean   Chile   Costa Rica   Cuba
     Morocco   Nepal   Russia   Scandinavia   Southwest USA   other: _____

Where did you buy your guidebook?   independent bookstore   college bookstore
        travel store   Internet   chain bookstore   gift   other: _____

Please fill this out and return it to **Let's Go, St. Martin's Press,** 175 Fifth Ave., New York, NY 10010-7848. All respondents will receive a free subscription to *The Yellow-Jacket*, the Let's Go Newsletter. You can find a more extensive version of this survey on the web at http://www.letsgo.com.